The Forbidden Lands

HAL LANGFUR

The Forbidden Lands

Colonial Identity, Frontier Violence, and

the Persistence of Brazil's Eastern Indians, 1750–1830

STANFORD UNIVERSITY PRESS

Stanford, California

Stanford University Press
Stanford, California
© 2006 by the Board of Trustees of the
Leland Stanford Junior University

Library of Congress Cataloging-in-Publication Data

Langfur, Hal.
   The forbidden lands : colonial identity, frontier violence, and
the persistence of Brazil's eastern Indians, 1750–1830 / Hal Langfur.
      p.   cm.
   Includes bibliographical references and index.
   ISBN 0-8047-5180-3 (cloth : alk. paper)
   ISBN 0-8047-6338-0 (paper : alk. paper)
      1. Brazil—Territorial expansion.   2. Brazil—History—1763–1822.
3. Brazil—History—Empire, 1822–1889. 4. Minas Gerais (Brazil)—
History.   5. Land settlement—Brazil—Minas Gerais—History.
6. Violence—Brazil—Minas Gerais—History.   7. Indians of
South America—Brazil—Minas Gerais—History.   8. Blacks—
Brazil—Minas Gerais—History.   9. Brazil—Race relations.   I. Title.
F2534.L325 2006
981′51033—dc22

                                            2005037517

Original Printing 2006
Last figure below indicates year of this printing:
15   14   13   12   11   10   09

Typeset by TechBooks, New Delhi, in 10/12.5 Minion

FOR KERRY, BRIDGER, AND DEVON

Contents

Map, Illustrations, Figures, and Tables

Map

Illustrations

Figures

Tables

Acknowledgments

My first visit to Brazil many years ago began in the western border town of Corumbá, where my traveling companion and I boarded a train and crossed the great grasslands of Mato Grosso do Sul on our way to the Atlantic coast. Anyone would find that trip difficult to complete without experiencing some measure of awe at the beauty and vastness of the nation's interior. As a son of the western United States, I became irrevocably fascinated by Brazil's frontier history, although I as yet had little idea of its complexity. Ultimately, the contrasts between the North American history I knew and the South American history I came to know would prove as revealing as any commonalities. Even so, this book remains the result of questions that began to form as I watched the farms and ranches roll by from the open window of that train. Little did I imagine that I was heading in the same direction, west to east, chosen by or forced upon many of the individuals who would inhabit my research as I traced their movements through the forests, mountains, and river valleys of tropical Portuguese America during the eighteenth and early nineteenth centuries.

From its inception a decade ago at the University of Texas, this project benefited from the insight and rigor of mentors Richard Graham, who counseled me to let it steep, and Sandra Lauderdale Graham, who urged me to be bold. I followed the former advice perhaps too well, and hope I incorporated the latter well enough. Alida Metcalf also became an incisive critic and steadfast supporter from an early stage, as did Mary Karasch, Judy Bieber, and Barbara Sommer, all of whom have themselves advanced the study of Brazilian frontier and indigenous history. At a crucial juncture, Laura de Mello e Souza, as a visiting scholar, shared her unrivaled knowledge of the history of colonial Minas Gerais, the gold-mining region at the center of this study, as well as invaluable sources from her research in progress. Similarly, John Monteiro, first on a visit from Brazil where he has helped transform the field of colonial ethnohistory, suggested important avenues of investigation, as he has done many times since.

I benefited from the encouragement and constructive criticism of my colleagues in the History Department at the University of North Carolina at Wilmington, where I spent five productive years, especially Robert Toplin, Michael Seidman, and Susan McCaffray. Kathleen Berkeley, in her capacity as department chair and unstinting friend, marshaled an ample share of her prodigious energies in support of the project. Norman Fiering was instrumental in providing a year of further research and writing at the John Carter Brown Library at Brown University, a matchless environment for scholars studying the early modern Atlantic world. Other individuals who at one point or another offered intellectual guidance include Susan Deans-Smith, Enylton de Sá Rego, David Montejano, Gunther Peck, Myron Gutmann, Starling Pullum, Hendrik Kraay, Matthew Edney, A.J.R. Russell-Wood, Valéria Gauz, Matthew Restall, and Neil Whitehead. Stuart Schwartz and Bert Barickman combed the entire manuscript in its penultimate form, making recommendations that greatly enhanced the final version.

Repeated research trips to Brazil have brought me in contact with numerous friends and scholars whose practical assistance, camaraderie, and expertise I have treasured. In each of these realms, I owe particularly large debts—which show no signs of diminishing—to Maria Leônia Chaves de Resende in São João del-Rei and Valter Sinder and Vania Belli in Rio de Janeiro. José Bessa Freire provided the opportunity to discuss my work with the members of his Programa de Estudos dos Povos Indígenas at the Universidade do Estado do Rio de Janeiro. Antonio Carlos de Souza Lima placed the library and other resources of the Museu Nacional at my disposal. Manolo Florentino and Júnia Ferreira Furtado steered me to important sources in Rio de Janeiro and Belo Horizonte, respectively. I also wish to thank José Celso de Castro Alves, Dona Jarice Ferreira de Andrade, Luiz Carlos Villalta, Douglas Libby, and Izabel Missagia de Mattos for extending their aid, ideas, and friendship. Many Brazilian archivists and library professionals, whose institutions are listed in the bibliography, greatly facilitated my research. Of the few I can name here individually, my special thanks go to Carmen Tereza C. Moreno, Vera Lúcia Garcia Menezes, Pedro Tortima, Alda Maria Palhares Campolina, and Monsenhor Flávio Carneiro Rodrigues. Expert research assistance was provided in Mariana's archives by Maria Teresa Gonçalves Pereira. In Lisbon, Tiago C.P. dos Reis Miranda, Virgínia Maria Trindade Valadares, and James Wadsworth were particularly generous.

With research sites on three continents, this undertaking would not have been possible without the financial and institutional support of the University of Texas, the University of North Carolina at Wilmington, the John Carter

Brown Library, the Tinker Foundation, the Conference on Latin American History, the David L. Boren NSEP Graduate International Fellowship Program, the Andrew W. Mellon Foundation, the National Endowment for the Humanities, and the American Historical Association. The University at Buffalo – SUNY supported the acquisition and reproduction of images to complement the text. The *Hispanic American Historical Review*, *The Americas*, and *Ethnohistory* published portions of several chapters in earlier forms. I wish to thank the editors for permission to use expanded versions of that material. Norris Pope and John Feneron at Stanford University Press guided the final publication process with their renowned expertise and enthusiasm.

The completion of a book of this sort presupposes a commitment that inevitably involves those who are closest to its author. As such, I counted repeatedly on the support of both sides of my family, particularly my parents, Bert and Rosalyn Langfur, my sister, Meg Langfur, and my wife's parents, Michael and Laing Reynolds. Finally, there are those patient few who live with the project on a daily basis as it ends up taking longer and demanding more than anyone expected. Whatever has come of this effort would have amounted to far less without the love and cherished companionship of Kerry Reynolds, my wife and finest critic, my partner on that train trip across Brazil, and ever since. It is to her and to our dear children, Bridger and Devon, who joined our journey along the way, that I dedicate this book.

A Note on Conventions

For textual consistency, I have adopted contemporary Brazilian orthography but retained diverse original spellings, grammar, and punctuation in citations of historical manuscripts and imprints. The names and spellings of indigenous groups follow those most widely used by Brazilian scholars, although they too vary widely in the notes according to the original sources. The *real* (pl. *réis*) was the basic unit of currency in colonial Brazil. One *mil-réis* equaled one thousand *réis* and was written 1$000. One *conto de réis* (or simply one *conto*) equaled one thousand *mil-réis*, and was written 1:000$000. Throughout the second half of the eighteenth century, the Portuguese Crown set the value of one *oitava* of gold (an eighth of an ounce) at 1$200 in Minas Gerais.

The Forbidden Lands

Introduction

A Forgotten Frontier in Colonial Brazil

A S R E V O L U T I O N A R Y sentiments stirred on both sides of the Atlantic in 1789, the governor in charge of Brazil's great inland mining district, the captaincy of Minas Gerais, hurried to increase military forces at strategic points. Having discovered a conspiracy by local plutocrats who planned his assassination, an armed uprising against the Portuguese Crown, and the declaration of an independent republic, Governor Luís Antônio Furtado de Mendonça, the Viscount of Barbacena, set in motion a plot of his own. The supposed sighting of hostile Indians along the captaincy's primary road and escape route, which ran south out of the Minas highlands to the colonial capital of Rio de Janeiro, provided Barbacena the excuse he needed to reinforce captaincy troops on patrol. A second pretext came from unauthorized prospectors rushing to stake claims at two remote gold and diamond strikes, where hundreds had "gathered tumultuously." The conspicuous need to police these migrants, disperse them if necessary, apprehend smugglers, and prevent others from following their path would help conceal the governor's ruse as he requested two infantry companies dispatched from the capital by Viceroy Luís de Vasconcelos e Sousa. The governor was well aware of the "suspicion that any extraordinary movement of troops would cause." Scheming to make his false orders widely known, he revealed his true intentions only in secret communications with the viceroy, his uncle. Barbacena calculated that local inhabitants, accustomed as they were to the use of troops to control unconquered Indians and vagabond fortune seekers, would not divine his true purpose—the arrest of the conspirators and their removal from the mining district. The success of his ploy can be measured, at least in part, by the subsequent swift capture of the rebellious cabal.[1]

Unfolding amid momentous transformations in the Atlantic world, the nativist intrigue known as the Inconfidência Mineira has preoccupied generations of historians seeking to understand the demise of colonial rule in Portuguese America. Long seen as a heroic first step toward Brazilian independence in 1822 and its participants elevated as national icons, the plot would later suffer the skeptical reevaluation of scholars less dazzled by the motives of its self-interested wealthy backers, who stood to profit from a tax rebellion. Despite such close inspection, the governor's deceptions involving Indians and uprooted miners never prompted a second scholarly thought. After all, they were minor machinations in the overall plot and its official suppression. Yet they raise an intriguing question about the broader contours of life in the mining district during the final decades of the eighteenth century.

Why was it that, counter to everything canonical scholarship would indicate, the movements of Indians and frontier migrants supplied the governor with his most plausible official cover for the deployment of Portuguese troops? Evidently, the inhabitants of Minas Gerais would have believed many other things about the region's autonomous Indians: that many were cannibals, that their presence on the periphery of the settled mining district prevented new discoveries of gold, emeralds, and diamonds, and that the conquest of these lands would restore Minas Gerais to a grandeur that had faded with the exhaustion of the great mineral deposits that first attracted a flood of settlers to the region early in the century. Residents of the captaincy's traditional mining towns would also have recognized in the constant and often unlawful movements of prospectors a persistent drive to occupy still-unsettled areas and establish in them the slave-based mining operations that had enriched their predecessors. These ongoing concerns about Indians and frontier conquests, matters conventionally considered affairs of the distant past, point to the central subject of this study.

Atlantic Connections, Academic Ruptures

The following chapters consider the curious history of a mining and farming frontier that expanded not westward into the heart of colonial Brazil but eastward from the mountainous interior back toward the Atlantic coast. They explore the accompanying surge in interethnic violence that engulfed the eastern forests of Minas Gerais, the colony's most populous captaincy, with just under 400,000 inhabitants in the 1780s, nearly half of them slaves and a third of them free persons of color—in both cases, more than in any other region.[2] They comprise one of the few sustained scholarly examinations of any portion of Portuguese America's sprawling frontier. Focusing on the racial, ethnic, and geographic relations of the whites, free blacks, slaves, and Indians who inhabited this slowly receding wilderness, they challenge prevailing depictions of Brazil's inland colonization. A traditional preoccupation with coastal events and export-led development has deprived this centuries-long frontier history of anything approaching the intensive study it merits. To admit how little is still known about the settlement of this great inland swathe of the Americas is nothing short of astonishing.

The first step toward an adequate analysis requires connecting two realms often considered separately and even antithetically: the early modern Atlantic system and the frontier regions that formed along its perimeter. This bifurcation of academic inquiry has produced some surprising lapses. For example, my emphasis on independent Indians sets this work apart from a historiography routinely dismissive of their enduring significance throughout the colonial period, which ended with independence from Portugal in 1822. Equally, my scrutiny of the inland movements of peoples of African origin distinguishes this work from studies that bind slavery to the coastal plantation economy and reduce Brazil's frontier history to a dyadic contest between Europeans and Indians when the latter are not entirely ignored. To account for pervasive archival evidence linking these phenomena, which is fundamentally also the link between the frontier and the Atlantic world, I have sought to re-conceptualize the colony's internal consolidation, elaborating an approach for understanding the stark conflicts it engendered. Briefly stated, my overarching argument is that the key to the relentless violence that accompanied frontier incorporation can be found in the incompatible ways in which Luso-Brazilians, Afro-Brazilians, and seminomadic indigenous peoples sought to territorialize their distinctive societies—that is, to construct, sustain, reproduce, and protect those societies in an unsettled tropical and subtropical environment. Understood in this way, I propose that frontier conflict constituted a defining feature not only of Brazil's transition from colony to independent nation but also of its relationship to a wider world. In this respect, Brazil deserves a prominent place in any thorough understanding of the hemispheric sweep of internal colonization in the Americas.

In addition to these fundamental issues, the scholarly concerns that inform this book emerge from the efforts of a growing cohort of historians, ethnohistorians, and anthropologists newly attentive to Brazil's indigenous history. Renderings of Brazil's past have typically diminished the historical contribution of the first of three peoples—Indians, Europeans, and Africans—whose labors, conflicts, and creative energies created Portugal's New World colony. As new questions regarding the colony's internal dynamics have come to the forefront in recent years, researchers have begun to grapple more systematically with Indians and their role in Brazil's territorial and social formation.[3] Their combined efforts might now fairly be classified as Brazil's "new" Indian history, except that no "old" Indian history ever coalesced—making current contributions, still few in number, all the more noteworthy. This book extends these efforts to the regional transformation in Minas Gerais that gathered force as the occupants of the mining district began to disperse after 1750. This migration, because of its historical idiosyncrasies, has eluded proper recognition as the primary instance of frontier expansion in late colonial Brazil. The resulting scholarly neglect, exacerbated by the dismissive slant on native peoples, has left the region's indigenous history utterly ignored.[4]

Another corpus of work this book engages is extensive research on the settled towns and mining camps of colonial Minas Gerais, if not its frontiers. In recent years, this endeavor has produced a veritable scholarly renaissance.[5] This activity stems in part from a renewed conviction, to use a metaphor applied by the Crown's colonial secretary, that the "soul" of Portuguese America lay not along the coast in the eighteenth century but inland.[6] Coastal events, particularly the fortunes of Brazil's export-oriented tropical plantation complex, while providing the customary focus of scholarly production about the colonial period, accounted for just one aspect of an economic and social matrix integrally linked to the interior. Benefiting from but identifying a fundamental flaw in the forceful new research on Minas Gerais, the present study insists that decisive events took place not only beyond the coast but also beyond the confines of the mining district's primary productive sites. The history of Minas Gerais and its ties to the rest of the colony can be fully understood only by reference to the wilderness that surrounded these mining centers and their agricultural hinterlands.

Beyond such connections, I hope to convince the reader that the historical issues at stake transcend the boundaries of this region, however important it might have been, and of Portugal's colony as a whole. In this larger realm, revisionist research focusing on frontiers elsewhere in the Americas, especially those that developed around the same time, represents a final body of scholarship incorporated in the pages that follow. In dialogue with this material, I seek to link regional, Brazilian, Latin American, and Atlantic histories.[7] Eighteenth-century Minas inhabitants referred to the mountains, forests, and river valleys to the east of the mining district as the Eastern *Sertão*. Over the course of this study, much will be said about the elusive meaning of the word *sertão* and its plural *sertões*. The term can be adequately translated into English as *wilderness, backlands*, or *frontier*. In the colonial period, usage was not confined geographically, as it now often is, to description of the semiarid, sparsely settled rural zones of northeastern Brazil. In the colony, the sertão described unsettled regions throughout Brazil's immense interior. During the second half of the eighteenth century, the portion of that interior called the Eastern Sertão became one of the many frontier zones that formed on the periphery of consolidating states and market economies throughout Latin America and the Atlantic world. The history of this zone resists the kind of stage-by-stage analysis, whether as progressive triumph or catastrophe, until recently favored by frontier historians.[8] For decade after decade, colonization led neither to the successful establishment of a sedentary settler society nor to the final subjugation of the region's indigenous peoples. In other words, not merely historical idiosyncrasies but theoretical and methodological insufficiencies explain why historians have seldom recognized the Eastern Sertão as a frontier at all.[9]

The advances and reversals of settlement characteristic of this area and others like it have prompted some scholars to see the long-incomplete incorporation of the Brazilian interior as a negation of the usual frontier dynamic or, to use the terminology some have preferred, as a "hollow frontier." For instance, one historian has argued that a Brazilian "pioneer frontier" can hardly be said to have existed at all until the 1930s when industrialization prompted rapid expansion into the wilderness.[10] The trouble with such views stems from a failure to understand territorial incorporation as a multidimensional process that involved not only conquest but also, depending on the time and place, successful resistance, cooperation, mediation, and negotiation, and that produced prolonged periods of stalemate and equilibrium. To confine frontier history to only those periods when colonists succeeded is to write history from the limited perspective of the intruding society. A more comprehensive and historically precise approach conceptualizes frontiers not merely as the leading edge of European expansion but as zones of contact, conflict, and interaction, albeit often unequal interaction, between and among cultures. While the penetration of market capitalism into remote environments was central to the dynamic connecting the frontier to Atlantic commerce, this expansion occurred, more often than not, in fits and starts, advancing and receding, and requiring a long period of gestation. Despite the teleological conventions of much of the historiography, the frontier was not that distant place where European-based capitalism and imperial administration finally achieved dominance but, rather, exactly where they as yet failed to do so. This characteristic explains why those inhabiting the eastern reaches of Minas Gerais felt the pressures of frontier expansion well before the region experienced rapid economic growth and effective incorporation into either an export economy or a consolidated domestic market.[11] In short, fundamental to the perspective orienting this book is the assumption that the frontier constituted that geographic area remote to settled society but central to indigenous peoples, where such consolidation was not yet assured and where the outcome of multiethnic cultural encounters remained in doubt.

At the outer reaches of an expanding capitalist and imperial system, frontier migrants were thrust into precarious circumstances in peripheral zones

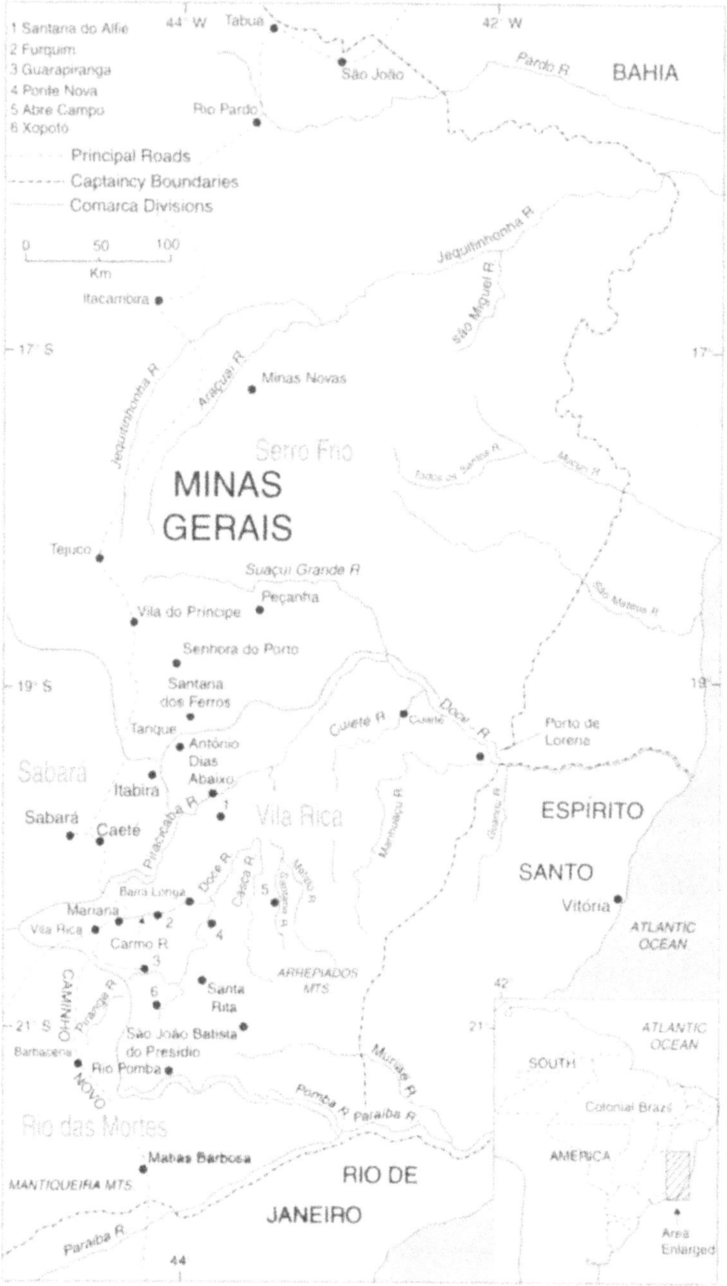

1 Santana do Alfie
2 Furquim
3 Guarapiranga
4 Ponte Nova
5 Abre Campo
6 Xopotó

Principal Roads
Captaincy Boundaries
Comarca Divisions

0   50   100
Km

44° W   Tabua
42° W

BAHIA

São João
Pardo R.

Rio Pardo

Jequitinhonha R.

São Miguel R.

Itacambira

17° S   17°

Araçuaí R.

Minas Novas

Jequitinhonha R.

Serro Frio

MINAS
GERAIS

Todos os Santos R.

Mucuri R.

Tejuco

Suaçuí Grande R.

Peçanha

São Mateus R.

Vila do Príncipe

Senhora do Porto

19° S   19°

Santana
dos Ferros

Tanque

Antônio
Dias
Abaixo

Cuieté R.   Cuieté

Doce R.

Porto de
Lorena

Sabará

Itabira

Piranga R.

Vila Rica

Manhuaçu R.

ESPÍRITO

Sabará   Caeté

Doce R.

Casca R.

Matipó R.

Guandu R.

SANTO

Barra Longa

Mariana

Vila Rica   2

Carmo R.

5

Gualaxo R.

Vitória

ATLANTIC
OCEAN

3   4

42°

6   Santa
Rita

ARREPIADOS
MTS.

CAMINHO

Pitanga R.

21° S   21°

ATLANTIC
OCEAN

São João Batista
do Presídio

Barbacena

Rio Pomba

Muriaé R.

SOUTH

NOVO

Pomba R.   Paraíba R.

Colonial Brazil

Rio das Mortes

Matias Barbosa

AMERICA

MANTIQUEIRA MTS.

RIO DE

JANEIRO

Paraíba R.

44

Area
Enlarged

MAP 1. The Eastern Sertão, Minas Gerais, Brazil, ca. 1800 (all boundaries were disputed).

inhabited by natives throughout the Atlantic world. Another great rift in the historiography of the colonial Americas has consistently severed the study of frontiers from that of settled enclaves and thus the history of independent native societies from that of peoples occupying plantation and mining zones, where African slaves, their captive descendants, free persons of color, detribalized Indians, and poor whites comprised the primary work force.[12] The framework employed in this book explains why these peoples frequently occupied overlapping territories and why scholars have missed much of this complex process in the Brazilian interior. Failing to find a dramatic westward movement comparable to the far more thoroughly studied North American frontier experience, a process wrongly considered archetypal, historians have stumbled. They have overlooked the plodding, multidirectional, ethnically complex patterns of territorial incorporation central to the peopling of Portuguese America.

After the Fall

By the time the wilderness known as the Eastern Sertão became the object of intense official interest, the apex of the mining boom had come and gone. Beginning in the 1690s with the discovery of the most extensive gold strikes the Americas had ever known, the rush to exploit Brazil's southeastern interior resulted in an unprecedented economic expansion, producing a complex inland urban society and a rich Baroque culture. Two hundred years after the colony's discovery in 1500, the first great wave of Portuguese immigrants crossed the Atlantic in pursuit of opportunity and riches. During the first six decades of the eighteenth century, more than half a million colonists emigrated from Portugal and its Atlantic islands to Brazil. Tens of thousands of them and, in even greater numbers, the African slaves they purchased pressed inland from the seaboard. A small minority amassed fortunes from the alluvial deposits that sustained this bonanza. The population of European descent swelled from an initial handful of adventurers, cattle ranchers, and speculators. That of African descent grew even faster, eventually forming the largest regional captive population in Portuguese America, which, as a whole, received by far the greatest overall slave influx of any American colony. The number of free persons of African descent also ballooned as it did in most slaveholding societies, the result of migration from Brazil's plantation zones, of miscegenation, whether consensual or forcible, and of accumulated manumissions. Mining camps burgeoned at Sabará, Mariana, Caeté, and Vila Rica, to name only a few of the most prominent sites. Vila Rica blossomed into the gilded capital of the mining district. To the north at Tejuco, diamonds were discovered in 1729, adding still greater impetus to the windfall that transformed the colony and the transatlantic commerce that linked it to Europe and Africa.

The name bestowed on the region, Minas Gerais, meaning the general mines, reflected with fitting transparency the zone's importance to the world beyond the colony. The district's cataract of precious metal and stones flooded the South Atlantic economy, restructured the Portuguese overseas empire, salvaged a declining Iberian kingdom, and nourished the burgeoning Industrial Revolution in England, Portugal's exigent ally to the north. In the colony itself, economic power shifted decidedly toward the mining region and Rio de Janeiro, the port city through which the bulk of the bullion, immigrants, slaves, trade goods, and contraband passed. However, before the Portuguese Crown fully acknowledged these changes and transferred the colony's capital from Salvador da Bahia to Rio de Janeiro in 1763, the inevitable depletion of the mineral washings was well underway. Considerable economic diversification cushioned the blow, particularly in the form of market-driven farming and ranching developed over time to meet the demands of a growing population. Nevertheless, the exhaustion of the mines produced economic havoc. First felt on a large scale around the middle of the century and intensifying over several decades, the slump brought with it marked social dislocation and political discontentment.

Another crucial consequence of the economic slide was that long after the search for gold purportedly ended and the concerns of colonists turned elsewhere, the inhabitants of Minas Gerais continued to scour outlying lands for new mineral deposits. Wherever these failed to materialize, they looked to the same surrounding lands for pastoral, agricultural, and commercial alternatives. This movement into the wilderness originated not from a scantily settled area in the remote interior but rather from what was by 1750 a relatively well-developed demographic crossroads, constituting during the second half of the century the colony's single largest captaincy with a fifth of Brazil's total population. Similarly, the interactions this movement produced among Portuguese settlers, slaves, free blacks, and Indians were not minor oddities arising in a far-off corner of the colony but phenomena occurring in its heart or, as the Crown minister preferred, its soul.

Like the gold nuggets and precious gems that occasionally still surfaced in newly discovered ravines and riverbeds, the questions that impel this study arise from the gaps that separated expectation from outcome in the pursuit of post-boom frontier conquest and settlement. Why would colonial society prove so difficult to replicate in this wilderness? If established society represented the colonial order and the sertão its antithesis, how did the struggle to tame the wilderness shape the local, colonial, and transatlantic culture of territorial expansion? Such questions provoke others. How was frontier conquest imagined and effected? How was it opposed? Who provided the labor? What sort of set-tlers participated? What became of the Indians? Why did some cooperate, how did others resist, and when did those who chose the course of violence finally submit? What did this violence say about frontier cultural exchange? What drove the whole process in the first place? And why have historians left it virtu-ally unrecorded? I have sought the answers to these questions on both sides of the Atlantic in the dispersed, fragmented, sometimes intractable, but nonethe-less copious archival materials documenting the eastward-moving frontier that formed after the middle of the eighteenth century in the forests separating the settled mining district from the Atlantic seaboard.

The gradual colonization of the Eastern Sertão was part of a much larger migratory process whose history, taken as a whole, remains poorly understood. Beginning no later than the 1750s, local elites, slaves, impoverished settlers, and seminomadic indigenous peoples engaged in a contest for land, labor, and re-sources, radiating outward from the mining district's major towns in several directions at once. Throughout the vast sertões of Minas Gerais, this conflict sometimes smoldered and sometimes flared. A slow-moving, often inconspic-uous dispersion from urban into hinterland areas and from hinterlands into wilderness, this transformation depended on the actions of the powerful and the poor, the free and the enslaved. Each had their own reasons for journeying to the frontier, each made their own claims on unsettled land, and each confronted indigenous groups who saw them as invaders. By probing the relations of those who encountered and struggled with one another along the eastern extremes of this larger migratory flow, I attempt to rethink the process of Brazilian internal territorial consolidation.

Local inhabitants responded actively to the economic disarray and social dis-juncture that followed the quickening disappearance of accessible gold. Among other responses, they joined the migration to the west, to the south, and—for the purposes of this study—to the east into lands officially sealed off a half-century earlier to thwart the flow of contraband gold and diamonds out of the mining district to seagoing smugglers. Along with most contemporary Minas historians, I reject the long-established view that the economic crisis left the re-gion in a state of virtual collapse. The rich corpus of new and neglected sources assembled for this study demonstrates that frontier conquest played a critical role in responding to the crisis and shaping Brazil's late colonial history. Ac-cordingly, this book moves beyond a historiography that has long subordinated the subject of internal colonization to that of Brazil's export complexes—sugar, gold, coffee, cotton, cacao, rubber, and cattle—under the erroneous assump-tion that the frontier advanced only when transatlantic trade and, later, domestic industrialization propelled inland movement. The evidence presented reveals the historical salience of internal colonization precisely between two export booms—gold and coffee—a period traditionally treated as one of stasis and decadence.

Together, Luso-Brazilian settlers and Afro-Brazilian freemen and slaves, encroaching on highly mobile aboriginal peoples, forged a complex, conflict-ridden frontier social order in which all of these groups challenged each other and the colonial administration by turning motion and geography to their advantage. The violence accompanying this history stemmed from the mutually exclusive ways in which these groups struggled to secure their prerogatives. Severed from a mining economy in turmoil and often in search of basic subsistence, farmers and small-stakes miners, many of them persons of color, dispersed into zones bypassed more than half a century earlier by the gold rush and then placed off-limits by the Crown. Such migrants posed a direct threat to elites engaged in their own effort to seize territory. Lands deemed "vacant" and "virgin," like their geographic correlates in North America, became the object of a drive by the locally powerful to enlist the state in frontier conquests as an antidote to social and economic displacement.[13] When official conquest began, however, these lands proved to be already occupied—albeit sparsely—not only by the captaincy's own straying subjects but also by aboriginal groups determined to defend their domain from invasion. Over the course of the second half of the eighteenth century and the first two decades of the nineteenth, the rugged Eastern Sertão became the portion of the encircling Minas frontier where indigenous resistance peaked.

My delineation of varied native responses to this predicament depends, as it must, both on a specific methodology and on the possibilities and limitations of the extant archival material. It presupposes an understanding of Brazil's native peoples not as culturally pristine aboriginals but as full and deft participants in the contested process of territorial consolidation. This study is not a history of a particular indigenous group or native point of view per se but of the contact and connections among diverse groups of Indians, Portuguese colonists, and peoples of African descent. Part of the reason so little has been written about Brazil's colonial Indians, especially those independent peoples who inhabited the sertão, is that the sources are not only disjointed but also so difficult to decode. Written almost entirely by colonists, they simply do not allow for an unadulterated reconstruction of native perspectives. Only in rare instances do they even identify individual Indians by name. Nevertheless, with the focus fixed on contacts, connections, conflicts, and relationships, a rich story emerges situated at the nexus of the various peoples who encountered one another on the frontier. Worth remembering is that the sources are also far from transparent when conveying colonial perspectives. Not only did those who were literate portray Indians—and, for that matter, non-literate settlers and slaves—with a jaundiced eye, they also depicted themselves with predictable indulgence. The application of an ethnographic sensibility to the world these sources echo uncovers multiple meanings attached to the shared experience of interethnic commerce deep in the forests. Such an approach, to use anthropologist Richard Price's formulation, "need know no geographical or typological boundaries: historical studies of 'primitives' or 'the civilized'... (and especially their respective interactions), come equally under its purview."[14] This insight encourages persistence in the face of the analytical difficulties surrounding non-literate historical subjects. Renderings of all parties must be treated with skepticism; restricting the field of analysis to those portrayed impartially would produce histories of none. Access to the Eastern Sertão would remain just as colonial authorities intended—strictly controlled.

In pursuing these lines of inquiry, I have divided my analysis into two parts. Part I, "Colonization," explores how local officials, influential elites, and frontier settlers of varying economic, social, and racial status reinterpreted or ignored Crown proscriptions that designated the eastern forests as the "Forbidden Lands." They tested, chipped away at, and ultimately helped reverse the Crown policy that placed the Eastern Sertão off-limits. As Chapter One demonstrates, the emergence of this frontier was far from a predetermined development in a progressive advance into the interior. The zone as a field of conquest and colonization had to be conceptualized and constructed both geographically and discursively. It had to be occupied, militarized, pacified, panned, sluiced, and planted. This could occur only in accordance with the fears, desires, imaginings, policies, and cumulative and contradictory actions of those who perceived something of value in a place previously considered beyond the limits of colonial activity. Mapmakers proved critical to the formation of the zone as a frontier, as did colonists' preconceptions about natives and nature, and the eastern Indians and wilderness in particular.

Rejecting a monolithic conception of the colonial state, Chapter Two highlights issues over which Crown and captaincy diverged with respect to lands beyond the edge of settled society. Tensions between governing the colony and the captaincy showed the extent to which local events rather than royal fiat determined the direction of frontier and indigenous policy. Soon after the middle of the eighteenth century, local authorities began to invoke a Crown policy formulated to "liberate" the colony's settled indigenous population but they transformed this policy into the legislative basis for the conquest of unsettled, seminomadic groups. Minas officials also began to establish and defend small outposts of controlled settlement in the sertão. They used a royal crackdown on the free poor to round up laborers, especially those of African descent, to advance the goal of frontier conquest. Reflecting a changing colonial identity vis-à-vis the frontier, events in this distant wilderness began to impinge on metropolitan authority, erode established territorial boundaries, and undermine Crown dictates. As Lisbon clung to the Forbidden Lands policy banning access to the Eastern Sertão, captaincy elites adopted a competing conquest mentality with territorial divisions constructed along racial fault lines. What I have chosen to call an emergent "racial geography"—a conception of territorial incorporation infused with racialist assumptions—defined activities deemed disparately appropriate and inappropriate for those of European, African, and Indian origin who inhabited specific regions of the frontier. No matter how insistently colonial elites described the sertão as "virgin" or "wild," the region was anything but an undifferentiated, uninhabited expanse awaiting European settlement. It consisted of various interpenetrating zones, ranging from the outer edge of the settled mining district, where nascent villages represented the eastward extension of Brazil's slaveholding society into the wilderness, to the innermost reaches of coastal forests still dominated by natives. Between these extremes lay a zone where neither slaveholder nor Indian held sway. Still largely beyond the limits of established authority, this intermediary zone in particular revealed the strains between Crown and captaincy visions of the frontier, that is, the dissimilarities between their contradictory racial geographies.

Two chapters examine the formidable difficulties encountered transporting lusophone society into the wilderness and reconstructing it according to models employed in mining and plantation zones. Chapter Three considers episodes from individual settlers' lives and contextualizes them with census and land tenure data. Just as captaincy authorities pursued objectives that diverged from royal intentions, frontier landholders failed to conform to the dream officials nurtured of revitalizing Minas Gerais by conquering new lands rich in mineral wealth deep in Indian territory. Slaveholding colonists favored a more secure alternative: cautious expansion into fertile, less isolated stretches of the sertão that promised safe subsistence or agricultural profits. On lands located within reach of transportation routes and commercial networks, slaves could be redeployed from failing mining operations to extract gains by supplying foodstuffs to a growing colonial population. The expansion of these agricultural hinterlands occurred according to a common pattern by which squatters came to occupy territory still vulnerable to Indian attack. As the threat from such resistance diminished, as trails and roads improved, and as pastures and fields were cleared, planted, and valorized, early settlers found themselves displaced by subsequent waves of colonists. Directly or indirectly, even settlers who eschewed lands vulnerable to Indian raids ended up provoking them because the relentless search for secure colonial domain intensified pressure on the territory seminomadic natives required for survival.

Chapter Four focuses on the most marginalized group of frontier migrants: impoverished, rootless, free individuals, often the descendants of slaves or former slaves themselves. The opulence of the mining boom disguised the poverty and tenuous social status characteristic of all but the most fortunate. During the ensuing bust, those who were poor but free suffered greatly and were among the first to disperse. Denounced as "useless people" and "vagabonds" for abandoning established society to venture to the frontier, these settlers resisted the repressive tactics of a state that sought to control their movements and labor. Journeying outward from the mining district, their migration—like that of colonists of greater means—presaged a regional economic shift from mining to agriculture, along with attendant changes in social relations. Only when the risk of Indian attacks had been substantially reduced did settlers with sizeable slaveholdings successfully establish themselves in outlying lands. Where free poor Afro-Brazilian migrants arrived first, additional tasks confronted mining and farming elites, and the state authorities who arrived in their wake. Determined to transform land into profitable resources, they strove to mold transient subsistence farmers into compliant workers, disciplining them and fixing them to the land as dependents, compelling them to labor for the state, or chasing them away to replace them with slaves. Both the legal and informal imposition of racial categories on frontier activities, the further elaboration of a racially specific geography of conquest, proved central to this project.

Rather than discuss slaves in a separate chapter, I have treated them as the pervasive presence that they were, involved to varying degrees with all other sectors of society and in all aspects of the settlement process and thus a concern of each of these chapters. Some slaves, like those who helped found the wilderness outpost of Cuieté, journeyed with their masters to the frontier. Others were forced by the state to serve alongside the free poor on military expeditions sent out to conquer new lands or to retaliate against hostile natives. Some were killed by Indians while laboring in fields, forests, or mineral washings. Others were armed by their masters to protect those laboring. Runaway slaves also set out for the frontier, their treacherous journey culminating, when successful, in the founding of remote maroon settlements. In turn, these fugitives became targets of whites seeking to tame the frontier. The very fact that this was a slave-owning society proved decisive to the course of frontier settlement, as masters calculated how to use to the greatest advantage their investment in captive human capital and as Indians learned how to take advantage of those calculations.

Of course, the entire settlement process looked very different to the Indians, a reality that informs Part II, "Confrontation." As subjects of historical and anthropological research, the natives of this zone, like those throughout the colony during this period, have been virtually forgotten. And yet numerous aboriginal groups, among them the Puri, Pataxó, Maxakali, and above all the seminomadic peoples the Portuguese first called the Tapuya, later the Aimoré, and later still the Botocudo, blocked settlement and exploration. Between the 1750s and 1808, colonists mounted dozens of military and paramilitary expeditions to neutralize Indian resistance east of the mining district. Aggression against the natives persisted as what remained of the royal ban on settlement gradually collapsed. Then, following the 1808 arrival in Rio de Janeiro of the Crown and royal court that fled Napoleon's invasion of Portugal, Prince Regent João declared open war on the Botocudo and others Indians condemned as cannibals or otherwise hostile, officially sanctioning their slaughter and enslavement.

Chapter Five demonstrates that the militarization of this conflict began a full half-century earlier, another testament to the gaps between Crown and captaincy policy. Despite royal prohibitions and at times despite their own profound misgivings, virtually every governor of Minas Gerais from the 1760s on pursued a policy of violent Indian conquest at one time or another. None commanded the military resources and only a few possessed the unabashed anti-Indian conviction of the prince regent. Nevertheless, the fact that the conflict commenced long before he declared war demands a rethinking of the basis of this action. Far from a sudden reversal marking the deterioration of relations between a strengthening colonial state and the remnant of once numerous Brazilian Indians, the military action capped a long history of conflict caused by settler and state incursions into the Eastern Sertão. This chapter details this long assault sponsored by the captaincy government, especially in the form of wilderness expeditions known as *bandeiras* (literally, banners). During the half-century prelude to declared war, these expeditions institutionalized the mounting military threat. Committed more than other less fortunate colonists to the constituted centers of settled, urban authority, the regional elite lagged behind impoverished migrants seeking to put distance between themselves and the oppressive structures of a slave-owning society. As economic problems deepened with the sharp decline in gold production, established miners, ranchers, farmers, merchants, and even clergymen sought to salvage their languishing fortunes by enlisting the state to conquer and safeguard new lands. The revival of the bandeira, a mobile institution of conquest first employed in Portuguese America in the sixteenth century, served this advance. It did so long after the historiography asserts that the bandeira era had closed. As the decades passed, the aggressive push into Indian territory gradually relinquished its ties to a bygone golden age and emphasized the burgeoning commerce of the Atlantic world that could be tapped by opening the river valleys leading out of the mining district to the sea.

For native peoples, intensive bandeira activity and the settler influx it accompanied forever broke the protective isolation of the Eastern Sertão. With the geography of the conflict demarcated, its chronology revised, its ideology articulated, and its mechanisms clarified, two chapters elucidate how, from the far side of the frontier, various native groups experienced and, to the extent sources allow, understood the eastward migration and its militarization. Chapter Six considers the pitfalls of relying too heavily on conventional sources, namely the published accounts of European naturalists and colonial memorialists, to understand developments in the forests. Unexplored archival materials provide alternative narratives that make better sense of the options available to natives. Even as captaincy policy hardened, numerous indigenous groups found ways to maintain peaceful, cooperative relations with settlers and soldiers alike. When such accommodation failed, Indians tenaciously resisted invasion of their domain. They felt the effects of state-sponsored aggression near the wilderness outposts now established by the captaincy government. Even more disruptive was the slow-moving invasion of slaveholding colonists on the very edge of the mining district. Despite a mounting state of calamity, natives took advantage of still salient prohibitions on uncontrolled settlement and, more generally, of the contradictions in Crown and local policy, as well as the vulnerabilities of a society dependant on slavery. Their actions belie the common supposition that violent indigenous resistance had become all but ineffectual by the late colonial period. At the same time, they created a refuge, insecure though it may have been, in increasingly remote forests. In each instance, they struggled to prolong their own survival and did so at times with marked success but also at great cost.

Chapter Seven presents the pervasive violence in the eastern forests as, paradoxically, evidence not of the cessation of cultural exchange but as a primary mode of interethnic commerce. The peculiarities of the encroaching slaveholding Luso-Afro-Brazilian society presented Indians with specific opportunities to impede expansion. They did so by understanding their adversary's culture and translating that understanding into acts orchestrated to achieve the greatest possible effect. Settlers, soldiers, and Indians alike learned and appropriated the rules and techniques of barbarous conduct from one another according to fear-laden assumptions about their respective adversaries. Warring parties found in terror an essential language of contact and communication. This chapter explores this dynamic by disaggregating various types of reported native atrocities. Attacks on property and possessions, on slaves and settlers, and on soldiers in the field are considered as separate issues, each revealing another aspect of the cross-cultural meanings associated with frontier violence, including those attached to the alleged practice of cannibalism. These observations are then extended to retaliatory attacks launched by the Portuguese and characterized by the same inclemency they denounced in their adversaries' actions.

The final chapter, an exploration of the 1808 war and its immediate aftermath, begins by focusing on the sustained ability of the Indians to force settlers to retreat from previously unicorporated lands. Beyond resisting incursions, they attacked weak points on the edge of colonized territory. Close analysis of the geography of the conflict illustrates that this characteristic held true not only for lands recently settled but also those occupied by the Portuguese for decades. More than any other single affront, this strike at the colonial claim to territorial dominion, a claim formalized in royal land grants, demonstrated enduring native proficiencies and convinced captaincy authorities to transform what they described as defensive war into an openly offensive posture. After decades of reluctance, Crown officials now concurred, relinquishing all remaining allegiance to their obsolete policy of maintaining the Forbidden Lands off-limits and, at least at the moment of crisis, all adherence to their official rhetoric of benevolence. Reinterpreting these early nineteenth-century developments in light of the long buildup to declared war, this chapter stresses the many historical continuities of the military response. At the same time, it argues that the coordinated reaction by Crown and captaincy distinguished the 1808 war from an earlier period during which these two seats of colonial authority often strained against one another when crafting policies pertaining to unsettled lands and unconquered indigenous peoples. The policy of military invasion remained in place until 1831 even though its failings quickly became apparent.

In a concluding section, the ambiguous outcome of even this unified drive to subdue remaining strongholds of native resistance informs a series of final considerations about the significance of the frontier in late colonial Brazil. Phrasing the issue in this way echoes, ironically, the famous essay of Frederick Jackson Turner, the towering figure of North American frontier scholarship whose work energized generations of disciples and, later, revisionists not only in the U.S. but also Latin America. Because writing about the frontier inevitably means writing about the birth of the nation-state, one element of its significance must always be the place it occupies, or fails to occupy, in the national psyche and a nationalist historiography. I therefore take up the question of scholarly ambivalence about Brazil's frontier experience along with the subtle process of forgetting about that experience. Both are byproducts of insistent pessimism about the nation's territorial formation, profoundly shaped by racial and economic hierarchies. In this context, I find further cause to reflect on the important implications of Brazilian internal colonization for comparative frontier and Atlantic studies.

The territorial dynamic forged by these multiple phenomena must be understood as part of a broad, ongoing, frequently unsuccessful effort by colonial administrators and the local elite to exert control over the Minas frontier and its straying peoples, be they natives, runaway slaves, or migrating subsistence farmers cut loose from a disintegrating gold-mining complex. The increasing inability to cordon off the Eastern Sertão as restricted territory betrayed the tensions between the Crown, its captaincy governors, their civil and military officials, and the vassals they governed. The presence of slaves as an essential component of the frontier labor force deeply influenced landholders' calculations about the merits of advancing eastward into unincorporated forests. The long struggle to bend free persons of color to the demands of colonization efforts further complicated colonization. Seminomadic aboriginal peoples who had long found a refuge in the Eastern Sertão exercised their own options concerning the proper use of this territory. Frictions stemming from the formation, reproduction, maintenance, and self-defense of these various groups in the wilderness—in short, the discordant territorialization of their respective cultures—accounted for the conflicts documented in this study.

To support this view, the chapters that follow probe beyond the laws, decrees, and official ideologies promulgated by the Crown and its ministers, privileging instead the local origin of frontier policy. They do so by employing diverse unpublished sources from numerous local, state, and national archives in both Brazil and Portugal, including records of frontier expeditions, military correspondence, manuscript maps, property surveys, land grant titles, local census data, wills and testaments, post-mortem estate inventories, judicial proceedings, settlers' petitions, dispatches from Indian villages, ecclesiastical documents, and marriage, birth, and baptism records. The study thereby pinpoints the contact and clash of cultures on the frontier as the source from which official policy emerged rather than the other way around. It stresses the persistence of frontier violence as central to the history of a region and period long considered quiescent in this regard.

The frontier scrutinized in this book bordered Brazil's great gold and diamond fields and divided the South Atlantic's two major mercantile entrepôts, Rio de Janeiro and Salvador da Bahia. As Crown officials recognized, the zone was of singular importance for the entire colony for its geographic and economic cohesion and for its integration into the Atlantic system. Illuminating these connections while applying a more flexible conception of Brazilian territorial incorporation, the following analysis helps situate the Eastern Sertão among other frontiers located at key points along the American perimeter of the Atlantic world, especially those zones where African and indigenous peoples together formed part of the cultural matrix. While every one of these frontiers remained distinct, each also responded to a larger historical process in which states, settlers, slaves, and Indians struggled for control of land, labor, and resources adjoining the wider world.

PART ONE

Colonization

CHAPTER 1

Uncertain Refuge

The Shifting Geography of a Frontier in the Making

A S IN OTHER regions south of the Amazon Basin, Brazilian Indians all but vanish from accounts of the history of Minas Gerais the moment they no longer serve as a foil for the exploits of *bandeirantes*, the famed coastal adventurers whose pursuit of native slaves led to the mineral discoveries of the late seventeenth century.[1] The ensuing rush to the gold fields, which quickly turned to African slaves to replace detribalized natives as laborers, unfolds in historical narratives virtually devoid of indigenous peoples. By the third decade of the eighteenth century—as one historian puts it, articulating a common working assumption—gold seekers had "already penetrated practically all of the forests and sertões, expelling and/or decimating the great majority of the indigenous population."[2] Given this perspective, the absence of Indians from what is known about colonial Minas Gerais becomes understandable if no less misleading. Other topics predominated as scholars focused on the opulent apex of the gold cycle, on the export as opposed to internal economy, on urban rather than rural society, and on the overshadowing presence of the foiled Inconfidência Mineira.

By mid-century, as the gold boom subsided, surviving natives just beyond the fringe of the mining district were becoming the great nemesis of settlers bent on occupying new lands and discovering new sources of wealth, which they hoped would restore their languishing fortunes or simply provide for their subsistence. This was especially true of the Indians who inhabited the Eastern Sertão, first among them the Botocudo. Since the sixteenth century, the region had nourished rumors of untapped riches in gold, diamonds, and emeralds.[3] After the gold boom ended, convinced that the eastern lands would return the captaincy to its former prosperity, government officials became no less determined than many settlers to neutralize Botocudo resistance. As colonists both rich and poor pushed into zones bypassed by the gold rush, they invaded lands the Botocudo and other groups controlled, provoking violent clashes and, ultimately, the prince regent's declared war in 1808.[4] Unmentioned in standard histories of the era, however, is the fact that the war against the Botocudo had its violent origins in expansionist policies set in motion a half century before the royal declaration.

The origin and chronology of the assault on the Indians of the Eastern Sertão are not the only formulations requiring historical reassessment. Crown and local attitudes toward Indians—which were seldom the same—also need to be reexamined, as do notions of geography and regional identity that gave rise to the renewed colonization effort in the direction of the coast. Changes in the region unfolded in a fluid context in which interdependent yet irreconcilable positions concerning the significance of Indian territory vied for predominance and to whose opposing ends Crown policy often proved equally adaptable. Before conquest became legitimate, the policy that forbade activity by colonists in the eastern forests had to be challenged, as did prevailing indigenous policy. Geographic space itself had to be culturally reconstituted, the sertão transformed from a savage wilderness into a beckoning frontier, from an accepted barrier blocking the passage of gold and diamond smugglers into a fertile, gold-laden cornucopia, an Eden or Eldorado, promising sustenance and riches to those who dared seize them. This transformation, like the conquest it engendered, occurred gradually and unevenly, with the notion of the frontier as a desirable deterrent enduring, in a weakened form, into the nineteenth century.

The Formation of a Colonial Frontier

Unlike the Aztec, Maya, and Inca civilizations of Mesoamerica and western South America, the native peoples of Portuguese America, particularly those living beyond the coast, have never attracted the scholarly attention they warrant. Unlike their seminomadic counterparts in inland North America, they have rarely been portrayed as integral, even in counterpoise, to Brazil's late colonial or postcolonial history. Their significance has been ignored with respect both to what they were, adepts of an environment through which the Portuguese moved only inexpertly, and what they were not, a malleable workforce readily molded to the demands of a colonial labor regime. Their multiple and radically divergent cultures and histories, the influence they exerted on colonial development, the intricacies of their highly effective resistance to conquest, and their importance for even a rudimentary comparative understanding of the formation, expansion, and circumscription of the early modern Atlantic world remain poorly understood.[5] Their absence from the history of Brazil's most important colonial zones is part and parcel of this neglect.

Although scholars of a later era posited the Indian's disappearance from Minas Gerais soon after the onset of settlement, inhabitants of the captaincy knew otherwise, to their great consternation, especially those who migrated outward from the urban mining centers as the decline following the bonanza became pronounced. West of the mining district, beyond the São Francisco River, the Kayapó formed a barrier to settlement well past the beginning of the nineteenth century. One official in 1807 described this border area between Minas Gerais and the captaincy of Goiás as an unsettled expanse inhabited solely by "wild heathens who cause great damage to travelers who pass through those lands."[6] South and southeast of the mining district, along its border with the captaincies of São Paulo and Rio de Janeiro, lived the Coropó and Coroado. From the seventeenth century and likely earlier, pressures from settlers in the coastal Campos dos Goitacases region of the lower Muriaé and Paraíba River valleys reverberated inland through this zone. According to some accounts, the Goitacá Indians, from whom the coastal plain took its name, had conquered the inland Coropó and Coroado. According to others, these groups themselves were fragments or "mixtures" of Goitacá bands forced to flee the colonized littoral.[7] During the late 1750s, as the search for gold-bearing and agricultural lands in southeastern Minas intensified, these Indians fought displacement in what one of the era's most respected observers described as a "barbarous and bloody war."[8] Throughout subsequent decades, they responded to settler incursions with a combination of resistance and accommodation. Coroado hostilities in the captaincy of Rio de Janeiro appear to have increased toward the end of the eighteenth century, suggesting that some bands were pushed out of Minas Gerais entirely, prompting clashes with coastal settlers.[9]

However, it was particularly to the east of the central mining district that numerous Indian groups continued to keep the expansionist ambitions of late colonial Minas society in check. Like the Coropó and Coroado—speakers of associated but mutually unintelligible languages of the Macro-Gê linguistic stock—these eastern groups shared many cultural traits, leading contemporaries and, later, historians to confuse one with another. During the second half of the eighteenth century, their world came to be defined not only by confrontations with colonists but with each other as well. As in many regions on the edge of expanding European empires, interethnic and even internecine warfare, catalyzed by competition for dwindling resources, typified the Eastern Sertão as a threatened zone of refuge.[10]

Along with still-independent Coroado Indians, the Puri resolutely held the southern reaches of the tropical and subtropical forests separating Minas Gerais from Brazil's Atlantic coast. Puri domain stretched from the Paraíba River to the low mountains of the Mantiqueira range and the upper tributaries of the Doce River. Reputed to be cannibals, they engaged in perennial conflict with the Coroado and, subsequently, with rivals to the north as their respective territories diminished. In addition to the Puri, ranging roughly from south to north from the Doce to the Pardo River valleys, the Makoni, Malali, Maxakali, Panhame, Kumanaxó, Monoxó, Kutaxó, Kopoxó, Pataxó, and Kamakã inhabited the forests dividing Minas Gerais from Espírito Santo and Bahia's southern *comarcas* (judicial districts) of Ilhéus and Porto Seguro, including portions of the Doce, São Mateus, Mucuri, Jequitinhonha, and Pardo River valleys.[11]

Finally, vying for the territory of these groups and moving across a vast expanse of mountainous terrain extending from the Pomba River north to the Pardo River and beyond, the Aimoré or Botocudo, as they were increasingly called after the middle of the eighteenth century, blocked exploration and settlement. Portrayed both by contemporaries and historians as inveterately hostile, even to other Indians, the Botocudo can be better understood as acting with marked success to secure limited land and natural resources under the pressures of colonization. East of Minas Gerais' border, a boundary then still ill-defined, they controlled much of the interior of Espírito Santo and southern Bahia until well into the nineteenth century. Along with the Puri, they continued to conduct raids in the vicinity of the port city of Vitória. Effective colonization remained limited to a coastal strip rarely extending inland more than four leagues (26 km), according to the French naturalist Auguste de Saint-Hilaire, who traveled throughout the region in the 1810s. As late as 1838, when a well-informed friar set out to the south from Bahia along the coastal route, the Botocudo and others still prevented access to substantial sectors of the highlands beyond the seaboard.[12]

The Portuguese applied the name Botocudo generically to a variety of groups believed, probably erroneously in some cases, to be common descendants of the Aimoré, inland natives who had for two centuries all but stifled settlement of coastal Ilhéus, Porto Seguro, and Espírito Santo before seeking safe haven from the Portuguese deeper in the interior. These groups generally spoke derivatives of the Macro-Gê languages.[13] At times, the Portuguese classified groups like the Pataxó, Maxakali, and Makoni as Botocudo subgroups; other times, they considered them distinct. To this day, no scholarly consensus has emerged.[14] Vexed by the difficulty of systematically distinguishing the various Botocudo "tribes" with their "diverse customs" despite extensive direct contact with them, Saint-Hilaire wrote, "In truth, there exists no bond among all those [groups] that constitute, as a whole, the [Botocudo] nation."[15]

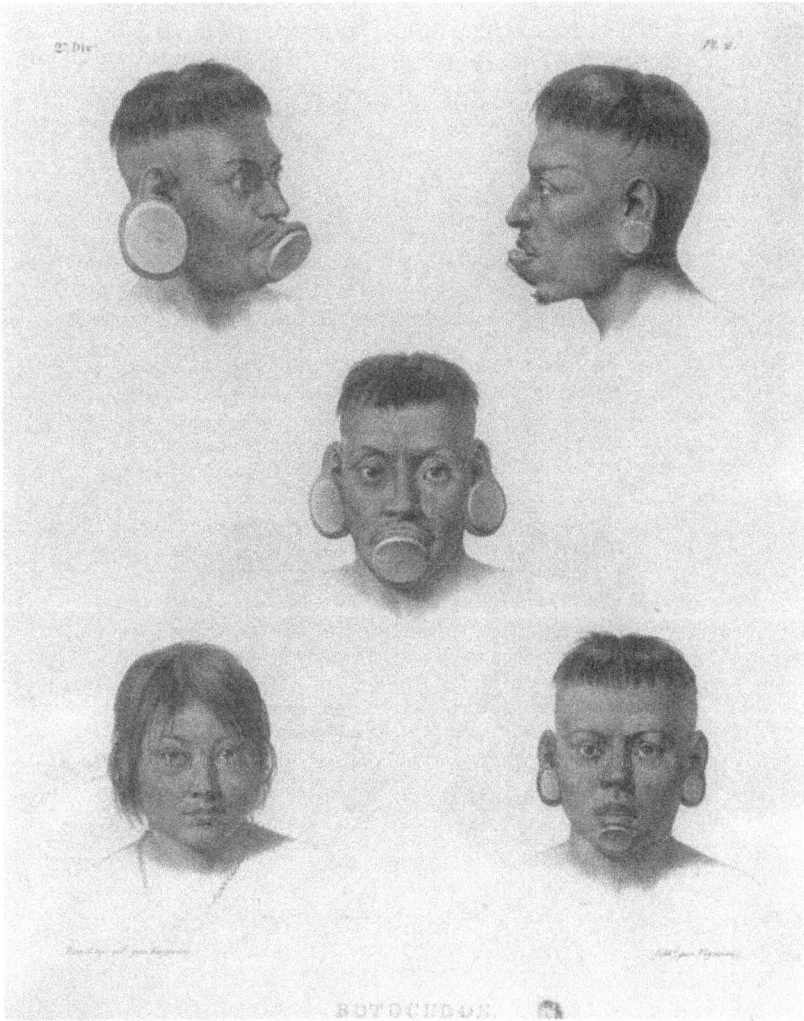

ILLUSTRATION 1.1. The German artist Johann Moritz Rugendas drafted these portraits of Botocudo after traveling to frontier garrisons along the edge of native territory in the 1820s. Viewed as archetypal savage hostiles throughout the colonial period, the Botocudo blocked settlement of Brazil's Atlantic forest, opposition first seen as useful but later condemned

SOURCE: [Johann Moritz] Rugendas, *Voyage pittoresque dans le Brésil*, trans. Mr. de Colbery (Paris: Engelmann, 1835). Biblioteca Nacional, Rio de Janeiro.

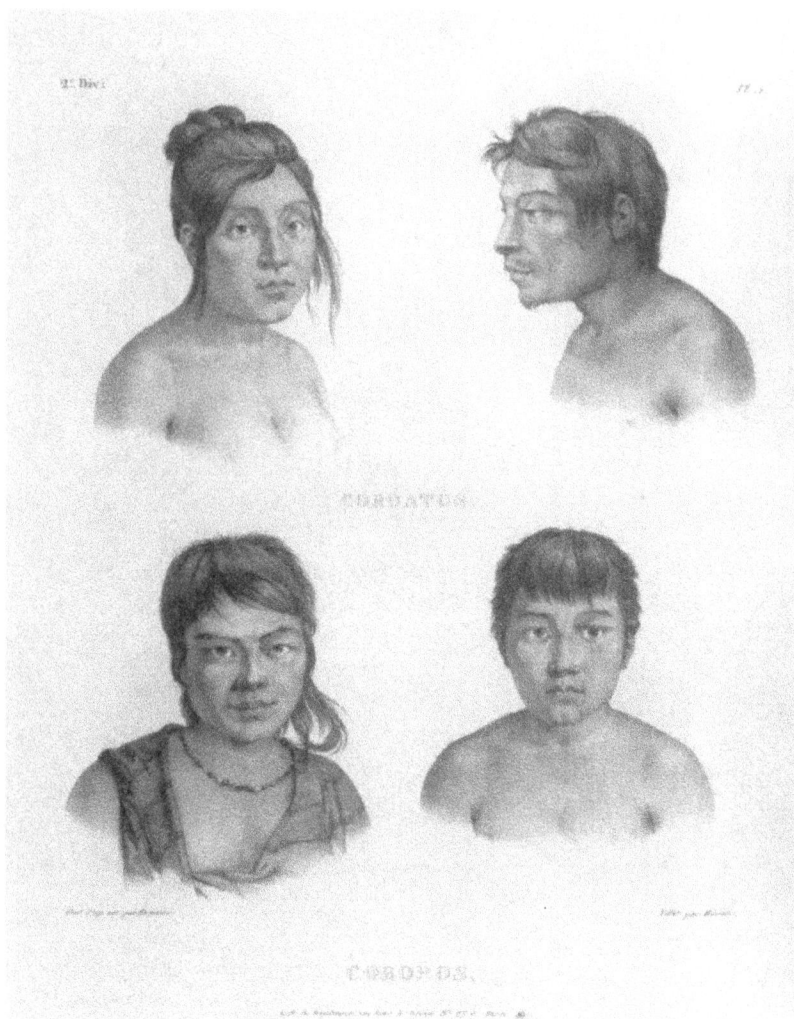

ILLUSTRATION 1.2. The Coroado and Coropo found themselves caught between the fast-growing southeastern captaincies of Rio de Janeiro and Minas Gerais. Faced with extermination, many chose to enter colonial society
SOURCE: Rugendas, *Voyage pittoresque*. Biblioteca Nacional, Rio de Janeiro.

That the name Botocudo had a less than reliable ethnological basis is clear from its origin, even though it must still be employed as colonial sources provide no alternative. According to most scholars, it derived from *botoque* or *batoque*, the Portuguese word for a barrel lid thought to resemble the ornamental wooden

ILLUSTRATION 1.3. Like the Botocudo, the Puri were assailed as irredeemable adversaries of Portuguese settlers
SOURCE: Rugendas, *Voyage pittoresque*. Biblioteca Nacional, Rio de Janeiro.

disk that many, but not all, of these Indians inserted in their ear lobes and lower lips.[16] Other experts cited the adaptation of names the natives used for their own lip and ear ornaments, *betô* and *betô-apôc*, respectively. Another explanation attributed the name to an elision of the Portuguese words *boto* (bulky object) and *côdea* (crust) in reference to the group's supposed corpulence and habit of

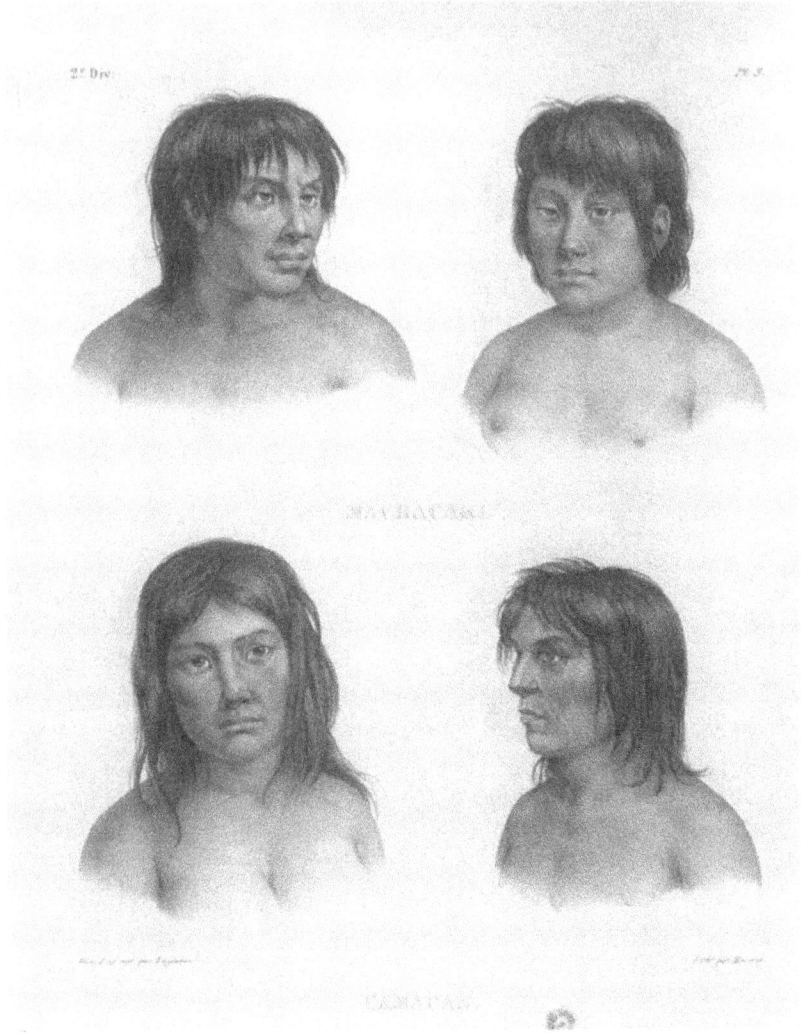

ILLUSTRATION 1.4. Among the numerous ethnic groups occupying the forests sep-
arating inland Minas Gerais from coastal Bahia and Espírito Santo, the Maxakali and
Kamakã struggled against both settler incursions and Botocudo raids
SOURCE: Rugendas, *Voyage pittoresque*. Biblioteca Nacional, Rio de Janeiro.

covering their bodies in hardening copal resin as protection against mosquitoes.
An English merchant who resided in Brazil between 1808 and 1818 offered a
particularly fanciful etymological theory. The Botocudo Indian acquired his
name, the traveler wrote, because of his practice, when in flight, of endeavoring

"to reach the brow of a hill little encumbered with wood, where, dropping on his breech, he puts his head between his knees, and his arms round his ankles." In this position, "being nearly as round as a ball, he precipitates himself from the brow, and rolls speedily to the bottom. From this circumstance . . . the Indians take their modern name of Booticudies, or Butucudies, a barbarous word, half Tupi, half Portuguese, signifying fallers by the breech."[17]

Similar disagreements and essentializing pronouncements pervade the ethnological literature on the Botocudo. Scholarly descriptions of their skin color are another case, with specialists describing the Botocudo on various occasions as "whiter than most other Brazilian Indians"; "not merely light or dark ruddy-brown, but almost quite white, and cheeks even pink"; "yellower than Guaraní"; "nearly as light as the Portuguese"; "whitish yellow"; "light, some even white, with red cheeks"; and "yellowish." Collecting these and other expert opinions and proffering his own, a nineteenth-century British anthropologist concluded the following about the Botocudo complexion:

I have heard it . . . spoken of as a drab, a fawn, a buff, a chamois, a light leathery-brown, and so on. But I consider that the yellowish tinge . . . is unmistakable, and it is this very yellow complexion which, combined with [other] features, imparts both to the Guaraní-Tupi and to the Botocudo that decidedly Mongolic look which has been noted by most observers.[18]

If such assessments verge on the preposterous, so did the colonial habit of grouping diverse peoples together under the rubric of a single, reductive name. In practice, when colonists used the term Botocudo, they collapsed many distinct ethnic groups into one, usually referring to nothing more specific than any one of the numerous indigenous bands of the Eastern Sertão that refused to submit to Portuguese subjugation. The primary exception occurred when colonists sought to focus attention on a particular group, for instance, singling them out as enemies not only of the Portuguese but of other indigenous groups. Thus, in 1800, the priest Francisco da Silva Campos petitioned the Crown for greater aid in the struggle to Christianize Indians, horrified that those whom he labeled the Botocudo had "destroyed through warfare" a series of other "nations" in order to "eat them." Those victimized, he said, included the "Mandali [Malali?], Maxakali, Pendi, Capoxi [Kopoxó], Panhame, . . . Monoxó, [and] Pataxó."[19] The generic term Botocudo, in other words, was synonymous with incorrigible enemy.

The classificatory ambiguity pervading the sources points to what anthropologists describe as coerced tribalization. Like other groups destabilized by colonial expansion in innumerable frontier regions throughout the Americas, the Botocudo *became* an ethnic group to a significant degree as a result of this process.[20] In conjunction with the gradual formation of the frontier itself, they coalesced as an identifiable people largely as a product of their contact with, struggle against, and representation by encroaching settlers. Ethnogenesis, in a word, occurred as colonists ascribed supposed preexisting cultural affinities and affiliations to what were, in fact, distinct indigenous communities.

The persistence of inadequate renderings of these groups in the historiography derives from a dearth of ethnographic studies extending into the second half of the twentieth century. By then, the near extinction of the region's natives and their languages had occurred. Apart from the broadest of characteristics, therefore, frustratingly little has been reported about the historical conduct of the Botocudo and others, a problem the second half of the present study in particular seeks to address. For the present, it suffices to make note of their

ILLUSTRATION 1.5. A Botocudo family on a journey, ca. 1815
SOURCE: Maximilian, Prinz von Wied, *Travels in Brazil in the Years 1815, 1816, 1817* (London: Henry Colburn, 1820). The John Carter Brown Library at Brown University.

ILLUSTRATION 1.6. Puri natives in their shelter, ca. 1815
SOURCE: Maximilian, *Travels in Brazil.* The John Carter Brown Library at Brown University.

seminomadic hunting and foraging, their proclivity for fissuring into small bands, their determined territoriality, and their frequent conflicts with neighboring groups. Mobility and fragmentation themselves help explain the nature of their resistance to colonization, which took the form of isolated ambushes and flight far more frequently than large-scale warfare. Furthermore, the impulse to resist sprang from the most fundamental need to retain an expanse of territory sufficient to ensure physical, social, and cultural reproduction.[21]

As a consequence of such conduct, Portuguese territorial incorporation had stalled in the rugged, forested sertão separating the mining camps from the Atlantic coast, and Indians, especially the Puri, Botocudo, and Pataxó, remained dominant throughout the second half of the eighteenth century. Their persistent presence was in no small part a function of Crown policy. Soon after bandeirantes from São Vicente (later São Paulo) made the first discoveries of significant mineral wealth in the 1690s, the Crown sealed off the Eastern Sertão. The aim was to prevent the smuggling of gold and diamonds to the coast by those seeking to evade heavy taxation. As far as some of the Crown's closest advisors were concerned, such deviousness characterized virtually everyone living in the mining district. Accusations of smuggling, ceaseless over the course of the eighteenth century, required "the most scrupulous investigation," Brazil's viceroy avowed, because "the spirit of the people of Minas is utterly rebellious and lacking in sincerity."[22] Therefore, at least in theory, trade and other overland traffic between the captaincy and the coast were restricted to just three roads rigorously patrolled by soldiers: the first leading southwest to São Paulo and the port of Parati; the second heading south to Rio de Janeiro, the so-called Caminho Novo; and the third leading northeast to Bahia and Pernambuco. Topography largely dictated the location of these routes. Attempts to penetrate the sertão at other points, particularly by way of the most direct route of cutting across Espírito Santo from the Atlantic coast, proved impracticable because of the inaccessibility of the mountains and forests, the lack of easily navigable rivers, and the absence of settlers—out of fear of hostile Indians—to provision travelers. In any case, this is how one contemporary described the problem of access to the mines at the beginning of the eighteenth century.[23] But the determination of the Crown to control smuggling, monitor the flow of gold out of the mines, reap its requisite royal fifth on gold production, and tax exports and imports (including slaves) meant that natural barriers evolved quickly into legal prohibitions.[24]

The state-sponsored formation of a buffer zone free from unauthorized activity additionally served to protect Portugal's New World riches from the predatory inclinations of imperial rivals. France, the most aggressive of Portugal's South Atlantic challengers in the sixteenth and early seventeenth centuries, rekindled Portuguese apprehensions about the vulnerability of the colony just as the gold rush entered its climactic phase. In 1710, a French expeditionary force of some 1200 soldiers led by Jean-François du Clerc staged a doomed invasion of Rio de Janeiro. A year later, the famed Breton corsair René Duguay-Trouin, with nearly 4000 troops, briefly captured and then plundered the coastal city, which had fast become Brazil's leading port for exporting gold and importing slaves and supplies destined for Minas Gerais. In the case of the first attack, forces dispatched from the mining district—composed largely of armed blacks—expelled the French, who had miscalculated that the port would be emptied and thus weakened by the exodus inland to the mines. In the second case, Minas troops again responded zealously but arrived too late to protect the city. These incidents made manifest the urgent need for an effective defensive cordon around the mining district to secure it against Portugal's European enemies.[25]

Spain's longstanding designs on Brazil's contested southern borderlands similarly assumed more pressing significance with the discovery of gold. The threat of a Spanish invasion from the south aimed at seizing the mining zone troubled Portuguese officials not only throughout the first half of the eighteenth century but even after the production of gold began to wane. In negotiations leading to the signing of the Treaty of Madrid in 1750, Portugal ceded to Spain the southern fortress and settlement of Colônia do Sacramento, across the River Plate estuary from Buenos Aires. The move elicited dire warnings from the colony's displaced governor, who predicted that the concession would throw open "the

ILLUSTRATION 1.7. In the eighteenth century, the Portuguese Crown restricted the travel of residents of the mining district to a few authorized routes
SOURCE: Rugendas, *Voyage pittoresque.* Biblioteca Nacional, Rio de Janeiro.

door to which until now our Colônia was the key." The concession would guarantee unhampered access to the "road that runs directly to the sertão of that unknown land" and from there directly to the treasures of Minas Gerais. Alexandre de Gusmão, Portugal's lead negotiator, dismissed such claims. He insisted that Portugal had retained its commitment not only to block access to the mines and prevent smuggling out of them but also to deny the Spaniards and all other European competitors a coastal foothold from which they could "flood Brazil with [imported] contraband and cause us other harm." Provisions in the treaty that strengthened Brazil's southern defenses were more critical for protecting the mining district than the relinquished territory. "Instead of delivering the keys to our mines," Gusmão insisted, "we have to the contrary acquired in that region greater security for them."[26]

Whether for or against the treaty provisions, both arguments rested on the mercantilist orthodoxy that the district should remain closed to all but Portuguese merchants, settlers, soldiers, and government officials. It should be sealed off from the chaotic currents of South Atlantic commerce and imperial competition while simultaneously fortified against internal attempts to circumvent royal control. Prohibitions on all movement through the sertão encircling authorized inland settlements served this dual purpose. A full century would pass after the discovery of gold before the Portuguese Crown would begin to reconsider its insistence on severing all unregulated links between the mining district and South Atlantic commerce. At stake during this prolonged period, as local authorities and the restive peoples they governed tested that policy ever more aggressively, was nothing less than the fate of a massive region, its land and resources, its would-be settlers, its indigenous inhabitants, and, together, their articulation with and relationship to that wider Atlantic world.

Within Minas Gerais itself, just as the discovery of gold determined which regions of the captaincy would become densely populated, the absence of discoveries left other areas all but untouched by colonists where initial exploration failed to uncover accessible mineral wealth. As settlement patterns took shape, the Crown imposed its policy of prohibiting access to these unoccupied zones. Over time, major portions of the unsettled border areas circumscribing the mining district came to be known as the Forbidden Lands.[27] When Minas officials employed this designation, they sometimes referred to the southern reaches of the captaincy. There, the heavily traveled routes to Rio de Janeiro and São Paulo as well as constant pressure from settlers to open new lands made restrictions on movement imperative in the view of authorities bent on surveillance. But it was to the east, the region separating the mining district from Espírito Santo and Bahia, where the connection between the presence of Indians and the prohibition on settlement became most tightly drawn. Mountainous territory covered by dense, primeval forests, this "sertão of the eastern parts," as one governor explained, had been cordoned off and labeled the Forbidden Lands "in accordance with the theory that the said sertões serve as a natural barrier that protects this captaincy against smuggling."[28]

The susceptibility of this verdant sertão to any number of activities incompatible with the dictates of strict colonial supervision meant that the eastern region was among the first to be set off-limits after the gold strikes. In 1700, as news of the discovery of gold rapidly spread, construction of a road linking the mines with the Espírito Santo coast began and then, two years later, abruptly halted on Crown orders. From one point of view, the project made sense. Promising a direct route to the mines, traversing a distance from east to west of some 330 kilometers between the coast and Vila Rica, the road could have served as the primary or even sole access to the mines, all traffic being monitored as it passed through the fortified gateway port of Vila Nova do Espírito Santo (later Vitória). But the opposing view, which prevailed, was that opening this road would make the supervision of all routes more difficult.[29] Addressing these concerns, a 1701 royal edict criminalized all communication, even the transport of cattle and provisions to miners, through the unsupervised coastal forests as far north as Bahia.[30] That the Crown experienced some difficulty stopping what it had begun is clear: Acting on royal authority, the governor of Espírito Santo was forced in 1704, 1710, and again in 1712 to reaffirm the suspension of all exploration or road building in the region.[31] The discovery of precious gems at Tejuco in 1729 brought particularly draconian proscriptions on unofficial activity of any kind throughout what became Brazil's renowned diamond-mining district, which included northern reaches of the Eastern Sertão.[32] Movement away from the captaincy's existing mining camps, particularly colonists' penchant for rushing to remote new sites of rumored gold and diamond discoveries, became the target of royal restrictions in 1730. Soon thereafter, the Crown issued a charter in 1733 (reconfirmed in 1750) that prohibited the opening of new roads to the mines from any direction, not just the east. The first order stipulated banishing to Portuguese Angola those who illegally entered the diamond district; the second, punishing as smugglers anyone who traveled along unauthorized routes. Violators had their possessions seized as presumed contraband and divided equally among the royal treasury and any informants whose collaboration led to arrests.[33] Not until a full century after the initial prohibition did the Crown change positions and finally permit the construction of a number of roads cutting through the Eastern Sertão to the coast, including a route descending the Doce River basin, passing from Vila Rica to Vitória through the heart of Indian territory.[34]

The perimeter of a territory as vast as the Eastern Sertão was impossible to patrol, but colonial authorities did what they could to enforce the ban. In 1761, for example, Governor Gomes Freire de Andrada, the Count of Bobadela (1735–52, 1758–63), learned of the discovery of gold at Cuieté, far to the northeast of Vila Rica. The gold was unearthed by the explorer Domingos José Soares and a dozen of his companions, who formed a bandeira and descended the Doce River. Proceeding eastward to the coast, where they presented a quantity of gold dust to authorities in Vitória, Soares and part of his band were promptly imprisoned for venturing off established roads to prospect in prohibited zones. Five more associates arriving later learned of the arrest and fled north up the coast to the settlement of São Mateus, a town on the river of that name described by their accuser as a bastion of fugitives, smugglers, and murderers, among whom these men were to be included for daring to cross the Eastern Sertão. The town acquired this reputation, at least in part, because it served many other wrongdoers, according to one Minas official, as a stopping point on the contraband route linking the mining district to Atlantic smuggling networks. "One should fear and take precautions against all sorts of smuggling," he said, warning authorities in 1770 that various trails used by outlaws and Indians alike cut through the eastern forests. Avoiding capture by "seeking the most out-of-the-way places," smugglers descended the river valleys to the coast "without impediment" and "free of risk" before heading north, eventually to the port of city of Salvador in Bahia, aided by poor villagers along the way who supplied them with food.[35]

To the south, similar violations also occurred with some regularity, repeatedly provoking renewed efforts by the captaincy government to seal off the forests. In 1778, for instance, Governor Antônio de Noronha (1775–80) learned that one of his district military commanders, without authorization, had allowed a number of men to form and arm a bandeira to enter a mountainous region between the Doce and Paraíba Rivers. Implicated in the illegal action were the militia officer Captain Francisco Pires Farinha and his brother, Manoel Pires Farinha.[36] In charge of a group of settled Coropó and Coroado Indians at the newly established parish of São Manuel da Pomba (Rio Pomba), the Farinhas found their strength bolstered by an influx of settlers to an area until recently dominated both by these Indians and the Puri. Emboldened, they sought to explore outlying zones, including those set off-limits. Noronha reacted after the bandeira, probably manned by settled Indians, set out in search of "a great stretch of open country thought to be rich" in mineral wealth. The governor chastised his district commander and Captain Farinha alike for sanctioning the expedition and thereby potentially opening a route for contraband. Only with Noronha's express permission were bandeiras to be allowed to "penetrate the forests of that sertão," which, the governor reminded his commander, "serve as a wall" separating the captaincy from the coast. Anyone who persisted in such activity would be considered a criminal and imprisoned. Some officials, including those in Lisbon, feared that acculturated Indians in contact with colonists in this zone might be abetting the movement of contraband through the forests.[37]

In this way, over time, the geographic basis of the mining district's settlement patterns and access routes merged with the spatially specific application of colonial power to determine the boundaries of those lands occupied by colonists and, conversely, those where indigenous peoples found refuge and remained dominant. The Crown intentionally sought to turn the zone between the Atlantic and the inland mining district into a kind of forested no-man's-land, peopled by native antagonists whose enmity, forged over the course of two previous centuries of conflict with coastal settlers, would prevent unauthorized access to and smuggling from the mines to the coast.[38]

Crown legislation and the zeal of local governors had to go only so far in constructing such a barrier. The best defense against smuggling was the untracked wilderness itself and its reputedly savage denizens. Although official concerns about illicit activity in the region would never ease entirely, colonial authorities remained convinced that their prohibitions were largely successful, certainly far more so than measures taken to stop contraband along authorized routes like the Caminho Novo. Governor Noronha could declare in the late 1770s that "through the [eastern] forests the smuggling of gold is impracticable given that the nature of the said forests, their breadth, and the wild Indians who inhabit them make impossible the criminal pretension of smugglers in those parts."[39]

Cartography and Conquest

Maps of the region help gauge the effectiveness of this barrier. They reveal how the Eastern Sertão had acquired an ambiguous status as Indian territory over a long period beginning in the sixteenth century. Moreover, they offer a glimpse into the conceptual framework government authorities and their informants projected onto distant forests, mountains, and river valleys. They reveal the changing way this unsettled space was culturally constructed, encoded, and represented, whether through valorization of its resources, demonization of its native inhabitants, or a combination of the two.[40] By the end of the eighteenth century, the official patrons and elite authors of these visual documents had embraced the Enlightenment aspiration for comprehensive and technically perfected cartographic depictions. In the case of the Eastern Sertão, this endeavor promised substantial rewards, as an imprecisely mapped region presumed rich in unearthed minerals revealed its treasures. Not surprisingly, the maps resulting from this effort, many of which remained in manuscript form, represented far from objective spatial renderings. This flaw developed because those who commissioned and crafted these works sought a particular sort of knowledge about territory they hoped to incorporate. Furthermore, they were acutely concerned, to apply the insight of one scholar of Enlightenment cartography, "with the legitimation, reproduction, and perpetuation of a given social order."[41]

The hopes, expectations, fears, and ethnocentrism of colonists were often more in evidence than topographical accuracy, as the creators of these maps sought to possess graphically a territory that remained beyond their grasp physically. With each added detail, each refinement in technique, mapmakers documented and disseminated new knowledge that unwittingly amounted to a challenge to the very royal injunctions that initially infused the eastern forests with special significance. The extensive cartographic oeuvre produced by these regional mapmakers portrayed this frontier as it acquired form in the imagination as well as on the ground. It did so in a constant tug-of-war between Crown prohibitions and the countervailing interest in exploring and exploiting the zone. Mapping reflected this latter interest, but it also prefigured and impelled it.

A preoccupation with depicting the continental interior and its indigenous inhabitants had become evident in the work of famed Portuguese cartographers within the first decades of what began as a sluggish effort to colonize Brazil. As early as 1519, they ornamented their drawings of Brazil's interior with images of Indians pictured as both docile creatures and industrious workers, sometimes nude, sometimes donning elaborate, multicolored garments made of feathers. They drew natives laboring with axes supplied by Europeans, cutting brazilwood, flanked by monkeys and parrots. They linked Indians immediately and inextricably to the extraction of tropical commodities, all three of these forest products—brazilwood, monkeys, and parrots—having entered European markets ahead of Brazilian sugar, whose export had only just begun.[42] Not until the middle of the sixteenth century did representations of Portuguese America's interior begin to bear markings of the most rudimentary topographic features, namely the Amazon River and the River Plate. Scenes of cannibalism, reflecting a more bellicose native demeanor, also first appeared on maps, thereafter becoming commonplace.[43] Surely by chance rather than design did some of the century's most gruesome cartographic scenes appear on a 1562 map in virtually the same zone that would become Brazil's mining district. Naked natives were pictured roasting human body parts on spits, dismembering a corpse splayed on a table, suspending pieces of flesh from the branches of trees, and boiling severed limbs in a great cauldron placed over a raging fire.[44]

Representations of hidden mineral wealth in Brazil's Indian-dominated interior appeared on maps more than half a century before the actual discovery of major gold deposits. Cosmographer João Teixeira Albernaz I included more than one reference to "gold mines" on his 1627 atlas of Brazil. He also drew and labeled the *Serra de Esmeraldas* (Emerald Mountains) in the interior of Bahia, rising up from the coastal plain and extending far southward to the Doce River. In the rugged zone that the Crown would set off-limits after 1700, this royal mapmaker thus gave visual form to reports of a series of epic sixteenth-century expeditions that entered this region in search of precious stones and metals. Such activity would be pursued with redoubled intensity during the second half of the seventeenth century as many of the expeditions departing from the southern captaincy of São Vicente set the stage for the great mineral discoveries of the 1690s. The positioning of indigenous groups on Albernaz's map underscored the perception that access to the anticipated wealth in these alluringly named mountains remained blocked. The Tamoio occupied the land to the south and the Tupinambá the land to the north.[45]

This mapmaker's son, João Teixeira Albernaz II, appears to have made the first prominent cartographic reference to the Indians that would later come to be known as the Botocudo. He referred to them as the Aymore (Aimoré), employing the Tupi name for these non-Tupi peoples, which meant "thief," "killer," or simply "evil one." On his 1666 map of Brazil's central coast, the younger Albernaz drew a range of mountains in the interior of Porto Seguro, labeling them the *Serra dos Aymores*.[46] By then, the Indians who descended from these forested mountains to raid coastal towns and plantations were feared above all others and blamed for depopulating the great stretch of coastline between the mouths of the Pardo and Paraíba Rivers. On maps, in other words, the conviction that Indians formed a barrier to exploration beyond Brazil's central coast and, even more irksome, to the wealth such exploration would surely yield had begun to take visual form.

As late as 1706, Portugal's leading cosmographers had not yet incorporated evidence of the great initial gold strikes on their maps of Brazil.[47] Despite intense official interest in the stream of gold beginning to flow from the Brazilian interior, this discrepancy was to be expected. Portuguese cartography emphasized charting the coast for navigators, not mapping the interior. Even so, descriptions of Indians and untapped riches had already become permanently coupled on maps of the region that would now be designated prohibited territory by the Crown. An ethnography of unfulfilled conquest and a cartography of imagined wealth had converged.

The Portuguese were not alone in their dreams. The same motifs dominated maps of the region authored elsewhere in Europe. Drawn in the first half of the seventeenth century, a map by the master Dutch cartographer Willem Janszoon Blaeu retained the scenes of native atrocities in the Brazilian interior and divided the space just inland from the coast into numerous regions identified by the indigenous groups dwelling in them. The Eastern Sertão bore Indian names from north to south: the Guaymure and the Aymure [Aimoré] (west of Bahia); the Apiapetang, Tapuia [Tapuya], and Margaia (west of Espírito Santo); and the Molopaque and Tououpinanbauti [Tupinambá] (northwest of Rio de Janeiro). During the second half of the century, Joan Blaeu, Willem's son, continued this practice, representing interior river basins with slightly more detail and eventually altering the names of some indigenous groups. The territory controlled by the Indians the Portuguese would later name Botocudo extended far to the west of the São Francisco River, although there is no reason to believe that Blaeu based the extent of their dominion on anything but speculation.[48] On a map of South America engraved in London that circulated widely in the 1720s, the headwaters of the Doce River corresponded with an area labeled as the site of "mines discovered" by the sixteenth-century bandeirante Sebastião Fernandes Tourinho. To the north lay "parts unknown" and to the south, the territory of the "Tupinimbes." Cartographer Herman Moll, claiming access to "the newest and most exact observations," described this map as a rectification of notorious[ly] false" maps engraved and published by "ignorant pretenders."[49] Still devoid of evidence of inland settlement even though the rush to unearth riches had by then lured tens of thousands of migrants and their slaves to Minas Gerais, another map authored by Georg Seutter and distributed in Eastern Europe after 1730 identified the colony's entire immense interior simply as "barbarous Brazil."[50]

At about the same time, a pair of British geographers elaborated on such depictions, melding mapmaking with lurid textual descriptions of Indian savagery. Inland from Brazil's central coast, wrote Charles Brockwell in his 1726 study, *The Natural and Political History of Portugal,* resided hostile natives he called the Guamures.

They devour their own Offspring, and rip up Women with-child to eat the Faetus, and drive Flocks of Men like Herds of Cattle to devour them. They are of a Gygantick Stature, and are said to have been expell'd from their native Country by their Enemies; they wander up and down having no settled Habitations, lying like brute Beasts in the open Fields, their Weapons are large Bows with long Arrows, they never fight openly, but lie in Ambuscade, taking Men by Surprize.[51]

Two decades later, Emanuel Bowen, a British mapmaker and self-described "geographer to His Majesty," evidently relied on Brockwell's natural history for the description of the region published in his monumental *Complete System of Geography.* The map of Brazil he included retained notes on Tourinho's inland gold discovery. Standing between those riches and the South Atlantic were the Aimoré, whom he described as Brazil's "fiercest and most barbarous Indians." They "hunt men as we do wild beasts, and eat all they kill or take," he wrote.

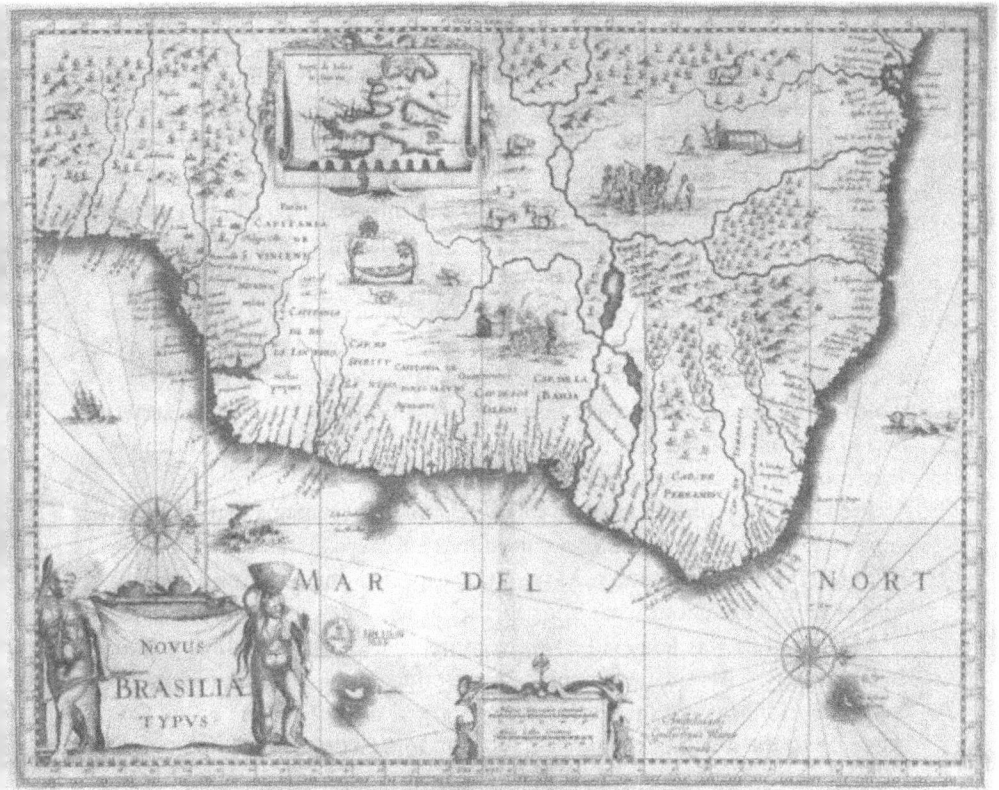

ILLUSTRATION 1.8. Well before the development of Brazil's gold and diamond fields, this Dutch map of Brazil depicted native atrocities and imagined inland regional ethnic divisions [1631?]
SOURCE: Willem Janszoon Blaeu, "Novus Brasiliae Tipus," [1631?]. Biblioteca Nacional, Rio de Janeiro.

"They are even said to eat their own children, and even rip them out of their pregnant women."[52] In much of Europe, no less so than in Minas Gerais, all manner of horrific conduct could be imputed to the alien inhabitants of this scarcely explored geographic zone.

Published European maps evoked the geopolitical importance authorities on both sides of the Atlantic attached to the region. Comprising much of the bulge of Brazil, this forbidden expanse jutted far out into the ocean, sometimes in exaggerated fashion. It constituted a kind of *cordon sanitaire* protecting the colony's great interior mineral wealth. It lay strategically between the distant commercial centers of Salvador da Bahia and Rio de Janeiro, the two major terminals of the South Atlantic slave and commodity trade. Whether pictured as featureless and colorless or inhabited solely by Indians, the zone was not meant by mapmakers to be considered autonomous merely because it remained unoccupied and ungoverned. Rather, lands like these were colonial domain but "until the present still to be occupied," as one legend identified other blank regions on a Portuguese map produced in 1750.[53] Beyond the reach of colonization, such lands were not beyond official claims and imperial aspirations. Portugal had not relinquished its designs on the Eastern Sertão just because it had never been surveyed. Depictions of the territory remained amorphous, particularly on published maps, even as the most precise cartographic rendering of Portuguese America yet progressed in connection with negotiations between Spain and Portugal leading up to the treaties of Madrid (1750) and San Ildefonso (1777), which formalized South American borders. Even on these maps, the Eastern Sertão was still divided into the same archaic ethnic territories the Dutch had used more than a century earlier.[54]

Even as royal prohibitions were solidified, no doubt remains that some new exploration and settlement had occurred in the Eastern Sertão during the first half of the eighteenth century. As might be expected, the resulting accumulation of knowledge about what one geographer termed "the unknown spaces" of Minas Gerais was less evident on comprehensive maps portraying Brazil in its entirety.[55] A 1746 cartographic "description of the continent of meridional America," for instance, erroneously showed the headwaters of the Doce River far to the north of their actual location in a territory inhabited only by "Topiques," or Tupi-speaking peoples. The inaccuracy, both topographic and ethnographic, occurred even though the anonymous mapmaker had based his work on information gathered from "the most experienced *sertanejos*," that is, men of the sertão or backwoodsmen.[56] More narrowly focused and thus less prone to imprecision, manuscript regional maps show that local knowledge of the eastern forests was gradually expanding. By the 1730s, the most prescient among the colony's geographers already surmised that any future occupation of the zone would likely advance not from the coast but in a reverse direction from the increasingly populous interior mining district.[57] Evidence of this advance appeared on an unpublished map dating from the 1750s, when the major discoveries of the gold cycle were already a thing of the past, their alluvial deposits increasingly exhausted. Even at this early stage of the economic crisis that would ensue, regional officials had intensified their gaze on the Eastern Sertão. This map showed many of the Doce River's numerous tributaries. East of Mariana a few towns and parishes marked the landscape, including those of Furquim, Guarapiranga, and Antônio Dias Abaixo. To the north, the parish of Peçanha appeared along the Suaçuí Grande, a major tributary joining the Doce

River roughly halfway along its descent to the sea. A note on the map pinpointed "fields of emeralds," which the unidentified mapmaker described, without irony, as "still to be found." He made no mention of Indians. The barrier that specific native groups posed to settlement was not yet the well-defined, geographically specific problem it would become by the late 1760s. This was also the case on a map illustrating an expedition Governor Luís Diogo Lobo da Silva (1763–8) led in 1764 through the sertão south and west of Vila Rica, a map that also included the Eastern Sertão, to which Silva would turn his attention in constructing an aggressive Indian policy.[58]

Despite signs of increasing exactitude, large portions of the Eastern Sertão remained unmarked, labeled simply "terra incognita," on an undated manuscript map apparently drawn no later than the 1760s. At least in the mind of this anonymous mapmaker, much of the region had been sealed off so well that it could be represented only by reference to the unknown, revealing its secrets no more than had been the case on the earliest maps of Brazil. Nevertheless, on another regional map completed in 1767, marks appeared in an otherwise vacant landscape denoting Indian encampments. As official interest grew with respect to the restricted Eastern Sertão, the presence and precise location of Indians there became an increasingly pertinent subject. Penned in the middle of a nearly featureless expanse, a note by the unknown author of this map described the Botocudo there as "wild heathen" who were impeding attempts to secure the settlement of Cuieté.[59]

Between 1777 and 1780, José Joaquim da Rocha completed the most detailed series of maps of Minas Gerais to date, along with an accompanying text. A Portuguese military engineer, cartographer, and geographer ordered to Minas Gerais by King José I (1750–77) in the 1760s, Rocha invested his work with an Enlightenment passion for vanquishing the unknown. Like other geographers of his era, he fixed his scientific attention on regions beyond the boundaries of incorporated colonial domain, seeking to give them visual form. He strove to illuminate the topographical mysteries these zones encompassed, to classify the unfamiliar autochthons dwelling in them, and, inseparably, to impose an order on these lands and peoples in accordance with European ideals. Like other military men in the inland captaincy, he linked reconnaissance and cartography to the defense, administration, and imperial control of a region strategically critical because of its mineral wealth. He had never balked at the risks this mission demanded of him, he once wrote, appealing to the captaincy governor for fair remuneration. His work had exposed him repeatedly to the threat of "being devoured by beasts while penetrating the densest sertões, with no other interest than the usefulness of service to my Sovereign."[60] Rocha perceived his cartographic enterprise as the foundation for rational recommendations about the captaincy's post-boom malaise, one of the most urgent (in his mind) being the occupation of the Eastern Sertão, which concealed the captaincy's "most precious treasure." He was convinced these hidden riches remained "still to be found, for lack of anyone willing to risk the conquest of the barbarous heathen Botocudos, who are the dominant ones in those sertões, inhabited also by a great variety of other heathen nations."[61]

On a map encompassing the entire captaincy, Rocha depicted a near absence of European settlement in the southeastern and eastern reaches of the captaincy, except for the towns—like so many beads on a string—along the Caminho Novo. Indian encampments were the primary features drawn in the unsettled eastern periphery, apart from schematically rendered forests, mountain ranges, and rivers. Similar sites appeared on the more detailed maps that Rocha drafted of the individual comarcas. Minas Gerais then had four of these judicial districts: Vila Rica, Serro Frio, Rio das Mortes, and Sabará. In the eastern reaches of the northeastern comarca of Serro Frio, Rocha drew groups of red dots to indicate the existence of native villages, describing one of them as the dwelling place of the "heathen Panhame who eat other nations." On the map of the southeastern comarca of Vila Rica, roads now extended into the Doce River watershed all the way to three settlements deep in the forest, São Manuel dos Coroados (Rio Pomba), Abre Campo, and Cuieté.

Rocha adorned his regional maps with elaborate, outsized cartouches depicting Indians in various insinuative poses. Melding the mythological with the historical, these drawings—even more overtly than the maps they decorated—betrayed the tension in Rocha's work between unembellished scientific formality and undeterred imaginings. Infused with symbolism, the cartouches made manifest the colonial endeavor to extend lusophone culture, society, and governance spatially over the unincorporated areas and peoples at the rim of the settled mining district. They bore witness to the colonial imperatives of possession and domination.[62] On the map of the comarca of Sabará (more commonly called Rio das Velhas), a naked warrior crouched and drew his bow, aiming a serrated arrow at a cartographer in Portuguese military dress. The earnest, industrious European soldier, evidently Rocha himself, was pictured preoccupied by the task of plotting compass points, unaware of the threat to his life, single-mindedly carrying Enlightenment praxis into the tropical forest. In radical contrast to the angry warrior, a drawing of a bejeweled Indian princess covered the upper half of the comarca of Vila Rica map. Breasts bared and patterned after the mythical figure America who appeared on innumerable eighteenth-century maps, the young woman sat in a clearing at the edge of the forest. With one hand she motioned freely to an opening in the trees, a gesture of welcome; with the other, she grasped a cornucopia overflowing with fruits of the sertão.[63]

More than simply the artifice of a lone cartographer, Rocha's illustrations represented two sides of an image dear to the Minas elite: an image of Indians as both savage sentinels and naive deliverers of nature's abundance. By no coincidence did Rocha imagine the former as male and the latter as female. Masculinized savagery elevated its own defeat to a prerogative of European heroism and manly honor. Feminized nature encouraged mercantilist infatuation, similarly inviting conquest.[64] Nor by chance did these illustrations capture an emerging vision of the forbidden Eastern Sertão in which the geographic barrier mandated by the Crown increasingly appeared to be an obstruction to the acquisition of hidden riches and the gratification of colonial desires. With the determined action of virile, enlightened colonists, of men undaunted by the irrational violence of Indian warriors, of settlers willing, as Rocha himself put it, "to risk the conquest of the barbarous heathen," the captaincy's post-boom plight would be assuaged. Bountiful, pliant nature would bear fruit and restore Minas Gerais to its former grandeur.

As Rocha made visible the growing anxiety regarding unconquered Indians in eastern Minas Gerais, another mapmaker documented in even greater detail the ongoing, albeit dilatory, penetration of the Eastern Sertão. Although unfinished, as evidenced by half-drawn cartouches and crossed-out and corrected topographic labels, a series of maps by this anonymous figure depicted the advance of colonists who sought subsistence where they failed to find substantial gold, much less glory. These maps identified a still greater number of rivers and their tributaries and delineated many previously unmarked trails linking settlements both new and old. Two trails headed eastward into the sertão from the royal road between Tejuco and Itacambira. Another cut through the forest separating Mariana and Guarapiranga. An interconnecting web of more than half a dozen trails tied together hamlets to the east of Guarapiranga. Two unnamed settlements along the Casca River were linked by a path that continued far down the Doce River watershed to Cuieté. Yet another route veered off in the direction of the upper Casca River to a site labeled "Quilombo," the Portuguese name for a runaway slave community.[65]

To assume that many minor trails and ill-fated settlements escaped the notice of even the most diligent mapmakers seems fair. Even the routes that did enter the cartographic record belied the claim that transport to and from the captaincy could be effectively monitored along its three official thoroughfares. This pertained as well to the official position articulated by the Crown and many captaincy authorities, despite evidence to the contrary, that access to the forests

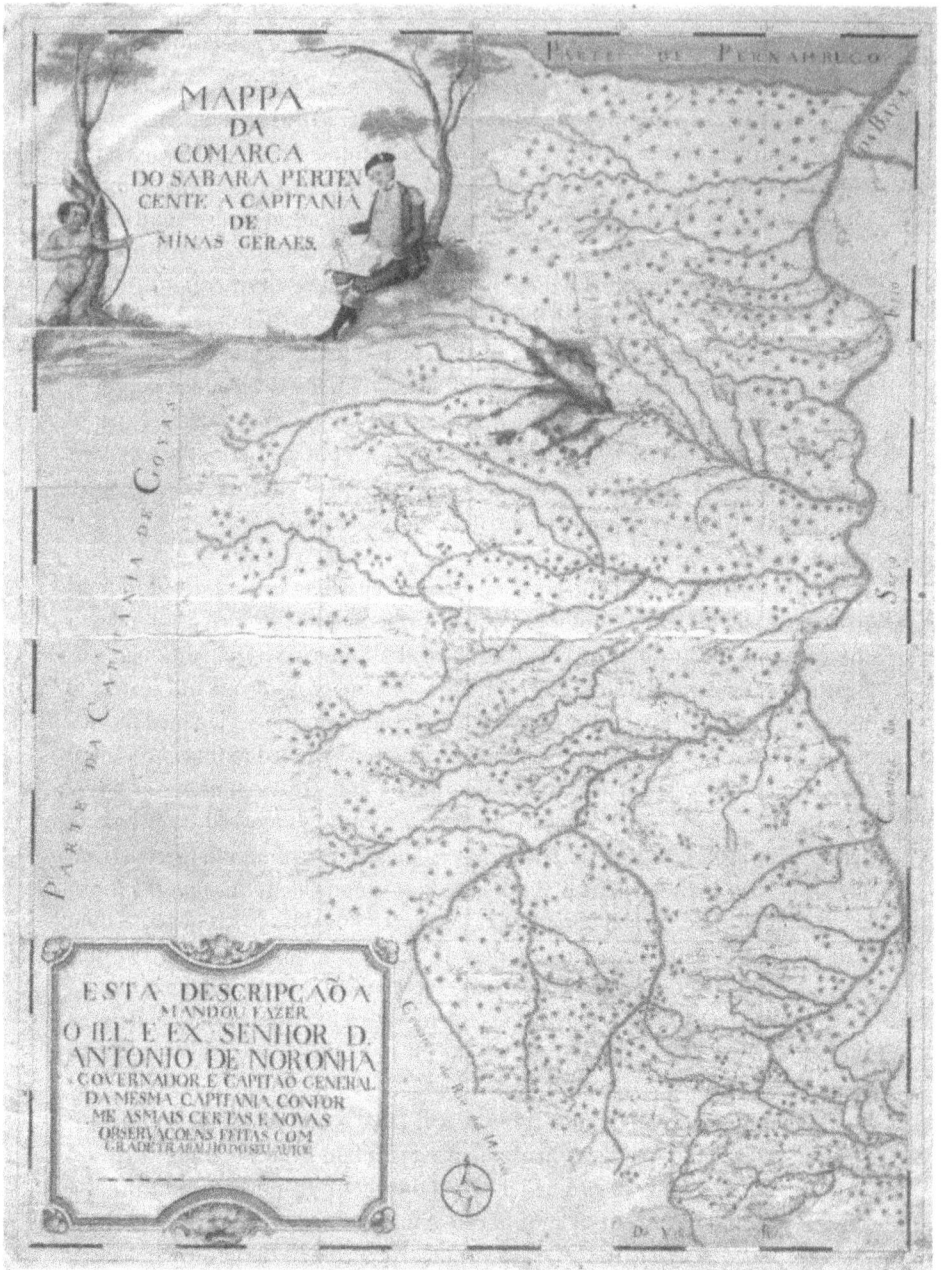

ILLUSTRATION 1.9. This early map of the Sabará region exemplifies the impulse to comprehend the mining district's little-known periphery. The elaborate cartouche portrays the supposed antipathy between native savagery and western rationality, 1777 SOURCE: José Joaquim da Rocha, "Mappa da comarca do Sabará pertencente a capitania de Minas Geraes." Biblioteca Nacional, Rio de Janeiro.

of the Eastern Sertão had been effectively stanched. A few perceptive individuals willing to expose these fallacies realized that royal prohibitions could only inadequately be enforced given the measureless distances of the Minas hinterlands. Alexandre de Gusmão, the brilliant Brazilian-born diplomat and private secretary to José I in Lisbon, had asserted as early as 1750 that the Crown would have to do far more to crack down on contraband as the existing ban on road construction was ineffectual. Minas Gerais, he wrote, had been "penetrated everywhere by trails." A "cordon" of guards comprising "many thousands of men" would no longer be enough to prevent smuggling out of the mining district.[66]

As the illusion of successful geographic containment faded still further after the turn of the nineteenth century, and as attention turned to protecting frontier migrants who might contribute to the captaincy's economic recovery, the official preoccupation with Indians grew increasingly explicit on manuscript regional maps. One detailed map depicted the northern portion of the sertão separating Minas Gerais from Ilhéus and Porto Seguro. The map testified not only to the tenacious Indian presence in the region, and not only to the mounting pressure from settlers, but also to the way that Indians were more unambiguously than ever portrayed as a barrier to legitimate settlement. The map mentioned the plight of *fazendas* (farms) near Peçanha subject to the "invasion of numerous heathen of the Tocoió nation" (apparently a Botocudo subgroup). Elsewhere were zones described as places where "a multitude of heathen Botocudo and others roam," or where the "wild and heathen Pataxó" disrupted settlement, or where the "heathen Amburé [Aimoré] customarily rob fazendas." Also depicted were villages of Tupinambá and Kamakã, both labeled as "fugitives," suggesting they had once occupied lands nearer to Portuguese settlements but had now retreated into more remote reaches of the sertão, seeking refuge in isolation as relations with encroaching settlers hardened.[67] As late as 1810, another anonymous mapmaker described the Eastern Sertão as a territory "in which the heathen Botocudo roam." To their south was territory "peopled by the wild Puri heathens" and "dominated by heathen Guarulho." They had similarly sought sanctuary in isolated forests, ascending the Pomba and Muriaé Rivers from Rio de Janeiro into Minas Gerais, where they had become, according to the mapmaker, the "sole adversary of the Botocudo." It was an erroneous assertion; the Puri, Coroado, and Coropó also clashed with the Botocudo in the same zone. The mapmaker's narrative of interethnic turmoil derived from well known texts of an earlier period. Most notable among these was the *Ensaio econômico* (1794) by the Brazilian and later Portuguese bishop José Joaquim da Cunha de Azeredo Coutinho, who glorified efforts to clear the zone of Indians who fought settlers encroaching from the coast, Coutinho's own family among them.[68]

What maps revealed to be the evolving interconnections of political borders, frontier settlement, and ethnic conflict informs a final observation about the way that these neglected visual documents made conspicuous much that remained obscured in other archival sources. All of these maps showed that no exact political boundary between Minas Gerais and Espírito Santo had been established, so unexplored and unknown was the intervening territory, despite the persistent but haphazard attempts at settlement. In 1780, having completed his ambitious mapping project, Rocha wrote that "between the captaincy of Minas Gerais and that of Espírito Santo there is no known division other than the Ilha da Esperança," a small island along the Doce River. No other border had been established because these were "scarcely penetrated sertões peopled by heathens of various nations."[69] Twenty years later, a rigorous military map of the course of the Doce River pictured the same island and a nearby waterfall between the Manhuaçu and Guandu tributaries, which the mapmaker, Lieutenant Colonel João Baptista dos Santos e Araújo, labeled the "dividing line of the two captaincies." But the lack of such a line immediately to the north and south was further evidence that the administrative boundary had been located only at this single spot.[70] Legislation meant to define and formalize the border, authored in 1800 and confirmed by royal edict in 1816, failed to settle what would evolve into a long dispute between the captaincies that would remain in litigation until the twentieth century. Throughout this period, the contested region would bear the simple designation, "Aimoré Territory."[71]

The connection between Indians and missing borders was again no accident. The unsurveyed division between captaincies, the absence of a line drawn on maps to distinguish one colonial jurisdiction from another, attested both to a vacuum of colonial power and to the continued dominance of the Indian. The captaincy's western border was also not a well-defined dividing line but rather "unsettled sertões" kept vacant by the often hostile Kayapó. The same was true of portions of the southern border with São Paulo, where the Kayapó impeded exploration and colonization at least until the early 1770s.[72] Even the internal divisions between individual comarcas, especially where they coincided with the eastern wilderness, were still "uncertain," lamented Governor Noronha in 1779, because they had been established at a time when these lands were "unsettled, unknown, and inhabited by savage Indians, just as part of them still remain."[73] Above all, the lands between Minas Gerais and the coastal captaincies constituted an uninhabited "desert," as one contemporary put it.[74] There, in place of a formal border, the Crown and, with varying degrees of cooperation, captaincy officials had attempted to create another sort of jurisdictional authority—one of enforced absence.

In the process, they fashioned imaginary lines no less significant than political borders, lines that separated the established mining territory from Indian domain and Indian domain from the thinly settled coast. These lines, shifting over time, divided and defined identities, both regional and colonial, in accordance with patterns as old as the Portuguese colonization of Brazil itself. The boundaries between settled and nomadic societies—between commercial and kinship-based economies, between (in terms used by colonists) the Christian and the heathen, the civilized and the savage—emerged from and then reinforced the oppositions central to the fluid dynamics of frontier containment and conquest on the eastern edge of the mining district. A territory long deemed terra incognita thus assumed a significance far beyond the geographic confines that gave rise to its sparse settlement pattern and to the concerns over smuggling and surveillance that prolonged its status as a frontier. Slowly taking shape, configured and reconfigured by a progression of mapmakers, the region emerged topographically, discursively, and pictorially in conjunction with the ever-present conflict between the colonial "self" and the indigenous "other." Restrictions on the region's settlement came to represent the contested limits of state power. The maps that made this process visible contributed to its gathering import. They illustrated a nexus of economic aspiration, political consolidation, and ethnic and cultural antagonism as these impulses assumed territorial form throughout the peripheral spaces of the Eastern Sertão.

Heathens and Hidden Gold

As close analysis of the cartographic record substantiates, no matter how determined the Crown policy of cordoning off the region, no matter how unequivocal the assertions by captaincy officials guaranteeing the policy's implementation, ample reason exists to question the supposed impenetrability of this imposing expanse of wilderness and Indians. This truth militates against accepting as historical fact the geographic divisions colonial officials managed, only with partial success, to impose in practice. This truth does not suggest the divide they sought to enforce was entirely or even primarily imagined, a mere fiction captaincy governors created in their eagerness to reassure a Crown obsessed with preventing contraband. In the Eastern Sertão, as in all early modern frontier settings on the rim of the Atlantic world, geographic and especially cultural boundaries turned out to be extraordinarily difficult to consolidate and maintain. The lines separating colonist from Indian proved highly unstable, and the official ban on crossing into Indian territory played no small role in creating the conditions for its own violation. Both the ban and the cultural cleavages that were its counterpart accentuated the most threatening depiction of the Indian and, alternately, the most enticing image of the land Indians occupied.

The more the Portuguese succeeded in creating a zone—even the perception of such a zone—off-limits to settled, "civilized" society, the more the Indians who lived there would be categorized as "uncivilized," no matter whether they resisted, fled, tolerated, or welcomed the presence of colonists. To the degree the Indians were identified with the impenetrable "interior of the sertões," they would be seen as a part of savage nature, as "wild" and "inhuman," as "irrational beasts" or even "more fearful than the beasts themselves."[75] Differentiating the useful threat they posed to renegade smugglers from the intolerable impediment they represented to settlers became increasingly difficult. As a local priest wrote, the Indians occupying the Eastern Sertão were "perverse bandits," "enemies," and otherwise "malefactors" who "scandalously persist in being our execution-ers and the capital enemies of the civil and human contract."[76] Of course, he overlooked the fact that it was precisely these characteristics that were supposed to serve official purposes. But such purposes did not preclude a concomitant outrage at the Indian presence. Captaincy officials themselves came to view the Indians as indomitable not because they were—in many instances, they demon-strated a willingness to cooperate when conditions suited them—but precisely because of the prohibitions designed to cordon off their territory. The more the Indians seemed to exercise unchallenged control of the Eastern Sertão, the more they inspired terror in the minds of colonists, officials included. A policy designed to create a barrier to smuggling also created fear, racial polarization, and an irrepressible impetus for conquest.

Another consequence of the ban on entering the Eastern Sertão, and another way it undermined itself, was the status the region acquired—nothing short of mythical—of a place of unparalleled fecundity. As long as substantial portions of the region remained terra incognita, unexplored and unknown, and aggres-sively portrayed as such, colonists could sustain the same longings and fantasies that drove the conquest of the Americas from the beginning, inscribing them on the still unconquered mountains, forests, and river valleys separating the mining district from the sea. Colonists came to prize the region in direct proportion to the impenetrability of the barrier, both real and perceived, created by its in-digenous occupants. The notion of terra incognita melded seamlessly with what the Portuguese referred to as "*haveres incognitos*," unknown riches presumed to be concealed by Indians in their mysterious dwelling places.[77] As indicated, on maps this preoccupation took the form, for example, of the note describing emeralds "still to be discovered."[78] The sertão would be described as "salubri-ous" and laden with "hidden wealth," holding the promise of future settlement and abundance and simultaneously as a place "infested by the Puri," as though they were so many ants or mosquitoes, or as a place corrupted by a pervasive "fear of the wild Indians of the Botocudo nation" and thus uninhabitable.[79]

Extolling the economic potential of the Eastern Sertão in 1798, the memorialist José Eloi Ottoni prophesied the discovery of riches surpassing all of the gold and diamonds previously extracted from Minas Gerais. "The greatest treasures are yet to be discovered," he wrote. The Indians themselves had transmitted news of this untapped wealth, not only mineral but agricultural, whose existence had been confirmed by backwoodsmen who visited the Indians in their villages. "The fertility of the soil," continued Ottoni, "is such that the greater part of our crops grow spontaneously without cultivation, requiring only the provident effects of wise nature, which, perhaps anticipating the inertia of the Indians, conserves for the benefit of humanity the root and the seed." Left alone, the fruits of the earth came "at their proper time to produce in their own season. What incomparable wealth agriculture promises us in that land!" If the mere presence of Indians was enough to elicit outrage, the possibility that they were preventing the Portuguese from obtaining concealed riches went beyond all toleration. To rectify the unacceptable, Ottoni called on the Crown to promote a new era of the bandeira, encouraging a new generation of explorers to enter the forests in search of gold: "I would be in favor of animating the bandeiristas [*sic*], stimulating the project of making new discoveries by means of favors, privileges, and grants conceded to those who, inflamed by patriotic zeal, enter into the forests." The result would be the definitive Portuguese possession of the Eastern Sertão and the ushering in of an era of unprecedented prosperity. Ottoni's image echoed a central myth that galvanized the European conquest of the New World and particularly Brazil, that of the existence of and consequent search for an earthly paradise, a lost Eden, especially one whose fecundity rendered human labor unnecessary. It also spoke to another powerful and paradoxical belief, that the Indians who occupied that paradise consorted with the Devil.[80]

Economic hardship in the post-boom mining district contributed to proposals like Ottoni's, which advocated the abandonment of what by his time was a century-old policy of sealing off the Eastern Sertão. That he identified the Indians who controlled the territory not as unwitting accomplices in the Crown's efforts to control contraband but as backward savages blocking the discovery of new sources of wealth can be attributed to the pressing problem of counteracting the disintegration of the gold economy. The depletion of the mines made it increasingly difficult for colonists, whether they were individual settlers or captaincy authorities, to abide by the territorial restrictions established by the Crown.[81] Indeed, migration to the frontier must be understood in the context of the various economic activities—including ranching, agriculture, small-scale commerce, light manufacturing, and interregional trade—that revisionist scholars have identified as strategies successfully adopted to counter mining's decline and ameliorate its traumatic consequences.[82] Drawn to the sertão by images of undiscovered wealth, many colonists were also impelled there by precarious economic conditions.

By the beginning of the nineteenth century, a growing consensus identified the opening of both the Doce and Jequitinhonha River valleys, not only to gold and diamond exploration but to all manner of commerce, as nothing less than a necessity for future prosperity. This conviction extended beyond Minas Gerais to Crown ministers in Lisbon and to captaincy officials in Espírito Santo and Bahia.[83] "Everything will take on a new vigor," wrote the naturalist José Vieira Couto, calling for the development of these commercial corridors to the sea in a report to the Crown on stimulating the Minas economy. The activity of farmers, miners, and merchants in these regions would "fill the coffers of the state," he asserted. "What abundance, what new sources of wealth! And today these rivers serve only as drinking places for the ugly monsters and dispersed bands of barbarous people who inhabit their shadowy banks."[84] The long-held notion that the wilderness barrier served the interests of the state was now rapidly giving way to the view that little had been attempted by way of territorial expansion, that Indian resistance was largely responsible for frustrating moves to exploit the region's wealth, and that trade with the coastal population and the Atlantic world, not hidden gold, held the key to restoring the captaincy to its former prosperity. Expressing the frustrated sense of land-locked isolation and the deprecating view of the Indians that went hand in hand with this perspective, Couto described the Eastern Sertão as "an extensive cordon of dense forests inhabited solely by barbarous and wild peoples," which "runs along the entire eastern side" of the captaincy and which "prevents communication" between Minas Gerais and the Atlantic coast.[85]

A revulsion of Indians, an Edenic vision of nature, and a sense of economic calamity combined in the form of increasingly strident reports outlining how to reverse the captaincy's alleged descent into decadence by focusing on lands still controlled by Indians. In 1805, Basilio Teixeira Cardoso de Sá Vedra Freire wrote one such diatribe to the monarch's Overseas Council. One key to bolstering the captaincy economy, wrote Freire, was to focus on lands the Botocudo dominated. The "wildest" Indians of Brazil, the Botocudo, continued to occupy an "immeasurable territory," especially along the banks of the Doce River. This land was "constantly reputed to be very rich in gold and very fertile in every kind of crop," Freire continued. "Once the heathens are expelled, the river opened up, and settlements made capable of resisting the same heathens," the region would provide a dwelling place for the "many laborers, either useless or harmful, who impregnate this captaincy." Freire reported with evident outrage the tale of a parish vicar who attempted with some companions to expand their land holdings into the sertão but Botocudo "incursions" forced them to retreat after enduring "many losses and cruel deaths." The Crown, he insisted, should come to the aid of such individuals.[86]

Writing to the governor two years later, Diogo Pereira Ribeiro de Vasconcelos called for the Doce River to be opened to navigation in accordance with a plan previously initiated but implemented with little success. Recognizing that barriers both "moral and physical" stood in the way, he nevertheless urged officials to move aggressively. "Incalculable are the advantages in terms of exports and imports that can come to the captaincy by way of navigation" of the rivers linking Minas Gerais to the coast, argued Vasconcelos, a Portuguese-born member of the local elite who occupied numerous high government posts. "Apart from commerce, we would equally obtain the vast riches that cover those lands." The entire region through which the Doce flowed constituted nothing less than "a new India," so abundant were its precious stones and metals. No previous governor had succeeded in securing and populating the region, Vasconcelos continued, conveniently ignoring the history of Crown prohibitions on settling the region. Travel along the Doce River remained blocked by the "hostilities of cannibals," which could be countered once and for all only with "sufficient military force." A military solution would guarantee settlement of the riverbanks and safe portage around impassable falls and rapids. All peaceful methods, however, were doomed to failure. "The Botocudo, devourers of animals of their same species, insensible to the voices of reason and humanity that invite them to participate in society, should be offensively hunted down and run through with knives, until such evils subject the remainder of them to their obligations." The use of force would "effect what through kindness we have been unable to achieve," Vasconcelos continued, and he concluded with what he called a general rule: "Force is appropriate for men incapable of education and principled action."[87]

Such arguments contributed to a hardening of indigenous policy during the final years leading up to the 1808 declared war, convincing top administrators of the Portuguese empire that the Indians, living as they did "among the wild animals of Brazil," as one priest submitted in a passionate appeal to the Crown, did not "understand their own unhappiness." They were "victims of a stupidity inherited from their parents" and would never become fully human until they engaged in "the commerce of policed nations, living content under the happy vassalage of the Crown of Portugal." [88] Yet a striking incongruity exists between these belated calls for conquest and the events that preceded them. On the imperial level, the Crown policy of maintaining the sertão as a barrier to contraband continued in force, although feebly, until the early nineteenth century. On the regional level, the systematic military conquest of the Eastern Sertão began in the mid-1760s. The long-standing royal prohibition did not stop local authorities from responding to the pressures of an increasing number of miners, farmers, and ranchers, especially in the face of dwindling gold production, by forging an incompatible policy of opening the territory to exploration and settlement. All activity in the region, every facet of relations among the state, settlers, and Indians, would be informed by the inevitable tensions inherent in these opposing objectives.

This analysis should not suggest that Crown prohibitions had no effect at all; in fact, their continued potency tended to limit the range of possible relations between the Portuguese and Indians, elevating oppositional and violent interactions above all others. As a paradoxical result of the Forbidden Lands policy, recourse to force came to define the period, the region, and the nature of attempts initiated locally to explore and occupy the zone. Nor should this interpretation be construed as implying that violence was a new phenomenon in this zone. Inland native forest dwellers clashed with the coastal Tupinambá Indians before the Portuguese ever arrived. They did so also with the inhabitants of the first seaboard settlements in the sixteenth century, an encounter that had driven many Indians deeper into the forests in the first place, causing them, as one eighteenth-century observer wrote, to "desert the seashore...and retreat into sertões made inaccessible by distance, mountains, and impenetrable forests."[89] They subsequently fought with bandeirantes who explored the region during the sixteenth and seventeenth centuries and with prospectors, farmers, and ranchers who probed the eastern edge of the mining zone during the first half of the eighteenth century.[90] However, the assault on Indian territory in the second half of the century exceeded in magnitude and destructive consequences all of these earlier conflicts as an organized and prolonged effort to incorporate the zone into the colonial domain developed for the first time, despite Crown restrictions.

CHAPTER 2

Ordered Space, Disorderly Peoples

Challenging Portugal's Frontier Policies

T HE COLONIAL AMBIVALENCE over opening and occupying the Indian lands of the Eastern Sertão resulted in a progression of conflicts. As historical actors worked at cross-purposes, they set in motion a process as entangled and forbidding as the tropical forests they found so fascinating. Considered together in the broad context of the second half of the eighteenth century, the actions of captaincy governors revealed a basic truth. From the 1760s forward, notwithstanding continual delays, hesitations, temporary reversals, and contradictory pronouncements, the Crown-appointed leaders of the inland mining district's colonial administration pursued a pattern of invading indigenous territory and attacking its seminomadic occupants. Deeply rooted cultural preconceptions nurtured the making of maps and the crafting of discourse that linked Indians to undiscovered wealth. Moreover, images and words did not circulate in isolation. Resolute action undergirded both of these expressions of regional transformation, setting the course for the attempted occupation of the Eastern Sertão. Having contrived a cultural construct of a wilderness both alluring and appalling, local authorities would not be content merely to ponder this creation and remain confined to previously settled areas. As their new vision of the Eastern Sertão took hold, they set out to secure and subdue the unknown spaces they perceived as a panacea to present ills. Cautiously yet doggedly, questioning, circumventing, and ultimately undermining Crown restrictions on eastward expansion, they set in motion the conquest of a wilderness they increasingly infused with significance.

Remarkably little of the attendant frontier activity has been recorded in regional or national histories. A few prominent examples of standard scholarly perspectives will serve to illustrate this lapse. Kenneth Maxwell, whose study of

Minas Gerais during the second half of the eighteenth century retains its defining historiographical status, wrote briefly but unequivocally: "The River Doce valley was the undisputed territory of the ferocious Aimoré [Botocudo] Indians." Before Maxwell, the distinguished Brazilian scholar Caio Prado Júnior offered somewhat greater detail. The sertão separating Minas Gerais from the coast, he asserted, "remained under the near-absolute dominion of the Indians, who preserved their independence from the Contas River to south of the Doce." Apart from the northern diamond district centered on Minas Novas and some minor gold-mining activity in the vicinity of Peçanha, the Eastern Sertão was "a desert," the Crown having "completely closed off the region" to prevent smuggling. North of the Paraíba River valley, "the forests remained intact, occupied solely by tribes of savage Indians." Only at the end of the century, according to Prado, did any significant advance into the sertão east of Minas Novas occur. Expansion in the Doce River region began only after the beginning of the next century. The "bellicosity" of the Indians who roamed these zones, attacking settlers both in Minas Gerais and along the coast, would not be countered by the Portuguese in a "general and systematic action" until the early nineteenth century, that is, until the 1808 military assault. In turn, Prado took his cue from earlier scholars such as Diogo de Vasconcelos, considered the founder of the modern historiography of colonial Minas Gerais. Writing in the early twentieth century, Vasconcelos described the eastern forests as "rigorously conserved, access to them impeded as a barrier against smuggling, and for this reason called Forbidden Lands." Finally, statements like these originated in official colonial-period sources— the 1780 historical geography of the cartographer José Joaquim da Rocha, for instance, which described the Botocudo as "absolute dominators" of the forests around Cuieté.[1]

Turning to the realm of frontier policymaking, this chapter proposes a very different analysis of developments that defined the half-century preceding the prince regent's 1808 declaration of war against the region's indigenous inhabitants. It does so with the objective of correcting the customary inattention to the enormous effort devoted to and multiple conflicts engendered by late colonial territorial expansion. Efforts by captaincy governors and their administrative subordinates, beginning in the 1760s, amounted to the very thing historians have contended the era lacked: a methodical and prolonged, if not always consistent or successful, scheme to colonize the Eastern Sertão. Even though regional authorities could not count on unequivocal royal support for their plan—which would come only later—they displayed a perennial and decisive "bellicosity" of their own, predating the Crown's, as they embarked on a campaign to project colonial society into the Eastern Sertão. The success of this campaign hinged on incapacitating the region's native population. Animated by crystallizing, spatially specific images of heathens and hidden gold, compelled to answer to settler demands, determined to avoid post-boom social, political, and economic upheaval, local officials set out to transform this forested geographic space into a field of conquest. In so doing, they exposed the limits of royal authority by refashioning Crown indigenous and frontier policy to serve captaincy needs.

By probing this divergence between Crown and captaincy, thereby rejecting all presumptions of a monolithic colonial administrative apparatus, this chapter explores the local innovations upon which the occupation of the Forbidden Lands found its footing. The relationship between the state and the Indians represented only one component of what amounted to a transatlantic tug-of-war over the frontier's status and significance. That is, the modification in Minas Gerais of Crown indigenous policy was one aspect of a much broader elaboration of a new locally based frontier project. No less vital to this project was the need to encourage, direct, monitor, and discipline frontier settlers. As Minas authorities narrowed their sights to Indian lands in hopes of reclaiming a golden age perceived as vanishing, official action concerning settlers concentrated on two distinct social sectors. First, captaincy officials sought to identify and safeguard settlers of comparatively significant means and to make sure that they occupied the sertão in ways consistent with the colony's traditional extractive, mercantile origins and its dominant slave-based social order. Second, where such settlers were in short supply as a consequence of obstacles that hindered the extension of that desired order into the wilderness, authorities turned to an otherwise suspect sector of the colonial population to advance this task. They strove to deploy, often at great distances from the mining district's settled areas, a coerced, compliant legion of workers who were free but poor and largely of African descent. As in the case of Crown policies regarding Indians, those governing the status of both slaveholding society and this marginalized underclass were subject to adaptation and revision by Minas officials bent on promoting the colonization of selected sectors of the Eastern Sertão.

Whether aimed at indigenous seminomads, landholders and their slaves, or landless free laborers, the local variants of royal policies presupposed the imposition of a set of elaborate social controls designed to reconfigure territory previously lying outside the captaincy ambit. Indians would be forced to relinquish key portions of their as yet unincorporated lands. Frontier slaveholders and their captive workers would have to conform to established regimes that regulated their activities in the captaincy's settled zones. The highly mobile free poor—the vagabonds (*vadios*) and "useless people" (*os inúteis*), as the Portuguese elite called them—would be located, pursued, rounded up, and

ILLUSTRATION 2.1. The mining district racial hierarchy: slaves washing for dia-
monds along the Jequitinhonha River, ca. 1808
SOURCES: John Mawe, *Travels in the Interior of Brazil, Particularly in the Gold and
Diamond Districts of that Country* (London: Longman, et al., 1812). The John Carter
Brown Library at Brown University.

transported to designated mining and agricultural sites, and then finally fixed in place in regions still subject to Indian hostilities. In short, several categories of peoples inclined to disorder, by official standards, would be controlled by imposing established structures, both social and spatial, on certain areas of the frontier. If Indians were to remain anywhere near these zones—the same lands from which Crown policy had long encouraged them to repel Portuguese trespassers—they would have to learn new lessons about the consequences of hostile behavior. If slaveholders, their slaves, and accompanying unattached free laborers were to enter these restricted areas, they would do so under carefully regulated conditions and the closest official surveillance.

Pursuing these objectives, captaincy authorities reshaped, sometimes unintentionally, the prevailing frontier policies of the Portuguese Crown and, in the process, the very nature of the Forbidden Lands. The locally driven social and geographic restructuring of the frontier entailed pushing the eastern edge of the settled mining district outward toward the Atlantic coast. As slaveholders searched for new mineral deposits or redeployed their bondsmen from mining into agricultural enterprises, they would consolidate an outlying hinterland in newly incorporated tracts of the eastern forests. Society in this hinterland would be divided as strictly as possible into Portuguese masters and African slaves. This binary model was held up by authorities as an ideal in previously settled zones, even if they could never entirely create it in practice. The freeborn poor, a primary cause of the model's insufficiency, would preferably attach themselves to property owners as dependents, which the Portuguese called *agregados*. Beyond this hinterland, farther to the east, officials would work to establish a transitional zone peopled by expendable poor freemen, condemned and coerced as vadios, who would labor in areas too dangerous for slaveholders and their costly captive workforce. At sites even more remote, where gold or precious stones were discovered, isolated outposts structured to replicate colonial society would be established for slaveholders and defended, once again, by the marginalized free poor. Elsewhere, the wilderness between the hinterland, the frontier outposts, and the Atlantic coast would continue to be preserved as a no-man's-land in accordance with royal dictates (see Figure 2.1). This reconfiguration of territory that the Crown and its ministers in Lisbon had sought to keep entirely off-limits represented a substantially idealized creation of captaincy officials, much as maps of the sertão portrayed largely imagined constructions of space. Landholding settlers, landless migrants, and Indians themselves would insist on pursuing incompatible territorial ambitions. For this reason, a key feature of the new policies promulgated by the captaincy administration was that they set in motion conflicts involving all sectors of this nascent frontier society.

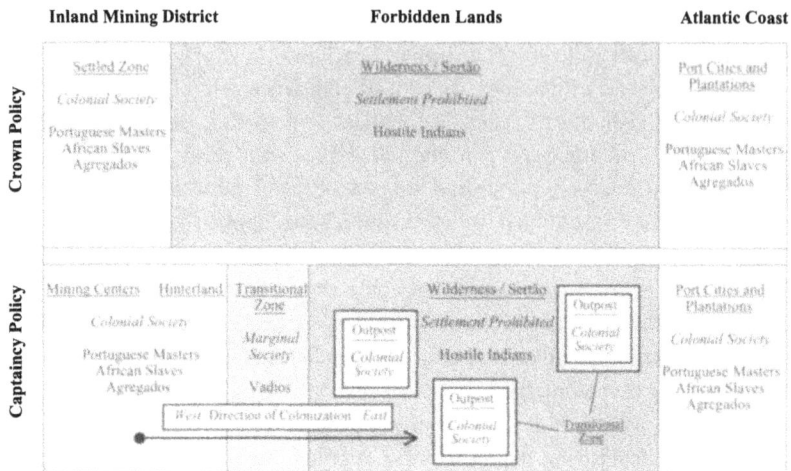

FIG. 2.1. Divergent Crown and Captaincy Frontier Geographies, ca. 1770

NOTE: Colonial authorities defined agregados as free, landless, dependents. Vadios were also free and landless, but autonomous and thus a threat to the social order; even more than agregados, they were assumed to be poor and of African descent.

Recasting Crown Indian Policy

Out of the pliant corpus of colonial indigenous legislation, Minas officials forged the legal authority they required to justify the occupation of the Eastern Sertão even as Crown territorial prohibitions explicitly forbade such a project. In the early 1760s, Governor Silva interpreted the existing laws governing Indian relations as comprising part of what he called his "royal orders" to march into the untracked forests.[2] The indigenous policy operating at the time had been formulated during the previous decade, beginning in April 1755 with a royal edict designed, in the contradictory spirit of Portuguese enlightened despotism, to end racial persecution of the native peoples of the Amazon Basin while speeding their assimilation. Emblematic of a long tradition of paternalistic legislation benevolent in word but repressive in deed, the edict outlawed the use of the derogatory term *caboclo* (half-breed), encouraged mixed-race marriages between Indians and whites, and sought to eliminate the stigma attached to children of such miscegenation, promising them preferential treatment in the allocation of royal favors as well as equal eligibility for "any employment, honor or dignity."[3] On June 6, 1755, José I promulgated a second law, the so-called Law of Liberty, that restored to the Indians, specifically those living in Jesuit-controlled *aldeias* (villages), "the liberty of their persons, possessions, and commerce."[4] The law swept aside, at least on paper, what the monarch deemed to be the abusive practices, including forced labor and enslavement, that these Indians had been subjected to for more than two centuries. Granted political autonomy and ownership of their village land, they could now (theoretically, at least) choose to work for whomever they chose, and at fair wages. The reform's hidden agenda then became clear: On June 7, the king stripped the Jesuits of all temporal powers they exercised over Indian villages, restricting the missionaries to ecclesiastical activities alone, and threw open the villages to trade with the outside world.[5] For the Indians, as one historian of the Amazon has observed, this putative "emancipation" represented little more than a legal device to speed their "forced integration" into colonial society.[6]

As legislation advanced by the king's autocratic minister Sebastião José de Carvalho e Melo, future marquis of Pombal (1750–77), Indian liberation was designed to check the wealth and power of the Jesuits, to bolster the ailing economy of northern Portuguese America, and to secure geopolitical advantage against the Spaniards in the strategic Amazon Basin following the conclusion in 1750 of the Treaty of Madrid's border negotiations. But Francisco Xavier de Mendonça Furtado, Pombal's brother and the governor of the Amazonian captaincies Grão Pará and Maranhão, also wished to guarantee colonists access to Indian labor. In May 1757, he issued his own lengthy set of policies known as the *Diretório dos índios*, or Indian Directory, effectively nullifying native autonomy by appointing outside lay directors to oversee village life in place of the Jesuits, whom he accused of making themselves "masters of the sertão." Deemed to lack the "necessary aptitude required to govern themselves," the Indians would now be subject to the rule of directors named by the governor himself. The directors would "Christianize and civilize these hitherto unhappy and wretched peoples," teaching them the essential skills of trade and agriculture that would hasten their transition to secular governance and allow them to shed the "ignorance and rusticity to which they find themselves reduced." The Indians would thereby become "useful to themselves, to the colonists, and to the state." Under the guise of enlightened action, Furtado sought in the Directory to eradicate the isolation of the Amazon's village Indians and to exploit them as efficiently as possible as a workforce. The new system ushered in an era at least as repressive as the one Indians had confronted under the rule of the Jesuits, who were then expelled from Brazil in September 1759.[7]

Little has been written about the implications of this legislation for non-Amazonian Brazil.[8] Formally enacted by the Crown and extended to the remainder of Portuguese America by charter in August 1758 and in the *Direção* legislation of May 1759, the Directory remained the backbone of indigenous policy until it was abolished in 1798. In many regions of Brazil, its precepts continued in force well into the nineteenth century.[9] Yet historians have not pursued its effects, subject perhaps to the misconception, articulated by such influential scholars as Capistrano de Abreu, that "in the rest of Brazil, Indian affairs were no longer a matter of concern, and the violence against them was not as great as farther north."[10]

Quite to the contrary, in Minas Gerais the Law of Liberty, the Directory, and the Direção had far-reaching consequences when applied by local officials, providing the legal framework for unremitting violence. Nowhere were the implications of such legislation—drafted with settled village Indians in mind— for the subjugation of still-nomadic forest Indians more evident than on the eastern periphery of the mining district. At the time of the legislation's extension to the rest of Brazil, Silva, who would assume his post as governor of Minas Gerais in 1763, was serving as governor of the northeastern captaincy of Pernambuco, where he received the Direção and supervised the conversion to the Directory system of 54 Indian villages, homes to the descendants of natives forcibly resettled by the Portuguese in the sixteenth and seventeenth centuries.[11] In Minas Gerais, where the primary problem he would face involved not village Indians but independent seminomads still occupying the unsettled sertão, he set out to adapt Crown policy to suit local conditions.

In the official government register outlining the basis for his actions, Silva established legitimacy for a policy of military conquest by citing three documents. The first was the order he received as governor of Pernambuco in 1758, in which the Crown instructed him to take steps, in accordance with its earlier decrees, to restore liberty to the Indians in Pernambuco's aldeias while placing them under the civil authority of white directors. These officials were to give settled Indians "all of the support and protection they needed until they were entirely established in the tame and peaceful possession of these liberties." In each village, land was to be protected in the form of a royal grant (*sesmaria*) conceded to the Indians for the benefit of farming and trade. Aldeias were converted into official townships and assigned Portuguese toponyms to replace their "barbarous" indigenous names. Secular rather than religious authority would govern these settlements. The second document reaffirmed the end of missionary rule in all Indian villages on the eve of the Jesuits' expulsion. The third was a letter from Furtado, now in Portugal as a minister to the king, dated February 12, 1765, two years after Governor Silva assumed leadership of Minas Gerais. The letter communicated the monarch's permission to proceed with an attempt begun the previous year to distribute goods among certain Indians of the Eastern Sertão to "establish some trade" along its rivers, specifically the Doce and Piracicaba. Furtado told Silva that the king would underwrite expenses incurred in the effort. He also urged the governor to "work to whatever extent possible to establish with the same Indians civil townships, applying all means judged necessary" to secure this end. The king, he averred, was convinced that in addition to possible profits accruing from trade, other benefits existed that were "still more important, both temporal as well as spiritual, that will follow from our becoming familiar with and associating with these heretofore unfortunate peoples who, because of the tyranny with which they have always been treated, find themselves in the ignorance in which they were born." Condemned to their miserable fate, these Indians had degenerated into the Portuguese's "capital enemies, lost souls, depriving the state of the great advantages it could derive from them."[12] Even the Crown itself, Silva must have gleaned from this communication, was prone to contradictions on the subject of whether Indians in the Eastern Sertão should be left completely alone and whether activity there was entirely forbidden.

Furtado did not elaborate on what he meant by "all means judged necessary." Based on his accompanying phrases, that he meant something short of military confrontation should have been evident. His language mirrored that which he and other officials had developed over the years to manage relations between village Indians and settlers in the Amazon region.[13] His injunction to concentrate on "becoming familiar with and associating with these heretofore unfortunate peoples" indicates that he had more moderate methods in mind than did Governor Silva.

Additional correspondence between the two men captures how the gap between Crown and captaincy frontier and indigenous policy continued to widen. To some degree, this discrepancy was a natural consequence of the always incomplete flow of detailed information out of the remote sertão to the seat of the captaincy administration in Vila Rica, and from there across the Atlantic to Lisbon. But Governor Silva's hand in tailoring that information to suit his purposes is evident in every exchange of letters. He conveyed to Furtado only those specifics that would secure royal support for his aims, which in turn were a response to mounting pressure from settlers to seize land controlled by Indians. He dispensed with particulars that would have clarified the risks involved, notably that the execution of his plan was virtually certain to provoke a violent confrontation with the Puri, Botocudo, and other groups accustomed to the absence of settlers in the eastern refuge zone.

In March 1764, as one of his first acts after assuming his duties as governor, Silva laid out his comprehensive vision for the colonization of the Eastern Sertão in a letter to Pombal's brother. He began by describing his first encounter with the natives of Minas Gerais. Venturing out of the wilderness that separated the mining district from Rio de Janeiro, more than 50 "savage Indians" had journeyed to Vila Rica and presented themselves to him on two separate occasions. He identified them as Coropó, Guarulho, and Croá. (In the case of the third of these ethnic groups, the governor probably meant Croato, a common eighteenth-century designation for the Coroado Indians of the upper Doce River tributaries.) All three groups were among the more than 150 Indian "nations," he wrote, that lived in the unsettled southeastern region bounded to the south by the Mantiqueira Mountains, to the north by the Doce River, and to the east by the Serra do Mar, the mountains of the sea—that is, Brazil's great coastal escarpment. The Indians had come to ask the governor for two things: tools and baptism. He ordered the distribution of agricultural implements without hesitation, but baptism was more problematic. With no priest at hand who understood their languages, the adults could not undergo the religious instruction required to receive this sacrament. The vicar of Vila Rica thus restricted baptism to the children alone, and the Indians returned to the forests. Intrigued by these events, Silva began consulting a number of "experienced backwoodsmen" who had participated in expeditions to the region. They shared their knowledge of the great expanses of fertile land lying to the east, of the innumerable rivers and streams promising alluvial gold, and of the "great quantity of numerous nations of heathen" that lived there, "destitute" of all teachings of the Catholic faith.

The prospect of harvesting riches as well as errant souls prompted the governor to propose a fundamental reshaping of the Crown's Forbidden Lands policy. He called on Lisbon to incorporate these previously restricted reaches of unsettled territory. Colonial authority over the zone should extend eastward from the inland capital of Vila Rica to the very brink of Brazil's inhabited coastal zone. This plan, he argued, accorded with the Crown's stated indigenous policy. After "reducing the heathen to the bosom of the church," he would set out "to civilize" them, while "making use of their great utility for the benefit of the people and His Royal Treasury." In other words, Indians, once integrated, would themselves help extract the region's copious wealth. That wealth would occur "in the form of gold, which initial tests had turned up along the headwaters of the rivers and in many other places in that country, as well as that which would naturally be discovered at the edges of the mountain ridges, which promise more than just minor riches."

Naturally, the Crown was worried about any breach in the wilderness buffer zone created decades earlier to protect the mining district and to keep the lusophone inhabitants of Minas Gerais in their proper place. According to Silva's plan, therefore, this colonizing project would commence only after troops from the mining district had secured the area's far eastern perimeter. Two detachments of soldiers would march into the sertão to take up positions guarding mountain passes, the route down the Doce River, and other strategic points through which smugglers might attempt to escape to the coast. Assuming the information he had gathered on gold and Indians proved accurate, the governor then envisaged the eventual formation of an unbroken chain of "Indian towns and settlements" along the inland edge of the coastal range. These settlements would be established near enough to one another that militias formed from their inhabitants could readily patrol the intervening distances. Under competent command, together with regular soldiers, these forces would interdict "all smuggling of gold and diamonds without augmenting the already onerous expenditures of the royal treasury." Finally, anticipating another possible royal objection, Governor Silva pledged to pursue his goal with methods that avoided the "destructive form with which the first settlers of this land tyrannized" the Indians. He also repudiated the "criminal ambition that everyone always demonstrated in reducing them to slavery."[14] Almost a year later in his letter of February 12, 1765, when Furtado authorized the governor to proceed and promised him financial support, it was on the assumption that peaceful methods would guide this foray into the sertão and that the region's Indians themselves sought some sort of interchange.

What Furtado, Pombal, and the Crown did not know in Lisbon was that Governor Silva had already embarked on the course of armed conquest. Correspondence between the governor and local officials mark 1764 as the year he ordered a series of military expeditions provisioned to combat the "wild heathen" of the Eastern Sertão. These and subsequent military operations will be analyzed in detail in a subsequent chapter. For present purposes, the emphasis is that Silva did not volunteer this information to the Crown. In May 1765, he received a particularly grave report of Indian hostilities from settlers on the eastern edge of the mining district. Yet when he wrote back to Furtado in July 1765 to acknowledge the Crown's support for his venture, he mentioned nothing of this mounting conflict involving settlers, soldiers, and Indians. Rather, he simply pledged to proceed with the Crown's instructions to "civilize, Christianize, and associate with" the Indians.[15]

This omission was not simple subterfuge. The governor probably assumed that Lisbon would sanction his methods even when he resorted to military action. This interpretation is supported by the tenor of Crown indigenous policy in other regions of the colony. A compilation of pertinent legislation lists orders relating only to settled Indians during the 1760s and early 1770s: the payment of Indian salaries by those contracting their labor services in the captaincies of Pernambuco and Paraíba do Norte, restrictions on their movement along trade routes in São Paulo, and allotment of land in their aldeias and the transformation of these Indian villages into civil townships, also in São Paulo.[16] As in Minas Gerais, local officials in other captaincies—not the Crown—signed off on orders authorizing violent conquest during the second half of the eighteenth century. Such was the case of new conquests originating in São Paulo, where in 1771,

Luís Antônio de Souza Botelho, the morgado de Mateus, who governed that captaincy between 1765 and 1775, armed and mobilized 60 soldiers to subdue Indians along the border between São Paulo and Rio de Janeiro. In a separate action, he also granted special exemptions to members of an expedition ordered to combat Indians along the border between São Paulo and Minas Gerais. In the Amazon region, too, locally formulated policies that were tantamount to offensive military action and couched in the language of "just war" governed the conflict between mutually hostile Portuguese settlers and Indian groups such as the Mura and Xavante during this period.[17] Captaincy authorities preempted the Crown in these cases, but apparently did so assuming they acted in accordance with Lisbon's wishes.

The most immediate royal precedent for such aggressive operations into the sertão against defiant Indians was the 1755 Law of Liberty itself. Although focused on settled Indians, the law contained provisions for incorporating natives "living in the darkness of ignorance" in the "interior of the sertões" far removed from the Jesuit missions of the Amazon that were to be turned into civil townships. The law called for these independent Indians to be settled in aldeias, Christianized by missionaries, and encouraged to engage in agriculture and trade. It also stipulated that local authorities guarantee that these natives, like those already settled, "maintain the liberty of their persons, possessions, and commerce," rights that were not to be "interrupted or usurped under any policy or pretext." Individuals caught perpetrating acts of violence against the newly settled Indians were to receive prompt punishment.[18]

In Minas Gerais, Governor Silva did not hesitate to ignore such subtleties. Basing his actions on the three documents cited, taking full advantage of Furtado's vague instructions and imagining that the task at hand differed little from the orders he previously imposed on village Indians elsewhere, the governor resolved to "proceed with the execution of [royal] orders," repeating what he "had done in Pernambuco" to secure the "reduction of the wild Indians who infest" the captaincy of Minas Gerais. As such, he pursued what he conveniently construed to be the wishes of a Portuguese monarchy that sought to "convey the law of God to the barbarous nations, reducing them to the Catholic faith and to the true knowledge of His Holy Name."[19]

A concurrent response from the captaincy church hierarchy highlights the expediency of this locally orchestrated approach to Indians and the eastern frontier. As noted, the Directory had been devised for Indians settled in aldeias. On receiving orders from Lisbon to enforce the Jesuit purge and mission secularization at the heart of that policy, the captaincy's first diocesan bishop, Dom Frei Manuel da Cruz, responded from his ecclesiastical headquarters in Mariana with thinly disguised bafflement at the Crown policy's apparent inapplicability to local circumstances. First, a Jesuit presence had never been established in Minas Gerais. Second, "in this bishopric there are at present no Indian aldeias," he replied to Lisbon. "But if ever there should be any during my time," he respectfully promised, "I stand immediately ready to execute His Majesty's orders."[20]

In sharp contrast, Governor Silva had no intention of remaining idle, known Indian villages or not. For him, the Crown's new Indian policy assumed the pressing status of a call to action. The roving native bands of Minas Gerais, he reasoned, would first have to be settled to implement that policy. They would have to be gathered in villages, forcibly if necessary, submitting to what the governor and his contemporaries freely called "conquest." Only then might their privileges, guaranteed by the 1755 law, be conferred. Yet in explicit reference to and de facto rejection of that law, he ordered captaincy troops to "block the liberty" exercised by the forest Indians, countering their resistance with military force.[21] That is, Indians would first have to be subdued and settled so that they could later be liberated.

Although invoking royal orders, Silva revealed his willingness to act in circumvention of the stated intent of Crown indigenous policy and to exceed the apparent reach of Furtado's direct instructions. The Indians of the Eastern Sertão, the governor believed, had demonstrated themselves to be utterly intractable. His actions made clear that their legislated liberty was not to be construed as the freedom to maintain a traditional, itinerant existence. Rather, it simply implied their right—or, more accurately, their obligation—to contribute to colonial society as loyal, sedentary, industrious Christian vassals. Such was the local origin of the policy of violent conquest of peoples and lands that the Crown would continue to maintain were off-limits except for a few strictly controlled exceptions. To the great detriment of the Indians of the eastern forests, Silva's essentially antithetical interpretation of royal legislation would, in one form or another, remain in effect in Minas Gerais throughout the ensuing decades, leading directly to the prince regent's 1808 declaration of war.

As the anthropologist Beatriz Perrone-Moisés has deduced, many apparent contradictions in the colonial indigenous legislation of the Portuguese Crown can be resolved by distinguishing those policies intended for pacified, settled Indians from those meant for refractory nomads.[22] Governor Silva's sleight-of-hand, transmuting a policy meant for incorporated natives into one targeting still-independent groups, demonstrated the degree to which legislative distinctions could hinge not on the Crown's perspective but on local exigencies and opportunities. Without a change in the royal ban on frontier colonization, the captaincy administration had taken decisive steps toward redefining the status of Indians in the Forbidden Lands and their suitability for legitimate conquest.

Structuring Frontier Settlement

The recasting of the captaincy's Indian policy rested, in turn, on the need to respond to settlers venturing into the sertão in search of basic subsistence and profit. Without direct Crown authorization, the idea of military deployment to secure specific frontier settlements prompted Governor Silva to take action. In 1764, the governor first provisioned and the following year deployed a series of armed expeditions that officials, as was their custom, referred to as bandeiras in the tradition of the great exploratory and slaving parties of the sixteenth and seventeenth centuries. The stated motive prompting this action was to "hinder the pillage" of the "wild heathen," who "year after year" and at numerous locations had attacked fazendas and other lands conceded to frontier settlers in the form of royal grants. The Indians had committed "such hostilities as murder and the destruction of cattle, crops, and fazendas." They had engaged in looting and arson, burning settlers' fields and houses. Not only had they harmed property owners and others in the region but, as long as their attacks went unchecked, they threatened "the ruin" of neighboring hinterland areas dangerously near to the central settled zones of the mining district. In particular jeopardy was the remote mining camp of Cuieté, where Indian raids forced settlers to flee from promising gold-mining operations.[23] Reacting violently to settler incursions, the Botocudo Indians had "infested"—as farmers and miners in the area put it, using the same vocabulary favored by captaincy officials—substantial stretches of the Eastern Sertão. The Indians fought savagely and, at least for the present, victoriously, first attacking Cuieté and then brazenly challenging the permanence of outlying parishes within the *termo* (municipal district) of Mariana, one of the captaincy's oldest and most important jurisdictions and the seat of its highest ecclesiastical authority.[24]

Although reports of Indian attacks reached Vila Rica from various locations, Governor Silva took as one of his prime objectives the need to secure the defense and expansion of settlement at Cuieté. Like the river along which it lay, Cuieté took its name from a Tupi word for bottle gourd, a shape associated with a nearby rock formation.[25] The drive to found a mining camp and, secondarily, a self-sustaining agricultural settlement at Cuieté had a long history, so long that it preceded the Crown's barring of exploration, mining, and other activities in the Eastern Sertão. Crucially, for this reason, contemporaries saw little contradiction between sustained attempts to promote settlement there and such prohibitions. And yet, as much as any single frontier initiative, the determination to establish, protect, and develop Cuieté as a productive mining camp galvanized Silva's actions and those of his successor, Governor José Luís de Meneses Abranches Castelo Branco e Noronha, the Count of Valadares (1768–73). The push to settle Cuieté, along with a number of other frontier outposts, seriously undermined the opposing commitment to enforcing the royal ban on settler activity in the sertão. The presence of settlers at this exposed and inaccessible site placed them at perpetual risk to native hostilities, prompting further armed confrontations and efforts at territorial consolidation each time soldiers came to the mining camp's defense.

Although the sources are vague as to the precise routes of early exploration parties, scholars generally identify the settlement of Cuieté, which lay along the banks of the river of the same name, 240 kilometers northeast of Vila Rica, as the approximate site of some of the initial discoveries that first sparked the gold rush. Especially during the immediate post-boom period, the mining camp and its environs assumed an almost mythical status in the minds of those who sought to restore the golden glow of previous decades to a captaincy perceived as suffering a desperate decline. The mapmaker José Joaquim da Rocha expressed this perspective, describing Cuieté as a place whose distinctiveness lay in a volatile combination of Indians and gold. Of all the "rugged and never penetrated sertões" traversed by bandeirantes from São Paulo in the seventeenth century, he wrote, the "most notable" was a region called Casa da Casca, where an Indian village stood at the site later called Cuieté. In 1693, Antônio Rodrigues de Arzão, a native of São Paulo, led a bandeira of 50 men to the region in search of Indian slaves. After descending the Doce River to the coast, he presented authorities in Espírito Santo with gold he had unearthed, becoming (according to Rocha) the first to announce the discovery of the precious metal that would soon provide the basis for bestowing the name Minas Gerais on the entire region. Although further bandeirante exploration depended on the capture and aid of numerous Indians from the Doce River watershed, rapidly the search for gold itself and not the acquisition of Indian slaves became the primary objective. The great mineral deposits that ultimately fueled the boom period would be found farther inland, leaving the remote streams and forested ravines around Cuieté scarcely explored along with the rest of the Eastern Sertão. Thus bypassed, the forests always retained their promise of future riches.[26]

Attempts to establish a permanent settlement on the banks of the Cuieté River dated from no later than the 1740s.[27] Local lore identified Captain Pedro de Camargos and his family as among the first to secure a foothold. They explored the region in 1746 and 1747, discovering traces of gold along various streambeds. Only after receiving permission from Governor Silva's predecessor, the Count of Bobadela, were these earliest settlers allowed to remain in the area. Bobadela stipulated that they postpone all mining activity for one year to devote their energies to agriculture to provide for their subsistence. Thus established, they sought to prevent others from following their path. Those who attempted to do so complained of being barred from entering this distant stretch of the Doce River by aggressive members of the family. Intimidated not only by such opposition but also by the difficulty of travel and transport to the region, some settlers retreated. Others eventually managed to establish themselves, including, according to one 1770 account, some who were "married, single, white, and of every other color," accompanied by "a priest who administered the sacraments for them." They, too, withdrew in the end, hastened by fears of the Botocudo, who had killed a number of their slaves. Those who lost slaves included such prominent individuals as the *capitão-mor* (militia commandant) of Mariana José da Silva Pontes, the officer Custodio de Sá Ferreira, and the priest João Nunes da Gama. Meanwhile, Captain Camargos held on without slaves, relying instead on "persons dependent on him," perhaps allied Indians, to secure his place in the wilderness. In this way, he managed to extract sufficient gold to warrant remaining in the area despite the constant threat of Indian attack.[28]

Governor Silva took credit for being the first to promote the permanent settlement of Cuieté, even though officers in the field traced the earliest efforts to his predecessor. By the time Silva assumed leadership of Minas Gerais in 1763, most of the earlier activity had come to a halt, threatening to undo all efforts to maintain a presence at this remote site. The intensification of violent opposition by the Botocudo and "other nations" had made exploiting the modest mineral wealth known to exist there impossible. The search for the great untapped deposits thought to be awaiting discovery in the surrounding hillsides and riverbeds would have to be delayed indefinitely. In the context of the Directory legislation, which stipulated the transformation of native aldeias into Portuguese townships, the potential demise of a Portuguese settlement at the hands of Indians, even one as tenuously established as Cuieté, struck an ambitious Crown agent like Governor Silva as the most ironic and appalling of possibilities. He determined not only to retaliate by sending out a series of armed bandeiras, the beginning of a sustained military assault, but also to impose a secure, recognizable, and remunerative colonial order on this insecure site.[29]

Committed to protect, monitor, and tax settlers who migrated there, Silva appointed Captain Paulo Mendes Ferreira Campelo to the post of regent governing the forests centering on Cuieté. The position gave the captain an authority over the zone exceeded only by that of the governor himself. He would be the first of several officers promoted to this status and charged with administering extensive areas of the Eastern Sertão. His orders clarified that the responsibilities of a regent, who answered directly to the governor, encompassed all manner of military and civil governance, including command of army and militia forces, tax collection, food and commodity distribution, commercial regulation, Indian relations, and measures to counter smuggling.[30]

Once invested with such authority, given the practical and political hazards of his assignment, Campelo must have reacted with some anxiety to the orders he received from Silva in early June 1765 at the end of the rainy season. Not only did those orders expose him directly to the danger of Indian adversaries, they also placed him directly at the center of the emerging contradictions in royal policies, captaincy necessities, and settler intentions. After all, those same hostile Indians were supposed to keep unauthorized persons from pursuing objectives similar to the ones the governor now assigned him. The orders instructed him to leave Vila Rica and proceed immediately to the vulnerable mining camp at the heart of the otherwise forbidden reaches of the eastern forests. There, near the confluence of the Doce and Cuieté Rivers, he was to select a level, well-watered site as close as possible to the gold deposits around which colonists had gathered. To guarantee the survival of the mining camp, Campelo was to make sure that fertile farmland lay within easy reach of the chosen site. At a suitable location, he was to raise a great pole from which he would measure one-half league (3.3 km) in each of the cardinal directions, delimiting the boundaries of the new settlement. After settlers and their slaves cleared enough land of its luxuriant flora, they were to erect a church facing a central square. Buildings housing military, fiscal, and other essential administrative offices would follow. The square would stand at the focal point of nine roads, each of a width precisely specified by the governor. Community pasturage and a public commons would be set aside and surveyed. On the periphery of town, Campelo was to cede to settlers ample land on which to build their own homes. The height of these dwellings, the direction they faced, and their facades would be standardized to achieve maximum order and conformity. The commander, in short, was to structure the ideal space of a Portuguese settlement in the wilderness.[31]

Apart from emphasizing the power of church and state, the town design was meant to order social relations and daily conduct within its confines, as well as settlers' relationship to the unsettled, restricted, Indian-dominated lands beyond. As in other frontier regions of colonial Brazil, the regulation of property rights provided the mechanism for this task.[32] In effect, settlers were to be as carefully surveyed and partitioned as the village plots, agricultural lands, and mining claims they received. Campelo would keep a list of the name, filial relations, and geographic origin of every arriving migrant over the age of 14. He would form able-bodied men into a town militia organized according to race and legal status, with separate companies composed of whites, free mulattos, and free blacks.[33]

More than any other economic pursuit in the colony, mining required a strict ordering of wealth-bearing space, and Cuieté was no different in this regard. As in other mining camps, gold deposits discovered along the many ravines, streams, and rivers in the area would be subject to official inspection and division into individual claims. The richest of claims would be allotted to the Portuguese Crown and then auctioned off to the highest bidder. Other choice plots would be reserved as a reward for the discoverers of particular deposits in general accordance with the royal mining code that had governed such matters since the beginning of the eighteenth century. The remainder would be divided among free settlers according to a lottery, each one receiving two claims, plus an additional one for each slave owned. By this system, authorities reasoned, slave owners would be able to extract sufficient gold to purchase provisions to feed their captive workers.[34]

Practical considerations notwithstanding, Campelo's founding ritual based on rigid orders also ensured that preexisting individual wealth and power would gain a privileged presence, reinforced by the hierarchical allocation of space, as this territory was drawn into the colonial fold. The economic, juridical, social, and racial hegemony of slave owners would in this way take root in the remote forests. The more slaves they owned, the more land and gold they merited. The spontaneous, lawless, untamed nature of the mining camp, its intrepid denizens, and the encircling forest would thus be subdued in accordance with practices perfected over the preceding decades in the mining district's central urban zones.[35] The sertão would be recast into a productive colonial domain.

The problem was that Cuieté and other settlements like it lay impossibly far from the nearest colonial centers of power, a distance only exaggerated by the tortuous intervening terrain. The administrative challenge created by this separation meant that despite the outward projection of a sanctioned village layout, landscape, architecture, and social structure, Cuieté and other frontier outposts would never become ordinary colonial settlements. Even the governor's original orders made this evident, despite their normative veneer. They stipulated that those who came to live in the town would not be allowed to travel elsewhere without first returning to Vila Rica to obtain official authorization. The hope was to stifle the flow of contraband gold from a place whose geography was still so poorly understood that the site had only begun to appear on captaincy maps.[36] If violated, this provision called for the arrest and imprisonment of offenders. A related measure required miners to appear every Sunday before Commander Campelo and two of his subordinates to sign a declaration stating how much gold each had extracted during the previous week. The miners could retain the amount of gold dust deemed necessary to provide for themselves and their slaves, but any excess had to be registered and deposited, to ensure proper taxation, in an official strongbox with three locks whose keys were held separately by each of the three officials. Moreover, the marginal nature of the first settlers gave such restrictions their particular urgency. Most of the migrants lamented their present "indigence," borne of unhappy economic circumstances in the villages and towns they left behind to migrate to this distant place. In the surrounding gold diggings, they hoped to remedy their poverty. Although eager to advance this aim, Governor Silva intended to make sure that they did not do so at the Crown's expense.[37]

The interplay of imposing distances, strict government surveillance, and wrenching economic insecurity was not the only threat to the smooth functioning of conventional colonial models. The presence of indigenous antagonists in the dense forest that all but enveloped the incipient mining camp gave early settlers direct and discouraging experience of the pitfalls of taking up residence there. If the village center laid out by Campelo represented a spatial projection of the colonial order, the surrounding Indians portended its negation. Along with the resident militia, therefore, extra troops would be stationed in Cuieté from the outset to defend against the constant "hostilities of the wild and savage heathen." Other soldiers were to advance into the forest to engage them in battle.[38]

The founding of a new settlement in such a remote place would thus depend not only on the ability to reproduce the society and economy that sustained colonists in previously settled areas. The two great perils to these structures, unruly settlers and uncivilized Indians, would also have to be actively reduced to submission. The hierarchies of colonial society would not only have to be transported into the wilderness but also fortified against opponents who seemed arrayed against them. A year and a half after he issued his original directives, Governor Silva expressed hope that this transformation would soon be achieved. He predicted that the first settlers and the slaves they brought with them would be able to "harvest food in superabundance" from the region's fertile land, food enough to encourage others to flock there in pursuit of similar rewards. News of the wealth of the area and the governor's proclaimed commitment to protect inhabitants from the Indians would encourage, he was convinced, a gathering stream of migrants (he called them "voadores," literally, flying ones), who would settle the zone for the benefit of future generations.[39]

In another setting, nothing unusual would have been noted about the governor's plan; however, with the mounting of military expeditions against the natives of the Eastern Sertão as well as the increasingly frequent comings and goings of settlers and soldiers, the incompatibility of royal and regional policy became ever more apparent. The policy gap would widen even though officials on both sides of the Atlantic downplayed and even ignored its significance. The comparison of sources produced at the Crown and captaincy levels makes clear the fact that royal authorities had only the faintest notion of the extent of local actions designed to open up territory and to conquer Indians—again, precisely those Indians who were supposed to keep the sertão free from unauthorized colonists. Apprised by the Count of Valadares of ongoing efforts to consolidate Cuieté's settlement in a letter dated April 1772, Pombal delayed seven months before belatedly instructing the governor to proceed but with caution. He emphasized the importance of measures to "prevent the acts of gold and diamond smuggling that people might commit in the area of Cuieté, the Doce River, and nearby places." Further, he stressed the indispensability of the governor's avowed commitment to impose "a total prohibition on anyone at all traveling to the mentioned sites or entering there under any pretext."[40] As far as Pombal understood, the region remained closed to all but Portuguese soldiers and perhaps a few closely supervised miners dispatched personally by the governor. His response betrayed Lisbon's understandable ignorance of events not merely across the Atlantic but also on the remote frontier. Even in Rio de Janeiro, a much closer locus of royal power, Brazil's viceroy, the Marquis of Lavradio (1769–79), adhered to the old assumptions. He personally had called off a planned conquest of "barbarous Indians" between the Paraíba and Doce Rivers, because "the king had prohibited entering into and founding establishments" in those lands, reputed to be rich in gold and diamonds.[41]

In the inland mining district, governors did not entirely abandon the prohibitions on eastward frontier expansion. Rather, they perennially found themselves caught between the impulse to restrict travel through the sertão and the desire to promote its exploration in hopes of discovering new mineral reserves. They resolved this conflict by attempting to impose the kinds of draconian regulations implemented at Cuieté on the sertão as a whole. A vast portion of the eastern wilderness became known simply as the Conquest of Cuieté (*Conquista do Cuieté*), not to be confused with the mining camp that bore this name. In this much larger region, Governor Antônio de Noronha sought to negotiate the contradictions between Crown and captaincy imperatives by encouraging limited exploration while instructing his military commanders to monitor all persons entering and leaving the region, a veritable impossibility given the area's size.[42] By the time he appointed João da Silva Tavares regent of the Conquest of Cuieté in 1779, the region was understood to comprise the land bounded to the south by the Arrepiados Mountains; to the east by the still largely unexplored borderland with Espírito Santo, including the Guandu River basin, which would ultimately fall within Espírito Santo's jurisdiction; to the north by the Jequitinhonha River valley; and to the west by the towns and villages of the settled mining district—in short, much of the eastern third of the captaincy.[43]

As evidence of ongoing attempts to monitor while reordering this sprawling wilderness, Regent Tavares, like Campelo before him, was invested with extraordinary powers. He assumed complete judicial authority to apprehend and jail those accused of crimes—among them, that of unauthorized movement. He became arbiter of land disputes between settlers. He oversaw commerce, controlling the functioning of all stores and warehouses and the licensing of merchants. Civilians entering the area were required to present Tavares with a "passport" issued by the governor or risk being arrested. Only clergy were exempt from this regulation, but even they were escorted out of the sertão to episcopate headquarters in Mariana where they were subject to punishment if they entered the Conquest of Cuieté without official documents. No one was to leave the region without Tavares' permission as well as an exit passport issued by him "showing urgent and legitimate cause."[44]

All gold extracted from deposits within the Conquest of Cuieté was to be transported directly to the royal smelter in Vila Rica under the supervision of an official guide appointed by the regent. Tavares would submit quarterly reports on the amount of gold extracted. He would make sure that no smuggling occurred, especially in the direction of Espírito Santo, limiting the number of boats on navigable stretches of the Doce River to those absolutely necessary for local transport and commerce. Descending the river to the Ilha da Esperança, the small island lying at the western edge of the captaincy of Espírito Santo, was expressly forbidden. Local inhabitants who passed that point would be presumed smugglers and taken prisoner. Tavares was to prevent the opening of any new roads or trails, except for one connecting Vila Rica and the town of Cuieté itself, whose construction Governor Noronha sponsored himself. Anyone caught clearing paths, making their own way through the forest, or ascending the Doce River from the coast was to be arrested immediately. The official objective, briefly stated, amounted to nothing less than preventing "the communication between the inhabitants of one settlement and another" throughout the Conquest of Cuieté.[45]

To initiate post-boom colonization of Minas Gerais' eastern wilderness in the 1760s, Governor Silva, apparently without the slightest intentional disloyalty, had effectively reconstituted Crown indigenous policy to suit the pressing requirements of captaincy governance. Concomitantly, he attempted to substitute limited, strictly monitored and controlled settlement for the Crown's longstanding prohibition on colonization to the east. As increasing activity led to further commitments of local resources and military might in restricted areas, he and his successors unwittingly made a mockery of royal regulations formulated to restrain frontier expansion. In this way, over time, captaincy authorities presided over the imposition of a new spatial and, ultimately, geopolitical order on lands once a refuge for unincorporated Indians. That these officials never perceived their own actions as disobedient should be clear from what they sought to achieve: the replication in the wilderness of structures that had traditionally served the colony's dominant society in settled settings both urban and rural. That these actions would engender substantial conflict should also be apparent, as key portions of Indian territory were reordered into a defensible hinterland and into fortified frontier outposts.

Controlling Unauthorized Migrants

In addition to devising the legal basis for an assault on the Eastern Sertão and creating structures upon which slaveholding society could be gainfully established in conquered lands, Minas authorities grappled with a third critical challenge related to frontier policymaking. This final realm of official innovation targeted a rapidly growing free population of African descent, the heirs of what by mid-century were several generations of miscegenation and manumission in the mining zone. The resulting policies shared key features with those devised to govern both Indians and slaveholding settlers. For instance, the task of controlling free persons of color on the frontier similarly entailed the molding of royal regulations to suit local objectives. Measures adopted to deploy these individuals as a frontier labor force similarly undermined Crown restrictions on activity in the sertão. Moreover, the determination to establish this marginalized population in its proper place similarly presupposed the reordering of territory in accordance with preexisting hierarchies that sustained unequal social and racial relations in the colony's settled areas. No less than Indians, slaveholders, and slaves, those individuals descended from slaves or themselves freed from slavery pursued their own objectives on the frontier. In response, captaincy officials strove to force them to conform to plans that would unite these disparate sectors of society seamlessly and remuneratively in the bid to extract resources from the Eastern Sertão and extricate Minas Gerais from its post-boom malaise.

In 1766, Governor Silva received an order from the king instructing him to crack down on the "cruel and atrocious offenses that vadios and criminals have committed in the sertões of this captaincy, where they live as beasts separated from civil society and human commerce."[46] Issued simultaneously to the governors of various captaincies, the directive corresponded to a move by José I to halt demographic dispersion throughout Brazil. The royal anxiety about unsupervised migration had both immediate and deep historical origins. Long before the arrival of the Portuguese on Brazilian shores, anxious European elites, responding to the breakdown of feudal society, had defined vagrancy and vagabondage as forms of direct resistance to the established order. The founding of New World colonies with their immense territories—which left church and state authority attenuated—gave new meaning to these concerns, particularly during periods of social and economic upheaval. In Minas Gerais, the need early in the eighteenth century to assemble a stable workforce deep in the colony's interior had only intensified the conviction that poor, non-slave migrants posed a dire threat to constituted authority. The presence of such migrants in the mining district often seemed more menacing than that of slaves who, by definition, were less mobile and thus more firmly bound to the mercantile labor regime. For Minas officials, the dislocations associated with the unraveling of the mining complex exacerbated these fears.[47] Worth noting is that on the eve of the gold rush in the 1690s, during an earlier period of economic hardship then engulfing Brazil's agricultural export sector, comparable dispersion from settled zones into the hinterlands had troubled colonial authorities. The Crown responded in similar fashion, attempting to congregate straying subsistence farmers in sanctioned towns and villages.[48] These parallel circumstances underscore one of the primary but least understood characteristics of frontier formation in Brazil and other American colonies, that cycles of economic privation as well as those of expansion propelled the peopling of unsettled territory.

The 1766 edict corresponded with a royal campaign to assemble sufficient recruits for forces deployed against the Spaniards in a deepening conflict along Brazil's southern border. In São Paulo, where greater proximity to the borderlands made the urgency of military readiness all the more apparent, the order prompted the morgado of Mateus to intensify forced backcountry recruitment efforts. He forbade inhabitants from "deserting the places in which they lived" to enter the surrounding forests without official permission.[49] Received in Minas Gerais amid the captaincy's mounting economic crisis, the order took on another meaning, resonating with the anxieties and ambitions of members of a white elite eyeing outlying lands in search of new sources of wealth. To control these lands, they would have to subdue not only the indigenous hunters and gatherers who stood in their way but also the free poor migrants who wandered this way and that as squatters and petty prospectors.

José I, with his own eye on the colony as a whole, aimed the 1766 directive at all "infamous and pernicious vadios," that is, individuals "found living in the ... sertões as vagabonds."[50] The derogatory Portuguese term *vadio*, uttered ceaselessly during this period by Crown and captaincy officials alike, can be translated as idler, vagrant, or vagabond, the latter best conveying the connotations of rootlessness, mobility, and criminality in documents from this period referring to impoverished denizens of the sertão. Portuguese law defined a vadio as "any man who does not live with a landowner or master, who has no occupation at which he labors and earns a living, [and] no employer, or who does not engage in some sort of business of his own."[51] A respected dictionary of the era relied on this legal definition, adding that a vadio was equally someone "not rooted in the land."[52] Hence, to wander inevitably raised suspicions of mis-conduct, but to be settled did not by itself dispel those suspicions. As long as a poor individual remained autonomous—devoted, for example, merely to his own subsistence or that of his family—official doubts persisted. The vadio was cast, in short, not merely as unsettled, unemployed, and uncivilized, like the beasts to which the Portuguese monarch compared these individuals, but also as unmastered, even in the event of being both settled and employed. To master the autonomous poor, both in the process and for the purpose of conquering unincorporated lands, would in this context come to constitute a third pillar of frontier policymaking in Minas Gerais, along with the conquest of Indians and the consolidation of slaveholding society in the wilderness.

The king's edict also specifically targeted those caught farming at so-called "sítios volantes." Like the term vadio, this phrase betrayed the intense preoccupa-tion with mobility that coincided with captaincy purposes. Sítio, from the Latin situs, meaning site or location, was used then, as now, to denote a small farm, the place that a farmer cleared and cultivated. The oxymoron sítio volante—translating literally as a flying or moving farm, a place that was not a place at all—bespoke the transient, roving nature of migrant agricultural practices.[53] The pervasive use of slash-and-burn subsistence farming, which kept settlers moving in an endless advance on uncleared, uncultivated land, militated against royal designs to control demographic dispersion.

Just as they abhorred native nomadism, Minas authorities, like their counter-parts elsewhere in the colony, came to associate the habitual mobility and rustic isolation of impoverished migrants with all manner of vice. They condemned the wandering poor for neglecting religious obligations, for vagrancy, and for criminality, concubinage, and incest. Conversely, these prejudices served to ex-clude and justify the repression of those for whom settled agricultural or urban life and the morality of dominant society remained unattainable or undesir-able because of poverty's dislocations. The royal edict, along with its political, military, and economic purposes, responded to a state of affairs in which many rural dwellers rarely saw a priest, in which baptisms were often delayed until adulthood, and in which couples lived together for years, often for their entire conjugal lives, without formalizing their union in the church.[54] The wilderness was awash in "the tears of countless peoples excluded from the bosom of the church," as one priest with 20 years' experience ministering to souls in the sertão described the situation in an eloquent plea for support written to the Crown. The lack of clergy sufficient for the task meant that the most rudimentary teachings of Christian morality never reached the Portuguese-speaking inhabitants of the sertão, whose "miserable state" was such that they resembled "a new species of heathen in their customs, with the only difference being that they are baptized."

And many of them were not; for such settlers, the priest continued, "there are no Sundays nor sacred days." They never attended Mass because they never had access to a priest who could celebrate it. As a consequence, corruption and criminality flourished: "homicides are continuous, concubinage universal, and all of these crimes go unpunished." The only recourse was to fortify the presence of the church in regions distant from the centers of colonial settlement.[55]

On this score, the highest officials of the colonial church also weighed in. The code drawn up to govern ecclesiastical affairs in Portuguese America at the beginning of the eighteenth century contained provisions singling out those settlers who abandoned their towns, villages, and parishes of origin to "wander from one place to another." Wherever they found themselves, such individuals were required by canon law to confess and take communion in the nearest church. Parish priests were ordered to monitor their presence and care for those who fulfilled their spiritual duties. The negligent, however, were to be barred from church grounds, refused the sacraments, and denied alms within parish limits. Marriage law itself regulated mobility. The church required painstaking and prolonged investigations of those seeking Christian marriages, routinely reaching across the Atlantic to probe ancestry, nativity, racial and ethnic origins, and changes of residence since birth. A central objective was to identify and spurn those who "licentiously practiced the vice of concupiscence and concubinage" and who "frequently left their legitimate wives and husbands" to remarry in the new places to which they migrated.[56] Like the paganism associated with indigenous wanderings, the threat to Catholic orthodoxy and civil authority posed by the non-sedentary frontier poor demanded a concerted response by church and state.

To express this impulse somewhat differently, the suppression of condemned behavior in distant places called for the conversion not only of marginal peoples but of the space itself through which they drifted.[57] The nettlesome sertão migrants linked to censured conduct would be, according to the king's order, "immediately compelled to choose settled places to live together in civil townships." These townships were to number at least 50 households, and they were to be administered by a full complement of public officials. Existing law gave new arrivals just 20 days to locate an established landowner or employer with whom to live and work. Further delay could result in arrest, a public whipping, and imprisonment. In the event that entirely new settlements formed in the sertão to accommodate errant migrants, officials were to divide available land in "just proportion" among the settlers. But small-scale landholding alone, as noted, would not suffice to legitimize a poor migrant's activities; that would result only with direct subordination to those deemed one's betters in the rural social hierarchy. Meanwhile, migrants who persisted in their nomadic ways, the king warned, would "be treated as highwaymen and common enemies" and "punished with all the severity of the law."[58] Spatial and territorial thinking, in short, infused the social and racial notions of proper place that pervaded official discourse on vadios.

This thinking was evident as well in those the king was careful to exclude from his crackdown. That his edict applied to various captaincies must be considered; he did not intend it to undermine the Forbidden Lands policy, which was specific to Minas Gerais. Even so, his exemptions would serve the purposes of those who wished to circumvent that policy. According to the king, first among legitimate sertão inhabitants were farmers (roceiros) who engaged in the provisioning of the colony's urban nuclei, as the contemporaneous usage of this Portuguese term implied, and who possessed cattle, slaves, and other accoutrements of authorized, permanent and, importantly, taxable agricultural and pastoral activity. These sanctioned sertão settlers constituted the very individuals "subject to being molested" by "those infamous and pernicious vadios." Also to be left at liberty to pursue their occupations in isolated reaches of the sertão were the rancheiros (inn-keepers) established along public roads. These individuals promoted commerce by providing "hospitality and comfort" to travelers. Finally, the king exempted members of authorized exploratory bandeiras from his order because they served a "useful and laudable" function, venturing into the sertão "in order to make new discoveries there." Not only did José I exclude these three groups, he also charged them with the task of rounding up all those not permitted to live and labor freely in, migrate to, or wander through remote lands. He invested them with "all of the necessary authority to capture and remit to public jails" anyone else inhabiting the sertão, whether they were discovered along public roads or in distant forests. The migrants need not have committed a specific crime; it was enough that they subsisted "without any permanent or solid dwelling"—like Indians—in lands outside the colony's incorporated realm.[59]

In post-boom Minas Gerais, as the autonomous poor scattered from failing mining operations, captaincy officials could call on the Crown's condemnation to classify nomadic behavior of any kind as open resistance to all manner of authority, both local and royal. Along the eastern edge of the mining district, these migrants could be corralled, impressed, and deployed in armed expeditions to "make new discoveries," in the king's words, or to contain indigenous peoples similarly damned for wandering from place to place. At frontier outposts like Cuieté, they could be employed for the same sort of risky military purposes or bound to the locally powerful as laborers, supplementing or replacing slaves, similarly mastered, contributing to the captaincy economy. In other words, mobility caused by marginalization would have regionally specific implications for the free poor, especially persons of color, as local authorities prodded and probed at the forbidden status of the frontier. Repudiating as resistance this essential subsistence strategy of the migrant poor, the Crown acted vigorously to thwart such wandering. On the other side of the Atlantic, captaincy officials saw an opportunity to use the Crown directive to buttress their campaign to extract riches from the Eastern Sertão. They perceived that by redirecting these migrants rather than halting them altogether, they could be enlisted, even if only by coercion, in frontier colonization schemes. As bandeira members exploring for hidden gold, as frontier troops fighting Indians, as impressed laborers opening trails, transporting supplies, and raising crops, even as squatters clinging to untitled land in areas still subject to Indian attack, they could be employed to secure promising sectors of the sertão.[60]

Faced with waning gold production and increasingly insistent demands from Lisbon to recapture the abundance of former years, Minas authorities weighed the Crown's insistence on restricting access to territory beyond the reach of the state. Finding this policy more and more wanting, they maneuvered to employ the free poor "useless ones" selectively in these lands in hopes of developing resources. A subtle reorientation of Crown intent was all that would be required to harness the mobile mass of frontier migrants for this purpose. The seizure of Indian land and the reordering of previously inaccessible territory into colonial villages, mining camps, and farmsteads would depend on measures to assemble a submissive, sedentary workforce. Success would require the imposition of the accustomed hierarchy of labor categories, racial and ethnic divisions, class and gender rankings, and religious and legal status that for more than two centuries had come to define colonial society in the settled urban and rural centers of Portuguese America.[61] Quite simply, the "useless ones" would not merely be useful but essential for the reproduction of that society on the frontier.

In zones targeted for incorporation, authorities would employ the power differentials inherent in these hierarchies to legitimize the often-violent suppression of conduct that challenged the colonial project. The conflation of suspect social and racial categories required for such control had firm royal precedent in Minas Gerais, a legacy elites would put to their advantage. A royal order issued in 1731 authorized the captaincy governor to take judicial action against unruly "bastards, *carijós* (persons of mixed Indian and European descent, that is, mestizos), mulattos, and blacks." A 1757 order stipulated that measures meant to control the actions of vadios also applied to the "excesses of mulattos, blacks, and freed slaves." Local authorities were authorized to arrest, pending verification, anyone whose status as free person or slave was in doubt. The king's 1766 order suppressing vadios would reinforce such doubts about all free persons of color who lacked permanent domicile, steady employment, or direct supervision, subjecting them to the threat of corporal punishment and imprisonment. In particular, the implied association of nomadism and rootlessness with resistance, whether by Indians or persons of African ancestry, linked outcasts in the minds and policies of those who would command their labor and dominate the lands they inhabited. Thus, in 1774, when a bureaucrat working for the captaincy administration indexed all laws extant in the government archives, he grouped together in one section legislation pertaining to "vagabonds, Indians, slaves, mulattos, [and] blacks."[62] Under a single heading, he articulated the nexus of status, race, and—pertinent especially in the sertão—mobility that marked those considered dangerous in the captaincy.

In her pioneering study of the captaincy's free poor population, historian Laura de Mello e Souza identified a number of ways in which such individuals were compelled to participate in the project of frontier expansion. They were recruited for expeditions to the sertão in search of gold and precious stones. They manned military garrisons in the eastern forests at places such as Abre Campo, Peçanha, and Cuieté, fighting Indians and protecting landholders and slave owners. They were transported to remote sites to labor at new mineral washings and on agricultural lands that settlers of greater means and independence eschewed. They were deployed in search of runaway slaves who sought the protection of the wilderness.[63] As these actions pertained to the Forbidden Lands policy, captaincy governors were once again deviating from the Crown's own purposes, using the sanctioned repression of those deemed unruly and unproductive to shore up moves to subdue Indians and protect settlers of greater status and means in the Eastern Sertão.

As the Crown pressed the captaincy to gather such individuals together in towns and villages, Minas governors insisted on deploying them at ever greater distances in the sertão. A little more than two months after the Crown issued its 1766 order, Governor Silva felt compelled to respond directly to Lisbon, writing Pombal's brother to explain the distinctive circumstances of the Minas sertão and to demand added nuance in Crown policy. First, he addressed the issue of criminals living in the sertão. He granted that some exercised "absolute power," emerging from the forests in armed raids to terrorize travelers and settled folk. But most of those who would be subject to the Crown's crackdown on vagabonds were of another ilk. In particular, he mentioned two areas east of the mining district in the vicinity of Antônio Dias Abaixo and Peçanha, as well as another site far to the west, where "a great number of fugitives" were congregated in small villages and dispersed in outlying farmsteads. Many were fleeing debts they could not pay or crimes they had committed in the settled regions of the captaincy. Most continued to work productively as farmers and miners under the supervision of local militia commanders whose orders they followed. Some who were able had even reached agreements with their creditors to pay off the sums they owed over time. The prospect of rounding up such individuals to send them to prison, as the royal pronouncement prescribed, made little sense, especially given the ease with which they could escape into "the sprawling sertões and forests." Furthermore, marginal men of this sort offered the Crown the "well known utility" of being willing to wander far into the forests, make mineral discoveries there, and attract other, more reputable settlers in their wake. Colonists who were "rich and established" refused to "subject themselves to the calamitous and miserable life and risks" assumed by men who had less to lose because of their misfortunes in settled society. Moreover, those fugitives who had committed truly "atrocious acts" tended to venture farthest of all into the remote sertão, making impracticable any effort by the state to apprehend them or even know their whereabouts.

Governor Silva proceeded to explain that the lands beyond the mining district's settled core also provided refuge to two other groups of outcasts not mentioned in the king's order, runaway slaves and hostile Indians. He made every effort, in accordance with existing laws, to apprehend the former and destroy their *quilombos* (maroon communities) so that the threat they posed would not increase. Nevertheless, he dismissed as "morally impossible" the prospect of "ceasing to have some [slave] fugitives in a land in which the great mass of inhabitants is composed of slaves." This circumstance was especially persistent because of the "impious treatment" most of their masters meted out. Any effective policy governing the sertão, he continued, would have to take into account the "wild Indians" who "committed killings, arson, and theft" in various river valleys of the Eastern Sertão and along the captaincy's western border with Goiás. Silva told Pombal's brother that he was currently engaged in efforts to "repel" these Indians through the deployment of armed expeditions while simultaneously attempting "by way of kindness and gentleness to reduce them to Christianity, obedience, and civility," despite the "habitual barbarity in which they exist."

Finally, with respect to the vadios singled out in the royal edict, the governor urged Lisbon not to encompass in its attempted purge those connected to the farms and mining operations that depended on these impoverished individuals for labor. As noted, the king's pronouncement itself made the same distinction, but Silva felt it necessary to reemphasize the point. Without that labor, the Crown would see its tax revenues from such operations decline and the working poor would lose their current means of subsistence. The Crown should therefore restrict its campaign to "those vadios with neither work nor occupation who wandered away from the mentioned forms of decent labor" and

ILLUSTRATION 2.2. A runaway slave hunter, many of whom were of African descent, returns from the forest with his captive
SOURCE: Rugendas, *Voyage pittoresque*. Biblioteca Nacional, Rio de Janeiro.

those who "moved continually from one place to another" and often became involved in illicit activities. Concerning even these clear-cut cases, the governor expressed doubts about the feasibility of the order because the captaincy's vastness, the distance between its settled areas, and what he called the "duplicity" of its extensive forests and open range complicated the task of identifying and apprehending "delinquent" individuals.

In this point-by-point response, Governor Silva in effect objected to every detail of the policy of consigning the countless marginalized inhabitants of the Minas sertão to the settled roles in towns and villages envisioned by the Crown. Either that policy was unworkable or it was decidedly counterproductive in the context of Silva's notions about how best to govern remote lands using the labor of this population. He concluded his reply by pledging his loyalty to the Crown, but he was clearly convinced that local exigencies took precedent over idealized policies drafted overseas. Like most of his successors, he would enthusiastically assume the authority stipulated in royal legislation to exert control over the captaincy's roving poor when and where this was possible; he also would not miss the chance to turn that authority to the purposes he deemed most pressing in territory the Crown continued to consider off limits.[64]

If Governor Silva was ambivalent about fulfilling the royal order to the letter of the law, so were his subordinate district commanders. Six years later, frustrated with this status quo, Silva's successor, the Count of Valadares, would admit to Colonial Secretary Martinho de Melo e Castro (1770–95) that the king's order had been utterly ignored by local officials. The consequences of such negligence, he maintained, were ongoing public disturbances, property crimes, and killings by the region's vadios. Despite the veiled criticism of his predecessor, Valadares continued to ascribe to Silva's belief that the Eastern Sertão, with its dangers and opportunities, offered the most promising environment for the labors of such individuals. He would pursue the practice of coercing them to work there under military supervision and impress them to man armed expeditions sent out to battle Indians.[65] So would his successors.

Out of the region's drifting, impoverished peoples, most of them of African descent, local authorities attempted to create an army of coerced individuals deemed fit for the hazards of frontier conquest. By the 1770s, members of this population had been pressed into service as occupants of a realm situated precariously between settled colonial society and unincorporated Indian territory. The Crown continued to think of the Eastern Sertão as a defensive cordon, protecting the traditional mining district from illicit access and egress. Meanwhile, captaincy governors acted to forge a transitional social and geographic space in which the free poor buffered sanctioned frontier settlers from native hostilities and insupportable hardship.

The reconfiguration of this space by captaincy authorities depended on the three fundamental spheres of a locally derived frontier policy. First, with respect to indigenous peoples, Minas officials replaced the Crown's policy of leaving Indians in place with one of violent conquest. Where native adversaries had once been encouraged to roam at will through the eastern forests to bar passage to the Atlantic seaboard, they now were to be cleared from selected sites that promised riches long-since anticipated on maps and in chronicles of early bandeirante explorations. Second, with respect to impatient slaveholders, local officials chipped away at the Crown's strict ban on eastward colonization. Where settlers of a favored social, economic, and racial sort had strayed into remote areas beyond the reach of the church and state, they now were to be protected while fastened to the administrative surveillance and regimentation of captaincy governance. Third, regarding the transient ranks of dispossessed Afro-Brazilians, officials reshaped Lisbon's concerns into a mechanism of frontier occupation. Where impoverished freemen had wandered through the forests as petty prospectors or subsistence farmers, they now encountered intense official pressure to act as labor and military fodder, bearing the brunt of Indian resistance to frontier colonization and thereby speeding the transformation of unincorporated lands into productive mining and agricultural grounds.

Propelling these changes was the desire to establish in the Eastern Sertão a privileged class of slave-owning frontier settlers consisting of farmers, ranchers, and miners, whose languishing fortunes led them to seek alternative sources of income. As the captaincy government strove to safeguard such settlers in Indian territory, and particularly as colonization plans ran up against the great obstacle of ongoing Indian resistance, officials turned to the autonomous poor, singling out those of African descent. The 1766 royal directive had emphasized that it was one thing for authorized, productive, tax-paying settlers to establish themselves in the sertão and quite another for the free poor to attempt to do so on their own without official supervision. In the hands of local authorities, this order conferred legitimacy on local moves that would undermine prohibitions against colonizing the captaincy's eastern forests. Over time, a new geography of conquest conceived along racial fault lines, a territorially specific mental and material construct that can best be termed a "racial geography," emerged against the backdrop of obsolete Crown restrictions. Instead of leaving hostile Indians at large in the Forbidden Lands, this new territorial vision required that they be pushed back from the mining district's hinterland and held at bay in the vicinity of frontier outposts. Transgressing royal prohibitions but doing so subtly and deferentially without risking serious rebuke, captaincy authorities promoted the creation of a frontier society erected as sturdily as possible on structures that had long supported social and economic hierarchies in the old gold-mining district. Wherever this incorporation of remote lands into colonial territory met with native opposition—which meant virtually everywhere to the east—those deemed vadios and useless ones would be mustered to drive forward the conquest so that mining, agriculture, and ranching could move eastward undisturbed.

Hardly surprising is that given these circumstances the Eastern Sertão became a crucible of racial conflict. Because the locally powerful perceived both seminomadic Indians and the black and mixed-race wandering poor as avatars of disorder, racial difference would figure prominently in policies devised to advance frontier conquest. The local elite thought schematically about social difference despite constant evidence that the crude categories they sought to impose did not match the complexities of late colonial society. The struggle to colonize the eastern forests spurred captaincy officials to delineate (often in inchoate form) and then act on (often in inconsistent ways) what they took to be the appropriate conduct of whites, blacks, Indians, and mixed-race individuals in specific geographic areas. The unequal power relations upon which the colony was built shaped this territorialization of racial difference and the course of frontier conquest, incorporation, and settlement. As this process unfolded, the region that the Crown had set aside as an undifferentiated, unsettled, and uninhabitable expanse gradually took form as a series of zones whose characteristics imposed very real if always contested confines on social and racial relations. Along the eastern edge of the settled mining district, newly cleared farmland, expanding parish boundaries, and developing hamlets and villagers extended Brazil's slaveholding society into the wilderness. Deep within the tropical forests, seminomadic natives continued to prevail, skirting or confronting isolated frontier outposts. Interlacing the entire territory lay transitional zones that neither slaveholder nor Indian effectively dominated. Especially to these zones, captaincy authorities consigned the free persons of color they considered expendable.

This racial geography—or rather, this alternate racial geography that supplanted the Crown's—would establish the possible and permissible activities of Europeans, Africans, and Indians who moved through particular areas of the Eastern Sertão. Destined to change the lines and legends on maps, this altered view of unincorporated lands would create the boundaries, both social and spatial, both practical and imagined, that defined the accompanying struggle over the legitimate function, the official status, and, quite literally, the proper place and position of the various peoples inhabiting the captaincy's eastern frontier. The most violent theater of that struggle pit colonists against Indians. But before the nature of this brutal conflict can be fully perceived, certain essential obstacles to official intent remain to be explored. These obstacles arose when colonists themselves, be they slave owners and slaves or the impoverished freemen denigrated as vadios, refused to conform to the frontier policies that captaincy authorities sought to impose. For just as local officials molded Crown edicts to serve their own purposes, frontier settlers and wandering migrants influenced the practical application of captaincy colonization schemes.

CHAPTER 3

In the Eastern Forests

Territorializing Colonial Society

"COMMAND OVER SPACE," observes the cultural theorist David Harvey, "is a fundamental and all-pervasive source of social power in and over everyday life." Spatial experiences serve as a primary vehicle "for the coding and reproduction of social relations."[1] Given the manifest importance of land, distance, resources, market linkages, mobility, and geography to the colonial quest to absorb new territory, the lack of attention by historians of the Brazilian frontier to basic spatial considerations is surprising. The drive to exert "command over space" on the eighteenth-century Minas frontier functioned on multiple levels. Maps, historical geographies, official pronouncements, and state policies evolved to represent in text and image, and to shape in form and practice, the changing significance of unincorporated and unfamiliar territory. Crown and captaincy diverged over the meaning of these changes. The formulation of indigenous policies suited to local conditions, the structuring of new hamlets and mining camps in the wilderness, and the regulation of unauthorized sertão migrants depended on contested conceptions of space. In turn all of these imperatives influenced the course of the lives of individual inhabitants of the sertão. As the divergence between Crown and captaincy played itself out in official discourse and direct state intervention, a new spatial context emerged for activities deemed acceptable in the territory lying to the east of the traditional mining district.

On the unofficial level, among those who never saw the manuscript maps that circulated among civil and military leaders and who never read the local literati's jeremiads on the receding gold cycle, the specific requirements of occupying new lands dictated responses that did not always neatly coincide with the plans of either royal or regional authorities. The willingness of settlers to assume the rigors of life in the sertão would be forged in countless direct experiences of the risks and rewards of clearing a tract of virgin forest or panning for gold along an unnamed streambed. That willingness, or its absence, turned on any number of considerations directly linked to spatial potentialities and limitations: the relative ease with which frontier migration could provide for individual or family subsistence, the availability of free and slave labor at remote sites, the access to regional markets, and the safety and range of communication and transportation networks. A settler's relocation to the sertão also depended on a certain confidence in private, collective, and military means to defend and secure lives and property at unaccustomed distances. It required an evaluation, whether adequately informed or not, of the relative strength of state authority on the frontier.

The history of the Eastern Sertão's formation as a frontier and its prolonged conquest cannot be explained by recourse to standard narratives of state-directed expansion and Indian resistance. Captaincy officials sought to establish a new social order for the Eastern Sertão, spatially no less than racially articulated, in which the proper place of wandering Indians, slaves, free persons of color, and migrating white settlers alike would be unambiguously determined. However, to confuse official policies with settler practice, to imagine that migrants to the sertão simply set out to do the state's bidding, would be a mistake. The fact that monarch and governor did not themselves always pursue shared purposes was enough to make such compliance impracticable. More to the point, settlers devised plans of their own, to varying degrees independent of the state. Their actions revealed just how different their conceptions of desirable territory, their practical approaches to its occupation, and their notions for transforming it into wealth-bearing space—in short, their territorialization of settler society—could be from official notions and policies. Portuguese settlers along with the slaves they transported to the sertão were themselves coauthors of frontier history. They did not wait for the captaincy government to clear the Eastern Sertão of Indians before migrating there, albeit in numbers that depended fundamentally on the specific destination at stake. Nor did they readily submit to official plans designed to regulate their movements and reap a portion of their rewards. Thus, a binary narrative juxtaposing the military assault on the Eastern Sertão and the ensuing indigenous response, without accounting for the multifaceted role of settlers, strips events of their nuance to such an extent that neither frontier expansion nor native conduct can be adequately understood. Such a narrative also risks the condescending tendency of historians and anthropologists who stereotype frontier settlers as "rough and uncouth" and motivated primarily by their "racial hatred of Indians," to cite just one example.[2] This limited perspective stems from historians' own prejudices, which are frequently confirmed by the elite, official sources they consult. In practice, colonists comprised a transformative force on their own, not so easily categorized, acting at times in accordance with but frequently in opposition to state-directed projects. Many considerations other than "racial hatred" determined their conduct on the frontier.

The actions of captaincy governors compelled the Portuguese Crown to grant exceptions to, tolerate local indifference about, justify violations of, and ultimately abrogate its own prohibitions against activity in the eastern forests. Likewise, power devolved even further to the separate sphere of migrant actions. Governors and their military and bureaucratic functionaries could form and promulgate policies regarding the frontier, frequently based on wishful thinking; they could explore and map the sertão; they could march armed expeditions into the wilderness; they could order Indians killed or put to flight. However, more than this would be required to annex and reorder the Eastern Sertão. Colonial society could not simply be imagined into existence. It had to be physically transported to the sertão, reconstructed on a foundation that would lend it permanence, and adequately protected against its adversaries, real or perceived. For this, the conduct of migrants proved critical from the outset, and more often than not, on their actions the success or failure of captaincy frontier policy turned. Just as local officials coaxed the Crown to change its approach, so did settlers alter the form and function of captaincy attempts to direct the incorporation and reorganization of alien space in the Forbidden Lands.

Sources hailing the successes and lamenting the tribulations of the state tend to be fundamentally misleading in this regard, portraying settlers as pawns. Even so, intimations of the influence of individual colonists on frontier poli- cymaking appeared consistently in official pronouncements. When Governor Silva launched his first military moves on the Eastern Sertão in the mid-1760s, for instance, he invoked with appalled indignation his responsibility to defend those driven to flee their lands by marauding Indians. This held true for settlers on the poorly defended outskirts of well-established mining and agricultural zones as well as for those cut off from such zones by great forested distances who were struggling to extract gold at remote sites like Cuieté. When Governor Noronha decided in the 1770s to form a corps of free men of color to combat Indians, he did so in response to raids on fazendas already scattered through- out the upper tributaries of the Doce River. When Governor Rodrigo José de Meneses (1780–83), later the Count of Cavaleiros, turned his attention in the 1780s to the Arrepiados Mountains, he traveled there accompanied by a great retinue of settlers pressing him for land in Indian territory. When his succes- sor, Governor Luís da Cunha Meneses (1783–88), later the Count of Lumiares, shifted the geographic focus of frontier policy yet again, he did so to keep pace with migrants flooding into the southernmost reaches of the Eastern Sertão. By the 1790s, as far as captaincy governors were concerned, all pretense of barring internal migrants from entering the eastern forests had vanished in the face of the need to keep pace with rapidly changing social, economic, and political circumstances in the colony. Instrumental in this change was the pressure frontier settlers exerted, even when few in number, on captaincy authorities to relinquish strict adherence to the policy of cordoning off the Forbidden Lands.

From their direct experience of the post-boom milieu, captaincy governors and their subordinates could not easily maintain the fiction that official measures, however rigid, to stanch the flow of contraband out of the captaincy would be sufficient to reverse the dramatic declines in gold production and royal revenues from mid-century highs. The search for new sources of wealth universally impelled these men, determining how favorably their regional leadership would be assessed by members of the imperial administration across the Atlantic. Not one of these governors could afford to ignore the potential that the unexploited resources of the Eastern Sertão held for endowing his sojourn in the colony with the sheen of success. Disproportionate claims concerning that potential, despite what in many cases amounted to modest returns, can be attributed to this eagerness to please the Crown even while modifying its policies. But beneath the play of rhetoric and ad hoc policymaking, governors did not always have their own way—any more than the Crown did—when dictating the course of frontier events. Without exception, they had to respond to colonists straining at the controls that both Crown and captaincy sought to implement. Just as monarch and governor often found themselves out of step with one another, so did governor and frontier migrant.

Reproducing Slaveholding Society in Unsettled Lands

If settlers were destined to seek their fortunes and risk their lives at a place like Cuieté, the dictates of colonial rule then required that their actions be regulated by the state. Social structures characteristic of life in the colony's settled zones would have to be transferred to the sertão. Throughout the colonial period, captaincy administrators—governors first among them—harbored a great mistrust of the mining district's inhabitants, considering them an unruly, libertine, even barbaric lot, drawn to the region by avarice and adventurism. This deep suspicion seemed all the more justifiably directed at those who ventured into the forests, preferring an abode far from the state's watchful gaze. Officials associated such migrants with the uncivilized seminomads of the surrounding sertão.[3] In this sense, the task of molding migrant society to the contours of centralized authority, of converting distant wilderness into ordered colonial space presented an enormous and urgent challenge. No small part of this challenge was the inconstant purpose of the migrants themselves. Seemingly, just as authorities caught up with them or sought to direct their energies, their determination to settle in a given place shifted to a new expanse of unclaimed forest rumored rich in gold.

From the earliest stages of the move to colonize lands lying east of the mining district, the destinations identified as auspicious by governors diverged from those selected by settlers. The case of Cuieté exemplifies the problem. After the middle of the eighteenth century, a series of governors focused on Cuieté as one of the most promising, if most remote, sites in the sertão because of the supposed extent of its mineral deposits. That these captaincy administrators made some progress toward colonizing Cuieté was apparent by the end of the 1760s. In an informal census taken in 1769 or 1770, Commander Paolo Campelo counted just 23 *moradores* (inhabitants) of Cuieté, only one of them a woman; however, in keeping with standard colonial social categories, this figure probably represented only heads of household and landowners, almost all of them white slaveholders.[4] A simultaneous count of local militia members registered a larger male population, 37 whites and 15 free or freed mulattos and blacks. How many wives, sisters, children, dependents, free poor, and Indians had assembled in the town remains a mystery, their lack of status the probable explanation for their absence from Campelo's tallies. From the recorded origin of militia members, settlers clearly migrated from many places. Some moved into the forest from the urban nuclei of the central mining district—from places like Vila do Príncipe, Mariana, and Vila Rica. Others came from smaller mining camps on the eastern edge of that district. Some even journeyed from more distant cities, like Rio de Janeiro and São Paulo, and some from as far away as Portugal. Eighteen inhabitants possessed captive workers, ranging from 1 to 36 slaves each, for a total of 129. The amount of land under cultivation in the township and its vicinity stood at 37 *alqueires* (180 hectares) and the amount of gold extracted in 1767 at 1425 *oitavas* (178 ounces).[5] A small fortune had it belonged to a single person, this much gold could buy approximately 17 slaves.[6] However, it did not belong to a single person and individual accumulations remained less than impressive. All the same, a start had been made on incorporating this distant sector of the wilderness into the colonial domain, even without the Crown's full cognizance or consent.

The divergent aims of settlers became evident as the effort to promote the development of Cuieté persisted with increasingly disappointing results. One governor after another pursued the project. Prominent officers like Campelo devoted a good part of their lives to seeing it to fruition. Many slaves labored there, as did many coerced freedmen and condemned criminals. Some Indians even entered the settlement when they chose the path of accommodation. Long before war was declared in the nineteenth century against those Indians who opted to resist, numerous retaliatory raids had been staged to secure the mining camp. Yet as late as 1813, with the most violent stage of the conquest of the Eastern Sertão already in the past, census takers counted just 235 residents in Cuieté. A decade later, the tally had scarcely increased to 243.[7]

Few accounts make the frustrations if not futility of the effort more evident than that authored by Guido Thomaz Marlière, an officer who gained fame in the 1820s for his attempts to befriend and acculturate the Indians of the region. With more than half a century of striving come to naught, he described Cuieté as a decrepit mining camp fit only for the "banishment of malefactors." Hopes for a flourishing township that would anchor the development of the immense Eastern Sertão had been abandoned for a more prosaic goal, the maintenance of a penal colony. The site remained surrounded by wilderness "without any way out whatsoever, except by river." Not even that escape was possible for six months of the year when the water route became an impassable torrent. Even the penal colony had failed to thrive. In the past, the place served its disciplinary purpose well, "being surrounded by the heathen, cannibal [Indians], from whom not a single fugitive exile escaped without being eaten." By the 1820s, however, once the Indians still living in the surrounding forests were "friendly and tame," Cuieté had outlived its usefulness, Marlière concluded. Criminals exiled to the wilderness could count on the Indians to guide them out of the forests. The only thing left for the few remaining settlers was to reestablish themselves at a more auspicious point downriver and turn the site into a mission village for tame Indians.[8]

The failure of Cuieté and a number of other isolated settlements like it to take hold should not be misinterpreted. Captaincy authorities expended enormous effort and substantial resources to secure these sites, and they almost always did so in response to a preexisting settler presence, however tenuous. Although Governor Silva in his original orders to colonize Cuieté made much fanfare of the founding of a new, carefully planned township, the truth was that settlers had been in the area for as much as two decades before he took office. Reports of their flight from Cuieté, under the continuous threat of Indian raids, prompted the governor to defend the area militarily. At the same time, he sought to preempt the unregulated nature of migration to the area. Colonization schemes of this sort hinged ultimately on the willing presence of settlers. Migrants themselves largely determined whether frontier settlements took root. Lacking individuals, families, and their slaves to people the places captaincy officials designated as sanctioned nodes of development, no amount of state-directed effort would prove effective. The stagnation of Cuieté demonstrated that settlers balked at official plans, even as governors strove to keep pace with post-boom demographic dislocation. As captaincy authorities tested and ultimately undermined prohibitions on colonizing the eastern forests, settlers remained one step ahead of local policymakers. Colonists quickly became disenchanted with sites too remote and precarious to support safe and profitable mining and agriculture. Crucially, they did not hesitate to take up the task of reproducing the structures of colonial society at locations they found favorable. As Crown and captaincy clung to their divergent imaginary geographies and backed contradictory projects to bring them into being, settlers complicated the colonization process by insisting on alternative visions of the sertão.

The contrasting perspectives that shaped the aims of Crown, captaincy, and settler had a direct bearing on the recreation of colonial society in the wilderness. The Crown sought to prolong prohibitions originating from the old gold mining complex, maintaining the position that the presence of Indians remained critical to blocking smuggling, which Lisbon's policymakers increasingly blamed for the lapse in declared production and tax revenues after the middle of the eighteenth century. Captaincy governors, better attuned to local conditions, understood that the mining economy's decline had more to do with exhausted gold deposits. They therefore perceived the territory east of the mining district as providing a different kind of solution to the captaincy's woes, a solution dependent on the discovery of new gold and diamond fields. As such, they too remained wedded to the established social and economic regime as a key to the future. By contrast, settlers focused on making their lives viable in the face of the pressing reality of changing circumstance. Some with the resources to pursue the old dream of mineral wealth carried that chimera into the sertão and found captaincy governors ready to back their efforts. But most settlers who looked eastward foresaw their immediate survival in agricultural production and thus directed their activity in the sertão toward the construction of a viable system for marketing foodstuffs to a growing captaincy and colonial population.

The owners of substantial numbers of enslaved laborers, who stood to gain the most from such commercial agriculture, would have been primarily, although not exclusively, white. By the late colonial period, a tradition of slaveholding by free persons of color had developed in Minas Gerais as elsewhere in the colony, but it remained a minority practice. Even when free Afro-Brazilians became slaveholders, persistent racial hierarchies meant that they owned far fewer slaves overall than their white counterparts. They were also not nearly as likely as whites to own slaves in the first place. The fact that they did at all speaks to the blurring of the idealized racial order authorities considered instrumental to frontier colonization.[9] At the same time, white slaveholders, as an absolute minority in an overall colonial population dominated by slaves and free blacks, would not have questioned the need to erect a frontier society firmly on racial hierarchies.

One such settler was Dona Anna Joaquina de Almeida. Her successful bid to secure a royal land grant (*sesmaria*) near the Pomba River in the late 1790s merits detailed examination because it sheds light on the experience of the majority of frontier settlers, those who headed east without venturing to sites as isolated, tenuous, and potentially dangerous as Cuieté. A historian of comparative frontiers once referred to individuals like Dona Anna, settlers of agricultural frontiers, as the "colorless many," contrasting them to the "colorful few" who made their mark by taking great risks.[10] In the Eastern Sertão, the most intrepid entered the historical record with comparative prominence, a minority arousing official attention by risking exposure to Indian attack or by claiming new gold strikes. Those less daring, of Dona Anna's ilk, lived out their lives in the sertão largely unnoticed, even though they were far more numerous and representative of the common migrant's experience.[11] This reality ultimately contributed to the failure of historians to recognize the extent of frontier expansion in late colonial Minas Gerais and elsewhere.

The experiences of such ordinary individuals can be reconstructed by assembling documentation they left behind in mundane forms that, as such, are indicative of everyday life on the frontier. For example, town notarial registers contain land grant requests, surveys, and titles; civil actions brought by property owners; records of credit; last wills and testaments; and post-mortem estate inventories. When linked with specific locations in the sertão identified in geographic records from the period, these sources can be cross-referenced with each other and with ecclesiastical documents registering births, baptisms, and marriages, which reveal the nativity, migration patterns, and familial networks of individual settlers. While generally too fragmented in frontier zones to allow for reliable quantitative analysis, such sources register important junctures obscured in the lives of otherwise anonymous settlers. Although no single account can give a comprehensive sense of the settlement process in all its variety, Dona Anna's experience is a useful starting point because it encompassed almost the entire period under study and coincided with important demographic and geographic developments between the 1750s and 1820s. The fact that this woman would manage to outmaneuver a long-established male rival in a property dispute serves as a reminder, particularly in a frontier world conventionally depicted as quintessentially masculine, that the settlement process could have unexpected outcomes.[12]

When Dona Anna died in 1817, followed just over a year later by her husband, Captain Francisco Soares Maciel, the couple's six surviving children inherited a sizeable estate.[13] Dona Anna had married in 1765 when she was 27, then living "in the company of her parents," and when Maciel was 33. Her new spouse had emigrated from Portugal and settled in the southeastern mining camp of

Xopotó, which by mid-century had passed the apex of the local gold rush that brought it into existence. Probably with the initial aid and influence of Dona Anna's father, a lieutenant, the couple managed to amass five major properties over the course of the following decades, despite royal regulations designed to prevent the ownership of more than one land grant. They had passed two of these sesmarias on to married daughters as part of their dowries. The remaining three properties, each in progressively remote areas, lay to the east of the central mining district, the most distant and least developed in the vicinity of Rio Pomba. The 15 slaves, draft animals, farm implements, planted fields, and tobacco and milling operations recorded in the couple's post-mortem estate inventory leaves no doubt that they profited handsomely from a growing market for foodstuffs in southeastern Minas Gerais.

In 1798, another prominent settler—also a lieutenant—mounted a challenge to this acquisition of frontier property, accusing Dona Anna of laying claim to land held by individuals who entered the southeastern forests decades earlier. The sesmaria in question lay along a creek feeding into a tributary of the Pomba River in hilly, fertile territory. Jurisdiction over the territory, which was itself at issue in the case as it was in many frontier land disputes, hinged on whether authorities in Rio Pomba, Xopotó, or Guarapiranga would exert greater sway over their superiors in Mariana, whose sprawling municipal district encompassed the region.[14] Just as settlers struggled with one another to claim land, district and sub-district officials vied for control over areas undergoing the process of colonial incorporation.

Dona Anna was one of many new settlers seeking land in the area. The surveyor who described the property she claimed noted that it abutted land already occupied by others, including another female landholder, several unrelated men, and Lieutenant Luis da Silva Pereira and José da Silva Pereira (probably brothers) who formally disputed Dona Anna's claim. Most of these neighbors were *posseiros*, squatters of varying means and thus unequal prospects of converting their holdings into sanctioned royal grants. Dona Maria's refined signature on her own sesmaria petition testified to the upbringing and resources that set her apart from most frontier settlers—especially women—in a society in which few females, even among the elite, ever learned to read and write.[15]

From the onset of the conflict, the Pereiras' hold on their land was clearly less secure than they imagined. Introducing an element of doubt, the surveyor of Dona Anna's claim described the adjoining land to the south as a tract "to which they say Lieutenant Luis da Silva Pereira has succeeded in obtaining a sesmaria title." Even less secure was the land to the north, a plot without formal title "on which they say Cipriana Maria da Conceição lives."[16] The surveyor did not indicate whether these neighbors had arrived in the area sooner or simply completed their surveys earlier. In Conceição's case, that a formal survey had been completed was not even clear. Yet both neighbors had stature enough at least to be noted by local authorities. That other even more marginal and inconspicuous settlers were not registered in such sources at all seems certain. Officials themselves recognized that many migrants along the eastern fringe of the mining district resided beyond the reach of church and state and thus beyond the bureaucracies that generated documents and archives.[17] The surveyor's ambiguity about Dona Anna's neighbors may have been an intentional equivocation to protect him from the consequences of allotting land no longer available. It may have been a ruse aimed at undercutting his client's potential legal rivals. More likely, it reflected genuine uncertainty about holdings acquired in a chaotic land grab occurring at the outer limits of the captaincy's administrative and judicial apparatus.

Two months after the Pereiras filed a formal protest charging Dona Anna with encroachment, she was awarded her sesmaria. After another two months, they were also each awarded a land grant but too late to avoid losing a portion of the property they claimed.[18] Acting on behalf of José Pereira, who was away prospecting for gold at another location, Lieutenant Luis Pereira attempted to substantiate their original claim by reference to official correspondence between several captaincy governors and a mulatto priest, who by the 1790s had become the most prominent early settler of the region. Extending over a period of more than two decades, the correspondence describes the arduous process of occupying territory controlled until the 1760s by Indians as well as the struggle of the region's first settlers to hold on to land they considered rightfully their own. The priest, Padre Manuel de Jesus Maria, became widely known as the "civilizer" of the Coroado and Coropó, Indians who roamed the Pomba River valley along with the less assimilable Puri. (More will be said about him in a later chapter.) For the present discussion, his importance lies in his defense of those who first moved into the southeastern wilderness from the captaincy's settled zones. For the Pereiras, however, his prestige would not prove sufficient to safeguard their land against Dona Anna's intrusion toward the end of the century.[19]

The Pereiras claimed to have been among the Portuguese migrants who, along with slaves and detribalized Indian porters, originally occupied the Pomba River valley under Padre Maria's leadership in the late 1760s. As the cleric set about establishing mission villages for the Coroado and Coropó, beginning the task of "Christianizing, civilizing, and reducing the Indians to the faith of Christ," the settlers who aided his efforts sought land upriver from the Indians. Together they had traveled first along an existing road as far as it took them, and then continued in canoes and overland without a road, carrying their supplies on their backs. Some earlier Portuguese settlement was apparent in the region, probably the result of similar activity initiated by the priest Ângelo Pessanha, who had ventured into Coroado and Coropó territory from the coastal plantation district of Campos during the previous decade.[20] Nevertheless, the route into these forests from the mining district had become virtually impassable by the late 1760s because most of those who previously claimed land there lived elsewhere. The few remaining settlers were "not disposed to work" and, in fact, sought to hamper the priest's efforts, apparently concerned about opening the area to interlopers. Padre Maria had thus enlisted others he described as "poor people" to build a new road to the site, but they had agreed to do so only on the promise of remuneration. To gain their allegiance, the indefatigable priest secured a promise from Governor Silva to grant them land for their efforts and to protect their claims against any others who might follow. As part of the priest's plan, these impoverished migrants would then supply the Indians with food from their new farms.[21]

Secured in this manner, the Pereiras' land lay just upriver from a tract set aside for the Indians. In keeping with practices dating to the sixteenth century, the Crown frequently granted natives who settled at mission villages a communal sesmaria of their own. Ostensibly a protective measure to provide farmland and prevent starvation, the policy in practice alienated far larger hunting and gathering grounds from the Indians, opening this land to colonization. It also helped concentrate groups of potential indigenous laborers at a single, manageable location.[22] Like many other frontier migrants participating in the initial expansion of settlement into the sertão, those who accompanied Padre Maria did not immediately obtain their own official land titles. But in instructions to the priest, and in further affirmation of the new racial geography then just beginning to take hold in the Forbidden Lands, Governor Silva confirmed the rights of those he called "civilized whites" as legitimate albeit untitled landholders. Their protection by the state would be their reward for "risking their lives in the service of the Indian conquest and the opening of roads" to the remote area, even though the construction of such roads was supposed to be banned by royal decree. As long as they did not "molest" the Indians in their new aldeias while contributing to their "reduction and Christianization," the new colonists could work their land without fear of the ambitions of future settlers. As always, the governor expressed his concern that the activity in the area not result in smuggling. Padre Maria, the settlers, and the lay directors who, in keeping with the 1757 Indian Directory legislation, would be placed in charge of the natives' civil affairs were to see to it that any individual engaged in such misdeeds be arrested immediately.[23]

Subsequent governors reaffirmed Silva's orders, reminded periodically by Padre Maria that the allotment of land was necessary to ensure that the initial settlers did not shrink from the effort required to carve a new parish and its Indian missions out of the wilderness. But authorities stopped short of granting sesmarias to formalize the transformation of native domain into Portuguese holdings. In 1770, for instance, the Count of Valadares barred the concession of sesmarias in the area pending a formal inquiry regarding the status of protected mission lands. In the early 1780s, Governor Rodrigo José de Meneses denied a petition by one of the most prominent early settlers who sought to convert his squatting rights into a land grant. The governor cited concerns that awarding sesmarias would impinge on tracts set aside for the Indians. Nonetheless, the original settlers remained "tranquil," Lieutenant Pereira would later maintain, confident that their promised privileges would be honored.[24]

As more and more migrants sought land in the area, the lack of formal title would prove decisive. In 1790, with Portuguese control of the area solidified, Padre Maria openly criticized the abrogation of guarantees made to him and his initial cohort. He reminded Governor Luís Antônio Furtado de Mendonça, the Count of Barbacena (1788–97), that he had "walked the entire way on foot, suffering hunger and hardships, and sleeping in the open" during his first expedition into the area. Over the short distance navigable by canoe, he had twice nearly drowned. Without the promise of protected land, those who had aided him never would have exposed themselves to the "great risks" posed by the "inconstancy of the Indians" or to the "afflictions" entailed in traveling to "regions so remote and dangerous." Now, more than two decades later, the Coropó and Coroado within the limits of Rio Pomba Parish had been "pacified," whereas Indians in neighboring districts not benefiting from similar efforts continued to engage in "treacheries." More than one road to Rio Pomba had been completed. With ready access now secured, "rebellious persons of poor conduct were entering [the area] on frivolous pretexts, as well as some rich settlers." They sought to "steal pieces of land from those same workers who had acquired them through their arduous effort and at great risk to their lives." They were also encroaching on the land set aside for Indians. Padre Maria insisted that the Directory's protective clauses required that this new wave of colonists be "thrown out of these lands, turning all of their handiwork over to the Indians." Furthermore, urgent measures were required to protect original settlers from this "unrest." Barbacena responded to the priest's appeal by ordering his district commanders to enforce the orders of his predecessors and "impede from this point forward any new establishments" sought at the expense of the Indians by anyone who could not demonstrate legitimate title to his or her land. The move did little to stem the tide.[25]

By the end of the 1790s when Dona Anna filed her petition for a sesmaria, the captaincy administration no longer put much stock in the agreements made three decades earlier. The mission Indians, Padre Maria, and the initial Portuguese migrants to the region would witness the expropriation of lands once guaranteed to them. Adopting a policy of granting sesmarias "throughout the captaincy, without exception," Governor Bernardo José de Lorena, the Count of Sarzedas (1797–1803), undermined any remnant of calm or pretense of orderly settlement. Profits to be made in the cultivation of tobacco, cotton, coffee, sugarcane, and other staples attracted thousands of settlers to the area. Further gains were to be made in the wild ipecac trade, as Indian laborers collected this medicinal plant widely used in the colonies and in Europe to induce vomiting and to treat colds, coughs, and fevers. No fewer than 40 sugar mills had sprung up in the region by the end of the century. According to Padre Maria, as he lamented in a letter sent directly to the colonial secretary in Lisbon, the land grab was driven by "jealous rivals who aspired only to annex his parish, divide the Indians, and usurp their best lands."[26]

At this juncture, the Pereiras filed their petition to formalize their squatters' holdings as a land grant. They feared that those now moving into the area, enjoying greater means and the advantages of cleared roads and pacified Indians, would drive out the early settlers altogether. Their fears proved justified: As their petition awaited action, Dona Anna secured the sesmaria that encompassed land they claimed as their own. With undisguised contempt regarding her appearance in the Rio Pomba region, Lieutenant Pereira complained that he "did not even know who she was."[27] In a futile effort to counter her claim, he pleaded with the governor to come to the site himself to allay any doubts, noting that the conflict over land in the area was more than a personal matter. Recent migrants were claiming sesmarias throughout the area without permission from the proper authorities. Not enough land remained to satisfy their demands without dispossessing the original settlers. If the governor did not intervene, land ownership would be determined not in accordance with fair precedence but rather in response to the speed with which individuals could move their claims through the captaincy bureaucracy.[28] At best, this practice would reduce the process to a contest of wealth and influence; at worst, to chaos.

The Pereiras received the official rejection of their complaint in late 1798, a day after Dona Anna paid a government surveyor to demarcate her plot. The local official who drafted the denial noted that the Pereiras had not sufficiently proven the merit of their "services conducted on behalf of the Indians," nor had they shown that the promises of past governors applied to the specific plot of land they claimed. As such, they had no legitimate priority over Dona Anna— in fact, quite the opposite. As the first to survey her tract and move a formal sesmaria request through official channels, Dona Anna would receive the royal land grant she requested.[29]

Her success, as well as the loss of those she displaced, points to a frontier settlement pattern underemphasized in high-level sources. As one of the three major properties still held by Dona Anna and her husband, Captain Maciel, on their deaths in the late 1810s, the Rio Pomba sesmaria represented part of a progressive family-based, market-oriented move into forestland increasingly distant from the captaincy's traditional population centers. Belying both the Crown's Forbidden Lands policy as well as the opposing preoccupation of captaincy governors with exploiting the eastern forests for their supposed hidden gold and diamonds, Dona Anna and Captain Maciel had made their way up in the world as farmers after the mining economy began its precipitous decline. Their most valuable holding, the fazenda in Guarapiranga Parish, while still encompassing some "virgin forests," was well-developed as a farm, producing corn, flour, and tobacco for the regional staples market. The couple's second fazenda lay within the village of Xopotó. Similarly devoted to foodstuffs production, it was assessed at just over half the value of the first farm. Finally, the Rio Pomba sesmaria, the least developed of the three holdings valued at less than a quarter of the primary farm, remained in the early stages of cultivation. Its forestland, second-growth scrubland, and cleared areas were not yet accompanied by any permanent structures substantial enough to be registered by the probate official who drafted the couple's post-mortem inventory. Notably, when listing the owners of properties bordering this sesmaria, the official did not mention Luís or José Pereira. Despite having legally secured a portion of the land they wanted, they had evidently moved on after losing their contest with Dona Anna at the beginning of the nineteenth century.[30]

With respect to the consequences for the region's indigenous hunters and gatherers, the ongoing replication of settled society and the extension of slave-based production into ever more distant reaches of the wilderness stood as the ultimate measure of the colonization process. Throughout the first half of the eighteenth century, migrants drawn by gold strikes to Guarapiranga Parish had encountered persistent native resistance. As the primary productive activity shifted to agriculture after mid-century, land-hungry settlers like Dona Anna and Captain Maciel continued to reshape the forests with consequences still more disruptive to the hunting and gathering practices of the Coropó, Coroado, Puri, Botocudo, and other seminomadic groups that had traditionally moved through the region.[31] The axes, saws, iron chains, scythes, hoes, handspikes, wedges, chisels, chopping blocks, shovels, and carts itemized in the couple's inventory, as well as the teams of mules and oxen, equipped the bonded laborers who transformed the forest into cleared, crop-yielding, profit-producing space. The 15 slaves belonging to the two settlers on their death made this metamorphosis possible and bore witness to its fruition.[32]

The dispute that arose over Dona Anna's land claim in Rio Pomba Parish produced a paper trail preserving extensive details about her family's frontier experience. Many others who received land grants also left evidence of similar eastward trajectories in the captaincy's notarial and ecclesiastical archives. As perhaps now evident, the acquisition of such grants frequently signified not the onset but the fulfillment of efforts to reshape the forest into productive land upon which enslaved laborers produced staples for a growing regional market. To examine another case, farmer Manoel Leitão de Almeida moved onto land along the Xopotó River years before the Crown granted him title to his property in 1774. By the time he applied for a grant measuring 11 square kilometers, he was long since "settled with draft animals and slaves on [this] sítio of cultivated lands." That he was among the first to settle this portion of the sertão was clear from the fact that his property was bounded on only one side by a neighbor, the rest of it opening onto the unclaimed wilderness.[33]

One of four children of Portuguese farmers, Almeida had emigrated from Lisbon, arrived in Rio de Janeiro in 1739 or 1740, and less than a year later made his way to Minas Gerais, settling in Guarapiranga Parish when he was approximately 15 years old. Ten years later, he entered church records, seeking marriage to 16-year-old Clara Pires Farinha, who had been born in Guarapiranga. By this time, Almeida was already active in the local provisioning economy but with only modest resources, owning just three slaves. He described himself as "making a living from tobacco farming," evidently on the same land he would eventually gain as a sesmaria, although not until almost a quarter-century later.[34] A few years after their marriage, the couple faced a challenge similar to the one that seems to have forced the Pereiras off their land. In this case, a squatter had moved onto a neighboring plot and then sold it, even before acquiring formal title. The purchaser, Dona Ângela Maria, converted the property into a legal sesmaria but in doing so claimed a portion of the land Almeida and his wife had already secured. Although the couple signed off on their new neighbor's official survey, they later claimed to have done so "out of fear," intimidated by a powerful former magistrate who backed Dona Ângela and whom they believed "would order some sort of violence done" to them if they refused. Whether the complaint they filed restored the entire portion of disputed land to them is not entirely clear from the documents; certainly, however, over the decades they held on to and profited handsomely from the bulk of their property.[35]

A decade after receiving title to his land, Almeida drafted his last will and testament, perhaps an ailing man as he died within two years. According to his post-mortem estate inventory filed in 1787, he and his spouse had an accumulated wealth characteristic of a couple of some means. As stipulated by Portuguese inheritance law, however, two-thirds of their estate would have to be divided evenly among their eleven children, a daughter and ten sons, the remaining third to be dispensed according to the couple's wishes. They had already bequeathed a second Xopotó sesmaria and four slaves to their daughter as part of her dowry. Another sesmaria, the most remote of the three, had been given to one of the sons—a priest—to provide for his support. Located in Rio Pomba Parish and carved out of "brute forests," this third land grant was surveyed, like the first, under frontier conditions with a single neighbor possessing title to bordering land. The rest of the abutting setters were described as squatters. By the time Almeida died, the first and most valuable property was bounded on three of four sides by titled land. Primarily a tobacco farm, it also contained "mineral-bearing lands," fields planted in other crops, and land set aside for the care of 100 pigs.[36] As additional evidence of the couple's financial success, their captive workforce had expanded from 3 to 22 slaves. Ranging from 1 to 70 years old, these slaves provided the unremunerated agricultural labor that kept the diversified homestead running profitably. Only eight were females, and only three of these were of childbearing age, the others being twelve years old or younger. The hardships associated with forced labor on the frontier can be inferred from the various debilities plaguing these slaves: 60-year-old Antônio was "broken"— that is, incapacitated—as was the infant Francisco; 40-year-old Miguel was "sick from an obstruction"; 20-year-old Maria was so ill that the probate official appraised her as valueless.[37]

Notwithstanding the image captaincy officials propagated of eastward frontier expansion producing mineral riches, accounts of the successes and travails of individual settlers and their slaves speak to the prominence of market-directed provisioning rather than mining. Downriver from Ponte Nova, in territory still plagued by Botocudo resistance, the priest João Ferreira de Souza, a native of the mining district, supplied the local market with his sugar and corn crop and his orchards. Forged out of the forest, this fazenda depended on the labor of 39 slaves at the time of its owner's death in 1776.[38] With surprising consistency and considerable irony, considering the dreams of fabulous hidden riches that drove captaincy policy, those who sought sesmarias to the east of the traditional mining centers rarely mentioned new mining operations. Instead, they spoke of farms for marketing produce and sometimes even of the need for fields substantial enough to feed hungry slaves once devoted to mining. At the headwaters of the Casca River, for instance, another priest, João Domingues Gomes, a native of the Minho region of Portugal who first settled in Furquim Parish in 1741, took possession of a land grant "facing the sertão" in 1790 when he was almost 80 years old. In his petition for this 11-square-kilometer tract, he stated that his property in the old mining camp of Sumidouro near Mariana no longer adequately provided for his captive workforce. Officials agreed on the merits of his request because he "found himself with numerous slaves" but "no farm-land with which he could provide for [their] sustenance."³⁹ In the same area yet another priest, who owned just two slaves, developed a homestead along the Casca River in the late 1770s. Although a church official referred to this cleric's poverty, Manoel Fernandes da Conceição did manage to extract more than mere subsistence from his land, selling surplus crops to other colonists.⁴⁰ Also along the Casca River, almost a generation earlier, Antônio Mendes da Fonseca began in the early 1760s to develop an agricultural operation that eventually became a land grant. An unmarried Portuguese immigrant who would rise to the rank of lieutenant by the time of his death in 1801, Fonseca had four children with the "crioula" concubine Joanna Fernandes. When he first filed a claim for his land at a time when royal policy still formally decreed the region off-limits, the surrounding forest was "very wild, without even a horse trail by which one could travel, or provisions for sustenance." The area remained "infested with heathens in the habit of killing any person" they encountered. Consequently, captaincy authorities could not reach the location to survey and validate land grants. This hazard explained why Fonseca and numerous other colonists, as he argued in a successful appeal to the governor, failed to complete the legal process necessary to validate their distant claims within the year-long period in which they were obligated to do so.⁴¹ Perhaps this is also why Minas officials took decades to understand that farming, not mining, would be the activity that ultimately sustained successful settlements in the eastern forests.

These sorts of colonization experiences reflected broader economic and de-mographic trends. This characteristic is clear even without access to comprehen-sive quantitative evidence, which the imperfect sesmaria data cannot provide. Refashioned into corn, sugar, and tobacco fields, peopled by migrants searching for alternatives to a languishing gold-mining complex, portions of the Eastern Sertão came to look and function nothing like the image of forests filled with heathens and hidden gold that permeated so much of the official discourse con-cerning the frontier. As governors imagined new mineral deposits unearthed in Indian territory, settlers endeavored to make a living from the land in the most practical ways possible. As late colonial memorialists fantasized about buried riches that would rekindle a receding golden age, settlers worked to feed themselves, their slaves, and the region's townsfolk and villagers. In much the same way that decrees dispatched from Lisbon were mismatched to the regional conditions besetting the mining district's governors, frontier policy forged in the captaincy capital was out of step with the actual transformation of the Forbidden Lands into productive, settled space. If the royal maintenance of a wilderness no-man's-land no longer reflected realities on the ground, neither did visions promulgated by captaincy officials of undiscovered gold and diamonds.

Both misrepresented the problems, import, and objectives of eastward-oriented settlers.

Population and Migration, Hinterland and Wilderness

When individual frontier experiences are situated in the broader context of large-scale internal migratory patterns, the disparity between official pronouncements and what actually occurred becomes unmistakable. Particularly between the 1760s and the early 1780s, at the height of the post-boom distress before a gradual recovery tied to further economic diversification took shape, captaincy authorities focused their attention on promising gold-mining sites like Cuieté and other remote outposts in the sertão. Framed in terms of sheer numbers of inhabitants, however, the failure of such frontier settlements to take hold can be understood in the context of migratory trends contingent on the ways colonists acted to pursue their own interests. The existing historiography provides little specific guidance concerning the magnitude of post-boom migration to the sertão.[42] With the help of census data, standard depictions of the post-boom geographic reorganization can be refined. Previously unpublished data allow certain demographic trends to be traced back close to the point at which the decline in gold production began to be felt on a comprehensive scale. At the same time, these data help clarify the limits of what can be known quantitatively about the captaincy's frontier population.

This analysis is an important issue because a fundamental measure of frontier incorporation was the extent to which state and church bureaucracies—which generated censuses as well as innumerable other historical sources—could extend their administrative functions over distant lands and peoples. Therefore, the following examination of census data is intended in part to help gauge the limits beyond which officials had trouble counting and even identifying people at the territorial margins of colonial society. Authorities had compelling reasons to tally these migrants. Only by doing so could they control them through taxation, military recruitment, and religious supervision, enlist them in state-directed colonizing endeavors, and protect them from Indians and each other.

The standard sources employed by historical demographers to study interregional migration during this period include censuses of varying precision conducted in 1776, 1786, 1808, and 1821.[43] These sources can be augmented with what is to my knowledge previously unanalyzed data located in one of Lisbon's primary repository of colonial records, the Arquivo Histórico Ultramarino. The additional data come from a number of summary manuscript censuses as follows: (1) A 1767 census with aggregate data enumerating households (fogos), adults (including civil status), children, slaves, free persons of color, dependents (*agregados*), priests, and total population for each of the captaincy's four comarcas. The figures presented in this census suggest that it significantly undercounted the Minas population. Nevertheless, assuming that all sectors of the population and all comarca jurisdictions were undercounted more or less equally, the data can be used to illuminate regional demographic shifts. (2) The original 1776 aggregate census. Previously, historians have cited this census only in its various published versions. The original manuscript version generally confirms the accuracy of the published data, apart from a few statistically insignificant discrepancies. It is mentioned here because it also includes age-distribution categories never published, which should prove useful to future historical demographers. (3) The four regional 1776 comarca censuses employed by officials when they assembled the captaincy-wide version of that year, which add refinements to the discussion of frontier race relations in the next chapter. (4) A slightly earlier, similarly detailed 1772 census from the comarca of Sabará.[44]

Not surprisingly, with minor, statistically insignificant exceptions, the comarca censuses excluded Indians as a distinct group. The process of purging Indians as a separate racial group, just as some wished to purge them from the Forbidden Lands, is explicit in the 1776 data and their subsequent use. Of the four comarca censuses of that year, only the one covering Serro Frio identified Indians separately—and then only 58 of them. This number was carried forward to the captaincy-wide manuscript census. But when the military engineer José Joaquim da Rocha employed the data a few years later in 1780, even those few Indians disappeared, included in the mulatto or mixed-race population that together he labeled *pardos*, the general designation for persons of color employed in all subsequent references to this data. Moreover, Rocha's use of the term entailed a further leveling of racial categories that became pervasive in the late eighteenth century. The individual comarca censuses employed seven separate racial designations, albeit with little consistency: for whites, *brancos*; for Indians, *índios*; and for non-whites of various racial, ethnic, and geographic origins, *pretos, crioulos, pardos, cabras,* and *mestiços,* terms whose meanings will be explained in greater detail in the next chapter. The 1776 aggregate census for the entire captaincy reduced the number of racial designations, combining mixed-race individuals of diverse origins and, in the process, demonstrating how racial categories were historically, socially, and bureaucratically constructed. Pretos and crioulos became simply pretos. Mestiços were subsumed under a single combined category labeled pardos and cabras. Índios, to the insignificant extent they were originally tallied, remained índios. When Rocha used the data in 1780, the leveling proceeded even further, as pardos, cabras, and índios became simply pardos. Subsequently, historians working with the 1776 data employed only the three remaining general categories—brancos, pardos, and pretos—ensuring the elimination of Indians from regional population studies. The decision to ignore this sector of the population extended not only to still-nomadic Indians who lived beyond the reach of the captaincy bureaucracy, which was to be expected. Also undifferentiated were those who inhabited state- and church-supported mission villages; so too were detribalized Indians and the more numerous mixed-race individuals of partial Indian descent living within colonial society, whom historian Maria Leônia Chaves de Resende has estimated to have comprised as much as 3% of the population of many Minas urban centers. Such acculturated groups were consistently counted as generic pardos, as was common practice elsewhere in Portuguese America.[45]

Historians have long known that the Minas population, the largest of any of Brazil's captaincies until the 1820s, continued to grow steadily during the second half of the eighteenth century and into the nineteenth, despite the dislocations caused by the exhaustion of alluvial gold deposits. Also not until this late date did the captaincy briefly relinquish its position as home to the greatest number of Brazilian slaves, although they were declining as a segment of the overall captaincy population. The free population of African descent grew especially fast. Adjusted to compensate for jurisdictional idiosyncrasies, the captaincy population stood at 341,769 in 1776; at 393,788 in 1786; at 433,049 in 1808; and at 580,786 in 1821.[46] Similarly adjusted, the 1767 population totaled 231,600.[47] As suggested, this final figure almost certainly represented a significant undercount, a fact that becomes apparent on calculating average annual rates of population growth. Between the 1767 and 1776 censuses, the jump in population would have required a yearly growth rate of 4.3%. Given the onset of the post-boom economic contraction, not to mention the radically smaller growth rates during the remainder of the century, this rapid increase defies reason. By comparison, the annual rate of population growth between 1776 and 1808 was a sluggish 0.7%.[48] The 1767 census, it must be concluded, counted most but not all of the Minas population.[49]

Another well-established fact remains valid for the entire period under study. On dividing the population into regions defined by Minas Gerais' four eighteenth-century comarcas—Vila Rica (southeast), Serro Frio (northeast), Rio das Mortes (southwest), and Sabará (northwest)—confirming the demographic center of the captaincy began, no later than the 1760s, to shift steadily over time away from the traditional mining towns toward the expanding agricultural and cattle-ranching areas of the south and southwest is possible (see Table 3.1 and Figure 3.1). Here another caveat is in order: The available data can offer only the roughest sense of this population shift from one region to another. Historians and demographers have been too sanguine about the reliability of figures tallying the number of inhabitants in individual comarcas and the captaincy

TABLE 3.1

Population and Annual Growth Rate of Minas Gerais by Region, 1767–1821

	1767		1776		1808		1821		Annual Growth Rate	
									1776–1808	1808–1821
Vila Rica	60,249	26.0%	78,518	23.0%	72,286	16.7%	78,863	13.6%	−0.3%	0.7%
Serro Frio	52,538	22.7%	80,894	23.7%	69,974	16.2%	94,296	16.2%	−0.5%	2.3%
Rio das Mortes	49,485	21.4%	82,781	24.2%	154,869	35.8%	236,547	40.7%	2.0%	3.3%
Sabará	69,328	29.9%	99,576	29.1%	135,920	31.4%	171,080	29.5%	1.0%	1.8%
Captaincy Totals	231,600	100.0%	341,769	100.0%	433,049	100.0%	580,786	100.0%	0.7%	2.3%

SOURCES: "Mapa geral de Fogos, Filhos, Filhas, Escravos, e Escravas, Pardos forros, e pretos forros, agregados, Clerigos, Almas, Freguezias, Vigarios . . . de toda a Capitania de Minas Gerais," 1767, AHU, Minas Gerais, cx. 93, doc. 58; "Resumo de todos os habitantes da Com.ca de Vª Rica . . . ," AHU, Minas Gerais, cx. 112, doc. 11, which slightly corrects previously published figures for Vila Rica, decreasing the total by 100 individuals; Bergad, *Slavery*, Table 3.3.

NOTE: The 1767 census undercounted the captaincy population, as noted in the text; thus, annual growth rates between 1767 and 1776 cannot be reliably calculated.

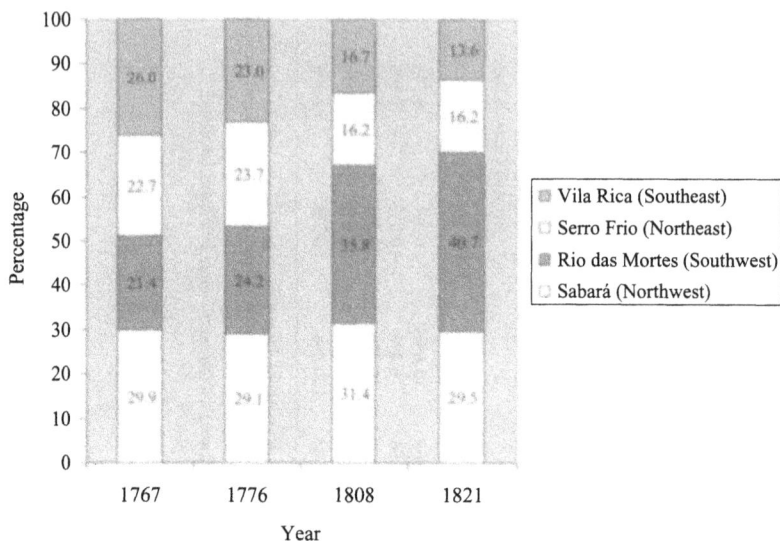

FIG. 3.1. Percentage Distribution of Population by Comarca (Region), 1767–1821
SOURCE: See Table 3.1.

as a whole. The inclusion of the new census data demonstrates such confidence to be misplaced. The clearest evidence to this effect comes from Sabará, where three different population counts conducted between 1767 and 1777 produced wildly divergent results. The total comarca population purportedly numbered 69,328 in 1767, dropped to 65,025 in 1772, then exploded to 99,576 just four years later in 1776.[50] Such swings testify, as the Portuguese immigrant, army officer, and early demographer Raimundo José da Cunha Matos bemoaned in the 1820s, to the "numerous uncertainties, diversity of calculations, and palpably manifest and absurd contradictions" inherent in the captaincy's colonial censuses.[51]

If such absolute numbers cannot be trusted as more than approximations, reaching conclusions based on the relative regional concentrations of the captaincy population and the changes in such concentrations over time remains possible. Between 1767 and 1776, the southeastern comarca of Vila Rica began to lose its hold on the overall Minas population, no doubt because of disruptions to the mining economy. After 1776, this demographic transformation gathered force. Both eastern comarcas, Serro Frio and Vila Rica, the latter now more rapidly than before, lost their traditional share of the captaincy population while the southwestern comarca of Rio das Mortes gained a disproportionate share. Between 1776 and 1808, moreover, both eastern comarcas experienced a net decrease in population, a trend that subsequently reversed itself as the nineteenth century advanced. The implication is that particularly during the four decades bounded by the censuses of 1767 and 1808, residents of the old gold-mining areas found themselves severed from their customary economic pursuits and forced to make a transition to new occupations, primarily in agriculture, and new locations, especially the south and southwest. That is to say, migration to the Eastern Sertão, while critical for understanding colonial Brazil's frontier and indigenous history, did not alter the direction of the largest number of migrants, who headed south. In doing so, many ended up—as will become evident—in the southern reaches of the Eastern Sertão in places like São João Batista do Presídio and Rio Pomba, where Padre Maria had unwittingly led the charge, followed by settlers like Luis and José Pereira and, later, Dona Anna and her husband Francisco Soares Maciel. Accounting for just 20% of the total captaincy population in 1767 as the mining boom began to fade, the southwestern comarca of Rio das Mortes doubled its share of the total to just over 40% in 1821. Particularly toward the end of this period, these southern areas of Minas Gerais found themselves drawn ever more firmly into the provisioning market and agricultural export economy centered on the fast-growing port of Rio de Janeiro, home to the exiled Portuguese court between 1808 and 1821.[52] For much of the second half of the eighteenth century, moves to the captaincy's eastern frontier occurred within the context of an overall population decline in the eastern comarcas of Vila Rica and Serro Frio. After 1808, demographic growth gradually returned to both comarcas. The dynamic expansion during this period of selected settlements in the eastern and especially southeastern forests is, in this sense, even more impressive because the larger jurisdictions around them were struggling, although the southeast by the turn of the century certainly benefited from the same expansion taking hold of the Rio das Mortes region.

Unfortunately, comprehensive data measuring intra- and interregional migration do not exist for the eighteenth century. Such figures are particularly spotty with respect to the settlement of the sertão. By definition, those who wandered into remote frontier zones tended to escape attempts by church and civil authorities to enumerate parishioners, taxpayers, and potential military recruits. The archipelagic character of colonial settlement in Minas Gerais, in which great seas of unsettled or lightly settled land separated urban islands, blurred the jurisdictional boundaries necessary to count rural migrants in any systematic way, as did the geographic incompatibility of ecclesiastical and secular jurisdictions. To complicate matters, as population growth and displacement occurred, a constant drawing and redrawing of lines defining judicial districts (*comarcas*), municipal districts (*termos*), sub-districts (*distritos*), and parishes (*freguesias*) took place. Population counts became more systematic only in the 1820s and especially the 1830s, producing detailed manuscript censuses that have provided surer footing for demographic historians of this later period.[53] But even then, the reliability of such figures with respect to sertão settlement remains suspect.

Despite these analytical hurdles, a great deal of anecdotal evidence and even some numerical measures point to significant dispersion away from urban centers, villages, and mining camps in the direction of the sertão. From the time some of the first significant gold deposits began to run out in the 1730s, Minas inhabitants responded by turning to agriculture and ranching in the western reaches of the captaincy along the upper São Francisco River. Even where mining camps flourished and urban centers developed around them, settlers occupied surrounding hinterlands as they realized the economic potential of provisioning miners.[54] By the 1760s, the development of agricultural and pastoral lands, along with the frontier settlement such development entailed, had spread across all regions of the traditional mining zone, affecting enslaved and free laborers alike. In a 1766 captaincy-wide census of slaves employed in agriculture, ranching, and mining, the shift was already dramatic, although the count must be taken as only partial, useful once again for its relative, not its absolute, numbers. Throughout the captaincy, even at this relatively early date, more Minas slaves worked outside the mining sector than within it. In the northeast, where the greatest imbalance developed, three out of four slaves labored in agricultural pursuits (see Table 3.2).[55]

As the shift away from mining became ever more pronounced, colonists turned to subsistence and provisioning activities, many of them beyond the reach of the civil and ecclesiastical bureaucracies that might have registered their presence. The frustrations expressed in 1823 by church officials who visited the outlying parish of Pomba betrayed the phantom presence of these often impoverished migrants. While the church emissaries tallied some 8,600 residents in

TABLE 3.2

Slaves Employed in Agriculture, Ranching, and Mining by Region, 1766

	Agriculture/Ranching		Mining		Total
Vila Rica	9,966	40.5%	14,617	59.5%	24,583
Rio das Mortes	9,266	60.8%	5,976	39.2%	15,242
Sabará	8,262	40.2%	12,301	59.8%	20,563
Serro Frio	8,591	76.2%	2,681	23.8%	11,272
Totals	36,085	50.4%	35,575	49.6%	71,660

SOURCE: Governor, "Resumo geral de Rossas, Lavras, Fazendas, e Escravos da Capitania de Minas geraes," [Vila Rica], 1766, AHU, Minas Gerais, cx. 93, doc. 58.

NOTE: Figures represent only a partial count of the captaincy's total population and thus are useful for their relative, not absolute, values.

this place they described as a settlement of "Indians" and "colonists," thousands more never entered the parish rolls. "How many never received the sacraments? How many failed to appear because of the distances? How many because they had nothing to wear! And how many because of sickness, or negligence, or for having sought succor in other places!" exclaimed one of the visiting clerics. "At present this parish must have no fewer than thirteen or fourteen thousand souls."[56] Church records produced in such circumstances frequently served as the basis for eighteenth-century censuses. The priest's plaint supports the conclusion that settlers living at any distance from parish churches were significantly undercounted.[57]

Employed to assess trends rather than absolute numbers, census data can nevertheless be used to document the expansion of settlements in the Eastern Sertão, especially during the early nineteenth century. Moreover, parish tallies made in 1818 and 1826, which the early demographer Matos considered the most accurate available, demonstrate the divergent fates of urban mining centers and rural agricultural settlements. As a general rule, the population of key urban centers on the edge of the eastern forests stagnated or declined. The sole exception was Vila do Príncipe, a town sustained by ongoing gold extraction and increasing foodstuffs and cotton production.[58] Primary rural parishes in or bordering the Eastern Sertão expanded in all cases and, in most, did so dramatically. The population of five such parishes grew at vigorous annual rates of 3% or greater. The most rapid influx of settlers occurred at São João Batista do Presídio, increasing from 2,783 inhabitants in 1818 to 4,089 in 1826 (4.8% annually). This parish was followed by Furquim, increasing from 5,210 to 6,942 (3.6%); Peçanha, from 1,236 to 1,600 (3.2%); Barra Longa, from 3,740 to 4,777 (3.1%); and Rio Pomba, from 11,571 to 14,704 (3.0%) (see Table 3.3). Other frontier settlements for which serial data are not available contained populations ranging from a mere 88 residents at Abre Campo in 1804 to more than 6,000 at Xopotó in 1819 (see Table 3.4).

Studying the demographic characteristics of a range of Minas population centers, historian Iraci del Nero da Costa analyzed additional data pertaining to two of these eastern settlements, Abre Campo and Furquim.[59] District commanders originally collected the data in 1804 as part of a captaincy-wide census ordered by the governor to identify residents who should be taxed.[60] The pitfalls of extending settlement eastward into the sertão were particularly evident in distant Abre Campo, whose meager 88 inhabitants expended much of their labor growing subsistence crops and guarding against Indian attacks in an attempt to exploit the region's gold deposits. The slaves and agregados of just three large landholders accounted for all but a handful of the mining camp's residents. The remainder included the three slaveowners themselves and three family members

TABLE 3.3

Population and Annual Growth Rates of Selected Urban and Frontier Parishes, 1818–1826

	1818	1826	Annual Rate of Population Growth
Urban Parishes			
Vila do Príncipe	11,555	16,000	4.1%
Sabará	9,055	9,012	−0.1%
Caeté	5,790	6,009	0.5%
Mariana	5,287	4,960	−0.8%
Vila Rica	8,658	8,377	−0.4%
Barbacena	14,229	12,205	−1.9%
Total	54,574	56,563	0.4%
Frontier Parishes			
Peçanha	1,236	1,600	3.2%
Antônio Dias Abaixo	3,656	3,765	0.4%
Barra Longa	3,740	4,777	3.1%
Furquim	5,210	6,942	3.6%
Guarapiranga	11,517	12,398	0.9%
São João Batista do Presídio	2,783	4,089	4.8%
Rio Pomba	11,571	14,704	3.0%
Total	39,713	48,275	2.4%

SOURCE: Compiled from Matos, *Corografia histórica*, vol. 2, pt. 4, 122–63.

NOTE: The data for urban Vila Rica include two parishes, Pilar do Ouro Preto and Nossa Senhora de Antônio Dias.

TABLE 3.4

Population of Other Selected Frontier Settlements

	Population	Year
Senhora do Porto	1709	1822
Cuieté	243	1823
Itabira	5608	1821
Abre Campo	88	1804
Santana do Alfié	654	1821
Ponte Nova	600	1823
Arrepiados	500–600	1823
Santa Rita	2251	1824
Xopotó	6000–7000	1819

SOURCES: All figures, except for Cuieté and Abre Campo, compiled from Trindade, *Visitas pastorais*, 95, 105, 160, 173, 181–82. On Cuieté, see Matos, *Corografia histórica*, vol. 2, 105. Trindade tallied Cuieté's population at 512 in 1819 (p. 170). On Abre Campo, see Costa, *Populações mineiras*, 108.

NOTE: All of these settlements lay within parishes listed in Table 3.3. Xopotó included two contiguous settlements, São José do Xopotó and São Caetano do Xopotó.

residing with one of them. In total, slaves numbered 58 (65.9%), agregados 24 (27.3%), and, as noted, the remaining free population just 6 (6.8%). Males significantly outnumbered females (65.9% to 34.1%). The imbalance derived not from the free sector, in which males comprised the minority (43.3%), but from the enslaved workforce, in which they outnumbered females by more than three to one (77.6% to 22.4%). Children under the age of 15 were almost nonexistent, numbering only 5 (5.7%).[61]

Such social organization was scarcely the basis for a thriving pioneer settlement, despite the substantial effort exerted by captaincy officials over the decades to make it prosper. Were comparable data available, they would likely show the demographic structure of other isolated and vulnerable mining camps of the Eastern Sertão—places like Cuieté, Santana do Alfié, Ponte Nova, and Arrepiados, all of which were subject to Indian raids—to be similarly unstable. While equally distant from a major urban market, the settlement of Peçanha, by contrast, had escaped such precarious conditions despite its history of Botocudo attacks. By the early nineteenth century, it had become part of an active hinterland, provisioning both Vila do Príncipe and Tejuco.[62]

The advantage gained from proximity to a major population center prevailed at Furquim, one of the captaincy's oldest mining camps. Over the course of the eighteenth century, Furquim developed into a well-integrated provisioning area for Vila Rica and Mariana, the latter just over 30 kilometers away. Furquim's metamorphosis paralleled the economic shift taking place throughout the captaincy, especially by the beginning of the nineteenth century, away from the gold complex toward what one historian has termed "mercantile subsistence agriculture," where the term *subsistence* is used in the broad sense employed by Brazilian scholars that includes marketing crops for consumption within the colony. Originally rooted in the foodstuffs markets required to sustain the old mining centers, this restructured slave-based economy continued to develop as the gold cycle ended but the colony's southeastern population increased. Farmsteads produced staples consumed and marketed locally, regionally, and, where transportation networks allowed, as far away as the coast. The provisioning economy lent greater stability to hinterland settlements, a fact reflected in their demographic profiles. Out of Furquim's total population of 2,309 individuals in 1804, slaves numbered 1,040 (45.0%), agregados 170 (7.4%), and the remaining free population 1,099 (47.6%). The proportion of males to females was significantly more balanced (56.7% to 43.3%), although once again the free population was more evenly distributed along gender lines (48.0% to 52.0%) than the enslaved population (67.3% to 32.7%). Children accounted for 665 individuals (29.3%), further attesting to this community's greater ability to reproduce and sustain itself (see Table 3.5 and Table 3.6).[63]

TABLE 3.5

Population of Abre Campo and Furquim by Civil Status and Gender, 1804

	Males		Females		Total	Percentage of Total Population
Abre Campo						
Independent Free Persons	4	66.7%	2	33.3%	6	6.8%
Agregados (free dependents)	9	37.5%	15	62.5%	24	27.3%
Total Free Persons	13	43.3%	17	56.7%	30	34.1%
Slaves	45	77.6%	13	22.4%	58	65.9%
Total Population	58	65.9%	30	34.1%	88	100.0%
Furquim						
Independent Free Persons	540	49.2%	558	50.8%	1,099	47.6%
Agregados	69	40.6%	101	59.4%	170	7.4%
Total Free Persons	609	48.0%	659	52.0%	1,269	54.9%
Slaves	700	67.3%	340	32.7%	1,040	45.0%
Total Population	1,309	56.7%	999	43.3%	2,309	100.0%

SOURCE: Calculated from Costa, *Populações mineiras*, 258, 278.
NOTE: For Furquim, the total number of independent free persons, and thus the total number of free persons and the total population, includes one individual of unknown sex, a statistically insignificant discrepancy.

TABLE 3.6

Population of Abre Campo and Furquim by Age Group, 1804

	Males		Females		Total Population of Known Age	Percentage of Total Population
Abre Campo						
Children (0–14)	2	40.0%	3	60.0%	5	5.7%
Productive Age (15–65)	51	67.1%	25	32.9%	76	87.4%
Elderly (over 65)	4	66.7%	2	33.3%	6	6.9%
Total	57	65.5%	30	34.5%	87	100.0%
Furquim						
Children (0–14)	365	54.9%	300	45.1%	665	29.3%
Productive Age (15–65)	823	56.3%	638	43.7%	1,461	64.3%
Elderly (over 65)	99	68.3%	46	31.7%	145	6.4%
Total	1,287	56.6%	984	43.3%	2,272	100.0%

SOURCE: Calculated from Costa, *Populações mineiras*, 259, 279.
NOTE: Excludes one person of unknown age in Abre Campo and 37 in Furquim.

Comparing similar data collected in 1804 in an urban district of Mariana, Costa demonstrates that the demographic differences between wilderness outposts like Abre Campo and hinterland settlements like Furquim stemmed, above all, from their primary productive activities. Furquim's stable demographic structure and dynamic population growth derived from two related

factors: First, commercial agriculture developed successfully alongside mining; second, the settlement became integrated into broader regional markets as
mining declined. Despite the decades devoted to its development, Abre Campo
remained an isolated and feeble mining camp. Work in the gold washings required a major simultaneous commitment of its largely enslaved labor force to
subsistence agriculture, but concomitant market incorporation never occurred.
The settlement's remoteness left its regional ties attenuated and its susceptibility
to Indian attacks undiminished. Such settlements attracted few settlers except
when mineral discoveries turned out to be substantial. Generally organized
around the few large holdings of a tiny elite, they relied on a disproportionate number of slaves and dependent agregados. Consistent with the extractive
labor regime, moreover, such frontier mining camps had fewer females among
both the free and enslaved. In contrast, as a once-booming mining camp much
closer to the captaincy's major urban centers, Furquim gradually made the transition away from mining toward the marketing of its farm products, as well as
to self-sustaining subsistence agriculture. Rudimentary urbanization occurred
and artisan activity thrived as the division of labor diversified. Furquim required proportionately fewer, although still substantial, numbers of slaves. It
also became home to many more women and children. In keeping with this
continuum, the fully urbanized realm of nearby Mariana had the lowest proportion of enslaved workers and the highest proportion of women of all three
population centers. Children in Mariana also comprised a healthy portion of
the population (see Figure 3.2).[64]

As noted, the lack of comprehensive census data of this sort was a function
itself of the frontier's imperviousness to projects designed to extend the reach of
church and state into the sertão. What can be learned quantitatively about frontier migration reflects what eighteenth-century governors and bishops could
themselves know. The boundaries of that knowledge attest to the difficulties
that authorities encountered measuring the tasks before them and consolidating
control over lives, labor, land, and resources in the sertão. With their imperfect
sense of the captaincy's mobile population, they could manage only inadequately
to influence settlers' movements. This reality led to official frustration that accounted in itself for periodic draconian attempts to exert more effective control.

By all indications, captaincy-directed projects to colonize the sertão in a manner officials deemed appropriate, orderly, and productive contrasted sharply
with the actions settlers took themselves. As the Crown balked at opening up territory considered strategically critical for protecting the mineral wealth that had
sustained the Portuguese Empire for much of the eighteenth century, captaincy
governors were at pains to insist that actions seeming to violate royal restrictions
derived from a loyal determination to supplement that wealth. Settlers weighed

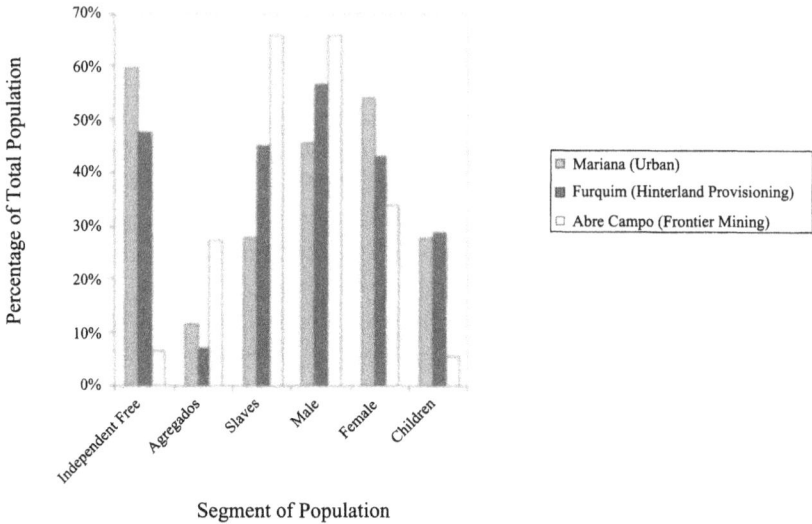

Segment of Population

FIG. 3.2. Demographic Structure of Selected Population Centers, 1804
SOURCES: Costa, *Populações mineiras*, 178–83; idem, *Minas Gerais: Estruturas popula-cionais típicas*, 89–98.

the prospects and perils of frontier colonization in more immediate terms. They did not shrink from seeking economic opportunities in the sertão. As a rule, when they settled on the frontier, they migrated not to its remote forests on the news of the latest gold strike but rather to its near periphery, advancing cautiously outward from the centers of long-established settlements, league by league. By maintaining ties to settled society, they mitigate the risks of encroaching on lands critical for native hunting and gathering, and the commercial prospects of foodstuff production offered an alternative to the ephemeral wealth of alluvial gold. In frontier zones emerging in urban hinterlands rather than the remote wilderness, settlers could hope to reap the benefits of an unexploited tract of land without completely severing connections to extended family, church, civil authority, and village markets. The accustomed structures of daily life in the mining district provided the model for such zones, as Indian lands were slowly remade to conform to them.

Squatters, Land Grants, and Frontier Incorporation

Colonial land-tenure policy fostered this territorial transformation on the rim of the mining district, thus helping to erode the Forbidden Lands policy. Across the Atlantic, where the specific geography of inland expansion could be apprehended only vaguely, Crown ministers failed to recognize how the laws and customary practices that regulated land acquisition undermined rather than preserved the status of the eastern buffer zone. Sanctioned methods of allocating royal land grants guaranteed that movement into the sertão, especially hinterland areas, would proceed unabated even as the Crown struggled to block or, where that was impracticable, strictly regulate incursions into Indian territory. One grant after another, restricted lands became colonial domain as settlers sought to legalize holdings they often first acquired as squatters.

Colonial land grant sources buttress the conclusions drawn from census data, further elucidating why much of the early pressure on Indians from frontier migration occurred on the near periphery of the Eastern Sertão, especially in its fertile southern areas, rather than at remote outposts deep in the forests. As with census figures, the quantification of this process, if only to the partial extent permitted by the sesmaria sources, provides a gauge of the intensity and continuity with which peripheral lands were incorporated. Rough numerical analysis also reveals the most active zones of internal colonization. Moreover, as sources generally unembellished by official polemics, land grant documents help distinguish quotidian practice from expansionist rhetoric.

The legal occupation of unsettled territory depended on Crown and captaincy policies that regulated the access to land. The economic changes that followed the decline of mining, the search for new sources of wealth, and the dispersion of peoples formerly concentrated in mining centers intensified the competition for lands on the fringes of settled zones. As the settler accounts that began this chapter make clear, those with resources substantial enough to be registered in the historical record gravitated toward commercial agriculture and sometimes even acquired farmland to feed their slaves. The most economically vulnerable of the migrants, the free poor, more commonly sought fertile plots simply to provide for themselves.

This post-boom reconfiguration occurred under the aegis of a system that held land to be the personal patrimony of the Crown. Throughout the colonial period, social status and service to the king had determined who received land grants and who did not. Land could not be purchased from the state; it was conceded as a royal gift. Through this system, the Crown secured political advantage with the colonial elite as well as the promise of future tax revenues. The size and location of tracts allotted depended on the prestige of individual colonists and their influence with the court and its colonial agents, the captaincy governor first among them. This did not stop grantees from selling sesmarias or parts of sesmarias to others; thus, over time, land became commodified, particularly along roads, in commercial farming districts, and on the outskirts of major urban concentrations. Farther into the sertão, where unsettled areas were plentiful, colonists more frequently acquired land by squatting. This unregulated side of the colonial land tenure system allowed powerful squatters to assemble vast holdings; it also left an opening for the free poor to occupy land that had no legal proprietor other than the Crown. On these plots, they grew corn, beans, and manioc to feed themselves and to barter or sell for other necessities.[65]

The territorial boundary at which settlers petitioned for and received such land grants was often the line that divided the well-off from the poor. On tenuous legal grounds, squatters, whether poor or not, claimed land rights by virtue of effective occupation and cultivation. They competed with those who then requested and received title to sesmarias. In Minas Gerais, the competition between the two proved particularly fierce in lands located along public highways, such as the Caminho Novo, in ranching country, and in agricultural lands producing crops for local and regional markets. Simple speculation was also a factor. One historian notes that many sesmarias were obtained by those who could sway Crown officials merely to "extort a settlement from genuine settlers who might later appear."[66]

Throughout the eighteenth century, a grantee's relative wealth and political influence determined the size of the sesmaria received, especially in the sertão, where untitled land remained plentiful. The largest grants went primarily to individuals expected to make them productive, at least eventually, through the use of slaves and other capital and thus profitable for the Crown. Other grants went to those whose prestige the Crown wished to recognize and enhance. Exceptions occurred, but they proved the rule. In 1783, for instance, Governor Rodrigo José de Meneses announced he would allot a number of sesmarias of limited size to impoverished migrants, many of whom possessed no slaves. The governor's proclamation specified the distribution of "sesmarias of a half-league of land."[67] As a rule, when authorities spoke of a sesmaria of a given size—in this case, one-half league—they meant a grant measuring one-half league (3.3 km) in length and width, that is, one-quarter square league (11 sq km). In practice, however, sesmarias of more than one square league, invariably bestowed only on those who owned slaves, were sometimes measured differently, so that a three-league grant might refer to land measuring three leagues in length and only one in breadth, or three square leagues (131 km²), rather than three-leagues on every side (392 km²). For example, the sesmaria allotted in 1752 to the cattle rancher Manoel da Silva de Almeida, an inhabitant of the sertão along the Velhas River in the northwestern comarca of Sabará, measured three leagues by one league.[68] The exact size of the tract in question can be known only when complete dimensions are noted explicitly in the sources. Grants of extraordinary size were frequently conceded in the early decades of the eighteenth century when unclaimed arable land still seemed limitless. In 1710, Manoel de Campos and Antônio Antunes Maciel received one such sesmaria near Jacuí, in the wilderness of what would become southern Minas Gerais when the inland mining district was made a captaincy in 1720. The area granted to the two men measured as much as one hundred square leagues (4,356 km²).[69] In an attempt to regularize and circumscribe the tenure system, a Crown order issued in 1725 stipulated a sesmaria of one-quarter square league (11 km²) as the standard allotment. A 1738 proclamation reaffirmed and elaborated on that order, declaring that henceforth sesmarias conceded in Minas Gerais would measure this same size, except those located in the sertão, which could measure as much as nine square leagues (392 km²); a subsequent 1744 iteration of the law removed this exclusion, theoretically limiting all land grants to the smaller, standard dimensions. Such legislation did not prevent wealthy and influential grantees from acquiring still larger tracts or more than one sesmaria in their own name or in the names of their relatives. One of the most successful beneficiaries of this practice was surely Ignácio Correa Pamplona, adept of the sertão, wilderness expedition leader, Indian killer, merchant, and confidant of a series of Minas governors, who himself acquired no fewer than eight royal land grants.[70]

After 1808, land grants comparatively modest in size became the norm. In 1817, for instance, the surveyor Francisco Gonçalvez Lima, charged with apportioning land seized from Indians in the Doce River basin, allotted a sesmaria to Dona Metilde Rosa da Silva e Buena. Lima called Buena a "new settler" (*novo colono*), a legal classification used to identify recipients of land grants conceded after the prince regent's declaration of war against the Botocudo. The land Buena claimed lay along a stream named the Onça Pequena in territory occupied by an army detachment deployed as part of the military mobilization. Measuring 750 square *braças* (2.7 km²), Buena's land was one of dozens of sesmarias granted along a road finally being opened between Minas Gerais and Espírito Santo through once-restricted territory now considered passable in the aftermath of the war. To the north, south, and west, Buena's land grant was bounded by tracts claimed by other settlers and to the east by the "depths of the forest." This is the extent of the information contained in Buena's sesmaria title.[71]

Despite the informality (some have said anarchy) surrounding land policy and ownership in colonial Brazil, those who were able to do so strove to legitimize their holdings, especially when competition from other settlers intensified. Accordingly, some 8,000 sesmarias were conceded in Minas Gerais during the eighteenth century and the early decades of the nineteenth century. These grants were recorded in the codices of the captaincy administration in registers of land grant titles (*cartas de sesmarias*), summary compendia that contain the recipient's name, the location of the grant, and its date, as well as certain standard prescriptions, notably that the owner cultivate a portion of the grant and pay a tithe in the form of a 10% tax on all crops produced.[72] This record-keeping at the captaincy level did not include much of the descriptive detail contained in sesmaria petitions dispersed in local notarial archives where additional documents, often in the form of legal challenges, were appended to the original cartas. Nonetheless, the abridged sources have the virtue of being collected comprehensively in a single place.

An index to this vast series of records, published in 1988, was heralded as a scholarly watershed that would allow historians to achieve a more complete mapping of the historical geography of Minas Gerais, a deeper understanding of the process of territorial occupation, and a clearer sense of the labor force utilized because of the requirement, generally enforced, that sesmaria holders own slaves.[73] Historians would eventually plot the incorporation of new lands and the expansion of slavery district by district, parish by parish, decade by decade.

The reason this promise has remained unfulfilled can be gleaned from a selective sample of this data, comprising more than 800 sesmaria grants.[74] The kind of historical mapping foreseen would have required that all or at least the large majority of the land grant titles contained specific information regarding the location of the grant. In practice, less than half (46%) of the sampled documents included the name of the municipal district (termo) in question, and less than a quarter (24%) the name of the parish (freguesia). Only this second unit is small enough to yield reliable conclusions about the precise direction and timing of territorial incorporation. Almost all (95%) of the titles sampled included yet another level of geographic reference, the *localidade*, or locale. Although intended by the scribes who drafted the documents to be even more specific than either the municipal district or parish reference, and no doubt widely intelligible at the time to captaincy residents familiar with local developments, most of this information is now hopelessly vague. For example, the title conceded to José Gomes de Araújo in 1767 stated merely that the land in question lay along the banks of the Casca River, offering no other information. Similarly, the land granted to Maria Brisida do Carmo in 1825 was identified only as situated in the sertão of the Doce River basin.[75]

This haziness should not imply that the data have no value. The dates on each document make possible charting the allocation of land grants by decade over the entire period between 1701 and 1836, when the first and last indexed sesmarias were conceded in Minas Gerais (see Figure 3.3).[76] The incorporation, valorization, and settlement of land proceeded throughout this period, even after the demise of the gold cycle, as indicated by the multiplication of sesmarias over the course of more than a century. Particularly intensive expansion occurred between 1740 and 1770, at the beginning of the nineteenth century, and again between 1815 and 1820. Although drawing conclusions about the relationship of this activity and the fate of frontier migrants and the indigenous peoples they displaced is tempting, this cannot be done definitively without more reliable

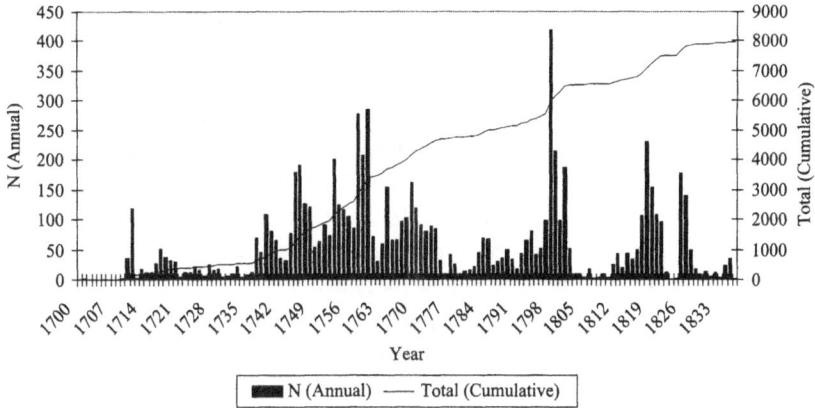

FIG. 3.3. Sesmaria Concessions, Minas Gerais, 1700–1836
SOURCE: Compiled from Leonardo Pires B. de Moraes, "Cronologia das cartas de sesmarias concedidas em Minas Gerais," Belo Horizonte, 1991, uncatalogued TS in reading room, APM.

information. For instance, unclear from the number of grants alone is how much of this activity occurred in cattle country to the west of the urban nucleus, how much to the south into lands previously cleared of their indigenous inhabitants, and how much toward the coast, advancing into the Eastern Sertão. In the latter case, however, clearly most if not all of the 489 sesmarias granted between 1824 and 1836 were located in territory until recently occupied by the Botocudo and Puri Indians. Although 1822, the year of Brazilian independence, is commonly thought to have brought the end of the colonial sesmaria regime, the new national government reinstated the system during this subsequent twelve-year period in Minas Gerais and neighboring Espírito Santo in order to appropriate Indian territory in the Doce River basin.[77]

Historians have assumed that the most rapid incorporation of land on the periphery of the mining district resulted from three activities in three separate zones: cattle ranching to the west and foodstuffs production to the south, both of which accounted for the particularly vigorous growth of the comarca of Rio das Mortes, and, to a much lesser extent, cotton farming to the northeast around Minas Novas.[78] Thus, for the 396 sampled titles that included municipal district information, the southern termos of Barbacena, São José, and São João del Rei together registered 59, 58, and 52 land grants, respectively, a combined 43% of the total. The termo of Mariana alone, however, accounted for 111 sampled land grants (28%), more than any other single municipal district and almost twice that of Barbacena, its closest rival. The only other termos to register more than

2% of the total were Caeté (not to be confused with Cuieté), which registered 39 (10%), and Sabará, which registered 24 (6%). Therefore, despite the imprecision of the documented locations, that the eastern outer reaches of Mariana's municipal district—which included settlements stretching along the sprawling upper tributaries of the Doce River from Xopotó to Abre Campo and Cuieté—corresponded with the zone of greatest conflict between colonists and Indians appears to have been no coincidence. In short, as the valorization and accumulation of land intensified in proportion to the concession of sesmarias, so did violent encounters of settlers and Indians. As the analysis of census data and migration trends illustrate, this process assumed its most forceful form in hinterland areas rather than on the more distant frontier.

Additional information gleaned from the sample of sesmaria titles includes data pertaining to the individuals who received land grants. A significant proportion (10%) of the grants went to men of military rank, ranging from sergeant to captain, positions often in the militia, not the army. Priests received 4% of all grants. Women acquired a full 9% and did so in a variety of capacities: as widows and heirs, as heads of households, and as the wives, sisters, and daughters of men seeking to extend family holdings by claiming more than one family land grant.

With respect to eastward migration, the key implications of this land grant data bear repeating, especially in the context of the population figures presented in the preceding discussion. Captaincy population growth combined with dispersion away from failing mining camps to encourage intensive land acquisition in specific sectors of the Eastern Sertão throughout the period under study. As migrants searched for remunerative ventures to replace the mining complex, they looked to commercial agriculture, particularly as the colony's southeastern regional markets expanded with the transfer of the colonial capital from Salvador to Rio de Janeiro in 1763, with the continued growth of the southern captaincies over the rest of the century, and, after 1808, with the economic impetus, voracious and Atlantic-based, of the Portuguese court's transfer to Rio de Janeiro. Crown policy forbidding settlement of the Indian lands east of the traditional mining district did not stem this activity. To the contrary, colonial land-tenure policy supported such territorial incorporation. The sesmaria regime favored the acquisition of holdings by those with slave labor forces geared toward the market. When profits made in gold production declined because of flagging mineral resources, entrepreneurial logic dictated the development of farmland and ranchland for the internal provisioning economy, which expanded in step with the colony's growing population. Ever since the early eighteenth century, Minas inhabitants had recognized the profits to be made in foodstuffs production. Well before the gold gave out, a substantial sector of the captaincy population devoted itself to farming and ranching. This long experience prepared the mining district's denizens for the changes following the economic dislocations of the second half of the eighteenth century. For the indigenous peoples of the Eastern Sertão, the effects of these changes were unmistakable. Even without the advent of spectacular new mineral discoveries, and even though remote mining camps like Cuieté and Abre Campo never fulfilled the promise officials ascribed to them, the inexorable incorporation of unsettled territory into the colonial domain gave rise to the most destructive era these Indians had ever faced.

The accounts of settlement activity reconstructed at the beginning of this chapter, despite their individual differences, exemplify the practical considerations that led most individual settlers fixed on reproducing slaveholding patterns to migrate to expanding hinterland areas, as opposed to more inaccessible destinations. In this overarching context, worth recalling are the choices made by Dona Anna. In the 1790s, she acquired a royal land grant in territory in the vicinity of Rio Pomba once controlled by the Coroado and Coropó. This and the other properties she assembled with her husband bore witness not to a reckless foray into isolated wilderness, and certainly not an uncouth aggressiveness spurred by racial hatred, but to a measured, progressive family-based accumulation of farmland oriented toward market production. Her presence at the southern reaches of the Eastern Sertão, her competition with other settlers to become the first to gain title to land squatters had previously secured from the natives, her family's dedication to corn and tobacco production, their substantial material possessions and sizeable enslaved labor force, even her status as a female sesmaria recipient placed her squarely within the profile of the thousands of migrants who moved outward and eastward from the traditional mining district.

In addition to the Crown and the captaincy government, slave-owning frontier migrants like Dona Anna shaped the conquest that unfolded progressively to the east of the traditional mining district after the middle of the eighteenth century. They did so in ways not always foreseen, understood, or effectively governed by the state. The Portuguese Crown persisted in seeing a territorial barrier whose impenetrable forests and hostile indigenous occupants protected the empire's inland riches. Captaincy authorities and elite memorialists continued to envision a battleground whose pacification would yield the discovery of new mineral reserves and a second golden age. However, settlers themselves made their choices in accordance with the existing structures of their slave-based colonial society. When they moved east, they sought destinations and routines most likely to guarantee security. They tended to move cautiously out from the edge of settled zones rather than risk their lives and livelihoods in the depths of the forest. They gravitated toward the clearing of fields and the planting of crops far more frequently than to the latest discoveries of alluvial gold or rumors of gold. They headed especially toward areas of the Eastern Sertão, where agricultural activity, transportation, communication, and market conditions proved most favorable. To return to David Harvey's formulation, they exerted whatever "command over space" they could muster as a source of power in their daily lives while laboring to reproduce the social relations they desired.

In the process, a slave-based society replete with the hierarchies and material trappings of life in the captaincy's older towns and villages gradually sank roots in the wilderness, often after substantial initial conflict—the displacement of Indians signaling only the beginning of colonial society's territorialization. The initial land-taking by individuals prepared to assume great risks set the stage for a subsequent transformation: the dislodging of original settlers by those with greater financial resources, larger workforces, and firmer links to state bureaucracy and market capitalism. The land that the first frontier migrants opened up, once defended against natives and cleared for agriculture, acquired greater value and attracted subsequent waves of colonists. Areas that proved resistant to such reconfiguration continued to vex captaincy authorities. If slaveholding settlers avoided them, an alternative source of transformative labor would be required. If Indians continued to have their way, a more clamorous rhetoric would be necessary. That rhetoric would seem justified and find a sympathetic audience because even settlers who avoided Indian conflicts ended up provoking them as the expansion of secure colonial domain diminished the territory hunters and gatherers required for survival. Colonization was always uneven. Certain areas of the sertão developed steadily while others stagnated. Some sectors, as will be seen, even fell back into Indian hands. The racial geography authorities sought to impose remained far from a fait accompli.

CHAPTER 4

The "Useless People"

Free Persons of Color and the Racial
Geography of the Frontier

I N   T H E   E A S T E R N Sertão, as well as in the other unsettled zones encircling the urban districts of late colonial Minas Gerais, attitudes about race
and proper place gave rise to policies governing labor and mobility, shaping
the incorporation of frontier lands. Efforts to curb post-boom demographic
dispersion centered not only on particular places but also distinct sectors of the
colonial population whose social and economic position was at issue. Specifically, for the purposes of the present chapter, the free poor—primarily persons of
African origin, those denigrated as the "useless people"—became the common
targets of such efforts with respect to frontier colonization schemes. Connected
to the intensive suppression of Indian nomadism that began during the second
half of the eighteenth century, this racialized conception of frontier geography
relegated persons of African descent not only to restricted locations within the
sertão but also to particular activities considered legitimate.

Since the early days of the gold and diamond rush, officials had tolerated
or even encouraged the hostility of Indians in the Eastern Sertão as a felicitous
impediment to the illicit transit of smuggled mineral wealth. This designation
of independent natives to a sanctioned geographic space required reassessment
in the post-boom era. As officials set their sights on the undiscovered treasures
of the Forbidden Lands, the nomadism of these Indians, their habit of living, as
one governor put it, "in a disorderly manner and without certain and constant
settlements," automatically set them at odds with the state.[1] The analogous
mobility of Afro-Brazilian frontier migrants branded them also as enemies of
the Crown and captaincy. Officials perceived nomadic behavior as a form of
resistance, ignoring the fact that movement away from the failing mining centers

had become, especially for the free poor, an essential survival strategy. In this way, attitudes about race, labor, and rootlessness shaped the settlement of remote lands as captaincy governors acted to control a mass movement, attempting to redirect Afro-Brazilian migrants so that they might serve elite purposes.

Despite the many differences separating Indians from the free poor in terms of their respective cultures, conduct, and status, they stood together in this sense as distinct from slaves. Chained to their masters, slaves remained captive precisely to the extent that they were stripped of their mobility. They journeyed to the frontier only in flight, thereby ceasing to be slaves, or when ordered by their masters to do so. Even those sent to work at distant mineral deposits on their own recognizance, as some were, remained bound to their owners by the backbreaking labor required to produce mandatory daily gold remittances. By contrast, the free poor could be doggedly itinerant, employing migration as one response to social marginalization. With this behavior in mind, a priest could reproach vagabond colonizers of the sertão as "a new species of heathen."[2] Also with this in mind, authorities sought to assemble the free poor and force them to toil in the sertão under controlled conditions that sometimes differed little from those governing the lives of bonded laborers. In this way, the powerful strove to make the free poor behave less like Indians and more like slaves. For their part, the free poor—like Indians—did not migrate only to resist a colonial project designed to form settled, stable, revenue-producing communities in the sertão. Often the basic need to secure subsistence led them to wander from one place to another. They did so in an atmosphere in which such movement routinely violated the limits defining the geographic and racial place assigned to them by the captaincy's white elite. Although cast in the same oppositional role as nomadic natives, the free poor often occupied a kind of buffer zone in which they bore the brunt of Indian resistance to frontier conquest. The evolving racial geography of the frontier, which divided indigenous peoples from the dominant slaveholding society, created this intermediary but frequently overlapping zone where free mulattos and blacks moved at their own peril, facing threat of Indian attack from one direction and official repression from the other.

Focused on labor coercion, the elite social and racial project took various forms. Some free poor frontier migrants deemed problematic by the state were conscripted to march out of the sertão and out of the captaincy to Brazil's southern border to bolster military forces arrayed against Spain in an imperial conflict over territorial claims. Others were rounded up and marched deeper into the eastern forests to combat Indians and capture runaway slaves. Civilian forms of disciplining free Afro-Brazilian labor were also employed. Many migrants who avoided military recruitment still found themselves forced to comply with official schemes to advance territorial expansion. Captaincy governors, district commanders, militia officers, and town officials confronted the situation by devising ways to enlist and redirect the energies of this mass of potential labor in motion. They sought to harness vulnerable individuals set adrift into the politically charged spaces of the sertão.

In addition to examining military and civilian solutions to this campaign, the present chapter elucidates some of the social constraints that determined how and where marginalized men and women who ended up on the frontier lived, labored, and formed families. It considers several state-directed projects in different frontier zones, all of them occurring in the 1780s, that reveal something of the range of this experience, including the obstacles faced by poor migrants trying to secure land in newly occupied areas. Although Minas officials considered allocating titled smallholdings to such settlers, the tenure system that concentrated land in the hands of the powerful prevailed in the end, barring the poor from securing ownership of the territory they settled.[3] In the most distant reaches of the sertão, where markets, commercial networks, land valorization, and stable land ownership had yet to take hold and where Indian resistance remained stubborn, state authorities pushed the poor to do their bidding, convinced that bonded laborers would be required to transform such regions into gold washings, farms, and ranches. Such laborers included not only slaves but also those who worked under various forms of peonage, servitude, or threat of punishment.[4]

The very fact that the state resorted to compulsion is evidence that the free poor often mustered the strength to resist official colonization projects. In more accessible, economically viable zones—to which the poor ventured willingly, even flocked, often outflanking the consolidation of state authority—squatters found at least temporary respite as subsistence farmers and small-stakes prospectors. Ultimately, like those compelled to labor for the state, they too suffered exclusion as a result of colonial policies that made land ownership dependent on royal favor, which in turn hinged on caste, class, and social prestige. In the interim, they carved out a significant space for themselves on the periphery of incorporated colonial domain.

The conduct of these frontier laborers demonstrates their reluctance to relinquish control over their lives. Some struggled to secure their independence; others, simply their personal and familial safety. They pursued their objectives even when authorities offered material incentives in exchange for their relocation to Indian territory. They thereby resisted the mercantilist logic that elevated economic productivity for the state above all other concerns. Where captaincy officials saw lands ripe for development (if only laborers could be found), the poor perceived the risk of injury and further subjugation; where the poor moved willingly into fertile zones, planting corn and other subsistence crops, authorities

ILLUSTRATION 4.1. Laboring on the Doce River, ca. 1815
SOURCE: Maximilian, Travels in Brazil. The John Carter Brown Library at Brown University.

feared a migration dangerously beyond state control. For poor families who already depended on patrons and landlords for their well-being, the security of the known seems to have outweighed the impersonal and uncertain advantages—including food, housing, and land—offered by officials to spur adherence to government territorial objectives. Notably, men and women who formed families found themselves more likely to achieve a modicum of independence on the frontier as compared to males who remained unattached. Considered a greater threat to the social order, the latter found themselves targeted by government and military leaders for participation in frontier labor schemes. Deemed skilled Indian hunters or otherwise willing risk-takers by those who wanted them to place their lives in jeopardy, the poor did not see themselves similarly.

The extent to which landless Afro-Brazilians resisted the imposition of colonization projects not of their own devising depended on many factors, as did their occasional success in winning concessions. In almost every case, official propositions had to be reconciled with the actions of these impoverished migrants, who had plans of their own. Their distinctive way of territorializing those plans, which often entailed moving across rather than settling down on the land, placed them somewhere between the ordered spaces of settled society and the unsettled lands of the frontier, between the Portuguese and the Indians, between the authority of the state and the autonomy of the forests.

Military Recruitment

The scope of the labor, mobility, and race problem, as governors and their district commanders saw it, can be measured—albeit roughly—by comparing to the rest of the captaincy the population of the southern comarca of Rio das Mortes, the regional pole attracting the largest number of internal migrants. That the vast majority of all internal migrants were of African descent is clear, given that this was also true of the captaincy population as a whole. The percentage of the total population composed of blacks and mulattos, both free and enslaved, increased from an already demographically dominant 77.8% in 1776 to a high of 81.9% in 1786, then declined somewhat to 72.1% in 1821 (see Table 4.1). Afro-Brazilians comprised the overwhelming majority of internal migrants to Rio das Mortes as well. During the 45 years separating the censuses completed in 1776 and 1821, the population of the comarca increased 186%—nearly tripling—from 82,781 to 236,547, while that of the rest of the captaincy increased just 33%, from 258,988 to 344,239. Although population figures from individual comarcas

TABLE 4.1

Estimated Population of Minas Gerais by Racial and Legal Category, 1776–1821

	1776		1786		1808		1821	
Whites	75,800	22.2%	71,248	18.1%	106,684	24.6%	161,800	27.9%
Free Mulattos	70,093	20.5%	87,217	22.1%	129,656	29.9%	177,274	30.5%
Free Blacks	38,764	11.3%	46,379	11.8%	47,937	11.1%	64,695	11.1%
Total Free Colored	108,857	31.9%	133,596	33.9%	177,593	41.0%	241,969	41.7%
Enslaved Mulattos	17,764	5.2%	22,104	5.6%	15,737	3.6%	23,215	4.0%
Enslaved Blacks	139,348	40.8%	166,840	42.4%	133,035	30.7%	153,801	26.5%
Total Slaves	157,112	46.0%	188,944	48.0%	148,772	34.4%	177,017	30.5%
Total Colored	265,969	77.8%	322,540	81.9%	326,365	75.4%	418,986	72.1%
Total Population	341,769	100.0%	393,788	100.0%	433,049	100.0%	580,786	100.0%

SOURCES: "Mapa dos habitantes atuaes da Capitania de Minas Geraes e dos Nascidos e falecidos no ano de 1776," AHU, Minas Gerais, cx. 110, doc. 59; "Resumo de todos os habitantes da Com.ᶜᵃ de V.ᵃ Rica...," AHU, Minas Gerais, cx. 112, doc. 11; Bergad, *Slavery*, Table 3.2. The first two sources, corrected for minor internal addition errors, slightly alter previously published figures, decreasing by 100 the total number of enslaved blacks in 1776. A statistically insignificant addition error has also been corrected for the 1786 figures provided in Bergad's Table 3.2.

TABLE 4.2

Estimated Population of Comarca of Rio das Mortes by Racial and Legal Category,
1776–1821

	1776		1821	
Whites	29,926	36.2%	86,201	36.4%
Free Mulattos			43,661	18.5%
Free Blacks			12,566	5.3%
Total Free Colored			56,227	23.8%
Enslaved Mulattos			9,195	3.9%
Enslaved Blacks			84,923	35.9%
Total Slaves			94,119	39.8%
Total Mulattos	15,794	19.1%	52,857	22.3%
Total Blacks	37,061	44.8%	97,489	41.2%
Total Colored	52,855	63.8%	150,346	63.6%
Total Comarca Population	82,781	100.0%	236,547	100.0%

SOURCE: "Mapa dos habitantes actuais da Com.ᶜᵃ do Rio das Mortes. . ."; AHU, Minas Gerais, cx. 112, doc. 11; "Mapa dos habitantes atuaes da Capitania de Minas Geraes e dos Nascidos e falecidos no ano de 1776," AHU, Minas Gerais, cx. 110, doc. 59; "População da província de Minas Gerais—1821," Matos, *Corografia histórica*, vol. 2, 55; Bergad, *Slavery*, Table 3.3.

NOTE: These data maintain consistent 1776 comarca geographic boundaries using methodology devised in Bergad, *Slavery*, Table 3.3. Legal category data were not recorded for Rio das Mortes in 1776. Racial category data were derived by calculating percentages from the manuscript comarca census of that year. Racial and legal category data for 1821 were derived similarly from the census of that year applied to the population living within the same geographic boundaries.

were approximate, especially in the eighteenth century, the substantial regional disparity can be attributed, as noted in the previous chapter, primarily to internal migration away from the waning centers of gold production, migration that was both free and, in the case of slaves, forced.[5] As the comarca's overall population grew, so did its population of African descent, increasing 184% from 52,855 to 150,346 over the same 45 years (see Table 4.2). In other words, tens of thousands of migrants were on the move in Minas Gerais during this period, the bulk of them people of color, at precisely the moment that local authorities were struggling to reestablish economic and social stability and incorporate portions of the Eastern Sertão in the midst of mining's deterioration.

The consequences became critical in 1776 when an open dispute developed between Governor Noronha and the viceroy in Rio de Janeiro as the governor resisted Crown military conscription efforts targeting the free poor. An intensification of hostilities between Portugal and Spain over Brazil's southern borderlands precipitated the dispute.[6] A focus of imperial rivalry throughout the colonial period, the borderlands region would in the nineteenth century become the Republic of Uruguay and major parts of the Brazilian provinces and, later, states of Paraná, Santa Catarina, and Rio Grande do Sul. Tensions over these lands peaked in the 1770s when the expulsion of the Spaniards from territory claimed by the Portuguese provoked Charles III to launch the largest military expedition Spain had ever ordered to the Americas. When this news reached Brazil in October 1776, Viceroy Lavradio sought additional troops to reinforce garrisons in Rio de Janeiro, believed to be a likely target of the impending attack. The viceroy called on Governor Noronha to march a cavalry regiment and as many recruits as he could muster from Minas Gerais to the coastal capital. He also ordered Noronha to ready militia corps based at strategic places in the captaincy, should the imperial conflict require further mobilization.[7]

Noronha balked at the viceroy's instructions to concentrate recruitment efforts on the captaincy's "least essential men and vadios." The governor warned that such an effort would cause "absolutely irreparable harm" to public security and to his determination to "extract [Minas Gerais] from the indigence that it suffers." The inland mining district differed from the rest of Brazil in this respect, Noronha argued, because "these vadios, who in other places would be prejudicial, here can be made useful."[8] Like many officials, Noronha blamed the economic difficulties peculiar to Minas Gerais on a shortage of labor, and he believed that the region's marginalized population, properly disciplined, would prove essential to alleviating these strains.[9]

Elaborating, he described the unique position of men labeled vadios in the mining district, a position he defined by linking imputed racial characteristics to an imagined geography. In essence, he argued that persons of color were peculiarly fit to do the state's bidding in the untamed spaces of the sertão. Identifying the kinds of men who would be subject to the viceroy's recruitment directive, Noronha asserted that apart from a small number of whites, the region's vadios were "all *mulatos, mestiços, cabras*, and *negros forros*." Elsewhere, he categorized them as "*pardos*" and "*crioulos*."[10] To understand the significance he attached to this state of affairs, a brief explanation of eighteenth-century Portuguese color, racial, and juridical classifications is in order. *Branco*, of course, meant white. Equivalent to its English cognate, *mulato* referred to persons of mixed European and African origin. *Pardo* was used interchangeably with *mulato*, although it also frequently designated persons of color more generally, with varying degrees of white, black, and Indian ancestry, making it the broadest of mixed-race categories. *Mestiço* and *cabra* carried this same general meaning and were similarly imprecise, although both could be used more narrowly to designate the mixing of mulatto and black or, more rarely, white and Indian, like the Spanish term *mestizo*. *Negro* meant black, as did *preto*, used less frequently, with both terms commonly reserved for slaves—more specifically, for slaves born in Africa. *Crioulo* referred to slaves born in Brazil, usually of African-born parents. *Forro* signified free or freed. Thus *negros forros, crioulos forros*, and *pardos forros* were all free blacks and mulattos, or in the broadest sense, free persons of color.

Characterizing vadios in these various ways, Governor Noronha called on this broader meaning in taking issue with the viceroy's orders.[11]

Such men, he explained, served a particular function in Minas Gerais, whether in the forests just beyond the perimeter of the mining district's hinterland or deeper in the wilderness at frontier outposts surrounded by hostile natives. Forcibly recruited men of color formed the squadrons deployed to "enter the forests to destroy the quilombos of fugitive slaves that have recently caused the most atrocious harm." These same "insolent men" were "sent to people remote places like Cuieté, Abre Campo, and other sites." They composed the squadrons used to defend settlers of a more desirable sort "from the invasions of barbarous heathen." And it was they who, "like beasts," according to the governor's geo-racial thinking, "penetrate the virgin forests in pursuit of these same heathen."[12] Their presence was required not only to further mining operations, Noronha wrote to one of Mariana's leading officials. They also served as an "obstacle preventing the heathen from penetrating [the] sertão and harassing the many fazendas that are to be found occupied and cultivated" in the environs of the upper Doce River tributaries. Were such sites to be abandoned, the Indians would surely proceed to attack the near hinterland of the mining district, disrupting the flow of essential provisions to Mariana.[13]

The extensive documentation stemming from the official struggle over the 1770s military recruitment campaign is worth pursuing because it illustrates the distinctive and frequently coerced role Minas authorities envisioned for the Afro-Brazilian population with respect to frontier colonization. Noronha would ultimately bow to the viceroy's demand for reinforcements drawn from this population. Even as he scrambled to respond, a company he had assembled of more than 200 of such soldiers was at work in the Eastern Sertão cutting a road through the dense forests separating the settled mining district from Cuieté.[14] As a result of the viceroy's call to arms, João da Silva Tavares, commander of military actions against the eastern Indians and the officer in charge of the road-construction project, was promoted to the rank of colonel and reassigned to direct the deployment of troops to São Paulo and the southern borderlands instead of to the Eastern Sertão. After the cessation of hostilities, he returned to his mission in Indian territory, appointed regent of the Conquest of Cuieté in 1779, continuing to draw on the same population of recruits.[15]

Noronha proved to be more determined to use the captaincy's recruits and overburdened military to patrol the Forbidden Lands—and to do so with troops he considered capable and well armed—than to fight the Spaniards, Portugal's principal external enemy. This preference is telling. To pursue his frontier policies, he was willing to sacrifice full compliance with the colony's reciprocal system of inter-captaincy aid as the need to combat the internal enemy, Indians and runaway slaves, limited the number and quality of troops he was prepared to spare. His actions underscore just how prominent a place the drive to conquer the sertão occupied in captaincy policymaking.[16]

Ironically, military conscription itself—or rather the flight from it—forced many of these individuals to the frontier in the first place. Throughout his tenure, Noronha, like other governors, habitually made Afro-Brazilians the target of forced recruitment efforts.[17] However, he knew that this policy prompted such men to flee their towns and villages and "desert into the sertão" to find refuge in distant forests. Fear of such flight on a massive scale led Noronha to warn of impending disaster when the viceroy ordered still more troops recruited in Minas Gerais as the fighting began in earnest in the south. The Spaniards captured Santa Catarina Island in late February 1777, followed by a nearby Portuguese garrison on the mainland in early March. Immediately thereafter, the viceroy called on Noronha to march no fewer than 4,000 soldiers overland from Minas Gerais to São Paulo and from there on to Rio Grande de São Pedro.[18]

The viceroy had ordered the governor to focus the recruitment campaign on vadios, men who would not be missed. Such men, the viceroy insisted, would learn proper discipline in the militia and return to Minas Gerais as better field workers and laborers. His call for reinforcements made explicit the racial categories he had in mind. Explaining the need for the thousands of Minas soldiers, Lavradio asserted that Minas Gerais was, more than any other captaincy, "filled with robust and strong persons accustomed to work in the field and forests." To make the best of these workers, the force would therefore be composed not merely of whites but also of "*negros, mulatos, cabras,* [and] *mestiços.*"[19] Governor Noronha knew the viceroy meant very few whites indeed: An overwhelming majority of men of color, who had always borne the brunt of forced military enlistment, would form the corps that eventually marched south.[20]

Short of men to meet the demand for troops, Noronha responded with the drastic measure of enlisting not only free men of color but slaves as well.[21] On March 20, 1777, he ordered regional authorities to "enlist half of the slaves held by every slave owner in the captaincy, without exception." Officers were to select "the most robust" enslaved males in every district, to arm them with spears and lances, and to prepare them to march south in the company of their masters or legitimate substitutes appointed in their stead. The order was to apply to slave owners of every sort, miners, ranchers, and planters alike, regardless of the number of slaves they held.[22] However, a week later, apparently facing mounting opposition to the order, the governor exempted certain owners and their slaves. He remained fearful that enlistment would prompt the flight of individuals to the sertão, but he also feared their absence from the sertão once they were rounded up and sent off to bolster Portuguese forces. The governor thus excused from impressment slaves and other manual laborers working in the most distant reaches of the captaincy, where he believed conscription would be especially disruptive, as well as those directly involved in the harvest currently in progress. Those exempted included free and slave laborers in the Eastern Sertão who worked on "fazendas lying along the forests that have a common boundary with wild Indians." Such individuals served as a defense against the "tyrannical attacks" of indigenous nomads, who could not "infest the interior of this captaincy as long as the said fazendas maintain a large number of laborers." Refusing to recruit them, the governor said he was unwilling to place local inhabitants at risk "of losing their lives and abandoning their fazendas" to raise the troops necessary to meet the viceroy's demands.[23] Despite the intensification of the external conflict with the Spanish, the internal threat from Indians continued to dictate the governor's actions. His actions presupposed a racially structured sense of frontier geography, in which Indians in remote regions threatened white landholders in more settled zones while a mass of slaves and free persons of African descent formed a buffer zone between the two.

Exemptions notwithstanding, by mid-May Governor Noronha had nearly completed the recruitment campaign. Slightly more than the requested number of soldiers (4,085 in all) had already marched to São Paulo or were about to leave. Almost all of them, the governor now confirmed, were "mulatos, mestiços, cabras, and negros," the final term employed instead of negros forros, perhaps a reference to the slaves among them. Whites had been withheld, the governor maintained, in case the viceroy should need them to defend Rio de Janeiro. Less than a fifth of the recruits bore firearms, attesting to the captaincy government's financial limitations and to the poverty of the recruits themselves, not to mention to concerns about arming slaves and men considered vagabonds with anything more than lances. In the meantime, enlistment was, as expected, taking its toll, causing "more than a little disquiet," wrote Noronha, "since the men most fit for the war have taken refuge in the forests."[24] With the recruitment campaign avoiding whites almost entirely, the governor's notion of fitness was clear: Fit men were not simply strong, experienced, courageous, or well armed; they were men of color.

The potential of forced, racially ordered recruitment to provoke turmoil in the sertão was epitomized by the events surrounding this mobilization. A sense of social volatility was palpable in official communication between the governor and regional officials. In possession of Noronha's recruitment order, the ouvidor (superior judge) of the comarca of Serro Frio queried the governor whether he meant to include even those slaves working in the captaincy's separately administered northeastern diamond district because the loss of their labor would prove extremely costly to the Crown. Meanwhile, slave owners in the region protested that some of the enlisted slaves believed they had been "freed and emancipated by this action." Others, the ouvidor warned, spoke "in secret of passing over to the enemy on the sly with the goal of freeing themselves from captivity." Whether attributable to elite fears or actual instances of insubordination, tensions were so high that he had refrained from punishing these insubordinate men "in order to avoid some sort of domestic war."[25] While waiting for a response to his query, the ouvidor nevertheless assured the governor that he was proceeding with the implementation of the recruitment order, assembling slaves into detachments of up to 30 soldiers each. Governor Noronha's reply was not recorded in the documentation consulted, but clearly he ultimately suspended enlistment within the diamond district. The force sent south was divided almost equally among recruits from the three comarcas Rio das Mortes, Vila Rica, and Sabará.[26] Absent were men from the captaincy's fourth comarca, Serro Frio, where the diamond district was located.

Noronha also suggested that increasing hostility among the captaincy's Indians was, as predicted, a result of this disruptive recruitment drive. Until the advent of the enlistment effort, he claimed, only the Botocudo Indians had harassed frontier settlers, but now the Puri had also become rebellious, "penetrating all the way to the fazendas of Abre Campo, where they had killed and robbed." In reaction, troops who might otherwise have been sent south were ordered to "enter the forests and destroy [Puri] villages, should these villages be discovered." According to the governor, another consequence of forced recruitment was the increasing flight of slaves and the resulting proliferation of quilombos. Noronha speculated that in the wake of the deployment of troops to the south, these runaways believed the captaincy had lost the force to oppose them.[27]

Ultimately, the sources do not specify what percentage of the force that marched to São Paulo actually consisted of those "insolent men" Governor Noronha identified as free Afro-Brazilian frontier inhabitants, hunters of Indians and fugitive slaves, itinerant denizens of the outermost fringe of colonial settlement. Nor can what percentage comprised slaves be determined, specifically those who worked the outlying fazendas subject to Indian attack. The documentary record does include descriptions of how these troops appeared to officials as they passed through São Paulo on the way south, affording ample illustration of both the penury that characterized their lives and the way they were reviled in racist terms. Recruits began arriving in late April in companies of more than 100. The governor of São Paulo, Martin Lopes Lobo de Saldanha, expressed unconcealed contempt on discovering how ill-equipped they were for battle. "These men arrive entirely nude or wearing nothing more than cotton drawers and shirts." The firearms, carried by a select few, were "broken" more often than not. The remaining troops bore "so-called lances," weapons so primitive that the governor said he did "not know what to call them." The men arrived "so lacking in all provisions," he wrote, that "they do not even carry mess pans or pots." In this condition, he warned, more would die of hunger and exposure en route to the chilly south than would ever reach the battlefield.[28]

Addressing these comments to the viceroy, Saldanha expressed even greater disdain for the soldiers to Lieutenant-General J.H. Böhm, the Austrian mercenary that the Portuguese placed in command of the southern forces, and to José Marcelino de Figueiredo, the governor of Rio Grande de São Pedro.[29] "By nature, they are all vile, without the least worth," he wrote. Only to obey the Crown's orders was he willing to "accept the shame" of sending them on to Rio Grande after "removing from their company all of those who are crippled, broken, and old, ranging from sixty to one hundred years of age, of whom there are a good number."[30] He thus began transferring the Minas troops south to the theater of conflict. Apprised of the governor's misgivings, the viceroy responded that he intended these soldiers not as a front-line corps but as men, in accordance with their function in Minas Gerais, who could move through surrounding forests with ease and thereby wreak chaos in the ranks of the enemy, perhaps by staging surprise raids. After 15 detachments of the soldiers had already marched south from São Paulo, General Böhm reported he that had no use for this sort of reinforcement, and Saldanha resolved to send the rest of the recruits back to Minas Gerais. Exasperated, he reported to Lisbon that he had taken this course of action to free his forces "from the starvation so many vagabond men were causing, without any function other than multiplying in this land a massive band of thieves and malefactors." He explicitly lamented the racial composition of the troops: They were "in greatest part blacks and very few whites," at a time when only well-armed, white soldiers could effectively serve the wartime requirements of the colony.[31]

In this way, the connections between frontier social relations, race, and labor continued to play themselves out even after these troops, or some portion of them, were pulled out of the Eastern Sertão and sent to the southern borderlands. In response to Saldanha's complaints about the lack of uniforms, firearms, food, and other basic supplies, Governor Noronha retorted that this was the way men of this sort were accustomed to living in the sertão. Lacking provisions and barely clothed, they nevertheless served their function in Minas Gerais. "It is in this manner," he repeated, that their squadrons "penetrate the virgin forests and deserted places of this captaincy to pursue the wild heathen and to extinguish the quilombos of blacks." He had therefore chosen to send them south in the same fashion, avoiding unnecessary expenditures on provisions with which they had no acquaintance in the first place.[32] Uniforms and equipment would have constituted a wasteful expense because these men had "no concern for honor and are inclined toward violence" and "might desert in great numbers" before arriving at their destination. The governor had not sent more firearms because to do so would have been to take them away from those who had greater need, among them squadrons that remained behind, deployed, he emphasized once more, to control unruly slaves and repel Indian attacks. Were Minas officials to ignore their "war" in the Eastern Sertão, the live of farmers and miners would be placed at risk, lands producing essential food supplies for the captaincy would be "abandoned and left uncultivated," and a "considerable part" of the region's agricultural and mining activity would cease.[33]

Immediately after Noronha wrote the governor of São Paulo about the need to protect Minas Gerais from its internal enemies, he issued a revealing pardon to those who had fled into the forests attempting to escape the march southward. To qualify for the pardon, deserters had to present themselves to authorities within one month and be willing to serve in new frontier squadrons, which Noronha ordered formed and, in contrast to the force marching against the Spaniards, armed with weapons adequate to the task. These "forest squadrons" would combat the forest adversaries who had made full compliance with the enlistment campaign so onerous. The squadrons would respond, he wrote to local military commanders, to the "atrocious crimes" that fugitive slaves had "recently committed in diverse regions of this captaincy." Most urgently, they would strike back against runaways in the termo of Mariana, who had "infested public roads and assaulted fazendas, butchering white men and violating women." They would also be charged with "pursuing the heathen" who had invaded homesteads along various tributaries of the Doce River, also with fatal consequences. The pardon would ensure that these squadrons would be as numerous and well-trained as possible. Like the corps sent south, their composition again demonstrated the racialized social dynamics of frontier conquest in Minas Gerais. White men "never entered these squadrons," even though some whites possessed the requisite experience of the forests. Instead, the units were composed of up to 30 men of color, commanded by an officer chosen from among their ranks who had the greatest knowledge of the sertão. The governor threatened to punish local commanders who failed to ensure that they were fully manned and thoroughly equipped and provisioned.[34] After the conflict with Spain calmed and the viceroy's recruitment campaign ended in August 1777, these squadrons would continue to function for years in the Eastern Sertão.[35]

Noronha's rationale concerning fitness, phenotype, and frontier geography derived from necessity and experience, according to José João Teixeira Coelho, another proponent of the use of the free colored population to conquer the eastern forests, as their status as proscribed territory became increasingly ambiguous. Having served three Minas governors before returning to Portugal to become a *desembargador* (supreme court judge), Coelho addressed the issue in a 1780 report he authored on governing the captaincy. The success of the conquest, he explained, "could not be achieved without the use of a corps of troops of this color (*qualidade*)." Under Governor Silva's tenure, Coelho recalled, the king's edict of 1766 had provided the legal basis for enlisting vadios, "the bane of all civilized nations," in the conquest of sertão. Silva's successor, the Count of Valadares, issued further orders to this effect in the early 1770s, believing that "it made more sense that these [frontier] troops be composed of vadios and miscreants than of men who were well bred and needed for the cultivation of land." Noronha was simply pursuing the same objectives, adopting methods his predecessors had demonstrated to be effective.[36]

Evidence to this effect spanned the entire period under study. From the beginning of the official push eastward, Governor Silva threatened those who attempted to absent themselves from frontier expeditions with imprisonment. He used this tactic to ensure the availability of a compliant group of recruits for military actions launched against the Indians.[37] His approach to Afro-Brazilians made evident the vulnerability of even the most established settlers of color who inhabited the sertão. For example, recruited to serve in action against the Indians at Cuieté, the freed slave José Martins Chavez petitioned the governor for an exemption on the grounds that he owned a fazenda. In other words, he was one of those colonists whom, when white, captaincy authorities considered legitimate transgressors of the Forbidden Lands policy. Military service, Chavez argued, would compromise his agricultural and mining activity, but the governor replied by calling into question the validity of Chavez's claim both to land ownership and special privilege. He ordered a local military commander to verify the title to his land. Regardless of the result, Chavez was to be compelled to join an expedition marching against the Indians. This duty, the governor insisted, "is not incompatible with the labor of agriculture and mining." If Chavez neglected his obligation, "failing to conduct himself with the obedience he owes his officers," he was to be subjected to the "punishment that he merits."[38] The response indicates the predominance, once again, of racial considerations in determining who would serve the conquest and who would reap its benefits. Chavez hoped his status as a productive settler would outweigh the stigma of his former enslavement; instead, that stigma drew the attention of expedition officers in the first place, cast him as a liar and shirker, and nullified any privileges he might have enjoyed as a property owner.

In this and many other cases, officials dispensed with the usual pretense of calling impressed men vadios and openly singled them out for their racial characteristics. When forest squadrons were reorganized and reinforced in the early 1790s as part of a plan to deploy a series of bandeiras against the Puri and Botocudo, Captain José Bernardino Alves Gundim proposed increasing their ranks with "all of the freed pardos and pretos" readily available.[39] He made no distinction whether these men were gainfully employed or not, owned land or not, worked for another landowner or not. It was enough that they were men of color and had once been slaves.

Free men of color and slaves frequently served on the same expeditions to the sertão, although in somewhat different capacities. For the series of bandeiras in which José Martins Chavez found himself forced to enlist in the 1760s, slaves worked in gangs of as many as 25 to open roads through the forest. The roads then made possible the movement of free Afro-Brazilians pressed into military service.[40] A dozen years later, following his efforts as military recruiter for the conflict with Spain, Colonel Tavares used his own slaves to extend by another 18 leagues (119 km) the road Governor Noronha had ordered built, which finally reached Cuieté. Relieved of duties at gold washings operated by Tavares, the slaves worked for more than a year on the project. As they cut the route "through virgin forests and sertões infested with heathen Botocudo," the slaves labored under the protection of squadrons of impressed colored soldiers, perhaps some of those troops sent home from the southern borderlands.[41] In both of these cases, soldiers who were legally free, but forced to enlist, protected slaves as they felled trees and cleared undergrowth. With roads constructed, the soldiers could then proceed to the heart of Indian territory to attack natives who were also legally free but subject to conquest.

At other times, when slaves were unavailable, nominally free men of color built the roads themselves. Governor Meneses found the labor of the men he called vadios to be particularly valuable in the construction of roads linking a number of towns in the captaincy. In 1781, he ordered officers to assemble crews of such men to work on the "opening of trails" to the Arrepiados region, trails that he deemed "necessary at the onset of the conquest" because they permitted transport and exploration for gold.[42] Meneses applied the same methods in the Cuieté region, ordering militia commanders throughout the captaincy to detain laborers and put them to work in the Forbidden Lands. In one instance, he "gathered the greater part of those soldiers and vadios who could be spared" from Cuieté and "made them work day and night" on a new, more reliable road leading from the town to the site of a promising gold discovery, which in the end yielded disappointing results.[43]

Affirming historian David Eltis' observation that in the early modern Atlantic system slave and non-slave labor functioned more "as part of a continuum than as polar opposites," projects like these tended to blur juridical distinctions.[44]

At times on the Minas frontier, the main characteristic that separated slave laborers from the free or freed recruits enlisted to advance eastward expansion was that one group bore arms whereas the other did not. Even this final difference sometimes disappeared. Together, soldiers, settlers, and their slaves, all of them armed, formed a retaliatory bandeira that marched into the forests in pursuit of the Botocudo after native hostilities forced the inhabitants of Itabira, Tanque, and Santana dos Ferros to abandon their farms and mines in 1794.[45] Convicted criminals, slaves, and enlisted Indians served jointly under the command of Quartermaster Elesbão Lopes Duro at a remote garrison on the Doce River just after the turn of the nineteenth century.[46] Moreover, the formal declaration of war against the Botocudo in 1808 did not dramatically change these labor configurations. A contingent of 35 foot soldiers and 78 "auxiliaries," both slaves and former slaves, formed a crew that opened a strategic road along the Jequitinhonha River in 1811 under the command of Lieutenant Julião Fernandes Leão.[47]

In some cases, a paucity of free or freed laborers required the use of slaves. Commander Francisco Álvares Pereira, like many officers, used his own slaves— under military escort—to transport munitions and provisions to the sertão. Pereira's slaves traveled by foot and by boat from Vila Rica to Cuieté in July 1770. He did not specify the number of slaves involved except to note that the party, which also included merchants, totaled 18 men and filled four canoes on the navigable stretch of the journey. Six months later, another party left Antônio Dias Abaixo for Cuieté. This time, Captain Manoel Martins da Costa escorted a priest destined to tend to settlers' spiritual needs. Three canoes carried an entourage of 22 persons. Seven merchants, whom Pereira identified as "whites," and their trade goods filled two more canoes. Thirty-six slaves joined the party on its trek.[48]

This kind of evidence, together with that describing the struggle to recruit troops for the conflict with Spain, gives voice to the drive to define and control race-specific labor in the Forbidden Lands. Together with the runaway slaves and Indians they were called on to track down and subdue, free persons of African origin were characterized, in the minds of urban authorities, by the disturbing ease with which they seemed to move through the unsupervised spaces of the sertão. More often than not, unfortunately, the way in which these people perceived themselves and the degree to which they resisted efforts by the state to monitor and direct their movements remain obscured in the official accounts in which such individuals make their appearance. The king denounced these men as "infamous and pernicious," the viceroy dismissed them as "lazy vagabonds," São Paulo's governor scorned them as "vile," and Minas officials condemned them as "beasts."[49] Documents drafted by such men and the officers who carried out their orders cannot be expected to distinguish between actual and perceived resistance.

Even if most of the free poor who ventured to the sertão drifted outward from the urban nucleus simply to guarantee a subsistence existence at a moment when former economic ties no longer did, migration and mobility themselves were perceived as threats by a captaincy government convinced that the efficient deployment of submissive laborers would be required to restore the region to a new golden age. In the service of this goal, those elsewhere deemed "useless" could effect the conquest of the Eastern Sertão, clearing designated sectors of Indians and runaway slaves so that mining, agriculture, and ranching could expand undisturbed. Determined to prevent the unsupervised migration of such marginal individuals to the frontier, captaincy authorities sought instead to conscript them for its state-led, militarized conquest. Mulatos, mestiços, pardos, cabras, pretos, and negros—these were the racial designations applied by officials to the groups considered suitable to serve as human fodder for the arduous and often violent advance of colonial society into the wilderness.

Deploying Civilian Labor

As civilian laborers, the mobile mass of free poor migrants to the sertão often experienced circumstances nearly as limiting as those endured by men enlisted in military operations against their will. This was particularly true of unattached males. Many were assembled and put to work in zones where voluntary settlers refused to venture. Men who escaped military impressment found themselves recruited nonetheless, as unskilled labor for state-sponsored mining, road-building, and agricultural projects. By contrast, impoverished squatter families sometimes enjoyed a more favorable outcome, even offered title to land they cleared and farmed. Between the solitary male laborer and the small-holding family, a spectrum of possible frontier experiences existed combining various degrees of compulsion and concession, of resistance and accommodation.

Governor Noronha's successor, Rodrigo José de Meneses, even more ambitious in his attempts to shape the conduct of the captaincy's free colored population, focused with particular energy on transferring laborers to zones designated for colonization. "One of the greatest concerns that has occupied me since I began governing this captaincy is that of putting vadios to work," he reported in 1781 to Colonial Secretary Martinho de Melo e Castro, now serving Queen Maria I (1777–1816), who had succeeded José I. The governor reasoned that once "subjected to work," these individuals would cease to provoke the social disruptions "to which their inclinations lead them." He sought to "put to good use" men who were "entirely useless to and a burden on the state." As registered in recruitment lists assembled by local militia commanders, these individuals were almost always blacks or mulattos.[50]

Like his predecessors, Governor Meneses used road-building in the sertão as a preferred method of imposing discipline, ordering militia commanders throughout the captaincy to take into custody individuals considered idle and send them to the Cuieté region where they could be put to work. After visiting the place himself in 1781 to acquire first-hand knowledge of its potential mineral reserves, he hatched an even more ambitious scheme. Reports circulating in the mining camp suggested that significant deposits of precious ore lay along the Manhuaçu River, some 50 kilometers upstream from its confluence with the Doce River. Meneses turned to the poor and marginalized to pursue his plan to exploit the discovery but only after first unsuccessfully trying to attract settlers of greater means to the region. "I have not ceased to publicize" news of these gold discoveries, he wrote in frustration, "to see if this will persuade some miners with large workforces to go there to establish themselves." By now accustomed to news of this sort from the Cuieté region amounting to little, and far more interested in agricultural opportunities at this stage of the post-boom era, such affluent colonists were united in their disinclination to comply. Meneses refused to resort to financial incentives as Noronha and previous governors had done, forgiving or postponing debts owed by those who agreed to migrate to the region. For Meneses, such measures amounted to a "transgression" against creditors. Besides, these steps had failed in the past: "Not even in this case," he lamented, did the desired colonists "resolve to go so far away to seek an uncertain remedy for their oppression."[51]

The governor found himself searching for some other approach to extract the region's mineral wealth in the context of a perceived labor shortage. He settled on ordering the arrest of the "sizable number of vadios who abound in this captaincy." They would be formed into quasi-military companies of 50 men, each captained by a "man of probity," who would "make them work for their own benefit," establishing mining operations whose gold would be remitted to Vila Rica. The Crown would subtract its royal fifth, each company leader would receive a tenth of the remainder, and the rest would be divided "among the vadios themselves, who in this way would be made into industrious men." The governor recognized the complexities of such a scheme, which would entail feeding and clothing the impressed workers, marching them to the easternmost edge of the captaincy, and supplying them with tools and other mining equipment. But he considered this the only practicable means of effecting the conquest of the region and a method that would "augment the royal fifth, occupy the vadios, make them useful to themselves and to the state, and free the people from the disturbances they cause."[52] The fact that Meneses wrote all of this enthusiastically to Colonial Secretary Melo e Castro in Lisbon showed that the era was all but over of professing that Crown prohibitions on eastward-directed colonization efforts remained in force. Yet the elusive dream of invigorating the Minas economy with hidden riches from the sertão lived on.

By June 1782, the governor reported substantial progress toward his goal. In another letter to the colonial secretary, he first emphasized the state of "discredit in which the improbable and imaginary projects for the settlement of Cuieté find themselves." He estimated that the royal treasury had "uselessly spent the fantastic fortune" of more than 50 contos on the region, or the equivalent of the sum needed to purchase some 500 healthy slaves. The expenditure had not yielded the "least profit," either for the Crown or for local inhabitants. The governor then outlined steps he had taken to implement his new plan to exploit the substantial gold deposits now thought to lie along the Manhuaçu River. That plan, he admitted, was based as much on "high hopes" as on any substantial and verifiable mineral deposits. But initial exploration had shown promise, and the governor was determined to unearth the area's gold or "dispel for the last time the illusion" of such bounty. Despite many warnings of the risks involved to his own reputation and personal fortune, the governor determined to pursue his plan, mounting a new sort of expedition to the sertão. Manned by civilians rather than soldiers, its purpose was not Indian conquest per se but the transfer of laborers to a remote worksite.[53]

Meneses appointed himself "chief" of this "involuntary society." Acting as personal guarantor, he set out to transport men and materiel to the region at no cost to the Crown. On credit to be repaid with the profits of anticipated gold production—and failing that, with his own funds—he purchased iron, steel, mining tools, gunpowder, buckshot, clothing, and "a thousand other supplies." To feed the workers, he ordered fields cleared and cultivated near Cuieté, which by mid-1782 had already produced a substantial crop of corn. Along the road leading from Vila Rica to Cuieté, which his predecessors had constructed, additional fields were planted and shelters constructed. At a bridge Governor Noronha had ordered built over the Doce River, Meneses based pack animals to haul supplies back and forth along the road. The governor based three of his own slaves at the site, including their leader, a mulatto "very adept in such transport." He even provided for spiritual matters. "To celebrate the divine offices in that sertão where new inhabitants were to establish themselves, a priest was necessary," he wrote to Melo e Castro. But he did not wish to burden the royal treasury even with the minimal expense of a priest's salary. Fortuitously, the governor discovered a "criminal priest" who had been jailed for two years. The bishop of Mariana agreed to the cleric's release when the governor promised to resolve his financial problems, indicating his crime involved outstanding debts. The governor also pledged to pay his stipend as expedition chaplain and supply a portable altar and other accouterments necessary to conduct Mass en route to the Manhuaçu River.[54]

Although the governor assumed ultimate financial responsibility, he envisioned covering all costs by mounting the expedition, as he put it, "at the expense of the interested parties," that is, the impoverished men he considered burdensome to society. His orders to commanders throughout the captaincy to assemble vadios for the task provided him a workforce of 200 men. He then invested his personal assistant, José Joaquim de Sequeira Almeida, with the "honorable commission" of becoming what the governor described as the "founder of a new colony" along the Manhuaçu. Should the expedition find the "wealth that had been promised," the endeavor would surely be "of great utility," attracting new settlers while ensuring that poor men deemed restive and rootless did "something advantageous for themselves, for the public, and for the royal treasury." The governor proposed leaving his orders in effect on a permanent basis so that, "at all times, all men who have no occupation or fail to practice the one they have" would be "remitted from every part of the captaincy" to go to work in the eastern diggings. Rather than continuing the customary practice of throwing such men in jail, officials would now have a means of putting them to work.[55]

To ensure the desired outcome, Meneses ordered Almeida not to depart from the new establishment without either leaving it "well consolidated" or having finally dispelled reports of the region's wealth. In either case, the governor was determined to shift the burden of the zone's development from the state to marginalized workers. Thus, Almeida was to dismiss all but the most essential military personnel in Cuieté and its environs, officers and soldiers alike. They constituted a drain on the captaincy's coffers, the governor argued, made worse by the practice of corrupt officials who inflated troop rolls by including the names of dead soldiers and slaves.[56]

Almeida reached the town of Cuieté, accompanied by his coerced workforce, and made preparations to proceed to the Manhuaçu River. The activity intrigued observers in the comarca of Serro Frio. Convinced that the government would not mount such an expedition "without the greatest certainty of its success," these individuals rushed to the Manhuaçu site to stake out mining claims.[57] Meanwhile, the governor broadened his search for laborers. He commanded militia officers in the cities of Vila Rica, Sabará, São João del Rei, and São José to redouble their effort. Despite the "continuous measures taken to extinguish vadios," he complained, "a great number of them still are to be found in this district." He issued another round of orders to arrest them and remit them to Vila Rica's jail, where they would await transfer to the eastern forests.[58]

Concerning the character of the men sent to the Cuieté region, little information is found. A few details emerge in isolated cases, always couched in the deprecating remarks of authorities and always reinforcing the conclusion that these were primarily men of color. For instance, Governor Meneses wrote of sending one group of individuals to Cuieté, including a black man he described as a "famous crook" who had posed as a government official to "extort money."[59] In another case, a militia captain described a man named João Vieira who had been arrested a second time after escaping a forced march to Cuieté. Vieira, he said, was a "half-breed" (cabra) and a "great vadio" who "went around robbing his neighbors continuously." He had "taken an honorable girl from the home of her parents and wanted to kill them for trying to impede him." He had "cut the hands of a slave" belonging to another militia captain, leaving the slave crippled. Most recently, he had tried to "injure with a knife" the brother of the corporal who had apprehended him.[60] These individuals garnered special mention in the sources because they were criminals and thus the harbingers of the penal colony that Cuieté would become. But many, perhaps most, of those rounded up for duty in the forest were not criminals but criminalized. Thus, Manoel Vieira was a Brazilian-born black condemned to labor because he did not "occupy himself with anything at all." Mulatto José Pereira's crime was that he had appeared in a certain district "after coming from another parish, and showed himself to be entirely inactive according to his custom." Antonio da Silva, a "half-breed" who arrived in the mining district from São Paulo, simply remained "without a place to live."[61] As vadios, their primary offense was to have found themselves among the un-mastered poor and thus to have fallen afoul of the dominant order.

The military cartographer José Joaquim da Rocha recorded further details regarding those men transported to the sertão. Local commanders, he wrote, had been ordered to "apprehend those insignificant persons whose vagabondage not only serves as a bad example to the rest but also causes disquiet and perturbation among the people." They were arrested, jailed, and marched "in great numbers" to Cuieté. They explored the Manhuaçu River as well as several other rivers and streams, all of which, despite initial optimism, produced insignificant returns. At some point in late 1782 or 1783, disillusioned, Governor Meneses ordered his involuntary expedition to retreat, "seeing that the promised riches were not found."[62]

Rocha might also have mentioned that the governor's labor force demonstrated little interest in doing the finding. Almeida was explicit on this matter. For instance, he recounted one incident in which a soldier charged with keeping watch over prisoners sent to the site had conspired to escape with them. He had promised them gunpowder, shot, and firearms to be stolen from other soldiers. He provided them a file to remove their chains. Those who refused to participate were to be murdered. But Almeida discovered the plot hours before its execution, extracting confessions from the prisoners. He had the lead soldier placed in chains, thrashed publicly, and condemned to labor alongside the others. His indignation was palpable as he reported to the governor, "These men, having been so well treated, live as though in desperation." Some days later, three prisoners managed to flee into the forest. Almeida ordered them pursued but to no avail. He did not worry about them returning to freedom because, he said, "it will be impossible for them to escape from the hands of the Botocudos."[63]

The perceived need for laborers at far-off outposts like Cuieté varied according to the presence, occasionally substantiated but more often imagined, of wealth-producing resources. The labor shortage constantly deplored by those in power derived not from a simple absence of workers. After all, with the mining economy in disarray and a growing captaincy population, free poor workers were in short supply only to the extent that they sought alternatives other than mining in places other than the depths of the eastern forests. Perhaps they had learned too well the lesson captaincy officials endeavored to teach about ferocious natives barring entrance to the Forbidden Lands. Without doubt, they knew that projects rigorously supervised by a state bent on enforcing racial and economic hierarchies did not bode well as the solution to their marginalized condition. The alleged labor shortage at precarious frontier outposts arose because authorities could not easily impose their vision of a secure, remunerative future on these workers, nor could colonists muster sustained enthusiasm for gold that could not be found, even when they were destitute and coerced.

Free Land

The captaincy government found altering the behavior of potential settlers possessed of their own notions regarding how the frontier might serve as an antidote to economic dislocation surprisingly difficult. Even when officials offered significant incentives, they had trouble luring migrants to zones considered too hazardous or otherwise unviable for commercial or subsistence farming. This was the case in the area that became known as the Conquest of Arrepiados, the mountainous region along the captaincy's southeastern border, another place where Governor Meneses pressured and often forced the captaincy's "useless people" to labor.

That the place remained dangerous as the governor hatched his plan, there can be no doubt. On one occasion, in an attempt to placate Indians in the area, soldiers at the presidio constructed at Arrepiados left some handkerchiefs and mirrors in the forest to demonstrate their "good intentions." Indians rebuffed the offer violently, surrounding more than 20 soldiers one morning as they were planting beans in an outlying field. Unarmed and without the padded cuirasses they wore when expecting trouble, the soldiers fled toward the presidio. Screaming in Portuguese, "All of you must die!" the Indians pursued, unleashing a flurry of arrows, striking one soldier in the leg. Once inside the stockade, the troops prepared a counterattack. But before they could strike, the Indians retreated into the forest but continued to make their presence known for several days. At that point, a detachment of 12 new foot soldiers arrived to reinforce the besieged presidio but most of them quickly deserted out of fear.[64]

In the context of such hazards, Governor Meneses reasoned that colonists might be attracted to the site with the incentive of freely conceded land. A poor man's marital status determined, as much as any other single factor, whether such state-supported settlement was an option, although compulsion played a role even when it was. Normally, single males—or rather, males the state considered single even though they may have been attached to female partners—were the primary targets of officials seeking mobile civilian laborers and soldiers alike. In 1781, the governor, having already found such men valuable in the construction of roads linking a number of towns, ordered those condemned as vadios to be arrested and employed in the "opening of trails" to the Arrepiados region, facilitating gold exploration.[65] However, to promote settlement, Antônio Veloso de Miranda, commander of Mariana's second auxiliary cavalry regiment, proposed a less coercive plan after the governor appointed him regent of this conquest, another sign of lapsing state restrictions on eastward colonization. On Miranda's recommendation, Governor Meneses made arrangements for passage to the zone of Gabriel José Francisco and his family, among the first settlers to participate in a scheme to "people that conquest with agregados" rather than vadios.[66] In other words, as opposed to the unattached wandering poor, free dependents were to serve the state as settlers. Officials distinguished such individuals by their more permanent ties to the land, to a fixed abode, to employers and patrons, and to other commitments, including marital and familial bonds. Usually agricultural workers, agregados depended on a landowner for permission to raise subsistence crops on an otherwise unproductive plot. The agreement made them less mobile, unruly, and threatening in the eyes of the elite because they were more easily supervised and controlled. By definition, they were not vadios because, although legally free, they had masters.[67]

At one point, Governor Meneses noted that among the men he was sending to Arrepiados were three "gypsies" (*ciganos*) who were not to be treated as common criminals if they demonstrated themselves industrious. In colonial Minas Gerais as in early modern Europe, to be labeled a gypsy was to run the risk of being persecuted for the very act of moving from place to place. But the fact that all three of these men were "married and with families" persuaded the governor to take a more lenient course: "If they want to accept settling down" in a way fitting of "members of a civilized nation," Meneses wrote, then Miranda was to grant them land in the form of titled sesmarias. They would thus be able to "subsist honorably." But if they persisted in their wanderings, Miranda was to "make them work, along with all the others, like perverse men who desire only to nourish their vices at the cost of civil society."[68]

To secure the relocation of agregados to Arrepiados, Governor Meneses sought to convince the landowners on whom these indigent families depended that they would be thereby relieved of an unwanted burden. He augmented this message with what can only be interpreted as an appeal to the agregados themselves, offering them inducements. Deploring the continual "vexation" and "great disturbances" such dependents provoked among "legitimate" landowners—meaning those who held royal land grants—the governor declared he intended to put an end to such "abuse" and its "pernicious consequences." However, as he did not wish to see these impoverished tenant farmers remain without land, he promised to provide them with "a more certain subsistence and a more solid, permanent, and tranquil establishment." To this effect, he ordered Miranda to resettle agregados "who present themselves with their families or farmhands."[69] Miranda would "freely" grant such individuals sesmarias, each measuring a half-league in breadth and depth (11 km^2). He would distribute seed corn and sufficient provisions for them to sustain themselves until the first harvest. In addition, settlers would receive assistance in building new homes. That is, they could anticipate "all of the acts of hospitality that men should expect who go to establish themselves under the most direct protection of the government." After maintaining a continuous presence for three years, as was the legal practice for all sesmaria recipients, they could expect to receive permanent title to their land.[70]

The governor ordered local militia commanders to help carry out the plan. According to their orders, infused with the same combination of compulsion and avowed benevolence characterizing colonial indigenous policy, commanders were to "oblige" such families, especially those who "caused the greatest vexation ... to go to the Conquest of Arrepiados," where they would be resettled "without being the burden they currently are on other inhabitants of the captaincy." They would benefit from a life "more worthy of free men" than the "servile dependence" that was their present condition. They would no longer need to rely on the "will of others" to grant them "a bit of land to cultivate the necessities of life."[71] In actuality, they would quickly discover the limited extent to which the governor's comparatively egalitarian proposals could be made to work. To Miranda, nine months earlier, the governor had expressed concern that migrants to the region would need temporary shelter and other provisions.[72] The sources do not show that such measures were addressed, and the plan to promote "voluntary" relocation of poor families began to unravel from the moment the governor implemented it. Meneses' effort to convince large landholders that tenant farmers constituted a drain on their personal resources belied the truth, which was that the well-to-do found the dependence of the poor to be an advantage more often than not. The hold that the landed exerted on tenant families, exercised both through paternalism and duress, proved stronger than state incentives designed to woo the poor away to the frontier.

By the beginning of 1784, lack of progress forced Meneses' successor, Governor Luís da Cunha Meneses, to resort again to a policy of open compulsion of marginalized men without families. To secure the "expansion of the conquests" and the further acquisition of "knowledge of the vast sertões of this captaincy," the new governor instructed district and militia commanders to "order to the Conquest of Arrepiados all vadios that exist in their districts, malefactors that cause disturbances, and anyone without certain abode." The reversal stemmed from the governor's conviction that distant regions like Cuieté and Arrepiados "could not be...settled without the security that animates men who enter those conquests." Such security could be achieved only through the initial labor of "men who, being useless, serve to perturb the people among whom they reside."[73] The governor did not specify whether such individuals would open the way for future settlement by fighting Indians, clearing land, building roads, transporting supplies, or manning frontier garrisons. Presumably, he was willing to see them to do all of these things. In the process, the experiment with settlement by impoverished settler families was abandoned. Suspect, solitary males again came to bear the onus of the occupation of remote territory.

If much turned on racial and economic standing in the hierarchical world of colonial Minas Gerais, as well as in the frontier settlement schemes therein devised, a settler's gender and civil status also mattered. Transferred from Europe and adapted to the conditions of Portuguese America, traditional notions defining the role of marriage and proper tasks for men and women determined the kind of treatment male and female settlers received from the state. Throughout the colonial period, officials fretted over how to populate an area as vast as the interior of Brazil. Population increase and the founding of permanent towns and villages were seen as central, not only to the defense of the colony but also its productive capacity. In the case of the Minas sertão, when even the boldest authorities proposed allocating land to the poor, they thought only of those who formed families. To ensure the permanence of new settlements, they focused on married couples as the basis of a community that could sustain and reproduce itself. To rely on men alone was to doom to failure the attempt to foster population growth and permanence in the countryside.[74] Marriage "constitutes the most solid basis of society," one governor of São Paulo observed at about this time. "All of the means that properly facilitate marriages will also promote settlement."[75] Perceived by authorities as the wellspring of the sedentary, moral, and economically productive life, settler families would enjoy benefits appropriate to that end.

By contrast, single males, especially those who were poor and non-white, had always been the primary targets of official sweeps through the Brazilian countryside to round up individuals deemed vagrants and criminals. The unattached, itinerant male, bound neither by legal matrimony nor the daily obligations of settled life, nor the demands imposed by civil, ecclesiastic, and military authorities, presented a direct challenge to colonization plans, not to mention an opportunity for labor recruitment. Most Minas officials concluded that their services could be best exploited on the frontier if they were removed from society and forced to labor in the most distant reaches of the sertão, still too inaccessible and prone to Indian attack to attract settler families.[76] These zones, along with others like them throughout the Americas, were thought of as distinctly male preserves even when women were present.[77]

For this and other reasons, the return to the use of coerced male laborers in Arrepiados cannot be attributed simply to the change in captaincy leadership from one governor to the next. Governor Rodrigo José de Meneses was a man of the Enlightenment, willing to consider the needs of the population at large to a degree not matched by his autocratic successor.[78] But under the supervision of military subordinates, the implementation of the original plan would have involved scarcely less coercion than did the arrest and transfer of solitary males to the frontier. The failure of freely distributed land grants to succeed as an incentive pointed to a fundamental wariness among the poor regarding state-directed frontier policies, true of settler families no less than single males. As a rule, impoverished subsistence farmers did not respond to promises of material advantages proffered by local militia commanders, who in the past had rarely demonstrated themselves to have the best interests of the poor in mind. Persistent Indian hostility, which captaincy officials since the 1760s had denounced to justify an advance on the Forbidden Lands, further undermined the plan to settle the Arrepiados region with marginalized families. The powerful liked to think of the poor as especially well-suited to the task of fighting Indians, but the poor apparently thought themselves no more proficient in this regard than anyone else. In fact, they were significantly more vulnerable—and probably understood this reality—because their lack of status meant they could not count on mobilizing the state and the military to come to their defense.

Forced Settlement

Events in a yet another frontier zone active in the 1780s provide a further context illuminating the state's struggle to maintain control over migrants to the sertão. In the southern Mantiqueira Mountains, where Indian resistance was not the factor it continued to be at both Cuieté and Arrepiados, Governor Rodrigo José de Meneses confronted the unauthorized migration of settlers of both meager and substantial means by attempting to regularize this dispersion through the concession of royal land grants. The course of settlement in this zone reinforces the conclusion that the power to organize labor in remote lands never rested entirely within the captaincy government's hands. To transfer workers and settlers to the loci of state-supported conquests was one thing, but to control their movement in zones to which they flocked on their own was quite another. In this sense, the Mantiqueira region developed in counterpoint to the Eastern Sertão. Far more accessible than either the Conquests of Cuieté or Arrepiados, the zone lay along the Caminho Novo, the primary overland commercial route linking Minas Gerais to the Atlantic coast. It was too far south to be considered the Eastern Sertão but it nevertheless bore the designation Forbidden Lands, as a border area between Minas Gerais and the captaincies of Rio de Janeiro and São Paulo, much of it still unsurveyed and unsupervised by the state and thus considered an open invitation to smugglers. In this southern region, the irreversible invasion of miners and farmers forced authorities to relinquish strict controls on frontier settlement to gain what advantage they could from the captaincy's migrating masses.

By the time the Minas government turned its attention to the incorporation and administration of the fertile Mantiqueira Mountains, effective occupation and settlement had already taken place outside the state's purview. This happened despite the fact that the region fell under the Crown's prohibitions on the settlement of outlying lands. News that settlers were nevertheless moving into the area began to circulate as early as the mid-1750s. In response, the prohibition on migration and settlement was affirmed, first by the captaincy government and then, in 1760, by the Crown's Overseas Council. By the 1780s, however, that the exodus of migrants southward from the mining nucleus could not be stopped had become clear. Desperate to maintain a modicum of control, Governor Meneses argued that the original prohibition had been "based on totally impracticable principles, whose observance would result in the ruin of this captaincy."[79] Summarizing the findings of a reconnaissance party ordered to explore the region, Meneses wrote that "the evil has already begun: the place has been invaded, dug up, and planted." The only thing left for the government to do, apart from formalizing land tenure, was to dispatch soldiers to patrol the region to prevent the movement of contraband.[80]

The governor's decision to "penetrate the wild sertões," once considered a vacant barrier to smuggling, came as a direct response, as the military mapmaker Rocha explained, to "the clamor of the people over the lack of gold-mining operations" still functioning profitably in the captaincy. But equally to the point was the fact that "the people" had already begun effective settlement of the zone, ignoring the Crown's Forbidden Lands policy. Sent off to the region in 1780, the governor's aide-de-camp Francisco Antônio Rebelo discovered at least eight established trails through the mountainous terrain. One of these he described as an "extremely wide and well traveled highway," which he followed for five or six leagues, finding it lined on both sides with settlers, their homesteads and fields, and even a few gold diggings.[81]

The appeal of the Mantiqueira region to settlers derived not only from the fact that the subjugation of the Indians inhabiting this southern area was by the final quarter of the eighteenth century virtually absolute. Far more accessible than either Cuieté or the Arrepiados Mountains, the zone's geographic position along the Caminho Novo placed it much closer to the rapidly growing city of Rio de Janeiro and its voracious market for basic provisions. Southern Minas Gerais also participated in coastal Brazil's generalized export-led "agricultural renaissance" during the final decades of the eighteenth century, an expansion further animated by the transfer of the Portuguese court to Rio de Janeiro in 1808. By the 1780s, the already burgeoning Brazilian capital created an expanding market for grain and cattle that left concerns about post-boom decadence in this southern sector of the captaincy largely relegated to the past. Frontier migrants streamed to the area, both east and west of the Caminho Novo, to participate not only in interregional trade but also in a growing intraregional agricultural, pastoral, and small-scale manufactures market. The region's fertile lands thus attracted not only subsistence farmers but also those seeking to profit from the trade route.[82] The roads Rebelo discovered in the area were undoubtedly traveled far more frequently by muleteers transporting staples to market than by gold and diamond smugglers.

Impressed by the region's potential for both illicit activity (if left unmonitored) and additional tax revenues (if properly administered) Governor Meneses journeyed to the region from Vila Rica in June 1781. Entering the southern forests, he discovered many miners already established and at work, in flagrant violation of Crown restrictions. Along the Peixe River, he encountered "innumerable people who solicited enough land to accommodate their slave holdings." More than 700 individuals submitted formal petitions for farmland and mineral claims. Denying these requests would, as the governor saw it, leave the region utterly unregulated, a sieve for smugglers. Convinced that the only remedy was to co-opt that which could no longer be reversed, he proceeded to partition the land in the form of sesmarias and appoint authorities to govern the region.[83]

A central problem Meneses confronted was ensuring that the poorest migrants to the zone did not end up, in his words, "discontented." Their "total exclusion" from land ownership in the area, he feared, would make them "more aware of their unhappiness." Without slaves and without the necessary funds to survey, register, and improve the land they occupied, these free poor could not meet the legal qualifications for receiving a sesmaria. Meneses therefore adopted an approach "not practiced until now" of allotting "half-sesmarias" of agricultural land. By this he seems to have meant sesmarias measuring one-half league in length and width (11 km^2) in contrast to the tracts of one square league (43 km^2) or more that were conventionally granted to slave owners in the sertão. Sesmarias of this size had certainly been allocated before. What was new in the governor's method was to do so to the benefit of non-slaveholders normally excluded from royal grants. He hoped in this way to occupy "useless individuals" who were a "burden on the state," employing once again those phrases so favored by authorities bent on labor discipline. As laborers on the land, he argued, they and their children would "work with more efficacy than slaves."[84] The unusual reference to children indicates the governor envisioned the same kind of family-based settlement he sought to promote in the Arrepiados region.

Meneses had earlier stipulated that these new land grants be demarcated and distributed among the poor only after the well-to-do had made their own claims.[85] With respect to both classes of settlers, there is reason to conclude that few of these families in the end ultimately gained title in this way. Authorities claimed that 700 petitions for land and mineral claims in the Mantiqueira Mountains were submitted in 1781. During the same year, similar requests by migrants to the Arrepiados Mountains totaled 373.[86] Local records survive for hundreds of mineral claims conceded in the Mantiqueira region, mostly concentrated in the hands of a select group of slaveholding colonists. They include 43 claims granted to Joaquim José da Silva Xavier, the dragoon officer and dentist known as Tiradentes (the tooth-puller), who was later implicated in the Minas conspiracy of 1789, executed, and eventually transformed into a hero of Brazilian independence.[87] But captaincy registries show no parallel burst in the allotment of land grants during 1781 or the several years that followed (see Figure 3.3). The sources consulted do not reveal whether Meneses simply could not move fast enough to effect the land distribution before the end of his term in 1783, whether his successor found the plan quixotic and reversed it, as in the Arrepiados Mountains, or whether other powerful interests stood in the way.

In any case, extralegal settlement in the once-forbidden Mantiqueira region continued apace. In the extreme south of the captaincy, it exacerbated a border dispute between Minas Gerais and São Paulo that had simmered throughout the second half of the eighteenth century. The conflict indicates the degree to which migration by settlers of all classes southward out of the urban mining nucleus challenged the state. In 1785, Governor Luís da Cunha Meneses ordered Brigadier Antônio José Dias Coelho to the border region to determine which lands belonged to Minas Gerais and which to São Paulo. Coelho carried orders to shut down all roads or trails circumventing the customhouses meant to regulate and tax commerce. The officer discovered that many residents of São Paulo had pushed into Minas Gerais, establishing farms; however, the migrants refused to obey Minas officials, claiming the territory lay in São Paulo's jurisdiction. The landholders imported slaves and provisions along a "clandestine road" that crossed the mountains without passing a customhouse where taxes could be assessed. They avoided paying church tithes and duties on merchandise, slaves, and livestock by claiming residence in Minas Gerais when questioned by São Paulo officials and residence in São Paulo when pressed by Minas officials. Coelho ordered a detachment of Minas soldiers to be based in the area. When he returned several years later at the behest of the governor, he found conflict in the region still intensifying. In their ongoing attempt to seize land without submitting to Minas authorities, the São Paulo migrants had taken up arms and were threatening Minas troops.[88]

The problem persisted into the nineteenth century. In 1812, the Minas governor Francisco de Assis Mascarenhas, the Count of Palma (1810–1814), sent a local judge, José Joaquim Carneiro de Miranda e Costa, to report on settlement along the São Paulo border. The information Costa gathered showed just how little authorities in the distant capital knew about outlying lands in their own captaincy. Costa described the roads, towns, and parishes in the region and the primary economic activities: the export of provisions to the city of São Paulo and the import of mules, slaves, salt, and other goods. None of this commerce produced revenue for the Minas government because local settlers still maintained they lived in São Paulo. When Costa proposed, in accordance with his orders, the construction of a new customhouse along the main road to collect duties, local residents again objected. Costa recommended nevertheless staking claim to the ill-defined border region and the income to be gained by effective taxation.

Farther to the east, along the border between Minas Gerais and Rio de Janeiro, migration to the sertão similarly continued to outpace the government's ability to maintain control or even stay informed. When in 1812 the prince regent ordered a new road opened from Rio de Janeiro to the town of São João del-Rei in southeastern Minas Gerais, Governor Mascarenhas had to dispatch another reconnaissance party to the area to determine the most appropriate route, given the lack of available topographic information. This does not imply that the region remained unsettled, for the lieutenant charged with the task was to inspect "all of the roads that... have been opened" to choose the one most appropriate for transporting provisions to the coastal capital. Settlement proceeded ahead of government control.[89] Throughout this period, officials continued—with rare exceptions—to refer to the southern sertão as lying within the boundaries of the Crown's Forbidden Lands.[90] The de facto occupation of the region by settlers made a mockery of that assertion.

Sources referring to the masses circulating on the fringes, both social and geographic, of Minas society raise as many questions as they answer. The dominant white population viewed the poor free colored population as a straying people whose undeterred, sometimes defiant migration stood as a threat to established labor regimes and the integrity of the settled urban nucleus. At the same time, they also viewed the presence of these migrants in peripheral zones as a necessary step toward effective territorial incorporation and economic productivity. Individuals who might otherwise have been considered "useless" served well to fight the frontier battles with Indians and the untamed wilderness that more prosperous settlers shunned.

Which of these apparently contradictory views of the free poor should be taken as paramount in seeking the origin of frontier land and labor policies? The free poor were considered unproductive and thus a burden on society; yet, in documents pertaining to their presence in the Cuieté, Arrepiados, and Mantiqueira regions, they occupy a conspicuous role in local settlement activity, transportation networks, and food production. Does this imply that in the absence of significant new mining strikes, frontier expansion in Minas Gerais during the second half of the eighteenth century was led by a silent army of dispossessed subsistence farmers, most of them of African descent? Were they therefore among the prime adversaries of the indigenous peoples of the Eastern Sertão? Where and how often on the frontier did they outpace both elite white slave owners and the intrepid officers and rank and file of the military expeditions that explored the region?

Minas officials complained constantly of a labor shortage in outlying areas. To what extent did that alleged shortage explain the complex process of territorial incorporation? Those who attempted to raise a labor force adequate to the demands of frontier conquest focused on differences in skin color and economic status to justify their draconian policies. They found it easier to arrest the disenfranchised and ship them off to remote areas threatened by hostile Indians than to offer incentives sufficiently attractive to promote settlement. Given such prejudices, what elements of elite discourse concerning the settlement of the frontier can be trusted? Officials made distinctions based not only on race and class but also gender. The presence or absence of women and children among the free poor inhabitants of the sertão had much to do with the tasks envisioned by the state for these masses and the zones in which their migration would be forbidden, tolerated, or compelled. The most distant and dangerous reaches of the sertão, like frontiers everywhere, became a bastion of male conquerors and laborers. This situation occurred not by geographic necessity but as a consequence of specific, historically determined decisions, policies, and attitudes about gender as well as race. To what extent did the free poor men and women of Minas Gerais submit to these prescriptions, defy them, or turn them to their own advantage?

The fragmentary nature of the documentation available does not inspire confidence that such questions will ever yield definitive answers. Impoverished migrants to the sertão generated even less commentary than the Indians themselves, whose violent opposition to colonization entered the archives as evidence of a savagery to be granted no quarter. As with Indians, the documentary traces pertaining to the free poor survived, more often than not, in the form of highly skewed accusations by literate settlers, military commanders, law enforcement personnel, captaincy governors, and other elites. Despite such methodological problems, a number of conclusions are warranted.

For the dominant members of Minas society, the mobility of a mass of poor frontier migrants—most of whom where mulattos and blacks—constituted an acute preoccupation because their unsupervised movement outward from the urban nucleus undermined the very basis of social control. In this context, regional elites turned to the conquest of unsettled or sparsely settled areas not only to satisfy territorial ambitions emerging from their search for new sources of wealth; they did so also to maintain control over this errant population, to regain access to their labor, to incorporate taxable settlers and commodities, and to secure an effective defense against restive Indians. Authorities thus moved inexorably to restrict not only the movement of smugglers, not only the nomadism of Indians, but also the wandering of dispossessed men and women, especially those of African origin, who were the most likely to be labeled vadios. Powerful colonists viewed all of these manifestations of unsupervised mobility as a menace to the existing social order, even though Indians and impoverished frontier migrants alike often had only their immediate survival in mind.

The efforts to settle the Cuieté, Arrepiados, and Mantiqueira regions with varying combinations of individuals deemed criminals, vadios, and agregados, with families or with men alone, highlighted the ongoing struggle to assemble a tractable labor force in zones far from the urban centers of the captaincy. Race and gender figured prominently in frontier policies devised to achieve economic gain and maintain authority. When families flocked to forbidden areas of the sertão, as they did in the Mantiqueira Mountains, the prohibitions on settlement collapsed in the face of mass disregard for the law. The state was reduced to a reactive stance, promising land to those who had already seized it even if such promises could not be fulfilled. When settlers refused to migrate to sites singled out for settlement, as they did in the case of the Arrepiados and Cuieté regions, authorities promptly resorted to coercion of the poor and especially of unattached males of African descent. Where the promise of substantial gold deposits or agricultural gains failed to materialize, or where ongoing Indian resistance made settlers balk, the state would require the services of this "involuntary society," again to invoke Governor Meneses' apt phrase, as the most ready means of ensuring the "expansion of the conquests." The members of this society took their place among the countless migrants who, since the earliest days of Portuguese overseas expansion, had been pressured, forced, or otherwise compelled to voyage to the outermost reaches of the empire.[91]

As with other themes arising in these chapters, the early historians of the captaincy help place this issue into relief. Writing in the 1780s about Governor Rodrigo José de Meneses, his contemporary José Joaquim da Rocha extolled the leader's "grand policy" of promoting the incorporation of the sertão surrounding the decadent mining district. The governor determined to "separate from the good in number those bad ones who perturb their tranquility." Among these individuals, he introduced "service and work, the only means to remedy one's condition." Feeding, clothing, and dispatching them to Cuieté to labor in the gold diggings and to earn a share of the profits, Meneses acted to transform them into settlers who would proclaim the advantages of migrating to the Eastern Sertão while "obscuring the obstacles." They would, the governor hoped, convince others of their kind to follow in their footsteps, migrants who would now, "without being forced, except by their own interests, penetrate those sertões and overcome the risks" of establishing themselves there. In this way, those condemned as vadios would "change their conduct," making themselves "extremely useful to the state." Royal revenues would increase, economic distress would be surmounted, and the "prosperous and happy state" of the captaincy would be restored, the sertão finally "opening its bowels and revealing the riches that until now have remained hidden."[92]

More than 20 years later, in 1807, memorialist Diogo Pereira Ribeiro de Vasconcelos would describe the inhabitants of Minas Gerais on the eve of the prince regent's declaration of war against the Botocudo Indians. Vasconcelos argued for the extermination of nomadic Indians, given the failure of persistent efforts to settle them in villages. Despite Rocha's prophesy of the transformative power of the frontier, Vasconcelos found the state of the local poor unredeemed.

He noted that the captaincy's population could be divided into slaves, freed slaves, and whites, and observed that the first of these groups formed "the laboring class" but lacked all "virtue." The second group he classified simply as "pernicious to the state" because they could not even be relied on to labor with due submissiveness. Apart from "a few other simple folk of different classes," whites were the only "useful vassals of the captaincy," but unfortunately, as Vasconcelos saw it, they were far outnumbered by peoples of African origin.[93]

Together, Rocha and Vasconcelos conflated notions of race and labor, of status and utility, of poverty and mobility. Such attitudes in the writings, policies, and actions of eighteenth- and early nineteenth-century Minas elites help explain how the sertão became a site for the conquest not only of Indians but also of the wandering poor, the captaincy's "useless people," as they were so often and ignominiously classified. Their plight was that of countless migrants propelled into territories where Europeans, Africans, and indigenous peoples met at the margins of the Atlantic world, as the political and economic beneficiaries of an expanding world economy sought to incorporate new lands to extend their power and accumulate wealth. Also from this perspective, the Forbidden Lands of the Eastern Sertão had more in common with other frontiers than scholars have previously understood. For those long accustomed to viewing the frontier as a place where free laborers occupied free land, the parallels have been difficult to grasp, another reason that the occupation of the Brazilian interior escaped their attention.[94] As with other frontiers, the history of the lands ringing the settled center of colonial Minas Gerais had less to do with the triumphant establishment of a free settler society than with the extension of unequal power relations into distant lands, crystallizing in racial domination and the exploitation of labor. In response, those excluded by this process marshaled their energies to resist subjugation in the interstices of a consolidating state and commercial economy. With these underpinnings of the internal colonization process articulated, turning to the violent confrontation that occurred to the east of the mining district is now possible, as Portuguese settler society, with its tenacious hierarchies and its latent and contested racial geographies, clashed with the indigenous peoples of the coastal forests.

PART TWO

Confrontation

CHAPTER 5

The Assault on the Eastern Sertão

T HE KIND OF LOCAL nuance surfacing in documents that found their way back to Vila Rica and Lisbon from the Eastern Sertão, the malleable nature of Crown and captaincy policy with respect to the frontier and its diverse inhabitants, the extensive activity in the forests of settlers both prosperous and poor, and, more fundamentally, the startlingly pervasive presence of Indians in archival sources during a period in which they were supposed to have been a long-forgotten concern—these phenomena demand a more thoroughgoing analysis than they have received in the historiography. A number of conventional assertions in particular require revision. First, given the official preoccupation with native resistance, the notion that Indians disappeared as active agents in the colony's history must be rejected. The act of "expelling and/or decimating" the indigenous population before and during the gold rush, to repeat a phrase emblematic of this standard view, need not entail ignoring the eastern seminomads; instead, it should direct attention to the isolated forests and river valleys where many of them took refuge.[1] Furthermore, given an unbroken record of overt violent conflict between the captaincy government, colonists, and Indians intensifying in the 1760s, the emphasis placed on 1808 as the pivotal year in relations between the colonial state and the hunters and gatherers of southeastern Brazil must be discarded.[2] The declaration of war issued in that year was significant for a number of reasons—one of the most important being its role in the final demise of the Crown's impulse to contain frontier settlement. But it did not mark the advent of a radically new kind of official violence against Indians in general or the Botocudo Indians in particular. Conflict between the Portuguese and the Botocudo, a perennial feature of the sixteenth and seventeenth centuries, did not thereafter vanish until it reemerged *ex nihilo* in 1808; rather, it began to gather force a half-century earlier as a consequence both of resurgent internal colonization tied to the decline of the central mining district and of the decidedly elastic character of Crown policy in the hands of local administrators. In declaring war against the Botocudo, Prince Regent João assumed royal responsibility for an ad hoc policy of violent conquest already in effect on the regional level.

Something more far-reaching was also at stake. The declaration of war pointed to the struggle to establish centralized power over regional authority characteristic of the formation of the Brazilian state in the early nineteenth century.[3] As with other administrative tasks in the distant colony, the responsibility of interpreting, implementing, and even forging state policy on both indigenous relations and internal territorial matters had devolved largely to the governors of individual captaincies rather than to the viceroy in Rio de Janeiro before the Crown transferred residence to Brazil. Only well into the nineteenth century, following national independence, would these largely autonomous regions submit in any unified manner to central authority, and even then local governments continued to set the course for indigenous policy. To remain fixed on the legislative machinations of the royal court, failing to search beyond the laws, decrees, and official ideology promulgated by the Crown, is to overlook the local origin of Indian and frontier policy. It is to miss the forging of cultural and regional identities that such policy embodied. It is to ignore the central importance of frontier conquest and native resistance to the history of a vital colonial region scholars have treated as a place effectively settled and purged of Indians within a few decades of the discovery of gold. In Minas Gerais, where Indians all but disappear from the historiography, only by crossing into the Forbidden Lands of the Eastern Sertão does one come face to face with the quotidian persistence of interethnic frontier violence.

One is easily misled by the many official sources that glossed over the history of this conflict, such as José Eloi Ottoni's 1798 call for expansion into the Eastern Sertão in which he urged the Crown to promote a new era of exploration and conquest led by brave bandeirantes. He referred to a few adventurers who formed bandeiras to search for gold and precious stones in the region.[4] For understandable reasons, given his purposes and preconceptions as a memorialist seeking solutions for the captaincy's economic woes, Ottoni grossly underestimated the energy, accomplishments, and disruptive incursions of preceding generations; however, like his elite precursors, he retained faith in the regenerative power of the wilderness expedition. Between 1755 and 1804, after which early mobilization in advance of the 1808 declaration of war transformed these expeditions into more conventional Crown-ordered military operations, at least 79 bandeiras set out for the Eastern Sertão, well-armed and ordered to brook no resistance from intransigent natives. Although further research will likely uncover still others, the peak of this activity will surely remain the 20 years between 1765 and 1785,

TABLE 5.1

Expeditions to the Eastern Sertão, 1755–1804

Years	Number
1755–59	2
1760–64	1
1765–69	24
1770–74	10
1775–79	14
1780–84	14
1785–89	0
1790–94	5
1795–99	3
1800–04	6
Total	79

SOURCES: AIHGB, Conselho Ultramarino, Arq. 1, 3, 8; APM, CC, cod. 1156; APM, SC, cods. 60, 118, 183, 200, 214, 224, 227, 259, 260, 276, 277; "Ordens..., 1768[–1771]," BNRJ, SM, CC, gaveta I-10-7; BNRJ, SM, cód. 2, 2, 24; BNRJ, SM, CV, cód. 18, 2, 6; RAPM 2:2 (1897): 315; Diogo Pereira Ribeiro de Vasconcelos, *Breve descrição*, 150–51; Diogo [Luís de Almeida Pereira] de Vasconcelos, *História média*, 206–08, 252; Barbosa, Dicionário histórico, 83; Castro, *Os sertões de leste*, 11–15; Resende, "Gentios brasílicos," 379–83.

NOTE: The 1775–79 quinquennial includes a series of expeditions that Governor Antônio de Noronha dispatched in 1776 to the upper Doce River to counter Indian attacks and track down runaway slaves. Without specifying an exact number, Noronha ordered "several expeditions," which have been counted as three. The final years leading up to the 1808 declaration of war against the eastern Indians have been excluded because an unknown number of expeditions began to mobilize in what Governor Pedro Maria Xavier de Ataíde e Melo described as "continuous patrols."

precisely the period during which the dislocations of the post-boom era became most severe (see Table 5.1).[5]

A term employed here in accordance with its appearance in archival sources, and not to be confused with the renowned raids led by São Paulo backwoodsmen primarily in the seventeenth-century, the bandeira in Minas Gerais during the second half of the eighteenth century tended to be of more limited scope in numbers of participants, duration, and distance traveled. A mobile frontier institution with its origins in the sixteenth century—and before that in the re-conquest of the Iberian peninsula from the Moors—these military and paramilitary expeditions reappeared, long after their purported demise, to become the Minas elite's favored means of frontier expansion by force. Such bandeiras could be either state-sponsored and manned by soldiers or privately (and sometimes illegally) organized and financed. They were dispatched to neutralize native resistance, to secure land, to search for new sources of mineral wealth, to clear authorized trails and roads, to reconnoiter rivers, to track down smugglers and runaway slaves, and to extend state authority over areas sparsely populated by subsistence farmers and unsupervised prospectors. Usually they combined more than one of these objectives, most common among them the pacification of Indian territory and the quest for gold.

ILLUSTRATION 5.1. A deadly encounter between soldiers and natives, ca. 1822
SOURCE: Rugendas, *Voyage pittoresque*. Biblioteca Nacional, Rio de Janeiro.

The task of forming, funding, provisioning, and deploying bandeiras, which often depended on the forced labor of slaves, free Afro-Brazilian conscripts, and detribalized Indians, required a considerable mobilization of regional resources and manpower. Although chronically short of funds, the captaincy government assumed this task with enthusiasm, endowing these eighteenth-century expeditions with a legality and legitimacy that their precursors often lacked. The historical memory of those who advocated their use invested the bandeira with the status of a ritual of conquest infused with symbolic meaning. The bandeira became fixed in the imagination of a local elite determined to retain and extend its hegemony over a region first traversed more than a century before by backwoodsmen from the coast who enslaved native populations and later discovered extravagant deposits of gold and diamonds. In less prosperous times, new expeditions served to reenact this heroic history, sustaining the same faith in

ILLUSTRATION 5.2. Hunting for game
SOURCE: Rugendas, *Voyage pittoresque*. Biblioteca Nacional, Rio de Janeiro.

conquest and yearning for wealth and glory that had impelled the colonization
of Brazil from its earliest days. The resurgence, frequency, and persistence of
such expeditions in the face of determined native opposition, royal trepidation,
and unimpressive material gains can thus be seen as central to the historical
memory and colonial identity of those who supported the conquest.[6]

Like others, Ottoni misunderstood the magnitude of what was by then a
decades-long expansion into the Eastern Sertão by soldiers and settlers and
its devastating consequences for unincorporated natives. The advance persisted
through virtually every governor's tenure until the end of the eighteenth century
and then proceeded unchecked into the nineteenth. In some cases, soldiers led
the march; in others, settlers did and then called on the military to defend with
bandeiras newly colonized territory subject to Indian attack. By Ottoni's time,
dozens of expeditions and hundreds of expeditionaries protecting thousands

ILLUSTRATION 5.3. A river crossing
SOURCE: Rugendas, *Voyage pittoresque*. Biblioteca Nacional, Rio de Janeiro.

of settlers had already plunged into the eastern forests to do battle with the Indians. They did so in circumvention and often contravention of all measures to keep the region off-limits but also as an unintended consequence of those very measures.

The same incongruity writ large would characterize the prince regent's 1808 declaration of war, announced with all the rhetorical trappings of a momentous change in colonial policy. To accept the thrust of the Crown's pronouncement is to see the armed assault as the moment at which relations irrevocably hardened between the state and the Indians, when tensions presumably long-since forgotten suddenly, almost unaccountably, re-ignited and provoked the ire of the colony's highest authority, the prince regent himself. He reacted by invoking the principle of "just war." Dating, like the bandeira, from the re-conquest era and applied to indigenous peoples throughout the Americas from the onset of colonization, the principle of "just war" invested the Crown with legal and theological authority to conquer and enslave Indians deemed hostile—and often anthropophagous. According to the most comprehensive compendium of indigenous legislation available, the monarch had not claimed this right in Brazil since the 1730s and never at all in Minas Gerais.[7] However, Crown and captaincy were two different entities, and the war against the Botocudo—extended officially in November 1808 to the Kaingáng of São Paulo and unofficially to the neighboring Puri in Minas Gerais as well as to other groups in the captaincies of Goiás, Piauí, and Maranhão—was anything but an anomalous eruption of violence.[8] Instead, it marked the royal endorsement and legitimization of a policy that had a long history in Minas Gerais.

Strikingly little of the violent activity that led up to 1808 has been recorded in regional, colonial, or national histories. The present chapter offers an alternate narrative of events during the half-century preceding the prince regent's declaration of war. It does so in considerable detail to correct the customary inattention to multiple conflicts engendered by territorial expansion in forests portrayed as banned by eighteenth-century contemporaries and subsequent historians. The related issue of selective historical memory will be taken up in the next chapter and again in the concluding discussion.

The Conquest of Cuieté

Following some initial tensions between settlers and Indians in southeastern Minas Gerais during the 1750s, the distant mining camp of Cuieté as well as its environs, the so-called Conquest of Cuieté, became the most prominent locus of these post-boom conflicts. Governor Silva took a keen interest in the region from the moment he assumed leadership of the captaincy in 1763. Prodded by outraged settlers who had drifted into the region and found themselves subjected to what they denounced as "notorious" and "constant" losses of property, including entire homesteads, Silva ordered some 150 armed men to march to Cuieté and its surrounding forests. Drawn from military and civilian populations alike, the troops were to repel the Indians, put an end to their hostilities, and reverse the territorial losses of colonists who had fled the area. The governor hoped to make this prized portion of the frontier safe for the benefit not only of settlers themselves but also the royal treasury because the mineral wealth and "commerce" that resulted from a secure frontier would generate revenues in the form of the royal fifth assessed on gold production and steep taxes levied on other profitable enterprises.[9] Whereas his predecessor, the Count of Bobadela, limited his actions at Cuieté to a defensive posture of protecting the few earliest settlers, Silva adopted an explicitly aggressive stance intended to quash Indian resistance. He sought, as one of his successors described it, to "reduce those

Indians to the Roman Catholic religion by means of military expeditions and to make them fit for society and useful to the state."[10] That is, they would become useful in some way other than in their prescribed role as savage guardians of the forests who kept smugglers and errant settlers at bay and preserved the status of the Forbidden Lands. In effect, the language of this mobilization relied on terms simultaneously applied to the autonomous Afro-Brazilians who would be enlisted as soldiers in this conquest.

Silva named Captain Antônio Cardoso de Souza commander of a series of military missions whose stated goal was to halt the "advances (*entradas*) and abuses" of the "heathen Botocudo and other barbarous and wild nations." The first of the two words he used to describe Indian rebelliousness was significant. Literally meaning entrance, the term *entrada* was commonly employed along with *bandeira* to describe the expeditions mounted by the Portuguese to enter and conquer the sertão. Applied in the reverse sense to Indian attacks on settlements, the term was far less common and suggested an invasion of or, as it has here been translated, an advance into territory the Portuguese considered their own. In short, the governor became convinced that the Portuguese were losing ground—an accurate assessment, as it turned out. Soldiers would therefore "reduce" these Indians "to peace and civil conformity" in accordance, asserted Silva, with royal orders. Souza and his fellow officer Captain Antônio Pereira da Silva, one of the region's most successful gold miners, were to lead separate bandeiras, which would advance on Indian territory. They were to engage the Botocudo and any other Indians judged responsible for attacks on settlers. Should peaceful means prove unconvincing, Governor Silva authorized Souza to "submit them to the stated obedience by means of force."[11]

Such phrases made apparent the euphemistic quality of what the governor described as a policy of "defensive war," by which he meant a war justified by Indian atrocities, specifically those of arson, theft, and murder.[12] Invoking defensive action in this way, he established a continuum with the policy of the Count of Bobadela but, just as importantly, initiated what became in practice a combative departure from that policy. Silva's language made this innovation more palatable to a Portuguese Crown ensnared by the contradictions of its own policies, officially treating Indians with enlightened benevolence, effectively sanctioning the conquest of those opposing incorporation, while theoretically depending on just such opposition to maintain the Eastern Sertão off-limits to colonists and contrabandists who threatened to breach the barrier between the inland mining district and the coast. Silva's pronouncements also prepared impatient colonists to shoulder the cost of such actions, men and women who for all practical purposes were challenging the Crown's geographic prohibitions by venturing to Cuieté, as well as by extending their holdings on the eastern edge of the traditional mining zone. They would be heavily taxed—contributing not only gold but provisions—to pay for the mobilization of the captaincy troops deployed to guarantee their safety.[13]

Whatever verbal somersaults were practiced in the captaincy capital of Vila Rica, soldiers in the field acknowledged the openly bellicose nature of their missions. For years, Captain Souza remained in the Eastern Sertão pursuing Indians not only under the orders of Silva but also of his successor, the Count of Valadares. Throughout this period, the captain understood his military objective to be nothing less than "to extirpate the fierce Botocudo."[14] These wandering sovereigns of the sertão had chosen not to submit willingly to the obedience captaincy authorities demanded. Hence, Souza and his co-commanders endeavored, as they jointly declaimed during a strategic gathering on the banks of the Doce River in 1769, to "engage them in a violent war and subdue them by any means necessary."[15]

The clearest and most detailed statement of Governor Silva's own intentions came in the form of the orders he issued to Captain Souza. In deploying troops against the Indians, the governor did not rule out the possibility of an amicable solution. But if Souza's forces encountered the slightest resistance—which, in fact, they would almost immediately—the governor instructed the captain to "cede to the violence necessary to subdue [the Indians]," given their rejection of peaceful relations and the "murders they [had] committed." The Botocudo were to be considered "declared enemies" of the Portuguese and, as such, "deserving of the punishment required to make them . . . obedient." Without such punishment, they would "continue in the darkness of savagery, repeating the . . . hostilities that are harming this captaincy and its inhabitants." Thus war, which the governor at times persisted in terming "defensive," was to be waged against these seminomads because they themselves had engaged in a "declared and unjust war." After bowing to the possibility of peace, in short, the governor set violence in motion. He summarized his approach as one of "attracting the Indians by means of kindness and gentleness and, if that proved ineffective, by means of force."[16] This stance and the actions it prompted amounted to nothing less than warfare, declared by the governor, ratified by his officers, reaffirmed repeatedly in the conduct of his successors, and, finally, almost a half-century later in 1808, adopted and extended by the Crown.

In 1765, Governor Silva ordered three initial bandeiras to march into the sertão in pursuit of the Botocudo and any other rebellious natives. The largest of these expeditions, with 100 soldiers under the command of Captain José Gonçalves Vieira, probably departed from the village of Santa Rita. The others, under the command of Captain Jerônimo Martins Gomes and Felix da Costa Ribeiro, consisted of 30 to 35 soldiers each and entered the eastern forests from Antônio

Dias Abaixo. Governor Silva ordered his commanders to converge on Cuieté, still referred to in one document by its old name, Casa da Casca, originally assigned by São Paulo bandeirantes. All of the officers bore the governor's idiosyncratic orders to "make the Indians peaceful and reduce them to obedience . . . seeking to do so by means of kindness and gentleness, without using force, except in cases of necessary defense, should the rebellion of the said Indians make [force] indispensable in order to submit them to the aforementioned obedience and to Christianity." Reducing this policy to its essence, one of the officers would later describe it as "Christianization by violence."[17]

Twice as many military expeditions set forth the following year, a year that merits scrutiny as one of the most active and most thoroughly documented. In February 1766, the governor ordered the first of these bandeiras, composed of 20 soldiers and 50 slaves, to open a new road through an area in the vicinity of Abre Campo subject to attacks by Botocudo, Puri, and an obscure group known as Taititûs. The governor hoped the existence of such a road would, according to his customary language, "block the liberty the Indians were gaining."[18] In April, when Silva ordered captains José Gonçalves Vieira and José do Vale Vieira to lead the year's most ambitious expedition, setting out from a point downstream from Guarapiranga with 138 troops, the governor's rhetoric hardened still further. That the Botocudo, Puri, and other groups had found wanting the state's overtures of kindness in exchange for submission became increasingly evident. Because these Indians failed to respond to "the soft approach," and in light of mounting losses by property owners, the governor instructed his officers to dispense with all pretense of peaceful approximation. The expeditionaries were to "strike back at the offensive and declared war" initiated by the Indians. Intending to match force with force, he ordered two more bandeiras dispatched: one with 30 soldiers, following a road leading to remote fazendas along the Casca and Matipó Rivers, and another composed of 54 soldiers based in Cuieté. Two months later, the governor ordered more than 40 additional troops under the command of Captain Antônio Pereira da Silva into action from the town of Antônio Dias Abaixo with orders to establish a garrison at Cuieté and then march against the Indians.[19]

At this point, in August, Governor Silva authorized Captain Souza, first mentioned in the sources simply as a resident of Rio Pardo in the captaincy's northeast, to lead a privately organized bandeira to "reduce the heathen to peace and discover the riches presumed to exist" in the Eastern Sertão. As usual, the conquest of Indians and the discovery of mineral wealth were inseparably linked.[20] Although no complete record remains of this bandeira, Souza appears to have been handsomely rewarded. Bearing a captain's commission and one of four officers allocated munitions for new operations in 1766 and 1767, he soon resurfaced in official documents, serving as the top field commander in the Eastern Sertão.[21] Also during this period, a new group of settlers reached Cuieté, migrating southward from Minas Novas. Plagued by Indian resistance along their route, including the death of one of their leaders at the hands of the Capoxó Indians, these migrants apparently abandoned plans to found a separate isolated settlement and instead followed their surviving leader to Cuieté, where they took up residence under the protection of Captain Souza.[22]

In subsequent years, the Count of Valadares pursued the incorporation of the Eastern Sertão with undiminished vigor and, like his predecessor, made the Conquest of Cuieté the focus of his military actions. By then, the name of the mining camp and its environs had come to refer to a substantially larger area thought to be rich in gold and likewise destabilized by native resistance perceived as atrocities. Soon after taking office, the Count of Valadares created two companies of 25 foot soldiers each, paid by the royal treasury and permanently deployed to "conquer the barbarous heathen dispersed over the vast region of Cuieté." These companies remained in existence for seven years, garrisoned at the settlement of Cuieté and leading the armed advance on the Eastern Sertão, until decommissioned by Governor Antônio de Noronha in 1775.[23] Under Valadares, Captains Souza and Antônio Pereira da Silva remained as field commanders. They led six of the thirteen expeditions into the eastern forests registered in the records of the Valadares government, and their corporals, André Sanches Brandão and Alexandre da Silva Guimarães, led another two. With military authority in the sertão now more firmly established, they were made accountable to Captain Paulo Mendes Ferreira Campelo, whom Governor Silva appointed the first of three regents of the Conquest of Cuieté, overseeing an immense unincorporated area.[24]

During Valadares' tenure, Souza described his military mission as one intended "to extirpate the fierce Botocudo."[25] The still more zealous Corporal Guimarães, who chastised Souza for his inaction and cowardice, echoed these words. Guimarães praised the soldiers under his own command as fighting to bring about "the extinction of the Indians, whether dispersed [in the forests] or living in aldeias, so that once they are extinct this great forest can be settled" for the Crown's benefit.[26] Such words represented more than mere bravado. As head of the captaincy, Valadares was far more discreet than his soldiers, speaking in sweeping terms of ensuring the "expansion" of the Conquest of Cuieté and along with it the "security of settlers and the common good of the people."[27] In the end, however, officers like Souza and Guimarães took their cue from the governor's unmistakably belligerent orders. Like Governor Silva before him, for Valadares the goal of destroying Indian resistance ultimately outstripped even that of finding gold, although both objectives remained intertwined, as always.

While urging Souza to be assiduous in his exploration for precious minerals, Valadares emphasized that this search was not "the principal objective at which to direct your course but rather solely the conquest of the barbarous heathen." Souza was to "reduce them to membership in Christian society in a kind and gentle fashion, or terrorize them with force and by any means necessary, when, as rebellious heathens, they do not wish to embrace our friendly treatment."[28] With such directives, that field officers did not hesitate to assert that Indian eradication lay at the heart of their mission in the sertão is no surprise.

Beyond Cuieté

Even if the Crown and its ministers had been fully aware of and correspondingly determined to stamp out all activities by Minas colonists in the sertão, little could have been done to reverse the process set in motion in the 1760s and 1770s. More cognizant of the changes taking place by the 1780s, in fact, the Crown chose to do little. The ongoing activity of settlers and troops, although never approaching the scale of the mass migrations more conventionally studied by frontier historians, made the interethnic violence that would occur virtually inevitable, embroiling the captaincy government in further measures to counter Indian aggression and protect specific locations vulnerable to attack. Lisbon continued to stress the need to maintain a geographic barrier structured to isolate a mining district whose decline in gold production court officials still blamed on smuggling and straying laborers. Captaincy governors acknowledged this need, affirmed it to a degree, and continued to take actions to enforce some restrictions on unauthorized activity in the zone but also sanctioned repeated exceptions to Crown restrictions. When imagined mineral wealth stirred dreams of revitalization, when promising discoveries were reported or even rumored, when settlers advanced ahead of civil authority, seeking gold, land grants to cultivate marketable foodstuffs, or squatters' plots to ensure basic subsistence, authorities in Vila Rica found containing the push eastward ever more counterproductive. The actions of Governor Silva and the Count of Valadares at Cuieté established a precedent that legitimated further state-sponsored colonization of the Forbidden Lands even as they and their successors continued to promulgate the increasingly untenable notion that all areas outside official purview remained closed. Occasional efforts to crack down on private expeditionary activity in the sertão were less a sign of the captaincy government's ambivalence about frontier conquest than of its drive to retain control over the process and reap its benefits.

Wherever the captaincy government projected its presence on the frontier, Indian resistance to the colonial project undergirded arguments justifying what amounted to yet another action undermining the status of the region as proscribed territory. In this respect, Governor Noronha proved to be as willing as his predecessors to conceive and enact colonization schemes and as unwilling to leave hostile Indians at large so that the sertão remained impassable. At the beginning of his term, he articulated a certain restraint, criticizing what he termed the "unjust" violence against Indians perpetrated by Governor Silva and the Count of Valadares. Considering the two companies of regular soldiers based in Cuieté ineffectual and a financial burden on the royal treasury, he decided to decommission them and create unpaid militia companies in their place. During his five-year tenure, however, Noronha carried out numerous military actions and not only those limited to the Cuieté area or even the Doce River watershed. For instance, he ordered officer João da Silva Tavares, later to succeed Campelo as Cuieté's regent, to "make war" on Botocudo who had pushed their way up the Muriaé River and were raiding vulnerable aldeias of settled Indians in the vicinity of Rio Pomba to the southeast.[29]

Meanwhile, despite the expense, the garrison at Cuieté survived and Noronha reinforced it by forming and deploying squadrons to "protect" the region from Botocudo hostilities. Consistent with policies set in motion over the previous decade, these squadrons were not merely defensive mechanisms. Composed of the impoverished free men of African descent, who at this time were also being targeted as recruits for the war effort against Spain, they were ordered "to penetrate" the surrounding forests in active pursuit of Indians.[30] More than once, the governor informed would-be settlers, fearful of risking their lives and property, that he had deployed new reinforcements to Cuieté, above and beyond these squadrons, to "counter the hostilities of the heathen."[31]

Noronha's most ambitious foray into the wilderness focused on the road connecting Vila Rica with Cuieté first begun by Governor Silva. So convinced was Noronha of the merits of pursuing the development of the distant mining camp and its environs that he singled out the completion and defense of the unfinished road as the "sole means by which to make the captaincy flourish and its inhabitants rich," which, he told the viceroy, constituted "the first object to which my incessant efforts are directed." Bypassing a dangerous and time-consuming river route, the road would secure the region's safe settlement, once and for all, he insisted. Construction dragged on for more than two years, impeded by the difficulties of rugged terrain and interminable rains. On its completion, despite continuing native resistance, the governor assured prospective settlers in a public proclamation that they could now establish themselves freely in Cuieté "without being hindered by the fear of Indians." They could count on the protection of the forces he had sent there "to defend the conquest."[32] His confidence, like that of his predecessors, in the ability of state intervention and government troops to neutralize the Indian threat would prove unjustified.

Closer to the captaincy's central settled zones, Noronha ordered military action as part of a coordinated effort to quell the resistance both of Indians and runaway slaves in the forests on the periphery of the termo of Mariana. When Indians "invaded" a number of fazendas situated along the upper tributaries of the Doce River, killing and robbing property owners, Noronha ordered forces normally reserved for fugitive slave hunts to enter the forests "in pursuit of the wild heathen." His willingness to embrace the imperatives of conquest and subdue the unincorporated peoples and places of key sections of the Eastern Sertão was evident in every aspect of his dealings with these squadrons. He doubled from 15 to 30 men the number of soldiers in each, he sought to ensure that they were adequately armed, and he reorganized them into a single, more centralized and efficient corps. He instructed commanders throughout the captaincy to enlist the most "robust" men available to serve in this corps, whose units were to be led by officers of color chosen from recruits who demonstrated the greatest knowledge of the forests. Any local commander unsuccessful in assembling forces adequate to the task would be subject to punishment.[33]

Governing after Noronha, Rodrigo José de Meneses furthered the commitment to frontier conquest as a means of rescuing the captaincy from decline, even beyond his various projects deploying Afro-Brazilian laborers to promising sites.[34] Pursuing improvements along the road to Cuieté, he created a company of soldiers to defend work crews pushing their way through the forest. Meneses supplied both workers and troops generously with provisions.[35] Nevertheless, he admitted to certain reservations about Cuieté, signaling a temporary change in direction that may have afforded Indians in the surrounding sertão some respite from the more aggressive policy of confrontation. At first, the governor spoke enthusiastically about the settlement, a place, he wrote, "where they assure me there is an abundance of gold that could lift this captaincy from the depression in which it finds itself."[36] Insisting in 1781 on traveling the new road to see the settlement himself, he could not conceal his disillusionment. Isolated, impoverished, a continuing drain on captaincy resources, and as vulnerable as ever to Botocudo attacks, Cuieté looked nothing like the El Dorado it was touted to be. Governor Meneses called it a "congress of wretches, without possessions, without slaves, and without gold other than that which circulates there from the royal treasury when the troops who are based there get paid." He retreated from the attempts of previous governors to attract settlers of significant means to the place and turned instead to the forced recruitment of vadios, those marginalized men deemed vagrants by officials desperate for frontier laborers. As previously noted, he also shifted attention to the more accessible Conquest of Arrepiados, becoming no less bent on its incorporation than his predecessors had been on Cuieté's.[37] As the completion of nearly a quarter-century of energetic if often

unsuccessful captaincy-sponsored colonization efforts approached, Minas officials finally arrived at the point at which they rarely fretted about justifying such
schemes to Crown officials in Lisbon still uneasy about smuggling, tax evasion,
and other unregulated activities in the eastern forests.

At Arrepiados, as elsewhere, the expansion Meneses sponsored stirred up
Indian resistance, this time among the Puri, which prompted further official
efforts at territorial consolidation. Soldiers there were garrisoned at a presidio
under the command of Antônio Veloso de Miranda, the third officer to be
appointed regent over a portion of the Eastern Sertão. The soldiers cleared fields
to grow provisions and opened a road to the region wide enough for horse travel,
and the governor kept them well-supplied with arms. Along one stretch of the
road, they noted the appearance of "trails and recent traces of the enemy." They
assumed Indians were reconnoitering troop movements or plotting raids on the
newly cultivated fields. "Clearly have [these Indians] shown their resentment
and the degree to which they seek our harm," Miranda informed the governor.
The priest Manuel Luís Branco, a veteran of previous Puri encounters, had been
charged with leading an initial expedition to explore the mountainous territory
for gold. He noted similar evidence of native unrest. "All of the savages of this
land are greatly agitated," he told Miranda. "They sound their trumpets every
night in order to threaten and terrorize . . . Numerous are the heathen," the priest
warned, "and at every step new vestiges are found."[38]

Like previous governors, Meneses again articulated the inescapable link between colonization plans and Indian submission. He ordered Branco to "domesticate" the Puri and to "pull them toward the true religion," using, where
possible, "extreme kindness." But he changed his emphasis after visiting the area
himself as part of the same first-hand inspection of the sertão that a month later
took him to Cuieté. In this case "accompanied by a great quantity of people"
eager to settle in the Arrepiados Mountains, he recognized that more direct
methods would be required. Gazing down from atop a high ridge at "sertões as
wide as the eye can see, peopled by diverse nations of wild Indians and beasts,"
he resolved to ensure the area's colonization whether or not the Indians cooper-
ated. The following day—evidently and, as it turned out, justifiably convinced
that he would face no opposition from the Crown—he conceded more than
300 land grants and mining claims to expectant settlers.[39] He advised Colonial
Secretary Martinho de Melo e Castro "that it will be necessary to put to flight"
the Puri and others "if it is not possible to domesticate" them.[40] The lack of
success in either approach to the Indians apparently contributed to the failure
of many settlers to remain on the land they received.

The governor recommended a similar solution for Cuieté, despite his qualms
about the merits of pursuing settlement there. Dismayed by the absence of

Portuguese inhabitants throughout the final two-thirds of the forest separating Vila Rica from Cuieté, he wrote to the secretary: "In this entire expanse of land, there is not even a single house, nor anyone who intends to settle there." Ignoring the history of royal restrictions on colonizing the Eastern Sertão, he blamed the widespread fear of the "heathen Botocudo, errant in those forests," for the failure of settlement to take hold. These Indians, "which they guarantee to be canni-bals," could readily be vanquished, he proposed, by deploying "a good number of armed men" who "could repel their forces by virtue of the advantageous difference that there is between our arms and those of the heathens."[41] Thus, under his leadership, the 20-year period of greatest bandeira activity stretched into the mid-1780s.

A comparative paucity of evidence of bandeira activity and conflicts between settlers and the seminomads of the Eastern Sertão characterized official sources produced during the decade following Meneses' departure from Minas Gerais. Accordingly, to posit that such conflict simply disappeared seems implausible given its persistence both before and after this lacuna. To be sure, an inclina-tion by captaincy officials to concentrate on less remote frontier zones not as susceptible to Indian attack was a feature of this period. Even more quickly than at Cuieté, enthusiasm for the Arrepiados conquest sputtered as initial gold discoveries failed to produce significant deposits and Puri resistance proved unrelenting.[42] The difficulty Meneses experienced corralling laborers willing to work in the zone also hurried the abandonment of the captaincy government's ambitious plans.

As an alternative, Governor Luís da Cunha Meneses emphasized opening— by official accounts, that is—the southernmost reaches of the Eastern Sertão, an area to the east of Barbacena and the Caminho Novo, where Crown prohibitions on settlement were being more brazenly than ever ignored by the invasion of frontier migrants profiting from foodstuffs production. This was the area of rapid colonization later known as the Zona da Mata, where Padre Manuel de Jesus Maria had been active among the Coroado and Coropó Indians since the early 1760s, and where Governor Noronha had ordered war waged against the Botocudo in the 1770s. By the 1780s, the Coroado and Coropó had been largely reduced to submission, many of them taking up residence at the state-controlled aldeias of Rio Pomba and São João Batista do Presídio. When officers were dispatched in 1784 to examine the region and to consolidate civil and military control, the settler invasion forced the governor to recognize the folly of imagining these fertile lands to be still off-limits. Subsequent census figures give some sense of this accelerating regional growth. By 1799, the parish of Rio Pomba, which then included both aldeias, was home to some 3,000 inhabitants. By the early 1820s, it had split into two parishes bearing the names of the two aldeias. More than 16,000 individuals inhabited these parishes, not including many unsettled and marginally settled Indians left uncounted by census takers. São João Batista do Presídio alone was home to 40 sugar plantations worked by a total of 245 slaves and 65 free laborers, bearing witness to the transformation long since underway. A parish census also included 845 settled Indians.[43]

For their part, settlers to the north did not stop invading Indian land just because official attention fixed on the more active, less distant locations of the captaincy's southeastern hinterlands. But without the kind of close government scrutiny that accompanied official colonization plans, fewer orders were sent, fewer reports written, and fewer accounts of clashes between settlers and Indians reached the capital, later to be preserved in the archives. This issue became especially influential during the political upheaval of the late 1780s that culminated in the Inconfidência Mineira. Reports of Indian resistance and renewed bandeira activity reappeared in government records just as calm returned to Vila Rica in the wake of the foiled 1789 nativist rebellion. The transmission, pertinence, and preservation of news of frontier conflict seemingly depended as much on the vigilance of officials in Vila Rica as on the actual presence of such turmoil in the sertão.[44]

Southern Minas Gerais' gradual economic recovery also provoked the diversion of attention, as the region profited from its connections to the coast and an expanding population. Those Coroado, Coropó, and Puri Indians who chose not to accept the subordinate status available to them in the southeastern, state-sponsored aldeias found themselves forced farther down the Pomba and Muriaé River valleys. There they were trapped between those migrants pressing outward from the old mining districts and those moving inland up the Paraíba watershed from the coastal sugar-producing Campos region. Accounting for the conduct of these Indians during this period, Manoel Martins do Couto Reis, a military officer who mapped and, in 1785, authored a natural history of Campos, wrote that the Coroado had retreated to the Pomba River valley from the Muriaé River valley, forced southward after military defeat by the Puri. Reis described the latter, themselves confronting the effects of shrinking territory, as "corpulent, audacious, fearless, vigilant, and of very traitorous principles, inclined to every sort of inhumanity." They "put to death every living thing they encountered," human or not, he wrote, even if they were harmless. As their refuge contracted, a significant number seem to have headed northward, contributing to conflicts throughout the upper Doce River watershed, both with other Indians competing for the same territory and with settlers, including those still established immediately to the north in the Arrepiados region.[45]

During this same period, another front of colonial expansion compressed traditional hunting and gathering grounds and exacerbated interethnic tensions still farther to the north. Since the 1760s, authorities in the captaincy of Bahia had taken measures to strengthen the fragile grip with which coastal settlers in the southern comarcas of Ilhéus and Porto Seguro clung to plantations exposed to Indian raids. One such measure, never effected, called for the conquest of the lower Doce River basin. Another project, initiated by the explorer Francisco Hernandes Teixeira Álvares before the Crown put an end to it, envisioned securing the subjection of the Pataxó Indians of the Mucuri River valley. Their defeat was to be achieved with the help of expeditions manned by settled village Indians engaged in a "continuous war" with these foes of the inland forests. During the final quarter of the eighteenth century, colonization in Ilhéus and Porto Seguro intensified as settlers drifted southward along the littoral to establish homesteads, where they cultivated crops to feed the urban population of Salvador, continuing to expand even though Rio de Janeiro had replaced it as the colonial capital. A road built from the upper reaches of the Pardo River cut through the forests eastward to the Bahian coast. The new route, authorities hoped, would facilitate the transport of timber, cattle, foodstuffs, and cotton from this fertile region. Overland exploratory expeditions also multiplied, along with river and navigation surveys. The veteran Indian fighter João Gonçalves da Costa embarked on a multiyear mission to subdue the Kamakã Indians north of the Pardo River. By 1782, combining persuasion and coercion, he claimed to have convinced 2,000 of them to take up residence in five villages rather than continue to "live unhappily in the...error of paganism." That these Indians sought Portuguese protection from attacks by Pataxó and Botocudo groups testified to the mounting pressure on the coastal forests and the Eastern Sertão as a whole. Maxakali and Malali Indians traumatized by Botocudo hostilities in the Jequitinhonha River valley reacted similarly.[46]

At a point located between these encroaching coastal population centers, increasing activity around the old port town of Vitória, capital of Espírito Santo, at the mouth of the Santa Maria da Vitória River, meant that Indians seeking refuge from these other conflicts would lose any semblance of safe haven they once enjoyed along the Atlantic seaboard. In 1779, for instance, members of the Vitória town council appealed to Maria I to protect them from constant raids to ensure that fazendas established upriver could get their produce to market. Efforts to develop the river basin had been stymied, its fertile valley left "uninhabited, at great loss and injury" to local colonists. Descending into the valley from the highlands along the border with Minas Gerais, the Botocudo, described as "the only barbarous heathens of these sertões known to eat human flesh," disrupted all efforts to transform the area into a thriving agricultural and logging center, from which not only Vitória but also Rio de Janeiro and Salvador could be provisioned. Providing an unusually detailed account of the

ILLUSTRATION 5.4. A Kamakã chief, ca. 1820
SOURCE: Jean Baptiste Debret, *Voyage pittoresque et historique au Brésil* (Paris: Didot Frères, 1834–1839). Biblioteca Nacional, Rio de Janeiro.

ILLUSTRATION 5.5. A Kamakã woman, ca. 1820
SOURCE: Debret, *Voyage pittoresque*. Biblioteca Nacional, Rio de Janeiro.

cannibalism for which the Botocudo were frequently condemned, town council members testified that one settler had recently had his hands torn off while still alive, others their heads. The natives had then placed their mouths on the open wounds of the victims and had drunk their blood. Causing "continuous deaths" of both settlers and their slaves, moreover, the Indians dismembered some corpses to carry them off for later meals. "Tame Indians" enlisted in the timber trade feared to venture inland, having sustained numerous attacks themselves. Far more settlers would face expulsion or death—indeed, the entire region might end up uninhabitable—unless the Crown acted immediately and forcefully, the officials warned. Queen Maria did take action, authorizing armed bandeiras to launch counter-attacks aimed at reducing the Botocudo in the area to a state of subjection.[47]

By the 1780s, throughout the coastal forests stretching from Salvador to Rio de Janeiro, all along the eastern limits of settled Minas Gerais—in other words, from every edge of the great swathe of wilderness originally placed off-limits to protect the gold and diamond discoveries that had once sustained the Portuguese Empire—Indians who refused to submit to diverse colonial incursions were being pushed northward from the Paraíba River basin, southward from the Pardo River basin, westward from the Vitória region, and, above all, eastward from the inland mining district. As the region's encircled seminomadic autochthons struck back in various places, their survival dependent on the control of territory extensive enough to hunt and forage, they found no respite. Arising from the changes of earlier decades, heightening the potential for violence, these encounters all but extinguished any remaining possibility that the Portuguese would restrain themselves from demanding further decisive action to pacify the Indians of the Eastern Sertão, whose restricted status had eroded irrevocably. A quarter-century of intensive colonial pressure had shifted power definitively away from the Indians.

Military Mobilization and the Reversal of Crown Policy

The 1790s witnessed a redoubled emphasis on eastward expansion in Minas Gerais. The captaincy government now rarely made a show of hampering private expeditions and unsupervised settler activity in the sertão. To the contrary, top officials expressed regret that perennial financial constraints prevented them from providing monetary backing to such useful undertakings. As the gold cycle receded definitively into the past, royal concern about the status of the Eastern Sertão as a no-man's-land waned. As native resistance persisted, captaincy officials became ever more forthright about the need for a coherent military policy to complete the incorporation of the forests separating the old mining district from the coast. The line between intermittent armed bandeira activity and full-scale military mobilization became increasingly blurred.

By the early 1790s, Brazil's eastern Indians were again being vilified by authorities in the Minas capital. In 1792, residents of Ponte Nova and Guarapiranga appealed to the governor, the Viscount of Barbacena, for permission to counter the "abuses and hostilities" of the Botocudo and Puri. Barbacena granted Joaquim Correia Mosso authority to lead "interested residents or other subjects readied by them" on a bandeira to "chase off the said wild Indians who infest their fields and dwellings."[48] In the parishes of Guarapiranga and Rio Pomba, where conflict had intensified in proportion to the mounting presence of frontier migrants, the governor acted to secure further settlement. Local residents complained of being "deprived of the force and authority sufficient to impede the abuses of the enemy." Landholders reported in 1794 that "barbarous Indians" had grown "bolder the less resistance they faced." For the past four or five years, they had staged repeated "invasions" in this southeastern region, resisting settlers "with great fury and violence."[49]

The timing of this complaint provides additional evidence that settlers' pleas for military support went unanswered for a number of years beginning in the late 1780s and that frontier conflict proceeded whether or not it came to the notice of inattentive authorities like Barbacena, infamous for his handling of the foiled anti-colonial rebellion during these years. Whatever his earlier preoccupations, Barbacena now approved a plan submitted by the local commander Captain José Bernardino Alves Gundim, who proposed redoubling efforts to curb Indian hostilities. As Governor Noronha had done nearly two decades earlier, Gundim called for the expansion of local military units and their consolidation into a single, well-paid corps that would repel the Indians by making "the necessary forays" into unsettled territory. Each expedition would be composed of 30 soldiers, an unspecified number of paid "tame Indians," probably conscripted from the aldeias at Rio Pomba and São João Batista do Presídio, and a commanding officer. Expeditions would be deployed as many as three times each year, not including emergency actions required to respond to random Indian attacks. They would march in April, when the Indians "set out to wander and raid"; in July or August, when they "lingered" at such activities; and in September, when they returned to "seek winter quarters in their aldeias and perpetrate their hostilities."[50]

The governor authorized Gundim to organize these bandeiras and to dispatch them under the command of José de Arrudo, who came recommended as a man "expert in the ways of the tame Indians and respected by them." The governor could not provide monetary assistance from the royal treasury. The plan's execution would be dependent upon the ability of local residents to finance and provision the expeditions. Gundim had anticipated this stipulation in his original proposal. Thus, the governor approved a mobilization "destined to chase off and intimidate" the Botocudo and the Puri. Soldiers, he cautioned, were to inflict "only that harm that is indispensable, preserving all moderation compatible with self-defense and the just execution of the mission." The plan was to remain in effect for one year, after which it would be subject to review and renewal if necessary.[51] The available evidence, fragmentary as is so often the case with events that occurred in the distant reaches of the Eastern Sertão, does not reveal whether these bandeiras continued to be deployed in subsequent years.[52]

What is apparent is that such conflict was not limited to the southeastern frontier. In the same year that Gundim's bandeiras set out, landholders with agricultural and mining properties in the districts of Itabira, Tanque, and Santana dos Ferros were forced to flee their farms and mining operations after what can only be described, even if the settlers exaggerated their account, as a major offensive by an unprecedented 2,000 Botocudo. Horrified frontier migrants implored Barbacena to dispatch government troops to the area. The governor responded, ordering soldiers, reinforced if necessary by local militia members, to escort residents back to their homes. After securing the settlements under siege, soldiers, residents, and their slaves were then ordered to advance into the forests to "pursue, attack, and apprehend or chase away the perpetrators of this extremely grave abuse."[53] Elsewhere, the governor pushed forward a system of constructing fortified presidios at strategic points as a line of defense against Indian attack. The first such establishments had been those built deep in the forests at Abre Campo in the 1730s, but later abandoned, and at Cuieté in the 1760s. Now, Barbacena set up at least three more at various sites along the upper reaches of the Doce River and its tributaries. That many more patrols routinely set out from these fortifications can be assumed.[54]

After the turn of the century, the conquest of the Eastern Sertão continued to command both official attention and substantial resources, as it had for all but a brief period between the mid-1780s and the early 1790s. Authorities reasserted their public demands for the destruction of nomadic Indians in strident terms reminiscent especially of the denunciations that had first prompted the bandeira offensive of the late 1760s and early 1770s. This increasingly aggressive posture, articulated during the tenure of Governor Bernardo José de Lorena, pointed forward, as well, to the war that would be declared during the subsequent administration of Governor Pedro Maria Xavier de Ataíde e Melo, the Viscount of Condeixa (1803–1809).

The Portuguese Crown now displayed a growing willingness to support a military solution regardless of its implications for opening up what could now in any case be described only as a former no-man's-land. To an extent, this reflected a shift in colony-wide indigenous policy. Abolishing Pombal's 1757 Indian Directory and its companion 1759 Direção legislation, alarmed by reports of corruption rife among the lay directors of the old Jesuit-run Indian villages in the Amazon basin and along the Atlantic coast, the Crown formally abandoned its 40-year-old Enlightenment-inspired indigenous policy in May 1798, although the status quo would survive locally in many areas of the colony for several decades. Prince João, who would become regent the following year, having assumed effective control of the monarchy in 1792 after madness incapacitated his mother Maria, reaffirmed the freedoms guaranteed in the Directory but disbanded Indian villages, furthering the process of territorial expropriation. He forbade offensive war against the Indians but permitted defensive military action.[55]

No sweeping royal pronouncement directly revoked the policy that established the eastern Forbidden Lands and preserved the presence of indigenous peoples in hopes of thwarting smugglers and other wayward vassals. Remnants of that policy also remained in effect. Nonetheless, decades of activity in the region, both authorized and unauthorized, along with an intensifying search for new commercial opportunities to replace the shrunken gold economy, gradually accentuated the obsolescence of the old restrictions. Emphasis shifted from blocking the flow of contraband to promoting—while retaining fiscal control over—the movement of marketable goods out of Minas Gerais to an awaiting Atlantic commercial complex by way of a network of customhouses along the Doce River. The emerging consensus among officials, eying the late-century boom in Brazilian agricultural exports, was that tax revenues from trade along the river would be sufficient to justify the expense of maintaining these outposts and wresting the watershed from its indigenous inhabitants.[56] As before, this final feat would prove far more difficult than Crown ministers, Governor Lorena, or any of their subordinates anticipated.

In May 1801, as a prelude to full-scale military mobilization, the Crown empowered Lorena to conduct offensive, as opposed to its long-invoked defensive, warfare against the Botocudo. The governor was to divide the vast area "infested" by these Indians into six military districts, each placed under the command of a trusted officer. This strategic scheme would form the basis for later troop deployments in 1808, when the prince regent formalized and generalized the declaration of war.[57] Lorena anticipated the new policy. In an effort begun as early as 1799, he had moved vigorously to secure the "opening of the Doce River" in collaboration with a powerful member of Minas Gerais' Portuguese-born elite, Antônio Pires da Silva Pontes Leme e Camargo, who in 1800 became governor of Espírito Santo as it was elevated from the status of Bahian comarca to an independent coastal captaincy.[58] Taking advantage of Crown support in 1801, apparently ignoring an earlier agreement defining the border between the two captaincies, Lorena quickly established the first customhouse far down the Doce River well beyond that line, east of the Doce's confluence with the Guandu River. Naming this forest outpost Porto de Lorena, he deployed a detachment of troops there to monitor commerce on the river and collect duties on all taxable goods.[59] After basing another detachment upstream near the town of Antônio Dias Abaixo, Lorena declared the river route to Espírito Santo "free of savages."[60] Once again, the claim was grossly premature.

Farther north and later the same year, Lorena invested Francisco Martins Penna, the ranking militia officer of the termo of Vila do Príncipe, with "all powers" necessary to push settlement more deeply than ever into the Eastern Sertão. The governor committed funds from the royal treasury to secure arms and ammunition.[61] At the end of 1801, Penna gathered together authorities from throughout the region and devised a plan to crush Botocudo resistance by opening two new roads running eastward from the periphery of already settled areas. Proposed as a protective barrier between the Indians and frontier migrants, the roads in fact penetrated directly into new territory not yet secured for settlement. Calculated to promote both agriculture and renewed gold mining in ever more remote regions, the plan sought to "strike back at the cruelties of the heathen Botocudo," who had continued to force settlers to flee their precarious homesteads. The southernmost of the two new roads would stretch through "virgin forest" from the town of Senhora do Porto to the Doce River and join an additional segment of road, providing the first reliable overland communications with Santana dos Ferros. Migrants first settled in Santana dos Ferros in the 1770s but were forced to flee in the face of the Botocudo offensive of 1794. The second more northerly road would incorporate, improve, and extend an existing route from Vila do Príncipe to Peçanha and, from there, proceed to the Suaçuí Grande River, navigable to the Doce River.[62] Farther downriver, the governor commissioned a new commanding officer at the Cuieté presidio and issued orders to "repel the attacks" that, he now acknowledged, the Botocudo had not ceased to stage, despite his earlier assurances about securing the river for navigation.[63]

The ongoing resistance meant that rather than just a tax collection point, the Doce River customhouse of Porto de Lorena quickly became a base for staging military operations against refractory Botocudo. Post commander Elesbão Lopes Duro supplied his troops by way of Antônio Dias Abaixo and assembled additional forces there to attack the Indians. In July 1802, for instance, he marched 42 soldiers to the struggling new settlement of Alegre, not far from Antônio Dias Abaixo, where the Botocudo had recently raided settlers' cattle. Tracking one group of natives through the forest to a collection of makeshift huts, the troops launched a surprise dawn attack, killing an unspecified number of Indians. Duro's description of the battle suggests dozens died in the ambush. Reporting this victory to the governor, the officer made it clear that such expeditions had become a standard feature of his duties, although their records have not survived.[64] Meanwhile, Lorena's praise for Duro, his soldiers, and his commanding officer made no secret of his bellicose posture, yet the governor also revealed the limits of this stance. Military actions against the Botocudo in the forests were "not presently our principal aim," he explained, which was rather to establish a sufficient military presence in the area to control river commerce.[65]

Settlers, soldiers in the field, and Lorena's successor, Governor Melo, knew that these two goals were inseparable, as Lorena undoubtedly did also. Under Melo, the militarization of the frontier intensified still further. Although the transition occurred gradually and inconsistently, the bandeira activity characteristic of preceding decades gave way to a new era. Wilderness expeditions—which had once depended more on captaincy than royal authority, which had thrived on the dream of hidden gold and diamonds in unexplored native territory, and which had often marched into the sertão on an ad hoc and sometimes even an extra-official basis—would now increasingly take the form of formal military maneuvers, sponsored, funded, and supervised by the Crown.

Thus in 1806, Governor Melo implemented yet another new plan to combat the Botocudo, a plan as openly offensive in its strategy as any since Governor Silva's in the 1760s but this time vetted far more thoroughly by royal authorities.[66] "Horrified to hear the cry of the wretched people" who established themselves along the edge of the eastern forests, Melo settled on what he considered the sole viable solution: "to remove the heathens, to the extent possible, and prevent their passage through the lands and settlements" of this territory. A direct prelude to the Crown's impending declaration of war, his orders called for the creation of new squadrons, totaling 130 soldiers, to oppose Botocudo "invasions." Soldiers were commanded to "bar the entrance" of natives to a wilderness expanse of unspecified extent, which the governor simply called "our interior." To do so, troops would traverse "in continuous patrols the banks and ports of the rivers that form our [eastern] borders and which readily reveal the trails of those [Indians] who pass there." The governor established three new garrisons and reinforced two others with the objective of strengthening the decades' old "defensive barrier against Botocudo attacks."[67] Militarily, the ground was now thoroughly prepared for the final assault on the Eastern Sertão, the one remembered at least in passing in the historiography, which would follow the prince regent's arrival in Brazil in 1808 and his declaration of war against the Botocudo.

To return to an earlier point about the gap between Crown and captaincy policy and the need to distinguish official pronouncements of either provenance from ongoing frontier praxis—that this was precisely the historical juncture at which conventional sources suggest indigenous relations began to deteriorate is no small irony. Around the turn of the nineteenth century, Minas memorialists well-known to captaincy historians—authors such as José Eloi Ottoni, José

Vieira Couto, Basilio Teixeira Cardoso de Sá Vedra Freire, and Diogo Pereira Ribeiro de Vasconcelos—issued their diatribes against official inaction and impotence in the face of what they deemed irrational native resistance and the still-untapped mineral and, with growing emphasis, agricultural riches of the great eastern forests.[68] From the 1760s, however, determined action to conquer the forest dwellers and incorporate their lands had become standard practice. By the memorialists' era, official resolve, even on the part of the Crown, to incorporate the Eastern Sertão had all but supplanted the older impulse to keep it unsettled.

An opportunistic reinterpretation of paternalistic indigenous policy had established the legality of the first assaults launched in conjunction with the search for remedies for the decaying gold-mining complex. The sites at the focus of this early post-boom aggression were those at which the nexus of imagined mineral wealth and scorned native persistence assumed geographic specificity. Restive colonists spurred captaincy governors to action. Over the decades, such action gradually persuaded the Crown in turn to relinquish strict adherence to its policy of restricting access to the Eastern Sertão. By the 1780s, a massive distribution of royal land could be implemented not far from the captaincy's eastern border at a place like Arrepiados, as if such restrictions no longer existed. Although this and similar projects deploying laborers and unleashing settlers often amounted to little because of undiminished native resistance, they nevertheless occurred in areas notoriously susceptible to the kinds of unsupervised activities authorities had traditionally cited as justification for banning frontier colonization. The direct and imperturbable manner in which these new activities were communicated to the Crown testified to the progressively altered status of a zone once considered impenetrable and inviolable. Subsequently, especially as the southern reaches of the captaincy shook off the receding effects of the mid-century depression, successful migration to the region east of the Caminho Novo gathered force and captaincy officials hastened to keep pace. By the beginning of the nineteenth century, the entire Eastern Sertão had become the object of wide-scale military mobilization aimed at linking inland population centers with the coast by way of the sertão's rugged river valleys.

From its distant throne, the Portuguese Crown learned to sanction such efforts, even if sometimes out of ignorance of their geographic import. Seemingly, little could be done in Lisbon to prevent governors, not to mention settlers, from straying into the eastern forests. For decades, those who gradually pushed back the boundaries of the Eastern Sertão proceeded even though the frontier failed to yield its dreamed-of golden treasure. In the process, as much by default as by design, a de facto reversal in Crown policy took place. At geographically critical points ranging from north to south, the Crown found itself enlisted in colonists'

once-illicit drive to occupy the Eastern Sertão and conquer its besieged aboriginal inhabitants. The war to resolve this conflict started decades before it was ever
declared. While independent Indians remained the enemy throughout, the goal
of their desired acquiescence had shifted. Once seen as preventing the revival of
a lost era founded on protected inland gold, they now barred the entrance to a
new world based on free-flowing Atlantic commerce.

CHAPTER 6

Sources of Conflict

The Elusive Evidence of Indian Incorporation
and Resistance

THE TITLE of this chapter is meant to be understood in its dual significance, encompassing issues both of historical origins and documentary corroboration. The phrase "sources of conflict" refers, first of all, to the origins of the violence that pit soldiers and settlers against Indians in the Eastern Sertão during the second half of the eighteenth century. Second, it points to the surprisingly intricate nature of surviving archival evidence. What would seem to be relatively unambiguous condemnations of Indian attacks composed by outraged colonists turn out to conceal a great deal of information about interethnic strife. Read closely, these sources—mundane in authorship if not subject matter—offer a corrective to the texts traditionally used to reconstruct the history of Brazil's indigenous peoples, especially accounts by European travelers and naturalists as well as formal reports by prominent Portuguese officials. On the surface, the sources of conflict appear obvious, constituting yet another episode in what historian John Monteiro has described disapprovingly as the "chronicle of extinction" that characterizes the greater part of the historiography pertaining to Portuguese America's native peoples.[1] Scratch that surface and the explanation of violence as conquest, transparent and uncomplicated, turns out to be a thin veneer. A historically specific explanation of deteriorating Luso-Indian relations is required as an antidote to sweeping generalizations.

More than a few unanswered questions compel such an approach. Was conflict, though pervasive, the only alternative in this frontier zone? Of course, it would not have been so had the wild no-man's-land remained truly impervious to colonization. Even as the Forbidden Lands policy gradually broke down, was cultural cooperation ever possible, even though one colonist after another argued it was not? When interethnic tensions did degenerate into violent confrontation, who initiated the ensuing attacks—Indians, settlers, or the state? What was the link between numerous hostile engagements and the remarkable increased activity of armed bandeiras? Were reports of Indian aggression fabricated by state authorities to justify invasion and eradication, or were the reports generally accurate and thus evidence of determined Indian resistance? On an even more basic level, is assessing the extent to which the extant sources exaggerate or, alternatively, underreport the number of clashes in the Eastern Sertão possible? Is more to be discovered in these accounts than their authors, all of them colonial intruders, intended?

The aggressive seizure of land from the seminomadic inhabitants of the Eastern Sertão demolishes the claim advanced by colonial officials and settlers that the Portuguese entered the wilderness as heralds of civilization, forced into violence only in self-defense when attacked by incorrigible savages. This posture rings as false in the case of Brazil's eastern forests as it does in the innumerable other instances in which colonists professed a similar moral high ground wherever they sought to establish themselves in the New World. In any haste to dispel this myth and reclaim something of the Indian experience, however, the opposite view, just as distorted and reductive, must not be assumed: that the natives were invariably blameless victims. To reject the assertion that they always initiated violent confrontations only to conclude that they never did so is to move no closer to a balanced understanding of the behavior and motives of either natives or colonists. This view of a reactive, helpless indigenous population misconstrues the chain of events that led to the eventual subjugation of the Indians of eastern Minas Gerais, underestimates the role of frontier violence, and strips the natives of the initiative they took, including their prolonged, extraordinarily effective resistance to conquest.

To be sure, the Coroado, Puri, Botocudo, Kamakā, Pataxó, Panhame, Maxakali, and every other regional ethnic group found themselves in the end outnumbered and outgunned, stricken by disease, and displaced in the face of dwindling land and resources. Even so, throughout their long struggle, they—like the colonists they battled—acted not only in desperate self-defense. This was particularly true in the case of the Puri and Botocudo, who staged numerous aggressive forays into territory recently settled and, in some cases, areas long-considered securely under colonial control. In short, the Indians were both victims and perpetrators of the violence that occurred. Even the closest scrutiny of sources written exclusively by colonists can only begin to explain how the Indians perceived this struggle; however, careful analysis clearly demonstrates that they conducted themselves in nothing like the random and irrational fashion their literate enemies condemned.

Elite Ethnography and Historical Memory

The protracted process of forgetting and recasting the events that led to the 1808 impasse and declaration of war began decades earlier. When in 1780 the cartographer José Joaquim da Rocha wrote an early history of Minas Gerais, he reviewed the actions of recent captaincy governors with respect to the Indians of the Eastern Sertão, pointing first to Governor Silva as a leader who in the 1760s had "taken great interest in the conquest of the heathen, making every effort to reduce them to the bosom of the church." This was true of those Indians who inhabited the forests of Cuieté, about whom Rocha offered few details, as well as those of the Pomba River valley, where the governor "ordered churches built and placed vicars in them to baptize and sustain those pagans on spiritual pasturage." That Governor Silva and, after him, the Count of Valadares had openly sought the extermination of the Botocudo and other seminomads who resisted subjugation went unmentioned in Rocha's account. Governor Noronha's subsequent actions, specifically his opening of the overland route to Cuieté, also had no implications worth noting for the region's Indians. For his part, Governor Rodrigo José de Meneses was to be praised for his bravery in personally venturing through Indian territory to Arrepiados and Cuieté to verify firsthand the progress of colonization and for seeking to "domesticate" the Indians who stood in the way of exploration and settlement.[2]

In Rocha's account, Meneses' encounter with some settled Indians in Cuieté was emblematic. Despite enjoying the protection of the presidio constructed there, these "tame" Indians lived "terrorized" by the wild Botocudo, not unlike the Portuguese colonists established in the area. When the governor arrived at the remote outpost after an arduous journey, the settled Indians rushed to greet him, "addressing him in their language and treating him as their Captain 'Torussu,'" a native term Rocha translated as "great captain, dominator of all others." Governor Meneses received the Indians with his "customary loving care," accepting gifts of game, forest fruits, and wild honey. Joyful and satiated, evidently after much feasting, "they paid tribute to him," staging ritual dances as "demonstrations of their pleasure." Moved by the "simplicity and innocence of those peoples," the governor accepted their gifts and offered his own in return—probably the typical cloth, mirrors, beads, and rosaries. Before leaving, he attended the baptism of an Indian girl who was "versed in the dogmas of religion," offering himself as godfather and bestowing the Christian name Maria de Meneses on the neophyte. In the course of these events, the governor proved his skill in "captivating the wills" of Indians who, "scorning their own hearths and the company of their own brethren, resolutely wish[ed] to follow him" as their new leader. When the time finally came for him to depart, "great effort" was required to convince the Indians not to leave with him. In the end, two of them could not be persuaded to remain behind.[3]

Rocha's account and others like it asserted this kind of conduct constituted the essence of Portuguese policy toward the natives of Minas Gerais: patience, paternal benevolence, concerned civility. From the distance of more than two centuries, seeing the guileless Indian faces as the governor descended from his mount, the ecstatic dancing, the eager children darting forward to touch the gold braid on his uniform or to kiss his hand in the traditional act of Luso-Brazilian deference is almost possible. Feeling the protective presence of the presidio troops who shouldered the burden of defending these miserable souls against the savage, anthropophagous Botocudo is almost reassuring. The governor departed Cuieté in this story as savior, not conqueror. Chroniclers crafted a narrative in which peaceful interactions between Indians and the Portuguese predominated, in which natives offered themselves up cheerfully as wards of the state, and in which those who did not were forcibly conquered only as a last resort, as if no alternative existed.

Even the ultimate call to violent action would be conveyed in the guise of frustrated resignation, the consequence of the refusal of some to accept the compassionate terms of colonial authority. Writing in 1807 as both captaincy historian and prominent public official, Diogo Pereira Ribeiro de Vasconcelos, for example, fixed on force as the sole viable solution only after he pored over many of the same government records employed in this study. His research turned up royal orders "worthy of the pious and enlightened sovereigns that imposed them." A string of governors had done their utmost to achieve peaceful relations with the natives. The Viscount of Barbacena worked tirelessly for the "happiness" of Indians. Governor Silva set an example "worthy of special commemoration" of the same humane zeal. Even Vasconcelos' contemporary, the belligerent Governor Melo, had done what he could to apply "kindness in reducing the savages to the church and state." Despite such efforts, all attempts to "settle the Indians in aldeias and civilize them" amounted to nothing. "There is no hand powerful enough, no eloquence capable of persuading them to abandon their ways and the dense woods in which they are born," Vasconcelos lamented. "The cannibal Botocudo does not allow for the conventions of peace and friendship."[4] The only rational response to such savagery, he reasoned, was violence.

This perspective exerted a pervasive influence on modern histories and ethnographies. Writing in the early twentieth century, the venerable historian Diogo Luís de Almeida Pereira de Vasconcelos emphasized the peaceful efforts of captaincy officials with respect to Indians, virtually to the exclusion of evidence to the contrary. The plentitude of such contradictory evidence in the government codices Vasconcelos examined makes one marvel at the degree to which the eighteenth-century view of seminomadic Indians as subhuman enemies of the state outlived its colonial exponents. Vasconcelos simply restates the colonial position: "What experience had demonstrated is that at no time was it possible to discipline the wrath of cannibals. If they did not find others to devour, they devoured themselves," he asserted. "Thus it would have been more humane to extinguish them than to leave them at large in deference to the theories of Jean Jacques Rousseau, allowing them to extinguish humanity." The violent acts of colonial officials and settlers went all but unmentioned. Vasconcelos maintained that by the time Governor Silva assumed office in 1763, relations with the Indians had stabilized, the years of raiding by bandeirantes having long-since passed. Peaceful interchange predominated as benevolent royal policies crafted to protect Indians were reciprocated with the enthusiastic response of many natives to the "spread of Christian settlement."[5] Given such obfuscation, the predominant absence—up to the present day—of native peoples from the historiography becomes more intelligible.

Even the relatively recent work (1965) of the regional scholar Oiliam José, author of the sole published book-length history of the Indians of Minas Gerais, lapsed on the subject of violent conquest. Praising Diogo Luís de Almeida Pereira de Vasconcelos for his "objectivity" with respect to indigenous history, José more than once blamed the Indians for their own demise. He insisted any analysis of the frontier conflict must begin with the "affection of the natives for their socio-cultural position" because "they accepted only imperfectly the life established for them by civilized men in aldeias." More often than not, the Indians fled from such settlements, "hiding themselves in the thickets of the forest, leveling the fields of white men, and placing themselves in a position of hostility to the processes of civilized work." Only in acts of vengeance did they cast off their "habitual indolence and become dangerous." Characteristically, José treated the declaration of war against the Botocudo in 1808 as an anomaly in which captaincy officials temporarily "abandoned good sense" and opted for force rather than maintaining their traditional emphasis on peaceful conversion. The historian suggested that frontier settlers were markedly less accommodating than the state; nevertheless, the short discussion he devoted to warfare emphasized conflict between one indigenous adversary and another rather than between colonists and Indians. The hostile acts of captaincy governors from the 1760s onward simply did not appear in José's account.[6]

This is not to suggest that evidence of cooperation over the decades, which will be considered in this chapter, is lacking. When historians used this evidence, including the story of Governor Meneses' ceremonious encounter with the settled Indians of Cuieté, they did so to support the contention that by the middle of the eighteenth century, the era of violent relations between settlers and indigenous peoples in Minas Gerais lay safely in the past. Compounding this error was the failure to examine the assertion that the Eastern Sertão remained a no-man's-land, off-limits to colonists and thus the wrong place to look for a violent frontier confrontation. A further historiographical inaccuracy was the astounding contention that the warfare of 1808 represented a solitary lapse in relations otherwise focused on peaceful conversion. Such notions collapse under the weight of the daily orders, reports, petitions, and informal complaints sent back and forth among governors, local military commanders, soldiers, priests, and frontier settlers. Although full of contradictions, these sources make manifest a legacy of brutal colonization as settlers vied to seize territory far removed from the seat of captaincy authority in Vila Rica. Virtually every captaincy administration supported these settlers in some form and, as the previous chapter demonstrated, initiated official incursions into the sertão.

During the early nineteenth century, an additional body of literature shaping what came to be known and remembered about the seminomads of the Eastern Sertão was published in a spate of accounts by European naturalists and other travelers who visited Brazil. Based on peregrinations along the Atlantic coast and inland to Minas Gerais itself, these authors relied, in the best instances, on first-hand contact with some of the region's indigenous groups and, in the worst, on mere hearsay. They have long provided essential source material for historians of Brazil, including the few who concerned themselves with its native peoples.[7] Yet, with rare exceptions, the eastern Indians encountered by these European writers were no longer independent masters of their own lives; rather, they were splintered, subjugated groups living in close proximity to white society in the wake of the prince regent's 1808 military mobilization. Settled and detribalized Indians have generated a fascinating literature of their own, crucial for revising misleading preconceptions that permeate the ethnographic literature about so-called "pure" or "un-contacted" Indians and their allegedly degraded brethren in colonial missions, villages, and towns.[8] The point here is not to dismiss as worthy subjects the Indians who provided nineteenth-century travelers with information but simply to emphasize that their experience should not be mistaken for those who either concurrently or in earlier decades lived autonomously in the eastern forests.

Furthermore, although these travelers' accounts generally evinced more interest in native cultures than documents drafted by colonists, they remained highly biased when not overtly racist, crafted to appeal to an emerging European scientific community as well as a growing popular audience with an appetite for vicarious foreign adventure. In the transatlantic representation of Brazilian Indians as quintessential primitives, these authors succeeded admirably. By the

ILLUSTRATION 6.1. A European depiction of the eastern Indians as savages, ca. 1820
SOURCE: Debret, *Voyage pittoresque.* The John Carter Brown Library at Brown University.

mid-nineteenth century, in no less iconic a work than *Madame Bovary*, for instance, Gustave Flaubert could mention the Botocudo in passing—by name only—assuming readers would understand the reference. At one point in the novel, the pharmacist Monsieur Homais, disturbed by his wife's unconventional methods in raising their children, chastises her with the query, "Do you intend to make Caribs or Botocudos out of them?"[9] While nineteenth-century naturalists may have afforded Brazil's Indians a certain renown, their quasi-scientific texts had clear limits when measured as a source of reliable evidence concerning the conflict with settlers.

The problem becomes apparent on selecting three writers whose works are considered among the most dispassionate and thus the most widely cited as early ethnographic sources on the Botocudo and other seminomads of the region. These three include the German geologist and mining engineer Baron Wilhelm Ludwig von Eschwege (1777–1855), who lived in Brazil between 1809 and 1821; the German naturalist Maximilian, Prince of Wied-Neuwied (1782–1867), who traveled there between 1815 and 1817; and the French botanist Auguste de Saint-Hilaire (1779–1853), who did so between 1817 and 1822.[10] Despite reputations for scientific zeal, none of these authors suppressed fundamental misgivings about the character of his native subjects.

An example from each will suffice, with descriptions in every case of violence attributed to the Botocudo. Unlike most of his ilk, Eschwege traveled a significant distance into Botocudo territory, navigating portions of the Doce River. He spoke of exposing himself to the "great danger of . . . being devoured by the Botocudo." Although he escaped this fate, he did so not without seeing "abominable scenes and robust men reduced to slices of roasted meat." With evident repugnance he claimed that he had once seen Botocudo Indians consume this "horrible food, freshly captured . . . constituted of hands, arms, and legs, barely scorched and not roasted."[11]

Maximilian's close study of groups of Botocudo in contact with soldiers and settlers along the Jequitinhonha River left the German prince highly skeptical about such portrayals of cannibalism. Nevertheless, he took an equally dim view of Botocudo culture. "As they are neither guided by any moral principle, nor subject to any social restraint whatsoever," he wrote, the Botocudo "yield entirely to their five senses and their instincts, just like jaguars in the forest. The irrepressible impulses of their passions, their vengeance and envy in particular, are as appalling . . . as they are apt to erupt, rapidly and unexpectedly." Expert at finding the most favorable moment to exact revenge, the Botocudo "never cease to retaliate for the most minor offense," Maximilian continued, pointing to their senselessness in combat.[12]

Saint-Hilaire, who traveled down the Jequitinhonha and up the Doce Rivers as well as along other stretches of Botocudo territory, described what he viewed as the propensity of these Indians toward violence. "They love war, and their various hordes combat one another continually." Like Eschwege and Maximilian, Saint-Hilaire denounced the colonists' abuses of the Botocudo, but his recipe for resolving the conflict revealed the limits of his own views on interethnic relations. Brazilian authorities, he advocated, should "seek to encourage legitimate unions of Botocudo damsels with free negro and mulato men" to "obtain, thereby, a mixed race, more capable than the Indians of resisting the superiority of the whites, a race that will be more in harmony with our degree of civilization."[13]

Given such undercurrents, that all three early Botocudo ethnographers offer one-sided narratives of the violent conflict between the Indians and their Portuguese antagonists is to be expected. Of the three, Eschwege's visit came closest to the height of the violence following the 1808 declaration of war. He reached Minas Gerais in 1811, charged with a range of official duties by the

Crown including devising a plan for enhancing navigation on the Doce River, authoring a new map of the captaincy, "establishing friendly relations with the anthropophagous Botocudo, and presenting uniform plans to civilize them."[14] Describing them as "indomitable and savage," feared even by other Indians as "ferocious animals," Eschwege observed that the Botocudo lived "at war with all of the tribes that they encounter, yet they [were] never seen in groups of more than thirty to fifty bowmen." Contrasting their tactics with those of Europeans, he wrote, "they avoid the open fight; on the contrary, they prefer an ambush from the underbrush and behind trees, from which they rarely strike a blow that misses." Success in combat depended on the disposition of the adversary: "Attacked valiantly, [the Botocudo] disperse and attempt to flee; however, seeing the enemy turn timid and indecisive in the course of combat, they turn around and are bolder."[15]

As noted, Eschwege's observations, like those of other prominent European visitors to the region, came during the years following the 1808 war. With the military occupation of the Eastern Sertão at its peak, the peculiarities of this historical moment limit the value of employing post-war portraits of Indian conduct to extrapolate back to a time before the war. The biases already noted, along with the authors' inattention to the historical origins of the conflict they witnessed, raise further doubts about the pertinence of their observations. Areas exist in which they provide indispensable material, for instance, pertaining to native material culture, the conduct and ongoing resistance of groups that suffered military defeat, and the attitudes of settlers and soldiers toward those Indians who became dependent on them immediately after the war, often as slaves. However, for an accurate understanding of conflict in the sertão before 1808, other sources must be consulted.

The alternatives are anything but unproblematic. Contemporaneity did not guarantee greater impartiality. Virtually without exception, a bevy of erudite Luso-Brazilian natural historians, public officials, and Crown advisers commissioned during the second half of the eighteenth and early nineteenth century to report on ways to stimulate Minas Gerais' post-boom economy blamed natives for the violence associated with expansion into the Eastern Sertão. Thus in 1780, Rocha wrote that experience had shown that the "wild Botocudo" could not be civilized and that "only with excessive effort will they be extinguished rather than tamed." In the 1790s, José Eloi Ottoni condemned the "stupidity" and "inertia" of the Indians. During the first decade of the nineteenth century, Basilio Teixeira Cardoso de Sá Vedra advocated that "the heathen" be "expelled" from the Eastern Sertão, while Diogo Pereira Ribeiro de Vasconcelos called for the application of "sufficient military force" to counter "the hostilities of cannibals."[16] Often at greater geographic remove from the scene of conflict than the European travelers of the following decades, writing in the interest of a government desperate to reverse declines in the mining economy despite the fact that the region's agricultural transformation had long-since begun to bear fruit, these colonial memorialists proved no more reliable than the foreigners when deciphering the origin, varieties, and extent of frontier violence in late colonial Minas Gerais.

That diverse sources generated in the heat of the frontier violence itself provide the most reliable record of events is more than a little ironic—the very sources composed with the intention of prompting a rapid military response, documents written primarily by or to obscure individuals, often low-level officials who displayed considerably less detachment than others involved in the conflict. Letters and daily orders from governors to military commanders in the field; their return replies and reports; appeals by priests active in the conversion and conquest of Indians; requisitions of war materiel, tools, and other supplies to placate pacified Indians; petitions from frontier residents pleading for military aid or for permission to mount their own retaliatory expeditions—these are the neglected sources that approach most closely the remote scenes of combat. Like other, more accessible sources, those produced in the sertão or in communication with officials and settlers based there contain an ample measure of fury, hyperbole, and prejudice. What distinguishes them from more polished reports is that they focus on particular incidents as they occurred in specific places. They include calls for vengeance but are also constructed, however tenuously, on a foundation of direct experience and immediate events, providing essential details about a profusion of violent engagements involving soldiers, settlers, and natives. The variety of reported incidents alone demonstrates that a full range of contributing factors was at work and that more than one outcome of the encounter in the sertão was possible.

Cooperative Enemies

To begin with, these sources demonstrate that instances of cooperation between Indians and the colonial state were not only possible but numerous. One of the most important examples was the ongoing Portuguese reliance on natives as a kind of wilderness guard. Unquestionably, this relationship was an odd sort of cooperation, one that depended on natives to oppose incursions into their territory to serve the interests of the state. Such conduct could as easily be defined as resistance but an equally odd resistance because it provided authorities with exactly what they sought. Indians, as their appropriate behavior was defined by the Forbidden Lands policy, were expected to protect the empire's gold and diamond treasures by denying renegade smugglers and clandestine prospectors passage through the Eastern Sertão. They were expected to make the same distinctions captaincy governors made between illicit movement through the forests and officially sanctioned settlement and exploration. In the first case, they were to act as unyielding sentinels; in the second, to allow unfettered access to their domain. Not surprising is that natives fulfilled neither expectation consistently, as neither was of their own creation, nor was one objective attainable without violating the other, nor were the captaincy and Crown consistent in the geographic construct this policy entailed. But this did not stop government officials from repeatedly acting on the assumption that Indians would behave as stipulated. The relationship of cooperative enemies evolved as a consequence of the contradictions inherent in viewing the land occupied by Indians as both a protective barrier against illegal activity and as a resource-laden panacea for the captaincy's economic woes. Cooperation depended on an alliance, albeit unspoken and never defined as such, in which government officials and military commanders cast natives as resisting common enemies, namely, contrabandists, vagabond settlers, and even runaway slaves. However, the relationship unraveled whenever and wherever the state's search for forest resources became paramount.

On diverse occasions, governors strove to sustain and reinforce the presumed savagery of native antagonists. In October 1765, just as Governor Silva was commencing his military advance on the sertão, he also took measures to thwart the actions of smugglers moving gold or diamonds through the district of Xopotó. These criminals were "crossing the forests" that lay between Minas Gerais, Espírito Santo, and Rio de Janeiro. Blatantly flouting royal orders prohibiting travel through this region, apparently undeterred by the threat of punishment, these criminals further outraged Silva by ignoring the "risk of falling into the hands of diverse nations of wild and savage Indians." He ordered Captain José Leme da Silva, who only months before had been assigned to aid Captain José Gonçalves Vieira on the year's largest expedition against the Indians around Cuieté, to drop all other duties to concentrate on apprehending these brazen smugglers. Acting to protect the natives who might end up victims of the crackdown, the governor stressed that the restrictions on civilian activity in the zone pertained only to "civilized people." Soldiers were to redouble their efforts, he ordered, apprehending all violators, "no matter what legal status or color they may be"; however, "wild Indians" were to be left unmolested.[17] Such distinctions based on racial difference more frequently provided the justification for the conquest of the sertão. In contrast, here they served to identify Indians as the sole actors, apart from the military, whose presence was not only permissible but desirable in certain unsettled lands. For Governor Silva and others, an important role remained for "wild Indians" as adversaries of those who disobeyed Crown restrictions on mobility.

Despite substantial evidence documenting his enthusiasm for conquest, the Count of Valadares, Silva's successor, went so far as to place limits on military maneuvers to ensure that Indians retained this role. The limits are evident even in documentation devoted primarily to the exigencies of conquest. As he acted to effect that conquest, Valadares strove simultaneously to rein in his top field commanders whenever their marches through the forest threatened to make permeable a wilderness theoretically still impenetrable. In November 1769, Captain Souza and Corporal Guimarães marched their troops out of Cuieté in the direction of the São Mateus River without the authorization of their commanding officer, Captain Campelo, after he had been appointed regent of the Conquest of Cuieté. Campelo reported the action to the governor, calling on him to demand that Souza halt what Campelo characterized as the pursuit of private gain. Souza seemed bent on opening a route to the sea, presumably to profit from smuggling or, should commerce along the route ever be permitted, from legalized trade. Campelo denounced the action as a violation of orders that prohibited navigation to the coast along rivers with headwaters in Minas Gerais.[18] The governor concurred. He issued urgent orders meant to ensure that the sertão remain impassable. In observance of the governor's action, Campelo took immediate steps in the town of Cuieté. He posted notices explicitly forbidding town residents from following Captain Souza in any attempt to navigate to the coast. He reiterated the prohibition on opening overland routes to Espírito Santo and he ordered that all such existing trails be shut down. Violators would be treated as smugglers in accordance with orders both from the governor and the Crown.[19]

To a large extent, these orders depended on Indian cooperation in policing the wilderness. In the forests, Campelo redoubled efforts to shut down "any and every road, trail, footpath, or track by which one could reach the captaincy of Espírito Santo, the littoral, or the sea." His reconnaissance of the region turned up no obvious routes used by smugglers. Instead, he complained that the effort to secure the area was frustrated by the presence of countless "trails on which dispersed or settled heathen customarily move about when hunting or carrying out the correspondence they ... have with various aldeias." So numerous were such trails, Campelo reported, that "it would be impossible to plug them all." His concerns raise the intriguing possibility that the use of an indigenous overland network, and possibly collaboration with supposedly hostile Indians, was necessary for successful smuggling through the sertão. Campelo acknowledged precisely this possibility when he enlisted settled Indians to impede smuggling through the region. He ordered one of his corporals, José Ferreira de Almeida, based at a settlement of "tame" Indians not far from Cuieté, to make sure that no one passed through the surrounding forests along native trails in an attempt to smuggle gold to the sea. Almeida was to pursue suspicious travelers with "the most capable Indians" from the village, arrest all offenders, and deliver them to Cuieté where they would be transferred under guard to Vila Rica.[20] Not only "wild Indians" but "tame" ones were in this way enlisted by the state. The state depended on their cooperation and, in the case of those still roaming the forests, placed limits on their conquest to foster this service.

Even men like Silva and Valadares, who stood among the captaincy leaders most committed to the idea of extracting wealth from the wilderness, drew the line—or at least strove to do so—at a point at which state-sponsored incursions into the Eastern Sertão threatened to compromise the barrier Indians were supposed to maintain against the flow of contraband and unsupervised movement. Governor Silva unleashed military raids against Indians when he judged them rebellious, but he ordered them to be left alone when what he deemed their savage ways advanced the goal of intimidating would-be smugglers. Valadares charged troops with the destruction of Indian antagonists but grew wary of his own officers when they became too mobile themselves, even though full mobility was essential to a successful military campaign against roving natives. If no one, not even a high-ranking field commander like Souza, was to travel the trails on which these natives moved, the conquest—even a limited conquest, if one can speak in such terms—suffered from a serious strategic compromise from the very start. If measures to curtail smuggling depended on the presence of "diverse nations of wild and savage Indians," the very nature of captaincy policy afforded indigenous peoples significant room to wander and remain autonomous.

In apparent consternation at the contradictions of this approach, Governor Noronha denounced the aggressive, expansionist policies of both his predecessors in 1775. That Silva and Valadares' actions had constituted a war against the Indians—an exceedingly ineffective, expensive, and "unjust" war—Noronha had no doubt. "Attacking Indian aldeias," government troops had acted with "inhumanity"; yet they had "not reduced a single Indian to true belief, nor found in the streambeds gold of any account."[21] However, subject to Lisbon's unremitting directives concerning the production of revenue and the reduction of smuggling, Noronha found himself forced to negotiate the same hazards, relying on native antagonists to fortify Crown policy.

Noronha's concerns about the humane treatment of Indians must be viewed skeptically given the other actions of his government. Although he may have possessed a somewhat greater inclination toward tolerance than his predecessors, the primary impulse behind his action was to cut royal expenditures and make certain that the Indian presence remain a barrier to unauthorized colonists. Choosing partial demilitarization as the mechanism to guarantee this end, reasserting the curious position that the absence of colonists in the wilderness—not only settlers but officers and their troops as well—preserved the integrity of the central mining district, Noronha abolished the two companies of salaried soldiers created years before by Valadares. In their place, he left an unpaid militia in Cuieté. The aggressive anti-Indian campaign of his predecessors led to the unacceptable consequence of "soldiers penetrating the forests that divide this captaincy from that of Espírito Santo, forests that serve as a defense and guard against gold and diamond smuggling." Rather than patrol the forest and launch offensive strikes against the Indians, the militia would now simply protect settlers living within town boundaries and on nearby fazendas. Noronha believed the militia would provide sufficient force "to repel Indian assaults and to preserve the tranquility of the settlement of Cuieté."[22]

Meanwhile, the Indian presence in outlying areas remained advantageous: "The aldeias of wild Indians that are situated in the forests that lead to the seashore make smuggling impracticable in that zone, and for that reason alone they should be preserved." Diminished military activity would result in the forest's Indians remaining "peacefully in their aldeias, as long as they do not give cause for waging an offensive war against them." Noronha's predecessors, as the preceding chapter indicated, believed that the Indians had given precisely such cause. And even for Noronha, this more cautious approach had its limits. Indians, he argued, could be "expelled" from the territory they occupied should population growth in the captaincy require incorporation of new lands for agriculture or should new gold discoveries occasion migration and settlement.[23] A relationship that could so readily swing from protection to expulsion spelled the Indians' eventual doom, but this eventual outcome should not cloud the fact that even in an environment dominated by violence, the Portuguese at certain times and in certain sectors of the Forbidden Lands struck a tacit compromise with the Botocudo, Puri, and others, fostering cooperation of an unusual sort, especially during the third quarter of the eighteenth century when Crown restrictions on the territory remained most potent.

Concerns about military maneuvers undermining the wilderness barrier continued to influence the actions of subsequent governors even as the gold cycle definitively waned. Such concerns serve to undercut linear, teleological explanations of the incorporation of this frontier. The few historians who in the past took notice of the captaincy's eastward expansion tended toward this sort of narrative. For example, one noted the "centrifugal movement" of population outward from the central mining district, especially eastward in the direction of the coast. But his account downplayed the barriers that stood in the way of progressive settlement, barriers not only posed by the Indians but also by the vacillation of the Portuguese Crown and the wariness of potential settlers. Another pair of scholars recognized that the frontier could advance and then retreat but offered no plausible explanation for such reversals. They identified significant conflict beginning only in the mid-1780s as the restrictions on wilderness settlement weakened.[24] Both versions missed the interplay of actors and objectives, of open opposition and begrudging accommodation, which undermined any all-out effort to vanquish the Indians and which produced the long-term ebb and flow of official activity in the sertão. Only over the course of many decades did colonization result in Indian defeat and effective occupation of the zone. In the broadest context, the process took several centuries if periodization begins with the stalled attempts of the earliest Portuguese colonists to push into the region from the coast and ends with the final incorporation of independent remnants of the Botocudo in the early twentieth century.

Intermingling on the Battleground

A more conventional form of unequal yet cooperative relations between colonists and Indians, interaction based on conduct other than overt violence, occurred in the southeastern reaches of the captaincy in lands occupied by the Coroado and Coropó. Inheriting from his predecessor a policy of supplying clothing, tools, and other provisions to those natives who peacefully presented themselves to authorities in Vila Rica, Governor Silva determined to extend such methods into the distant forests. This he did by establishing a large central mission village where natives of the Pomba River valley could settle and benefit from state financial support and protection. The governor's aim was to win access to their fertile, well-watered, and perhaps, he hoped, gold-laden territory without resorting to the military mobilization required to the north.

The first significant steps toward peaceful accommodation in this zone occurred in the late 1750s.[25] More than 30 kilometers beyond the village limits of Guarapiranga, a number of Indians emerged from the forests along the banks of the Xopotó River in October 1757. A few of them already spoke rudimentary Portuguese and explained to settlers in the area, including Francisco Pires Farinha, that they sought amicable relations.[26] Destined to become one of the region's local potentates, not least because of the role he played in settling these Indians, Farinha accepted these overtures, which he took as evidence of the natives' "desire to seek refuge in the bosom of our Catholic religion." The forest dwellers took this action in the wake of contacts with the priest Ângelo Pessanha and his brother Miguel, who had entered their territory from the coastal plantation region of Campos dos Goitacases, northeast of Rio de Janeiro. Farinha gleaned that the Pessanhas had requested authorization for the "reduction of the Indians." Yet much of what the Indians said was "confusingly conveyed" and "poorly understood," according to the Minas official who transmitted this news to the acting governor of Rio de Janeiro, José Antônio Freire de Andrade.

Farinha decided to make the best of a puzzling situation. Before the natives returned to the forest, he drafted a letter seeking further information that he sent with them to Padre Pessanha, the member of a prominent planter family from the coast and the maternal uncle of José Joaquim da Cunha de Azeredo Coutinho, who would become Portugal's last grand inquisitor.[27] Continuing to use the Indians as messengers, the priest replied that he had "hopes of domesticating the Indians and in this manner opening the door for the easy propagation of the evangelical law." In telling disregard for the policy designating this territory as a forbidden zone, he predicted that the endeavor would produce "great benefits" for the king and his vassals in the form of access to "so many sertões, mountains, and rivers that in all likelihood have copious gold," as well as other commercial potential. Padre Pessanha explained that his brother Miguel "knew the language of the Indians" and was familiar with their customs. They also intended to make use of the services of a second interpreter, "a slave named José of the Congo nation, very practiced in the language of the Indians." They planned to visit all known native dwelling places in the area, bringing those Indians who were most amenable to Vila Rica to initiate the undertaking. With this information, Farinha traveled the 100 kilometers from his farmstead to the captaincy capital in the company of the natives who transmitted the priest's message, which Farinha relayed to a royal treasury official. Together they drafted another letter to Padre Pessanha, expressing "how much it would please God and the king if he were to put into action the proposed project." In possession of this authorization, the Indians returned to the forests but were delayed for months as they cared for a member of their band who took ill. On finally receiving the reply, the Pessanha brothers set to work, leaving Campos in the direction of Minas Gerais, hoping to gather together those "heathens" in the area who "anxiously sought to follow [them] for the peaceful ends that they desired."

Their journey began in mid-October 1758, a full year after the Indians first made contact with Farinha. Joining the brothers from the beginning were twelve Indians, their African interpreter, and four other black slaves. The slaves carried firearms to protect the party. Paddling upstream in canoes on the Paraíba River, they stopped at the first Indian village they encountered, speaking with its headman, Ignacio, who was more than 80 years old and had been baptized years before but then "rebelled to come live in these sertões." Although the

Pessanha brothers expected an enthusiastic reception, the inhabitants of the village greeted them warily. The Indians' "disgust" stemmed from interactions they had with "less Catholic" Franciscan missionaries who warned them that colonists wanted to "deliver them to the whites in order to cut off their heads." Only the efforts of the slave interpreter eased their mistrust.

The party proceeded through many more native settlements, which they called aldeias, on their climb through the coastal escarpment into the highlands. The next three villages, like the first, lay outside the border of Minas Gerais. With the interpreter's aid, the expedition members were allowed to pass freely. In every case, some village residents joined the party, accompanying the travelers "with much happiness and pleasure." Entering Minas Gerais, they passed through another ten villages. In one, inhabited by about 30 natives, a "very elderly cacique" joined the expedition's ranks, announcing his intention to be baptized in Vila Rica. They reached Farinha's farm in mid-November, the number of Indians having grown to 52, including 14 women. Six days later, they arrived in Vila Rica, "producing in the people an astonishment equal to the novelty."

An official in the capital who witnessed their arrival described the encounter between the townsfolk and the native visitors from the sertão. The Indians did not "merit horror at first sight," but they "could not help but look strange because of the nudity of their bodies," especially the women. Delighted by the Indians' "great affability," authorities housed them at a military barracks and permitted them to demonstrate their prowess as archers, their ritual dances, and "all of the barbarous doctrines of their nature." Some traded beeswax and honey, others baskets, still others their bows and arrows, receiving knives and razors in return.

The cacique received particularly solicitous treatment. By his great age, authorities speculated that he might have been one of the original inhabitants of an Indian settlement located at the site of Vila Rica when bandeirantes first discovered gold there at the end of the seventeenth century. The headman was described as "circumspect, grave, and prudent," although the interpreter could understand little of what he said. The rest of the Indians "venerated his counsel" and indicated that he exerted influence among all of the area's native inhabitants. "As such," noted the official, "one presumes his friendship will be very useful for the rest of the conquest." The Portuguese came to describe him as the Indians' "principal cacique," apparently with a certain optimism, given that he had been the only headman from the various native villages to join the expedition. Gratified by his eagerness to "follow our religion," churchmen "instructed him extensively in the essential mysteries." Vila Rica's leading authorities accompanied him to his public conversion and baptism, Ouvidor Francisco Ângelo Leitão escorting him by hand, and the treasury official, Silvério Teixeira, agreeing to be his godfather. The ceremony proceeded with great pomp and solemnity, accompanied by music as the other Indians looked on. All of them had requested baptism, according to officials, but they were deemed insufficiently prepared for conversion. In honor of the Portuguese monarch, the chief accepted the Christian name José, which officials took as an act "auspicious of many great things to come." The bishop of Mariana apparently conducted the ceremony, as he did the baptism of a second Indian who received the sacraments just before dying, his fatal illness a harbinger of the less lofty consequences of this encounter. Nevertheless, on the day of the burial, nearly a week after the Indians arrived in the capital, they "departed for their villages, trusting in their friendship and full of hope" that the king would grace this exchange with his favor. They left accompanied by Padre Pessanha, who planned to await further instructions at Farinha's farm while his brother Miguel headed south along the Caminho Novo to inform authorities in Rio de Janeiro and seek Crown support for pursuing this experiment in the forest.

Apprised of these developments, Andrade, the acting governor, conveyed the news by letter to Lisbon, concerned enough about the implications of such action to seek the Crown's direct authorization. While awaiting a response, he gave Miguel Pessanha his provisional approval to continue work among the Indians, whom he identified as the Coroado.[28] As other contemporaneous sources clarify, they and the Coropó had come under extreme pressure at this time from Portuguese settlers moving into their territory from both the coastal plantation zones and the inland mining district. The competition for land produced what Pessanha's uncle, the grand inquisitor, would later label a "barbarous and bloody war."[29] Although Minas officials portrayed the Coroado and Coropó as having independently sought the blessings of church, Crown, and captaincy, authorities from the coastal zone described them as having rejected overtures by Minas settlers, whom they considered mortal enemies. Only when Padre Pessanha arrived on the scene did those in Minas Gerais sue for peace. According to this explanation, Pessanha, known for his friendly relations with the coastal Indians and possessed of "an almost inimitable art" for convincing "barbarous Indians" to obey him, accomplished what the settlers could not. By the time events came to the attention of Minas officials, the priest had already made more than one voyage into the mining district, "guided by the savages."[30] Just as with the disputed origins of violent conduct, disagreements over the causes leading Indians to seek accommodation were a perennial feature of Brazil's indigenous history, often rooted in competing bids for influence over "pacified" native groups and control of their territory.[31]

Andrade concluded from the information he received that to "settle into aldeias" those Coroado who lived within the confines of Minas Gerais would be possible. Without any irony regarding the fact that Miguel Pessanha had described them as already living in ten aldeias of their own, each with about two dozen individuals, Andrade added that the plan would require a great effort and significant expense "to oblige them to gather together into a single aldeia," where the work of converting them to Christianity could be effected. While speculating that the less tractable Puri to the north might also be settled through such an effort, Andrade admitted that the prospects in either case were complicated by the fact that "these Indians were very inconstant and change their point of view all the time." In fact, some of them were refugees from Jesuit aldeias along the coast of Espírito Santo where they had once settled peacefully. Andrade also expressed reservations about Miguel Pessanha's proposal to cut a road through the region to advance the work of conversion, to shorten travel time to Vila Rica, and to foster new mineral discoveries in the area. This aspect of the project risked causing great harm, he fretted, by opening a new route for contraband from the mining district to the sea.[32]

The documentary record on efforts to incorporate these Indians into settled society lapses for nearly a decade. Captaincy authorities shifted their attention farther north to the Conquest of Cuieté. For the time being, Crown concerns about smuggling through Coroado territory seem to have prevailed over the prospect of adding Christian souls to the church and undiscovered gold to the royal coffers. In the late 1760s, however, the project surfaced anew with Francisco Pires Farinha, now a militia captain, spearheading another drive to gather the Indians of southeastern Minas Gerais into villages where they could be more readily supervised, converted, and put to work. This time, he received the full backing of Governor Silva, eager to incorporate the eastern wilderness to counter the captaincy's gathering economic problems.

In accordance with the advent of Pombal's Indian Directory, Governor Silva appointed Captain Farinha to serve as commander in charge of all matters of civil governance pertaining to the natives of this zone. The mulatto priest Manuel de Jesus Maria answered the governor's call for a cleric to join the effort. In 1767, under orders to prevent the entrance of all other bandeiras except those granted express permission by the governor to explore for gold, Farinha assisted the priest in staging a wilderness expedition manned by slaves and domesticated Indians. As noted in the first chapter, future governors would have difficulties checking the ambitions of Farinha family members as they sought to control the region's resources. During these early years, however, the mission met with successes that Governor Silva claimed testified to his benevolent intentions, even as he mounted a military offense against the Puri and Botocudo to the north.

Padre Maria managed to establish a number of new native villages, not only that of São Manuel (Rio Pomba) but also one named São José do Paraopeba and another Espírito Santo. The governor used royal funds to pay for provisions requested by the priest. Gifts, including highly prized cotton, woolen, and linen cloth, were allotted to Indians who agreed to be baptized and married in the church. An incentive of extra linen, enough to make two shirts rather than the usual one, went to Indian women who married white men, again in pursuit of aspirations articulated in the Directory.[33] A document addressed to the treasury in 1771, characteristic of the priest's efforts, listed 69 Indians in need of clothing, including 20 men and women who were "still without names," that is, settled in the mission village recently enough that they had not yet been baptized. For more than 40 years, Padre Maria remained active in settling previously dispersed Coroado and Coropó. Acquiring the sobriquet "vicar of the Indians," he appealed to authorities repeatedly over subsequent decades to stanch subsequent waves of settlers encroaching on lands he considered part of the native villages. While he helped open the territory to settlers initially, he provided an alternative to the violent actions directed against the Puri and Botocudo to the north.[34]

At the close of the eighteenth century, Coroado aggression in the districts bordering Rio de Janeiro again became the focus of official concern. Some of the hunters and gatherers who, first, Padre Pessanha and, later, Padre Maria hoped to settle permanently in mission villages now apparently chose to flee Minas Gerais altogether. They fought with settlers pushing inland from the coast.[35] Meanwhile, those who remained in Minas territory found the villages formed for their conversion absorbed into the enveloping colonial society. One of the surest indications was their appearance in censuses that normally excluded them. For instance, an 1825 census of the parish of São João Batista do Presídio counted 553 detribalized Indians living in various familial and economic circumstances. An 18-year-old unmarried youth named João Índio worked as the sole farmhand in the household of a 75-year-old unmarried white woman. The eight-year-old Indian girl Eufrásia lived in the household of a white merchant, his wife, their four children, and their Brazilian-born slave. The four-year-old Indian Francisco, although legally free, was listed among the six slave children in the household of a white farmer who lived with his wife, daughter, granddaughter, another young married white woman, and two adult male slaves. Among the 116 households comprised entirely of Indians was one headed by 40-year-old Manuel Lemes and his 38-year-old wife, Rita. They had two daughters and three

ILLUSTRATION 6.2. Natives and settlers interact in the forest, ca. 1822
SOURCE: Rugendas, *Voyage pittoresque*. Biblioteca Nacional, Rio de Janeiro.

sons living with them, as well as another married couple and four others. Of the numerous Indian heads of household whose occupations were identified, every one was a farmer.[36]

Similar examples of natives entering into colonial society emerged at other locations in the eastern forests, including Cuieté, even though the town lay at the center of some of the fiercest conflicts. Even as Governor Silva unleashed his bandeira offensive in the 1760s, there official provisions allowed for the possibility of peaceful accommodation. Where feasible, soldiers and settlers were to "attract" Indians to "the peace and obedience" they owed the Portuguese Crown, seeking to "accommodate them in their separation from the darkness of heathenism." Only then would they "acquire the light of Christianity necessary to achieve

ILLUSTRATION 6.3. Indians who left the forest often settled in villages supervised by priests, ca. 1822
SOURCE: Rugendas, *Voyage pittoresque.* Biblioteca Nacional, Rio de Janeiro

eternal happiness." To diminish the potential for violence, the inhabitants of Cuieté, when not forced to fight, were to demonstrate amicable intentions. Specifically, they were to reassure uncertain Indians that the Portuguese did not seek "to usurp" native women and children. On joining settled society, natives would be allotted their own land sufficient to raise crops and livestock. No settler was to enslave the natives, no merchant to exploit them. Cooperative Indians would enjoy access to all "honors, jobs, and occupations" to which the Crown's paternal kindness entitled them.[37]

Priests sent to the site were charged not only with attending to the "spiritual needs" of settlers but also to the conversion of Indians who formed settlements on the periphery of the town.[38] The largest and most active of these Indian villages was named Larangeiras, home to Indians tallied by the priest Manoel Vieira Nunes to number 100 women, girls, and boys; 13 infants; and as many as 42 "warriors," although their numbers fluctuated widely, probably as they moved into and out of the settlement in accordance with their hunting rounds. Village occupants belonged to a variety of separate "nations," apparently Maxakali subgroups. Members of these groups were "married one with another," according to the priest. For remaining in the settlement and for their "obedience," they received food and gifts, including knives, machetes, hoes, and rosaries.[39]

Even though they conformed to one of the primary objectives of both Crown and captaincy indigenous policy by adopting sedentary habits, these Indians did not fit neatly into colonial categories. According to Nunes, all displayed peaceful intentions; however, some of the groups exhibited "good correspondence" while others displayed "little correspondence," suggesting that each may have had different objectives in submitting to Portuguese control. With respect to the less malleable natives, the priest betrayed a deep ambivalence: "If they cannot be judged friends," he wrote, "neither can they be called enemies, since they do not engage in hostilities against us." One could not have "total confidence" in any of the settled natives as they were "very inconstant," "indolent," and "distrustful."[40] Authorities must always assume, Nunes cautioned, "that necessity obliges them to seek our friendship." With Portuguese aid, they could "better retaliate against their enemies." The observation represented one of the rare documented instances in which a colonist recognized that native conduct depended on events deep within the forests over which the Portuguese had little knowledge or control, that natives were often inscrutable in their motives, defying official assumptions. The priest identified as adversaries of the settled groups the Botocudo (he used the name Aimoré) and the Capoxó, another Maxakali subgroup. The settled Indians of "good correspondence," Nunes reported, assisted in actions against these unsettled seminomads, whom he labeled "declared enemies" of the Portuguese and village natives alike.[41] The primary form such assistance took was joint participation in military operations. So vital was the cooperation of the settled "warriors" that two companies of captaincy troops made Larangeiras their base of operations, with the corporal José Ferreira de Almeida serving as the civil director of the village. In one of the few detailed descriptions of a joint maneuver, the village Indians comprised the bulk of an expedition mobilized in 1769. Twenty-seven of them accompanied Captain Alexandre da Silva Guimarães and 20 other soldiers in an attack on a Botocudo encampment. This joint force captured 32, killed three, and left others injured. Separate sources clarify that these "already conquered peaceful Indians" were active in numerous other expeditions from the very onset of the military assault on the Eastern Sertão in the 1760s.[42]

Ranging from cooperation to resistance, such a spectrum of conduct among native groups living virtually side-by-side characterized the situation still farther north as well. Describing the region surrounding the town of Minas Novas in 1778, members of Lisbon's Overseas Council observed that some parishes "bordered lands of the barbarous heathen." However, all parishes were "full of tame heathen, although baptized."[43] The final qualifier in this characterization suggests yet another outcome along the spectrum of possible conduct: Indians could abandon their nomadic ways, settle in villages, and accept the ministration of the church but still retain enough of their former ways to be seen by colonists as unredeemed heathens. After a surprise attack on a Botocudo encampment in 1802 in which dozens died, Quartermaster Elesbão Lopes Duro asked that his frontier garrison be supplied with more "tame Indians" of this sort than he already employed because they were particularly skilled in tracking and surrounding the elusive Botocudo. Governor Lorena denied the request, citing the expense of provisions. When Duro decided to relocate his remote post to a more secure point farther down the Doce River at the confluence of the Manhuaçu, he mentioned again that Indians were among his soldiers and boatmen. They provided labor for the move along with slaves and six convicted criminals brought from Cuieté.[44]

The possibility of this kind of exchange between Indians and colonists—unequal and often coerced but intensive exchange nevertheless—was not restricted only to groups more accommodating than the Botocudo. For instance, Governor Lorena sponsored initial moves to open, or perhaps deepen, a rift between bands officials referred to as the northern and southern Botocudo. The first subgroup inhabited the banks of the São Mateus River; the second, the Doce River basin. Lorena's strategy to set them against one another would later prove crucial to the prosecution of the war declared in 1808. Having made contact with the northern group, José Pereira Freire de Moura, an official charged with the administration of Indians in the region, reported that "as far as one can understand from their actions, they are declared enemies" of those who lived farther south. Possessed of a "good disposition," these northern groups had shown Moura wounds they suffered in clashes with the southern Botocudo, as well as arms they had captured that were clearly different from their own and known to be used by Botocudo in the vicinity of Cuieté and the Doce River. Given firearms, Moura assured Lorena that the northern Botocudo would "with pleasure offer themselves to aid the plan" to subdue the southern groups and would "place themselves in the position of guides." Moura predicted their assistance would prove crucial in pacifying the sertão.[45]

The potential for frontier interaction extended to labor arrangements as well. The priest Ângelo Pessanha became an active agent of such arrangements, moving northward after his initial efforts among the Coroado and Coropó to become a leader of the early colonization of the region around Cuieté. A member of a 1765 expedition to secure the "obedience" of the region's Indians, Pessanha turned over to military authorities an unspecified number of natives he characterized as "newly civilized or attracted to peace and friendship." Governor Silva ordered that they be treated humanely; specifically, settlers in the area were to pay the Indians a "fair wage" for their labor. For example, the governor explained that even when Indians required just half a *tostão* (50 reis) to cover the cost of food, employers were not to pay them less than twice that amount so that the Indians could use the surplus to purchase clothing and tools required for successful sedentary life.[46] In another case, letters written in 1772 by the governor to the vicar of Cuieté and the region's top military commander mentioned fields that had been prepared by soldiers and other local residents to provide food for the Indians settled there. These documents indicated that the natives earned the food by joining area road-construction projects.[47] Such arrangements would become still more common following the 1808 war, when authorities set up numerous native settlements in the Eastern Sertão for Botocudo brought to submission in that military campaign.[48]

Numerous references in sources such as these demonstrate that forms of interaction between indigenous populations and the Portuguese not directly predicated on violence were both possible and pervasive throughout the period under study. The types of cooperation discussed here may not have matched the intensive trade-based intermingling and exchange between indigenous peoples and colonists documented in other American frontier zones.[49] However, the fact that instances of collaboration existed at all in this eastern wilderness reveals that alternatives other than unchecked interethnic violence were available to colonists and the state, were employed by them, and were greeted with pragmatic if not always enthusiastic acceptance by some Indians. Furthermore, the persistence of cooperative relations, however limited, posed a challenge to official attempts to portray native and colonial societies as fundamentally and fatally adversarial.

Therefore, the role of violence in the colonization of the Eastern Sertão must be approached with great care. Despite often being the ultimate and predominant outcome of territorial incorporation, violence need not be considered inevitable. The degeneration of relations between the state, settlers, and particular groups of Indians into open warfare resulted from a specific social and historical conjuncture in a distinct region of the interior. Of course, the same occurred in many other places in Brazil and at many other times. Even so, when and where it did occur, the sources of violence were more complex than suggested by explanations assuming the innate, irrational militancy of the Indians or, for that matter, of the Portuguese.

The Origin and Extent of Interethnic Violence

What of the archival evidence pertaining to the origin of interactions that turned violent? The nature of this evidence requires a methodologically transparent response. Between 1760 and the declaration of war against the Botocudo in May 1808, 86 violent engagements involving Indians in the Eastern Sertão were reported in the records of the captaincy government (see Table 6.1). Over the course of this span of nearly half a century, only one five-year period (1785–1789) passed without a report of violence, yet the frequency of reports during the rest of the era proved highly erratic. Almost half of the 86 incidents occurred between 1765 and 1769, the period during which military operations against the Indians in the sertão reached their peak under Governor Silva and the Count of Valadares.

The sources documenting these many clashes do so in terms that make even this kind of rudimentary quantitative analysis a challenge. In some cases, only the vaguest mention of violence surfaces. For instance, Captain Campelo, then the region's top military commander, described an attempt by settlers to re-cultivate

TABLE 6.1

Violent Engagements with Indians in Eastern Sertão, 1760–1808

Years	Number
1760–64	3
1765–69	42
1770–74	1
1775–79	12
1780–84	5
1785–89	0
1790–94	7
1795–99	1
1800–04	11
1805–08[a]	4
Total	86

[a] This number does not include incidents after the Crown's declaration of war against the Botocudo on May 13, 1808. These figures count as two all engagements described in sources as multiple but whose total number is not specified. When multiple locations are mentioned, each counts as a single engagement.

SOURCES: APM, CC, cód. 1156; APM, SC, códs. 118, 224, 260, and 277; BNRJ, SM, II-36, 5, 32 and cód. 2, 2, 24, cód. 19, 3, 39, and cód. 3, 1, 35; APM, SG, cx. 11, doc. 55; BNRJ, SM, CV, cód. 18, 2, 6; RAPM 1:4 (1896): 781; Diogo Pereira Ribeiro de Vasconcelos, *Breve descrição*, 147–48; Diogo [Luís de Almeida Pereira] de Vasconcelos, *História média*, 203; Cambraia and Mendes, "Colonização," 142.

fields that former residents had abandoned fearing Indian attacks at the settlement of Cuieté.[50] The implication is that such fear derived from experience, and many sources report other attacks at the settlement halfway down the Doce River watershed. However, the document cited remains opaque. A formal letter to the governor in which the commander describes his frustrations at the slow pace of settling the sertão, it can be dated to the period soon after Valadares took office in 1768. The flight of settlers it mentions occurred at some unspecified point in the past, perhaps even before Campelo was named to his command by Governor Silva in 1765. The letter does not indicate what sort of violence occurred, for example, whether the supposed attacks were directed against soldiers or settlers, against persons or property, or whether they took place in the surrounding forest or within the confines of the town of Cuieté itself. Nor did Campelo state how many Indian raids occurred before settlers chose to flee. In such cases—and there are many—in which the ambiguity of the source rules out precise identification, the incident or implied incident has been excluded from the count of violent engagements. This is true also of cases like the one reported in 1769 by Cuieté's vicar, Manoel Vieira Nunes. Railing against the "unfaithful rebelliousness" of Capoxó Indians in the vicinity of the town, the priest accused them of having "assassinated some of our people."[51] Yet the vicar gave no date for the incident nor did he specify whether a single event or multiple attacks produced these deaths. Again the source defies quantification and has been excluded from the count.

Many reports cite multiple attacks but do not tally exactly how many occurred. In such instances, the most conservative approach has been adopted, assuming one violent incident per location cited and two if described in the plural, that is, as "attacks" in a single place. Thus a series of military expeditions deployed by Governor Silva in the 1760s responded not simply to a single Indian attack or a series of single attacks in several places but against attacks that he said were occurring "year after year" at sites throughout the Eastern Sertão.[52] The frequency of such reports of numerous but unspecified incidents provides the first piece of evidence suggesting that substantially more interethnic violence occurred in the Eastern Sertão than registered in the 86 cases that can be dated and linked to a particular location.

Further evidence concerning the origin and extent of the violence comes to light when the data on reported attacks are compared with those on expeditions to the Eastern Sertão (see Figure 6.1). The comparison reveals the exceedingly close correspondence between reported Indian attacks and the deployment of bandeiras. The spate of violent episodes documented between 1765 and 1769 comprised two separate onslaughts, the first coinciding with bandeiras dispatched during the final two years of Governor Silva's rule, the second with

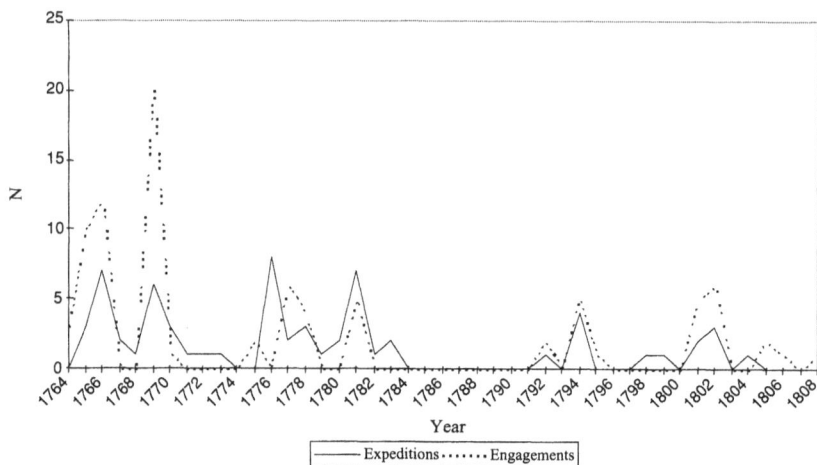

FIG. 6.1. Expeditions and Violence Compared, 1764–1808
SOURCE: See Tables 5.1 and 6.1.

similar activity during the second year of Valadares' term. Recall that both governors were particularly avid in their attempt to rejuvenate the captaincy economy
by way of new conquests. Together, the peak in violence during this five-year
period and the absence of aggressive acts during the nine-year stretch between
1782 and 1791 corresponded with the periods of greatest and least bandeira
activity, respectively. The same correspondence held true, on a relative scale,
for virtually every other period of intensification or diminution of bandeira
activity.

A variety of explanations are possible for the direct relationship between
violent incidents and bandeiras. First, the most skeptical hypothesis: In most
or at least many cases, violent incidents did not really occur at all but were
concocted by authorities as a pretext for dispatching troops to explore and
occupy the sertão. Without question, given the disparity between captaincy and
Crown objectives, governors needed some sort of justification for venturing into
territory set off-limits by Lisbon. The call to retaliate against Indian atrocities
provided precisely the required excuse. The need to counter native aggression
legitimized the allocation of substantial resources to form expeditions, which
could then search for new deposits of mineral wealth and seize new lands if the
search succeeded. Even so, the explanation that officials fabricated the violence
falls short. They may have exaggerated, and they unquestionably infused their
reports with a colonial bias, but they did not simply make up the relatively
specific accounts that have been included in this tally. Too many cases survive in

the archives, providing too many details over too long a period, to support such a conclusion. Despite the maddening vagueness of some reports, many contain ample specificity, providing more precise information than would reasonably be expected from falsified claims. Furthermore, because the burden of financing bandeiras often fell on the local residents living in the zones where the attacks were said to have taken place, that governors could have enlisted the necessary local participation without basing their appeals to these colonists on solid facts seems highly unlikely.

Several alternate possibilities explaining the correlation of bandeiras and violence are less easily assessed. The first assumes that violent incidents in almost every case provoked the government or local settlers to form retaliatory bandeiras. Expeditions marched immediately into the field, in other words, virtually whenever and wherever clashes occurred. The converse possibility is that when bandeiras roved the wilderness, they invariably provoked native resistance. Anecdotal evidence can be assembled to support both hypotheses. After the Botocudo and Puri conducted raids at the settlements of Ponte Nova and Guarapiranga, the Viscount of Barbacena authorized Joaquim Correia Mosso to lead a 1792 bandeira to "chase off" the perpetrators.[53] This was clearly an act of retaliation after the fact. By contrast, when soldiers set out to explore the Arrepiados forests in 1781, they were attacked by unidentified "heathens," probably the Puri.[54] This would seem to be an obvious case of the opposite circumstance, in which Indians struck at expeditionaries rather than the reverse. Thus, a third possibility suggests itself, a middle position that assumes both types of events occurred: violence elicited expeditions, and expeditions stirred up violence. All three possibilities share the supposition that in almost every case and every place, in accordance with the matching data, a direct relationship existed between frontier violence and the presence of bandeiras.

On closer examination, the data suggest still another interpretation (see Table 6.2, Table 6.3, and Table 6.4). In an overwhelming majority of cases (92%), Indians were reported to be the aggressors in these violent confrontations. In

TABLE 6.2

Identity of Aggressor

Aggressor	Number	Pct
Indians	79	92%
Soldiers	7	8%
Settlers	0	0%
Total	86	100%

SOURCE: See Table 6.1.

TABLE 6.3

Identity of Victims of Indian Attack

Victim	Number	Pct
Settlers	57	72%
Soldiers	16	20%
Settled Indians	4	5%
Unknown	2	3%
Total	79	100%

SOURCE: See Table 6.1.

only a handful of cases (8%) were soldiers said to have initiated hostilities. Of the entire 86 instances of violent conflict, not a single incident was attributed to the actions of settlers. This final point will be addressed shortly.

As for the victims of Indian attacks, settlers were named in almost three of every four cases (72%), soldiers in one of five (20%), and settled Indians living in their own villages in just a few (5%). Adding the 16 attacks against soldiers to the 7 attacks they initiated, the total number of clashes between Indians and soldiers amounts to 23, or slightly more than one-fourth of the total 86. The violence in the Forbidden Lands clearly stemmed from a conflict waged primarily between Indians and settlers, not Indians and soldiers. This was true even at an early stage when captaincy officials still took Crown restrictions on colonization very seriously and even though the sources highlight a connection between native violence and military deployment.

The point can be extended. Of the 16 attacks on soldiers, half occurred while they were based at presidios, the often less-than-impressive fortifications governors established as frontier garrisons. Two more attacks were directed against small groups of soldiers hunting or exploring in the vicinity of these presidios. Only on six occasions did Indians choose military expeditions in the field as the target of attack. The seven attacks against Indians initiated by such expeditions increase the number of violent engagements between Indians and military

TABLE 6.4

Objective of Indian Attacks on Soldiers

Target	Number	Pct
Presidio	8	50.0%
Expedition	6	37.5%
Individuals	2	12.5%
Total	16	100.0%

SOURCE: See Table 6.1.

expeditions to only 13 incidents, just 15% of the total. In effect, soldiers on expedition, touted throughout the period under study as the vanguard of the drive to subdue the natives of the Eastern Sertão, in fact saw negligible action in terms of documented military engagements. While the captaincy government threw its authority behind such expeditions and allocated considerable resources in deploying them, the primary violent conflict took place elsewhere between Indians and settlers at the far-flung farms and ranches of frontier outposts and along the expanding edge of hinterland townships and parishes. In both cases, it took place out of the immediate reach of the state's roving wilderness expeditions.

The direct correlation between the data on violence and bandeiras conceals this intermediary and most bloody stage of the conflict. Bandeiras did stir up Indian resistance but they generally did so in an indirect way. They were deployed when ongoing hostilities between Indians and settlers, in the opinion of the ruling governor and his commanders, merited resorting to the use of military force. In short, the link between violence and bandeira activity can be attributed to the nature of the sources themselves. These sources necessarily documented the attacks that prompted the government to act and warranted the accompanying expense and recruitment efforts. Such documents also provided a written rationale for the decision to flout, in an official and conspicuous fashion, the royal prohibition on the settlement and exploration of the Forbidden Lands as pressures within the captaincy transformed the Crown's frontier barrier into something more porous.

That many violent episodes went unreported also seems likely. When government officials were too preoccupied by other matters, when they were too saddled by debt, or when an incident because of its isolated nature went otherwise unattended, no documents were generated by the bureaucratic machinery set in motion by the mounting of a retaliatory bandeira. In particular, just as the number of bandeiras dropped off in the tumultuous years leading up to the 1789 nativist rebellion in Minas Gerais, so too did the number of reported violent engagements with Indians decline to zero as the captaincy government's attention became fixed elsewhere—namely, on its own political survival rather than on events in the distant sertão. The converse was also true. Thus, the five-year period in which almost half of the violent incidents occurred can be divided, as noted, into two different periods of activity corresponding to the offensive mobilizations of the administrations of Silva and Valadares. The remaining five years in which five or more attacks were reported—1777, 1781, 1794, 1801, and 1802—corresponded to similar aggressive actions by the captaincy government: the first with Governor Noronha's attempt to build a road to Cuieté, the second with Governor Meneses' drive to settled the Arrepiados region, the third with the Viscount of Barbacena's support of bandeiras in the vicinity of both

Guarapiranga and Santana dos Ferros, and the fourth and fifth with Governor Lorena's attempt to open the Doce River to navigation as the prohibition on activity in the Eastern Sertão increasingly gave way to schemes to promote commerce between the interior and the coast. In this way, reports of Indian violence corresponded almost exactly with the relative intensity of state-directed efforts to secure new areas of the frontier where, in most cases, settlers had already ventured.

Eliminating military expeditions as the primary source of this violence makes sense as well from the perspective of the Indian side of the conflict. After long experience dealing with colonists encroaching on their territory, Indians would have recognized the folly of engaging a well-armed military expedition in the field, except perhaps through the use of hit-and-run tactics. Far more frequently, they chose targets cautiously from among the isolated homesteads, farms and ranches, and even villages and towns along the shifting frontier between Portuguese and native territory. The use of bandeiras was an essential tactic of the state, lurching yet relentless, as it moved to incorporate the Eastern Sertão into the colonial domain; however, for the Botocudo, Puri, and other indigenous groups, soldiers on the march posed a comparatively modest threat. Settlers were more numerous by orders of magnitude; they were a more permanent fixture of the transformation occurring in the wilderness; they were proportionately more disruptive to nomadic ways; and yet they were far more vulnerable to attack than the well-armed soldiers who passed through native territory on intermittent expeditions and then disappeared. As Minas settlers in their various guises—rich, poor, black, white, free, and enslaved—repeatedly and increasingly crossed the boundaries established by the Crown between settled zones and Indian territory, they became the victims as well as perpetrators of interethnic violence.

Only an elite minority of these settlers possessed the resources to gain the attention of public authorities when Indians attacked. These cases, and these alone, were the ones that surfaced in the documentation pertaining to military expeditions sent out in response. Many incidents—perhaps most—went unreported. On some occasions, this problem was explicit in the sources. For instance, this was true of the 1794 case involving landholders in the parishes of Guarapiranga and Rio Pomba. When they finally enlisted Captain José Bernardino Alves Gundim to appeal on their behalf to the governor, they did so after enduring what the captain described as four or five years of repeated "invasions" by the Botocudo and Puri.[55] None of these preliminary attacks appear in the surviving sources nor, because of the lack of details, have they been counted among the 86 incidents for which specific dates and locations exist. Only when Captain Gundim finally submitted a formal petition directly to the governor, and only because the governor considered the complaint worthy of his attention, did evidence of what was apparently a sustained and bloody conflict between Indians and settlers in the two parishes become part of the archival record. Many other cases must have gone unrecorded, whether because they involved impoverished, illiterate settlers with no recourse to official channels, or because many single, isolated attacks failed to catalyze the kind of "great fury" that finally convinced Gundim to seek the governor's aid, or because the governor himself was unable to attend to every appeal by settlers and officials in the numerous distant outposts of lusophone settlement.

Finally, of all the distinctive characteristics of the documents describing interethnic violence in the sertão, the one that most clearly highlights how the very production of sources both molded and reflected the way officials understood the conflict is the utter absence of reported attacks initiated by settlers against Indians. The imbalance is simply impossible to credit. Like other peculiarities in the data, this silence does not point merely to the limitations of the sources— it also suggests paths to greater insight. After surmising that many individual attacks between settlers and Indians never appeared in government records, determining why those hostilities initiated specifically by colonists remained undocumented or were blamed on Indians is possible.

Consider the case of the private bandeira organized in 1766 by Antônio Cardoso de Souza, a future commander of Governor Silva's wilderness military assault, by then already in progress. From the document authorizing this expedition to the north of the Doce River basin, clearly Governor Silva maintained different standards for a private action like Souza's and the state-sponsored operations farther south, where the governor abandoned all pretense of a benevolent approach to the Indians. In granting his permission to stage a bandeira, the governor warned Souza to employ the "soft approach" or face the possibility that members of his bandeira would be punished. Violence was to be used only in self-defense to repel Indians who proved to be uncooperative.[56] Given that Souza and his soldiers were at the same time authorized to invade native territory deep in the forests, little effort would seem to have been required either to conceal the use of such violence or to provoke Indians to actions that justified retaliation.

A second case involving the same Farinha family active in the southeastern colonization effort provides further details of the dynamic that tended to silence settler aggression in the sources. Captain Francisco Pires Farinha, both a settler and an expedition leader, assisted Padre Pessanha in the 1750s. A decade later, he took charge of overseeing Indian relations throughout the Pomba River basin and protecting settlers on their initial forays into land controlled by the Coroado and Coropó Indians. Captain Farinha and members of his family then found themselves in a position to benefit from staging further incursions elsewhere in the zone. At least two of the Pires Farinha clan received royal land grants

in the region.[57] In 1778, Governor Noronha chastised the captain for permitting Manoel Pires Farinha to lead a bandeira into still-prohibited areas of the
southeastern wilderness, an action that threatened to open a contraband route
to Rio de Janeiro. The reprimand had no lasting effect. In 1781, this time without informing Governor Rodrigo José de Meneses, Manoel Farinha led another
unauthorized expedition into the region, attacking a group of Puri and killing
ten.[58] When the news reached Governor Meneses, he drafted a forceful rebuke
to Captain Francisco Farinha. Describing himself as "very displeased," the governor condemned the "impetuosity" with which Manoel Farinha's expedition
"threw itself on the Puri," even though the Indians had given no "immediate
motive for being treated as enemies." The governor had devoted all of his effort
"to show those miserable souls the amenity of our customs," he said, and it
was "against my intention that my subalterns give them occasion to judge us
disposed to take their lives and liberty from them." Although Meneses stopped
short of prohibiting the Farinhas from leading a subsequent expedition into the
same region, he warned against waging similar attacks "in any case other than
natural defense."[59] From Meneses' other actions, such as his aggressive efforts
to clear the regions around Arrepiados and Cuieté of Indians, clearly he was
willing to sanction violence when he considered Indians to be the aggressors.
Under such conditions, that settlers and soldiers not only learned to couch their
own aggression in terms of self-defense but often concealed it entirely seems
again a fair conclusion.

The denial of colonial responsibility for clashes with indigenous peoples
became a trope of conquest in frontier settings throughout the Americas. In
this sense, the surviving commentary on the events in the Forbidden Lands
comes as no surprise, whether penned by settlers, regional commanders, governors, or colonial literati. But the sources—especially the mundane sources—
demonstrate more than this, sometimes despite the intentions of their authors.
Paradoxically, they demonstrate primarily how much remained hidden. Subjected to careful analysis, their lacunae and biases made evident, they reveal that
interethnic strife in the Eastern Sertão proliferated to an extent even greater than
the many documented cases of violent incidents would suggest—although how
much greater must remain a mystery. The sources suggest consistent conceal-
ment of the provocative actions of settlers, encouraged by policies that permitted
retaliation in cases of self-defense. The accusations they conveyed to authorities
in Vila Rica regularly ignored a parallel history of cooperation with Indians, as
though no outcome other than open warfare was possible. At the same time,
they point to how much information likely never left the forests at all to be
preserved in the archives. Finally, they demonstrate how the particularities of

individual encounters were eclipsed by a discourse cast in the most totalizing terms.

Myths, wrote Roland Barthes, arise when events lose their historical specificity.[60] Distinct human acts and intentions, resulting from specific historical events, become subsumed by language that appears to state transcendent principles—in this case, the alleged innate incompatibility of Indians with and their hostility toward European society. To the extent that a measure of concrete detail survived in reports from the frontier, this common narrative tendency becomes evident, tying together the accounts by nineteenth-century European travelers and those by eighteenth-century regional historians and ideologues. Both sets of observers largely ignored the quotidian particulars of the violent conflict between settlers and Indians. Such fine points were overshadowed by the grandiose, dualistic rhetoric of social restraint versus savage depravity, of the Christian versus the heathen, of order versus chaos. Eschwege's shock at what he called "abominable scenes," Maximilian's condemnation of the natives' missing "moral principle," Saint-Hilaire's comments on their racial inferiority and their love of war—together such images created the impression of a conflict without immediate cause. From an even earlier historical vantage point, the memorialists Rocha, Ottoni, Sá Vedra, and Vasconcelos, employing similar terms, described a conflict similarly without solution except by way of the natives' forced eradication, removal, or submission. For both groups of writers, the violence endemic in the eastern forests assumed the form of an ageless contest between civilization and barbarism. For the Portuguese officials and experts whose duty it was to conjure up scenarios of future prosperity for the struggling captaincy, that contest pit an organized, government-led military advance on unincorporated territory against the random acts of irrational cannibals.

Ironically, the effect was to gloss over the extent of actual conflict on the ground. Favoring the universal to the particular, the period's most influential authors evinced little interest in individual instances of frontier confrontation. Placing the burden of conquest on the state, they relegated settlers to an incidental role in the battle for land and resources—more often than not to the role of victim. Contemporaneous texts written by those directly engaged in the conflict relied on similar images of the state, settlers, and Indians. Nonetheless, the reported incidents, while blamed virtually without exception on Indian savagery, contained evidence of settler initiative and culpability, although to exactly what degree is, in the end, again difficult to assess. Despite Crown restrictions, settlers of all classes were pushing slowly but relentlessly into Indian territory. Some sought gold, others simply subsistence on their own terms. The prominent presence of the state in the form of military expeditions and troops garrisoned at frontier presidios should not disguise the basic fact that violent clashes occurred not only between Indians and soldiers but also and especially between Indians and settlers.

A final finding requires a less painstaking reading of the sources. It is that native opposition to Portuguese territorial expansion persisted in a sustained, meaningful, and exceedingly disruptive fashion throughout the second half of the eighteenth century and beyond. If Portuguese behavior did not conform to the peaceful, civilized intentions colonists claimed for themselves, neither was the native response characterized by the passive acceptance of defeat.

CHAPTER 7

Cannibalism and Other "Abominable Scenes"

Frontier Violence as Cultural Exchange

A CCORDING TO STANDARD histories of colonial Brazil, by the second half of the eighteenth century, Indians had long ceased to pose any real threat to Portuguese territorial control. It is true that Indians could not have expelled the Portuguese from their vast American colony. Divided both by geography and ethnicity, they could not have done so in the sixteenth or seventeenth centuries either. However, on what were arguably the more important levels of local and regional governance, effective Indian pacification and Portuguese security still often appeared to be distant goals in the late colonial period. More than in any other major region, native raids on settlers, slaves, soldiers, and property in the eastern reaches of Minas Gerais seemed difficult—if not impossible—to check and capable of disrupting both Crown and captaincy projects.[1] To some Minas governors, field commanders, and high-ranking civilian officials, that hostile Indians might even overrun outlying settlements and attenuated military defenses on the eastern perimeter of the inland mining district seemed possible. These seminomadic hunters and foragers might then extend their depredations westward from their traditional dwelling places in the remote forests, attacking critical areas that had been settled during the mining boom of the first half of the eighteenth century. Indeed, the profusion of violent engagements enumerated in the previous chapter, in what must be considered a partial count, leaves no doubt that between the 1750s and 1808, Indians launched numerous raids testing the strength of both nascent and languishing mining camps and their surrounding agricultural lands. However plodding and uneven the occupation of Brazil's interior may have been during the colonial period, the advance of lusophone society into new lands defined the Portuguese presence in the Americas. The Forbidden Lands policy had constrained this process in the interest of social and economic control, attempting to structure the colony's geography along rigidly conceived racial lines. During the second half of the eighteenth century, seeking unsettled lands and new sources of wealth, Minas settlers and officials challenged these constraints, reinvigorated deeply ingrained expansionist patterns, and reshaped the Crown's vision of a coastal *cordon sanitaire.* As Indians fought back from territory still unconquered after more than two centuries of Portuguese presence, many Minas inhabitants became convinced and correspondingly alarmed that the indigenous occupants of Brazil's Atlantic forests placed their new advance at risk as they progressed haltingly back toward the coast from the settled interior into lands bypassed by the earlier wave of colonization.

Allowing for the inflammatory nature of lusophone sources documenting this cultural collision, clearly the threat of Indian attack became exceedingly problematic to those who dispersed from the old mining towns and entered the largely unexplored eastern forests in search of both undiscovered gold and basic subsistence. An Indian raid resulting in the burning of a farmhouse or a field, the theft of farm or mining implements, or the death of a family member or slave could have devastating consequences for colonists who, like rural dwellers on the periphery of settled zones throughout Brazil, led precarious lives. For military men ordered to protect such vulnerable individuals, or to retaliate for offenses already incurred, the peril that Indians posed proved no less menacing. Charged by captaincy governors with securing portions of the forests against native antagonists despite the royal policy of keeping hostile Indians in place, troops participated in comparatively few open battles but these few betrayed desperate tactics. More commonly, soldiers faced the constant, gnawing, unpredictable threat of an ambush or a single deadly arrow fired from the cover of the trees. For soldiers no less than for settlers, potent indigenous opposition discouraged any reckless movement into the Atlantic forests.

Dispassionate analysis of this violent episode in Brazilian history was stifled almost as soon as the period of greatest conflict concluded. By the middle of the nineteenth century, when Brazilian historians began to codify the colonial experience into a narrative that explained the emergence of a newly independent nation, native resistance to the colonization of the Eastern Sertão and other interior regions seemed futile and often scarcely worthy of notice.[2] Yet for much of the previous century, a violent insurgency wreaked havoc in this zone. A measure of its impact was the reversal of royal restrictions leading to the 1808 declaration of war on the region's aboriginal occupants. On the eve of that declaration, a key Crown minister explained that a coordinated military response was the monarch's final answer to the "deplorable harm that the heathen Botocudo," the zone's primary indigenous antagonists, "have caused the inhabitants of this captaincy." Experience had proven that the deployment of armed forces was the only way to "oppose the cruelty of those anthropophagous barbarians."[3] Like the Crown and its ministers, colonists who endured this opposition cast it as perverse and undifferentiated savagery, an inflammatory view no more adequate than the dismissive strains of the nationalistic historians who would soon follow. One must look beyond such characterizations to better understand the conflict and to assess the effectiveness and deficiencies of the adversaries involved.

At the same time, that violence did ultimately predominate as colonists encountered Indians in this zone is certain. The archival evidence testifies to the centrality of warlike conduct on both sides in defining the period leading up to the Crown's declaration of official war. As in other frontier zones, settlers and soldiers were never above employing tactics identical to those they deemed savage when used by their indigenous antagonists.[4] The bloody struggle that pit these peoples against each other took a variety of forms and disrupted internal territorial expansion in different ways. By carefully examining the violent comportment on both sides, this chapter illuminates how each employed these forms to achieve and communicate incompatible objectives.

More broadly, armed conflict did not represent the cessation of cultural interaction on this colonial frontier; rather, it frequently was an essential means by which that interaction occurred. This is not meant to suggest that violent resistance became the sole mechanism governing native actions. As previously demonstrated, instances of adaptation and cooperation, surrender, and peaceful incorporation occurred as well. Flight and nonviolent opposition offered still other options. Moreover, violent attacks on colonists drew on a logic internal to an indigenous society, one which can often be discerned only dimly. Native cosmology and prophesy, the ravages of epidemic disease, the claims of competing headmen and kin-ordered groups, revenge, the search for food, the demands of indigenous distribution networks for metal and other manufactured objects, and a centuries-long historical experience of violent clashes with Portuguese settlers also accounted for bellicose actions directed at late colonial intruders.[5] Without diminishing the importance of such dynamics, understanding them as indispensable components of the full spectrum of frontier behaviors and outcomes, this chapter reaches beyond a common but misleading approach to discord of this kind, which portrays armed conflict as the point at which intercultural commerce collapses.[6] To that end, the chapter situates warfare and violence within the realm of cross-cultural practice and analysis rather than viewing them as antithetical.

Frontier cultural exchange and military confrontation could be fundamentally intertwined. Violence could signal an intensification of interethnic relations rather than their dissolution. In this expanse of Portuguese America's immense unincorporated territory, mutual bloodshed and brutality came to constitute a shared language and praxis, at once symbolic and agonizingly concrete. For many decades, neither side in the conflict possessed sufficient force to prevail over the other. Even so, this relative balance of power did not foster the formation of a negotiated "middle ground," the metaphor historian Richard White introduced in his study of cultural relations between French and Algonquian peoples in North America's Great Lakes region, which historians hastily have adopted to explain frontiers throughout the Americas. Far from necessitating peaceful accommodation, the absence of decisive force in the case of the Forbidden Lands prolonged and elevated the violence until it defined the relationship and the era.[7] Conversely, neither did persistent conflict stem the process of transculturation through which the Indians selected, appropriated, transformed, and exploited materials and colonizing practices transmitted to them by the Portuguese.[8] If anything, this process accelerated amid the deadly disorder. The fact that it often did so for the specific purpose of orchestrating successful armed opposition does not mitigate the importance of such an exchange. Both colonists and natives crafted strategies calculated to strike fear and panic in their respective enemies in accordance with assumptions about one another's culture, society, and economy. Such strategies had long characterized the struggle between settlers and Indians in Brazil, but they assumed a new urgency and intensity in the face of the late colonial transformations that left residents of the mining district scrambling for secure economic footing in the eastern forests. As settlers pleading for royal assistance in the region described the situation even as early as 1750, the conflict produced an atmosphere in which "disturbances, deaths, and spoliation" left them constantly "intimidated and afraid."[9] Over the subsequent decades, opportunities for peaceful coexistence diminished while those for learning and practicing violence increased as the once-isolated Eastern Sertão and its inhabitants became engulfed by what can perhaps best be described as a culture of terror.

Violence against Property and Possessions

Finding themselves at a demographic and technological disadvantage, the Indians of the Eastern Sertão proved to be particularly adept at developing compensating collective military tactics. These tactics responded not only to eighteenth-century incursions from the mining district to the west but also to a far longer experience of battling sixteenth- and seventeenth-century settlers and, before them, pre-colonial Tupi peoples to the east along the coast.[10] Settlers could be forced to retreat and soldiers to abandon important military objectives when the right tactics were employed. As a result, securing this sector of Brazil's internal frontier proved to be far more difficult than colonial officials expected and more complicated than historians would later allow. Militarily these forest dwellers were throughout the eighteenth century no more the inevitable victims of the frontier's advance than they were the irredeemable savages of the colonists' imaginations. They did not always react violently to encroachment on their territory but they did so frequently enough, and with sufficient success, that this conduct must be taken seriously and, to the extent possible, understood on its own terms.

Importantly, recall that more than a dozen distinct Indian groups presented a barrier to colonial expansion to the east of the mining district. While the Botocudo became the most feared and infamous of these groups, they moved, hunted, and fought among many others. As the second half of the eighteenth century progressed, all faced a surging conflict with Portuguese settlers. Despite many shared cultural traits, these many groups also clashed increasingly with each other, fissuring into subgroups and rival clans. Resistance to colonial rule comprised only one part of a struggle among various competitors over territory. As in native refuge zones throughout the Atlantic world, imperial expansion intensified interethnic and intraethnic conflict by forcing opposing groups into smaller and smaller geographic confines. When colonists used the term Botocudo, they tended to fold these diverse peoples into a single generic enemy encompassing all of those who resisted conquest and incorporation. In other words, accompanying the external pressures on these native societies was a coerced process of tribal and ethnic formation. The Botocudo became the Botocudo, in this sense, as a result of an accelerating historical process that hinged on the degree to which colonial expansion destabilized the region.[11]

In the midst of this process and in keeping with Amerindian experience dating from the earliest arrival of Europeans, the various bands that opposed colonization in the Eastern Sertão discovered that they need not only target colonists per se. They found that the assault on their territory could be impeded and reversed not only by attacking individuals but also, and often more easily and effectively, by seizing or destroying property and possessions. Sometimes this meant stopping somewhere short of face-to-face combat—which came at great peril because settlers carried knives, axes, swords, and firearms—and striking at material belongings left unprotected. Sometimes it meant risking such combat and then extending an attack beyond human antagonists to include their houses, farms, and mining operations. Indians could burn crops and kill livestock. They could steal tools and other manufactured goods. More than incidental targets, such belongings comprised the very essence of the cultural matrix that distinguished settlers from the Indians, the material basis of colonial society and civilized identity.[12] When Indians seized and destroyed them, they

ILLUSTRATION 7.1. Pataxó with ax and knife, ca. 1815. European goods influenced native society even where Europeans themselves were not yet present
SOURCE: Maximilian, *Travels in Brazil.* The John Carter Brown Library at Brown University.

frequently dealt incapacitating blows, dislodging their adversaries and forcing them to abandon their holdings entirely.

The effects of property loss of this sort extended from the most vulnerable settlers to the Crown itself as forfeited taxes on agricultural and mineral production in the sertão diminished the royal treasury. Minas authorities emphasized this connection as they importuned the monarch for assistance. After visiting the southeastern parish of Guarapiranga in 1750, the bishop of Mariana urged King José I to take "prompt action to avoid the entire loss of that district, extremely abundant in farms, foodstuffs, and gold-mining operations." Mineral strikes were still being made in the region and new placer mines established. Once the Indians were either "chased off or made peaceful, that great sertão would become extremely fertile in every way." The bishop called on the king to respond quickly and forcefully by supplying settlers with powder and shot.[13] Over the ensuing decades, up to and including the Crown's decision to wage war in 1808, pleas of this sort reached the throne from every sector of the Eastern Sertão. Settlers in retreat from the forests north of the Doce River in 1796 spurred the town council of Caeté[14] to urge Lisbon to come to the rescue of those "fleeing death" who had "lamentably abandoned their fazendas." Town officials stressed these holdings served the public good by bolstering royal tax revenues as they beseeched the Crown to put an end to the "fury of the barbarous enemy." Although the response was characteristically delayed, nearly two years later Lisbon authorized the governor to take the action he deemed necessary to defend these settlers.[15]

For those preoccupied with expanding Minas' commercial, agricultural, and mining revenues, indigenous attacks on property came to be considered the primary factor hampering production and revenue collection to the east of the mining district. Articulating this view to Prince Regent João in 1801, Mariana town council members wrote that they would like nothing better than to contribute more generously to the royal fifth (*quinto*) that the Crown collected on mining gains and the tithe (*dízimo*) that it assessed on agricultural production. To the east of Mariana, however, this fiscal objective had been stymied by "the anthropophagous nations of the Puris and Botocudo," whose raids threatened to depopulate an extensive region stretching from the frontier parishes of Guarapiranga and Furquim to the Matipó River. Recently, these natives had forced the abandonment of as many as 80 fazendas dedicated to the production of foodstuffs. Settlers had been compelled to retreat to land long since stripped of precious minerals and fertile soil. The guaranteed dividend of a Crown-sponsored military response would be the restoration of taxes paid by these retreating colonists. Town councilors calculated that Mariana's annual contribution to the royal coffers would promptly increase by 50% or more once they secured the eastern territories under their jurisdiction, which included much of the sertão south of the Doce River. While they may have exaggerated, the claim revealed just how valuable they estimated their losses to be as a consequence of indigenous resistance.[16]

In 1806, on the eve of full militarization of the conflict, the captaincy's highest fiscal board—presided over by Governor Melo, who was instrumental in convincing the prince regent to declare war two years later—submitted a report to Lisbon railing against undeterred Indian raids. Hostile Indians continued to force settlers to "abandon their farming and mining fazendas after having cultivated these lands at the expense of their labor." The treasury board received numerous appeals from these settlers, which testified to the "excessive costs" to the Crown in the loss of tax revenues and in the attempt "to expand the captaincy in that direction." This argument, received approvingly by a leading Crown minister who decried the "barbarous cruelty of the anthropophagous Indians," would find its way into the text of the declaration of war after the Portuguese court had made its way to Rio de Janeiro. In that text, the monarch denounced Botocudo "invasions" that had combined to "devastate all of the fazendas" along stretches of the Doce River and its tributaries, driving landowners "to abandon them at great loss to themselves and to my royal Crown."[17] At these various levels, property loss both real and perceived, already incurred or feared in the future, became a decisive factor in disrupting the enterprise of colonial expansion.

More detailed documentation from the frontier helps clarify how native raiding, even when no casualties resulted, could communicate a powerful message to colonists, local and regional authorities, and the Crown. Official correspondence, low-level military communications, and settlers' petitions reveal that property loss and damage, often in tandem with physical injury or death, were the primary offense denounced by those whose homesteads suffered Indian attacks. Such property included livestock, cultivated fields, farmhouses, household possessions, and tools and weapons, which Indians looted or burned. In 1764, one such attack was instrumental in prompting the series of retaliatory expeditions dispatched by Governor Silva. Cited with particular frequency were the killing of cattle and the burning of fields, both in the vicinity of Cuieté and in zones nearer to Mariana and Vila Rica, the captaincy's most important urban centers.[18] In 1777, even after coordinated expeditions had been marching into the sertão for more than a decade, Puri raiders were reported to be slaughtering cattle and horses at will on fazendas outside a frontier presidio at Abre Campo. Settlers had retreated there after again coming under siege and abandoning their property at Cuieté.[19]

As indicated, not every action the Portuguese perceived as hostile held the same meaning for the native forest-dwellers. Although details concerning Indian objectives were always sparse in accusations recorded by colonists, a report condemning raids occurring just after the beginning of the nineteenth century revealed that attacks on livestock signified not only direct resistance to settler incursions but also a means of subsistence. Indians returned to their encampments after these raids, according to an officer in the field, to consume the stolen meat after roasting it on spits.[20] Repeated attacks on fields probably also served this double purpose—to weaken settlers and provision Indians—especially as the latter's control of sufficient territory for hunting and foraging became threatened. In 1778, Colonel João da Silva Tavares informed Governor Noronha of the "dangerous state" in which the presidio at Cuieté functioned. The squadron based there was too small and lacked sufficient ammunition. It was thus incapable of "repelling the attacks of Indians and defending the crops in the fields, the sole means of subsistence of the inhabitants of that presidio." Noronha took immediate action, ordering the colonel to march additional troops to the area post-haste. Fearing that the presidio might be "entirely destroyed by the Indians," he pledged to do everything in his power to put an end to the state of "calamity and disorder" fostered by the natives.[21]

Settlers' land, marriage, and probate records underscore the close connections between raids on property meant to satisfy native material needs, those designed to halt territorial invasion, and the meanings both types conveyed to colonists. These connections help pinpoint how and to what degree Indians could undermine the social and cultural order of the encroaching society. As settlers brought more things with them to the frontier, as they deemed a growing multiplicity of items essential to their survival, as they increasingly sought to replicate the material and social configurations of life in the colony's settled zones, they became ever more susceptible to this sort of assault. Indians could disrupt and disorient the lives of farmers, ranchers, and miners by severing the attachment they demonstrated to a seemingly endless variety of possessions in addition to crops and livestock.

When the Portuguese immigrant Carlos Leite de Araújo sought land in the sertão in the mid-1750s, he chose a spot on the periphery the settlement of Xopotó that would, over the coming decades, experience substantial territorial expansion and recurring conflicts with Indians. Along with many other newcomers, Araújo, a farmer and dry goods merchant then 27 years old, requested and received a sesmaria measuring one-half league in length and breadth (11 km²).[22] In the 1760s, he married Maria Joanna de São José, a native of Vila Rica who had moved to the outlying parish with her parents more than 15 years earlier.[23] He would turn his stake in the sertão into a respectable farmstead producing sugar and milled maize. Toward the end of his life in 1779, 18 slaves worked his fields, pastureland, banana grove, barn, and sugar mill.[24]

No record is found of Araújo's farm ever having suffered an attack. Rarely did official denunciations of such crimes ever specify individual properties thus affected. However, during the 1760s, just like the previous decade, surrounding districts suffered the "abandonment of a great number of … fazendas, mining operations, and fields" as a consequence of Indian raids.[25] Thus, Araújo's characteristic accumulation of material possessions provides a fair idea of what could be lost by settlers and gained by Indians in raids on the eastern edge of the mining zone's settled nuclei. To begin with, Araújo maintained significant stores of maize, beans, and rice, provisions that sustained his slaves and supplied his dry goods store. The agricultural labor regime required an array of tools and implements, including seven scythes, two machetes, seven hoes, a mallet, an axle, and a scale. To pull the cart that he owned, to operate his mill, to provide meat, and to facilitate trips to nearby Guarapiranga, Araújo kept several oxen, a pair of horses, a steer, two cows, two calves, and 28 pigs. Among his domestic possessions were two copper pans and a pot, a setting of six silver forks and spoons, pewter serving dishes and plates, a pewter basin and water pitcher, and a wooden table with two drawers. Still more precious belongings included a small collection of gold, diamond, and topaz jewelry, two pairs of silver buckles, a pair of silver spurs, a whip with a silver handle, a silver rapier with a shoulder sling, gold dust in sufficient quantity to buy a good horse, a picture frame decorated with enamel and gold braiding, and three images of saints adorning the interior of the estate's small chapel.[26]

Although Araújo apparently possessed no firearms, other settlers of similar means found them indispensable in the sertão along with a plethora of additional items exchanged by force in frontier raids. In 1768, the Portuguese immigrant Antônio José Peixoto and his wife, Ignácia Cordeira, received two contiguous land grants on opposite banks of the Casca River. When Cordeira died in 1786, her estate inventory listed two guns. She also owned six sheep, a compass, a chisel, a bronze mortar and pestle, several manufactured boxes, and two beds complete with pillows, cotton blankets, and sheets, along with many other items like those found at Araújo's farm.[27] Another female settler, Dona Anna Joaquina de Almeida, whose successful struggle for land was considered in a previous chapter, received her sesmaria along an upper tributary of the Pomba River in 1798. With her husband, Captain Francisco Soares Maciel, she came to hold enough gold to buy more than half a dozen adult slaves. She also owned a caldron, a wire bowl, a locking trunk, four collapsible beds, 13 leather chairs, 26 glass bottles, a loom, separate tool sets for a sawyer and a carpenter, a shovel, horseshoes, barrels, buckets, a pair of iron rails, a wooden tub, fencing material, an iron chain, a grater, a bronze bell, five lengths of fine cotton cloth, 40 lengths of coarser fabric, and a variety of garments and outerwear, to mention only those items not already cited in the previous two cases.[28]

In short, the developing frontier raiding economy tapped into a highly diversified market in commodities and manufactured goods that meant more to Indians than Portuguese characterizations of simple resistance suggested. Only in rare cases did contemporary Portuguese observers recognize this truth, however condescendingly. Bishop José Joaquim da Cunha de Azeredo Coutinho— the nephew of Padre Ângelo Pessanha and descendent of prominent sugar planters active in colonizing the coastal forests, a close advisor to the Crown by the 1790s, a member of Lisbon's Royal Academy of Sciences, and soon to be Portugal's last grand inquisitor—argued that material appetites were the key to civilizing intransigent Indians. "They have virtues, they have vices, they are full of ambition just like us." This fact was clear from their "excessive desire for goods," he advised the prince regent in 1794. Knives, machetes, glass beads, and other trifles held the status of "luxury" goods among these Indians. "They seek them out with as much diligence as civilized peoples, by which it is evident that they possess, just like us, the seeds of the passions and of ambition. Nothing more is necessary," he continued, "than the art of making those seeds sprout and of adding heat to those passions." Coutinho advocated introducing additional items to familiarize the natives with Portuguese material culture, thereby achieving their incorporation. Since the early eighteenth century, his ancestors in the coastal plantation zone of Campos successfully practiced this technique, developing a kind of marketplace on land they turned over to Indians along the Paraíba River. Natives from the sertão came to exchange goods with settlers, trading beeswax, honey, birds, wild game, and fire-resistant clay for machetes, scythes, knives, fishhooks, salt, and other items. The Indians also "rented themselves out" to lumbering operations for several days at a time to earn enough to purchase metal tools before returning to the sertão. The lesson to be learned was that "the shirt, the hat, the dress, trousers, [and] shoes, which they have disdained as superfluous things, and even as a heavy burden to carry through the forests and wilderness, will become useful to them, and necessary." Over time, they would learn that life dependent on such comforts was "incompatible with absolute liberty and with unlimited independence." Ample irony informed this perspective, advanced at a time when settlers on the Minas frontier, moving back toward the coast, were ever more enraged by Indians who seemed able to tap into this material culture without giving up their independence.[29]

Scholars have become increasingly practiced in assessing the integrity of the material culture that Indians struggled to preserve, managed to adapt, or rushed to abandon, depending on the exigencies of particular frontier encounters. In zones where cross-cultural trade or gift exchanges predominated, indigenous dependencies on Western goods developed and, as a consequence, pre-contact polities broke down. Alternatively, native societies found ways to exploit the market in such goods for their own benefit and strengthened their position vis-à-vis would-be colonizers. Despite the inclination to think of hostile seminomadic groups as insulated from such eventualities by their resistance, goods continued to change hands through raiding and similar transformations ensued.[30] Indians who raided establishments like those whose inventories are preserved gained access to far more than just the standard axes, knives, grain, and livestock commonly associated with frontier booty. The seizure of all kinds of other wares entailed adaptations that can only be imagined in the absence of sources describing the daily lives of natives who continued to seek refuge in the forests. Scholars know utilitarian steel blades and other metal tools galvanized indigenous trade networks even where European contact remained indirect or in its earliest stages.[31] The evidence from the Minas frontier indicates that such oddities as gold coins, silver buckles, pillows, pails, and leather whips did so, too.

Less frequently have scholars focused on the meaning of material effects for settler culture, which is necessary to tease out the full ramifications of Indian raids. Although individuals like Araújo, Cordeira, and Almeida were not wealthy by the standards of the colony's urban elite, the proliferation of goods and objects they possessed shored up the civilization they esteemed and gave it the concrete form that defined, by way of contrast, the Indian savagery they decried.[32] Such crimes had enormous material consequences as well as profound symbolic meanings for settlers whose cultural identities and social boundaries were externalized in the belongings they labored to accumulate at their far-flung homesteads. Settlers' possessions were, to an unappreciated degree, precisely the objectives at stake in frontier conflicts of this sort. They were, in the words of a historian of colonial North America who has studied this phenomenon, "a good part of what differentiated [settlers] from the Indians."[33] While frontier conflict had no special claim on pillage as a military tactic, such action took on distinctive meanings, forged in battle and ascertained through experience, because it involved adversaries who defined themselves so differently in relation to property and possessions. Bishop Coutinho surely captured something of the truth when he argued that Indians had no innate aversion to rudimentary material accumulation. But as independent seminomads, they exhibited nothing like the fundamental dependence on the landed property, permanent dwellings, livestock, and manufactured items that delineated slave-based settler society.

The extent to which Indians recognized the broad implications of their individual attacks cannot be certainly known, particularly because the surviving documents recount native actions, not thoughts, and only those actions that became visible to consistently unsympathetic colonial observers. As silent but wide-ranging witnesses to the consequences of their own raids, the seminomadic bands of the Eastern Sertão surely gleaned just how enmeshed in property and possessions settlers' lives were and just how destabilizing strikes could be against even seemingly insignificant items. To conclude otherwise, given their repeated experience of colonists' reactions, would require an unsustainable presumption of native ignorance. "Different cultures, different rationalities," as Marshall Sahlins once wrote, but rationality nonetheless.[34] Facing mounting aggression during the second half of the eighteenth century, the Indians honed their skills. By taking aim at things, they learned to deliver a potent message communicated in the distinct language of frontier material culture. They learned that by slaughtering a few head of cattle, looting iron tools from a barn, or setting fire to a field or outbuilding, they could often send settlers scurrying out of the forest. They may even have known that their message would be carried from frightened settler to frontier commander, from parish priest to bishop, from governor to monarch. What probably took longer to realize, as it dawned only gradually on authorities themselves, was that after mid-century, as lands once set off limits increasingly became the object of colonial aspirations and activity, the message thus conveyed assumed a new meaning. Acts once deemed savagery that benefited official policy by keeping straying settlers in place now seemed like savagery that could cripple the colonial project.

Violence against Slaves and Settlers

When Ignácia Cordeira received her land along the Casca River, the captaincy governor granted her request on the grounds that she owned "twenty-five slaves engaged in mining" but no land "on which to plant crops for their subsistence."[35] The fact that feeding slaves in an atmosphere of post-boom economic disjuncture could be a prime impetus for migrating to the Eastern Sertão points to another critical component of the resulting territorial conflict. Attacks on slaves who worked the fields and mineral washings of the region's isolated farms and alluvial gold deposits were at least as consequential to settlers as the theft and destruction of material possessions. Even if such attacks occurred less frequently, they resulted in not only the loss of life and labor but also the added cost of protecting slaves from raids. The sources suggest that Indians were cognizant of the variations in skin color, labor, and caste that structured colonial society and that they could single out slaves, the most valuable and vulnerable of assets, who far outnumbered the whites assembling them on the frontier. This abomination was cited as another justification for the military mobilization of 1764.[36] In the northern reaches of the sertão, to cite an example from the early nineteenth century, the German prince and naturalist Maximilian reported the case of an estate carved out of the forest where a slave had shot a Pataxó native, incensing the "savages, who to revenge themselves, attacked the negros in one of the plantations, and killed three of them with their long arrows." The value of the estate subsequently declined.[37] In a rare count of casualties, Baron von Eschwege, the German mining engineer, stated that during a five-year period, the Botocudo had "fallen on more than 300 free men and killed more than three thousand slaves," pursuing some colonists all the way to the coast. Unfortunately, he provided no specific dates or locations for his estimate of a ten-to-one casualty ratio of slaves compared to free settlers.[38]

While specific details are meager in the documentation, slave casualties occurred frequently enough that property owners made this loss a part of their calculations when deciding whether to settle in the sertão or to dispatch some of their bonded workforce there to labor at placer mines. Reflecting on the slow pace of development in Cuieté, the vicar Manoel Vieira Nunes wrote in 1769 that until the region's Indians could be subdued, the remote settlement would remain of "little or no utility" to the Crown. The viability of the place, he explained, depended on a basic financial reckoning made by slaveholders. Cuieté's perpetual vulnerability to Indian attack meant that the modest amount of gold extracted there did not compensate miners who were forced to "consume a great part of their earnings in the payment and purchase of guards" to protect slaves toiling in the fields and mining operations.[39] The situation had not changed a dozen years later when Governor Rodrigo José de Meneses traveled to Cuieté to assess the merits of continuing to promote its settlement. Again the present and potential profitability of the mining camp was at issue. One of his foremost objectives in visiting the site, the governor wrote, was to determine "if the quantity [of gold] that can be taken out" could offset the expense of conducting business in so distant a place. Expenses were significantly inflated not only by the exorbitant cost of importing commodities, which made their loss to Indians all the more injurious, but by the need to protect laborers through extraordinary means, namely, arming them. The governor sought to determine the expenses accruing from "the portion of slaves necessary to have under arms to defend themselves from the heathens, while the other portion works." Such considerations, he noted, "always enter into the calculations of miners and should equally be considered in the political calculus" of any decision by the government to subsidize and defend the struggling mining camp. The problem extended beyond Cuieté wherever slaveholders sought to secure new lands subject to Indian attack. The violence forced owners, as one priest described the situation to the prince regent at the beginning of the nineteenth century, to "employ part of their slaves and overseers in the defense of their properties, keeping them always armed." As a consequence, in the opinion of their masters, slaves became a clear target of native raids.[40]

By all indications, armed slaves became a fixture of life throughout the Eastern Sertão. From the sixteenth to the eighteenth century, the Spanish on Hispaniola; the Portuguese in coastal Brazil; the English in Massachusetts, Virginia, and North and South Carolina; the Dutch in New Amsterdam; and the French in Louisiana and Guiana all placed weapons in slaves' hands to defeat Native American foes.[41] In eastern Minas Gerais, during the final decades of the eighteenth century and the beginning of the nineteenth, individual settlers and the captaincy government did the same. The defense of established settlements and protection of fellow captives constituted just one aspect of the responsibilities assigned to slaves bearing firearms. They were also marched into the forest to wage direct combat with Indians. In the São Mateus River valley, for example, they followed their owner José de Souza Passos in "penetrating the wild forests" to attack the Botocudo in 1793. They joined soldiers and settlers on an expedition dispatched to counter the Botocudo attacks on Itabira, Tanque, and Santana dos Ferros in 1794. They also served and likely fought alongside frontier conscripts commanded by Quartermaster Elesbão Lopes Duro after the beginning of the nineteenth century.[42] The willingness of individual settlers, frontier commanders, and the captaincy government to give arms to men held in bondage betrayed the whites' desperation. For that matter, so did the willingness to place slaves, whether armed or not, in harm's way. The ability to disrupt the smooth functioning of the slave regime, to threaten slaves or to force them into unconventional and unprofitable roles, contributed significantly to the marked success Indians enjoyed in opposing the colonization of this frontier.

Settler probate records illustrated just how valuable slaves were to their owners and how ruinous their loss or injury could be. As in the captaincy's settled urban zone and throughout Portuguese America, slaves represented more often than not the primary capital investment of the landowners, mining claim holders, and even military men of the Eastern Sertão. Four years after the death of its owner in 1787, the estate of Captain José Leme da Silva was appraised in a postmortem inventory. Silva lived in Guarapiranga, whose environs, despite the town's decades-long existence as a mining and agricultural center, were the site of repeated Indian attacks in the 1750s, 1760s, and 1790s, and likely at other times given that the archives preserve only incomplete records of such places.[43] He had co-commanded one of the bandeiras ordered to retaliate against the Botocudo in 1765.[44] At a time when the average value of an adult slave in Minas Gerais stood at approximately 100 mil-reis or 100$000, the estate inventory valued the officer's slaves as follows: Paula of Angola, approximately 50 years old, 60$000; Grácia of Angola, 25 years old, 120$000; Antônio, Grácia's one-year-old Brazilian-born son, 35$000; André, of the "mocumbe nation," approximately 70 years old, 6$000; João of the Congo, 60 years old, 50$000; and Caetano of the Congo, approximately 25 years old, 135$000. Together, this human capital totaled 406$000. The only possessions of comparable worth were Silva's land and the structures built on it, including houses, a barn, and a *monjolo*, a water-driven mechanism used for pounding grain. These were valued at 400$000. The sum of his remaining possessions—for example, two horses, 48$000; 25 pigs, 7$500; a copper pot, 4$250; and five machetes, 2$100—came to 72$750, bringing the value of the entire estate to 878$750. In other words, almost half of his relatively modest material wealth derived from slaves. The loss of the most valuable slave alone—were he killed, for example, while clearing land at the edge of the estate—would have reduced Silva's net worth by more than a sixth. As in the case of material belongings, Indians acquired, through long experience, a sense of the value and vulnerability of such unprotected captives, whose labor sustained a system that in frontier zones made them moving targets.

In a second case, the somewhat better-off Manuel Luís Branco, the priest prominent in the conquest of the Arrepiados region, died in 1811 with an estate valued at 1:150$345, more than a quarter of this wealth counted in enslaved workers. Branco lived in Barra do Bacalhau, a subordinate parish of Guarapiranga. Apart from the land and houses he owned and a pocketwatch worth 120$000, slaves were the priest's most valuable possessions. After two were set free on his death, four remained: Manuel, 23 years old, 80$000, and Domingos, 30 years old, 90$000, both of them of "Benguela" provenance, as well as Joaquina, Domingos' 29-year-old Brazilian-born wife, 60$000, and Benedito, their ten-year-old son, 80$000.[45] Once again, the point is that a major investment was put at risk when slaves worked or fought in zones subject to Indian hostilities. Apart from taking the lives of property owners themselves, this threat was the Indians' most effective weapon. The imposition of a slaveholding regime represented the clearest sign of successful territorial incorporation and the culture of economic and racial domination that accompanied it. Acts of resistance that stopped, stalled, or simply increased the price of this outcome had consequences, again both symbolic and material, beyond the cost of human life itself.

As far as Portuguese colonists were concerned, of course, casualties they suffered themselves inflicted the highest costs. Such assaults were more likely to provoke an official response, commonly in the form of an expedition dispatched to avenge the crime. More than in the case of slaves, to provide at least a partial quantification of the extent of such casualties is possible. Of the 86 violent engagements with various Indians of the Eastern Sertão reported in the documentary record between 1760 and 1808, 57 cited settlers as opposed to soldiers or settled natives as the victims.[46] Numerous documents cited the occurrence of deaths and injuries but only rarely provided numerical data. In just five of the 57 documented attacks against settlers were casualty figures specified: a 1769 killing by unidentified Indians of a settler in the vicinity of Cuieté; a 1770 killing by Botocudo natives of three settlers along a tributary of the Cuieté River; a 1777 killing by Puri of a landowner near Abre Campo; and the deaths in early 1808 of more than 20 settlers, again at the hands of the Botocudo, in a hamlet on the edge of the Doce River basin.[47] In a notable exception to the usual ambush tactic, the largest, most sustained, and deadliest attack occurred during a five-day onslaught in 1794. A reported 2,000 Botocudo "destroyed and razed" houses, fazendas, and the main chapel in the town of Santana dos Ferros, killing 48 settlers.[48] Death or injury to settlers was mentioned in connection with another 25 attacks but without providing specific casualty figures. Despite the inherent quantitative limitations, clearly natives posed a very real threat, because more than half of all recorded attacks produced casualties.

As had been the case in such circumstances since the onset of colonization in the sixteenth century, casualties led to denunciations of cannibalism. This ultimate expression of corporal vulnerability figured prominently in the 1808 declaration of war against the Botocudo, an accusation essential to deeming the war just, as will become evident in the next chapter. Given the near absence over so many decades of direct archival evidence of Botocudo anthropophagy, allegations of routine cannibalism would seem to reveal more about the European imagination than Indian conduct. For the same reason, exactly to what extent or even whether the Botocudo, the Puri, and other groups in the region engaged in this act will likely never be known.[49] Some foreign visitors to Brazil accused settlers and officials of exaggerating this claim to justify the seizure of land. Others, including the usually meticulous Eschwege, gathered evidence to support the claim. Yet Eschwege's denunciation of "abominable scenes and robust men reduced to slices of roasted meat" bore the characteristics not of an eyewitness account but of the repetition of generic images of anthropophagi employed by some Europeans, and debunked by others, since colonization began in the sixteenth century.[50] Prince Maximilian reached perhaps the most evenhanded conclusion based on the greatest amount of information. Regarding the Botocudo and Puri, he wrote that "it is difficult to believe, as some affirm, that they eat human flesh as a matter of preference." He pointed out that against this conclusion stood the evidence that they kept alive at least some of the prisoners they captured. "There is no doubt, however, that out of revenge they devour the flesh of their enemies killed in battle."[51]

The German prince offered additional details about the Puri and Botocudo:

They are said to devour . . . human flesh out of revenge; but as for their eating their own deceased relations, as a last token of affection, according to the report of some early writers, no trace of such a custom is to be found, at least in our times, among the Tapuyas on the east coast. The Portuguese on the Paraíba [River] universally assert that the Puris feast on the flesh of the enemies they have killed, and there really seems to be some truth in this assertion . . . but they would never confess it to us. When we questioned them on the subject, they answered that the Botocudos only had this custom. [John] Mawe relates that the Indians at Canta Gallo ate birds without plucking them. I never saw a savage do this; they even carefully take out the entrails, and probably had a mind to amuse the English traveller by shewing him some extraordinary trick.[52]

Such "tricks" likely figured into reports on eating humans as well, although Maximilian did not make this connection. Hard evidence of cannibalism almost never surfaced, and verifiable facts had little bearing on either accusations or the policies based on them. Denunciations of cannibalism reached their greatest intensity preceding the two periods of full-scale military mobilization during the 1760s and the years following 1808, which calls attention to the way that they served European purposes. As had always been the case, the accusation proved to be a particularly effective means of articulating the radical differences between colonists and Indians when the former resorted to violence. To the extent that anthropophagy occurred, the practice probably also served the natives when they sought to underscore such difference for their own purposes. Considering the allegations by the Puri about Botocudo conduct, this seems to have held true not only between the Indians and the Portuguese but also between separate indigenous groups at odds with one another. Furthermore, some intriguing evidence—including Maximilian's assessment of Puri motives in the presence of the British observer—suggests that if and when the eastern Indians did practice cannibalism, they were seeking to give form to and thus exploit obvious European phantasms as opposed to engaging in a culturally intact, pre-contact ritual. If so, they had discovered yet another way to communicate through violence.[53]

Botocudo perceptions of European fears may have been honed by their own. When one of Brazil's finest ethnologists interviewed a handful of native survivors regarding their origin myths and religious belief in the mid-twentieth century, he learned that the Botocudo also dreaded being consumed, not only by wild animals but by cannibals. His native informant recounted the tale of an Indian, apparently a dark-skinned Botocudo, hunting alone in the forest. He came upon a group of unknown Indians identified as "the man-eating Tombrék." The cannibals killed the Botocudo, cut him open, removed his entrails, and dissected his body. When their chief arrived, "he examined the skin color of the slain man, which was dark, and said, 'Why did you kill him? He is a mulatto!' [He did not want his people to kill mulattoes, but only whites.]" Regretful, the Tombrék urged their chief to use his great powers to restore the man's life. The chief had them pile the viscera and slices of flesh together. He then began singing "and the man got up and remained standing upright. The chief bade him go; he took his bow and went home."[54]

A final passage by Maximilian complicates the matter still further:

That the Puris do in fact sometimes eat the bodies of their slaughtered enemies is attested by various witnesses in this part of the country. Father João, at St. Fidelis, assured us that he had once on a journey to the river Itapemirim found in the forest the body of a negro, who had been killed by the Puris, without arms and legs, and round which a number of carrion vultures had assembled. We have observed above that the Puris would never confess to us that they eat human flesh; but after the authentic testimonies that have been adduced, their own denial cannot have much weight. Our Puri too acknowledged that his tribe fix the heads of the enemies whom they have killed upon a pole, and dance round

ILLUSTRATION 7.2. A priest's painting of Botocudo cannibalism, 18th c
SOURCE: Alberto Lamego, *A Terra Goitacá á luz de documentos inéditos* (Rio de Janeiro: Garnier, 1913–1941).

them. Even among the Coroados in Minas Gerais, as Mr. Freyreiss [another European naturalist] affirms, a custom prevails of putting an arm or foot of an enemy into a pot of *caüi* [*cauim*], which is afterwards sucked out by the guests.[55]

The anecdote clarifies that any ability to authenticate cannibalistic conduct depends on accounts in which experts assessing the facts at the time rejected the reliability of the Indians themselves as authorities on their own cultural practices. In any event, far more certain than the ambiguous evidence on cannibalism was the corrosive power over colonists exerted by natives in general when they attacked property, possessions, and people.

The ability to endanger all of these components of the slave-based settler society radically altered the course of conquest. Although captaincy officials set their sites on the lands and resources of the Eastern Sertão, settlers who migrated there faced persistent, if intermittent, violent opposition. As was invariably the case in conflicts of this sort, exaggerations and biased portrayals of native hostilities colored colonial sources, serving (among other purposes) to encourage and justify state intervention. Moreover, the most brutal forms of violence could have multiple meanings for colonial and indigenous societies. Nevertheless, the archival record, read with caution, provides ample details to conclude that resistance was recurrent, prolonged, intentional, and effective.[56] Drawing on the experience of more than two centuries of contact first with coastal and later with inland colonists, the seminomadic indigenous occupants of the zone carefully orchestrated this resistance, their success measured in terms of the many decades they continued to forestall conquest after 1750. Over time, they learned that direct bodily attacks on slaveholders and landowners were far from the only way to disrupt incursions. Settlers' possessions were dear enough and their hold on new lands tenuous enough that theft, arson, vandalism, or the murder of a single slave could force the abandonment of nascent settlements. The peculiarities of the encroaching lusophone society presented Indians with diverse opportunities to impede expansion. They did so by understanding their adversary's culture and translating that understanding into acts crafted to achieve the greatest possible effect.

Violence against Soldiers

The conquest of this frontier might have progressed more rapidly had threatened settlers been able to count on effective military support; however, when field commanders retaliated against Indian depredations by marching troops into the forests, the Botocudo, the Puri, the Pataxó, and others found that they could foil standard military procedures and forestall anticipated outcomes. As in the case of settler incursions, the degree to which Indians managed to influence the dynamics of conquest is evident on the level of the dozens of individual military and paramilitary expeditions dispatched to the sertão for purposes ranging from exploration to combat. Had these expeditions proven more successful, providing Brazil's early historians with a heroic frontier narrative, perhaps their place in the collective memory of the mining district would have been more prominent. Instead, few of them achieved their avowed objectives, which almost always included pacifying hostile Indians. The persistence of native nomadism, the undeterred raiding throughout the period, and the recourse to declared war at the end of it together testified to the limitations of these armed expeditions to the sertão. So did the fact that only six of the 86 recorded clashes pitting Indians against the Portuguese between 1760 and 1808 involved native attacks on expeditions in the field. As noted, the vast majority involved settlers, not soldiers. But with so many expeditions marching through the sertão, Indians learned to respond to organized military force long before the Crown declared open war. Above all, they learned to avoid direct confrontations with soldiers. The extended period of training in counter-tactics helps explain why the 1808 warfare produced numerous informal clashes but few major battlefield triumphs for the Portuguese.[57]

Many silences suffuse the frontier dispatches, marching orders, officer correspondence, and casualty reports documenting the retaliatory expeditions. But even vague accounts testify to the effectiveness of Indian resistance. For example, a Makoni detachment dealt Captain Antônio Lourenço's 1766 bandeira an ignominious blow, surrounding soldiers en route to Cuieté and then forcing them to retreat, although additional details from the encounter are lacking.[58] In contrast, a violent engagement in 1769 between Indians and troops marching to Antônio Dias Abaixo under the command of Captain Alexandre da Silva Guimarães ended with some of the Indians in captivity. But in general, military expeditions were regularly stymied by the fact that, as one official report put it, the Indians were "raiders and have no fixed place."[59]

Another violent incident recorded in more detail than usual involved three soldiers, rather than a full-fledged expedition, ordered to explore the forests of the Arrepiados Mountains in 1781. One of the soldiers was ambushed and "pierced deeply" by an arrow. The offending "heathen," accompanied by other Indians, emerged from the forest to retrieve the arrow. As he yanked it from the soldier's body, the wounded man fired his gun, striking one of the assailants. The seriousness of the injury was apparent from "the great amount of blood that stained the leaves of plants and the path" in the direction that the Indians fled. As for the soldier's wound, "one judged that it had not cut through any of the viscera, since even though it was at first presumed mortal, it already appear[ed] to be healing" by the time the soldier's commanding officer reported the incident to the governor.[60] Random clashes with similarly ambiguous results continued to characterize engagements between soldiers and Indians even after the Crown prince declared war on the Botocudo in 1808.

Although the Portuguese were loath to recognize the fact, native hit-and-run tactics did not reflect a fixed cultural predilection. Maximilian, the most reliable ethnographer of the period, was one of few Europeans ever to observe the sort of combat the Botocudo waged among themselves, a highly ritualized, open-field, non-lethal exercise of martial prowess. His account of a battle that took place between rival bands bears quoting at length. Having settled at a Portuguese frontier garrison (*quartel*) after the most violent stage of the declared war concluded

ILLUSTRATION 7.3. Botocudo practicing ritualized violence, 1816. A very different kind of practice was required for successful combat against advancing colonial adversaries
SOURCE: Maximilian, *Travels in Brazil*. The John Carter Brown Library at Brown University.

in 1811, a group of Botocudo led by a headman whom the Portuguese knew as Captain Jeparack faced off in a territorial dispute against another group led by a Captain June:

The warriors of both parties uttered short rough tones of defiance to each other, walked sullenly round one another like angry dogs, at the same time making ready their poles. Captain Jeparack then came forward, walked about between the men, looked gloomily and directly before him, with wide staring eyes, and sung, with a tremulous voice, a long song, which probably described the affront that he had received. In this manner the adverse parties became more and more inflamed: suddenly, two of them advanced, and pushed one another with the arm on the breast, so that they staggered back, and then began to ply their poles. One first struck with all his might at the other, regardless where the blow fell: his antagonist bore the first attack seriously and calmly, without changing countenance; he then took his turn, and thus they belaboured each other with severe blows, the marks of which long remained visible in the large wheals on their naked bodies. As there were on the poles many sharp stumps of branches which had been cut off, the effect of the blows was not always confined to bruises, but the blood flowed from the heads of many of the combatants. When two of them had thus thrashed each other handsomely, two more came forward; and several pair were often seen engaged at once: but they never laid hands on one another. When these combats had continued for some time, they again walked about with a serious look, uttering tones of defiance, till heroic enthusiasm again seized them, and set their poles in motion.

Meanwhile, the women also fought valiantly; amidst continual weeping and howling, they seized each other by the hair, struck with their fists, scratched with their nails, tore the plugs of wood out of each other's ears and lips, and scattered them on the field of battle as trophies. If one threw her adversary down, a third, who stood behind, seized her by the legs, and threw her down likewise, and then they pulled each other about on the ground . . .

In this manner the combat continued for about an hour; when all appeared weary, some of the savages showed their courage and perseverance, by walking about among the others, uttering their tones of defiance. Captain Jeparack, as the principal person of the offended party, held out to the last; all seemed fatigued and exhausted, when he, not yet disposed to make peace, continued to sing his tremulous song, and encouraged his people to renew the combat, till we went up to him, clapped him on the shoulder, and told him that he was a valiant warrior, but that it was now time to make peace; upon which he at length suddenly quitted the field, and went over to the Quartel. Captain June had not shewn so much energy; being an old man, he had taken no part in the combat, but constantly remained in the back-ground . . .

The bows and arrows of all these savages had stood, during the whole combat, leaning against the neighbouring trees, without their touching them; but it is said sometimes to have happened, on similar occasions, that they have thrown aside the poles, and taken to their arms, for which reason the Portuguese do not much like to have such combats in their neighbourhood.[61]

Even as natives continued such practices among themselves, their tactics evolved over time in response to European enemies. This trend is apparent from settler descriptions of any number of Botocudo attacks, including those recounted to the British traveler John Mawe, who toured the mining district in 1808 and 1809. With increasing migration occurring to the settlement of Barra Longa and its vicinity, reported Mawe from this frontier township, "a sufficient force is always at hand to repel the savages; who, no longer daring to attack openly, now have often recourse to stratagem." The Botocudo had learned to apply in combat "arts requisite for catching the wild animals on which they subsist." Their methods were numerous:

Sometimes they render themselves invisible by tying branches and young trees about them, and fix their bows imperceptibly, so that, when a poor negro or white happens to pass near them, they seldom miss their aim. At other times they rub themselves with ashes and lie on the ground, or make pit-falls, in which they place pointed stakes, and cover them with twigs and leaves.

Rather than confront those with firearms, which in any case were neither plentiful nor reliable and "frequently altogether useless," the Botocudo fled into the forest, forcing soldiers to resort to unconventional tactics:

It sometimes, though rarely, happens that the soldiers surprise the aborigines, in which case no combat takes place; the latter run away as speedily as possible; and their pursuers, taking vengeance for injuries sustained, seldom give quarter. Those whom they make prisoners they are obliged to tie hand and foot, and carry on a pole to a place of security: if any one of them be loosed but for a moment, he bursts away, and flees into the woods like a tiger, leaving his pursuers behind.[62]

As in the case of Amerindian societies ranging from the Iroquois and Blackfoot, to the Comanche, Caribs, and Araucanians, ample reason exists to conclude that the natives of the Eastern Sertão devised their military methods not independently, as pristine cultural practice, but as a response to the futility of conducting open battles against gun-toting Europeans.[63] As Indians adjusted their tactics, and as Portuguese troops refashioned theirs accordingly, the process of transculturation quickened, rather than faltered, in the midst of military confrontation.

The fact that such conflict persisted after the most active phase of the war attests to the limits of military mobilization even when such action had full royal support. The creeping uncertainty of marching through dense tropical forests, which negated the advantage of firearms, left officers and their soldiers in a constant state of dread. Such was the case of an expedition led by Lieutenant João do Monte da Fonseca, commander of the second of what were ultimately seven army detachments deployed to patrol the Eastern Sertão in fulfillment of the 1808 declaration. It is instructive to trace the fate of this expedition to gain a better understanding of indigenous tactics.

Ordered to explore and attempt to navigate the Muriaé River from its headwaters in Minas Gerais to its confluence with the Paraíba River in the captaincy of Rio de Janeiro, Fonseca embarked with his soldiers on July 5, 1812.[64] Almost immediately, one of the expedition's canoes was destroyed when it plunged over a waterfall, dumping its load of ammunition and delaying the party eleven days while soldiers fashioned a replacement canoe in the field. When travel resumed on July 17, Fonseca's own canoe was swamped descending another falls, soaking the expedition's food supply. Nine days later, more canoes were shattered at still another falls, forcing a further delay to construct new vessels. On August 7, the soldiers got underway once more but only briefly. Attempting to descend another rapids, one of the boatmen had his leg crushed. The required amputation took place in camp before fellow soldiers carried him out of the forest on a hammock. In the meantime, another detachment, under the command of Lieutenant José Caetano da Fonseca, joined the ill-fated party.

On August 18, as the combined expedition recovered from the near loss of yet another canoe, José Fonseca spotted a lone Indian. The field commander shouted, pinpointing the man's position for his troops. Before they could react, the man dove into the river, swam the strong current, and disappeared on the far bank. The following evening, their caution heightened, the soldiers pitched camp along a trail used by the "savages," eventually identified in the expedition diary as Puri. João Fonseca sent out a patrol of seven soldiers in search of the enemy. Shortly thereafter, he discovered an Indian scout crouching along the riverbank. Spotting the same interloper, a foot soldier guarding the canoes fired twice. The first shot sent the native diving to the ground, perhaps wounded. The second shot, aimed at other Indians who rushed to his aid, missed its targets but struck and killed two of the dogs at their sides. Meanwhile, the patrol returned to report that they had found a group of deserted cabanas, which led them to surmise that the "barbarians" were lying in ambush.

The next day, August 20, the expedition proceeded downstream with great trepidation. They narrowly survived another stretch of rapids. Just as one of the canoes emerged from the torrent, seeking the safety of the nearest bank, an arrow struck one of its crew. A quickly formed patrol plunged into the forest to retaliate but the Indians had already dispersed. Increasingly agitated, fearing further attacks ahead, Lieutenant João Fonseca ordered some of his troops to march along the riverbank, watching for the first signs of resistance, while the remainder guided the boats downstream. The tactic did not prevent another soldier from being hit by an arrow. Again the commander sought revenge, dividing the troops into three groups in hopes of surprising their elusive foes by converging on them from several directions. Without being spotted, soldiers manning the first of these patrols discovered Indians lying in ambush just as the second patrol was about to walk into the trap. Gunfire followed, but only one Indian was killed. Soldiers seized his weapons and cut off his ears as trophies. The third patrol, João Fonseca's reported, "had even happier results." After "discovering the encampment of these barbarians," the soldiers waited for nightfall. As the Indians were "dancing unsuspectingly," presumably illuminated by the light of their campfires, the patrol attacked, killing seven, taking four prisoners, and putting the rest to flight.

Advancing farther down the Muriaé River, the expedition spied smoke in the distance on August 26 and braced for another ambush. Leaving their canoes under guard and proceeding by land, they came upon more deserted cabanas.

ILLUSTRATION 7.4. European visitors observe a Puri ritual dance, ca. 1822. The most deadly attacks on Brazil's Eastern Indians caught them unawares in their encampments, usually at night or at dawn
SOURCE: Rugendas, *Voyage pittoresque*. Biblioteca Nacional, Rio de Janeiro.

The sentinel left at the boats was the first to spot a "barbarian," an archer poised to shoot, but the soldier managed to fire first, forcing the Indian and his companions nearby to flee. Soldiers killed two more dogs belonging to the Puri. Finally, four days later, the expedition discovered evidence of a timber-cutting operation, the first sign of settlement advancing up the river valley from the coast. On September 1, soldiers verified the presence of settlers, reaching a sugar plantation. In total, over the final 60 kilometers of the Muriaé between its lower falls and its confluence with the Paraíba River, Fonseca counted 24 ranches, the majority of them newly established, including 17 with sugar mills. Noting the presence of substantial river traffic and trade, the lieutenant categorized the zone as a "new colony," a telling description given that he was emerging from Indian territory.[65] Indians in the zone were contending with settlers encroaching from the coast as well as the interior.

The outcome of the expedition's almost two months in the forest could hardly be termed decisive. Soldiers had navigated the Muriaé but had not demonstrated it to be, as Fonseca admitted with substantial understatement, "accommodatingly navigable." Had the more than one dozen waterfalls and rapids presented the only barrier, the commander might have emerged from the forest more sanguine. The land along both banks appeared fertile and the rock fragments he examined along the way promised alluvial gold. The problem, as Fonseca saw it, was that the Muriaé watershed remained "infested with Puri."

Tenaciousness of this sort, half a century after settlers and the state began coordinated attempts to secure portions of the Eastern Sertão, requires a reconsideration of the standard narratives of doomed native resistance. It also demands that close attention be paid to the adjustments both sides made in what became the routines of violence. Fonseca's predisposition to attack these Indians whenever possible leaves no doubt that, although the declaration of war pertained to the Botocudo, not the least hesitation existed about killing the Puri as well. Such behavior draws into question the repeated claim that the Botocudo were somehow fiercer, more savage, and thus more justifiably targets of official violence. Or to put this differently, any direct native resistance whatsoever warranted armed retaliation. Moreover, officials claimed that barbarous conduct was the target of Portuguese military maneuvers. In Fonseca's account, identifying other objectives is easy enough. These aims included gaining access to trade routes linking Minas Gerais to the coast, to land that promised agricultural and pastoral profits, and to elusive but always beckoning gold deposits. For their part, the Puri continued to impede the exploitation of these resources, even after the 1808 mobilization, just as the Botocudo did farther north. Using techniques carefully tailored to achieve the greatest effect with the least lost of life against an enemy that behaved in discernable ways and created specific tactical opportunities, Indians continued to impose significant restraints on declared military objectives and their attendant operations. The Puri, Botocudo, and others continued to defy the colonial order that military action was intended to impose. As frustration along with outrage mounted in the face of a conquest denied, the conflict took on a more foreboding aspect. The ongoing stalemate provoked ever greater excesses, especially when soldiers successfully applied the skulking, highly mobile, guerrilla-like methods learned, at least as Europeans imagined the tutelage process, from the Indians themselves.

Retaliation

As the Muriaé River expedition's final deadly ambush under the cover of darkness suggests, the inconclusive character of most official military action in the Eastern Sertão should not veil its occasionally devastating impact. Although Indians could frequently evade forest patrols and occasionally inflict significant damage of their own—although they could terrorize settlers into fleeing settled lands—they could not ultimately sustain their struggle to control the coastal forests. This truth hardly seems necessary to state. By the 1820s, as decades of violent conflict took their toll, the ability of Brazil's eastern Indians to oppose colonization with collective force had begun to deteriorate, which is not to say it had vanished, nor to discount the potency of other forms of resistance.[66] However, in the midst of the sustained conflict of the eighteenth and early nineteenth centuries, the persistence of native opposition increasingly dismayed those determined to secure the forests for safe settlement. From the lowest foot soldier to the highest-ranking captaincy officers, military men questioned and then refashioned unsuccessful methods in response to native intransigence. The result was the application of wilderness tactics that mirrored not only the practical methods adopted by Indians but also the inclemency that, according to the Portuguese, gave such methods their effect.

As is by now evident, lusophone colonization of the Eastern Sertão and aggression against its native occupants cannot be attributed to a dramatic change of strategy in 1808 when Prince Regent João declared open war on the Indians of this zone. By then, settlers and the state had applied violence in a determined fashion for a full half-century. In the mid-1760s, Governor Silva, the first captaincy leader to order systematic military action to counter Indian raiding to the east of the mining district, had grappled with the attendant tension between offensive and defensive action. This tension explains the apparent contradiction in the orders he issued field commanders to "make the Indians peaceful and reduce them to obedience . . . seeking to do so by means of kindness and gentleness, without using force, except in cases of necessary defense, should the rebellion of the said Indians make [force] indispensable in order to submit them to the aforementioned obedience and to Christianity."[67] When they rejected this "soft approach," the governor authorized his officers to "strike back at the offensive and declared war" that he said the Indians had initiated.[68]

This colonizing discourse, including the notion that Indians brought conquest on themselves, demands skepticism. Although these Indians produced no written record of their own, they did leave important clues to the influence they exerted on regional territorial incorporation. Despite the self-reflexive vituperations of field commanders, governors, and, finally, the prince regent, Portuguese sources document the changes that Indians forced in settlement patterns and Crown and captaincy policy. To disregard such changes is to underestimate the strength of indigenous resistance. Specifically in military operations, this transformation occurred at the highest strategic levels, leading Governor Silva, the prince regent, and a procession of officials over the intervening decades to forsake what they liked to term the Crown's peaceful approach and instead take up direct, offensive action.

In the field, tactical changes paralleled strategic ones. Like officers everywhere, field commanders in Minas Gerais preferred to engage in battles they were sure to win. Indigenous tactics of the kind classified as guerrilla warfare during a later period severely hampered the effectiveness of troops, as the account of Fonseca's Muriaé River expedition attests. This was true no matter how well-armed and adequately supplied soldiers were, and often they were neither. Officers found themselves compelled to practice ambush techniques of their own, perfected as assiduously as those employed by Indians, techniques that were otherwise anathema to European notions of honorable military engagement.[69] As one commander of the 1770s put it, victory in the sertão depended on retraining troops in the combat tactics of Indians "whose formula consists in ambushes and encirclements at appropriate times of the day."[70] In the 1810s, Maximilian observed this change, noting that only through "frequent practice" had soldiers learned to counter the Botocudo effectively in the forests. Even so, they "all confess that the Botocudos are far more expert hunters, and better acquainted with the forest than themselves; hence the greatest precaution is requisite in these engagements and enterprises in the woods."[71]

One early successful action was reported in 1769 with evident satisfaction by Cuieté's Vicar Nunes. While traveling in the vicinity of that frontier outpost, Nunes happened on a large number of Botocudo (he called them Amborés) encamped along a nearby stream. Without revealing himself, the priest sent out messengers by canoe, bearing word of the discovery to a nearby village in which so-called "domesticated" Indians lived, receiving food, clothing, and agricultural implements from the captaincy government. Apprised of the news, Captain Guimarães set out with 27 Indians. With an inconsistency of terms common to the frontier and its ambiguous social circumstances, the vicar identified these natives as "tame . . . warriors." By "tame," he meant their subordination to the state, not their unwillingness to fight, and Guimarães would exploit their expertise in moving about and conducting combat in the forest. The party captured 32 Botocudo, among them men, women, and children. They left behind three dead and an unspecified number of injured.[72]

How such successes were achieved can be gleaned from cases in which officers described surprising Indians in their encampments. By the tone in which the incidents were reported and the equanimity with which captaincy governors received the news, such ambushes came to be considered part of accepted military practice rather than misdeeds to be concealed, punished, or even reprimanded. Although officials registered no sense of contradiction, these actions clearly departed from the avowedly benevolent purposes of Crown indigenous policy.

Another such incident in 1769 occurred after the Count of Valadares ordered Captain Antônio Cardoso de Souza and the soldiers comprising his bandeira to explore the Doce River basin. Souza's precise orders would later come under scrutiny when he was accused of opening unauthorized routes through the forest for personal gain, that is, for plotting to move untaxed contraband into or out of the settled mining district or perhaps out of the forest itself. He claimed to have construed his orders as authorization to descend the length of the river after first exploring its tributaries. Among other tasks, he was to seek out "vestiges of trails, either new or old," opened by smugglers.[73]

The members of the expedition found nothing of interest, Souza reported, except the "many roads and trails of the fierce and malevolent Botocudo," whom his men twice engaged in combat. He provided few details about the first of these clashes but he described the second, more heated battle at length. Traversing a region of "rugged sertões through which the fierce Botocudo continually roamed," the expedition approached the Ilha da Esperança at what would later come to mark the official border dividing the captaincies of Minas Gerais and Espírito Santo. From a distance, soldiers noticed the smoke of Botocudo fires. Approaching within a few kilometers and then scouting ahead, they ascertained that the Indians had paused on their way north. Delayed by the arduous task of crossing the turbulent Doce River, they had fashioned wooden rafts from fallen trees. Careful to conceal themselves, the soldiers withdrew to an island less than two kilometers away and then marched within range of attack after nightfall.

As dawn broke, they moved to surround the sleeping Botocudo when, suddenly, the howling of dogs broke the silence. It was an unexpected betrayal. Alerted to the impending assault, hoping that the dwindling darkness would save them, the Indians snapped up their bows and arrows and began to disperse into the surrounding forest. Fearing disaster should they gain the protection of the woods, Souza decided to act. "God came to our aid," he wrote afterward, noting that more than 20 Indians died in the attack. Others escaped in random dashes through a break in the circle of fire, leaving the soldiers with only six prisoners—a woman and her three children, along with two other youngsters, both judged to be seven or eight years old. The uneven character of this battle was evident in its results: Souza expressed "great happiness" that "not one of our group was endangered."

As far as the commander was concerned, the battle was not over. From evidence left in the Botocudo encampment and along the trails on which they fled, he surmised that a great number of natives were present to the south, perhaps near the headwaters of the Guandu River. Emboldened, Souza determined to pursue these Indians to stop them from harassing residents of Cuieté and neighboring districts, where they had caused "numerous deaths," forcing area residents to "abandon their farms." He decided to "penetrate all of the forests" along the Guandu River until reaching its source, to "destroy any encampments that we may find," as well as to search for gold, "which they say exists in abundance along the sources and streams of the said river." However, his weary soldiers would accept neither cajoling nor outright commands. Forced to bow to their objections, he agreed to delay the new mission until he could supply them with fresh provisions.

Given the challenges of forest combat, why Minas officials—increasingly agitated about ongoing native opposition after the beginning of the nineteenth century—sought unequivocal royal support for fighting Indians not only with Indian methods but with Indians themselves is easy to understand. For instance, the Mariana town council insisted that "the defense of our colonists along the frontier of the sertão" could be guaranteed only by establishing a line of presidios manned by native hunters and soldiers. Such detribalized Indians were "the most appropriate ones to prevent the hostilities of the Puris and Botocudos."[74] Against these two "ferocious nations," the more sedentary Coropó and Coroado were considered, in the words of Padre Manoel de Jesus Maria, who after more than 30 years was still active in attempts to convert them, "the best guard[s]" in the captaincy's southeastern wilderness and "the best soldiers and boatmen for the navigation and defense of the Pomba and Paraíba Rivers." As Vicar Nunes' 1769 report made clear, field officers had made use of such "ethnic soldiers" from the earliest stages of their move into the Eastern Sertão, a tactic common to tribal zones targeted for colonial intrusion.[75]

"Tame Indians" enlisted as backlands soldiers participated in an 1802 ambush that seems to have been particularly bloody. Quartermaster Duro, the commander of the garrison established along the Doce River by Governor Bernardo José de Lorena, led a punitive bandeira consisting of 42 soldiers, including an unspecified number of natives, dispatched from Antônio Dias Abaixo.[76] Descending the Santa Barbara River (formerly the Piracicaba),[77] reaching the small settlement of Alegre, not far from the river's confluence with the Doce, Duro left part of his company behind to guard the expedition's canoes. Proceeding through the forest with 34 soldiers, he discovered eight abandoned native encampments that he estimated sheltered 60 to 70 Botocudo. Following a trail leading still farther into the forest, the company spotted the enemy one evening encamped beneath a high ridge. The soldiers concealed their presence throughout the night.

At dawn they attacked, managing first to slip "almost inside the huts" of the Botocudo before opening fire. Duro coolly noted that the soldiers demonstrated superior marksmanship. Everything was proceeding as planned when residents of Alegre, having secretly followed Duro's men into the forest, apparently accustomed to meting out punishment themselves, opened fire from the periphery of the battle. As a result, Duro's soldiers came under fire themselves. The commander screamed at the civilians to stop shooting but could not be heard above the fray. Many of the Indians, despite being surprised in their sleep, located their bows and managed to "shoot many arrows," although none struck its target. A corporal involved in the fight was "seized" by a wounded "savage." Commended by Duro for his particular bravery, he had to stab his assailant ten or twelve times before the latter finally fell dead.

Had it not been for the settlers' firing wildly, reported the quartermaster to Governor Lorena, "I certainly would have had the pleasure of sending Your Excellency a few live prisoners, even if only children." This he promised to do on another occasion. He had to content himself instead with forwarding other items: 67 arrows, six bows, and one knife. For live prisoners, he had to substitute pieces of dead ones: of the "various ears" cut from Indian victims and carried back to Alegre, Duro sent just one by way of courier to prove that "I have not failed in what I promised."[78] Finally, he ordered his troops to destroy the remaining captured weapons and to burn everything else. The success led Duro to request more "tame Indians" than those already being employed because they were particularly skilled in tracking and surrounding the nomadic Botocudo.[79]

In addition to the use of indigenous troops, other clues in the sources point to a convergence of native and Portuguese methods. For instance, the dogs noted by Fonseca, Souza, and others hint at the transcultural dynamism of frontier warfare. Although unmentioned or even explicitly denied as culturally compatible in later ethnographic literature, the custom of keeping dogs was adopted by these Indians evidently to pick up the scent of invaders and foil attempted ambushes. "The Indians are sometimes warned of the approach of the soldiers by their dogs and pigs, and then all of them flee—women, children, and the men themselves," observed the German artist Johann Moritz Rugendas, who visited a number of frontier presidios during his travels in Brazil between 1822 and 1825. Tellingly, when the officer and Indian expert Guido Tomás Marlière wrote a Botocudo vocabulary in 1833, he noted that the Indians had no word of their own for dog but rather employed the Portuguese word *cão*.[80] Field commanders like Souza and Fonseca overcame the disadvantage at which they conventionally fought in the forest by employing techniques they borrowed, or believed they were borrowing, from the enemy; the Botocudo and Puri, adopting this European custom, escaped greater losses by doing the same.

The use of ambushes, native soldiers, and domesticated dogs were not the only examples of cultural borrowings on both sides. Explaining his inability to pursue the Botocudo still deeper into the forest, Captain Souza noted that his men lacked provisions because so many natives had passed through the region that it was "barren of all forms of food," including wild game, hearts of palm, and other comestibles. Despite frequent denunciations of Botocudo cannibalism, of an enemy Souza described as "habituated since their creation to eat us," the Portuguese found themselves relying on the same sources of forest foods as their adversaries. While the soldiers resorted to native subsistence practices, the Indians turned to European manufactured goods. At the Botocudo encampment he attacked, Souza collected a cache of tools belonging to settlers, confirming accusations of thievery. Lieutenant Fonseca offered greater detail on a similar discovery. When his soldiers surveyed the native encampment they ambushed, they found what Fonseca described as a small farm. The patrol destroyed not only cabanas but also planted fields and returned from the action "weighed down with spoils." The captured items included machetes, knives, and hoes, bearing the identifying marks of local settlers and presumed stolen.[81] These Puri were apparently not precisely the isolated, primitive hunter-gatherers commonly portrayed in sources of the time and in later scholarly literature. European manufactured goods and even their application in small-scale agriculture had spread deeply into the forests, as might be expected given continuing native attacks on colonists and their property. These attacks not only represented resistance but also provisioned an indigenous raiding economy. Whether fighting settlers or troops, Indians did not cling to their pre-contact customs but responded to changing frontier circumstances, including the cultural and economic reconfigurations that access to such goods implied. The warring parties came to depend on the same basic provisions. Both resorted to hunting and gathering. Both used European goods. Moreover, these adaptations and borrowings were an outgrowth of, not counter to, the hostile relations that dominated the region during the period under study.

Such exploits by soldiers in the field offer a closer glimpse at the unremittingly violent character of encounters with the native inhabitants of the Eastern Sertão, especially those that occurred at the heart of Indian territory, beyond the fringe of advancing settlement. While documenting a determination to root out native resistance, these incidents also reemphasize that this resistance, whether against settlers or soldiers, persisted and remained potent enough to force changes in military policy and practice. Standard European tactics counted for little against a foe who knew the forest so well. The only significant combat successes reported came in the form of ambushes whose execution undermined all distinctions between the savage and the civilized. Scenes of unrestrained violence provide the starkest evidence of the extent to which those who moved through this zone, colonist and colonized alike, could be transformed even in defense of the norms and values that ostensibly defined their respective societies.

Faced with decade after decade of attacks and counterattacks, of sporadic yet prolonged armed conflict, of hostile acts that never approached the scale of more famous Indian wars but that relied nonetheless on unfettered cruelty, Crown officials, captaincy governors, their soldiers, and the settlers they aimed to protect struggled to find a vocabulary equal to this bloody confrontation. Frontier historians as well have found this dynamic difficult to describe. Having discredited a nationalist tradition that rendered histories of this sort triumphs over savagery, having recognized both the imperatives of conquest and the importance of indigenous agency, more recent scholarship has portrayed the frontier as a zone of cultural interaction. Many scholars now favor terms like *contact zone* or *middle ground* to describe the complex social relationships possible in a contested space, particularly where conquest was delayed or remained partial over long periods of time. But to use such terms in connection with the colonization of Brazil's Atlantic forest would be to speak in euphemisms.[82]

In the context of this protracted, desultory conflict, a more apt formulation would seem to be the "space of death," whose centrality to the colonial project Michael Taussig theorized. As such, the Eastern Sertão, when its combatants clashed, constituted a geographic space in which chaos flourished in proportion to the colonial drive to impose order. A "culture of terror" produced acts of "appalling violence and senseless brutality in a theater of sensual cruelty."[83] Rational explanation and action foundered on fears of dismemberment and cannibalism. Savagery imputed to Indians, born of a general horror of indigenous alterity and the perils of an alien environment, made colonists capable of almost any action, which in turn ensured that Indians would indeed respond savagely. Effective statelessness in a zone encircled by the state but not yet subject to its "enduring monopoly of violence" provided unconstrained latitude for atrocities on both sides.[84] Small-scale and even unsuccessful opposition could provoke ferocious retaliation. If racial hatred did not explain the mundane activities of most colonists as they went about their daily lives, clearing land, harvesting crops, and slowly pressing into the sertão, it figured prominently whenever they perceived a threat from Indians drawing near.

This is not to suggest dispensing with the scholarly concern for frontier negotiation and mediation; to the contrary, what is necessary for a complete explanation here is to extend this concern to the realm of violent acts. The emphasis on cultural interaction must be applied cautiously and appropriately in accordance with the peculiarities of the geographic zone and historical moment in question. It must be flexible enough to make sense of the contempt, coercion, and lethal impulses evident wherever Europeans intruded on indigenous peoples along the colonial frontier. Thus, if terms like *negotiation* and *mediation* are to be used to clarify events in the unconquered space of the Eastern Sertão, they must encompass the fact that armed conflict represented a principal currency of interethnic exchange.

Far from acting in cultural isolation, frontier adversaries appropriated the rules of violent conduct from one another in a realm permeated by fear. Indians found out about axes and guns, but they also discovered the astonishing esteem with which settlers prized their pigs, plates, and silver spurs. These items became easy prey. Where casualties were involved, the viability of entire settlements could be placed in doubt by taking aim not just at landowners but also at slaves, their most valuable and vulnerable asset. Soldiers themselves could be outwitted, outmaneuvered, and disabled one by one, if conditions proved favorable.

The extent to which the native application of such knowledge extended beyond individual clashes cannot be definitively determined. The Botocudo and other groups of the eastern forests had confronted settler incursions from the coast for more than two centuries before advances from the inland mining zone intensified after 1750. Native trails crosscut the eastern forests, permitting communication over a vast territory.[85] As seminomads, the Indians were in a better position than most colonists to understand the regional ramifications of the threat they faced and of the opposition they mounted in response. A dubious logic is therefore required to posit that Indians were ignorant of their actions' broad consequences. What was surely more difficult for them to fathom was the gradual shift in Portuguese policy, whereby resistance once expected, even desired, of them as a means of controlling straying settlers had become all but intolerable as the nineteenth century began.

Settlers and soldiers too, as has been seen, were capable of adjusting to the dictates of frontier conflict in the dense forest. The cycle of violence that resulted would persist until they ultimately shattered the ability of Brazil's eastern Indians to oppose them with organized force. In remote pockets of the Eastern Sertão, final "pacification"—the term that Brazilian officials would come to favor—did not occur until the early twentieth century.[86] Between the 1750s and the 1820s, a period during which Indians largely vanish from the historiography, violence dominated the region as effective conquest remained elusive. Mutual brutality came to constitute cultural commerce, as warring parties found in terror an essential means of communication and exchange.

CHAPTER 8

War

T HE MANEUVERS of soldiers on patrol provide a closer glimpse of the violent character of encounters with the Indians of the Eastern Sertão; however, the relative rarity of direct clashes between soldiers and natives underscores the fact that the primary locus of conflict was not deep in the wilderness but at the edge of colonial settlement, where settlers pushed slowly onto peripheral lands. They did so facing backwards, as it were, with their homesteads, family plots, farms, and livestock operations oriented toward the mining district's settled zones. As frontier land grant recipients who eyed the foodstuffs market as an outlet for slave-based production, or as impoverished subsistence squatters who balked at venturing too far into unprotected areas, they tended to move cautiously outward from towns and parishes onto lands just beyond the edge of established settlements. While they did not act in accordance with the grand schemes of governors and memorialists who imagined them unearthing gold and diamonds hidden deep in the tropical forests, they nevertheless disrupted indigenous territorial prerogatives with every wary step. Accordingly, the most startling testament to indigenous resistance was not the challenge Indians occasionally presented to soldiers dispatched to clear remote areas of hostile natives but the lasting barrier they maintained against tentative settler incursions. Not only did they impede the Portuguese frontier advance well into the nineteenth century but, in many cases reversed it, seizing territory long held or at least claimed by colonists.

Despite their problematic nature as sources, official reports of violent incidents yield substantial evidence of this consequence of indigenous opposition. In addition to the denunciations of attacks on persons and property considered in the previous chapter, another common refrain filled these reports. Native violence, authorities claimed, was not just exacting a heavy toll in terms of casualties and material possessions but was actually forcing the abandonment of numerous Portuguese settlements over entire stretches of the sertão. Fury over this fact, more than any other, repeatedly served to justify the use of retaliatory force. To a certain degree, officials could endure—indeed, were forced by limited government resources to endure—incidents of individual loss, whether civilian or military. However, when indigenous resistance threatened the integrity of territory considered settled and thus integrally part of the colony, they felt compelled to act. Uprooted vassals of the Crown forced to retreat from long-settled outlying areas had to be avenged. Military action was seen as a natural and required response to this affront. Of course, describing the predicament in this way, colonial authorities ignored the fact that fundamentally all settlers were invading and seizing land inhabited for centuries by the indigenous groups accused of hostilities and, more than this, land these groups had once been left to control as unconsulted allies in the attempt to cordon off the inland mining district. What officials labeled Indian aggression is, in many cases, better understood as an indigenous defense of long-held domain.

The sources demand allowing for the possibility that Indians periodically took the offensive, that officials were in fact reacting to attacks on areas settled for such a long time that these places came to be seen not as disputed frontier zones but as previously secured Crown property. Until the end of the eighteenth century, the fact that officials continued to see at least some role for Indians in occupying restricted lands to stem smuggling meant, conversely, that only rarely did they envision all indigenous control of territory as anathema. The use of force became necessary when Indians were perceived as having transgressed this distinction, as having crossed the boundary into land officials considered in possession of the Crown, the captaincy, and the Portuguese vassals who served them.

According to the same logic, considering a further possibility is essential: that Indians had their own military objectives, may have carefully orchestrated their attacks rather than simply engaging in isolated violent outbursts, and, more generally, may have enjoyed far greater success pursuing their territorial imperatives—even in the military sphere—than previously assumed. Throughout the colonial Americas, for that matter, such reframing of standard assumptions might help scholars better explain why seminomadic peoples evaded conquest so effectively—much more so than sedentary native societies. The usual reasons given for their resistance to defeat include their lack of permanent settlements that could be readily dominated, hunting and gathering practices that left no food surplus to be seized by invaders, the ecological constraints of their often marginal lands, great mobility that allowed them to retreat before advancing colonists, and a kin-ordered political economy that placed limits on the organization of labor, left them unprepared to deliver tribute, and inhibited the imposition of an alien centralized power.[1] These factors emphasize negative traits, characteristics non-sedentary societies lacked, and their tendency to react and retreat. The conduct of Brazil's eastern Indians suggests that more dynamic cultural practices were at work, factors that made seminomadic peoples more proactive as historical agents in the control of territory. In addition to their apparently sophisticated assessment of the strengths and weaknesses of frontier slaveholding society discussed in the previous chapter, the Gê-speaking groups of the Eastern Sertão found that many of the same characteristics that helped them defend themselves in remote forests also allowed them to pursue a broader strategy of combating colonists in settled zones long-since incorporated into the colonial realm. To acknowledge that Indians waged a war after their own fashion is to recognize more clearly the extraordinarily disconcerting opposition they mounted to the colonial project. To understand that their actions were, in many cases, effective enough to force colonists into full-scale retreat requires revision of the image of desperately fractured Indian societies rarely able to rise to their own defense.

Like colonists who flouted Crown restrictions on entering the Forbidden Lands, Indians also did not conform to the role the state prescribed for them. They did not stay within the boundaries of their territory as defined by the Crown any more than settlers stayed out. This was the other face of the conflict, as it took shape simultaneously in both colonial and native domain. Moving into Indian territory, settlers drew the captaincy into a war of extermination; crossing the opposite direction into settled zones, Indians reinforced the government's determination while asserting their own claims. The sallies of military expeditions into Indian territory belie insistent attempts to characterize the conflict as a defensive war, yet settlers frequently did find themselves attacked in zones in which Indian resistance genuinely seemed an invasion of colonial territory long ago incorporated. Indians defended themselves from the incursions of soldiers and especially settlers, but their range of tactics also encompassed striking brazenly into the other side of the frontier—that is, at least according to the way that captaincy officials constructed the frontier over time, its boundary advancing ever deeper into the forests.

In this sense, native resistance did not simply slow down the transformation of the region into settled agricultural zones, regional markets, and an imperial realm. The sources point instead to the inescapable conclusion that many sectors of the sertão thus transformed decades earlier fell back into Indian hands, at least temporarily. For government authorities and settlers alike, the ability of Indians to overrun significant expanses of long-settled territory—reversing the progress of the colonial project, striking at the basic underpinnings of both regional and colonial identity—was perhaps the most insistently harrowing threat of all. The forced retreat from areas whose occupation was often legitimized through royal concession, severing the consecrated land grant contract between monarch and vassal, represented a singularly grave and disorienting loss. It forced colonists to recognize that the natives, more than 200 years after explorers first crossed this portion of Portuguese America, still considered these mountains, forests, and river valleys their own, an assumption all the more galling because this land lay scarcely beyond the Atlantic seaboard. Indians thereby exposed as illusory the fundamental colonial assumption that this unsettled territory was merely virgin forest that could be cordoned off or cast open at will, available for the taking on the orders of the governor or Crown. Giving full form to a mélange of other outrages, this reality prompted the final coordinated offensive by Crown and captaincy enshrined in the 1808 declaration of war.

Unsettling the Land

The struggle to hold settled territory dated to the earliest days of the advance on lands to the east of the mining district. During the years before Governor Silva mounted the first military offensive of the mid-1760s, according to the bandeira captain, Antônio Pereira da Silva, settlers in Cuieté had been "routed" three times by "heathen so cruel that their tyranny extends to eating human meat." At the same time, Indians struck at numerous settlements all the way to Santa Rita, "where they had killed and robbed in such a manner that many farms remain deserted."[2] When the inhabitants of Antônio Dias Abaixo and other districts appealed to the governor for help in reclaiming Cuieté, they cited the considerable wealth of the region that had not been exploited out of "fear of the wild Indians of the Botocudo nation." The Botocudo had not only "infested" the region in response to attempts to settle it but had, through violent resistance, forced the withdrawal of "everyone who had transplanted themselves" to the forest mining camp. In their retreat, they had lost all of their possessions.[3] The governor accepted this version of events when he ordered expeditions dispatched to guarantee the exploitation of new mineral wealth.

Even more worrisome was the fact that the reach of Indian attacks extended disconcertingly close to the central settled regions of the captaincy. Indians had killed fazenda owners in such places as Guarapiranga, Xopotó, and Barra Longa. They had also attacked slaves and their foremen, raided cattle, and burned cultivated fields—in short, committing whatever "hostilities their barbarity inspired." They depopulated significant expanses and put at risk much of the periphery of the zone east of Mariana and Vila Rica. Forces had to be dispatched, the governor maintained, to put an end to these losses.[4] Shockingly, land abandoned by settlers included not merely marginal zones, tenuously appropriated by squatters, but tracts conceded by the Crown in the form of sesmarias.[5] As a consequence, in ordering an assault on the Eastern Sertão, Governor Silva argued not primarily for the need to make new territorial gains but to "strike back at the hostilities with which the wild Indians... have endeavored to cause [our] ruin, placing in total consternation the inhabitants of those distances."[6]

By 1766, Silva's initial mobilization had not thwarted such attacks. Residents of Furquim, Barra Longa, and Abre Campo sought government intervention in response to continuing hostilities that left a "great number" of inhabitants "cut off from the farmland they used to have."[7] Indians had perpetrated murder, theft, and arson at fazendas along the Piranga River and, perhaps still more threatening, the Carmo River, which flowed through Mariana before descending into the sertão. Neighboring districts suffered the "abandonment of a great number of... fazendas, mining operations, and fields."[8] Once again, Governor Silva ordered bandeiras into action, citing the temerity displayed by Indians in their "successive and repeated attacks," particularly the daring they demonstrated by "infesting" holdings not far from Vila Rica and Mariana.[9]

Both by the variety of sources and their persistence over time, reports on Indian successes in holding and even gaining territory represented more than merely the contrivance of those who wished to invade their territory (see Table 8.1). In 1769, well after the attempt to secure Cuieté had begun, Captain Campelo complained that progress was being hampered by "the great multiplicity of heathen in this sertão." "At every step," he noted, settlers and soldiers "run up against immense encampments [of Indians]," presenting a formidable barrier to the peopling of the region and to making it useful to the Crown.[10] For his part, Captain Silva reported that local inhabitants in or on the edge of Indian territory remained petrified and had not returned to take up their abandoned habitations. "Ultimately," he lamented, "everything is just as it was in the beginning."[11] Campelo submitted an impressive list of settlements subject to attack by the Botocudo and the Puri. In addition to Cuieté, Santa Rita, and Abre Campo, the list included "many deserted farms and solitary settlements" along

TABLE 8.1

Objectives of Indian Attacks on Settlers

Settler Target	Number	Pct
Established settlement	32	56%
New settlement	25	44%
Total	57	100%

SOURCE: See Table 6.1.

rivers and streams all the way from the western bank of the Casca to the eastern bank of the Guandu, and from the southern tributaries of the Doce River to zones lying beyond its northern banks.[12]

None of the intensive military operations concentrated between 1765 and 1773, nor subsequent actions over the following decades, would undermine the Indians' ability to take the offensive, at least from time to time. Indian gains were reported throughout the rest of the eighteenth century. During the administrations of governors Noronha, Rodrigo José de Meneses, Mendonça, and Lorena, the Botocudo and other groups continued to attack fazendas along the Rio Doce and its tributaries, forcing their abandonment. Resistance also was fierce in southern Bahia during this period. Crown officials reported that settlers fled from territory long occupied in the vicinity of the Rio das Contas because of Pataxó raids.[13]

During Noronha's tenure in the late 1770s, the fatal attack by the Puri near Abre Campo provided more than the usual amount of detail concerning setters' struggle to hold territory. Even so, the incident again underscores the limits on any precise understanding of native grievances. However the Puri may have rationalized their actions, their point of view was silenced by strident denunciations followed by the official preoccupation with organizing a retaliatory expedition. This was one of a series of attacks that local officials reported they had insufficient military force to quell. The incident occurred on February 13, 1777.[14] A little more than four kilometers from the presidio of Abre Campo, the Puri attacked the fazenda of the well-to-do landholder, Manoel Pinto Guimarães. The attack came after several weeks of mounting Indian hostilities in the zone. The Puri had repeatedly raided the settler's livestock and had destroyed fields he had planted. On the day of the attack, Guimarães had been working with his slaves and some farmhands in his fields when he was killed without warning, his chest pierced by an arrow, one of a "mass of arrows" shot by the "heathen Puri." One of the farmhands was also struck and wounded. A local commander said many others would have been killed had one of Guimarães' slaves not managed to shoot and kill the leader of the attacking band. Although they outnumbered the settlers, the Puri retreated on seeing their headman slain, an event believed to have saved the lives not only of the field workers but of the rest of those living at the fazenda, one of only two in the region.

The attack and the ongoing raids around the presidio signaled real vulnerability. José do Vale Vieira, identified in the sources as the presidio's conservator, requested permission to arm at his own expense six men to guard his own fazenda and to oppose the Puri in the forests. Decrying the "cruelty of that inhuman nation," Governor Noronha assented, admitting that the presidio in its current state presented no effective barrier to the Puri. He called the maintenance of the presidio a matter of the utmost importance to the security of the captaincy's settled nucleus. He feared the Puri would seize the initiative and "penetrate" the region encompassing the entire expanse between Abre Campo and the Piranga River, attacking fazendas and townships already established there, placing at risk the "abundance of foodstuffs" with which these settlements provided Mariana and its environs. Not only was a certain amount of gold being extracted from the region, the presidio was meant to protect "the many fazendas that are to be found inhabited and cultivated in the vicinity of the Casca River." Were these fazendas to be deserted, the native advance westward would be far easier. The task of apportioning the slain man's property among his heirs should be conducted with the region's territorial integrity in mind, Noronha cautioned. Part of the "new and useful settlement" that formed around the presidio, his fazenda should remain undivided even if inheritance law dictated otherwise. Authorities should not permit Guimarães' heirs to remove the slaves that cultivated the land and worked the mill at the fazenda because doing so would place the property's future in jeopardy and with it, the future of the settlement.

Absent from the agitated official letters sent back and forth in the wake of this attack was mention of just how tenuous the settlement of Abre Campo had been for decades. It was first occupied in 1734 when the explorer Matias Barbosa da Silva assembled a group of 70 associates and 50 slaves, led a bandeira to the site, attacked the Botocudo, and constructed the presidio. Under continuous native threat, however, colonists soon evacuated; others returned in 1755. They followed Vieira, who would later seek to avenge Guimarães' death. Opening a horse trail to the site of the abandoned presidio, Vieira claimed to be the region's first conqueror, founder, and permanent settler. Over the next decade, he and others were twice expelled by Indian attacks, the second time witnessing their homes and two chapels burned to the ground; however, each time they returned in greater numbers until in 1770, Vieira finally declared the settlement established.[15] The concern over Guimarães' land suggests authorities were not yet convinced.

Elsewhere, settlers intermittently found themselves "reduced to the necessity of vacating... their fazendas, abandoning them and the furniture and comforts that the property provided them" when "invaded by the Botocudo Indians." As noted, the largest and deadliest attack uncovered in the sources occurred in 1794 when a reported 2,000 Botocudo killed 48 persons in Santana dos Ferros. Panicked settlers informed the Viscount of Barbacena that "the strength of those dwelling there is not enough... to resist the invasion."[16] To the south, where resistance similarly remained fierce, more than 50 fazendas had been "entirely evacuated," while others were on the verge of abandonment in the early 1790s.[17] Along the Onça Grande and Onça Pequeno Rivers, settlers at more than 70 fazendas established in the wake of Governor Noronha's drive to settle the region in the 1770s were forced in 1795 and 1796 to "abandon their establishments to escape the voraciousness of the Botocudo."[18] To the north, the Botocudo continued to prevent exploration along the São Mateus River. In 1780, Rocha wrote that discoveries of major deposits of gold and precious stones could not be exploited. "These riches are still yet to be, for lack of anyone willing to risk the conquest of the barbarous Botocudo heathen, dominant in those sertões."[19]

By 1792, in and around Peçanha, the Maxakali (including members of the Monoxó, Panhame, Makoni, and Capoxó subgroups) and the Malali had for four or five years been converging on settled lands, apparently in search of Portuguese protection. Founded long before in 1758 at the site of a village of Monoxó Indians, Peçanha attracted migrants from Vila do Príncipe and its environs. Some of the Indians there intermingled with the settlers; others remained at a distance in outlying lands. The latter were now forced to abandon these lands as they were overrun by the Botocudo, who were themselves being pushed north by other settlers. "Without the forces to make [the Botocudo] go back" into more distant forests, the Maxakali and Malali were now fleeing the sertão in unprecedented numbers, according to Peçanha's priest and schoolmaster, João Pedro de Almeida, who made an appeal for military intervention to Vila do Príncipe's town council that was forwarded to the governor. Settlers in Peçanha were increasingly intimidated by this aggressive northward migration of the Botocudo, "the most barbarous nation that there is in this New World." Their hostile advance, the priest argued, was keeping settlers from developing a region rich in gold.[20]

After the beginning of the nineteenth century, Indian territorial assertiveness did not abate. In 1801, local authorities reported that the Botocudo had "killed all of the residents" of fazendas along the "frontiers" (*fronteiras*) of the region between the Suaçuí Grande and Doce Rivers. The Botocudo did not hesitate to strike at the very center of villages established by settlers. Officials feared they would succeed in "unsettling" (*despovoando*) the region. Already the flight of settlers was causing "the abandonment of what had cost them many years of work and zeal by the sweat of their brow in new lands."[21] In 1806, parishioners in Santana do Alfié appealed to the regional vicar to send them a priest to tend to the religious needs of the village, which had been all but deserted out of fear of Indians surrounding the settlement.[22] On the eve of the war's declaration—according to the high-ranking captaincy official, Diogo Pereira Ribeiro de Vasconcelos—natives still barred the exploration for and exploitation of mineral wealth over a vast stretch of territory, including the Doce, Jequitinhonha, and São Mateus River valleys. The hostility of the Botocudo and other groups, he wrote, "blocked the continuous work that could be carried out in search of precious metals and stones over the space of more than fifty leagues [330 km] that stretch from the zone in which one works without risk [eastward] to the sea."[23] Measured as such, that expanse essentially corresponded to the entire distance between Vila Rica and the coast.

To reemphasize the key issue here, the curious thing about many of these instances of native violence is that they occurred in places settled long before by colonists, places where initial hostilities had long since subsided. Although Vasconcelos portrayed a sharp delineation between the captaincy's settled areas and the territory dominated by natives to the east, no such line existed any more in practice for Indians or settlers. The conflict at places like Cuieté constituted one end of a continuum. An isolated mining camp deep in Indian territory, Cuieté was first settled nearly two decades before the bandeira offensive of the late 1760s. From the onset of settlement until the 1808 war, it was never free from attack. Abre Campo was another such place. Although less than half Cuieté's distance from the urban centers of Mariana and Vila Rica, it was nevertheless another of the most isolated settlements in the Eastern Sertão. There settlers also did not easily establish themselves after initial exploration and conquests. From the 1730s to the 1770s, native resistance remained a fact. Peçanha was yet another remote settlement subject to the perennial threat of Indian hostilities from the time it was founded in the late 1750s until the war of 1808.

However, these distant outposts were far from the only places where authorities and settlers struggled to establish colonial dominion long after initial settlement. Indians turned their opposition on long-established settlements, raiding fazendas and mining operations in much more accessible places occupied for still longer periods, sometimes dating back to the beginning of the eighteenth century. Understanding this phenomenon requires close attention to the chronology and geography of the frontier conflict, aided by a series of historical geographies produced by local authorities beginning in the eighteenth century.[24] These compendia catalogued town, parish, and village names; listed the distances of these places from administrative centers; and, in many cases, provided dates of their initial exploration, settlement, and official recognition. When such information is matched with the sources documenting Indian resistance, a picture emerges of Indians combating settlers who were seemingly secure in previously incorporated zones. For example, sources from the second half of the eighteenth century mentioned attacks at the following sites that had first been settled years before: São Bartolomeu, just 15 kilometers from Vila Rica, a parish since 1716; Guarapiranga, first settled in the 1690s; Barra Longa, settled by the 1730s; Xopotó, established at the beginning of the eighteenth century; Furquim, a parish since 1724; Pomba, explored repeatedly during the first half of the eighteenth century; Itabira, settled during the first decade of the eighteenth century; and Antônio Dias Abaixo, settled as early as 1706 and quickly developed into a major mining center. Established later but nonetheless subject to attack decades afterward were townships like Santana de Alfié, settled in the early 1750s, and Santana dos Ferros, settled in the 1770s.

The finer details of settlement patterns remain inevitably vague in many of these outlying regions. Only in two of the cited cases—Abre Campo in the 1760s and Santana dos Ferros in the 1790s—did sources speak clearly of town centers being overrun. Moreover, what appears to have been a brazen attack on a long-standing settlement might in fact have been a defensive move by Indians against a few landholders or squatters attempting to enlarge their claims into unsettled forests on the outermost edge of such a settlement. Even in such cases, however, the attacks occurred in areas perceived as dangerously near to the established centers of longstanding parishes and townships. This was not a frontier that advanced rapidly, implacably, and in a single direction—toward the east. The boundary between Portuguese and indigenous peoples changed slowly and unevenly. Deep incursions into Indian territory occurred in some places, long standoffs and even reversals in others. With surprising frequency, settlers found themselves expelled from zones they had long before come to consider their own.

Enough evidence of settlers withdrawing from such areas survives to confirm that even as the Portuguese increased their military presence in the sertão, conquest remained a two-way process. As settlers and bandeiras pushed into new zones in search of undiscovered wealth, Indians forcibly held many of their advances in check and carried out raids on settlements in territory they once lost. As such, the causal chain of frontier conquest became far more fluid and complex than the mere collapse of seminomadic societies in the face of relentless settler and state incursions. Instead, a chronic state of conflict developed in which the Portuguese repeatedly failed to gain the upper hand, even in the midst of military mobilization. In some cases, a dynamic diametrically opposed to the customary one was at work, as the feeble existence of many settlements in the Eastern Sertão provided Indians an opening to make new territorial gains of their own.

The slanted, incomplete character of the documentary evidence—all of it written from the colonial perspective—irrevocably complicates and, in many instances, renders futile the effort to reconstruct the conduct of the nomadic indigenous peoples of the Eastern Sertão. Nevertheless, the sources have left enough traces to move beyond simplistic assessments of the fate of these native populations. Indians acted neither as the irrational savages the colonists portrayed them to be nor as mere victims overwhelmed by internal territorial expansion. Nor did the incorporation of the Eastern Sertão ever appear an accomplished fact in the eighteenth and early nineteenth centuries—not to settlers, not to the state, and not to natives. For more than half a century, the Indians answered lusophone encroachment along the periphery of the inland mining district, having already done the same for much longer along the coast, with strategies that stymied the colonial advance, insisting on the maintenance of a territory large enough to ensure their survival. Dispensing with the conventional view of the late colonial period is thus necessary. Inherited from the nineteenth century, this view holds that Indians "had ceased to be a threat to European occupation of Brazil." To quote a particularly prominent scholar, they had "become insignificant, anachronistic and rather pathetic."[25]

The extent and success of Indian offensive action are important not only for what they say about the Indians but also about the colonists. This resistance provided whatever justification the Portuguese needed to frame the military actions spanning the second half of the eighteenth century as a defensive necessity. It provided Prince Regent João with all the rationale he required to recast this military strategy once again in 1808 into an openly offensive policy. A regional historian in the 1830s understood the situation as follows: "The hostilities repeatedly committed by the barbarous Aimoré and by the Puri, and the vain efforts practiced to attract them to civilized life, *obliged Dom João*" [emphasis added] to order the governor of Minas Gerais to "launch forth into offensive warfare against the Botocudo, until they could be reduced to the terms of subjection and the state of agricultural or sedentary life" demanded by colonists.[26] By this formulation, Indian aggression alone forced the declaration of war. Forgotten were the decades of provocative actions by authorities and soldiers as they searched for gold and diamonds and the slow but persistent advance of settlers as they pushed slaveholding society eastward into the coastal forests. The prince regent now accepted the view that longstanding, highly effective, and once-desirable native opposition to the presence of colonists in the Forbidden Lands could no longer be tolerated, but he did so without acknowledging that this presence itself had been exacerbating tensions for decades.

From Defensive to Offensive Warfare

Prince Regent João declared war against the Botocudo Indians on May 13, 1808, just three months after arriving in Rio de Janeiro, expelled from Lisbon by Napoleon. By then, an uncompromising military offensive seemed the only answer to the outcry of those who labored unsuccessfully to settle the Eastern Sertão. Addressing the declaration to Governor Melo, the monarch wrote that his determination to act derived from "grave complaints" that had reached the throne about native atrocities throughout the eastern forests of Minas Gerais.

He condemned the "invasions that the cannibal Botocudos [were] practicing daily," especially along the banks of the Doce River and its tributaries. Not only had Indians managed to "devastate all of the fazendas located in those areas," and not only had they "forced many landowners to abandon them at great loss to themselves and to my royal Crown," they also dared to perpetrate "the most horrible and atrocious scenes of the most barbarous cannibalism." They "assassinated" Portuguese and "tame Indians" alike. They opened wounds in their victims and drank their blood. They dismembered them and consumed their "sad remains." Such conduct demonstrated, once and for all, "the uselessness of all human efforts" to civilize the Botocudo, to settle them in villages, and to persuade them "to take pleasure in the permanent advantages of a peaceful and gentle society." As a consequence, the monarch now declared the end of what he termed his policy of "defensive war." He replaced it with one of "just" and "offensive war," a war that would "have no end" until settlers returned to their habitations and the Indians, "moved by just terror," submitted to the rule of law, accepting settled life as "useful vassals," as other Indians before them had done.[27]

To prosecute the war, the governor of Minas Gerais was to deploy six detachments of foot soldiers, each responsible for a particular sector of those lands "infested" by the Botocudo. Selecting soldiers fit for such "hard and rugged" duty, the commanders of these detachments would form "diverse bandeiras" with which they would "constantly, every year during the dry season, enter into the forests" until they had effected the "total reduction of [this] . . . cruel cannibal race." Armed Indians captured in these actions would be considered prisoners of war and subject to a ten-year period of enslavement. They should be kept "in irons," the monarch instructed, if they showed "no sign of having abandoned their atrocities and cannibalism." Commanders would receive additional pay for each year in which they managed to keep the districts under their command free of attack not only by the Botocudo but also "any other wild Indians." Also meriting a bonus would be any commander who "captured and destroyed" more Indians than his fellow officers. Although the decree singled out the Botocudo, the Minas governor was to understand that it pertained to the "reduction and civilization . . . of other Indian races" as well.[28]

A final section of the royal edict dealt with the related matters of exploration, settlement, and development. The monarch ordered the Minas government to secure—again, once and for all—the uninterrupted navigation of the Doce River. Exploration efforts were to be redoubled with reconnaissance parties sent out every three months to examine different segments of the river. The state would now move to "favor those who wish to go to settle those precious gold-bearing lands, abandoned today because of the fear that the Botocudo Indians cause." Settlers would enjoy a ten-year exemption in paying the tithe collected by the government for the church. They would be excused from the payment of all debts owed the Crown for a period of six years. Commanders would distribute among them sesmarias allotted from lands "recovered" from the Botocudo. Furthermore, no taxes would be imposed on goods imported to and exported from the region for a full decade.[29]

How deeply this declaration drew on the past half-century should by now be evident. The language of the edict can be tied to a report by the prince's emissary, Luís Tomás Navarro de Campos. Campos traveled the overland route from Bahia to Rio de Janeiro in April 1808 and conveyed to the monarch the opinion of the militia commander Francisco Alves Tourinho, whose 22 years of experience with the Botocudo and other indigenous groups in southern Bahia led him to conclude that "violence is the most appropriate means of rendering these lands tranquil and fit for settlement."[30] Given that the prince regent issued his edict to the governor of Minas Gerais, however, the influence of increasingly impatient Minas officials must be given primary weight. José Eloi Ottoni called on the Crown as early as 1798 to sponsor a new era of bandeira-led conquest in the Eastern Sertão. Basilio Teixeira Cardoso de Sá Vedra Freire advocated the expulsion of the Botocudo in 1805. Two years later, Diogo Pereira Ribeiro de Vasconcelos stressed the need to open the Doce River to navigation and to secure the region for settlement. To do so, the "hostilities of [the] cannibals" would have to be countered with "sufficient military force," as all previous peaceful overtures had failed. At the beginning of the nineteenth century, Minas officials already referred to state actions in the region as a "war." They had done so as well nearly half a century earlier.[31]

The declaration's language and intent were strikingly similar to official denunciations that framed the conflict from the beginning of its intensification after the middle of the eighteenth century. In the mid-1760s, Governor Silva, the first Minas governor to take systematic military action to counter Indian raiding to the east of the mining district, grappled with the same tension between offensive and defensive action. The field commanders he dispatched to the sertão carried with them orders imbued with this contradictory discourse, directing them, as noted earlier, to "make the Indians peaceful and reduce them to obedience ... seeking to do so by means of kindness and gentleness, without using force, except in cases of necessary defense, should the rebellion of the said Indians make [force] indispensable in order to submit them to the aforementioned obedience and to Christianity."[32] When they refused to respond to this "soft approach," the governor told his officers to "strike back at the offensive and declared war," which he said the Indians had initiated.[33]

These calls to military action invoked the foundational lexicon of Iberian conquest in the Americas. At the same time, they underscore the function of language as "a mere screen for the brutal reality of power," as Stephen Greenblatt observed in writing about Spanish conquests, while providing convincing evidence that "the possession of weapons and the will to use them on defenseless people are cultural matters that are intimately bound up with discourse: with the stories that a culture tells itself, its conceptions of personal boundary and liability, its whole collective system of rules."[34] Both the governor and the prince regent, who consecrated either end of the period under study with bloodshed, portrayed an excruciating passage from reluctance to resolve, justifying violent means for benevolent ends. Both maneuvered across the shifting terrain dividing defensive and offensive action. Both referred to the legal precedent of just war while employing the compassionate vocabulary of kindness, gentleness, and obedience. Words both peaceable and violent coalesced, phrases united in their presumption of Indian subjugation, as authorities articulated evolving territorial ambitions and a colonizing discourse consonant with these aims.

By 1808, the Crown's support for offensive action was already a fait accompli. The Crown empowered the Minas government to conduct offensive warfare against the Botocudo as early as 1801, whereas similar orders went into effect in southern Bahia in 1806. Weeks before receiving the formal 1808 declaration, the Minas governor visited the court in Rio de Janeiro, bearing news of what War Minister Rodrigo de Souza Coutinho, the Count of Linhares, who had struggled with Crown policy regarding the Botocudo since being appointed colonial secretary in 1796, described as a "happy encounter with the Botocudo Indians," in which soldiers already patrolling the Eastern Sertão "had killed many" and taken 13 prisoners. In the process, soldiers also stripped the natives of an "immense plunder" they were said to have robbed from settlers in the vicinity of Ponte Nova. Still earlier, in March, Coutinho responded to reports of Indian hostilities from the town council of Caeté. The war minister made clear that the Crown supported greater diligence in implementing measures not only directed against such "incursions" but also the intent to "destroy" native villages, "if it were not possible to reduce them to some species of civilization." Hostile Indians were to be pursued and forced to flee from "all of our possessions," wrote Coutinho.[35]

The prince regent opened his 1808 declaration by describing acts of indigenous hostility. His account is notable for its portrayal of the Botocudo as brazen aggressors. They did not simply resist incursions into territory they controlled. Far more grievously, they dared to invade areas claimed by the Portuguese and already occupied by settlers. They did not simply prevent future gains but inflicted present losses on past achievements. Given that all of this land had at one time been the exclusive domain of the natives, and for much of the previous century been cordoned off by the Crown so that it would remain impassable, accusations of this sort might seem preposterous. Yet in the context of the regional perspective gradually appropriated by the Crown, the assertion carried real weight. For decades, settlers complained of being forced to abandon territory they came to consider their own. In settlement after settlement, places occupied for 30 years or more, they did in fact lose ground to Indians. As much as any other justification for war, this now stirred the Crown to act.

The prince regent proceeded to accuse the Botocudo of routine cannibalism. As was perennially the case with such accusations, the monarch had little evidence to support this claim. Only after the war was declared did the war minister order the Minas governor to send to the court, under strict security, one Botocudo male and one female "of the same species" to satisfy the monarch's "curiosity to see this cannibal race."[36] The less than conclusive efforts by European naturalists to document the practice would only come in subsequent years. In the past, authorities used the fear of cannibalism to discourage illicit activity by colonists in the Eastern Sertão. The prince regent's action marked the final moment of that era, decades in coming, as changing events slowly transformed Indian savagery from an asset into an outrage in the minds of those who set policy for the region. Now cannibalism came to play its more customary role in colonial conquest, as a legal basis for declaring a just war.[37]

Not only royal rhetoric can be traced back in a direct line to the escalation of conflict between settlers and Indians in Minas Gerais in the 1760s but also the specific material justifications for moving offensively as well as the means proposed to enact such a move. The prince regent's condemnation of native cannibalism, of their nomadism, of their occupation of gold-laden lands, of their uselessness to the Crown and society—all of these issues resonated with the past as did his decision to deploy armed bandeiras to bring a quick resolution to the problem. Even the tax and duty exemptions he granted hearkened back to policies attempted in the 1760s and 1770s. Meanwhile, navigation of the Doce River had been a formal government goal for at least a decade. In effect, the royal declaration of war was modeled throughout on captaincy policies that had been applied over and over again in the Eastern Sertão. More generally, it adhered steadfastly to a resilient colonial vision of the past that looked to the conquest of native domain as the proper function of government and the means to future prosperity.

In the Lair of the Beasts

Even as it drew on well-honed policies and practices, the declaration of war no longer recognized the opposing impulse to keep the Forbidden Lands off-limits in an attempt to monitor Crown subjects and protect precious resources. A dream of employing not only Africans but also Indians as laborers, whether enslaved or free, in a territory now definitively opened to settlement and commerce supplanted concerns about contraband escaping from a mining economy showing no sign of recovery.[38] In this departure from past ambivalence lay the essential innovation that freed the Crown and captaincy government to act with coordinated and unencumbered vigor in securing the unincorporated lands that separated the mining district from the Atlantic.

Accordingly, if continuities abound, they are not the sole guide to understanding events after 1808. The ensuing war might have looked similar in practice to previous assaults but it was a significant departure in scale. The wholesale slaughter of Indians spread rapidly through the forested regions of eastern Minas Gerais, inland Espírito Santo, and southern Bahia. Traveling in the area between 1815 and 1817, Prince Maximilian observed that "no truce was granted the Botocudo, who proceeded to be exterminated wherever they were encountered, without regard to age or sex." This "war of extermination," he wrote, "was maintained with the greatest perseverance and cruelty, since it was firmly believed that [the Botocudo] killed and devoured any enemy that fell into their hands."[39]

Soldiers, protected from neck to knees against native arrows by padded cuirasses, moved into the forests, taking up positions at frontier garrisons. Many of these garrisons were undermanned and poorly maintained, but between 1800 and 1850, they nevertheless multiplied to form an interconnecting line of 87 forts, stockades, and guard posts, stretching from south to north between the Doce and Pardo Rivers as well as along the region's major river valleys. Baron von Eschwege estimated the number of troops permanently deployed in the Eastern Sertão at four hundred in 1810, although 2,000 were reported to have been mustered for one of the war's largest expeditions under the command of Colonel Julião Fernandes Leão. From their posts they launched bandeiras, often reinforced by men from neighboring farms whose security in Indian territory depended on the military presence.[40] Rugendas, the German artist, described these raids:

They hunt the Indians, attacking them wherever they find them. They seek if possible to surprise them in their encampments. When discovered, they are surrounded during the night and at daybreak the still-sleeping Indians are fired upon from all sides. Surprised in this way, the savages attempt to escape by fleeing. As a rule, the soldiers massacre all who fall into their hands. Only very rarely do they spare the women and children, even when all resistance, which is often stubborn, has ceased.[41]

To refer to these ambushes, settlers adopted the phrase "to kill a village," a practice a number of contemporaries described with few variations. Sometimes soldiers and settlers would spare a number of Botocudo adults to act as porters for future expeditions. Frequently, the colonists allowed native children to live for the purpose of supplying an active trade in Botocudo youths. Seized in this way, purchased from their parents with trinkets or even captured and sold by enemy native bands, these children labored for settlers throughout the region. Their presence among the slave labor force was registered as far away as southern Bahia to the north and the coastal capital of Rio de Janeiro to the south. All of these practices persisted long after the government unceremoniously revoked the declaration of war in 1831, although the official military offensive largely ended by 1811 and milder legislation governing the treatment of the region's Indians was adopted by 1823.[42]

ILLUSTRATION 8.1. Burying the dead, ca. 1822
SOURCE: Rugendas, *Voyage pittoresque* Biblioteca Nacional, Rio de Janeiro.

The formation of dozens of hastily established state-controlled aldeias provides one measure of the disruption caused by the war to the Botocudo, whose population in the region extending from eastern Minas Gerais to the coast during this period was estimated at 20,000 individuals. These villages, a throwback to the Pombaline Directory system—which had been formally abolished in 1798—brought together natives forced out of the forests. In exchange for food, shelter, consumer goods, and protection from armed assault, the Indians submitted to the village regime, which included religious conversion and sedentary agricultural labor. Between 1800 and 1850, in the area bounded by the Doce and Pardo Rivers, 73 of these villages were formed and ultimately placed under the administration of the French émigré Guido Tomás Marlière, many of which would later evolve into townships.[43]

Botocudo resistance did not cease, neither during nor after the period of greatest military activity. Like their adversaries, the Botocudo continued to prefer ambushes to open combat. According to Rugendas, they occasionally succeeded in surprising soldiers, "chopping away the dense growth of the forest enough to launch their arrows with the greatest security, yet without making themselves visible." Soldiers caught without protective cuirasses on such occasions found themselves at great risk. Their firearms made little difference when the natives could not be seen.[44]

More commonly, however, the Botocudo avoided—as they always had—direct encounters with military units and struck instead at isolated fazendas established in contested zones. They also seem to have pressed eastward and northward. Reporting to the war minister, one close observer of the military action described long stretches of the Doce River basin as "forgotten and entombed" amid ongoing native hostilities. A state of complete decadence prevailed. Many troops posted to the zone deserted with the firearms they received from the state. Even Portuguese settlements within 15 kilometers of Vitória, the coastal capital of Espírito Santo, lived under the constant threat of native raids. One woman in the area had recently been "cut to pieces while still alive" and then "devoured by the ferocity of those cannibals." The same had happened to a number of settled, detribalized Indians. Newly opened roads had done nothing but provide the Indians with more rapid means of attack and retreat. Attempts to increase trade on the Doce River had been thwarted and commerce in Espírito Santo in general was "entirely paralyzed."[45]

In April 1809, the war minister ordered a retaliatory attack against a force of 600 Botocudo that emerged from the forest to raid settlers, resulting in the "devastation" of fazendas lying farther north along the São Mateus River. Seven years earlier in the same location, military patrols found only those Indians of "good disposition" referred to as the "northern Botocudo." Their belligerent cousins, officials surmised, had been pushed out of the Doce River valley by intensive military action and now had begun "to infest" the northern reaches of the captaincy.[46] More than two years after the war began, "continuous invasions" of this sort causing "grave harm to the people" settled along the Jequitinhonha River and in other northern locations prompted the creation of an additional detachment of foot soldiers. These soldiers were charged with clearing natives from "the entire forest stretching to the captaincy of Bahia," so that settler families established in that zone could "live in peace."[47] At even greater remove, Botocudo presumed to have been "expelled" from Minas Gerais were now accused of "practicing acts of great carnage" along the coast of southern Bahia.[48]

Between 1811 and 1813, officials moved to secure this northern frontier and open it to commerce by building a road along the Jequitinhonha River linking the town of Minas Novas with the Atlantic coast. Convinced that the conquest of the Eastern Sertão was nearing completion, Minas Governor Francisco de Assis Mascarenhas described the wilderness expedition that built this road as "the final bandeira sent out to discover the Americas."[49] The governor's grandiloquence notwithstanding, this would not be the final bandeira, nor would it signal the completion of the conquest, nor herald anything approaching the end of the conflict between the natives of eastern Brazil and colonists. Violence between soldiers, settlers, and Indians persisted into the 1820s and well beyond. In portions of the comarca of Porto Seguro, settlers still fearing Botocudo aggression failed to push more than two leagues (13 km) into the forests from the coast, even though maps of the region now pictured what one cartographer labeled the new "line of forts to repel the Indians." Subsequent maps drafted in the 1860s recalled those produced a full century before, describing extensive swathes of the Eastern Sertão as "unsettled lands" and "little-known forests inhabited by indigenes." By the 1880s, the great bulk of the estimated remaining 12,000 to 14,000 Botocudo were described by a contemporary anthropologist as "still in the savage state, forming the most numerous and one of the fiercest wild tribes in East Brazil" and still practicing cannibalism. The Indians remained in control of substantial territory, especially but not only to the north of the Doce River, until the early twentieth century.[50]

If the war of 1808 fails to provide a satisfactory endpoint to the history of indigenous resistance, neither does it mark with any precision the onset of successful lusophone settlement. To be sure, the most extensive state-directed march of settlers into the sertão to that date did follow soon after the declaration of war. During a one-year period between October 1809 and September 1810, more than 3,000 settlers entered portions of the Doce River valley under the protection of two of the detachments dispatched to secure the area. A total of 381 settler families received sesmarias along the river. Family members numbered 1,132 and were accompanied by 1,219 slaves and 658 agregados. By 1811, one group of settlers formally applied to found a township, complete with civil officials and a chapel constructed at their own expense.[51]

Once again carried away by a sense of triumph, Governor Mascarenhas, appropriating the language of an official he dispatched to inspect the military campaign's progress, described the lands these settlers occupied as lying at the very heart of Botocudo territory. "Never before had the inhabitants of this captaincy entered there," he wrote. Three years before, when war was declared, they would never have hoped that lands into which they previously pushed would be so quickly and completely "liberated" from the "barbarous incursions of the Indians," much less would they have expected to proceed still deeper into the forests, as they now did, "to form permanent agricultural and mining settlements at the center of the Indians' own dwelling places." Reporting to the Crown, the governor evoked a sense of finality:

The thick and extensive forests until now have served as the lair of beasts and of Botocudos, still more terrible than the beasts themselves. This territory will be transformed into delightful towns. Agriculture will prosper in these untilled and, for that reason, extremely fertile lands. Mining will revive, as in the first happy days of this captaincy. At the same time an active commerce will arise, the likes of which have never before been seen or hoped for.

"In the near future," the governor assured the prince regent, Minas Gerais would exceed the "splendor" it once enjoyed as Brazil's most important captaincy.[52]

Other events did not confirm this euphoric portrayal. Despite his enthusiasm, the governor found himself promising that he would "accelerate, to whatever extent possible, the conquest of lands that continue to be invaded by the Botocudo Indians, so that they can soon be distributed and put to good use by the inhabitants of this captaincy."[53] The pledge betrayed ongoing frustrations. Native resistance likely explained why only a small proportion of the sesmarias allotted in the Doce River basin following the declaration of war entered government record books. Of the 381 land grants reportedly distributed over a 12-month period, most appear to have been quickly deserted. During all of 1809 and 1810, only 14 sesmarias were officially recorded. Even allowing for the slow pace of government bureaucracy, the data do not suggest success. Only 164 land grants were allotted during the following five-year period from the beginning of 1811 to the end of 1815. Not until well after the military assault launched in 1808 was abandoned were large numbers of land grants recorded: 649 between 1816 and 1820, many of them in the Eastern Sertão.[54] At every turn, the attempt by contemporaries to claim final victory in the protracted battle for the sertão encountered obstacles. Anecdotes drawn from the north, south, and distant interior of the former Forbidden Lands make this clear.

To the north, signs of an unfinished conquest remained apparent in complaints drafted by such local officials as the members of the town council of Vila do Príncipe, the seat of government for the northeastern comarca of Serro Frio. At the height of the military occupation of the region in 1810, facing the latest royal orders to intensify recruitment in Minas Gerais, council members found themselves arguing a point that was virtually identical to that made by Governor Noronha more than three decades earlier. They pleaded with the prince regent not to remove a single man from the comarca because such recruitment would cause irremediable harm to a region "in the cradle of its birth." Just as Noronha had done, they based their argument for preferential treatment on an imagined racial geography. They insisted the enlistment of whites would be sheer folly because so few whites lived in the comarca and those who did were employed in productive agricultural and mining activities essential to the region's economic growth. To siphon off such men to the military would serve only to leave those whites who remained more vulnerable then ever, outnumbered as they were by their "enemies"—slaves and Indians. Portions of the region these officials governed were "situated in the center of the great forests [and] surrounded by Botocudo and other wild heathen." The Indians continued to commit "barbarous" crimes, even though the captaincy had mobilized for war. The bulk of the region's free population—described as mulattos, mixed-bloods, and creoles, many of them former slaves—were capable, the council members feared, of joining the Indians in rebellion. The prince regent rightly excluded "employed persons" from recruitment. But this was not enough as even unemployed individuals had a function in a conflict that was at once racial and territorial. "The vadios and useless ones, despite being among the excluded class because of the quality of their color, are in one form or another necessary in this land," they explained. Occupying a middle ground between whites and Indians, these poor subsistence farmers of African descent were invariably "the first to send news of insurrections and skirmishes" in outlying lands involving hostile groups, by which the town officials did not specify whether they meant rebellious Indians, runaway slaves, or both. Accustomed as these free persons of color were to "wandering the forests and enduring the rigors of the seasons and of hunger," they managed to survive and escape such violence more readily than others, carrying the news of wilderness disturbances with them back to settled areas. Conversely, such individuals were the first to flee to the forests when threatened by recruitment. Such evasion of military authorities already resulted in serious harm to agriculture in the region, leaving hunger and poverty in its wake. Prices of basic provisions had quadrupled, even quintupled, over the past two years as a result of this flight to the wilderness.[55] Although the members of the Vila do Príncipe town council might not have been aware that their language echoed that of their eighteenth-century precursors, they expressed the tenor of the preceding half-century perfectly. That is, they attempted to define and impose racial categories in conjunction with the perceived requirements of internal territorial consolidation. Meanwhile, resistance to this project—both perceived and actual—persisted unabated as a decisive determinant of life on the outer edges of the settled mining district.

To the south, where colonists had been developing the commercial provisioning economy for decades, conflicts hinging on the region's frontier conditions remained unresolved, eerily reminiscent of an earlier era. For example, along the Sem Peixe River (a tributary of the Doce River), Lieutenant José Joaquim de Barcellos struggled unsuccessfully against a woman and her two sons to hold onto a land grant he claimed to have occupied since the early 1780s but whose status was cast in doubt when Botocudo raiders forced him to abandon it. Barcellos held the land "in docile and peaceful possession," he alleged in a civil action, when in the 1820s, Joanna da Rocha and her sons burned, cleared, and cultivated a portion of it, acting as "despotic" trespassers. When a stray goat belonging to the lieutenant wandered onto these newly cleared fields, one of da Rocha's sons shot it in the head and threatened to slaughter the rest of the livestock. In her defense, da Rocha argued that she was "free to plant on any part" of the land because her grandfather, despite Barcellos' claim, in fact had held the original title to the land, land that she also maintained her family held for more than 40 years and that passed to her through inheritance. Barcellos responded by producing his title to the land, measuring approximately 4.5 square kilometers. He received the sesmaria not on his first arrival in the 1780s but as a "new colonist" in 1809 after the region had been secured following the declaration of war the previous year. But as it turned out, da Rocha's grandfather had held an earlier grant to the land as well as 80 mining claims along the Sem Peixe River. He also abandoned these holdings in the face of Botocudo hostilities, resulting in settler deaths. As the claimants assembled witnesses and documents to prove their respective cases, the suit dragged on for three years and through two appeals, advancing to the colony's high court in Rio de Janeiro. At one point, da Rocha was forced to prove that she was the legitimate heir of the man she claimed to be her grandfather because her grandmother had given birth to her children "as a single woman with various fathers." In the end, Barcellos lost his bid to evict da Rocha and her sons. A judge ordered him to pay a fine for his actions and to turn over a portion of the land grant, recognizing as "joint owners" the settlers he had accused of trespassing.[56]

Familiar struggles persisted deep in the forests as well. A European adventurer on a commercial mission to the mining district, apparently an Englishman who identified himself as X. Chabert, described an incident he witnessed as a participant on the major military expedition led by Colonel Julião Fernandes Leão in the early 1810s. At a point in the sertão about 170 kilometers from Minas Novas, the expedition happened upon rival bands of Botocudo and Puri preparing to do battle. Fearing their common enemy, however, they united against Leão's forces who engaged them in a series of clashes. Chabert was wounded during one battle, sustaining an arrow to the neck, and his servant was slain. The Indians "were all put to the bayonet without mercy." He claimed to have seen a young Indian boy creep away from the scene into a thick hedge "where, with his own nails and teeth, he was struggling to tear and devour his own flesh and limbs, rather than be made a slave of." Chabert was then astonished to see among the natives "a negro man" who threw himself on his knees before him, pleading in Portuguese for mercy. The black man kissed his hands repeatedly and grabbed him so tightly he had trouble freeing himself. The Portuguese soldiers wanted to kill the man along with the defeated Indians but Chabert protested and brought him before the commanding officer where he recounted how he had ended up among the natives. He was traveling through the sertão "in the service of a famous smuggler." Twenty-two of them, including his master, were captured by a band of Botocudo. Some were devoured immediately but the captives were too numerous to be disposed of in a single feast. He and the remaining prisoners were to be "spared for a day or two, at which period they were to share the cruel fate of their slaughtered companions." During this reprieve, the daughter of the band's headman had a dream that he was to become her husband. As a result, he ended up the sole survivor. In exchange, he was required to become a member of the band, "upon which occasion his chin and ears were perforated so as to admit the introduction of the plug of wood worn in those parts by the Botocudo." The marriage took place and the former member of the smuggling ring lived among the Indians until the day of the battle with Leão's soldiers. Recognizing the benefits to be gained from one who "was well acquainted with the haunts of the Botocudos, and their mode of warfare," Leão now spared his life a second time and made him part of the expedition.[57]

Events like these militate against concluding that the incorporation of the Eastern Sertão was assured, much less achieved, by the decision to go to war. The predicaments of local officials, frontier migrants, and soldiers on the march remained so similar to what had come decades before. Frontier land conflicts and smuggling refused to subside. Unsupervised Afro-Brazilians continued to move through the forests, distressing white authorities. Unexpected permutations of racial encounters continued to play out. Independent Indians endured. Violence and its studied praxis remained a central fact of daily life. By 1831, when the war on the Botocudo and other groups officially ended, the military phase of conquest had already given way to less organized and, importantly, less expensive methods. Eloquent diatribes condemning the use of military force—especially those put forth by Baron von Eschwege, the prominent foreigner, and José Bonifácio de Andrada e Silva, the éminence grise of independence-era politics—helped secure the Crown's sympathy, if not the approval of settlers and captaincy officials. Eschwege argued that the offensive war policy served only to deepen the Indians' hatred of colonists while encouraging the migration of settlers away from Minas urban centers to the sertão, from places where their labor was sorely missed to forests where they resided under a false sense of security. José Bonifácio famously proposed a less aggressive approach for Brazil's indigenous peoples, focusing on the re-establishment of the aldeia system, a change that effectively occurred under Marlière's supervision.[58]

One thing the war did put an end to was any vestige of the Forbidden Lands policy. Further royal edicts issued to the Minas and Espírito Santo governors in 1816 reasserted the Crown's new view, so long in developing. Having ascended from his position as prince regent to the throne following the death of his mother, João VI reiterated his full support for the long-held desire of Minas officials that these "lands so vast and fertile be placed under cultivation, while at the same time taking advantage of the mineral riches that in all probability can be expected to be encountered." The monarch ordered captaincy authorities to "promote with the greatest energy communication between [Minas Gerais] and Espírito Santo by way of many and different roads, as many as are judged appropriate." These roads should run not only from west to east but from north to south, crisscrossing the sertão to ensure "the security of those who establish themselves there," as well as the ongoing "progress of pacification and civilization of the Indians." All rivers were to be examined for possible navigation. Military barracks and shelters for travelers were to be erected at frequent intervals along primary transportation routes. Tax incentives would remain in place and land grants and mining claims would continue to be distributed to colonists who settled on land anywhere in the sertão not yet allotted to another. Smuggling, unmentioned in the edicts, was no longer a matter that troubled the king, who asked to receive an annual report on all progress in the zone. No longer would the eastern wilderness or its itinerant natives be cordoned off, the king continued, "out of reach of my vassals because of the dangers to which they were exposed,

ILLUSTRATION 8.2. A racially mixed expedition opens a new road along the Macuri River (1861) after the Crown lifted the last vestiges of formal prohibitions on travel through and colonization of the eastern forests
SOURCE: Maximilian, *Travels in Brazil.* The John Carter Brown Library at Brown University.

having been attacked by the ferocious and barbarous race of Botocudo Indians to the degree that my royal protection and defense could not be found throughout the region." The Botocudo and "other barbarous Indian races, which so merit my care" would now be "welcomed with kindness to the recognition of and subjection to my laws." Those who persisted in committing hostilities would be "promptly punished."[59]

Nevertheless, the conquest of the frontier remained far from complete. In fact, the Crown's pronouncements proved just that. More than half a century had passed since the economic disruptions that followed the collapse of the gold boom spurred settlers and captaincy authorities to breach the Forbidden Lands barrier, exploring the region, mobilizing troops to secure its incorporation, pursuing its indigenous inhabitants, assembling coerced laborers in its most distant forests, and—finally and most elusively—recreating the slave-based society characteristic of the settled inland mining district. More than half a century after this uninterrupted if uneven effort began, the assault on the Eastern Sertão led, inescapably, to inconclusive results. This ambiguous outcome prompts some final reflections on Brazilian frontier history.

Conclusion

Unfinished Conquests, Unwritten Histories

ONVENTIONAL FRONTIER histories depend, both for their narrative structure and explanatory power, on the presence of victor and vanquished. Whether cast as heroes or villains, pioneers or despoilers, settlers turn their back on settled society, endure great hardship, and ultimately struggle successfully, for good or ill, to establish themselves in previously inaccessible lands. Nature and natives—the two are often confused, even indistinguishable—pose a formidable barrier to this movement outward from the settled centers of colonial or national society. As a result of the accidents of history and geography, this migration in the Americas frequently takes the form of a movement from east to west, so that conquest, pioneering, and distance traveled inland from the Atlantic seem mutually contingent, each the measure of the other. The significance attached to the inevitable clash between frontier migrants and those they encountered differs according to the historian's vision. The expansion of European civilization into unincorporated territory; the rise of new regional identities distinct from Old World, urban, or coastal precursors; the penetration of peripheral zones by a capitalist world economy; the economic, racial, or sexual domination of native peoples—these meanings become tropes applied variously by frontier scholars. In virtually every case, the incorporation of the frontier is understood as ultimately achieved, even if resistance continues within the framework of the consolidated states and societies that emerge from the preceding era of territorial expansion and cultural encounter. Even to recognize a region as a frontier is difficult until the advance of soldiers, merchants, miners, ranchers, farmers, shopkeepers, prostitutes, teachers, and missionaries prevails, or nearly prevails, until these diverse participants in conquest establish a sedentary society.

Exactly this moment of closure is missing in the territorial process examined in this study. The narrative rendered in these chapters might be brought to a close in a variety of ways. It might end with the profitable absorption of certain southern reaches of Minas Gerais into an agricultural and ranching matrix tied to provisioning the royal court in Rio de Janeiro after 1808. It might end with the rise of a coffee export economy in areas of the sertão suited to that crop's commercial cultivation after the middle of the nineteenth century. It might be extended to that distant point in the early twentieth century when the final instance of violent native resistance was recorded. Yet any one of these endpoints would impose a teleological order on events that had no such unity for those who lived through them. This problem is least troublesome in the choice of 1830 as a final juncture, linked to the winding down of the most violent phase of the conflict that began in the 1750s. Certainly, many clashes between settlers and Indians would follow but the climactic era of the state-sponsored assault on the Eastern Sertão had come to an end: first, with the conclusion of the Crown's declared military offensive around 1811, then with the return in the mid-1820s to the state-controlled aldeia system styled on Pombaline-era legislation, and, finally, with the formal revocation of the 1808 declaration of war in 1831. However, this periodization should not obscure one of the primary lessons gleaned from the history recounted here: Neither the Indians nor the settlers nor the agents of captaincy and Crown, despite an official penchant for hyperbole and finality, ever believed during the span of 80 years between 1750 and 1830 that the incorporation of the frontier was definitively achieved.

A similar insight has contributed to an outpouring of revisionist scholarship by historians of the North American frontier. "There was no conceptual problem in getting the frontier opened—with the arrival of white people in territory new to them or with the discovery of unexploited resources," writes historian Patricia Limerick. "The problem came at the other end. There is simply no definition of 'the closing of the frontier' that is anything but arbitrary and riddled with exceptions and qualification."[1] For more than a century, historians have accepted or, depending on their inclination, whittled away at the notion that America's frontier closed around 1890, the date proposed by Frederick Jackson Turner, who relied on census data showing that settlers had occupied almost every corner of the United States.[2] For better or worse, no such convenient juncture presents itself in the Brazilian case. The intractability of the periodization problem has tended to obscure the salience of the frontier for understanding Brazilian history.

This is one explanation for the lack of attention to events in places like the Eastern Sertão, where "getting the frontier opened" represents no less a historical problem than declaring it closed. Bandeirantes first made their way through the Doce River valley in the sixteenth century. The region was sealed off by the Crown at the beginning of the eighteenth century. Settlers began moving determinedly into the region despite this prohibition after the middle of the eighteenth century. The Crown declared the Doce River open to navigation and its great watershed available for settlement at the start of the nineteenth century. Where in these events lay the beginnings of the frontier? Unable to locate the start or finish of a period of effective exploration, conquest, and settlement, scholars resorted to questionable formulations, such as the "hollow frontier," which—as noted in the introduction—contrasted Brazil with a "full" or "solid" archetype, often explicitly the western United States. More commonly, they neglected the long history of internal colonization altogether.

Of course, the question of timing points to a more basic one. To define when something happened, one must first form a clear idea of exactly what this something entails. Here, the very meaning of the term *frontier* comes into question. In Turner's nationalistic conception, it represented, among diverse and often contradictory meanings, "the existence of an area of free land, its continuous recession, and the advance of American settlement westward." Turner claimed that these attributes of the frontier "explain American development."[3] To understand American history, he wrote, one should look not east toward the nation's political and industrial centers or, earlier, toward Europe, but west toward the frontier. "The true point of view in the history of this nation is not the Atlantic coast, it is the Great West." Turner famously argued that the exceptional nature of America's democratic institutions and the independent character of its people were forged on a continually advancing frontier, which he also defined as "the outer edge of the wave [of westward settlement]—the meeting point of savagery and civilization."[4]

Any suggestion that such a notion made sense of the history of Latin America has been considered almost universally absurd. Turner wrote as a privileged citizen of a nation fast on its ascent toward a position of dominance. His theories reflected a utopian understanding of the frontier process in fostering that rise and, as such, offered little insight when applied to the Latin American case. Certain scholars saw parallels but these thinkers generally came from outside Latin America, such as the American historians Herbert Bolton, Walter Prescott Webb, and the less well-known—but, in Brazil, arguably more influential—J.F. Normano and Roy Nash, and the British historian Alistair Hennessy.[5] With few exceptions, historians from Latin American rejected Turner's theories. They noted that little free land ever became permanently available to common settlers, that the Andes and other geographic barriers presented insurmountable obstacles to continental expansion, and that inland settlement rarely if ever led to the kinds of benefits Turner attributed to frontier expansion. The frontier, if it could be said to have existed at all, was more commonly a source of exploitation and injustice.[6] As a result, for much of the twentieth century, the study of Latin American frontiers claimed few enthusiasts and languished.

This proved to be the case for historians in Brazil, even though the phenomenon of frontier settlement had been, as the late Warren Dean once noted, "even more long-lasting and influential in Brazilian history than in that of the United States."[7] Most Brazilian historians continued to employ the term *frontier* in its European sense, meaning a border between two nations. The closest equivalent to the Turnerian concept was the sertão, construed as the wilderness or, especially, as the untamed, uncivilized interior, which scholars rendered in historical opposition to the coastal strip where the bulk of Brazil's population resided—along with most of its intellectuals. Some of these thinkers invested the sertão with nationalistic significance, particularly when stressing the need to draw the interior into a Europeanized nation-state. Seldom did they identify the sertão with democratic attributes.[8] Far more than the North American frontier, the sertão was seen as sinister, arid, inaccessible, and backward, the site of tragic Indian defeats, ominous miscegenation, disorienting distances, exploitative land barons, and arbitrary attempts by an autocratic state to establish authority.

If this view echoed many of the elite diatribes about the sertão and its marginalized denizens elaborated in the foregoing chapters, it similarly accorded with Eurocentric racial theories, ascendant in the eighteenth century, based on the Enlightenment writings of Montesquieu, Comte de Buffon, Adam Smith, Adam Ferguson, William Robertson, and others, who maintained that persons of color were a product of harsh environments and thus better able than whites to function in forbidding geographic zones. It also presaged the pseudoscientific racial geographies proposed by nineteenth- and early twentieth-century thinkers, who blithely consigned regions, nations, and entire continents to their unequal fates in accordance with the skin color of the peoples inhabiting them and who exerted no small influence over the way elite Brazilians viewed the rustic interior of their own new nation. The deprecatory eighteenth-century discourse undoubtedly informed nineteenth- and twentieth-century debates about Brazil's uncertain future as an independent nation, considering its mixed racial identity. The extent to which such ideas percolated up from the multiracial caldron of colonial life and from the sertão in particular, given the evidence presented in this study, indicates that local experience as much as alien theories informed elite views.[9]

The most famous Brazilian text concerning climate, race, and the nation's interior is Euclides da Cunha's *Os Sertões* (1902). In this classic depiction of the nineteenth-century inland inhabitants of the nation's northeast, written within a decade of Turner's most influential work and translated as *Rebellion in the Backlands*, da Cunha identified the peasants who settled the sertão as "the very core of our nationality, the bedrock of our race," from which a new, distinctly Brazilian people would emerge. And yet, in practically the same breath, he condemned them as savage, mixed-race degenerates, beings "on the lowest rung of our racial ladder." His views expressed a profound ambivalence about the sertão and its settlers. An intellectual strain long characteristic of the white elites of Brazil's coastal cities, this point of view further explains why few Brazilian intellectuals showed interest in the history of inland settlement.[10] The writer Clodomir Vianna Moog went so far as to lament that those who settled the Brazilian frontier were not more like their North American counterparts. Comparing the bandeirantes of Brazil and the pioneers of the United States, he contrasted "the fundamental differences of motives in the settlement of the two countries." The pioneers, he proffered, were driven westward by a "spiritual, practical, and constructive spirit in the development of North America," while the Portuguese assumed a "predatory, extractive, and almost secondarily religious spirit in the development of Brazil." The difference left Brazil "lacking in moral initiative and public spirit."[11] Moog's formulation was no less mythical, no less reductionist, and no more satisfying than Turner's.

Antecedents of this dim view of Brazil's frontier past pervade the colonial sources, and this intellectual legacy persists in modern scholarship about the colonial era. Beyond the derogatory, racist phrases used to describe the native hunters and gatherers of the Eastern Sertão, countless insults directed at colonists, especially those of African origin, similarly cast eighteenth-century frontier migrants in the objectionable light of elite disdain. From the earliest days of the gold rush, those who departed the coast for the distant mineral washings shocked high-ranking commentators as "vile people," as "licentious and unchristian," as "criminals, vagabonds, and malefactors," as "unruly and uncontrolled," to cite a few of the slurs marshaled by Brazil's governor general João de Lencastre in 1701.[12] When they found themselves among the few favored with royal land grants, settlers in the eastern forests sometimes denied they lived in the sertão. They drew a distinction between their privileged landholding cohort and the landless migrants they considered their inferiors. According to this connotation, the sertão was a place inhabited by those of less fortunate standing whose land claims were not likely to be honored, not legitimate in the first place, or at least not yet formalized.[13] The sertão became a measure of status, of a certain level of culture and civilization, or—more precisely—of the lack thereof. For a minister of the eighteenth-century royal court in Lisbon, the sertão might encompass all of Brazil; for a denizen of the colony's coastal cities, it comprised all territories inland; for the barons of the Minas gold boom gathered in Vila Rica and other major towns, it encircled the settled mining district; and for the large-scale, market-oriented, slaveholding farmers of the eastern forests' newly cleared hinterlands, it lay just over the ridge beyond their property lines. The sertão was anywhere but here. It was the unstable rim that gave form and meaning to the secure, civilized center.

Such views proved tenacious as post-independence intellectuals grappled with the significance of their nation's vast and sparsely settled interior. Da Cunha and Moog's concerns were shared by the preeminent twentieth-century historian of the Brazilian frontier, Sérgio Buarque de Holanda. Studying colonial attempts to traverse and settle the region between São Paulo and Mato Grosso, Brazil's far west, he described the bulk of the population active in this Herculean effort as "criminals and vadios," "poor human material," "individuals little accustomed to any useful occupation," and as an "immense population in flux, without a clear social position, living parasitically at the margin of regular and remunerative activities."[14] That the specific mechanisms of frontier settlement, particularly during the colonial period, failed to capture the interest of more than a few Brazilian historians is little wonder.

A deep-rooted inattention to indigenous history ran parallel to this tendency to discount what happened in the backlands as the province of uncouth and violent rustics. Where the plantation and, in the eighteenth century, the mining complexes took hold, scholars fixed their gaze on the most dynamic centers of economic production. Even though independent Indians continued to occupy forests, mountains, swamps, and river valleys not far beyond the perimeter of cane fields and mineral washings, they disappeared from sight. Meanwhile, those historians who eventually took the dispossessed of the mercantilist system as their subject tended to focus, understandably, on the colony's enormous population of African slaves. Natives made their narrative flourishes on the coast to marvel at or oppose the colony's first settlers, but then they vanished into the sertão. They reappeared in a few innovative studies of the Amazon Basin but remained, until quite recently, veritable nonentities elsewhere. As a rule, with the professional definition of their discipline at stake, historians passed over and even scorned the study of Indians, considering such research a matter for anthropologists. In turn, for much of the past century, anthropologists concentrated their efforts on peoples construed as isolated remants without a discernable history or as static primitives for whom history did not matter. However, eventually disenchanted with their own presuppositions, anthropologists began to ask historical questions, becoming some of the first scholars to consult the colonial archives. Such documentary work proved daunting, with sources dispersed on two continents and, in Brazil alone, scattered among distant and sometimes disorganized national, state, and local archives. In short, the history of Brazil's native peoples, like the frontier itself and its hard-scrabble settlers, remained for all practical purposes unwritten and unremembered.

To return to the paradigmatic hold Turner's ideas exerted over scholars of the American West, perhaps predictable was that the most urgent impulse for historical revisionism in the realm of frontier studies arose from within that camp. Since the 1950s, and with increasing force since the 1980s, American historians have dismantled Turner's hypotheses, abandoning his unequivocally heroic vision of westward expansion. They have called into question his progressive, romantic perspective and replaced it with an approach that resonates more compellingly with the history of Latin American colonization.[15] As Limerick notes, the revisionists oppose as nationalistic and often racist the older notion of the frontier as it implies "the area where white people get scarce." They frequently dispense with the term *frontier* altogether and instead employ "invasion, conquest, colonization, exploitation, development, [and] expansion of the world market" to describe a process involving "the convergence of diverse people . . . and their encounters with each other and with the natural environment."[16]

Although the present study has, for the sake of convenience and intelligibility, retained the term as well as the equally fraught notion of the sertão, it has also asserted an open-ended understanding of the frontier, conceptualizing what occurred in the interior of Portuguese America as part of a broad process of colonization and, concomitantly, of the elaboration of social and territorial hierarchies based on power, wealth, status, and race. It has characterized the incorporation of the frontier as a product of tensions between those historical factors specific to the region and its inhabitants and those that dictated the region's changing place in a larger world.[17] Focusing on these tensions has provided the analytical lens necessary first to identify and then make sense of a frontier like the Forbidden Lands. In this sense, the appropriate analytical context was conceived to be the contest over land, labor, and resources characteristic of regions on the periphery of consolidating early modern states and market economies. Without surrendering its uniqueness, the history of the territory separating Brazil's inland mining district from the Atlantic coast then comes to resemble that of other frontiers lying to the west, or the east—the direction does not matter—of settled areas throughout the Atlantic world.

By way of policies governing indigenous relations and especially through prohibitions banning access to Indian domain, the Portuguese Crown sought to regulate access to the Eastern Sertão. It did so according to mercantilist logic, convinced that the gold and diamonds pouring like a cascade off the colony's central plateau had to be walled off and protected for the sake of the empire. By the second half of the eighteenth century, the Forbidden Lands policy had irrevocably altered the fate of the region's seminomadic indigenous occupant as well as its would-be Luso-Brazilian, Afro-Brazilian, free, enslaved, and fugitive settlers. The policy strictly proscribed their relationship to the commerce and culture of the Atlantic world and established the conditions by which those restrictions would be challenged. Notwithstanding the Crown's desires, captaincy officials, landed settlers, squatters, and Indians themselves acted on alternative conceptions of appropriate territorial boundaries. Minas governors devised a substitute frontier racial geography for the Crown's, whereas colonists and natives pressed claims of their own. As the century advanced, race relations, settlement patterns, regional identity, and the fundamental articulation of the sprawling eastern forests with the wider Atlantic world would be altered more thoroughly by these local imperatives than by the political and economic programs of the Portuguese metropolis.

The act of sealing off the rugged lands separating the mining district from the Atlantic seaboard lent great import to the correspondence between those lands and the indigenous cultures that had sought refuge there since the sixteenth century from coastal settlers. From this fateful act onward, the region's history would be bound to a process whereby native and colonial identities became entwined in a territory defined by peculiar rules. Even basic ethnic divisions distinguishing the zone's diverse indigenous groups were altered as well as hierarchies defining the encroaching colonial society. These social groupings reflected preexisting categories but this should not hide the profound degree to which the separate historical roles of the Botocudo, the Puri, the Coroado, African slaves, poor subsistence farmers, soldiers, miners, and land grant recipients were forged in response to the gradual breakdown of restrictions on colonizing the eastern forests.

Effective colonization, as those in positions of authority saw it, presupposed the correlation of each set of actors with a particular position in the territory at stake. The historical importance of this requirement is why this study has stressed the social and cultural formation of the frontier as a precursor to its incorporation, rejecting any notion of a preordained conquest or of a frontier that existed, a priori, simply by virtue of the fact that European and non-European peoples encountered each other within its geographic limits. Because native groups inhabited unconquered and unknown lands, they would be condemned as savages. Because impoverished persons, especially persons of color, moved through such lands without supervision, they would be criminalized as vagabonds. When favored land grant recipients complained of threats to their fields, livestock, and slaves, they would command official attention. These social categories thus served to "organize the space and history of the frontier," to borrow the terms used by an ethnohistorian who has found a similar process at work in colonial Spanish America. They served to "prepare the terrain for a more efficient, appropriate, and [putatively] just enterprise of colonization and pacification."[18]

Ethnic and social labels themselves developed for this purpose. This is evident in the progression from Tapuya, the earliest name applied indiscriminately in the sixteenth century to Brazil's non-Tupi-speaking inland seminomads, to the more territorially specific term Aimoré, which faded from use over the course of the eighteenth century, to the still more narrowly focused ethnonyms Botocudo, Puri, Coroado, Pataxó, and many others, which from the eighteenth to the twentieth centuries were employed to differentiate with varying degrees of imprecision between the diverse native occupants of the eastern forests. These terms evolved in the discourse of state agents, reflecting the give-and-take between increasing knowledge of the sertão and its inhabitants and the use of that knowledge to forward colonizing projects by assigning groups to fixed territories. The phenomenon was not limited to Indians. Terms used to describe the landless poor (*vadios*), settlers producing for the market (*fazendeiros*), land grant owners (*sesmeiros*), and frontier expeditionaries (*bandeirantes*) all developed distinct meanings, spatially and socially, with respect to the specific objectives of late colonial frontier projects.

If internal territorial consolidation went hand in hand with rigid conceptions of a social and racial group's proper place in the frontier hierarchy, it did so according to idealized schemes inscribed in incompatible Crown and captaincy policies. Both sets of policies collided with the disobliging reality of daily events in the forests. Those who encountered each other in the eastern wilderness adapted to necessities not foreseen in either Lisbon or Vila Rica, imposing unanticipated limits on official projects. Everywhere testing and reshaping the confines of state-directed containment and colonization plans, Indians and settlers invested the territorialization process with far greater complexity than did royal ministers and governors.

In 1808, bowing to the pressure of local officials, the Crown finally legitimized the reversal of its Forbidden Lands policy, which captaincy officials, land grant recipients, and mobile subsistence farmers had challenged for more than half a century. It did so in the face of external forces as well. The colonial determination to preserve a no-man's-land between the mining district and the coast collapsed under the pressures of a changing world as well as changing local conditions. No longer was the fear of smuggling through the region paramount but rather the need to incorporate this territory without further delay into the Atlantic economy. Its rivers would now be used to move goods out of and into the interior. Its fertile land would be used to grow crops, planted, harvested, and transported by slaves and the free poor, and exported whenever possible to Brazil's burgeoning coastal cities and then overseas. The sertão would take its place, as one Minas commentator mused on the eve of independence in 1821, as part of Brazil's "immense territory now laid open and worked over," a transformation three centuries in the making, "brought about by African labor." Five years earlier, articulating the perspective of an outsider looking in, Englishman Henry Koster, himself with substantial experience in Minas Gerais, had used similar terms. "Brazil is thus laid open," he wrote, describing the anticipated windfall effect of commercial agreements signed between Great Britain and Brazil in the early nineteenth century, a diplomatic reflection of this same great if gradual shift.[19]

Viewed in its broadest context, the history of the region—with its belated, lurching, incomplete integration into the colonial domain and Atlantic world—parallels that of many marginal zones. Increasingly, historians have focused on these zones as they come to recognize the role of local conditions in mediating the transition to a capitalist economy and a postcolonial nation state. They are finding that the ebb and flow of colonization turned on the actions and preconceptions of settlers and natives as often as on the policies drafted across the ocean in Portugal, Spain, England, and elsewhere. "The struggle between metropolitan plans and local purposes is," as one of these historians writes, "coming to dominate newer scholarship."[20]

The history of the unsettled interior of Portuguese America leads to questions that might otherwise remain obscured with respect to frontier settlement, questions this study has only begun to answer, about the multidirectional nature of internal colonization; about the corresponding and relative mobility of Europeans, Afro-Brazilians, and Indians; about the use of indigenous, free poor, and slave labor in frontier regions; about the connections between geography and the formation of racial identities; about the power and limitations of the state in territorial conquest; about the character and variety of native responses and the persistence of native resistance. The aboriginal occupants and encroaching settlers of Atlantic world frontiers contended with these dynamics in peripheral zones throughout the Americas. Those who encountered each other in the Forbidden Lands of the Eastern Sertão added their distinctive responses to the global process of territorial integration, a process in which they both often flouted royal designs.

The history of the Eastern Sertão demonstrates that internal colonization can take place in conditions not commonly considered conducive to this process. After 1750, Brazil's inland urban mining district provided neither the rapidly expanding export complex nor the burgeoning industrial economy that usually propelled frontier expansion. Instead, demographic dispersion followed economic turmoil. Far from stifling migration to the frontier, these factors impelled it as officials and settlers sought an antidote to the problems they faced in remote lands where some hoped to reclaim past prosperity and where others hoped simply to make do. Taken together with the concurrent migrations outward toward the captaincy's south and the west, whose histories remain to be told, the expansion into Minas Gerais' eastern forests formed part of the most important frontier movement in late colonial Brazil. The absence of this development from virtually every modern rendering of Brazilian history derives from causes present at the very outset of the colonization process. The coercive means the state adopted to assemble laborers in remote forests and river valleys undermined any lasting sense of the transformative power of the frontier. When new settlements finally took hold, they depended on the same slave-labor regime that defined the colony since the sixteenth century. Alternately, the opposition settlers encountered to their territorial invasion not only slowed the process of incorporation but even reversed it in areas where natives most successfully mustered their strength. When settlers fled frontier zones they had colonized decades earlier, they abandoned not only their gold diggings, land grants, farms, and ranches, but also their claims to a triumphant past. When historians skirted this history as inconclusive, they denied Brazil the central place it merits in the field of comparative frontier studies

Ultimately, in a migration that continues to this day, Brazilian settlers would come to occupy a land mass approaching continental proportions, effecting an interior expansion equal in magnitude to and much longer in duration than the one that swept across North America. Yet the inequitable process of territorial consolidation did little to foster the emergence of a transcendent, unifying notion of the frontier in which civilization could be construed as having overcome savagery. Brazil's most durable myths of national identity—and the historical narratives deployed in their service—would therefore have to be sought somewhere else.

REFERENCE MATTER

Appendix

Governors of the Captaincy of Minas Gerais, 1750s–1820s

Governor	Beginning of Term
José Antônio Freire de Andrada, Second Count of Bobadela[1]	February 17, 1752
Gomes Freire de Andrada, Count of Bobadela	April 28, 1758
Antônio de Desterro, Bishop of Rio de Janeiro, et al.[1]	January 1, 1763
Luís Diogo Lobo da Silva	December 28, 1763
José Luís de Meneses Abranches Castelo Branco e Noronha, Count of Valadares	July 16, 1768
Antônio Carlos Furtado de Mendonça	May 22, 1773
Pedro Antônio da Gama Freitas[1]	January 13, 1775
Antônio de Noronha	May 29, 1775
Rodrigo José de Meneses, Count of Cavaleiros	February 20, 1780
Luis da Cunha Meneses, Count of Lumiares	October 10, 1783
Luís Antônio Furtado de Mendonça, Viscount of Barbacena	July 11, 1788
Bernardo José de Lorena, Count of Sarzedas	August 9, 1797
Pedro Maria Xavier Ataíde e Melo, Viscount of Condeixa	July 21, 1803
Francisco de Assis Mascarenhas, Count of Palma	February 5, 1810
Manoel de Portugal e Castro	April 11, 1814[2]

[1]Interim administration.

[2]On September 21, 1821, following Brazilian independence, Castro became the President of the Provisional Government of the Province of Minas Gerais.

Notes

The following abbreviations are used in the Notes:

ABNRJ	*Anais da Biblioteca Nacional do Rio de Janeiro*
ACMM	Arquivo da Câmara Municipal de Mariana
ACSM	Arquivo da Casa Setecentista de Mariana
ADIM	*Autos de devassa da Inconfidência Mineira* (Belo Horizonte, 1976–1983)
AEAM	Arquivo Eclesiástico da Arquidiocese de Mariana
AHEx	Arquivo Histórico do Exército, Rio de Janeiro
AHM	Arquivo Histórico Militar, Lisbon
AHU	Arquivo Histórico Ultramarino, Lisbon
AIHGB	Arquivo do Instituto Histórico e Geográfico Brasileiro, Rio de Janeiro
ANRJ	Arquivo Nacional, Rio de Janeiro
ANTT	Arquivo Nacional do Torre do Tombo, Lisbon
APEB	Arquivo Público do Estado da Bahia, Salvador
APM	Arquivo Público Mineiro, Belo Horizonte
ATC	Arquivo do Tribunal de Contas, Lisbon
BLAC	Benson Latin American Collection, Univ. of Texas, Austin, TX
BNL	Biblioteca Nacional, Lisbon
BNRJ	Biblioteca Nacional, Rio de Janeiro
CC	Arquivo Casa dos Contos
CHNPA	*Cambridge History of the Native Peoples of the Americas*, vol. 3, *South America*, ed. Frank Salomon and Stuart B. Schwartz (Cambridge, 1999)
CM	Cartografia Manuscrita
CP	Coleção Pombalina
CV	Arquivo Conde de Valadares
DB	Documentos Biográficos
DH	*Documentos históricos*
DI	*Documentos interessantes para a história e costumes de São Paulo*
ER	Erário Régio

GMD	Geography and Map Division
HSAI	*Handbook of South American Indians*, ed. Julian H. Steward; 7 vols. (New York: Cooper Square, 1963)
JCBL	John Carter Brown Library, Providence, RI
JGP	Junta do Governo Provisório
LC	Library of Congress, Washington, DC
OLL	Oliveira Lima Library, Catholic University of America, Washington, DC
MM	Arquivo Morgado de Mateus
MRSJ	Arquivo do Museu Regional, São João del-Rei
RAPM	*Revista do Arquivo Público Mineiro*
RIHGB	*Revista do Instituto Histórico e Geográfico Brasileiro*
SC	Seção Colonial
SCP	Seção Colonial e Provincial
SG	Secretaria do Governo
SI	Seção de Iconografia
SM	Seção de Manuscritos
SP	Seção Provincial

Notes to Introduction

1. Governor to Viceroy, Cachoeira do Campo, 6 May 1789, *Anuário do Museu da Inconfidência* 2 (1953): 49; Governor to Colonial Secretary, Vila Rica, 11 Jul 1789, ibid., 72. Kenneth R. Maxwell mentions this incident in his classic history of the Minas conspiracy, *Conflicts and Conspiracies: Brazil and Portugal: 1750–1808* (Cambridge: Cambridge University Press, 1973), 154.

2. Selecting from a number of contemporary estimates, Hugon favors the following figures for Brazil's total population: 1.5 million in 1750, 1.9 million in 1776, 2.5 million in 1780, 4.0 million in 1808 (a figure roughly equivalent to the U.S. population at the turn of the nineteenth century), and 5.0 million in 1825. More cautious, Alden estimates the population in 1800 at somewhere between 2.0 and 3.0 million. Minas Gerais remained the most populous captaincy in Brazil throughout the late colonial period, home to roughly one-fifth of the colony's total population. Slaves accounted for 188,944 (48.0%) and the free colored for 133,596 (33.9%) of the 393,788 inhabitants of Minas Gerais in 1786. The absolute number and overall percentage of slaves decreased to 177,017 (30.5%) of a total captaincy population of 580,786 in 1821, whereas the free colored population continued its rapid growth to 241,969 (41.7%). See chap. 4, Table 4.1. See Hugon, *Demografia brasileira* (São Paulo: Universidade de São Paulo, 1973), 36–37; Altiva Pilatti Balhana, "A População," in *O Império Luso-Brasileiro, 1750–1822*, ed. Maria Beatriz Nizza da Silva (Lisbon: Editorial Estampa, 1986), 33–36; Manolo Florentino, *Em Costas Negras: Uma história do tráfico de escravos entre a África e o Rio de Janeiro (séculos XVIII e XIX)* (São Paulo: Companhia das Letras, 1997), 38–40; Dauril Alden, "The Population of Brazil in the Late Eighteenth Century: a Preliminary Survey," *Hispanic American Historical Review* 43:2 (May 1963): 173–205; *idem*, "Late Colonial Brazil, 1750–1808," in *Colonial Brazil*, ed. Leslie Bethell, 284–343 (Cambridge: Cambridge University Press, 1987); Laird W. Bergad, "Demographic Change in a Post-Export Boom Society: The Population of Minas Gerais, Brazil, 1776–1821," *Journal of Social History* 29:4 (Summer 1996): 895. Also see Table 4.1.

3. On the growing interest in Portuguese America's internal workings, see Stuart B. Schwartz, "Somebodies and Nobodies in the Body Politic: Mentalities and Social Structure in Colonial Brazil," *Latin American Research Review* 31:1 (1996): 113–34.

4. Important overviews encapsulating the revitalized scholarship on the colony's indigenous peoples include Manuela Carneiro da Cunha, ed., *História dos índios no Brasil* (São Paulo: Companhia das Letras, 1992); Frank Salomon and Stuart B. Schwartz, eds., *CHNPA*, vol. 3, *South America* (Cambridge: Cambridge University Press, 1999), including the bibliographic essays by John M. Monteiro, pt. 1, 1015–23, and by Robin M. Wright with Manuela Carneiro de Cunha, pt. 2, 373–81. More specific contributions that have been particularly influential include John M. Monteiro, *Negros da terra: Índios e bandeirantes nas origens de São Paulo* (São Paulo: Companhia das Letras, 1994); Ronaldo Vainfas, *A heresia dos índios: Catolicismo e rebeldia no Brasil colonial* (São Paulo: Companhia das Letras, 1995); Ronald Raminelli, *Imagens da colonizacão: A representação do índio de Caminha a Vieira* (Rio de Janeiro: J. Zahar, 1996); Pedro Puntoni, *A Guerra dos Bárbaros: Povos indígenas e a colonização do sertão nordeste do Brasil* (São Paulo: Hucitec, 2000); Maria Regina Celestino de Almeida, *Metamorfoses indígenas: Cultura e identidade nos aldeamentos indígenas do Rio de Janeiro* (Rio de Janeiro: Arquivo Nacional, 2002); Nádia Farage, *As muralhas dos sertões: Os povos indígenas no Rio Branco e a colonização* (Rio de Janeiro: Paz e Terra and Anpocs, 1991); B.J. Barickman, "'Tame Indians,' 'Wild Heathens,' and Settlers in Southern Bahia in the Late Eighteenth and Early Nineteenth Centuries," *The Americas* 51:3 (January 1995): 326–27; Alida C. Metcalf, "Millenarian Slaves? The Santidade de Jaguaripe and Slave Resistance in the Americas," *American Historical Review* 104:5 (December 1999): 1531–59; Rita Heloísa de Almeida, *O Diretório dos Índios: Um projeto de "civilização" no Brasil do século XVIII* (Brasília: Universidade de Brasília, 1997); Ângela Domingues, *Quando os índios eram vassalos. Colonização e relações de poder no Norte do Brasil na segunda metade do século XVIII* (Lisbon: Comissão Nacional para as Comemorações dos Descobrimentos Portugueses, 2000). For initial treatments of a number of themes explored in this study, also see Hal Langfur, "Uncertain Refuge: Frontier Formation and the Origins of the Botocudo War in Late-Colonial Brazil," *Hispanic American Historical Review* 82:2 (May 2002): 215–56; *idem*, "The Return of the Bandeira: Economic Calamity, Historical Memory, and Armed Expeditions to the Sertão in Minas Gerais, 1750–1808," *The Americas* 61:3 (January 2005): 429–61; *idem*, "Moved by Terror: Frontier Violence as Cultural Exchange in Late-Colonial Brazil," *Ethnohistory* 52:2 (Spring 2005): 255–89.

5. Points of entry to an extensive literature on eighteenth-century Minas Gerais include C.R. Boxer, *The Golden Age of Brazil, 1695–1750: Growing Pains of a Colonial Society* (Berkeley, CA: University of California Press, 1969); A.J.R. Russell-Wood, "Colonial Brazil: The Gold Cycle, c. 1690–1750," in *Cambridge History of Latin America*, vol. 2, ed. Leslie Bethell (Cambridge: Cambridge University Press, 1984), 547–600; Maxwell, *Conflicts and Conspiracies*; Donald Ramos, "From Minho to Minas: The Portuguese Roots of the Mineiro Family," *Hispanic American Historical Review* 73:4 (1993): 639–62; Júnia Ferreira Furtado, *O Livro da Capa Verde: O regimento diamantino de 1771 e a vida no Distrito Diamantino no período da real extração* (São Paulo: Annablume, 1996); Luciano Figueiredo, *O avesso da memória: Cotidiano e trabalho da mulher em Minas Gerais no século XVIII* (Rio de Janeiro: José Olympio, 1993); Kathleen J. Higgins, *"Licentious Liberty" in a*

Brazilian Gold-Mining Region: Slavery, Gender, and Social Control in Eighteenth-Century Sabará, Minas Gerais, (University Park, PA: Pennsylvania State University Press, 1999); Marco Antonio Silveira, *O universo do indistinto: Estado e sociedade nas Minas setecentistas (1735–1808)* (São Paulo: Hucitec, 1997); Laura de Mello e Souza, *Desclassificados do ouro: A pobreza mineira no século XVIII*, 3rd ed. (Rio de Janeiro: Graal, 1990); *idem, Norma e conflito: Aspectos da história de Minas no século XVIII* (Belo Horizonte, Brazil: UFMG, 1999); Laird W. Bergad, *Slavery and the Demographic and Economic History of Minas Gerais, Brazil, 1720–1888* (Cambridge: Cambridge University Press, 1999).

6. Colonial Secretary, "Instruções (minuta) diversas dadas ao Visconde de Barbacena, Luís Antonio Furtado de Mendonça," 29 Jan 1788, AHU, Minas Gerais, caixa 128, doc. 18. As though expressing the same ambivalence of historians who later emphasized Brazil's coastal history to the detriment of its internal realm, Colonial Secretary Martinho Melo e Castro struck the term "soul" (*alma*) from this draft of his lengthy instructions to the new governor-designate of Minas Gerais, describing the region instead as "one of the most important of all the other captaincies that compose the dominions of Brazil and Portuguese America." For the text's final version, later published, see *idem*, "Instrução para o Visconde de Barbacena," *RIHGB* 6 (1844): 3–59. By way of comparison, Laura de Mello e Souza, the eminent historian of Portuguese America, once affirmed that Minas Gerais "was the synthesis of the colony" in the eighteenth century. Upon further reflection, she qualified this statement: "I am now certain, there was no single colony, but various ones, distinct from one another and, most of the time, hardly connected. Be that as it may, if Minas did not synthesize, such a synthesis being impossible, it expressed in a highly privileged form the contradictions of colonial life." Laura de Mello e Souza, introduction to Silveira, *O universo do indistinto*, 13–14. See also Maxwell, *Conflicts and Conspiracies*, 107.

7. The pervasiveness of such zones in late colonial Latin America and the value of comparing their histories have become increasingly evident to historians. Regions attracting study include, among others, northern Mexico, central and southern Argentina, southern Chile, central Brazil, and eastern Paraguay. See the essays collected in Donna J. Guy and Thomas E. Sheridan, eds., *Contested Ground: Comparative Frontiers on the Northern and Southern Edges of the Spanish Empire* (Tucson, AZ: University of Arizona Press, 1998).

8. Important efforts to conceptualize the process of frontier incorporation in Brazil include: Mary Lombardi, "The Frontier in Brazilian History: An Historiographic Essay," *Pacific Historical Review* 44 (November 1975), 437–57; Leo H. Waibel, "As zonas pioneiras do Brasil," *Revista Brasileira de Geografia* 17 (October–December 1955): 389–417; Warren Dean, "Ecological and Economic Relationships in Frontier History: São Paulo, Brazil," in *Essays on Frontiers in World History*, ed. George Wolfskill and Stanley Palmer (Austin, TX: University of Texas Press, 1981), 71–100; Seth Garfield, *Indigenous Struggle at the Heart of Brazil: State Policy, Frontier Expansion, and the Xavante Indians, 1937–1988* (Durham: Duke University Press, 2001). On the colonial period, see J. Capistrano de Abreu, *Caminhos antigos e povoamento do Brasil* (1930; reprint, Belo Horizonte, Brazil: Ed. Itatiaia, 1989); Sérgio Buarque de Holanda, *Caminhos e fronteiras* (Rio de Janeiro: José Olympio, 1957); James Lockhart and Stuart B. Schwartz, *Early Latin America: A History of Colonial Spanish America and Brazil* (Cambridge: Cambridge University Press,

1983), chap. 8; Alida Metcalf, *Family and Frontier in Colonial Brazil: Santana de Parnaíba, 1520–1822* (Berkeley, CA: University of California Press, 1992); and A.J.R. Russell-Wood, "Frontiers in Colonial Brazil: Reality, Myth and Metaphor," in *Society and Government in Colonial Brazil, 1500–1822* (Aldershot, UK: Variorum, 1992).

9. For frontier studies specific to Minas Gerais, see Percy Alvin Martin, "Minas Gerais and California: A Comparison of Certain Phases of Their Historical and Social Evolution," in *RIHGB*, tomo especial, *Congresso Internacional de História da América* 1 (1922): 250–70; Manuel Cardozo, "The Brazilian Gold Rush," *The Americas* 3:2 (1946): 137–60; Waldemar de Almeida Barbosa, *A decadência das minas e a fuga da mineração* (Belo Horizonte, Brazil: Universidade Federal de Minas Gerais, 1971); Laura de Mello e Souza, "Violência e práticas culturais no cotidiano de uma expedição contra quilombolas, Minas Gerais, 1769," in *Liberdade por um fio: História dos quilombos no Brasil*, ed. João José Reis and Flávio dos Santos Gomes (São Paulo: Companhia das Letras, 1996), 193–212; Judy Bieber, *Power, Patronage, and Political Violence: State Building on a Brazilian Frontier, 1822–1889* (Lincoln, NE: University of Nebraska Press, 1999); *idem*, "Postmodern Ethnographer in the Backlands: An Imperial Bureaucrat's Perceptions of Post-Independence Brazil," in *Latin American Research Review* 33:2 (1998): 37–72. On the Eastern Sertão, see Paulo Mercadante, *Os sertões do leste; estudo de uma região: A mata mineira* (Rio de Janeiro: Zahar Editores, 1973); Celso Falabella de Figueiredo Castro, *Os sertões de leste; Achegas para a história da Zona da Mata* (Belo Horizonte, Brazil: Imp. Oficial, 1987); Ricardo de Bastos Cambraia and Fábio Faria Mendes, "A colonização dos sertões do leste mineiro: Políticas de ocupação territorial num regime escravista (1780–1836)," *Revista do Departamento de História—FAFICH/UFMG* 6 (July 1988): 137–50; Angelo Alves Carrara, *Estruturas agrárias e capitalismo; Ocupação do solo e transformação do trabalho na zona da Mata central de Minas Gerais (séculos XVIII e XIX)* (Mariana, Brazil: EdUFOP, 1999), esp. 14–20.

10. On the "hollow frontier" formulation, see Warren Dean, "The Frontier in Brazil," in *Frontier in Comparative Perspectives*, Working Papers, no. 188 (Washington, DC: Latin American Program, The Woodrow Wilson Center, 1990), 23; Richard M. Morse, introduction to *The Bandeirantes: The Historical Role of the Brazilian Pathfinders* (New York: Alfred A. Knopf, 1965), 10; Arthur S. Aiton, "Latin-American Frontiers," in *Where Cultures Meet: Frontiers in Latin American History*, ed. David J. Weber and Jane M. Rausch (Wilmington, DE: Scholarly Resources, 1994), 19–25. On the 1930s "pioneer frontier," see Joe Foweraker, introduction to *The Struggle for Land: A Political Economy of the Pioneer Frontier in Brazil from 1930 to the Present Day* (Cambridge: Cambridge University Press, 1981).

11. Scholars instrumental in developing the notion of frontiers as zones of cultural contact include Patricia N. Limerick, *The Legacy of Conquest: The Unbroken Past of the American West* (New York: W.W. Norton & Co., 1987), 26–27; Mary Louise Pratt, *Imperial Eyes: Travel Writing and Transculturation* (London: Routledge, 1992), esp. 1–11; David J. Weber, *The Spanish Frontier in North America* (New Haven, CT: Yale University Press, 1992), 11; Weber and Jane M. Rausch, introduction to *Where Cultures Meet*; Richard White, *The Middle Ground: Indians, Empires, and Republics in the Great Lakes Region, 1650–1815* (Cambridge: Cambridge University Press, 1991), esp. x, 52; Daniel H. Usner, Jr., *Indians, Settlers, & Slaves in a Frontier Exchange Economy: The Lower Mississippi Valley*

Before 1783 (Chapel Hill, NC: University of North Carolina Press, 1992); Cynthia Radding, *Wandering Peoples: Colonialism, Ethnic Spaces, and Ecological Frontiers in Northwestern Mexico, 1700–1850* (Durham, NC: Duke University Press, 1997). On the uneven advance of capitalism, see Eric R. Wolf, *Europe and the People without History* (Berkeley, CA: University of California Press, 1982), 308. On the late eighteenth-century transition to capitalism in southeastern Minas Gerais, see Angelo Alves Carrara, *Estruturas agrárias.* Elsewhere, I have applied this analytical framework to the study of frontier conflicts in the Brazilian state of Mato Grosso at the turn of the twentieth century. See Hal Langfur, "Myths of Pacification: Brazilian Frontier Settlement and the Subjugation of the Bororo Indians," *Journal of Social History* 32:4 (Summer 1999): 879–905.

12. For a recent collaborative attempt to help close this divide, see Matthew Restall, ed., *Beyond Blacks and Reds: African-Native Relations in Colonial Latin America* (Albuquerque, NM: University of New Mexico Press, 2005). For the Brazilian case, see Stuart B. Schwartz and Hal Langfur, "Tapanhuns, Negros da Terra, and Curibocas: Common Cause and Confrontation between Blacks and Indians in Colonial Brazil," in ibid., 81–114. Also see Metcalf, *Family and Frontier.* Studies concerning North America that are salutary in this regard include Usner, *Indians, Settlers, & Slaves;* Jane G. Landers, ed., *Colonial Plantations and Economy in Florida* (Gainesville, FL: University Press of Florida, 2000); Gary B. Nash, *Red, White, and Black: The Peoples of Early America,* 4th ed. (Englewood Cliffs: Prentice-Hall, 1999); James F. Brooks, ed., *Confounding the Color Line: The Indian-Black Experience in North America* (Lincoln, NE: University of Nebraska Press, 2002).

13. For use of the terms "virgin land" and "virgin forests," see, for example, Governor to Viceroy, Vila Rica, 19 Nov 1776, BNRJ, SM, cód. 2, 2, 24, fol. 53; Governor Noronha to Governor Saldanha, Vila Rica, 13 May 1777, BNRJ, SM, cód. 2, 2, 24, fols. 114v–16v; Francisco Martins Penna to Governor, Tejuco, 17 Dec 1801, APM, SC, cód. 277, fols. 99v–100v. Also see Henry Nash Smith, *Virgin Land: The American West in Symbol and Myth* (New York: Vintage Books, 1957).

14. Richard Price, *Alabi's World* (Baltimore, MD: Johns Hopkins University Press, 1990), xvi.

Notes to Chapter 1

1. The primary exceptions to this predisposition in the Minas historiography are Maria Hilda Baquiero Paraíso, "O tempo da dor e do trabalho: A conquista dos territórios indígenas nos Sertões do Leste," (Ph.D. diss., Universidade de São Paulo, 1998); [Hal] Langfur, "The Forbidden Lands: Frontier Settlers, Slaves, and Indians in Minas Gerais, Brazil, 1760–1830," (Ph.D. diss., University of Texas, 1999); Maria Leônia Chaves de Resende, "Gentios brasílicos: Índios coloniais em Minas Gerais setecentista," (Ph.D. diss., Universidade de Campinas, Brazil, 2003); and two works by the regional historian Oiliam José, *Marlière, O Civilizador* (Belo Horizonte, Brazil: Ed. Itatiaia, 1958) and *Indígenas de Minas Gerais* (Belo Horizonte, Brazil: Imp. Oficial, 1965). The present chapter develops themes first presented in Hal Langfur, "Uncertain Refuge: Frontier Formation and the Origins of the Botocudo War in Late Colonial Brazil," *Hispanic American Historical Review* 82:2 (May 2002): 215–56. For a brief discussion of scholarship on the Indians of Minas Gerais, see José, *Historiografia mineira,* 2nd ed. (Belo Horizonte, Brazil: Imp.

Oficial, 1987), 336–38. On the absence of Indians in the historiography of eighteenth- and nineteenth-century Brazil, see Barickman, "'Tame Indians,'" 326–27.

Sources on the raiding by *bandeirantes* of native groups in Minas Gerais, as well as on the early exploration and occupation of the region in general, include Augusto de Lima Júnior, *A Capitania das Minas Gerais*, rev. ed. (Belo Horizonte, Brazil: Ed. Itatiaia, 1978); Afonso de Escragnolle Taunay, *História geral das bandeiras paulistas*, 11 vols. (São Paulo: Imp. Oficial, 1924–50), vols. 9–10; *idem, Relatos sertanistas* (Belo Horizonte, Brazil: Ed. Itatiaia, 1981); Diogo [Luís de Almeida Pereira] de Vasconcelos, *História antiga de Minas Gerais*, 4th ed. (Belo Horizonte, Brazil: Ed. Itatiaia, 1974); Francisco de Assis Carvalho Franco, *Dicionário de bandeirantes e sertanistas do Brasil: Século XVI, XVII, XVIII* (Belo Horizonte, Brazil: Ed. Itatiaia, 1989).

2. Carla Maria Junho Anastasia, introduction to *Breve descrição geográfica, física e política da Capitania de Minas Gerais*, by Diogo Pereira Ribeiro de Vasconcelos (1807; reprint, Belo Horizonte, Brazil: Fundação João Pinheiro, 1994), 15. John Monteiro notes the dearth of research on the role of native populations during the early years of the gold rush, *Negros da terra*, 210 n. 3. Also see Renato Venâncio Pinto, "Os últimos carijós: Escravidão indígena em Minas Gerais: 1711–1725," *Revista Brasileira de História* 17:34 (1997): 165–81.

3. For example, see Sebastião da Rocha Pitta, *Historia da America Portugueza, desde o anno de mil e quinhentos do seu descobrimento, até o de mil e setecentos e vinte e quatro* (Lisbon: Academia Real, 1730), 113–15; Francisco Tavares de Brito, *Itinerario Geografico com a Verdadeira Descripção dos Caminhos, Estradas, Rossas, Citios, Povoações, Lugares, Villas, Rios, Montes, e Serras, que ha da Cidade de S. Sebastião do Rio De Janeiro até as Minas Do Ouro* (Seville: Antonio da Sylva, 1732), 24–25.

4. For the prince regent's declaration of war against the Botocudo, see "Carta Régia (royal edict) ao Governador e Capitão General da capitania de Minas Gerais sobre a guerra aos Indios Botecudos," 13 May 1808, in *Legislação indigenista no século XIX: Uma compilação (1808–1889)*, ed. Manuela Carneiro da Cunha (São Paulo: Universidade de São Paulo, 1992), 57–60. For a manuscript version of the war declaration, see "Carta Régia do principe regente D. João VI [*sic*], dirigida a Pedro Maria Xavier de Ataide e Mello, governador de Minas Gerais ordenando que forme um corpo de soldados pedestres para lutar contra os índios Botecudos," Rio de Janeiro, 13 May 1808, BNRJ, SM, doc. I-28, 31, 20. An identical copy sent to the governor of Minas Gerais is published as "Sobre os Botocudos," *RAPM* 4:3–4 (1899): 783–86.

5. A telling measure of the persistent lack of attention to these native societies on the part of both scholars and students in the U.S. is the mere handful of references to them in the most widely used English-language, college-level textbook on colonial Latin America. See Mark A. Burkholder and Lyman L. Johnson, *Colonial Latin America*, 5th ed. (Oxford: Oxford University Press, 2004). Another prominent textbook characterized by a complete disregard for Brazilian Indians, despite its inclusive title, is John E. Kicza, *The Indian in Latin American History: Resistance, Resilience, and Acculturation*, rev. ed. (Wilmington, DE: SR Books, 2000). Kicza's still more recent work of even broader scope, which he describes as "profoundly comparative," remedies this problem only slightly, devoting a few pages to the coastal Tupi peoples but none to Brazil's inland natives. See Kicza, *Resilient Cultures: America's Native Peoples Confront European Colonization, 1500–1800* (Upper Saddle River, NJ: Prentice Hall, 2003), esp. 2, 157–61.

6. Vasconcelos, *Breve descrição*, 51; also see Robert H. Lowie, "The Southern Cayapó," *HSAI*, vol. 1, 519–20; Odair Giraldin, *Cayapó e Panará: Luta e sobrevivência de um povo Jê no Brasil Central* (Campinas, Brazil: UNICAMP, 1997); Mary C. Karasch, "Interethnic Conflict and Resistance on the Brazilian Frontier of Goiás, 1750–1890," in *Contested Ground*, 115–34. Throughout, I have translated the Portuguese term *gentio* as heathen. On the term's origin, relationship to the English word *gentile*, and usage in colonial Brazil, see Barickman, "'Tame Indians,'" 327 n. 6.

7. Although remaining territorially and, in many respects, administratively part of the captaincy of Rio de Janeiro during this period, the coastal Campos dos Goitacases sugar-producing district north and south of the Paraíba River was placed under the judicial jurisdiction of the captaincy of Espírito Santo between 1753 and 1832. In turn subordinated to Bahia for most of the eighteenth century, Espírito Santo gained administrative independence in 1800. On the Campos region, see José Carneiro da Silva, *Memoria topographica e historica sobre os Campos dos Goytacazes com uma noticia breve de suas producções e commercio* (1819; reprint, Rio de Janeiro: Typ. Leuzinger, 1907), 25–27, 43; Alberto Lamego, *A Terra Goitacá á luz de documentos inéditos*, vol. 2 (Rio de Janeiro: Garnier, 1913–41), 457–59, 505–06; Silvia Hunold Lara, *Campos da violência: Escravos e senhores na Capitania do Rio de Janeiro, 1750–1808* (Rio de Janeiro: Paz e Terra, 1988), esp., 130, 360; Sheila de Castro Faria, *A Colônia em movimento: Fortuna e família no cotidiano colonial* (Rio de Janeiro: Ed. Nova Fronteira, 1998), esp. 27–35. On Espírito Santo administration, see Dauril Alden, *Royal Government in Colonial Brazil with Special Reference to the Administration of the Marquis of Lavradio, Viceroy, 1769–1779* (Berkeley, CA: University of California Press, 1968), 39–40; Maria Beatriz Nizza da Silva, ed., *Dicionário da história da colonização portuguesa no Brasil* (Lisbon: Verbo, 1994), 310; Paraíso, "O tempo da dor," 165. Created in 1709 from the old captaincy of São Vicente, the captaincy of São Paulo and Minas Gerais endured for just over a decade until 1720, when Minas Gerais became a separate entity. In 1748, the new captaincies of Goiás and Mato Grosso were similarly detached from São Paulo, which was then subordinated to the captaincy of Rio de Janeiro, becoming a *comarca* (judicial district). In 1765, São Paulo again became a captaincy in its own right, remaining as such until 1822 when it became a province.

8. José Joaquim da Cunha de Azeredo Coutinho, *Ensaio economico sobre o comercio de Portugal e suas colonias oferecido ao serenisimo Princepe do Brazil, Noso Senhor* (Lisbon: Academia Real das Ciências, 1794), 65. Also see "Requerimento de D. José Joaquim da Cunha de Azeredo Coutinho a rainha D. Maria I," ca. 1794, in Lamego, *A Terra Goitacá*, vol. 2, 505–06.

9. Alfred Métraux, "The Purí-Coroado Linguistic Family," in *HSAI*, vol. 1, 523–30; José Ribamar Bessa Freire and Márcia Fernanda Malheiros, *Aldeamentos indígenas do Rio de Janeiro* (Rio de Janeiro: Programa de Estudos dos Povos Indígenas, Universidade do Estado do Rio de Janeiro, 1997), 21–25; José de Souza Azevedo Pizarro e Araújo, *Memórias Históricas do Rio de Janeiro e das provincias annexas a jurisdicção do vice-rei do Estado do Brasil*, vol. 5 (Rio de Janeiro: Imp. Régia, 1820–1822), 288–89, 295.

10. For example, see William Balée, "The Ka'apor Indian Wars of Lower Amazonia, ca. 1825–1928," in *Dialectics and Gender: Anthropological Approaches*, ed. Richard R. Randolph, David M. Schneider, and May N. Diaz (Boulder, CO: Westview Press, 1988), 155–69; Radding, *Wandering Peoples*, 275–79; Thomas Biolsi, "Ecological and Cultural

Factors in Plains Indians Warfare," in *Warfare, Culture, and Environment*, ed. R. Brian Ferguson (Orlando, FL: Academic Press, 1984), 141–68; R. Brian Ferguson and Neil L. Whitehead, "The Violent Edge of Empire," in *War in the Tribal Zone: Expanding States and Indigenous Warfare*, ed. idem (Santa Fe, NM: School of American Research Press, 1992), 1–30. Concerning scholarly disagreement over linguistic commonalities among groups classified as Gê speakers, see Norman A. McQuown, "The Indigenous Languages of Latin America," *American Anthropologist*, New Series, 57:3, pt. 1 (June 1955): 501–70, esp. 560.

11. Alfred Métraux and Curt Nimuendajú, "The Mashacalí, Patashó, and Malalí Linguistic Families"; and Alfred Métraux, "The Purí-Coroado Linguistic Family," in *HSAI*, vol. 1, 541–45 and 523–30, respectively; Paraíso, "O tempo da dor," 4–5; Silva, *Memoria topographica e historica*, 27. On the subordinate administrative status of the formerly independent captaincies of Ilhéus and Porto Seguro during this period, see Alden, *Royal Government*, 39–40; Barickman, "'Tame Indians,'" 334.

12. Nara Saletto, *Transição para o trabalho livre e pequena propriedade no Espírito Santo*, (Rio de Janeiro: Universidade Federal do Rio de Janeiro, 1991); Auguste de Saint-Hilaire, *Viagem ao Espírito Santo e Rio Doce*, trans. Milton Amado (Belo Horizonte, Brazil: Ed. Itatiaia, 1974), 14; and on Bahia, Barickman, "'Tame Indians,'" 357–65; Frei Ludovico de Leorne, Descripção topographica do que ha de notavel de poder ser inserido no novo Diccionario entre a Barra do Rio de Contas, e a do Rio de Belmonte..., São Pedro d'Alcantara, 12 Dec 1838, APEB, SCP, maço 5308. On intertribal warfare as a product of the contest for scarce resources, see Richard White, "The Winning of the West: The Expansion of the Western Sioux in the Eighteenth and Nineteenth Centuries," *Journal of American History* 65:2 (1978): 319–43.

13. Scholars now recognize dozens of distinct Macro-Gê languages. See Freire and Malheiros, *Aldeamentos indígenas*, 6–8.

14. For contrasting positions, see ibid.; Paraíso, "O tempo da dor," 4–5.

15. Auguste de Saint-Hilaire, *Viagem pelas províncias do Rio de Janeiro e Minas Gerais*, trans. Vivaldi Moreira (Belo Horizonte, Brazil: Ed. Itatiaia, 1975), 251 n. 360.

16. See José, *Indígenas*, 13–37; Métraux, "The Botocudo," in *HSAI*, vol. 1, 531–40; Nelson de Senna, "Principaes povos selvagens que tiveram o seo 'habitat' em territorio das Minas Geraes," *RAPM* 25:1 (1937): 337–55; Maximilian, Prinz von Wied, *Viagem ao Brasil*, trans. Edgar Süssekind de Mendonça and Flávio Poppe de Figueiredo (Belo Horizonte, Brazil: Ed. Itatiaia, 1989), 283–84. Among others who recognized that the Botocudo were not the only natives in the region to don lip and ear plugs, the European traveler X. Chabert noted that some Pataxó "pierce the lower lip and the ear, in imitation of the Botocudos, and wear a small piece of reed in the little aperture." See X. Chabert, *An Historical Account of the Manners and Customs of the Savage Inhabitants of Brazil; Together with a Sketch of the Life of the Botocudo Chieftain and Family* (Exeter, UK: R. Cullum, 1823), 20.

B. J. Barickman recently revived a long-standing debate as to whether the Botocudo in fact descended from the Aimoré. The link, he notes, is based on slim linguistic evidence. Barickman, "'Tame Indians,'" 335 n. 29. A more fundamental issue is that both names, Botocudo and Aimoré, were used interchangeably in Portuguese documents from the mid-eighteenth century onward, neither of them with any real precision. The latter designation, which also appears in sources as Aimboré, Amburé, and Imburé, was applied no less generically than the name Botocudo. Neither term was used, as scholars have long recognized, by the Indians to identify themselves. Instead, they used Gren, Krakmun, Naknenuk, and other names, referring to particular subgroups. But these more specific terms almost never entered into the documentary record before 1800 in Minas Gerais. The Portuguese rarely concerned themselves with native preference or, for that matter, with the differences, sometimes minor, sometimes considerable, between one subgroup and another. Accordingly, in most cases the sources leave no alternative but to use the generic name Botocudo.

17. Lamego, *A Terra Goitacá*, vol. 1, 17 n. 8; John Luccock, *Notes on Rio de Janeiro and the Southern Parts of Brazil; Taken During a Residence of Ten Years in that Country, from 1808 to 1818* (London: Samuel Leigh, 1820), 301. Also see A.H. Keane, "On the Botocudos," *Journal of the Anthropological Institute of Great Britain and Ireland* 13 (1884): 199–200, including n. 5.

18. Keane, "On the Botocudos," 204.

19. Petition of Padre Francisco da Silva Campos to Prince Regent, [1800], in *RAPM* 2:4 (1897): 692.

20. Ferguson and Whitehead, "The Violent Edge of Empire"; Neil L. Whitehead, "Tribes Make States and States Make Tribes: Warfare and the Creation of Colonial Tribes and States in Northeastern South America," in *War in the Tribal Zone*, 127–50.

21. See Paraíso, "O tempo da dor," 3–5; Robin M. Wright with Manuela Carneiro da Cunha, "Destruction, Resistance, and Transformation—Southern, Coastal, and Northern Brazil (1580–1890)," in *CHNPA*, vol. 3, *South America*, ed. Frank Salomon and Stuart B. Schwartz (Cambridge: Cambridge University Press, 1999), pt. 2, 340–45. Ramos, among other anthropologists, raises legitimate concerns about describing any of Brazil's native peoples as nomadic or even seminomadic. She notes that in the Americas, the words "suffered a slippage of meaning from a technical concept related to a mode of livelihood . . . to a moral judgment—a wandering tribe of Indians. This semantic meta-morphosis would not be particularly problematic if it had not been appropriated by the dominant society to despoil dominated Indians." While I have opted along with many other scholars to retain the term *seminomadic*, I do so in a fashion that makes colonial preconceptions against mobility a central feature of my analysis. See Alcida R. Ramos, *Indigenism: Ethnic Politics in Brazil* (Madison, WI: University of Wisconsin Press, 1998), 35.

22. Viceroy to Marquis of Angeja, Rio de Janeiro, 12 Jun 1778, AHM, divisão 2, seção 1, cx. 1, no. 28.

23. "Informação sobre as Minas do Brasil," [ca. 1700], in *ABNRJ* 57 (1935): 167–68. For detailed descriptions of the routes to Rio de Janeiro and São Paulo published at the height of the mining boom, see Francisco Tavares de Brito, *Itinerario geografico*, 2–9.

24. For statistics on gold production, Crown revenues, the royal fifth, and other taxes and levies in Minas Gerais, see Boxer, *Golden Age*, 333–50; Souza, *Desclassificados do ouro*, 43–9; and Maxwell, *Conflicts and Conspiracies*, 245–54.

25. Francisco Xavier de Menezes, *Relaçam da vitoria que os portuguezes alcançàraõ no Rio de Janeyro contra os francezes em 19. de Setembro de 1710* (Lisbon: Antonio Pedrozo Galraõ, 1711), JCBL; Boxer, *Golden Age*, chap. 4.

26. Gusmão to Antonio Pedro de Vasconcelos, Lisbon, 8 Sep 1751, in Cartas de Alexandre de Gusmão, Menistro [sic] de Estado particular de Sua Mag.ᵉ Fedelissima o Senhor Rey Dom Joam 5°, MS, Lisbon, JCBL, fols. 51–53v.

27. On the use of the term by officials both in Brazil and Portugal, see, for example, Governor to Colonial Secretary, [Vila Rica], 3 Jun 1781, APM, SC, cód. 224, fol. 29v; Governor to Colonial Secretary, Vila Rica, 31 Dec 1781, ibid., fols. 62–62v (first of four letters of this date written by the governor to the colonial secretary); would be Prohibited Areas; however, Forbidden Lands better conveys the colonial connotation in English. Although the term was applied most commonly to the southeastern portion of Minas Gerais now known as the Zona da Mata, I have used it more broadly, having documented similar restrictions pertaining to the entire Eastern Sertão. Paraíso studies the portion of this area lying to the north of the Doce River, primarily during the nineteenth century, referring to it as the "zona tampão" or buffer zone. See Paraíso, "O tempo da dor," esp. 2–4, 84–97.

28. Quoted in Diogo [Luís de Almeida Pereira] de Vasconcelos, História média de Minas Gerais, 4th ed. (Belo Horizonte, Brazil: Ed. Itatiaia, 1974), 275.

29. João de Lencastre to Crown, Salvador da Bahia, 12 Jan 1701, in Os manuscritos do Arquivo da Casa de Cadaval respeitantes ao Brasil, vol. 2, ed. Virginia Rau and Maria Fernandes Gomes da Silva (Coimbra, Portugal: Atlântica, 1955–1958), 14–17. This letter written by the governor general of Brazil indicates that authorities significantly underestimated—at 40 leagues (264 km)—the distance between the coast and the central mining fields. A road of that length, even if direct, would have reached eastward from Vitória only to approximately Abre Campo, which at the time remained unsettled. In practice, any such route would have had to skirt difficult terrain, probably following the course of the Doce River, as was the case with the road that finally did connect Vitória and Vila Rica in the early nineteenth century. The main highway that now links Vitória to Ouro Preto (Vila Rica) stretches 450 km. Also see Abreu, Caminhos antigos, chap. 4; and Boxer, Golden Age, 43.

30. Carta Régia to governor general, Lisbon, 7 Feb 1701, AHU, Bahia, cx. 123, doc. 78.

31. Silva, Dicionário da história, 309. See also Afonso de Escragnolle Taunay, História das bandeiras paulistas, 3rd ed. (São Paulo: Edições Melhoramentos, 1975), vol. 1, 325.

32. On the social and administrative history of the diamond district, see Furtado, Livro da Capa Verde; Maxwell, Conflicts and Conspiracies, esp. 45–46, 110–11; Alden, Royal Government, 12–13, 400–01; Boxer, Golden Age, chap. 8; Joaquim Felício dos Santos, Memórias do Distrito Diamantino da Comarca do Serro Frio (Província de Minas Gerais), 4th ed. (1868; reprint, Belo Horizonte, Brazil: Ed. Itatiaia, 1976); Wilhelm Ludwig von Eschwege, Pluto brasiliensis, vol. 2, trans. Domício de Figueiredo Murta (Belo Horizonte, Brazil: Ed. Itatiaia, 1979), 115–60; José Vieira Couto, Memória sobre a Capitania das Minas Gerais; seu território, clima e produções metálicas (1799; reprint, edited by Júnia Ferreira Furtado, Belo Horizonte, Brazil: Fundação João Pinheiro, 1994), 83–89; José João Teixeira Coelho, "Instrucção para o governo da capitania de Minas Gerais," 1780, RIHGB 15 (1852): 399–581, esp. 438–47. Documents pertaining to the discovery of diamonds and the origin of the diamond district administration have been collected and published in RAPM 7:1–2 (1902): 251–370.

33. Carta Régia to Governor of Rio de Janeiro, Lisbon, 8 Feb 1730, AHU, cód. 610, fols. 103–03v; Governor, Bando (proclamation), Vila Rica, 7 Jan 1732, AIHGB, Conselho Ultramarino, Arq. 1, 3, 3, fols. 1–4; Alvará (royal charter), 27 Oct 1733, AHM, divisão 2, seção 1, cx. 1, no. 15; and Alvará, 3 Dec 1750, AHU, cód. 610, fols. 103v–04v.

34. Eschwege, *Pluto brasiliensis*, vol. 1, 117. The road down the Doce River valley appeared first on "Mapa da capitania de Minas Geraes," 1810, BNRJ, SI, arc. 32, 4, 20. The year 1810 marked the beginning of a burst of road-building activity farther to the north as well, including the construction of a route from the town of Ilhéus inland along the Pardo River, a route between the towns of Belmonte in Porto Seguro and Minas Novas in Minas Gerais, and a route between the towns of Portalegre in Porto Seguro and Minas Novas. To the south, the situation was no different, as the Crown approved additional road construction related to provisioning the court in Rio de Janeiro, including a road between Rio Pomba and the coastal Campos region, cutting though Coroado and Puri territory. For accounts of contacts between road builders, settlers, and the Botocudo, see *Idade de Ouro do Brasil* (Salvador), 17 Dec 1811, 2–3; 20 Dec 1811, 3. Also see Barickman, "'Tame Indians,'" 355; Caio Prado Júnior, *Formação do Brasil contemporâneo*, 20th ed. (São Paulo: Brasiliense, 1987), 243–47; Alcir Lenharo, *As tropas da moderação: (O abastimento da Corte na formação política do Brasil, 1808–1842)* (São Paulo: Símbolo, 1979), chap. 2; Silva, *Memoria topographica e historica*, 27.

35. Francisco [de Sales] Ribeiro to Governor, n.p., 24 Jul 1761, AN, cód. 807, vol. 5, fols. 81, 85; João da Silva Pereira de Souza to Governor, Cuieté, 3 Feb 1770, BNRJ, SM, CV, cód. 18, 2, 6, doc. 267.

36. Governor Noronha identified Manoel Pires Farinha as the captain's son; however, Governor Rodrigo José de Meneses and the captain himself referred to Manoel as his brother. See Governor to Jozé Leme da Silva, Vila Rica, 27 Jul 1778, and to Francisco Pires Farinho, Vila Rica, 27 Jul 1778, BNRJ, SM, cód. 2, 2, 24, fols. 164–65v; Governor to Francisco Pires Farinho, Cachoeira, 13 Nov 1781, APM, SC, cód. 227, fols. 13–13v; Petition of Francisco and Manoel Pires Farinho to Queen, prior to 11 Dec 1782, AHU, Minas Gerais, cx. 118, doc. 96. On the spelling of this surname, see 353 n. 26.

37. Governor to Jozé Leme da Silva, Vila Rica, 27 Jul 1778, and to Francisco Pires Farinho, Vila Rica, 27 Jul 1778, BNRJ, SM, cód. 2, 2, 24, fols. 164–65v; Colonial Secretary to Governor, Salvaterra de Magos, 26 Jan 1785, AHU, cód. 610, fols. 104v–06v. Also see Waldemar de Almeida Barbosa, *Dicionário histórico-geográfico de Minas Gerais* (Belo Horizonte, Brazil: Ed. Itatiaia, 1995), 286–87; and Castro, *Os sertões de leste*, 11–15.

38. See Paraíso, "Os Botocudos e sua trajetória histórica," in *História dos índios no Brasil*, 415.

39. Governor, "Plano Secreto para a nova Conquista do Cuieté," [Vila Rica], [ca. August 1779], BNRJ, SM, cód. 2, 2, 24, fol. 230v.

40. See Walter D. Mignolo, "Misunderstanding and Colonization: The Reconfiguration of Memory and Space," in *Le Nouveau Monde, Mondes Nouveaux: L'experience americaine*, ed. Serge Gruzinski and Nathan Wachtel (Paris: EHESS/CNRS, 1996), 271–93; Edward W. Said, *Orientalism* (New York: Vintage Books, 1979), chap. 1, pt. 2; Barbara E. Mundy, *The Mapping of New Spain: Indigenous Cartography and the Maps of the Relaciones Geográficas* (Chicago: University of Chicago Press, 1996), xii–xiii; Raymond

B. Craib, "Cartography and Power in the Conquest and Creation of New Spain," *Latin American Research Review* 35:1 (2000): 7–36; J.B. Harley and David Woodward, eds., *The History of Cartography*, vol. 1 (Chicago: University of Chicago Press, 1987), xvi; John L. Allen, "Mapping the Plains and Prairies, 1800–1860," in *Mapping the North American Plains: Essays in the History of Cartography*, ed. Frederick C. Luebke, Frances W. Kaye, and Gary E. Moulton (Norman, OK: University of Oklahoma Press, 1987), 41–62. For an overview of the mapping of North American frontier zones during the same period, see Seymour I. Schwartz and Ralph E. Ehrenberg, *The Mapping of America* (New York: Harry N. Abrams, 1980), chaps. 7, 8. Also see Matthew H. Edney, *Mapping an Empire: The Geographical Construction of British India, 1765–1843* (Chicago: University of Chicago Press, 1997); Laura Hostetler, *Qing Colonial Enterprise: Ethnography and Cartography in Early Modern China* (Chicago: University of Chicago Press, 2001).

41. See Matthew H. Edney, "Reconsidering Enlightenment Geography and Map Making: Reconnaissance, Mapping, Archive," in *Geography and Enlightenment*, ed. David N. Livingstone and Charles W.J. Withers (Chicago: University of Chicago Press, 1999), 166, as well as the other essays in this collection.

42. Lopo Homem-Reinéis, "Atlas de 1519," facsimile, Armando Cortesão and Avelino Teixeira da Mota, *Portugaliae Monumenta Cartographica*, vol. 1 (Lisbon: Imp. de Coimbra, 1960), pl. 22. On the trade in brazilwood, monkeys, and parrots, see A.J.R. Russell-Wood, *The Portuguese Empire, 1415–1808: A World on the Move* (Baltimore, MD: Johns Hopkins University Press, 1998), 128. On the first appearance of Brazilian sugar on the Antwerp market in 1519, see Stuart B. Schwartz, *Sugar Plantations in the Formation of Brazilian Society: Bahia, 1550–1835* (Cambridge: Cambridge University Press, 1985), 16.

43. See Lopo Homem-Reinéis, "Planisfério de 1554," facsimile, *Potugaliae Monumenta Cartographica*, vol. 1, pl. 27; and the three maps by Diogo Homem, "Atlas de doze folhas," 1558; "Atlas de 28 folhas," 1568; and "Atlas de dezanove fohlas," ca. 1565, ibid., vol. 2, pls. 108, 131, 176.

44. Diego Gutiérrez, "Americae sive quartae orbis partis nova et exactissima descritio . . . " Antwerp, 1562, Lessing J. Rosenwald Collection, GMD, LC.

45. João Teixeira Albernaz I, "Atlas do Brasil com dezanove cartas," 1627, facsimile, *Potugaliae Monumenta Cartographica*, vol. 4, pls. 453, 455. Inland Brazil was not the only place Portuguese cartographers represented as terra incognita, rich in gold. Albernaz I himself made similar notations on his maps of southern and eastern Africa. Albernaz I, "Taboas Geraes de Toda a Navegação . . . ," Lisbon, 1630, MS, GMD, LC. Leaders of early bandeiras to the interior of southern Bahia, Porto Seguro, and Espírito Santo included Francisco Bruzza de Spinozza (1550s), Vasco Rodrigues Caldas (1560s), Martim Carvalho (1560s), Sebastião Fernandes Tourinho (1570s), Antônio Dias Adorno (1570s), João Coelho de Sousa (1570s and 1580s), his brother Gabriel Soares de Sousa (1590s), Diogo Martim Cão (1590s), Marcos de Azeredo Coutinho (before 1611), the Jesuit priest Inácio de Siqueira (1630s), Domingos de Azeredo Coutinho and Antônio de Azeredo Coutinho (sons of Marcos de Azeredo Coutinho, 1640s and 1650s), Agostinho Barbalho (1660s), Fernão Dias Pais (1670s), Rodrigo de Castelbranco (1680s), Manoel de Borba Gato (1680s), Antônio Rodrigues de Arzão (1690s), and Bartolomeu Bueno de Siqueira (1690s). Their adventures were featured in histories written throughout the colonial

period. See [Gabriel Soares de Sousa], *Noticia do Brazil, descripção verdadeira da costa daquelle estado, que pertence á coroa do Reino de Portugal, sitio da Bahia de Todos os Santos,* vol. 3, pt. 1 of *Collecção de noticias para a historia e geografia das nações ultramarinas, que vivem nos dominios portuguezes, ou lhes são visinhas* (1587; reprint, Lisbon: Typ. da Academia Real das Sciencias, 1825), 57–59; Sebastião da Rocha Pitta, *Historia da America Portugueza,* 113–15; Brito, *Itinerario Geografico,* 24–25; [Manuel Aires de Casal], *Corografia brazilica, ou relação historico-geografica do Reino do Brazil,* vol. 1 (Rio de Janeiro: Imp. Regia, 1817), 357; Ferdinand Denis, *Résumé De L'Histoire Du Brésil, Suivi Du Résumé De L'Histoire De La Guyane,* 2nd ed. (Paris: Lecomte Et Durey, 1825), 77, 144–45; Raimundo José da Cunha Matos, *Corografia histórica da Província de Minas Gerais (1837),* vol. 1 (São Paulo: Ed. Itatiaia, 1981), 329–44. Also see John Hemming, *Red Gold. The Conquest of the Brazilian Indians, 1500–1760* (Cambridge, MA: Harvard University Press, 1977), 93–96, 156, 378–80; Russell-Wood, *Portuguese Empire,* 103; Lima Júnior, *A Capitania das Minas Gerais,* 18–34; Franco, *Dicionário de bandeirantes.*

46. João Teixeira Albernaz II, "Costa dos Ilheos ao Rio de Santo Antonio," 1666, facsimile, *Potugaliae Monumenta Cartographica,* vol. 5, pl. 565G.

47. José da Costa Miranda, "Planifério de 1706," facsimile, *Potugaliae Monumenta Cartographica,* vol. 5, pl. 574.

48. Willem Janszoon Blaeu, "Novus Brasiliae Tipus," [1631?], BNRJ, SI, arc. 9, 11, 39; Johannes [Joan] Blaeu, "Brasilia," 1657; and Ioanne Blaev [Joan Blaeu], "Nova et Accurata Brasiliae," [ca. 1660], Rare Books Room, BLAC. The latter was apparently engraved for Blaeu's famed 1662 world atlas. See Rodney W. Shirley, *The Mapping of the World: Early Printed World Maps, 1472–1700* (London: Holland Press, 1984), 449–51.

49. Herman Moll, ". . . Map of South America, According to the Newest and Most Exact Observations," [London], [1709–1720], JCBL.

50. Georg Matthaeus Seutter, "Rencens elaborata Mappa Geographica Regni Brasiliae in America Meridionali . . . ," Augsburg, ca. 1730, JCBL.

51. Charles Brockwell, *The Natural and Political History of Portugal . . .* (London: T. Warner, 1726), 322–23.

52. Emanuel Bowen, *A Complete System of Geography, Being a Description of All the Countries, Islands, Cities, Chief Towns, Harbours, Lakes, and Rivers, Mountains, Mines, Etc., of the Known World . . . ,* vol. 2 (London: William Innys, et al., 1747), 535. For Bowen's map, see "A New & Accurate Map of Brazil," in ibid., between p. 520 and 521.

53. "Mapa dos confins do Brazil com as terras da Coroa de Esp.ª na America Meridional," 1751, GMD, LC, photostat. The source of this copy is itself a manuscript copy of a 1750 original.

54. Ibid., and Juan de Cruz Cano y Olmedilla, "Mapa Geográfico de America Meridional," [Madrid], 1775, JCBL. Also see Thomas R. Smith, "Cruz Cano's Map of South America, Madrid, 1775: Its Creation, Adversities and Rehabilitation," *Imago Mundi* 20 (1966): 49–78. On the Madrid and San Ildefonso treaties, see, among others, Alden, *Royal Government,* 86–95, 262–67. On the cartographic inaccuracies influencing the negotiations surrounding the first of these treaties, see Mário Clemente Ferreira, "Uma ideia de Brasil num mapa inédito de 1746," *Oceanos* 43 (July–September 2000): 184–95.

55. Brito, introduction to *Itinerario Geografico.*

56. "Descripçam do Continente da América Meridional que nos pertence com os rios, e montes, que os certanejos mais experimentados, dizem ter encontrado, cuja divizão se faz," 1746, Colecção Guita e José E. Mindlin, São Paulo, facsimile, Comissão Nacional para as Comemorações dos Descobrimentos Portugueses, *Brasil-brasis: Cousas notaveis e espantosas (A construção do Brasil: 1500–1825)* (Lisbon: Comissão Nacional para as Comemorações dos Descobrimentos Portugueses, 2000), pl. 69; Ferreira, "Uma ideia de Brasil."

57. Brito, *Itinerario Geografico*, 25.

58. "Mapa da região banhada pelo Rio Doce e seus afluentes, na Capitania de Minas Gerais," ca. 1758; and "Carta geographica que comprehende toda a Comarca do Rio das Mortes, Villa Rica, e parte da Cidade de Mariana do Governo de Minas Geraes," ca. 1764, fascimiles, Isa Adonias, ed., *Mapa: Imagens da formação territorial brasileira* (Rio de Janeiro: Fundação Emílio Odebrecht, 1993), pls. 152, 153.

59. The first of these maps, untitled, BNRJ, SI, arc. 9, 2, 7A, is erroneously catalogued as a copy of José Joaquim da Rocha, "Mappa da Capitania de Minas Geraes...," 1777, BNRJ, SI, arc. 1, 2, 28, from which it in fact differs. The second map is "Carta geographica da capitania de Minas Gerais e partes confinantes," 1767, BNRJ, SI, arc. 17, 5, 12.

60. Rocha to Governor, Vila Rica, 1 Apr. 1786, in Brazil, Minas Gerais, Câmara dos Deputados, *Autos de devassa da Inconfidência Mineira*, 2nd ed., vol. 5 (Belo Horizonte, Brazil: Imprensa Oficial, 1976–83), 48 n. 1. Also see Maria Efigênia Lage de Resende, introduction to *Geografia histórica da Capitania de Minas Gerais*, by José Joaquim da Rocha (1780; reprint, Belo Horizonte, Brazil: Fundação João Pinheiro, 1995), esp. 17–29, 49–59; Charles W.J. Withers and David N. Livingstone, introduction to Livingstone and Withers, *Geography and Enlightenment*, 1–28. On the importance of military engineers in eighteenth-century Brazil, see Roberta M. Delson, "The Beginnings of Professionalization in the Brazilian Military: the Eighteenth Century Corps of Engineers," *The Americas* 51:4 (April 1995): 555–74; Maria Beatriz Nizza da Silva, *A cultura luso-brasileira: Da reforma da Universidade à independência do Brasil* (Lisbon: Ed. Estampa, 1999), 71–73; Beatriz Siqueira Bueno, "Desenho e desígnio: O Brasil dos engenheiros militares," *Oceanos* 41 (January–March 2000): 8–38; Walter Rosa, "No primeiro dos elementos: Dados para uma leitura sintética do urbanismo e da urbanística portugueses da Idade Moderna," ibid., 40–58. On the Enlightenment in Minas Gerais and Brazil, see José Ferreira Carrato, *Igreja, iluminismo e escolas mineiras coloniais* (São Paulo: Nacional, 1968); Maria Beatriz Nizza da Silva, *A cultura luso-brasileira*, esp. 183–203; Sergio Paulo Rouanet, "As Minas iluminadas: a Ilustração e a Inconfidência," in *Tempo e história*, ed. Adauto Novaes (São Paulo: Companhia das Letras, 1992), 329–45.

61. Rocha, *Geografia histórica*, 132–33.

62. See Edney, "Reconsidering Enlightenment Geography and Map Making," 168–76; G.N.G. Clarke, "Taking Possession: The Cartouche as Cultural Text in Eighteenth-Century American Maps," *Word and Image* 4:2 (April–June 1988): 455–74.

63. In 1777, Rocha drafted a preliminary version of "Mappa da comarca do Sabará pertencente a capitania de Minas Geraes," BNRJ, SI, arc. 30, 1, 33. His 1778 maps include "Mapa da capitania de Minas Geraes com a deviza de suas comarcas," "Mappa da comarca do Serro Frio," "Mappa da comarca da Villa Rica," "Mappa da comarca do Rio das Mortes,"

and "Mappa da comarca do Sabará." The Arquivo Histórico do Exército in Rio de Janeiro holds the originals of these maps, facsimiles of which have been published as flyleaf inserts in Rocha's historical geography, completed two years later, *Geografia histórica*. North American regional maps from this period display similar topographic markings, settlement notation, and Indian imagery. For example, see John Mitchell, "A Map of the British and French Dominions in North America with the Roads, Distances, Limits, and Extent of the Settlements," 1755; Henry Timberlake, "A Draught of the Cherokee Country," 1765; and Thomas Hutchins, "A Topographical Plan of that part of the Indian-Country through which the Army under the Command of Colonel Bouquet marched in the Year of 1764," 1765, facsimiles, Schwartz and Ehrenberg, *Mapping of America*, pls. 96, 106, 107.

64. On gendered European views of nature and colonialism, see Elizabeth A. Bohls, "The Aesthetics of Colonialism: Janet Schaw in the West Indies, 1774–1775," *Eighteenth-Century Studies* 27:3 (Spring 1994): 363–90; Pratt, *Imperial Eyes*, chap. 5, 213–16; Richard C. Trexler, *Sex and Conquest: Gendered Violence, Political Order, and the European Conquest of the Americas* (Ithaca, NY: Cornell University Press, 1995). For Brazilian perspectives on this subject, see Ramos, *Indigenism*, 164–66.

65. "Colecção de quatro mapas da capitania das Minas Gerais abrangendo os territórios banhados pelos rios S. Francisco, Guarapiranga, dos Corvados, Paraopeba, das Velhas, Gualaxo, Pardo, Pardo pequeno, Arrasuali, Giquitinonha, Tucambira, Assu (*sic*), etc., " ca. 1780–1800, AHU, CM, Minas Gerais, nos. 1172–75. For numerous instances of Minas towns founded on sites once called "Quilombo," see Barbosa, *Dicionário histórico-geográfico*, 276–77. On runaway slave communities in colonial Minas Gerais, see Carlos Magno Guimarães, *Uma negação da ordem escravista: Quilombos em Minas Gerais no século XVIII* (São Paulo: Icone, 1988); Flávio dos Santos Gomes, "Seguindo o mapa das minas: Plantas e quilombos mineiros setecentistas," *Estudos Afro–Asiáticos* 29 (March 1996): 113–42.

66. Alexandre de Gusmão, "Reparos sobre a despozição da Lei de 3 de Dezembro de 1750, a respeito do Novo Methodo da Cobrança do Qunto do Brazil, abolindo o da Capitação," Lisbon, 18 Dec 1750, fol. 117, Cartas de Alexandre de Gusmão, Menistro [*sic*] de Estado particular de Sua Mag.e Fedelissima o Senhor Rey Dom Joam 5°, Codex Port. 5, MS, JCBL.

67. "Comarcas de Porto Seguro e de Ilhéus," ca. 1807, facsimile, Adonias, *Mapa*, pl. 145.

68. "Mapa da capitania de Minas Geraes," 1810, BNRJ, SI, arc. 32, 4, 20. As Coutinho had it, the Ouetacázes (alternatively, Goitacá or Goitacázes) Indians had attacked the Botocudo at the behest of his own forebears, members of the Campos sugar-planting elite. Guarulho was a term used by some to designate descendants of the Goitacá, by others to refer generically to various Indians groups residing in this region. See Coutinho, *Ensaio economico*, 65–66. On Guarulho origins, see Manoel Martinz do Couto Reys, *Manuscritos de Manoel Martinz do Couto Reys, 1785* (Rio de Janeiro: Arquivo Público do Estado do Rio de Janeiro, 1997), 72; José, *Indígenas*, 28–29. For a sixteenth-century denunciation of the bellicose, cannibalistic conduct of the Goitacá Indians in terms almost identical to those that would later be used to describe the Botocudo, see Araújo, *Memórias históricas*, vol. 2, 140 n. 11.

69. Rocha, *Geografia histórica*, 77–78.

70. "Carta da Viagem que pelo Ryo Doce athé às Escadinhas fez o Tenente coronel João Baptista dos Santos e Araujo . . . ," 1800, AHU, CM, Minas Gerais, no. 1176.

71. See Carta Régia [to Governor of Minas Gerais], Palácio do Rio de Janeiro, 4 Dec 1816, JCBL; Carta Régia [to Governor of Espírito Santo], Rio de Janeiro, 4 Dec 1816, JCBL; *Dicionário geográfico brasileiro* (Porto Alegre, Brazil: Ed. Globo, 1972), 192. On similar uncertainties regarding ecclesiastical jurisdictions and boundaries, see Raimundo Trindade, *Arquidiocese de Mariana: Subsídios para sua história,* 2nd ed. (Belo Horizonte, Brazil: Imprensa Oficial, 1953), 82–90.

72. On indigenous resistance along the São Paulo border, see Jerônimo Dias Ribeiro to Morgado de Mateus, Registo de Itupeva, 11 Jan 1766, 29 Nov 1768, BNRJ, SM, MM, I-30, 16, 9 docs. 1, 9; "Ordem mandando municiar aos Soldados que vão conquistar os Indios da Piedade," São Paulo, 6 Jun 1771; and "[Ordem] dando izenções aos que forem combater contra os Indios, nas divisas com Minas Geraes," São Paulo, 6 Jun 1771, *DI* 33 (1901): 10–11. Maps of these southern and southwestern frontier zones in late-colonial Minas Gerais showing similar expansion into the sertão, Indian persistence, and rudimentary knowledge of borderlands, include "Mapa da freguezia da Manga," ca. 1764; Manuel Ribeiro Guimarães, "Mappa da Conquista do Mestre de Campo Regente [Chefe de Legião] Ignacio Correya Pamplona," [1784]; Francisco de Sales, "Mappa de toda a extensão da Campanha da Princeza feixada pelo Rio Grande, e pelos registos, que limitão a capitania de Minas . . . ," 1799, AHU, CM, Minas Gerais, nos. 1158, 1165, and 1170, respectively.

73. Governor, "Bando para a devizão das comarcas," Vila Rica, 5 Oct 1779, BNRJ, cód. 2, 2, 24, fols. 223v–24v. In this decree, Noronha established new borders between what were then the captaincy's four comarcas: Vila Rica, Sabará, Rio das Mortes, and Serro Frio. The decree is published in Theophilo Feu de Carvalho, *Comarcas e termos: Creações, suppressões, restaurações, encorporações e desmembramentos de comarcas e termos em Minas Geraes (1709–1915)* (Belo Horizonte, Brazil: Imp. Oficial, 1922), 64–66.

74. The quotation is taken from the title of the manuscript, Manoel José Pires da Silva Pontes, "Extractos das viagens feitas no deserto, que separa as povoações da provincia de Minas Geraes, e as povoações do littoral nas provincias do Rio de Janeiro, Espirito Santo, e Bahia," n.d., BNRJ, SM, cód. 5, 3, 40.

75. Governor to Jozé do Valle Vieira, Vila Rica, 4 Mar 1777, BNRJ, SM, cód. 2, 2, 24, fol. 88; Governor to Commander, 3rd Detachment (*Divisão*), Vila Rica, 7 Mar 1812, BNRJ, SM, cód. 1, 4, 5, doc. 271; Paulo Mendes Ferreira Campelo to Governor, Cuieté, 4 Apr 1770, BNRJ, SM, CV, cód. 18, 2, 6, doc. 237; Pedro Afonso Galvão de São Martinho to count of Linhares, Vila Rica, 29 Jan 1811, BNRJ, SM, I-33, 30, 22, doc. 1. The portrayal of indigenous Americans as bestial, inhuman, and naturally inferior to Europeans had a long history in Portuguese, Spanish, and English America that preceded and then competed with the enlightenment notion of the "noble savage." See Antonello Gerbi, *The Dispute of the New World: The History of a Polemic, 1750–1900,* rev. ed., trans. Jeremy Moyle (Pittsburgh, PA: University of Pittsburgh Press, 1973), 63–67; Laura de Mello e Souza, *O diabo e a Terra de Santa Cruz: Feitiçaria e religiosidade popular no Brasil colonial* (São Paulo: Companhia das Letras, 1986), 49–72.

76. Manoel Vieyra Nunes, "Termo de reunião de conselho," Barra das Larangeiras, 5 Jul 1769, BNRJ, SM, CV, cód. 18, 2, 6, doc. 192.

77. See, for example, "Ordens sôbre arrecadação e despesas, 1768[–1771]," 6 Aug 1768, BNRJ, SM, CC, gaveta I-10-7, doc. 1.

78. "Mapa da região banhada pelo Rio Doce e seus afluentes, na Capitania de Minas Gerais," ca. 1758, Adonias, *Mapa*, pl. 152.

79. Pontes, "Extractos," BNRJ, SM, cód. 5, 3, 40, fols. 19v; "Ordens sôbre arrecadação e despesas, 1768[–1771]," 30 May 1770, BNRJ, SM, CC, gaveta I-10-7, doc. 55; and "Petição que fizerão e assignarão os moradores das freguesias ostilizadas," ca. May 1765, APM, CC, cód. 1156, fol. 9. See also Cambraia and Mendes, "A colonização."

80. Jozé Eloi Ottoni, "Memória sobre o estado actual da Capitania de Minas Gerais," Lisboa, 1798, in *ABNRJ* 30 (1908): 313. On the search for Eden in the Americas, see Sérgio Buarque de Holanda, *Visão do Paraíso: Os motivos edênicos no descobrimento e colonização do Brasil* 4th ed. (São Paulo: Companhia Editora Nacional, 1985). On the merging of that myth with notions of native diabolism, see Souza, *O diabo*, 32–72. Also see Ramos, *Indigenism*, chap. 2. For the North American counterpart to the paradise myth, in which the western frontier was portrayed as the "garden of the world," see Smith, *Virgin Land*. Pre-romantic notions of nature's abundance were expressed with increasing vigor by North American writers, painters, politicians, and propagandists in the final decades of the eighteenth century. See Gerbi, *Dispute*, 245–50.

81. For an analysis of the decline or *decadência* following the gold cycle during the second half of the eighteenth century, see Souza, *Desclassificados do ouro*, chap. 1. On the broader colonial economic crisis, of which the decline in mining was but one part, see Fernando A. Novais, "Brazil in the Old Colonial System," trans. Richard Graham and Hank Phillips, in *Brazil and the World System*, ed. Richard Graham (Austin, TX: University of Texas Press, 1991), 11–55; idem, *Portugal e Brasil na crise do antigo sistema colonial (1777–1808)*, 2nd ed. (São Paulo: Hucitec, 1981); José Jobson de A. Arruda, *O Brasil no comércio colonial* (São Paulo: Ed. Ática, 1980), esp. 115–20, 317–18, 655–62. Also see Kenneth Maxwell, *Pombal: Paradox of the Enlightenment* (Cambridge: Cambridge University Press, 1995), 131–36, and idem, *Conflicts and Conspiracies*, esp. chap. 2.

82. See Figueiredo, *O avesso da memória*; Furtado, *O livro da capa verde*; Douglas C. Libby, *Tranformação e trabalho em uma economia escravista: Minas Gerais no século XIX* (São Paulo: Ed. Brasiliense, 1988), esp. 13–15; idem, "Reconsidering Textile Production in Late Colonial Brazil: New Evidence from Minas Gerais," *Latin American Research Review* 32:1 (1997): 88–108; Angelo Alves Carrara, "Agricultura e pecuária na Capitania de Minas Gerais (1674–1807)," (Ph.D. diss., Universidade Federal do Rio de Janeiro, 1997); Souza, *Norma e conflito*, 159–60; Warren Dean, *With Broadax and Firebrand: The Destruction of the Brazilian Atlantic Forest* (Berkeley, CA: University of California Press, 1995), 92, 111; João Luís Ribeiro Fragoso, *Homens de grossa aventura: Acumulação e hierarquia na praça mercantil do Rio de Janeiro (1790–1830)* (Rio de Janeiro: Arquivo Nacional, 1992), 104–12; Lenharo, *As tropas da moderação*, chap. 2; Amilcar Martins Filho and Roberto B. Martins, "Slavery in a Nonexport Economy: Nineteenth-Century Minas Gerais Revisited," *Hispanic American Historical Review* 63:3 (August 1983): 539–40; Robert W. Slenes, "Os múltiplos de porcos e diamantes: A economia escravista de Minas Gerais no seculo XIX," *Caderrnos IFCH UNICAMP* 17 (June 1985): 39–80; Bergad, *Slavery*, 16–25.

83. For views expressed in Lisbon, Espírito Santo, and Bahia, see Luís de Vasconcelos e Sousa to Junta da Fazenda of Minas Gerais, [Lisbon], 16 Jan 1807, ATC, ER, cód. 4074; Anon. to Crown, Discursos sobre a decadencia em que se acha a nosa America relativos aos seos estabalecimentos e comerçio, [n.p., second half of 18th c.], ANTT, Papéis do Brasil, maço 78, nos. 14, 18; Anon. to Queen, Considerações sobre o estado dos sertões brasileiros, [n.p., end of 18th c.], ibid., no. 22; [Governor of Espírito Santo to Governor of Minas Gerais, Quartel da Vitória, 23 Apr 1800, AHU, Espírito Santo, cx. 6, doc. 438; Memoria sobre a abertura do Rio Doce, e sua navegação... e Extração das Madr^{as}ao Longo delle..., [1804?], APEB, SCP, maço 585.

84. Couto, *Memória*, 80.

85. Ibid., 53.

86. Basilio Teixeira Cardoso [de] Sá Vedra Freire, "Informação da capitania de Minas Gerais," Sabará, 30 Mar 1805, BNRJ, SM, cód. 3, 1, 35, fols. 10–11. This manuscript was published under the same title in *RAPM* 2:4 (1897): 673–83.

87. Vasconcelos, *Breve descrição*, 144–49, 157.

88. Anon. to Queen, Considerações sobre o estado dos sertões brasileiros, [n.p., end of 18th c.], ANTT, Papéis do Brasil, maço 78, no. 22.

89. António [Nunes] Ribeiro Sanches, Discurso sôbre a América portugueza, 3 Dec 1763, OLL, cód. 84, 23.

90. On the early history of Portuguese conflict with the inland indigenous inhabitants of Brazil's central coast, see, for example, Schwartz, *Sugar Plantations*, 29, 32–33, 45–46, 53; Hemming, *Red Gold*, 93–96, 172–73; Barickman, "'Tame Indians,'" 329–31; Paraíso, "Tempo da dor," 74–84.

Notes to Chapter 2

1. Maxwell, *Conflicts and Conspiracies*, 85; Prado Júnior, *Formação do Brasil contemporâneo*, 76–78, 103; Vasconcelos, *História média*, 275; Rocha, *Geografia histórica*, 192.

2. For examples of the governor's repeated references to the Crown's legal authority upon which he based his actions, see "Providencias tomadas para a catechese dos Indios no Rio Doce e Piracicaba, Vila Rica, 1764–1767," APM, CC, cód. 1156, fols. 1–4.

3. Alvará, 4 Apr 1755, quoted in John Hemming, *Amazon Frontier: The Defeat of the Brazilian Indians* (Cambridge, MA: Harvard University Press, 1987), 1–2.

4. "Ley porque V. Magestade ha por bem restituir aos Indios do Grão Pará, e Maranhão a liberdade das suas pessoas, bens, e commercio na forma que nella se declara," Lisbon, 6 Jun 1755, facsimile reprint in Carlos de Araújo Moreira Neto, *Índios da Amazônia: De maioria a minoria (1750–1850)* (Petrópolis, Brazil: Ed. Vozes, 1988), 152–63.

5. Hemming, *Amazon Frontier*, 1–2.

6. Moreira Neto, *Índios da Amazônia*, 164.

7. For the full text of the Diretório, see "Directorio que se deve observar nas Povoaçoens dos Indios do Pará, e Maranhão em quanto Sua Magestade não mandar o contrario," (Pará, 1757), facsimile reprint in Moreira Neto, *Índios da Amazônia*, 165–203, quotations 166–68. Furtado's accusation is quoted in Colin MacLachlan, "The Indian Labor Structure in the Portuguese Amazon, 1700–1800," in *Colonial Roots of Modern Brazil*, ed. Dauril Alden (Berkeley, CA: University of California Press, 1973), 209. Additional scholarship on the Directory includes Almeida, *O Diretório dos Índios*; Domingues,

Quando os índios eram vassalos; Barbara A. Sommer, "Negotiated Settlements: Native Amazonians and Portuguese Policy in Pará, Brazil, 1758–1798" (Ph.D. diss., University of New Mexico, 2000); Hemming, *Amazon Frontier*, 4–7, 11–16, chap. 3; Barickman, "'Tame Indians,'" 337–51; Beatriz Perrone-Moisés, "Índios livres e índios escravos: Os princípios da legislação indigenista do período colonial (séculos XVI a XVIII)," in *História dos índios no Brasil*, 115–32; Colin MacLachlan, "The Indian Directorate: Forced Acculturation in Portuguese America (1757–1799)," *The Americas* 28:4 (April 1972): 357–87; and João Capistrano de Abreu, *Chapters of Brazil's Colonial History, 1500–1800*, trans. Arthur Brakel (New York: Oxford University Press, 1997), 155–65. On Indian emancipation and the expulsion of the Jesuits, see also Maxwell, *Conflicts and Conspiracies*, 17, 30. For a useful index by year, subject, and ethnic group of legislation pertaining to Brazilian Indians, see Beatriz Perrone-Moisés, "Inventário da legislação indigenista, 1500–1800," in *História dos índios no Brasil*, 529–66. On nineteenth-century legislation, see Cunha, *Legislação indigenista*.

8. Exceptions include Barickman, "'Tame Indians,'" 337–51; and Mary C. Karasch, "Catequese e cativeiro: Política indigenista em Goiás, 1780–1889," in *História dos índios no Brasil*, 397–412; Paraíso, "Tempo da dor," 104–22.

9. The first of these documents is Alvará, 17 Aug 1758, facsimile reprint in Moreira Neto, *Índios da Amazônia*, 165–203, quotations 166–68. For the full text of the Direção, see "Direção com que interinamente se devem regular os indios das novas villas e lugares erectos nas aldeias da Capitania de Pernambuco e suas annexas," in *RIHGB* 46:1 (1883): 121–69.

10. Abreu, *Chapters*, 156.

11. The villages are listed in Abreu, *Chapters*, 164–65. On the conquest of Pernambuco's native population, see, for example, Hemming, *Red Gold*, chap. 8, 302–11, 351–61.

12. In order, these three documents were two Cartas Régias (royal decrees), both dated 14 Sep 1758, and Francisco Xavier de Mendonça Furtado to Governor, [Lisbon], 12 Feb 1765. They occupy the first pages of a manuscript codex, the remainder of which contains documents related to Governor Silva's attempted conquest of the Indians of the Eastern Sertão. See "Providencias tomadas para a catechese dos Indios no Rio Doce e Piracicaba, Vila Rica, 1764–1767," APM, CC, cód. 1156, fols. 2–3v. For the copy sent to Portugal of the third document, see Furtado to Governor, [Lisbon], 12 Feb 1765, AHU, cód. 610, fols. 31–31v.

13. See Domingues, *Quando os índios eram vassalos*, 336–37.

14. Governor to Furtado, Vila Rica, 1 Mar 1764, AHU, Minas Gerais, cx. 83, doc. 16.

15. "Lista das pessoas que devem e tem obrigação de concorrerem para embaraçar o corso com que o gentio Sylvestre está todos os annos entrando pelas fazendas e sesmarias da Beira do Rio Doce...," Vila Rica, 9 May 1765, APM, CC, cód. 1156, fol. 4; "Petição que fizerão e assignarão os moradores das freguesias ostilizadas," ca. May 1765, ibid., fols. 9–10; Governor to Furtado, Vila Rica, 6 Jul 1765, AHU, Minas Gerais, cx. 83, doc. 16.

16. For the legislation pertaining to Pernambuco and Paraíba do Norte, see ruling of Overseas Council, Lisbon, 11 Oct 1764, *DH* 92 (1951): 75–76. For São Paulo, see "Portaria para que nenhú Soldado q' estiver de Guarda nos Reg.^{os}desta Cap.^{nia} deixe passar Indio algum com cargas," São Paulo, 15 Jan 1767; "Ordem p.^{a} o Director da Aldea dos Pinhr.^{os} mandar medir as terras pertencentes á d.^{a} Aldea," São Paulo, 17 Jul 1767; "Ordem p.^{a} se

medirem as terras pertencentes á Aldea de S. Miguel," São Paulo, 29 Jul 1767; and "Ordem para se formar Villa da Aldea de Nossa Snr.ª da Escada," São Paulo, 14 Aug 1767, *DI* 65 (1940): 148, 172, 175–76.

17. On São Paulo, see "Ordem mandando municiar aos Soldados que vão conquistar os Indios da Piedade," São Paulo, 6 Jun 1771; and "[Ordem] dando izenções aos que forem combater contra os Indios, nas divisas com Minas Geraes," São Paulo, 6 Jun 1771, *DI* 33 (1901): 10–11. Also see Perrone-Moisés, "Inventário da legislação," 558. On the Amazon, see Marta Rosa Amoroso, "Corsários no caminho fluvial: Os Mura do rio Madeira," and Aracy Lopes da Silva, "Dois séculos e meio de história Xavante," in *História dos índios no Brasil*, 303–09, 363.

18. "Ley porque V. Magestade ha por bem restituir aos Indios do Grão Pará, e Maranhão a liberdade das suas pessoas, bens, e commercio na forma que nella se declara," Lisboa, 6 Jun 1755, in Moreira Neto, *Índios da Amazônia*, 161–62.

19. "Providencias tomadas para a catechese dos Indios no Rio Doce e Piracicaba, Vila Rica, 1764–1767," APM, CC, cód. 1156, fols. 1–2, 4.

20. For a published copy of this exchange of letters, see Colonial Secretary to Bishop of Mariana, Lisbon, 31 Jan 1758; Bishop of Mariana to Colonial Secretary, Mariana, [after 31 Jan] 1758, in Trindade, *Arquidiocese de Mariana*, 129 n. On the Jesuit absence from the mining district, a result of royal restrictions placed on clergy suspected of engaging in smuggling, see Dauril Alden, *The Making of an Enterprise: The Society of Jesus in Portugal, Its Empire, and Beyond, 1540–1750* (Stanford, CA: Stanford University Press, 1996), 597.

21. Governor, "Orden para a entrada dos corpos de gente para a civilização dos gentios silvestres Purîs e Buticudos," Vila Rica, 21 Apr 1766, APM, SC, cód. 118, fols. 148–50v; and Governor to Antônio Pereira da Silva, Vila Rica, 28 Jun 1766, APM, SC, cód. 118, fols. 171v–72.

22. Perrone-Moisés, "Índios livres."

23. "Lista das pessoas que devem e tem obrigação de concorrerem para embaraçar o corso com que o gentio Sylvestre está todos os annos entrando pelas fazendas e sesmarias da Beira do Rio Doce...," Vila Rica, 9 May 1765, APM, CC, cód. 1156, fol. 4.

24. "Petição que fizerão e assignarão os moradores das freguesias ostilizadas," ca. May 1765, APM, CC, cód. 1156, fols. 9–10.

25. On the origin of Cuieté's name, see "Memoria dos trabalhos statisticos e topograficos das margens do Rio Doce, e seus principaes confluentes, tirados pelo Alferes Francisco de Paula Mascarenhas, na viagem que fez ao Arraial de Cuithe," Ouro Preto, 1832, *RAPM* 3:1 (1898): 60; Matos, *Corografia histórica*, vol. 1, 77.

26. Rocha, *Geografia histórica*, 78–81. On the debate concerning whether Arzão was in fact the first to discover gold in Minas Gerais at Cuieté or some other location, see Franco, *Dicionário de bandeirantes*, 42–44.

27. Joaquim Ribeiro Costa, *Toponímia de Minas Gerais* (Belo Horizonte, Brazil: Imprensa Oficial, 1970), 215.

28. [Antônio Pereira da Silva] to Governor, n.p., ca. 1770, BNRJ, SM, CV, cód. 18, 2, 6, doc. 329; Antônio Cardozo de Souza to Governor, n.d., ibid., doc. 290. Governor Noronha later provided a less detailed account of the earliest settlers at Cuieté. See Governor to Colonial Secretary, Vila Rica, 25 Jul 1775, AHU, Minas Gerais, cx. 108, doc. 48. My

translation of the Portuguese terms *qualidade* as *color* or, when used synonymously, *race* follows that of Brazilian historical demographers, as does my translation of *condição* as *legal status* (i.e., free, freed, or enslaved). See, for example, Libby, *Tranformação e trabalho*, 30.

29. Governor, "Instrução que hade observar o Comandante distinado para o Destricto do Cuyeté a respeito do Arrayal que nelle se estabalece e de todos os moradores que no mesmo quizerem rezidir," Vila Rica, 4 Jun 1765, BNRJ, SM, CV, cód. 18, 2, 6, doc. 203. On the foregoing discussion concerning Cuieté's origins, see also Langfur, "Return of the Bandeira."

30. Governor Noronha appointed João da Silva Tavares regent of the Conquest of Cuieté in 1779; two years later, Governor Rodrigo José de Meneses designated Antônio Veloso de Miranda regent of the Conquest of Arrepiados. Campelo recounted the history of his own 1765 appointment, 1767 confirmation, and command at Cuieté in Campelo, "Representação," n.d., BNRJ, SM, CV, cód. 18, 2, 26, doc. 198. For his initial orders from Governor Silva, see Governor, "Instrução que hade observar o Comandante...," Vila Rica, 4 Jun 1765, BNRJ, SM, CV, cód. 18, 2, 6, doc. 203; and Governor to Campelo, Vila Rica, 21 Jun 1767, ibid., doc. 204.

31. Governor, "Instrução que hade observar o Comandante...," Vila Rica, 4 Jun 1765, BNRJ, SM, CV, cód. 18, 2, 6, doc. 203. This document did not mention Campelo by name, but his own correspondence made clear that he received the governor's orders and assumed command of Cuieté in 1765. See Campelo to Governor, n.p., n.d., ibid., doc. 198.

32. On the relationship between urban space and territorial conquest in colonial Brazil, see the essays collected in *Oceanos* 41 (January–March 2000); Ronald Raminelli, "Simbolismos do espaço urbano colonial," in *América em tempo de conquista*, ed. Ronaldo Vainfas (Rio de Janeiro: Jorge Zahar Ed., 1992), 163–75; Roberta Marx Delson, *New Towns for Colonial Brazil: Spatial and Social Planning of the Eighteenth Century* (Ann Arbor, MI: University Microfilms International, 1979). On frontier property rights, see Monteiro, *Negros da terra*, 107–13.

33. Governor, "Instrução que hade observar o Comandante...," Vila Rica, 4 Jun 1765, BNRJ, SM, CV, cód. 18, 2, 6, doc. 203.

34. Ibid. The division of land into mining claims at Cuieté generally conformed to the royal mining code of 1702 but also relied on later innovations that favored the Crown while extending to all slaveholders certain advantages previously reserved for those with more than a dozen slaves. The original code stipulated that the initial discoverer enjoyed the right to select the first claim. The second was then allotted to the Crown; the third, again, to the discoverer. Subsequent claims were divided according to a lottery system. The original code, moreover, allocated an entire mining claim (*data*) only to those with more than a dozen slaves but just a fraction of such a claim to those with fewer slaves. See "Regimento Mineral," 19 Apr 1702, *RAPM* 1:4 (1896): 675. Boxer presents a slightly different apportionment scheme in *Golden Age*, 52. Variations apparently stem from the fact that different versions of the code have been published, including Francisco Ignacio Ferreira, *Repertorio juridico do mineiro. Consolidação alphabetica e chronologica de todas as disposições sobre minas, comprehendendo a legislação antiga e moderna de Portugal e do Brasil* (Rio de Janeiro: Typ. Nacional, 1884), 200–08; Damião Peres, *Estudos de história*

luso-brasileira (Lisbon: n. p., 1956), 53–63. Also see Afonso de Escragnolle Taunay, *História geral das bandeiras paulistas*, vol. 9, 244–48; Francisco Vidal Luna and Iraci del Nero da Costa, *Minas colonial: Economia & sociedade* (São Paulo: Livraria Pioneira, 1982), 3–4; Francisco Vidal Luna, *Minas Gerais: Escravos e senhores: Análise da estrutura populacional e econômica de alguns centros mineratórios (1718–1804)* (São Paulo: Instituto de Pesquisas Econômicas, 1981), 38–40.

35. The official insistence on regularizing Cuieté's urban space challenges the conventional scholarly view that, in contrast to colonial settlements throughout Spanish America and along Brazil's Atlantic coast, the mining camps, villages, and towns of Minas Gerais were distinctive in their unconstrained, informal origins, free from the heavy-handed intervention of centralized power. For the traditional view, see Sylvio de Vasconcellos, *Arquitetura no Brasil. Pintura mineira e outros temas* (Belo Horizonte, Brazil: Escola de Arquitetura da Universidade Federal de Minas Gerais, 1959), 3–6. For revisionist counterpoints, see Cláudia Damasceno Fonseca, "Agentes e contextos das intervenções urbanísticas nas Minas Gerais do século XVIII," in *Oceanos* 41 (January–March 2000): 84–102; Delson, *New Towns for Colonial Brazil*, esp. chap. 1, 29–52. For Spanish-American comparisons, see Fernando de Terán, ed., *La Ciudad Hispanoamericana: El Sueño de un Orden* (Madrid: Centro de Estudios Históricos de Obras Públicas y Urbanismo, 1989); Zelia Nuttal, "Royal Ordinances Concerning the Laying out of New Towns," *Hispanic American Historical Review* 4:4 (November 1921): 743–53; Richard Kagan, *Urban Images of the Hispanic World, 1493–1793* (New Haven, CT: Yale University Press, 2000); Valerie Fraser, *The Architecture of Conquest: Building in the Viceroyalty of Peru, 1535–1635* (Cambridge: Cambridge University Press, 1990).

36. The first appearance coincided with the governor's orders. See "Carta geographica da capitania de Minas Gerais e partes confinantes," 1767, BNRJ, SI, arc. 17, 5, 12.

37. Governor, "Instrução que hade observar o Comandante . . . ," Vila Rica, 4 Jun 1765, BNRJ, SM, CV, cód. 18, 2, 6, doc. 203.

38. Ibid.

39. Governor to Campelo, Vila Rica, 29 Nov 1766, BNRJ, SM, CV, cód. 18, 2, 6, doc. 206.

40. Pombal to Royal Treasury Board of Minas Gerais, Lisbon, 19 Nov 1773, ATC, ER, cód. 4073.

41. Viceroy to [Tomás de Almeida], Rio de Janeiro, 26 Mar 1773, in Luís de Almeida Portugal, *Cartas do Rio de Janeiro, 1769–1776* (Rio de Janeiro: Instituto Estadual do Livro, 1978), 117. Lavradio's full name was Luís de Almeida Portugal Soares Alarcão Eça Melo Pereira Aguilar Fiel de Lugo Mascarenhas Silva Mendonça e Lencastre; however, scholars generally employ the abbreviated Luís de Almeida Portugal or, more simply, the Marquis of Lavradio, the title he used when signing letters and documents.

42. Governor to Commander at Antônio Dias Abaixo, Vila Rica, 26 Aug 1776, BNRJ, SM, cód. 2, 2, 24, fols. 9–10.

43. Governor, "Intrucções que se derão ao Regente João da Silva Tavares," Vila Rica, 7 Sep 1779, BNRJ, SM, cód. 2, 2, 24, fol. 226, 228.

44. Ibid., fol. 226v. The passport mechanism is also mentioned in Governor, "Plano Secreto para a nova Conquista do Cuieté," [Vila Rica], no later than August 1779, ibid., fol. 230.

45. Governor, "Intrucções que se derão ao Regente João da Silva Tavares," Vila Rica, 7 Sep 1779, BNRJ, SM, cód. 2, 2, 24, fols. 227–27v.

46. Ordem Régia (royal order), Palácio de Nossa Senhora da Ajuda, 22 Jul 1766, BNRJ, SM, cód. 36, 9, 28, doc. 1.

47. For the seminal treatment of vadios and the free poor in colonial Minas Gerais, including elite assumptions concerning their potential utility, see Souza, *Desclassificados do ouro*, esp. 51–71, 124–25, 215–22. I have benefited greatly from Souza's insights and revisited some of her sources in an effort to extend her observations with respect to the settlement of the Eastern Sertão. See also Stuart B. Schwartz, "Elite Politics and the Growth of a Peasantry in Late Colonial Brazil," in *From Colony to Nation: Essays on the Independence of Brazil*, ed. A.J.R. Russell-Wood (Baltimore, MD: Johns Hopkins University Press, 1975), 133–54, esp. 152. For a synthesis of recent scholarship on controlling vagrants and vagabonds in early modern Europe through penal servitude, military service, incarceration, and exile to overseas colonies, see Julius R. Ruff, *Violence in Early Modern Europe, 1500–1800* (Cambridge: Cambridge University Press, 2001), 112–13, 226–28.

48. Nestor Goulart Reis Filho, *Contribuição ao estudo da evolução urbana do Brasil (1500/1720)* (São Paulo: Livraria Pioneira Editôra, 1968), 73–75.

49. Governor, "Bando para que nenhua pessoa possa dezertar dos Citios em que viverem," Vila de Santos, 25 Feb 1766, *DI* 65 (1940), 48–49; Heloísa Liberalli Bellotto, *Autoridade e conflito no Brasil colonial: o governo do Morgado de Mateus em São Paulo: 1765–1775* (São Paulo: Conselho Estadual de Artes e Ciências Humanas, 1979), 175–76.

50. Ordem Régia, Palácio de Nossa Senhora da Ajuda, 22 Jul 1766, BNRJ, SM, cód. 36, 9, 28, doc. 1.

51. *Ordenações e leys do reyno de Portugal confirmadas e estabelecidas pelo Senhor rey D. João IV* (Lisbon: Mosteiro de S. Vicente de Fóra, 1747), Liv. 5, Tit. 68.

52. See Antonio de Moraes Silva, *Diccionario da lingua portugueza*, tomo 2, (Lisbon: Typ. Lacerdina, 1813), 825–26.

53. Ordem Régia, Palácio de Nossa Senhora da Ajuda, 22 Jul 1766, BNRJ, SM, cód. 36, 9, 28, doc. 1. For discussion of sítios volantes and roving peasant farmers in the captaincy of São Paulo, where in the 1760s an economic crisis similarly prevailed, see Alice P. Canabrava, "Uma economia de decadência: Os níveis de riqueza na Capitania de São Paulo, 1765/67," *Revista Brasileira de Economia* 26:4 (October–December 1972): 103–04; Sergio Buarque de Holanda, "Movimentos de população em São Paulo no século XVIII," *Revista do Instituto de Estudos Brasileiros* 1 (1966): 55–111; Bellotto, *Autoridade e conflito*, 172; Maria Beatriz Nizza da Silva, *Sistema de casamento no Brasil colonial* (São Paulo: T.A. Queiroz, Universidade de São Paulo, 1984), 20–22; Alida Metcalf, *Family and Frontier*, 122. Also see Francisco da Silveira Bueno, *Grande dicionário etimológico-prosódico da lingua portuguêsa*, vol. 7 (São Paulo: Edição Saraiva), 3777.

54. For official concerns about mobility and moral laxity, see Maria Beatriz Nizza da Silva, *Vida privada e quotidiano no Brasil na época de D. Maria I e D. João VI* (Lisbon: Editorial Estampa, 1993), 135–36; *idem, Sistema de Casamento*, 18–22, 48–49; Mary del Priore, *Ao sul do corpo: Condição feminina, maternidades e mentalidades no Brasil Colônia* (Rio de Janeiro: José Olympio, 1993), 44–45. On the morality and social conventions of the free poor in colonial Minas Gerais more generally, see Figueiredo, *O avesso da memória*; Silveira, *O universo do indistinto*; Souza, *Desclassificados do ouro*.

55. Anon. to Queen, Considerações sobre o estado dos sertões brasileiros, [n.p., end of 18th c.], ANTT, Papéis do Brasil, maço 78, no. 22.

56. Sebastião Monteiro da Vide, *Constituições primeyras do Arcebispado da Bahia* (Lisbon: Pascoal da Sylva, 1719), Livro 1, Título 38, 71; Título 70, 131–32.

57. See the essays in James Muldoon, ed., *The Spiritual Conversion of the Americas* (Gainesville, FL: University Press of Florida, 2004), esp. *idem*, "Introduction: Seeking Spiritual Gold in the New World"; Amy Turner Bushnell, "'None of These Wandering Nations Has Ever Been Reduced to the Faith': Missions and Mobility on the Spanish American Frontier"; and Daniel T. Reff, "Making the Land Holy: The Mission Frontier in Early Medieval Europe and Colonial Mexico." See also John M. Howe, "The Conversion of the Physical World: The Creation of a Christian Landscape," in *Varieties of Religious Conversion in the Middle Ages*, ed. James Muldoon (Gainesville, FL: University Press of Florida, 1997), 63–80.

58. Ordem Régia, Palácio de Nossa Senhora da Ajuda, 22 Jul 1766, BNRJ, SM, cód. 36, 9, 28, doc. 1; *Ordenações e leys*, Liv. 5, Tit. 68. For the establishment of townships in São Paulo during the same period, including those along the border with Minas Gerais, see Bellotto, *Autoridade e conflito*, 171–202. For the case of southern Bahia, see Barickman, "'Tame Indians,'" 331.

59. Ordem Régia, Palácio de Nossa Senhora da Ajuda, 22 Jul 1766, BNRJ, SM, cód. 36, 9, 28, doc. 1. On the meaning of the term *roceiro*, see José João Teixeira Coelho, "Instrucção para o governo da capitania de Minas Gerais," 1780, *RIHGB* 15 (1852): 360, 452.

60. See Souza, *Desclassificados do ouro*, 71–90.

61. See the trenchant analysis in Schwartz, *Sugar Plantations*, chap. 9, in which Schwartz employs the term "colonial slave society" to describe the product of these imbricated social hierarchies. On the mounting elite fear that a fast-growing, poor population of color would undermine social stability during the second half of the eighteenth century, see *idem*, "Elite Politics."

62. "Colecção sumaria das proprias Leis, Cartas Regias, Avisos e ordens que se acham nos livros da Secretaria do Governador desta Capitania de Minas Gerais, deduzidas por ordem a titulos separados," [Vila Rica], [1774], *RAPM* 16:1 (1911): 331–474, quotations 448–51. For the original manuscript with the same title—which provides the place and date of production—see ibid., BNRJ, SM, cód. 1, 2, 6. Authorship of this key document for the captaincy's legal and administrative history can be attributed to José João Teixeira Coelho. In 1780, as a Portuguese magistrate, Coelho discussed composing this work during two of his eleven years of government service in Minas Gerais. The index in turn served as a basis for the famous set of instructions he authored for future governors of the captaincy. See Coelho, "Instrucção para o governo da capitania de Minas Gerais," 1780, *RIHGB* 15 (1852): 255–481. Coelho describes composing the 1774 legislative index on p. 258. The 1780 instructions were also published in *RAPM* 8 (1903): 399–581.

63. Souza, *Desclassificados do ouro*, 75-90. On runaway slaves in Minas Gerais, see Guimarães, *Uma negação da ordem escravista*.

64. Governor to Francisco Xavier de Mendonça Furtado, Vila Rica, 8 Oct 1766, AHU, Minas Gerais, cx. 89, doc. 8.

65. Governor to Colonial Secretary, Vila Rica, 9 Jun 1772, AHU, Minas Gerais, cx. 102, doc. 56.

Notes to Chapter 3

1. David Harvey, *The Condition of Postmodernity: An Enquiry into the Origins of Cultural Change* (Oxford: Basil Blackwell, 1989), 226, 247.

2. Hemming, *Amazonian Frontier*, 99, 181. Also see Ramos, *Indigenism*, 76.

3. Silveira, *O universo do indistinto*, pt. 1, chap. 3; Souza, *Norma e conflito*, 85–90.

4. This use of the term *morador* referred broadly to a settler, inhabitant, or resident of a village or town, in this case apparently denoting only members of the mining camp elite. In the rural sphere, the term was also sometimes used interchangeably with *agregado*, that is, a landless agricultural dependent living on another's estate. See Schwartz, *Sugar Plantations*, 24, 434, 578.

5. Campelo, "Lista da Companhias Ordenansas de pe deste Arraial de N. Senhora da Conceição do Cuyethe," Cuieté, n.d., BNRJ, SM, CV, cód. 18, 2, 6, doc. 230; [Campelo], "Lista dos moradores do Cuyaté com os numeros dos Escravos," Cuieté, n.d., ibid., doc. 228.; [Campelo], "Lista dos moradores que plantarão neste Arraial," Cuieté, n.d., ibid., doc. 232; Domingos Francisco Rodrigues, "Lista do ouro que sahio deste continente do Cuyeté de que pasou guia o Cap.[am] Paulo Mendes Ferreira Campelo as pessoas abaixo declaradas neste Anno de 1767 para o de 1768," Cuieté, n.d., ibid., doc. 221. For the value of one *oitava* of gold (an eighth of an ounce), which between 1751 and 1803 the Crown set at 1$200 in Minas Gerais, see "Mappa do Rendimento que produzio o Real Quinto do Oiro na Cappitania de Minas Geraes desde o anno de 1700 a 1781 a saber," *RAPM* 8 (1903): 578; Maxwell, *Conflicts and Conspiracies*, 245.

6. By 1770, in an atmosphere of falling prices prompted by a contracting mining economy, the value of all slaves between 15 and 40 years old in Minas Gerais averaged approximately 100$000, with males costing about 15% more than females. In coastal Bahia, for which reliable figures also exist, a healthy male slave purchased for field-work in the 1780s also cost about 100$000. Prices in rural Rio de Janeiro appear to have been lower. An adult male slave born in Africa cost, on average, 73$000 in 1790, 87$000 in 1800, and 95$000 in 1810, while those born in Brazil cost less in 1790 (60$000) but more in 1800 and 1810 (101$000 and 105$000). See Bergad, *Slavery*, 163–76; *idem*, "After the Mining Boom: Demographic and Economic Aspects of Slavery in Mariana, Minas Gerais, 1750–1808," *Latin American Research Review* 31:1 (1996): 67–97; B.J. Barickman, *A Bahian Counterpoint: Sugar, Tobacco, Cassava, and Slavery in the Recôncavo, 1780–1860* (Stanford, CA: Stanford University Press, 1998), 139, Fig. 10.; Florentino, *Em Costas Negras*, 300. For more on slave prices in Minas Gerais, also see Oiliam José, *O negro na economia mineira* (n.p., 1993), 163–72; A.J.R. Russell-Wood, *The Black Man in Slavery and Freedom in Colonial Brazil* (London: Macmillan Press, 1982), 109; Town Council to Governor, Vila Rica, 5 Aug 1789, *RAPM* 4:3–4 (1899), 790–91.

7. "Dados estatísticos sôbre a receita e despesa da administração da capitania de Minas Gerais," 1813, BNRJ, SM, II-36, 9, 19; Matos, *Corografia histórica*, vol. 1, 105. The date of the census employed by Matos (1823) is specified in an editor's note on p. 100.

8. Guido Thomaz Marlière, "Reflexões sobre os Indios da Prov.[a] de Minas Geraes," Quartel Central do Retiro, 7 Mar 1826, *RAPM* 11 (1906): 84–85. For a biography of this energetic official, see José, *Marlière, O Civilizador*.

9. Using census data from 1831, a time when free blacks had made even greater strides in becoming integrated into Minas' market economy, Klein, Paiva, and Luna found that freedmen headed 43% of slaveholding households in the old mining center of Sabará and 12% in the southern agricultural region of Campanha. However, they held far fewer total slaves than their white counterparts, owning just 24% and 8%, respectively, of all slaves in the two locations. The divide was even more skewed throughout São Paulo during the same period, where freedmen comprised 6% of all slave owners and held 3% of all slaves. Herbert S. Klein and Clotilde Andrade Paiva, "Freedmen in a Slave Economy: Minas Gerais in 1831," *Journal of Social History* 29:4 (Summer 1996): 933–62; Francisco Vidal Luna and Herbert S. Klein, *Slavery and the Economy of São Paulo, 1750–1850* (Stanford, CA: Stanford University Press, 2003), 175. For similar findings from Bahia, see See B.J. Barickman, "As cores do escravismo: Escravistas "pretos," "pardos" e "cabras" no Recôncavo baiano, 1835," *População e Família* 2 (1999): 7–59.

10. Walter Nugent, "Frontiers and Empires in the Late Nineteenth Century," in *Trails*, 171–72.

11. Notable exceptions to the absence of common settlers in the historiography include Barbosa, *A decadência*, and Carrara, *Estruturas agrárias*, for eighteenth- and nineteenth-century Minas Gerais; Márcia Maria Menendes Motta, *Nas fronteiras do poder: Conflito e direito à terra no Brasil do século XIX* (Rio de Janeiro: Arquivo Público do Estado do Rio de Janeiro, 1998), for nineteenth-century Rio de Janeiro; and Thomas H. Holloway, *Immigrants on the Land: Coffee and Society in São Paulo, 1886–1934* (Chapel Hill, NC: University of North Carolina Press, 1980), for twentieth-century São Paulo.

12. The most extensive scholarly literature on frontier gender relations pertains to the western United States. "Of all the regions people have imagined within the boundaries of what is now the United States," writes historian Susan Johnson in a particularly insightful essay, "no place has been so consistently identified with maleness—particularly white maleness—as the region imagined as the American West." See Susan Johnson, "A Memory Sweet to Soldiers: The Significance of Gender in the History of the American West," *Western Historical Quarterly* 24:4 (November 1993), 495.

13. Except where otherwise specified, the account of Dona Anna and Captain Maciel's experience derives from the following sources: Inventory of Francisco Soares Maciel and Anna Joaquina de Almeida, 1819, ACSM, 2° ofício, cód. 117, auto (act) 2352; *processo matrimonial* (marriage proceedings), Francisco Soares Maciel and Anna Joachina de Almeida, 1765, AEAM, armário 3, pasta 287, processo 2869; sesmaria of Anna Joaquina de Almeida, 1798, ACSM, 1° ofício, cód. 2, auto 87. Appended to the sesmaria document are four petitions related to Almeida's successful claim on this land, including petition of Luis da Silva Pereira and Joze da Silva Pereira, [Xopotó?], [1798]; and petitions of Manuel de Jesus Maria to Governor Silva, [Rio Pomba], with governors' replies, Vila Rica, 2 Mar 1768, 29 Jul 1768, 8 Mar 1790.

14. Manuel de Jesus Maria to Colonial Secretary, Rio Pomba, 27 Aug 1799, BNL, CP, cód. 634, fol. 573–73v. For another copy, see ibid., AHU, Minas Gerais, cx. 149, doc. 62.

15. On female literacy during a slightly later period, see Sandra Lauderdale Graham, *Caetana Says No: Women's Stories from a Brazilian Slave Society* (Cambridge: Cambridge University Press, 2002), 101–04.

16. Sesmaria of Anna Joaquina de Almeida, 1798, ACSM, 1° ofício, cód. 2, auto 87.

17. José da Santíssima Trindade, *Visitas Pastorais (1821–1825)* (Belo Horizonte, Brazil: Fundação João Pinheiro, 1998), 173.

18. Sesmarias of Luis da Silva Pereira and Jozé da Silva Pereira, 1798, APM, SC, cód. 271, fols. 261–62.

19. On Padre Maria and his activities among the Indians, in addition to the documents cited previously detailing the conflict between Dona Anna and the Pereiras, see Petition of Padre Manoel de Jesus Maria to King, [Mariana?, ca. November 1768], ANTT, Ordem de Cristo, Padroado do Brasil, Bispado de Mariana, maço 5; "Ordens sôbre arrecadação e despesas, 1768[–1771]," 23 Jul and 8 Aug 1770, 18 Feb 1771, BNRJ, SM, CC, gaveta I-10-7, docs. 56, 71; Manoel de Jesus Maria to Governor, Rio Pomba, 27 Aug 1799, BNL, CP, cód. 634, fol. 573–73v ; Saint-Hilaire, *Viagens pelas províncias*, 276–77; Castro, *Os sertões de leste*, 11–15, esp. transcription, p. 14 n. 4, of royal order dated 20 Oct 1779. For an original manuscript of this final document, see APM, SC, cód. 220, fols. 44v–45. Also see Vasconcelos, *História média*, 205–10; Mercadante, *Os sertões do leste*, 40–42.

20. On Pessanha's activities, see [Governor?] to [José Antônio Freire de Andrade], Vila Rica, late November 1758, AIHGB, Conselho Ultramarino, Arq. 1, 3, 8, fols. 164v–67v; Sylverio Teixeira to [José Antônio Freire de Andrade], Vila Rica, 25 Nov 1758, ibid., fols. 163v–64v; José Antônio Freire de Andrade to Thomé Joaquim da Costa, Rio de Janeiro, 4 Jan 1759, ibid., fols. 162v–63v. On the priest's reputation as an adept among "savage" Indians in the Campos area, see Reys, *Manuscritos*, 29. Also see chap. 6 in this study.

21. Petition of Manuel de Jesus Maria to Governor Silva, [Rio Pomba], no date, with governor's reply, Vila Rica, 2 Mar 1768, appended to sesmaria of D. Anna Joaquina de Almeida, 1798, ACSM, 1° ofício, cód. 2, auto 87, fols. 11v–12v.

22. Schwartz, *Sugar Plantations*, 41–47; Monteiro, "Crises and Transformations," 999–1000.

23. Petition of Luis da Silva Pereira and Joze da Silva Pereira, [Xopotó?], [1798], appended as a protest to sesmaria of D. Anna Joaquina de Almeida, 1798, ACSM, 1° ofício, cód. 2, auto 87, fols. 9–10; petition of Manuel de Jesus Maria to Governor Silva, [Rio Pomba], no date, with governor's reply, Vila Rica, 2 Mar 1768, appended to ibid., fols. 11v–12v.

24. Petition of Manuel de Jesus Maria to Governor Silva, [Rio Pomba], no date, with governor's reply, Vila Rica, 29 Jul 1768, appended to sesmaria of D. Anna Joaquina de Almeida, 1798, ACSM, 1° ofício, cód. 2, auto 87, fol. 12v; petition of Luis da Silva Pereira and Joze da Silva Pereira, [Xopotó?], [1798], appended to ibid., fols. 9–10. Also see Resende, "Gentios brasílicos," 120–26.

25. Petition of Manuel de Jesus Maria to Governor Mendonça, [Rio Pomba], no date, with governor's reply, Vila Rica, 8 Mar 1790, appended to sesmaria of D. Anna Joaquina de Almeida, 1798, ACSM, 1° ofício, cód. 2, auto 87, fols. 14–15.

26. Manuel de Jesus Maria to Colonial Secretary, Rio Pomba, 27 Aug 1799, BNL, CP, cód. 634, fol. 573–73v. On the ipecac trade, see Henry Koster, *Travels in Brazil* (London: Longman, et al., 1816), 381.

27. Petition of Luis da Silva Pereira and Joze da Silva Pereira, [Xopotó?], [1798], appended as a protest to sesmaria of D. Anna Joaquina de Almeida, 1798, ACSM, 1° ofício, cód. 2, auto 87, fols. 9–10.

28. Ibid.

29. Ibid.

30. Inventory of Francisco Soares Maciel and Anna Joaquina de Almeida, 1819, ACSM, 2° ofício, cód. 117, auto 2352.

31. Resende, "Gentios brasílicos," 57-58; Pinto, "Os últimos carijós," 173.

32. Inventory of Francisco Soares Maciel and Anna Joaquina de Almeida, 1819, ACSM, 2° ofício, cód. 117, auto 2352.

33. Sesmaria of Manoel Leitão de Almeida, 1774, ACSM, 1° ofício, cód. 1, auto 29.

34. Processo matrimonial, Manoel Leitão de Almeida and Clara Pires Farinha, Guarapiranga, 1750, AEAM, armário 6, pasta 675, processo 6748. This document identifies Clara's last name as Farinha, whereas two other sources employ a spelling that was likely erroneous, Farinho. See testament of Manoel Leitão de Almeida, 1785, ACSM, 2° ofício, cód. 75, auto 1626; inventory of Manoel Leitão de Almeida, 1787, ibid.

35. Petition of Manoel Leitão de Almeida and Clara Pires Farinha, no date, ACSM, 1° ofício, cód. 4, auto 140, fol. 15.

36. Testament of Manoel Leitão de Almeida, 1785, ACSM, 2° ofício, cód. 75, auto 1626; inventory of Manoel Leitão de Almeida, 1787, ibid. The second Xopotó sesmaria appears to have been granted to Clara Pires Farinha in 1773. See sesmaria of Clara Pires Farinho, 1773, APM, SC, cód. 172, fol. 200v.

37. Testament of Manoel Leitão de Almeida, 1785, ACSM, 2° ofício, cód. 75, auto 1626; inventory of Manoel Leitão de Almeida, 1787, ibid. On the poor health and diet of Brazilian slaves, see, for example, Schwartz, *Sugar Plantations*, 368–71; Julita Scarano, *Cotidiano e solidaridade: Vida diaria da gente de cor nas Minas Gerais, século XVIII* (São Paulo: Brasiliense, 1994), 38–52.

38. Inventory of João Ferreira de Souza, 1777, ACSM, 2° ofício, cód. 46, auto 1045; João Ferreira de Souza, De Genere et Moribus, Camargos, 1749, AEAM, armário 5, pasta 818.

39. Sesmaria of João Domingues Gomes, 14 Oct 1790, ACSM, 2° ofício, cód. 8, auto 268; João Domingues Gomes, De Genere et Moribus, Sumidouro, 1750, AEAM, armário 5, pasta 800; testament of Padre João Domingues Gomes, 26 Mar 1802, AEAM, pasta 570. For another example of a land grant conceded to provision slaves, this one in Guarapiranga Parish, see sesmaria of Domingues Lopes de Mattos, 13 Jul 1775, ACSM, 1° ofício, cód. 1, auto 41.

40. Manoel Fernandes da Conceção, De Genere et Moribus, Sumidouro, 1778, AEAM, armário 9, pasta 1497.

41. Sesmaria of Antonio Mendes da Fonseca, 1760, ACSM, 1° ofício, cód. 5, auto 223; Inventory of Antonio Mendes da Fonseca, 1801, ACSM, 1° ofício, cód. 42, auto 956.

42. Important studies of the demography of colonial Minas Gerais include Bergad, *Slavery*; Iraci del Nero da Costa, *Vila Rica: População (1719–1826)* (São Paulo: Instituto de Pesquisas Econômicas, 1979); *idem, Populações mineiras: Sobre a estrutura populacional de alguns núcleos mineiros no alvorecer do século XIX* (São Paulo: Instituto de Pesquisas Econômicas, 1981); Luna, *Minas Gerais: Escravos e senhores*. A more recent study discussing the captaincy's rural demography and economic history is Carrara, "Agricultura e pecuária," esp. chap. 2 for the termo of Mariana.

43. For the published 1776 census, see "Mapa dos habitantes atuais da Capitania de Minas Gerais e dos nascidos e falecidos no ano de 1776," in Rocha, *Geografia histórica,*

182. For 1786, see "População da Provincia de Minas Geraes, 1786," *RAPM* 4:2 (1889), 294. This census did not categorize aggregate captaincy data according to region and thus is of little use for quantifying migration. The 1808 data are found in APM, Caixas Avulsas, cx. 77, docs. 61, 63, 65, 69, 72, 74–75, 77–80, 82, and 84. I have relied on the published version of these data available in Bergad, *Slavery*, App. B, Table B.2. For the 1821 census, see ibid., vol. 2, 57–63, also published in Bergad, *Slavery*, App. B, Table B.3.

44. For the 1767 manuscript, see "Mapa geral de Fogos, Filhos, Filhas, Escravos, e Escravas, Pardos forros, e pretos forros, agregados, Clerigos, Almas, Freguezias, Vigarios . . . de toda a Capitania de Minas Gerais," 1767, AHU, Minas Gerais, cx. 93, doc. 58. For the 1776 aggregate manuscript census, see "Mapa dos habitantes atuaes da Capitania de Minas Geraes e dos Nascidos e falecidos no ano de 1776," AHU, Minas Gerais, cx. 110, doc. 59. For the 1776 comarca censuses, see the packet of documents containing "Resumo de todos os habitantes da Com.ᶜᵃ de V.ᵃ Rica . . . "; "Mapa dos habitantes actuais da Com.ᶜᵃ do Rio das Mortes . . . "; "Mapa Geral dos moradores da Comarca do Serro Frio . . . "; "Rellação dos habitantes da Comarca do Rio das Velhas [Sabará]," AHU, Minas Gerais, cx. 112, doc. 11. For the 1772 census of Sabará, see "Rellação abreviada das Pessoas existentes nas Freguezias da Comarca do Sabará, Minnas [*sic*] Geraes," 1772, AHU, Minas Gerais, cx. 104, doc. 61.

45. On the population of detribalized "colonial Indians," those living within the towns and villages of the mining district, see Resende, "Gentios brasílicos," 159–87. Using parish registers, Resende estimated that such Indians averaged 3% of the inhabitants of selected settlements in southern Minas Gerais during the eighteenth century. In parishes on the edge of the eastern forests, this percentage could be substantially higher. Such was the case in São João Batista and its sub-district of São Januário, where in 1825 settled Indians, identified in a parish census, comprised 14% and 21% of the population, respectively. See Angelo Alves Carrara, ed., *Uma fronteira da Capitania de Minas Gerais. A freguesia de São João Batista do Presídio em 1821* (Mariana, Brazil: Universidade Federal de Ouro Preto, 1999), 108–09. For a parallel process of racial leveling elsewhere in Brazil, see Muriel Nazzari, "Vanishing Indians: The Social Construction of Race in Colonial São Paulo," *The Americas* 57:4 (April 2001): 497–524.

46. I have benefited from methodologies previously developed to adjust the 1776 census, which excluded the northeastern district of Minas Novas, and to maintain consistent comarca boundaries over time. See Bergad, *Slavery*, esp. 89 n. 27 and notes to Table 3.3. The focus of a jurisdictional dispute between the captaincies of Minas Gerais and Bahia, Minas Novas, lay within the civil boundaries of Minas Gerais for most of the second half of the eighteenth century but in the ecclesiastical jurisdiction of Bahia. On the history of this dispute, see Matos, *Corografia histórica*, vol. 1, 190–92. Access to the manuscript censuses cited above has led me to decrease slightly, by 100 males in the comarca of Vila Rica, the 1776 population figure used by Bergad, which was based on published data that contained an addition error. I have also corrected statistically insignificant errors made by Bergad in tallying the total captaincy population in 1786 and 1821. See Bergad, *Slavery*, Table 3.2.

47. Using Bergad's methodology to account for Minas Novas (see preceding note), I have increased the 1767 manuscript tally of 208,600 by 23,000 to arrive at this total.

48. Bergad, *Slavery*, 97.

49. The inconsistencies of the 1767 figures require rejecting as unreliable, pending the discovery of further archival evidence, two additional contemporaneous estimates of the captaincy's eighteenth-century population, for which, to my knowledge, historians have not located substantiating manuscripts. The first estimated a population of 226,666 in 1751; the second, 400,000 in 1768. See Minas Gerais, Departamento Estadual de Estatística, *Annuario estatístico, anno II (1922–1925)* (Belo Horizonte, Brazil: Imp. Official, 1929), 9, cited in Bergad, "Demographic Change," 899; and Matos, *Corografia histórica*, vol. 2, 53.

50. See "Mapa geral de Fogos, Filhos, Filhas, Escravos, e Escravas, Pardos forros, e pretos forros, agregados, Clerigos, Almas, Freguezias, Vigarios . . . de toda a Capitania de Minas Gerais," 1767, AHU, Minas Gerais, cx. 93, doc. 58; "Rellação abreviada das Pessoas existentes nas Freguezias da Comarca do Sabará, Minnas [*sic*] Geraes," 1772, AHU, Minas Gerais, cx. 104, doc. 61; "Rellação dos habitantes da Comarca do Rio das Velhas [Sabará]," 1776, AHU, Minas Gerais, cx. 112, doc. 11.

51. Matos, *Corografia histórica*, vol. 2, 71. On the uneven quality of later Minas census data dating from the 1830s, see Libby, *Transformação e trabalho*, 28–31.

52. These conclusions derive from several assumptions: that non-slave foreign immigration had little bearing on population figures until Europeans began migrating to Brazil in significant numbers in the second quarter of the nineteenth century; that slave imports during this post-boom period remained low; and that little variation occurred from region to region in the rate of natural population increase. Even as late as 1872, census figures revealed that nearly 96% of the Minas population had been born within Minas Gerais. See Hugon, *Demografia brasileira*, 182; Bergad, *Slavery*, esp. 98–102, 112, 217–18; Alden, "The Population of Brazil." Southern Minas had supplied the mining camps with foodstuffs throughout the eighteenth century. During the final decades of the century, interregional and extra-captaincy markets propelled the rapid growth of this region. Over the course of the nineteenth century, the southeastern region known as the Zona da Mata—that is, the southern reaches of the Eastern Sertão—would become the most dynamic in Minas Gerais as coffee production for export outpaced the urban provisioning economy. A similar move to coffee, on a smaller scale, occurred in the southwest after 1870. See Carlos Magno Guimarães and Liana Maria Reis, "Agricultura e escravidão em Minas Gerais (1700/1750)," *Revista do Departamento de História—FAFICH/UFMG* 2 (June 1986): 7–36; Fragoso, *Homens de Grossa Aventura*, 104–18; Libby, *Transformação e trabalho*, 43–44.

53. For a brief bibliography of this demographic work, see Herbert S. Klein and Francisco Vidal Luna, "Free Colored in a Slave Society: São Paulo and Minas Gerais in the Early Nineteenth Century," *Hispanic American Historical Review* 80:4 (November 2000): 913 n. 1.

54. Barbosa, *A decadência das minas*, chaps. 2–3; Mafalda P. Zemella, *O abastecimento da Capitania das Minas Gerais no século XVIII*, 2nd ed. (São Paulo: Hucitec, 1990); Carrara, "Agricultura e pecuária"; Cláudia Maria das Graças Chaves, *Perfeitos negociantes: Mercadores das Minas setecentistas* (São Paulo: Annablume, 1999); Bergad, *Slavery*, 7–8.

55. Governor, "Resumo geral de Rossas, Lavras, Fazendas, e Escravos da Capitania de Minas geraes," [Vila Rica], 1766, AHU, Minas Gerais, cx. 93, doc. 58.

56. Trindade, *Visitas pastorais*, 173.

57. Notations on the 1776 manuscript censuses of both eastern comarcas, Serro Frio and Vila Rica, make explicit reference to the ecclesiastical origin of their data. See packet of documents containing "Resumo de todos os habitantes da Com.ᶜᵃ de V.ᵃ Rica..."; "Mapa Geral dos moradores da Comarca do Serro Frio...," AHU, Minas Gerais, cx. 112, doc. 11

58. On Vila do Príncipe (or Serro), see Bergad, *Slavery*, 19, 49; Johann Emanuel Pohl, *Viagem no interior do Brasil*, trans. Milton Amado and Eugênio Amado (Belo Horizonte, Brazil: Ed. Itatiaia, 1976), 370; Saint-Hilaire, *Viagem pelas províncias*, chap. 14. On expanding cotton production during the early nineteenth century, especially in the northeastern region including Vila do Príncipe, Minas Novas, and Peçanha, see also Libby, *Transformação e trabalho*, 189–96.

59. Costa, *Populações mineiras*, 108–10, 116–29, 234–35, 258–62. For the Abre Campo and Furquim censuses used by Costa, see "Relação do Districto do Sertão do Abre Campo," 20 Aug 1804; "Relação circunstanciada de todos os individuos existentes no districto do Furquim," Furquim, 28 Aug 1804, ANRJ, CC, cx. 247, pacote 3. Costa also analyzed data for Vila Rica, Mariana, and its neighboring Passagem de Mariana, as well as the rural districts of Capela do Barreto, Gama, São Caetano, Nossa Senhora dos Remédios, and Santa Luzia.

60. Herculano Gomes Mathias, *Um recenseamento na Capitania de Minas Gerais, Vila Rica—1804* (Rio de Janeiro: Arquivo Nacional, 1969), vii.

61. Costa, *Populações mineiras*, 108–10, 258–60.

62. On Peçanha, see Saint-Hilaire, *Viagem pelas províncias*, 177

63. Costa, *Populações mineiras*, 116–18, 278–79; Libby, *Transformação e trabalho*, 14.

64. Costa, *Populações mineiras*, 178–83; *idem, Minas Gerais: Estruturas populacionais típicas* (São Paulo: EDEC, 1982), 89–98.

65. Costa, *Minas Gerais: Estruturas populacionais típicas*, 78–82; Stanley J. Stein, *Vassouras: A Brazilian Coffee County: The Roles of Planter and Slave in a Plantation Society* (Cambridge, MA: Harvard University Press, 1958; Princeton, NJ: Princeton University Press, 1985), 10–12.

66. Dean, *With Broadax and Firebrand*, 149. For regional variations, see Stein, *Vassouras*, 10–15; Metcalf, *Family and Frontier*, 50–51, 53, 60, 68, 125–26; Warren Dean, *Rio Claro: A Brazilian Plantation System, 1820–1920* (Stanford, CA: Stanford University Press, 1976), 10–12; Thomas H. Holloway, *Immigrants on the Land: Coffee and Society in São Paulo, 1886–1934* (Chapel Hill, NC: University of North Carolina Press, 1980), 112–13; Barickman, *A Bahian Counterpoint*, 105–08.

A number of studies employ sesmaria petitions and grants to document the occupation of land, often without adequately exploring their problematic use as sources. Emphasizing the expansion of cattle ranching, Waldemar de Almeida Barbosa studied the incorporation of land along in São Francisco River and Goiás border in Minas Gerais during the eighteenth century. See Barbosa, *A decadência*, chaps. 2–5. More recently, and with greater sophistication, Angelo Alves Carrara used sesmaria data to study the captaincy's territorial consolidation. For the early and late eighteenth century, respectively, see Carrara, *Contribuição para a história agrária de Minas Gerais* (Mariana, Brazil: EdUFOP, 1999), and *idem, Estruturas agrárias*. Mário Neme examined colonization of the interior of São Paulo, noting that a mass of backwoodsmen, peasants, free and freed persons of African descent, and acculturated Indians formed the "vanguard" that took possession of remote lands during the second half of the eighteenth century, that few gained formal title to this land through sesmarias, and that most were later displaced by more powerful settlers who did. See Mário Neme, *Apossamento do solo e evolução da propriedade rural na zona de Piracicaba* (São Paulo: Fundo de Pesquisas do Museu Paulista da Universidade de São Paulo, 1974), 77–78. Concentrating on the first half of the eighteenth century, many Minas royal land grant titles (*cartas de sesmarias*) were published in *RAPM*, vols. 2–7, 9–12, 14–20, 24. On the incomplete nature of these published records, however, see Carrara, *Contribuição para a história agrarian*, 9–11.

67. Governor, Bando, 29 Apr 1783, APM, SC, cód. 227, fol. 71.

68. Sesmaria of Manoel da Silva de Almeida, 1752, *RAPM* 20 (1924): 580–81.

69. Sesmaria of Manoel de Campos and Antonio Antunes Maciel, 1710, summarized in *RAPM* 21:2 (1927): 283.

70. See royal order to Governor, Lisbon, 20 Nov 1725, *RAPM* 30 (1979): 228; Governor, Bando, 8 Aug 1738, summarized in "Indices dos livros do Archivo Publico Mineiro," *RAPM* 20 (1924): 420. For the 1744 order, see Francisco Gregorio Pires Monteiro Bandeira, Indice cronológico das Leys, Alvarás, Cartas Regias, Decretos, Avizos, e Provizoens, que se expedirão para a Provedoria, e Junta da Real Fazenda da Capitania de Minas Geraes, Título 18, No. 2, 1770, OLL, cód 4. For the estate inventory describing Pamplona's various holdings, see Inventory of Ignácio Correa Pamplona, 1821, fol. 4, MRSJ, Fundo Cartorial, Livro de testamentos, no. 14. On Pamplona's life in the sertão, as well as his notorious actions as an informer and probable participant in the 1789 plot against the captaincy government, see Souza, "Violência e práticas culturais"; José Cláudio Henriques, "O Bairro de Matosinhos no Inconfidência Mineiro," *Revista do Instituto Histórico e Geográfico de São João del Rei* 7 (1992): 110–13; Maxwell, *Conflicts and Conspiracies*, 152–68, 189, 193.

71. Sesmaria of Dona Methildes Roza da Silva e Boena, APM, SP, cód. 36, fols. 5v–6v.

72. "Introdução," *RAPM* 37:1 (1988), 11–13. The citation refers to the first of a two-volume set containing a published index of these grants. The team of researchers that conducted this effort tallied 7985 sesmarias. Using the same data, arranged chronologically rather than alphabetically, Leonardo Pires B. de Moraes counted 8000 grants. See Leonardo Pires B. de Moraes, "Cronologia das cartas de sesmarias concedidas em Minas Gerais," Belo Horizonte, 1991, uncatalogued TS in reading room, APM. The origin of this statistically insignificant discrepancy (0.02%) remains unclear. More recently, researchers have identified still more Minas land grants, not included in this index, contained in the codices of other local and state archives. See Carrara, *Contribuição para a história agrarian*, 9–11.

73. Caio César Boschi, preface to *RAPM* 37:1 (1988): 8–9.

74. Using SAS software, I sampled data for 855 sesmarias, approximately 11% of the total number of grants.

75. The index citations to these land grants, respectively, are *RAPM* 37:1 (1988): 59; *RAPM* 37:2 (1988): 19. The original codex citations are APM, SC, cód. 156, fol. 14v; APM, SP, cód. 36, fol. 64.

76. A comparatively small but unknown number of sesmarias were conceded earlier, starting in 1674, by external authorities before Minas Gerais became a captaincy. See Carrara, *Contribuição para a história agrarian*, 21–22.

77. "Introdução," *RAPM* 37:1 (1988), 12.

78. Boschi, preface to *RAPM* 37:1 (1988): 8.

Notes to Chapter 4

1. Governor to Francisco Pereira de Santa Apolonia, Vila Rica, 16 Jul 1777, Vila Rica, BNRJ, SM, cód. 2, 2, 24, fols. 128–28v.

2. Anon. to Queen, Considerações sobre o estado dos sertões brasileiros, [n.p., end of 18th c.], ANTT, Papéis do Brasil, maço 78, no. 22. On gold remittances from slaves ordered to labor at mining sites on their own recognizance, see Higgins, *Licentious Liberty*, 68, 70.

3. In North America, frontier settlers of uncertain means were more commonly able to acquire titled smallholdings. For an insightful comparison, although drawn from a later period, between land policies in Brazil and the United States, see Emilia Viotti da Costa, "Land Policies: The Land Law, 1850, and the Homestead Act, 1862," in *The Brazilian Empire: Myths and Histories* (Chicago: Chicago University Press, 1985), 78–93.

4. Cf. Howard R. Lamar, "From Bondage to Contract: Ethnic Labor in the American West, 1600–1890," in *The Countryside in the Age of Capitalist Transformation: Essays in the Social History of Rural America*, ed. Steven Hahn and Jonathan Prude (Chapel Hill, NC: University of North Carolina Press, 1985), 293–324.

5. While Bergad finds that white mobility exceeded that of free blacks and mulattos in the southern reaches of the captaincy, this fact did not ameliorate official concerns about rootless persons of color and may well have exacerbated them by adding to the overall demographic flux. Accordingly, efforts to restrict mobility led officials to monitor the movements not only of the free poor but of the frontier elite in this southern region. Merchants and other travelers moving along authorized routes through the sertão complained of constant searches and inordinate delays. Those traveling the Caminho Novo to and from Rio de Janeiro not only faced two formal searches at garrisons established along the route but also impromptu inspections by soldiers ordered to patrol the road continually. Their vociferous complaints led to the closing of one of the formal search points in 1778. See Petition of travelers of road to Rio de Janeiro, Vila Rica, 4 Jan 1778, and Jozé João Teixeira to Governor, Vila Rica, 5 Jan 1778, BNRJ, SM, cód. 19, 3, 39, fols. 73v–74; Governor, "Despacho que se profferio em Requerimento dos Viandantes do Caminho do Rio de Janeiro...," [Vila Rica], 8 Jan 1778, BNRJ, SM, cód. 2, 2, 24, fol. 152. Also see Bergad, *Slavery*, esp. 98–102, 112, 217–18.

6. On military recruitment during the colonial period, see Silva, *Sistema de casamento*, 56–58, 189; *idem*, *Vida privada*, 135. For insights from the nineteenth century, see esp. Joan E. Meznar, "The Ranks of the Poor: Military Service and Social Differentiation in Northeast Brazil, 1830–1875," *Hispanic American Historical Review* 72:3 (August 1992): 335–51; Hendrik Kraay, "'The shelter of the uniform': The Brazilian Army and Runaway Slaves, 1800–1888," *Journal of Social History* 29:3 (Spring 1996), 637–57; *idem*, "Reconsidering recruitment in imperial Brazil," *Americas* 55:1 (July 1998): 1–33; *idem*, *Race, State, and Armed Forces in Independence-Era Brazil, Bahia, 1790s–1840s* (Stanford, CA: Stanford University Press), 2001.

7. For a comprehensive treatment of this border conflict, see Dauril Alden, "The Debatable Lands," pt. 2 of *Royal Government*. On the effects of the recruitment campaign in Minas Gerais, see Souza, *Desclassificados do ouro*, 85–89. For published correspondence on recruitment and related issues exchanged by Pombal, Lavradio, military commanders, governors, and other officials, see José d'Almeida [Correa de Sá], *Vice-reinado de D. Luiz d'Almeida Portugal, 2° marquez de Lavradio, 3° vice-rei do Brasil*, vol. 214 of *Biblioteca Pedagogica Brasileira, Brasiliana, Serie 5.a* (São Paulo: Ed. Nacional, 1942), 145–398, esp. Viceroy to Governor Noronha, Rio de Janeiro, 19 Oct 1776, 364–67. Also see Coelho, "Instrucção," 355–56.

8. Governor to Viceroy, Vila Rica, 19 Nov 1776, BNRJ, SM, cód. 2, 2, 24, fols. 51–52. This was not the first time that vadios had been impressed in Minas Gerais to be marched south against the Spaniards. The Crown ordered the same action taken in 1725 while mounting a military expedition to Montevideo. Ordem Régia, Lisbon, 8 Aug 1725, *RAPM* 30 (1979): 216. Another royal order nine years later authorized the governor to transfer to the south any "freed blacks and mulattos, idlers, and vadios" convicted of crimes. Summary of royal order, 24 Nov 1734, "Colecção sumaria," 450. For the origins of the forced settlement of the borderlands region by Portuguese and Brazilian criminals, which dated to 1689, see Alden, *Royal Government*, 70–71.

9. The governor's logic drew on and sustained the myth that blamed the mining sector's decline on a paucity of workers, thereby obscuring the fact that once-productive sources of gold had been depleted. Alden, *Royal Government*, 209. For a contemporary account ascribing the economic crisis in Minas Gerais to a shortage of slave labor, see Coelho, "Instrucção," 257, 377–79. For another, criticizing military recruitment for draining the labor supply, see Anon. to Crown, Discursos sobre a decadencia em que se acha a nosa America relativos aos seos estabalecimentos e comerçio, [n.p., second half of 18th c.], ANTT, Papéis do Brasil, maço 78, nos. 14, 18.

10. Governor to Viceroy, Vila Rica, 19 Nov 1776, BNRJ, SM, cód. 2, 2, 24, fol. 53. For Noronha's use of the terms *pardo* and *crioulo* to describe this population, see, for example, Governor to Francisco Joze de Aguilar, Vila Rica, 11 Jan 1777, ibid., fols. 80v–81; Governor to Ouvidor (superior judge) of Vila do Príncipe, 9 Apr 1777, Vila Rica, ibid., fols. 104–06.

11. On defining racial categories in colonial Minas Gerais, see the entries for individual terms in Waldemar de Almeida Barbosa, *Dicionário da terra e da gente de Minas* (Belo Horizonte, Brazil: Imp. Oficial, 1985). On such terms in Portuguese America more generally, see Muriel Nazzari, "Vanishing Indians"; Stuart B. Schwartz, "Brazilian Ethnogenesis: Mestiços, Mamelucos, and Pardos," in *Le Nouveau Monde, Mondes Nouveaux: L'experience americaine*, ed. Serge Gruzinski and Nathan Wachtel (Paris: EHESS/CNRS, 1996), 7–27. Although the evidence from colonial Minas Gerais remains to be systematically analyzed, elsewhere in the colony racial and color classifications tended to disappear from baptismal and marriage records of persons of color two or more generations removed from slavery, marking—or rather, unmarking—their gradual incorporation into the social world of the free. However, the practice in such sources was the exception. When written by non-ecclesiastical authorities, both in Minas Gerais and elsewhere, sources of the sort I have used in the current discussion continued to emphasize racial and color categories even for individuals not classified as such in church records. See

Faria, *A Colônia em movimento*, 135–39. After 1850, with the end of the trans-Atlantic slave trade to Brazil and the continued rapid expansion of the free colored population, many other forms of documentation ceased classifying by race and color those who were free. See Hebe Maria Mattos, *Das cores do silêncio: Os significados da liberdade no Sudeste escravista—Brasil século XIX*, 2nd ed. (Rio de Janeiro: Ed. Nova Fronteira, 1998), chap. 5.

12. Governor to Viceroy, Vila Rica, 19 Nov 1776, BNRJ, SM, cód. 2, 2, 24, fol. 53.

13. Governor to Ignacio Jozé de Souza Rabelo, Vila Rica, 28 Feb 1777, BNRJ, SM, cód. 2, 2, 24, fol. 89v.

14. Governor to Viceroy, Vila Rica, 19 Nov 1776, BNRJ, SM, cód. 2, 2, 24, fol. 53.

15. Governor, "Conta que foi inclusa nas ditas cartas do sr. Marquês de Pombal e Martinho de Melo sobre a extinção das duas companhias de pedestres do Cuieté," Vila Rica, 25 Jul 1775, APM, SC, cód. 212, fols. 72–73; Governor, Attestation (*certidão*) concerning the actions of João da Silva Tavares, Vila Rica, 20 Jan 1779, BNRJ, SM, cód. 2, 2, 24, fols. 199v–200v.

16. Governor to *capitães-mores* (militia commanders), Vila Rica, 15 May 1777, with accompanying edict, BNRJ, SM, cód. 2, 2, 24, fol. 121v–24. Also see Diogo [Luís de Almeida Pereira] de Vasconcelos, *História média*, 227–30; Maxwell, *Conflicts and Conspiracies*, 63–64.

17. For example, see Governor to Francisco Joze de Aguilar, Vila Rica, 11 Jan 1777, BNRJ, SM, cód. 2, 2, 24, fols. 80v–81.

18. Viceroy to Governor, 13 Mar 1777, Rio de Janeiro, BNRJ, SM, cód. 19, 3, 39, fols. 55v–58v. For Noronha's reply, see Governor to Viceroy, Vila Rica, 20 Mar 1777, BNRJ, SM, cód. 2, 2, 24, fols. 95v–96v. Also see Alden, *Royal Government*, 250–51. For preparations to receive, feed, and help transport these troops by officials in São Paulo, see Governor of São Paulo to Governor of Minas Gerais, São Paulo, 2 Apr 1777, *DI* 42 (1903): 222–23. This episode is also discussed perceptively in Souza, *Desclassificados do ouro*, 85–89.

19. Viceroy to Governor, Rio de Janeiro, 2 Nov 1776 and 13 Mar 1777, BNRJ, SM, cód. 19, 3, 39, fols. 49v, 57.

20. Governor to Viceroy, Vila Rica, 30 Mar 1777 and 13 May 1777, BNRJ, SM, cód. 2, 2, 24, fols. 95v–96v, 112v–13v.

21. The action preceded two instances of similar recruitment during wartime emergencies in nineteenth-century Brazil. After the Independence War in Bahia (1822–1823), the government purchased the freedom of slaves who enlisted to fight the Portuguese. During the Paraguayan War (1864–1870), it compensated masters whose slaves, on being freed, enlisted. In this eighteenth-century instance, however, no discussion of emancipation or compensation entered the documentary record. See Kraay, "'The Shelter of the Uniform,'" 639.

22. Governor to Ouvidores, Vila Rica, 20 Mar 1777, BNRJ, SM, cód. 2, 2, 24, fols., 98–101.

23. Governor to Circuit Judge (*juiz de fora*) of Mariana, Vila Rica, 27 Mar 1777, BNRJ, SM, cód. 2, 2, 24, fols. 101v–2v.

24. Governor to Viceroy, Vila Rica, 13 May 1777, ibid., fols. 112v–13v.

25. Joaquim Cassemiro da Costa to Governor, Vila do Príncipe, 2 Apr 1777, BNRJ, SM, cód. 19, 3, 39, fols. 59–60.

26. Vasconcelos, *História média*, 228.

27. Governor to Viceroy, Vila Rica, 13 May 1777, BNRJ, SM, cód. 2, 2, 24, fols. 112v–13v.

28. Governor Saldanha to Viceroy, São Paulo, 23 Apr 1777, *DI* 42 (1903): 245–46.

29. On Böhm, see Alden, *Royal Government*, 52; on the pseudonymous Figueiredo, whose given name was Manuel Jorge Gomes de Sepúlveda, see ibid., 449–50.

30. Governor Saldanha to Böhm, São Paulo, 30 Apr 1777, *DI* 42 (1903): 251–52. For similar statements to Figueiredo, see *idem* to Figueiredo, São Paulo, 30 Apr 1777, *DI* 42 (1903): 253–54.

31. Governor Saldanha to Colonial Secretary, São Paulo, 2 Aug 1777, *DI* 28 (1898): 342–44.

32. Governor Noronha to Governor Saldanha, Vila Rica, 13 May 1777, BNRJ, SM, cód. 2, 2, 24, fols. 114v–16v. This letter is published in *DI* 17 (1895): 290–93.

33. Governor Noronha to Governor Saldanha, Vila Rica, 13 May 1777, BNRJ, SM, cód. 2, 2, 24, fols. 114v–16v. For additional published correspondence among these authorities concerning the recruitment, transport, and alleged character of the Minas troops, see *DI* 17 (1895): 285–90, 297, 302, 308, 324–25; *DI* 42 (1903): 239, 251–52, 254–56, 260–61, 273–76, 280, 283–84, 288–89. Also see Alden, *Royal Government*, 250–51.

34. Governor to Capitães-mores, Vila Rica, 15 May 1777, with accompanying edict, BNRJ, SM, cód. 2, 2, 24, 121v–24.

35. For the letter informing Governor Noronha that hostilities with the Spaniards had been suspended, along with the transfer of troops from Minas Gerais to the south two months before the signing of the treaty of Santo Ildefonso in October, see Viceroy to Governor, Rio de Janeiro, 11 Aug 1777, BNRJ, SM, cód. 19, 3, 39, fol. 70v. On the treaty, see Sérgio Buarque de Holanda, ed., *História geral da civilização brasileira*, tomo 1, *A época colonial*, vol. 1, *Do descobrimento à expansão territorial*, 5th ed. (São Paulo: DIFEL, 1976), 375–76; Alden, *Royal Government*, 263–67.

36. Coelho, "Instrucção," 347–48.

37. Governor, "Portaria para Antonio Pereira da Silva...," Vila Rica, 28 Jun 1766, APM, SC, cód. 118, fol. 172.

38. Governor, "Deferimento que S. Ex.ª fes sobre o Requerimento de Joze Miz Chavez, pardo forro...," Vila Rica, 15 Apr 1767, APM, SC, cód. 60, fols. 140–41v.

39. Gundim, "Plano...a respeito da providencia que se deve dar as hostalidades e invazoens dos Indios barbaros no seu respeitivo Destrito," Mariana, [1794], APM, SC, cód. 260, fol. 52.

40. Governor, "Para a expulção dos Indios de S. Jozé da Barra Longa...," Vila Rica, 20 Feb 1766, APM, SC, cód. 118, fol. 133v.

41. Governor, Attestation (*certidão*) concerning the actions of João da Silva Tavares, Vila Rica, 20 Jan 1779, BNRJ, SM, cód. 2, 2, 24, fols. 199v–200v.

42. Governor to Colonial Secretary, Vila Rica, 31 Dec 1781, APM, SC, cód. 224, fols. 76–76v (second letter of this date).

43. Governor to Colonial Secretary, Vila Rica, 31 Dec 1781, APM, SC, cód. 224, fols. 83v–86 (third letter of this date).

44. David Eltis, "Labour and Coercion in the English Atlantic World from the Seventeenth to the Early Twentieth Century," *Slavery & Abolition* 14:1 (1993): 207–08.

45. Petition of João Damaceno dos Reis Vidal and other landholders with governor's reply, Vila Rica, 1 Nov 1794, APM, SC, cód. 260, fols. 42v–43.

46. Duro to Governor, Antônio Dias Abaixo, 15 Jul 1802, APM, SC, cód. 277, fols. 111v–12v; Governor to Duro, Vila Rica, 13 Aug 1802, ibid., fols. 112v–13.

47. Leão to Prince Regent, Quartel Geral de Palma, 1 Oct 1811, BNRJ, SM, cód. 8, 1, 8, doc. 75.

48. Pereira to Governor, Antônio Dias [Abaixo], 4 Jul 1770 and 18 Oct 1770, BNRJ, SM, cód. 18, 2, 26, docs. 172, 177.

49. Ordem Régia, Palácio de Nossa Senhora da Ajuda, 22 Jul 1766, BNRJ, SM, cód. 36, 9, 28, doc. 1; Viceroy to Governor Noronha, Rio de Janeiro, 2 Nov 1776, BNRJ, SM, cód. 19, 3, 39, fol. 49; Governor Saldanha to Böhm, São Paulo, 30 Apr 1777, DI 42 (1903): 251–52; Governor Noronha to Viceroy, Vila Rica, 19 Nov 1776, BNRJ, SM, cód. 2, 2, 24, fols. 52–53.

50. Governor to Colonial Secretary, Vila Rica, 31 Dec 1781, APM, SC, cód. 224, fols. 76–76v (second letter of this date). For sample recruitment lists, see João da Sylva Brandão to Governor, São Caetano, 17 May 1780, APM, SG, cx. 10, doc. 15.

51. Ibid.

52. Ibid.

53. Governor to Colonial Secretary, [Vila Rica], 24 Jun 1782, APM, SC, cód. 224, fol. 210v.

54. Ibid., 211v.

55. Ibid., 211v–12v.

56. Ibid., 212v–13.

57. Ibid.

58. Governor to Capitães-mores of Vila Rica, Sabará, São João del Rei, and São José, Caxoeira, 30 Nov 1782, APM, SC, cód. 227, fol. 47.

59. Governor to José Joaquim de Sequeira e Almeida, [Vila Rica], 25 Jun 1782, APM, SC, cód. 227, fol. 31.

60. Gonçalo Teixeira de Carvalho to Governor, Ponta do Morro, 16 Jun 1783, APM, SC, cód. 237, fols. 14v–15.

61. Brandão to Governor, São Caetano, 17 May 1780, APM, SG, cx. 10, doc. 15.

62. Rocha, Geografia histórica, 195–96.

63. Almeida to Governor, 21 Jul 1782, Boca do Bananal, APM, SG, cx. 12, doc. 18.

64. Miranda to Governor, 15 Dec 1781, Barra do Bacalhau, APM, SG, cx. 11, doc. 55.

65. Governor to Colonial Secretary, Vila Rica, 31 Dec 1781, APM, SC, cód. 224, fols. 76–76v (second letter of this date).

66. Governor to Miranda, Vila Rica, 18 Oct 1782, APM, SC, cód. 227, fol. 38v.

67. On the social status of agregados, see Richard Graham, Patronage and Politics in Nineteenth-Century Brazil (Stanford, CA: Stanford University Press, 1990), 20–21.

68. Governor to Miranda, Vila Rica, 14 Aug 1782, APM, SC, cód. 227, fol. 33v; Souza, Desclassificados do ouro, 197–99.

69. The reference to farmhands suggests that some agregados had dependents of their own.

70. Governor, Bando, 29 Apr 1783, APM, SC, cód. 214, fols. 16–16v.

71. Governor to José da Silva Pontes, Vila Rica, 26 Jun 1783, APM, SC, cód. 227, fol. 71.

72. Governor to Miranda, Vila Rica, 18 Oct 1782, APM, SC, cód. 227, fol. 38v.

73. Governor, Circular issued to militia and district commanders, Vila Rica, 7 Jan 1784, APM, SC, cód. 241, fols. 8v–9.

74. On peasant families in the frontier community of colonial Santana de Parnaíba in São Paulo, see Metcalf, *Family and Frontier*, chap. 5. From a growing literature on marriage in colonial Brazil, see Maria Beatriz Nizza da Silva, *Sistema de casamento*; Priore, *Ao sul do corpo*; Muriel Nazzari, *The Disappearance of the Dowry: Women, Families, and Social Change in São Paulo, Brazil (1600–1900)* (Stanford, CA: Stanford University Press, 1991); Faria, *A Colônia em movimento*. On marriage in urban Minas Gerais, see Donald Ramos, "Marriage and the Family in Colonial Vila Rica," *Hispanic American Historical Review* 55:2 (May 1978); *idem*, "Single and Married Women"; *idem*, "A Social History of Ouro Preto: Stresses of Dynamic Urbanization in Colonial Brazil, 1695–1726," (Ph.D. diss., University of Florida, 1972); and *idem*, "Vila Rica: Profile of a Colonial Urban Center," *The Americas* 35:4 (April 1979): 495–526. On marriage among slaves and former slaves, see Sandra Lauderdale Graham, "Honor Among Slaves," in *The Faces of Honor: Sex, Shame, and Violence in Colonial Latin America*, ed. Lyman L. Johnson and Sonya Lipsett-Rivera (Albuquerque, NM: University of New Mexico Press, 1998), 201–28; *idem*, *Caetana Says No*, 1–73.

75. Governor, "Memória econômico política da Capitania de São Paulo," *Anais do Museu Paulista* 15 (1961), 94.

76. Silva, *Sistema de casamento*, 18–22, 48–49; Del Priore, *Ao sul do corpo*, 44–45; Stuart B. Schwartz, "The Formation of Colonial Identity in Brazil," in *Colonial Identity in the Atlantic World, 1500–1800*, ed. Nicholas Canny and Anthony Pagden (Princeton: Princeton University Press, 1987), 22–24. For similar notions about frontier families and the role of marriage elsewhere in the Americas, see Kathleen M. Brown, *Good Wives, Nasty Wenches, and Anxious Patriarchs: Gender, Race, and Power in Colonial Virginia* (Chapel Hill, NC: University of North Carolina Press, 1996), 80–83.

77. Cf. Johnson, "A Memory Sweet to Soldiers," 495; Limerick, *Legacy of Conquest*, 48–54. Other works I have found valuable for understanding gender relations in the context of frontier incorporation include Elizabeth Jameson, "Women as Workers, Women as Civilizers: True Womanhood in the American West," in *The Women's West*, ed. Susan Armitage and Elizabeth Jameson (Norman, OK: University of Oklahoma Press, 1987), 145–64; Peggy Pascoe, *Relations of Rescue: The Search for Female Moral Authority in the American West, 1874–1939* (New York: Oxford University Press, 1990); Sarah Deutsch, *No Separate Refuge: Class, Culture, and Gender on an Anglo-Hispanic Frontier in the American Southwest, 1880–1940* (New York: Oxford University Press, 1987); Antonia Castañeda, "Women of Color and the Rewriting of Western History: The Discourse, Politics, and Decolonization of History," *Pacific Historical Review* 61 (November 1992): 501–33. For colonial Spanish America, frontier race and gender relations figure prominently in Ramón Gutiérrez, *When Jesus Came, the Corn Mothers Went Away: Marriage, Sexuality, and Power in New Mexico, 1500–1846* (Stanford, CA: Stanford University Press, 1991); and for Minas Gerais, see Higgins, *Licentious Liberty*.

78. On Rodrigo José de Meneses' attempts to reform the captaincy government in accordance with Enlightenment principles, see Vasconcelos, *História média*, 244–50; Furtado, *Livro da Capa Verde*, 189–99. Furtado also considers Cunha Meneses' subsequent policies as governor, 200–16, as does Maxwell, *Conflicts and Conspiracies*, 99–100.

79. Governor to Colonial Secretary, [Vila Rica], 3 Jun 1781, APM, SC, cód. 224, fol. 29v.

80. Governor to Felix Vital Noge, [Vila Rica], 14 Jul 1780, APM, SC, cód. 224, fol. 37.

81. Rocha, *Geografia histórica*, 189.

82. Bergad, *Slavery*, 127, 166, 194; Alden, *Royal Government*, 44–6, chap. 13; Jeffrey D. Needell, "Provincial Origins of the Brazilian State: Rio de Janeiro, the Monarchy, and National Political Organization, 1808–1853," *Latin American Research Review* 36:3 (2001): 134; Mercadante, *Os sertões do leste*, 25–26; Cambraia and Mendes, "A colonização dos sertões do leste"; Lenharo, *As tropas da moderação*, 58–59; Kirsten Schultz, *Tropical Versailles: Empire, Monarchy, and the Portuguese Royal Court in Rio de Janeiro, 1808–1821* (New York: Routledge, 2001), chaps. 2 and 4. Between 1780 and 1821, the population of the captaincy of Rio de Janeiro doubled to 333,000. Between 1808 and 1821, the population of the city of Rio de Janeiro did the same, doubling to 80,000. See "Mappa geral das cidades, villas e freguezias que formão o corpo interior da capitania do Rio de Janeiro," 1780, *RIHGB* 47:1 (1884), 27–29; Joaquim José de Queirós, "Mappa da população da côrte e província do Rio de Janeiro," 1821, *RIHGB* 33:1 (1870), 135–42.

83. Rocha, *Geografia histórica*, 190–92.

84. Governor to Colonial Secretary, Vila Rica, 31 Dec 1781, APM, SC, cód. 224, fols. 62–62v (first letter of this date).

85. Governor to [?], [Vila Rica?], 30 Jun 1781, APM, SC, cód. 224, fols. 65–65v.

86. Rocha, *Geografia histórica*, 190–92.

87. Livro de registro da guardamoria do Distrito da Serra da Mantiqueira abaixo até o Paraibuna, São João del-Rei, 1778, BNRJ, SM, I-3, 17, 15.

88. Antônio José Dias Coelho to Governor, Vila Rica, 5 Oct 1812, BNRJ, SM, cód. 8, 1, 8, doc. 95. For more details on tax collection along the border between Minas Gerais and São Paulo border, see Coelho, Documentos referentes ao pagamento dos direitos reais pelos habitantes das Capitanias de São Paulo e Minas, ben como aos limites das mesmas, 1806–1812, BNRJ, SM, cód. II-31, 19, 18. For published letters from São Paulo on the ongoing border dispute, see Count of Sarzedas to Count of Galveas, São Paulo, 25 Mar 1733, *DI* 41 (1902): 46–47; Governor Saldanha to Governor Noronha, São Paulo, 6 Feb 1778, *DI* 43 (1903): 138–43; *idem* to Governor Rodrigo José de Meneses, São Paulo, 2 May 1780, *DI* 43 (1903): 325. In 1765, Governor Silva of Minas Gerais traveled a circuitous route said to extend 380 leagues (nearly 2500 km) from Vila Rica to the region in an earlier attempt to regularize the administration of the border and put an end to suspected gold smuggling to São Paulo. See ruling (*consulta*) of the Overseas Council, 17 Sep 1767, Lisbon, AIHGB, Conselho Ultramarino, Arq. 1, 2, 6, fols. 89v–93, published in *RAPM* 15 (1910): 463–65. For documentation pertaining to the period 1766–73, again from the São Paulo side, see BNRJ, SM, MM, docs. I-30, 26, 11; I-30, 14, 37; I-30, 16, 9; I-49, 3, 17; I-30, 15, 34; I-30, 16, 4; I-30, 25, 12; I-30, 16, 30; I-30, 17, 6. Two of these documents discuss the violent resistance to settlers by Kayapó Indians in this borderland area. See BNRJ, SM, MM, docs. I-30, 16, 9 no. 21; I-30, 15, 20 no. 5.

89. Governor to Felipe Joaquim da Cunha, 14 Sep 1812, BNRJ, SM, cód. 1, 4, 5, doc. 483.

90. For a late example, see José Joaquim Carneiro de Miranda e Costa to Governor, Campanha da Princesa, 22 Oct 1812, BNRJ, SM, cód. 8, 1, 8, doc. 94.

91. On the history of Portuguese forced migration, see Souza, *Desclassificados do ouro*, 57–60; Schwartz, "The Formation of Colonial Identity," 21.

92. Rocha, *Geografia histórica*, 196.

93. Diogo Pereira Ribeiro de Vasconcelos, *Breve descrição*, 157–58. Vasconcelos is not to be confused with the twentieth-century Minas historian Diogo Luís de Almeida Pereira de Vasconcelos. See bibliography for their respective works.

94. Revisionist studies that examine bonded frontier labor, upending the traditional emphasis on free land, free labor, and frontier democracy, most famously asserted by Frederick Jackson Turner and his disciple Walter Prescott Webb, include Melvyn Dubofsky, "The Origins of the Western Working Class, 1890–1905," *Labor History* 7 (Spring 1966): 131–54; Joe Foweraker, *The Struggle for Land*; Lamar, "From Bondage to Contract"; William H. McNeill, *The Great Frontier: Freedom and Hierarchy in Modern Times* (Princeton, NJ: Princeton University Press, 1983); Carlos Schwantes, "The Concept of the Wageworkers' Frontier: An American-Canadian Perspective," *Western Historical Quarterly* 18 (January 1987): 39–55; Gunther Peck, *Reinventing Free Labor: Padrones and Immigrant Workers in the North American West, 1880–1930* (Cambridge: Cambridge University Press, 2000). Also see Frederick Jackson Turner, "The Significance of the Frontier in American History," in *idem, The Frontier in American History,* (originally a paper read at the American Historical Association meeting in Chicago, 12 Jul 1893; New York: Henry Holt, 1920), 1–38; Walter Prescott Webb, *The Great Frontier* (Boston: Houghton Mifflin, 1952), esp. 411–13. The issue is taken up again in the conclusion of the present study.

Notes to Chapter 5

1. The quotation is from Anastasia, introduction to Diogo Pereira Ribeiro de Vasconcelos, *Breve descrição*, 15.

2. For instance, Moreira Neto attributes the 1808 declaration of war against the Botocudo to the arrival in Brazil of the Portuguese Court, whose "new policy of oppression" reverted to sixteenth- and seventeenth-century precedents. See Moreira Neto, *Índios da Amazônia*, 32. This perspective also surfaces in the recent study by Paraíso, who considers 1808 a year of "radical changes" in state indigenous policy. See Paraíso, "O tempo da dor," 191. Other examples of scholars' treatment of the decree and the war that followed include Barickman, "'Tame Indians,'" 359–62; Oliveira Lima, *Dom João VI no Brasil,* 3rd ed. (Rio de Janeiro: Topbooks, 1996), 487–93; Hemming, *Amazon Frontier,* 91–93, 99–100; and Paraíso, "O tempo da dor," 211–51.

3. On the belated rise of centralized authority in Rio de Janeiro during the transition from colony to nation, see esp. Roderick J. Barman, *Brazil: The Forging of a Nation, 1798–1852* (Stanford, CA: Stanford University Press, 1988).

4. Jozé Eloi Ottoni, "Memoria," *ABNRJ* 30 (1908): 317.

5. See Langfur, "Return of the Bandeira." Most of the data in Table 5.1 was first presented in Langfur, "Forbidden Lands," chap. 2, and *idem,* "Uncertain Refuge." Maria Leônia Chaves de Resende, studying detribalized Indians living in the towns and villages of colonial Minas Gerais, subsequently identified 12 additional expeditions to the Eastern Sertão. I then identified another three, bringing the total to 79. Resende's fine study, which encompasses all of Minas Gerais over the entire colonial era, lists yet another 14 expeditions heading to other destinations or occurring during earlier or later periods for

a grand total of 93. Further research will likely uncover still others. See Resende, "Gentios brasílicos," 379–83.

6. Hal Langfur, "The Return of the Bandeira." Much of the subsequent evidence used in this chapter was first presented in this article, although for different thematic purposes.

7. On the historical origin and frequent invocation in the sixteenth and seventeenth centuries of "just wars" against the Indians of Portuguese America, see Perrone-Moisés, "Índios livres e índios escravos." For the best inventory of indigenous legislations, see *idem*, "Inventário da legislação indigenista," a catalogue of colonial indigenous legislation, according to which the penultimate instance of a just war declared by the Crown occurred in 1739, against the Guegué and Akroá Indians of Maranhão. See Ordem Régia, 16 Apr 1739, summarized in "Inventário da legislação," 556. Also see Mercio P. Gomes, *The Indians and Brazil*, trans. John W. Moon (Gainesville, FL: University Press of Florida, 2000), 60–64. For an analysis of English and Spanish notions of just war, see Jill Lepore, *The Name of War: King Philip's War and the Origins of American Identity* (New York: Knopf, 1998), 106–13.

8. On the war's extension to these other groups, see Lima, *Dom João VI no Brasil*, 487; Hemming, *Amazon Frontier*, 93, 112–13. For the royal declaration of war against the Kaingáng, see Carta Régia, 5 Nov 1808, in Cunha, *Legislação indigenista*, 62–64. A long history set the pattern for Portuguese military actions that were first directed against one indigenous enemy and then expanded to encompass neighboring groups. For example, see Mathias C. Kiemen, *The Indian Policy of Portugal in the Amazon Region, 1614–1693* (New York: Octagon Books, 1973), 22.

9. "Petição que fizerão e assignarão os moradores das freguesias ostilizadas," ca. May 1765, APM, CC, cód. 1156, fols. 9–10.

10. Governor [Antônio de Noronha], "Conta que foi inclusa nas ditas cartas do sr. Marquês de Pombal e Martinho de Melo sobre a extinção das duas companhias de pedestres do Cuieté," Vila Rica, 25 Jul 1775, APM, SC, cód. 212, fols. 72–73.

11. Governor, "Instrução que hade seguir o Cap.^{am} Antônio Cardozo de Souza," [Vila Rica], [ca. 1767], BNRJ, SM, CV, cód. 18, 2, 6, doc. 293. For records of gold extracted from the Cuieté region by Captain Silva in 1767, see Domingos Francisco Roiz, "Lista do ouro que sahio deste continente do Cuyeté de que pasou guia o Cap.am Paulo Mendes Ferreira Campelo as pessoas abaixo declaradas neste Anno de 1767 para o de 1768," ibid., doc. 221.

12. Ibid.

13. The tax records are registered in "Providencias tomadas para a catechese dos Indios no Rio Doce e Piracicaba, Vila Rica, 1764–1767," APM, CC, cód. 1156, fols. 2–3v.

14. Antônio Cardozo de Souza to Governor, Vitória, 15 Sep 1769, BNRJ, SM, CV, cód. 18, 2, 6, doc. 301.

15. [Manoel Vieyra Nunes], "Termo de reunião de conselho," Barra das Larangeiras, 5 Jul 1769, BNRJ, SM, CV, cód. 18, 2, 6, doc. 192. Such language, as well as its codification in this *termo* (official pronouncement), echoed words set down more than two centuries before in the Spanish *Requerimiento*, or Requirement, one of the founding texts of the conquest of the Americas. Drafted in 1513, the Requerimiento was a speech read to Indians or, in their absence, to the forests, rivers, and beaches they inhabited to make legal the

commencement of Spanish hostilities. For a brief discussion and English translation of one of the multiple versions of this protocol, see Lewis Hanke and Jane M. Rausch, *Latin American History: The Colonial Experience*, rev. ed. (New York: Markus Wiener Publishing, 1993), 89–91. A more extensive discussion can be found in Patricia Seed, *Ceremonies of Possession in Europe's Conquest of the New World, 1492–1640* (Cambridge: Cambridge University Press, 1995), 69–99. For an instructive comparison between the Requerimiento and early documents of English colonizers in North America, see Urs Bitterli, *Cultures in Conflict: Encounters Between European and Non-European Cultures, 1492–1800*, trans. Ritchie Robertson (Stanford, CA: Stanford University Press, 1989), 119–22.

16. Governor, "Instrução que hade seguir o Cap.^{am} Antonio Cardozo de Souza," [Vila Rica], [ca. 1767], BNRJ, SM, CV, cód. 18, 2, 6, doc. 293. Crucial for understanding the nature and exact timing of the assault on the Eastern Sertão, these orders are undated but were likely issued in conjunction with the allocation of weapons to Souza's soldiers in 1767. See "Relaçao das Armas de fogo que se entregarão aos Cap.^{ens} abaixo declarados," n.d., ibid., doc. 268. This document also bears no date, but it specifies the year in which weapons were distributed as 1767.

17. Governor to Treasurer, Vila Rica, 28 Jul 1764, APM, SC, cód. 118, fol. 65v; Governor, "Rellação do que se deve apromptar na Provedoria da Fazenda Real para a expedição que se fás contra o Gentio," ibid., fols. 65v–66; Governor, "Instrução que hade observar o Comandante distinado para o Destricto do Cuyeté a respeito do Arrayal que nelle se estabalece e de todos os moradores que no mesmo quizerem rezidir," Vila Rica, 4 Jun 1765, BNRJ, SM, CV, cód. 18, 2, 6, doc. 203; [Antônio Pereira da Silva] to Governor, n.p., ca. 1770, BNRJ, SM, CV, cód. 18, 2, 6, doc. 329.

18. Governor, "Para a expulção dos Indios de S. Jozé da Barra Longa . . . ," Vila Rica, 20 Feb 1766, APM, SC, cód. 118, fols. 133–33v. Mentioned extremely rarely in the sources, the Taititûs do not appear in the most extensive catalogue of the indigenous groups of Minas Gerais. See José, *Indígenas*, 37.

19. Governor, "Orden para a entrada dos corpos de gente para a civilização dos gentios silvestres Purîs e Buticudos," Vila Rica, 21 Apr 1766, APM, SC, cód. 118, fols. 148–50v; Governor to Antônio Pereira da Silva, Vila Rica, 28 Jun 1766, APM, SC, cód. 118, fols. 171v–72.

20. "Requerimento de Antonio Cardozo de Souza, morador no Rio Pardo da Co- marca de Serro Frio, respectivo sobre a rodução de Indioz que circulão a Otinga," [1766], APM, SC, cód. 60, fol. 86; Governor to Souza, Vila Rica, 29 Aug 1766, ibid., fols. 86–86v. Souza's destination, identified as Otinga in this source, may well have been the territory near the confluence of the Jequitinhonha and Araçuaí Rivers where the town of Itinga later formed following subsequent exploration in the early nineteenth century.

21. The other three officers receiving weapons were the captains Jerônimo Martins Gomes and Francisco Alvarez Pereira and the *sargento-mor* João da Silva Tavares. "Relaçao das Armas de fogo que se entregarão aos Cap.^{ais} abaixo declarados," n.d., BNRJ, SM, CV, cód. 18, 2, 6, doc. 268. Souza is identified as field commander in Governor, "Instrução que hade seguir o Cap.^{am} Antonio Cardozo de Souza," [Vila Rica, ca. 1767,] BNRJ, SM, CV, cód. 18, 2, 6, doc. 293.

22. João da Silva Pereira de Souza to Governor, Cuieté, 25 Nov 1769, BNRJ, SM, CV, cód. 18, 2, 6, doc. 264.

23. Patent of Antônio Pereira da Silva, Vila Rica, 2 Oct? 1768, Registo de patentes de officiaes, 1769[sic]–1770, BNRJ, CC, film MS-252, vol. 192, fol. 109v; Governor, "Conta que foi inclusa nas ditas cartas do sr. Marquês de Pombal e Martinho de Melo sobre a extinção das duas companhias de pedestres do Cuieté," Vila Rica, 25 Jul 1775, APM, SC, cód. 212, fols. 72–73.

24. Campelo, "Representação," n.d., BNRJ, SM, CV, cód. 18, 2, 26, doc. 198; Governor, "Instrução que hade observar o Comandante distinado para o Destricto do Cuyeté a respeito do Arrayal que nelle se estabalece e de todos os moradores que no mesmo quizerem rezidir," Vila Rica, 4 Jun 1765, ibid., doc. 203, and Governor to Campelo, Vila Rica, 21 Jun 1767, ibid., doc. 204.

25. Antônio Cardozo de Souza to Governor, Vitória, 15 Sep 1769, BNRJ, SM, CV, cód. 18, 2, 6, doc. 301.

26. Furious at what they considered the lack of success in achieving this goal, Guimarães and his subordinates opted for the drastic measure of filing a formal eleven-point complaint against Captain Souza, denouncing him as a "cowardly" commander, "unworthy and useless for his lack of economy and prudence," who left his men vulnerable and dispirited in the face of the enemy. Petition of Alexandre da Sylva Guimarães and soldiers to Paulo Mendes Ferreira Campelo, Cuieté, 12 Nov 1769, BNRJ, SM, CV, cód. 18, 2, 6, doc. 251.

27. [Manoel Vieyra Nunes,] "Termo de reunião de conselho," Barra das Larangeiras, 5 Jul 1769, BNRJ, SM, CV, cód. 18, 2, 6, doc. 192.

28. Governor, "Memoria do que deve observar na derrota que tem de seguir o Capitam Antonio Cardozo de Souza para a Conquista do Gentio a que vai destinado, e do que hade praticar," Vila Rica, 9 Apr 1769, BNRJ, SM, CV, cód. 18, 2, 6, doc. 306.

29. Governor, "Conta que foi inclusa nas ditas cartas do sr. Marquês de Pombal e Martinho de Melo sobre a extinção das duas companhias de pedestres do Cuieté," Vila Rica, 25 Jul 1775, APM, SC, cód. 212, fols. 72–73; Diogo [Luís de Almeida Pereira] de Vasconcelos, História média, 203.

30. Governor to Viceroy, Vila Rica, 19 Nov 1776, BNRJ, SM, cód. 2, 2, 24, fols. 52–53.

31. Governor, Bando, Vila Rica, 15 Mar 1776, APM, SC, cód. 50, fols. 168v–69; Governor, Bando, Vila Rica, 29 May 1779, BNRJ, SM, cód. 2, 2, 24, fols. 222–22v. Copies of these edicts can also be found in APM, SC, cód. 214, fols. 2v–3, 7–7v.

32. Governor to Viceroy, Vila Rica, 19 Nov 1776, BNRJ, SM, cód. 2, 2, 24, fols. 52–53; Governor to João Rodrigues de Monteiro, Vila Rica, 3 Sep 1778, ibid., fol. 178; Governor to João da Silva Tavares, 8 Sep 1779, Vila Rica, ibid., fols. 228v–29v; Governor, Bando, Vila Rica, 15 Mar 1776, APM, SC, cód. 50, fols. 168v–69; Governor, Bando, Vila Rica, 29 May 1779, BNRJ, SM, cód. 2, 2, 24, fols. 222–22v. See also Vasconcelos, História média, 235–36.

33. Governor to capitães-mores, Vila Rica, 15 May 1777, with accompanying document, Bando, BNRJ, SM, cód. 2, 2, 24, fol. 121v–24.

34. Some scholars date the expiration of Meneses' term at 1782, when he received orders to proceed to the governorship of Bahia. As with many captaincy governors,

however, the actual transfer of power occurred significantly later. Meneses remained in charge of Minas Gerais until October 10, 1783, when his successor, Luís da Cunha Meneses, who had been named to the post more than a year before on July 19, 1782, took office. See Queen to Luís da Cunha de Meneses, Palacio de Queluz, 19 Jul 1782 and Colonial Secretary to Luís da Cunha Meneses, Palacio de Queluz, 25 Aug 1782, *RAPM* 25:2 (1937): 252–53. This second source is a facsimile reprint of the manuscript codex, "Livro das posses dos senhores governadores, 1721–1827," APM, SC, cód. 25.

35. Vasconcelos, *História média*, 252.

36. Governor, "Exposição ... sobre o estado de decadencia da Capitania de Minas-Geraes e meios de remedial-o," Vila Rica, 4 Aug 1780, *RAPM*, 2: 2 (1897): 314.

37. Governor to Colonial Secretary, Vila Rica, 31 Dec 1781, APM, SC, cód. 224, fols. 80v–86 (third letter of this date).

38. Veloso de Miranda to Governor, Presídio dos Arrepiados, 1 Nov, 23 Nov 1781, APM, SC, cód. 224, fols. 79–80v. Miranda's rank and commission as the region's top commander are recorded in Governor to Colonial Secretary, Vila Rica, 31 Dec 1781, APM, SC, cód. 224, fols. 74–78 (second letter of this date). Maximilian identified native "trumpets," fashioned out of the tails of armadillos, as in use among the Botocudo in the early nineteenth century. See Maximilian, *Viagem ao Brasil*, 292. Branco referred to these instruments by the Portuguese word *buzina* (horn or trumpet); Maximilian used the same term, as well as the Botocudo name, *cuntschung-cocann*. A Portuguese translation of Maximilian's German phonetic spelling of the Botocudo original, the term's appearance in manuscript and published primary sources exemplifies the linguistic hazards of identifying the cultural artifacts and practices of these Indians. Maximilian also provides a sketch of this and other Botocudo implements, ornaments, and arms, pl. 14, n. 1, between pp. 324 and 325.

39. Governor to Colonial Secretary, Vila Rica, 31 Dec 1781, APM, SC, cód. 224, fols. 74–78 (second letter of this date); Rocha, *Geografia histórica*, 191–92. The governor spoke of "more than three hundred land grants"; Rocha specified 373 land grants and mining claims.

40. Governor to Colonial Secretary, Vila Rica, 10 Apr 1781, APM, SC, cód. 224, fol. 20–20v.

41. Meneses also mentioned the problem of tropical fevers that attacked those who entered the zone. These, he argued, would disappear with settlement, as the clearing of forests allowed the air "to rarify more easily" and the channeling of streams did away with stagnant waters and their "infected vapors" that "were continually corrupting the atmosphere." Governor to Colonial Secretary, Vila Rica, 31 Dec 1781, APM, SC, cód. 224, fols. 80v–81 (third letter of this date). The governor's favorable assessment of the possibility of military conquest was directed to a Portuguese court increasingly willing to consider such aggressive tactics in other regions of the colony. In the 1780s, demands by colonists in the Amazon Basin for access to more indigenous labor than provided by village Indians under the Directory system led the Crown to reinstate the practice of privately organized *descimentos* (literally, "descents"), that is, raids on and resettlement of independent forest Indians. See MacLachlan, "Indian Labor," 213.

42. Miranda to Governor, Presídio de São Lourenço, 20 Nov 1783, APM, CC, film 523, *planilha* 20023, *item* 2. Also see Barbosa, *Dicionário histórico-geográfico*, 30.

43. Vasconcelos, *História média*, 274–76; Barbosa, *Dicionário histórico-geográfico*, 286–87; 370; Trindade, *Visitas pastorais*, 50; Carrara, *Uma fronteira da Capitania de Minas Gerais*. On the exclusion of unsettled Indians from local censuses, see ibid., 9 n. 8.

44. Conspirators taken prisoner after the failed 1789 plot were finally transferred from Vila Rica to the vice regal capital of Rio de Janeiro for a final round of interrogation in July 1791. Sentencing occurred in April 1792, followed by the execution of Tiradentes. Throughout this period, tensions remained high in both Minas Gerais and Rio de Janeiro, and trade between the two urban centers was severely disrupted. Maxwell, *Conflicts and Conspiracies*, 192, 195.

45. For examples of these conflicts, see Governor to Francisco Pires Farinho, Cachoeira, 13 Nov 1781, APM, SC, cód. 227, fols. 13–13v; Veloso de Miranda to Governor, [Presídio dos] Arrepiados, 23 Nov 1781, APM, SC, cód. 224, fols. 79v–80v; Petition of Jozé Bernardino Alves Gundim, Mariana, [1794], APM, SC, cód. 260, fol. 51v; Petition of Padre Francisco da Silva Campos to King, [1800], in RAPM 2:4 (1897): 685–88. On the warfare between the Coroado and Puri, persisting at least into the 1810s, see Reys, *Manuscritos*, 72; Silva, *Memoria topographica e historica*, 27; Mercadante, *Os sertões do leste*, 31–2; Maximilian, Prinz von Wied, *Travels in Brazil in the Years 1815, 1816, 1817* (London: Henry Colburn, 1820), 108–09. On economic development and demographic expansion in the Campos region after 1770, see also Jozé Caetano de Barcelos Coitinho to Governor, São Salvador, ANTT, Papéis do Brasil, cód. 13, fols. 174–75 with appended manuscript census; Alden, *Royal Government*, 356; Lara, *Campos da violência*, 131–34; Faria, *A Colônia em movimento*; Maximilian, *Travels in Brazil*, 100–03.

46. Petition of Francisco Hernandes Teixeira Alvares to Governor of Bahia, São Mateus, s.d.; and Ouvidor to João Gonçalves da Costa, Cairu, 4 May 1790, APEB, SCP, maço 602-2. For Costa's earlier activity among the Indians in the region, see Governor to Ouvidor, Salvador da Bahia, 23 Feb 1782, and Costa to Ouvidor, Victória, 30 Jul 1783, ANTT, Papéis do Brasil, Avulsos 2, doc. 9; Ouvidor to Governor, et al., Cairu, 6 Aug 1783, ibid., doc. 10. Also see Paraíso, "O tempo da dor," 152–63; Barickman, "'Tame Indians,'" 352–57.

47. *Câmara* (Town Council) to Queen, Vitória, 8 May 1779, in Lamego, *A Terra Goitacá*, vol. 3, 447–51.

48. Governor, "Portaria para Joaquim Correya Mosso commandar hum Esquadra para afugentar os Indios Bravos," Vila Rica, 9 Jul 1792, APM, SC, cód. 259.

49. Petition of Jozé Bernardino Alves Gundim, Mariana, [1794], APM, SC, cód. 260, fol. 51v.

50. Gundim, "Plano . . . a respeito da providencia que se deve dar as hostalidades e invazoens dos Indios barbaros no seu respeitivo Destrito," Mariana, [1794], APM, SC, cód. 260, fols. 51v–52v. The aldeias referred to in this source, autonomous native encampments sometimes distinguished in the sources and especially the secondary literature as *aldeamentos*, are not to be confused with the state- and church-controlled missions at Rio Pomba, São João Batista do Presídio, and other sites.

51. Dispatch in reply to petition of Jozé Bernardino Alves Gundim, Mariana, 2 Sep 1794, APM, SC, cód. 260, fol. 52v. The description of Arrudo is from Gundim's "Plano," fol. 52, and the reference to the Puri can be found in Gundim, "Lista dos moradores do Turvo, destrito pobre que voluntariamente concorrem como interessados para a despeza

das expediçoens que se hão de fazer contra os Indios Poris e Boticudos," n.p., [1794], APM, SC, cód. 260, fols. 53–53v.

52. Cautious use of the evidence, therefore, required that Table 5.1 include only the three 1794 expeditions approved in the original plan.

53. Petition of João Damaceno dos Reis Vidal and other landholders with governor's reply, Vila Rica, 1 Nov 1794, APM, SC, cód. 260, fols. 42v–43.

54. Some sources state that Barbacena erected as many as six presidios. Diogo Pereira Ribeiro de Vasconcelos specifically identified three: Belém, on the Doce River east of Antônio Dias Abaixo, and Casca and Santana, on the rivers bearing the same names. Vasconcelos, *Breve descrição*, 155. See also Pedro Maria Xavier de Ataíde e Melo, "Sobre os Botocudos," Vila Rica, 1 Feb 1806, *RAPM* 3:3-4 (1898), 744; Cambraia and Mendes, "A colonização," 143.

55. Hemming, *Red Gold*, 60.

56. Governor, Bando, 30 Mar 1801, APM, SC, cód. 214, fols. 22v–23v. For one typical plan to extract lumber from the Doce River basin, see Memoria sobre a abertura do Rio Doce, e Estração das Madr^{as} ao longo delle..., [1804?], APEP, SCP, maço 585. For statistics on the decrease in gold production and increase in agricultural exports during these years, see "Statistical Appendix," in Maxwell, *Conflicts and Conspiracies*, esp. graphs A, B, E, F, G, and I.

57. Vasconcelos, *Breve descrição*, 155 n. 24. The 1808 declaration, then, constituted an expansion of this order, as well as similar ones issued to Bahian authorities in 1801 and 1806. See Barickman, "'Tame Indians,'" 360 n. 98; Paraíso, "Os Botocudos," 416; Moreira Neto, *Índios da Amazônia*, 32; Prado Júnior, *Formação do Brasil contemporâneo*, 103.

58. Governor to Luís Pinto de Souza Coutinho, Vila Rica, 17 Apr 1801, APM, SC, cód. 276, fols. 82v–83. On Pontes' efforts to increase commercial traffic on the Doce River and quell Indian resistance in Espírito Santo, see Maria Stella de Novaes, *História do Espírito Santo* (Vitória, Brazil: Fundo Editorial do Espírito Santo, 1968), 105–09; Paraíso, "O tempo da dor," 165–70.

59. Governor to Antônio da Silva Brandão, Vila Rica, 10 Feb 1802, APM, SC, cód. 277, fol. 103v.

60. Governor to Luís Pinto de Souza Coutinho, Vila Rica, 17 Apr 1801, APM, SC, cód. 276, fols. 82v–83.

61. Governor to Francisco Martins Penna, Vila Rica, 26 Jan 1802, APM, SC, cód. 277, fols. 100v–01.

62. Francisco Martins Penna to Governor, Tejuco, 17 Dec 1801, APM, SC, cód. 277, fols. 99v–100v; Barbosa, *Dicionário histórico-geográfico*, 133.

63. Governor to Manoel Rodrigues da Medeiros, Vila Rica, 14 Aug 1802, APM, SC, cód. 277, fols. 111–11v.

64. Duro to Governor, Antônio Dias Abaixo, 15 Jul 1802, APM, SC, cód. 277, fols. 111v–12v.

65. Governor to Duro, Vila Rica, 13 Aug 1802, APM, SC, cód. 277, fols. 112v–13; Governor to Brandão, Vila Rica, 13 Aug 1802, APM, SC, cód. 277, fol. 113.

66. For the entire text of the plan, see Pedro Maria Xavier de Ataíde e Melo, "Sobre os Botocudos," Vila Rica, 1 Feb 1806, *RAPM* 3:3-4 (1898), 743–48.

67. Ibid., 744; Vasconcelos, *Breve descrição*, 152–55.

68. Ottoni, "Memória," 313; Couto, *Memória*, 53, 80; Freire, "Informação da capitania de Minas Gerais," Sabará, 30 Mar 1805, BNRJ, SM, cód. 3, 1, 35, fols. 10–11; Vasconcelos, *Breve descrição*, 144–49, 157.

Notes to Chapter 6

1. John M. Monteiro, "The Heathen Castes of Sixteenth-Century Portuguese America: Unity, Diversity, and the Invention of the Brazilian Indians," *Hispanic American Historical Review* 80:4 (November 2000): 718.

2. Rocha, *Geografia histórica*, 153–54, 158, 159 n. 26a.

3. Ibid., 192–93.

4. Diogo Pereira Ribeiro de Vasconcelos, *Breve descrição*, 156.

5. Ibid., 204.

6. José, *Indígenas*, 67–70, 142–43, 204.

7. For the most prominent example of scholarship relying on travelers' accounts as a basis for Brazilian indigenous history, see Hemming, *Amazon Frontier*. Chaps. 5 and 18 focus on the Botocudo and other groups of Brazil's central Atlantic coast. On nineteenth-century travel accounts, with specific attention to women as both writers and subjects, see June E. Hahner, ed., *Women through Women's Eyes: Latin American Women in Nineteenth-Century Travel Accounts* (Wilmington, DE: Scholarly Resources, 1998), xi–xxvi. Also see Paulo Berger, *Bibliografia do Rio de Janeiro de viajantes e autores estrangeiros, 1531–1900*, 2nd ed. (Rio de Janeiro: SEEC-RJ, 1980); Regina Horta Duarte, "Facing the Forest: European Travellers Crossing the Mucuri River Valley, Brazil, in the Nineteenth Century," *Environment and History* 10 (2004): 31–58; Karen Macknow Lisboa, *A nova Atlântica de Spix e Martius: Natureza e civilização no viagem pelo Brasil (1817–1820)* (São Paulo: Hucitec, 1997); Pratt, *Imperial Eyes*. On the early historiography of Brazilian Indians, see Monteiro, "Heathen Castes."

8. For example, see Nazzari, "Vanishing Indians"; Resende, "Gentíos brasílicos"; Sommer, "Negotiated Settlements"; Maria Regina Celestino de Almeida, "Os índios aldeiados no Rio de Janeiro colonial: Novos súditos cristãos do Império Português," (Ph.D. diss., Universidade de Campinas, Brazil, 2001); Stuart B. Schwartz and Frank Salomon, "New Peoples and New Kinds of People: Adaptation, Readjustment, and Ethnogenesis in South American Indigenous Societies (Colonial Era)," in *CHNPA*, vol. 3, pt. 2, 443–501; Serge Gruzinski, *The Mestizo Mind: The Intellectual Dynamics of Colonization and Globalization* (New York: Routledge, 2002); John M. Monteiro, "Entre o etnocídio e a etnogênese: Identidades indígenas coloniais," (paper presented at the Latin American Studies Association Conference, Dallas, TX, March 27–29, 2003). On detribalized Indians in contemporary Brazil, see Jonathan W. Warren, *Racial Revolutions: Antiracism & Indian Resurgence in Brazil* (Durham, NC: Duke University Press, 2001).

9. Gustave Flaubert, *Madame Bovary*, trans. Mildred Marmur (New York: Signet Classic, New American Library, 1964), 125.

10. The most relevant works by European naturalists on Brazil's eastern Indians include Eschwege, *Brasil, Novo Mundo*, trans. Domício de Figueiredo Murta, Coleção Mineiriana, Série Clássicos (Belo Horizonte, Brazil: Fundação João Pinheiro, 1996); *idem*, *Pluto brasiliensis*; Maximilian, *Viagem ao Brasil*; Saint-Hilaire, *Viagem pelas províncias*; and *idem*, *Viagem ao Espírito Santo*. Hemming provides brief biographies and a helpful

chronology of these and other explorers, naturalists, and adventurers in *Amazon Frontier*, 483–511.

11. Eschwege, *Pluto brasiliensis*, vol. 1, 43; *idem, Brasil, Novo Mundo*, 240 n. 61.

12. Maximilian, *Viagem ao Brasil*, 292.

13. Saint-Hilaire, *Viagem pelas províncias*, 257, 276.

14. Eschwege, *Pluto brasiliensis*, vol. 1, 42.

15. Eschwege wrote this passage about the Aimoré Indians, but he assumed the Botocudo and the Aimoré to be one and the same. See Eschwege, *Brasil, Novo Mundo*, 239 n. 59.

16. Rocha, *Geografia histórica*, 192; Ottoni, "Memoria," 312; Freire, "Informação da capitania de Minas Gerais," Sabará, 30 Mar 1805, BNRJ, SM, cód. 3, 1, 35, fol. 11; Vasconcelos, *Breve descrição*, 148–49. Some of these reports, along with others not discussed here, were ordered drafted by the Portuguese colonial secretary Rodrigo de Sousa Coutinho as part of his effort to formulate a "grand plan" to revive the ailing Minas economy and, even more broadly and urgently, to retain Crown control over Portugal's restless American colony. Kenneth R. Maxwell, *Conflicts and Conspiracies*, 207–13.

17. Governor to Jozé Leme da Sylva, Vila Rica, 8 Oct 1765, APM, SC, cód. 118, fols. 116v–17.

18. Campelo to Governor, Cuieté, 16 Nov 1769, BNRJ, SM, CV, cód. 18, 2, 6, doc. 194.

19. Decree by Campelo, Cuieté, 30 Jan 1770, ibid., doc. 235.

20. Attestation (*certidão*) of [Paulo Mendes Ferreira] Campelo, Cuieté, 6 Feb 1770, ibid., doc. 234.

21. Governor, "Conta que foi inclusa nas ditas cartas do sr. Marquês de Pombal e Martinho de Melo sobre a extinção das duas companhias de pedestres do Cuieté," Vila Rica, 25 Jul 1775, APM, SC, cód. 212, fols. 72–73.

22. Ibid.

23. Ibid.

24. See Prado Júnior, *Formação do Brasil contemporâneo*, 76; 102–03; Cambraia and Mendes, "A colonização," 138–43.

25. Unless otherwise indicated, the following account is based on two manuscript letters: [Governor?] to [José Antônio Freire de Andrade], Vila Rica, late November 1758, AIHGB, Conselho Ultramarino, Arq. 1, 3, 8, fols. 164v–67v; Sylverio Teixeira to [José Antônio Freire de Andrade], Vila Rica, 25 Nov 1758, AIHGB, Conselho Ultramarino, Arq. 1, 3, 8, fols. 163v–64v. By all contextual clues, the author of the first letter would seem to have been the Minas governor, the Count of Bobadela.

26. Farinha's surname often appears in the sources spelled Farinho. I have standardized the name in the main text using the more common spelling, Farinha, but have left the different spellings intact in citations.

27. On Pessanha's relationship to Portugal's last grand inquisitor, see Coutinho, *Ensaio economico*, 64.

28. José Antônio Freire de Andrade to Thomé Joaquim da Costa, Rio de Janeiro, 4 Jan 1759, AIHGB, Conselho Ultramarino, Arq. 1, 3, 8, fols. 162v–63v.

29. Coutinho, *Ensaio economico*, 65. Also see "Requerimento de D. José Joaquim da Cunha de Azeredo Coutinho a rainha D. Maria I," ca. 1794, in Alberto Lamego, *A Terra Goitacá*, vol. 2, 505–06.

30. Coutinho, *Ensaio economico*, 64; Reys, *Manuscritos*, 29 n. 93.

31. See Langfur, "Myths of Pacification."

32. José Antônio Freire de Andrade to Thomé Joaquim da Costa, Rio de Janeiro, 4 Jan 1759, AIHGB, Conselho Ultramarino, Arq. 1, 3, 8, fols. 162v–63v.

33. No such incentive was offered to Indian men, marriages between indigenous males and white females being as unpalatable to officials in the 1760s as they were to Saint-Hilaire decades later when he called for the union of Botocudo women and free blacks.

34. Petition of Padre Manoel de Jesus Maria to King, [Mariana?, ca. November 1768], ANTT, Ordem de Cristo, Padroado do Brasil, Bispado de Mariana, maço 5; Ordens sôbre arrecadação e despesas, 1768[–1771]," 23 Jul and 8 Aug 1770, 18 Feb 1771, BNRJ, SM, CC, gaveta I-10-7, docs. 56, 71; Saint-Hilaire, *Viagens pelas províncias*, 276–77; Castro, *Os sertões de leste*, 11–15, esp. transcription, p. 14 n. 4, of royal order dated 20 Oct 1779, describing the priest's activities. For the original manuscript, see APM, SC, cód. 220, fols. 44v–45. Also see Diogo [Luís de Almeida Pereira] de Vasconcelos, *História média*, 205–10; Paulo Mercadante, *Os sertões do leste*, 40–42.

35. See Araújo, *Memórias históricas*, 288–89, 295.

36. For the manuscript 1825 census, see ACMM, cód. 398. For the published census, see Carrara, *Uma fronteira da Capitania de Minas Gerais*, 12, 20, 52–53, 60–73, 108–09. Also see *idem, Estruturas agrárias*, 17–18.

37. Governor, "Instrução que hade observar o Comandante distinado para o Destricto do Cuyeté a respeito do Arrayal que nelle se estabalece e de todos os moradores que no mesmo quizerem rezidir," Vila Rica, 4 Jun 1765, BNRJ, SM, CV, cód. 18, 2, 6, doc. 203.

38. The first of these priests was Manoel Vieira Nunes, vicar of Cuieté, who arrived in the settlement no later than March 1769. The second, arriving in 1770, was Domingos da Silva Xavier, brother of Joaquim José da Silva Xavier, the famous Tiradentes or "Tooth Puller," the sole conspirator executed in the aftermath of the 1789 Inconfidência Mineira. Xavier apparently replaced Nunes. See [Manoel Vieyra Nunes] to Campelo, Cuieté, [ca. 11 May 1769], BNRJ, SM, CV, cód. 18, 2, 6, doc. 187; Nunes, et al., "Lembrança do Gentio que se acha na Aldeya das Laranjeiras em que entrão as nações segt.s, monoxos, cumunoxoes, maxacalins cujas nações se achão cazadas humas com outras," [Barra das Larangeiras], [5 Jul. 1769], ibid., doc. 190. On Xavier's departure for Cuieté, see Francisco Álvares Pereira to governor, Antônio Dias Abaixo, 18 Oct 1770, ibid., doc. 177; "Ordens sôbre arrecadação e despesas, 1768[–1771]," 3 Jul 1771, BNRJ, SM, CC, gaveta I-10-7, doc. 72.

39. Manoel Vieyra Nunes, et al., "Lembrança do Gentio . . . ," [Barra das Larangeiras], [5 Jul 1769], BNRJ, SM, CV, cód. 18, 2, 6, doc. 190; Nunes, et al., "Lista da Ferramenta, e Rozarioz que se repartirão pellos Indios de paz chamados manaxois, e munuxois, e muxacalins todos moradores na Aldeya das Laranjeiras que se componham de corenta e dois homens da guerra pouco mais ou menos . . . ," ibid., doc. 191.

40. Nunes to Governor, [Cuieté?], [1769], BNRJ, SM, CV, cód. 18, 2, 6, doc. 321.

41. Ibid. The Capoxó were more commonly referred to as Coropoxó. See José, *Indígenas*, 23.

42. Nunes, et al., "Lista da Ferramenta . . . ," [Barra das Larangeiras], [5 Jul 1769], BNRJ, SM, CV, cód. 18, 2, 6, doc. 191; [Nunes] to Campelo, Cuieté, drafted no later than 11 May 1769, ibid., doc. 187; Governor, "Memoria do que deve observar na derrota que

tem de seguir o Capitam Antonio Cardozo de Souza para a Conquista do Gentio a que vai destinado, e do que hade praticar," Vila Rica, 9 Apr 1769, ibid., doc. 306. On the subject of Indian soldiers and laborers enlisted by the captaincy government, see also Resende, "Gentíos brasílicos," 303–17.

43. Ruling of Overseas Council, [ca. 1778, Lisbon], *RAPM* 15 (1910): 482.

44. Duro to Governor, Antônio Dias Abaixo, 15 Jul 1802, APM, SC, cód. 277, fols. 111v–12v; Governor to Duro, Vila Rica, 13 Aug 1802, ibid., fols. 112v–13.

45. Jozé Pereira Freire de Moura to Governor, Onça, 2 Oct 1802, APM, SC, cód. 277, fols. 117–18.

46. Governor to Francisco Pires Farinha and Deonizio Alvez Guimaraens, Vila Rica, 13 Jun 1765, APM, SC, cód. 118, fols. 103v–04.

47. Governor to Vicar, Vila Rica, 24 Jun 1772, APM, SC, cód. 183, fol. 14; Governor to Paulo Mendes Farinha, Vila Rica, 24 Jun 1772, ibid., fol. 15–15v.

48. Judy Bieber, "The Aldeia System Reborn: Botocudo Communities on the Espírito Santo-Minas Gerais Frontier, 1808–1845" (paper presented at the Latin American Studies Association Conference, Chicago, September 24–26, 1998).

49. Examples of such findings are numerous in the North American historiography, including William Cronon, *Changes in the Land: Indians, Colonists, and the Ecology of New England* (New York: Hill and Wang, 1983); White, *Middle Ground*; James H. Merrell, *The Indians' New World: Catawbas and Their Neighbors from European Contact through the Era of Removal* (New York: Norton, 1991); Usner, *Indians, Settlers, and Slaves*; Gutiérrez, *When Jesus Came*; Cynthia Radding, *Wandering Peoples*.

50. Campelo, "Representação," n.d., BNRJ, SM, CV, cód. 18, 2, 6, doc. 198.

51. Manoel Vieyra Nunes to Governor, [1769], [Cuieté?], BNRJ, SM, CV, cód. 18, 2, 6, doc. 321.

52. Governor, "Lista das pessoas que devem e tem obrigação de concorrerem para embaracar o corso com que o gentio Sylvestre esta todos os annos entrando pelas fazendas e sesmarias da Beira do Rio Doce . . . ," Vila Rica, 9 May 1765, APM, CC, cód. 1156, fol. 4.

53. Governor, "Portaria para Joaquim Correya Mosso commandar hum Esquadra para afugentar os Indios Bravos," Vila Rica, 9 Jul 1792, APM, SC, cód. 259.

54. Antônio Veloso de Miranda to Governor, [Presídio dos] Arrepiados, 23 Nov 1781, APM, SC, cód. 224, fols. 79v–80v.

55. Petition of Jozé Bernardino Alves Gundim, Mariana, [1794], APM, SC, cód. 260, fol. 51v.

56. "Requerimento de Antonio Cardozo de Souza, morador no Rio Pardo da Comarca de Serro Frio, respectivo sobre a rodução de Indioz que circulão a Otinga," [1766], APM, SC, cód. 60, fol. 86; Governor to Souza, Vila Rica, 29 Aug 1766, ibid., fols. 86–86v.

57. In 1773, Clara Pires Farinho received a sesmaria land grant along the Xopotó River and in 1786, the priest Martinho Pires Farinho received one along the headwaters of the Turvo River in Rio Pomba Parish. See sesmaria of Clara Pires Farinho, 1773, APM, SC, cód. 172, fol. 200v; sesmaria of Martinho Pires Farinho, 1786, APM, SC, cód. 234.

58. This was one of many cases in which an expedition was termed an *entrada*, rather than *bandeira*. Another term used in this document is *escolta* (escort), suggesting the expedition's military or paramilitary character.

59. Governor to Francisco Pires Farinho, Cachoeira, 13 Nov 1781, APM, SC, cód. 227, fols. 13–13v.

60. Roland Barthes, *Mythologies*, trans. Annette Lavers (New York: Hill and Wang, 1972), 142. Here I also draw on Richard Slotkin, *The Fatal Environment: The Myth of the Frontier in the Age of Industrialization, 1800–1890* (New York: Atheneum, 1985), chap. 2. The study of frontier mythology has generated a substantial literature pertaining to westward colonization in both the U.S. and Brazil. For a comprehensive treatment of the U.S. case, see the trilogy Slotkin, *Regeneration through Violence: The Mythology of the American Frontier, 1600–1860* (Middletown, CT: Wesleyan University Press, 1973); *idem, The Fatal Environment*; and *idem, Gunfighter Nation: The Myth of the Frontier in Twentieth-Century America* (New York: Atheneum, 1992). On Brazilian frontier mythology, see Candice Vidal e Souza, "A noção de fronteira e espaço nacional no pensamento social brasileiro," *Textos de História* 4:2 (1996): 94–129; *idem, A pátria geográfica e litoral no pensamento social brasileiro* (Goiânia: Universidade Federal de Goiás, 1997); Janaína Amado, "Construindo mitos: a conquista do oeste no Brasil e nos EUA," in *Passando dos limites*, ed. Sidney V. Pimentel and Janaína Amado (Goiânia, Brazil: Universidade Federal de Goiás, 1995), 51–78; Robert Wegner, *A conquista do oeste: A fronteira na obra de Sérgio Buarque de Holanda* (Belo Horizonte, Brazil: Universidade Federal de Minas Gerais, 2000); Nísia Trindade Lima, *Um sertão chamado Brasil: Intelectuais e representação geográfica da identidade nacional* (Rio de Janeiro: Revan, 1999); Mary Lombardi, "The Frontier in Brazilian History: An Historiographic Essay," *Pacific Historical Review* 44 (November 1975): 437–57. For competing frontier myths arising from the conquest of the Bororo Indians of Mato Grosso, Brazil, see Langfur, "Myths of Pacification."

Notes to Chapter 7

1. On the salience of regional as opposed to centralized governance during the late colonial period, see Barman, *Forging of a Nation*; Richard Graham, "Constructing a Nation in Nineteenth-Century Brazil: Old and New Views on Class, Culture, and the State," *Journal of the Historical Society* 1:2–3 (Winter 2000/Spring 2001): 17–56. In a shortened and somewhat altered form, the argument advanced in this chapter was first presented in Langfur, "Moved by Terror."

2. On depictions of Indians in nineteenth-century Brazilian historiography, see John M. Monteiro, "The Heathen Castes." On eighteenth-century elite views in Minas Gerais, see Souza, *Norma e conflito*, 91–94.

3. Colonial Secretary to Governor, Palácio de Nossa Senhora da Ajuda, 13 Nov 1807, AHU, cód. 611, fols. 105v–06.

4. Studying the process of territorial incorporation to the west rather than the east of the mining district during the same period, Laura de Mello e Souza identified a similar violent impulse. See Souza, "Violência e práticas culturais."

5. Recent works exploring alternative understandings of indigenous resistance include Michael F. Brown, "On Resisting Resistance," *American Anthropologist* 98:4 (December 1996): 729–35; Neil L. Whitehead, *Dark Shamans: Kanaimà and the Poetics of Violent Death* (Durham, NC: Duke University Press, 2002); Monteiro, "Entre o Etnocídio e a Etnogênese." Also see the essays collected in *CHNPA*, vol. 3, *South America*.

For a seminal early study examining this theme in the North American context, see White, "Winning of the West." For evidence concerning epidemic disease as a perennial killer of settlers and thus, undoubtedly, of natives in the eastern wilderness, see, for example, Araújo, *Memórias Históricas*, vol. 3, 137; Duarte, "Facing the Forest," 39. For more general consideration of European diseases among hunting and gathering societies, see John H. Bodley, "Hunter-gatherers and the Colonial Encounter," in *The Cambridge Encyclopedia of Hunters and Gatherers*, ed. Richard B. Lee and Richard Daly, 465–72 (Cambridge: Cambridge University Press, 1999. For specific reference to the natives of coastal Brazil, see Noble David Cook, *Born to Die: Disease and New World Conquest, 1492–1650* (Cambridge: Cambridge University Press, 1998), esp. 148–54. From the 1550s onward, writes Cook (p. 150), "the coastal strip was swept by wave after wave of epidemic disease," leading many natives to flee inland.

6. Exceptions to this interpretive tendency exist, to be sure. See esp. the essays collected in Ferguson and Whitehead, *War in the Tribal Zone*; also see the collection of articles on warfare and violence published in *Ethnohistory* 46:4 (Fall 1999); and Whitehead, *Dark Shamans*, esp. 232–43.

7. While my intention is not to contest the suitability of White's formulation for the specific case he studies, he unnecessarily opposes violence and cultural interaction when he characterizes the "middle ground" as contingent on "the inability of both sides to gain their ends through force," White, *The Middle Ground*, 52.

8. For the origin of the concept of transculturation, see Fernando Ortiz, *Cuban Counterpoint: Tobacco and Sugar*, trans. Harriet de Onís (Durham, NC: Duke University Press, 1995), 97–103. My use of the term also draws on Pratt, *Imperial Eyes*, esp. 6; Henry F. Dobyns, "Military Transculturation of Northern Piman Indians, 1782–1821," *Ethnohistory* 19:4 (Fall 1972): 323–43; Francis Jennings, "A Growing Partnership: Historians, Anthropologists and American Indian History," *Ethnohistory* 29:1 (1982): 21–34, esp. 28–29; Abril Trigo, "On Transculturation: Toward a Political Economy of Culture in the Periphery," *Studies of Latin American Popular Culture* 15 (1996): 99–118.

9. Petition of the inhabitants of Guarapiranga Parish to King, Guarapiranga, before 16 Mar 1750, AHU, Minas Gerais, cx. 55, doc. 25.

10. These early conflicts are discussed in John M. Monteiro, "The Crises and Transformations of Invaded Societies: Coastal Brazil in the Sixteenth Century," in *CHNPA*, vol. 3, pt. 1, 973–1023.

11. Ferguson and Whitehead, "The Violent Edge of Empire"; Neil L. Whitehead, "Tribes Make States and States Make Tribes."

12. See Lepore, *The Name of War*, chap. 3.

13. Bishop of Mariana to King, Mariana, 16 Mar 1750, AHU, Minas Gerais, cx. 55, doc. 25.

14. A major gold-mining center, Caeté should not to be confused with the frontier outpost of Cuieté.

15. Câmara to Queen, Caeté, 3 Dec 1796, AHU, Minas Gerais, cx. 142, doc. 53. The Crown's response is noted in this document's margin.

16. Câmara to Prince Regent, Mariana, 30 Dec 1801, AHU, Minas Gerais, cx. 160, doc. 82.

17. Treasury Board (*junta da fazenda*), Report (*termo*) to Prince Regent on Botocudo hostilities, Vila Rica, 1 Feb 1806, AHU, Minas Gerais, cx. 179, doc. 36. This document was published as Governor, "Sobre os Botocudos," Vila Rica, 1 Feb 1806, *RAPM* 3:3-4 (1898), 743–48. On the economic and administrative importance of the Minas Treasury Board, see Maxwell, *Conflicts and Conspiracies*, 44–45. For the response to this report, see Luís de Vasconcelos e Sousa to Junta da Fazenda of Minas Gerais, [Lisbon], 16 Jan 1807, ATC, ER, cód. 4074. Also see the declaration of war, "Carta Régia (royal order) ao Governador e Capitão General da capitania de Minas Gerais sobre a guerra aos Indios Botecudos," 13 May 1808, *Legislação indigenista*, ed. Cunha, 57–60.

18. Governor to Treasurer, Vila Rica, 28 Jul 1764, APM, SC, cód. 118, fol. 65v; Governor, "Instrução que hade observar o Comandante distinado para o Destricto do Cuyeté a respeito do Arrayal que nelle se estabalece e de todos os moradores que no mesmo quizerem rezidir," Vila Rica, 4 Jun 1765, BNRJ, SM, CV, cód. 18, 2, 6, doc. 203.

19. Governor to Jozé do Valle Vieira, Vila Rica, 4 Mar 1777, BNRJ, SM, cód. 2, 2, 24, fol. 88.

20. Duro to Governor, Antônio Dias Abaixo, 15 Jul 1802, APM, SC, cód. 277, fols. 111v–12v. For additional examples of Indian raids on settler property, see Governor, "Orden para a entrada dos corpos de gente para a civilização dos gentios silvestres Purîs e Buticudos," Vila Rica, 21 Apr 1766, APM, SC, cód. 118, fol. 148v; Paulo Mendes Ferreira Campelo to Governor, n.p., [ca. 1769], n.d., BNRJ, SM, CV, cód. 18, 2, 6, doc. 198; Governor to Capitães-mores, Vila Rica, 15 May 1777, BNRJ, SM, cód. 2, 2, 24, fol. 122; Joam Pedro de Almeida to Senate of Vila do Principe, Peçanha, April 1792, *RAPM* 1 (1896): 781; petition of Jozé Bernardino Alves Gundim, Mariana, [1794], APM, SC, cód. 260, fol. 51v; petition of João Damaceno dos Reis Vidal and other landholders with Governor's reply, Vila Rica, 1 Nov 1794, APM, SC, cód. 260, fol. 42v.

21. Governor to Tavares, Vila Rica, 11 Apr 1778, BNRJ, SM, cód. 2, 2, 24, fols. 159–60.

22. Sesmaria of Carlos Leite de Araujo, 1754, ACSM, 1° ofício, cód. 7, auto 307.

23. Processo matrimonial, Carlos Leite de Araujo and Maria Joanna de São Joze, 1762, AEAM, armário 2, pasta 156, processo 1558.

24. Inventory of Carlos Leite de Araujo, 1779, ACSM, 1° ofício, cód. 95, auto 1975.

25. Governor, "Orden para a entrada dos corpos de gente para a civilização dos gentios silvestres Purîs e Buticudos," Vila Rica, 21 Apr 1766, APM, SC, cód. 118, fols. 148–50v.

26. Inventory of Carlos Leite de Araujo, 1779, ACSM, 1° ofício, cód. 95, auto 1975.

27. Sesmaria of Ignacia Cordeyra, 1768, ACSM, 1° ofício, cód. 3, auto 91; sesmaria of Antonio Joze Peixoto, 1768, ACSM, 1° ofício, cód. 7, auto 293; inventory of Ignacia Rodrigues Cordeyra, 1786, ACSM, 1° ofício, cód. 100, auto 2084.

28. Sesmaria of Anna Joaquina de Almeida, 1798, ACSM, 1° ofício, cód. 2, auto 87; inventory of Francisco Soares Maciel and Anna Joaquina de Almeida, 1819, ACSM, 2° ofício, cód. 117, auto 2352.

29. Coutinho, *Ensaio economico*, 30–31, 37. On Coutinho's life, see Lamego, *A Terra Goitacá*, vol. 2, 370 n. 509; Silva, *A cultura Luso-Brasileira*, 198–200.

30. See, for example, Richard White, *The Roots of Dependency: Subsistence, Environment, and Social Change among the Choctaws, Pawnees, and Navajos* (Lincoln, NE: University of Nebraska Press, 1983); Richard W. Slatta, "Spanish Colonial Military Strategy and

Ideology" and Kristine L. Jones, "Comparative Raiding Economies, North and South," both in *Contested Ground*, 83–96, 97–114, respectively; and Louis de Armond, "Frontier Warfare in Colonial Chile," reprinted in *Where Cultures Meet*, 115–22. For other Brazilian regions in which settlers during later periods displaced Indians of the same Macro-Gê linguistic stock as those of the Eastern Sertão, see Langfur, "Myths of Pacification"; Seth Garfield, *Indigenous Struggle*, esp. 77–88, 112–23.

31. Ferguson and Whitehead, "The Violent Edge of Empire," 10–11.

32. Notions of civilization held dear by the Minas elite, as well as omnipresent threats to those notions, including the menace of the encircling sertão, are discussed in Silveira, *O universo do indistinto*, pt. 1, chaps. 2–3; Souza, "Tensões sociais em Minas na segunda metade do século XVIII," in *Norma e conflito*, 83–110; Souza, "Violência e práticas culturais."

33. "These were not simply material differences," writes historian Jill Lepore, "they were cultural, for every . . . frock coat was stitched with threads of civility, each thatched roof rested on a foundation of property rights, and every cupboard housed a universe of ideas." See Lepore, *Name of War*, 79.

34. Marshall Sahlins, *How "Natives" Think: About Captain Cook, for Example* (Chicago: Chicago University Press, 1995), 14. Also see Brown, "On Resisting Resistance," 731.

35. Sesmaria of Ignacia Cordeyra, 1768, ACSM, 1° ofício, cód. 3, auto 91.

36. See, for example, Governor to Treasurer, Vila Rica, 28 Jul 1764, APM, SC, cód. 118, fol. 65v; Governor, "Instrução que hade observar o Comandante distinado para o Destricto do Cuyeté a respeito do Arrayal que nelle se estabelece e de todos os moradores que no mesmo quizerem rezidir," Vila Rica, 4 Jun 1765, BNRJ, SM, CV, cód. 18, 2, 6, doc. 203.

37. Maximilian, *Travels in Brazil*, 210. On relations between blacks and Indians during the colonial period, see Schwartz and Langfur, "Tapanhuns, Negros da Terra, and Curibocas."

38. The work in which the estimate appears was published in 1824, three years after Eschwege left Brazil, and some indication exists that the casualty figure refers not to the Eastern Sertão as a whole but only to the coastal regions of Porto Seguro and Ilhéus, which he described as "in the greatest part depopulated and desolated by these barbarians." See Eschwege, *Brasil, Novo Mundo*, 239 n. 59.

39. Manoel Vieyra Nunes to Governor, [Cuieté?], [1769], BNRJ, SM, CV, cód. 18, 2, 6, doc. 321.

40. Governor to Colonial Secretary, Vila Rica, 31 Dec 1781, APM, SC, cód. 224, fol. 81v (third letter of this date); Petition of Padre Francisco da Silva Campos to Prince Regent, [1800], RAPM 2:4 (1897): 687.

41. Instances of arming slaves occurred often enough in frontier zones throughout the Americas to warrant more scholarly attention. See John Thornton, *Africa and Africans in the Making of the Atlantic World, 1400–1680* (Cambridge: Cambridge University Press, 1992), 141, 149–50; Peter M. Voelz, *Slave and Soldier: The Military Impact of Blacks in the Colonial Americas* (New York: Garland Publishing, 1993), 103–04; T.H. Breen and Stephen Innes, *"Myne Owne Ground": Race and Freedom on Virginia's Eastern Shore, 1640–1676* (New York: Oxford University Press, 1980), 25; Ira Berlin, *Many Thousands Gone: The First*

Two Centuries of Slavery in North America (Cambridge, MA: Belknap Press of Harvard University Press, 1998), 88–89.

42. Governor to Colonial Secretary, Vila Rica, 18 Jun 1798 [including documents recording events in 1793], AHU, Minas Gerais, cx. 145, doc. 5; Petition of João Damaceno dos Reis Vidal and other landholders with governor's reply, Vila Rica, 1 Nov 1794, APM, SC, cód. 260, fols. 42v–43; Duro to Governor, Antônio Dias Abaixo, 15 Jul 1802, APM, SC, cód. 277, fols. 111v–12v; Governor to Duro, Vila Rica, 13 Aug 1802, APM, SC, cód. 277, fols. 112v–13.

43. Inventory of José Leme da Silva, 1791, ACSM, 1º ofício, cód. 84, auto 1795. On Indian attacks at Guarapiranga, see "Lista das pessoas que devem e tem obrigação de concorrerem para embaraçar o corso com que o gentio Sylvestre esta todos os annos entrando pelas fazendas e sesmarias da Beira do Rio Doce...," Vila Rica, 9 May 1765, APM, CC, cód. 1156, fol. 4; Governor, "Instrução que hade observar o Comandante distinado para o Destricto do Cuyeté a respeito do Arrayal que nelle se estabalece e de todos os moradores que no mesmo quizerem rezidir," Vila Rica, 4 Jun 1765, BNRJ, SM, CV, cód. 18, 2, 6, doc. 203; Governor, "Instrução que hade seguir o Cap.ᵃᵐ Antonio Cardozo de Souza," [Vila Rica], n.d., ibid., doc. 293; Governor, "Portaria para Joaquim Correya Mosso commandar hum Esquadra para afugentar os Indios Bravos," Vila Rica, 9 Jul 1792, APM, SC, cód. 259; Petition of Jozé Bernardino Alves Gundim, Mariana, [1794], APM, SC, cód. 260, fol. 51v.

44. Governor, "Instrução que hade observar o Comandante distinado para o Destricto do Cuyeté a respeito do Arrayal que nelle se estabelece e de todos os moradores que no mesmo quizerem rezidir," Vila Rica, 4 Jun 1765, BNRJ, SM, CV, cód. 18, 2, 6, doc. 203.

45. Inventory of Manuel Luís Branco, 1811, ACSM, 1º ofício, cód. 112, auto 2307.

46. See previous chapter.

47. [Manoel Vieyra Nunes], "Termo de reunião de conselho," Barra das Larangeiras, 5 Jul 1769, BNRJ, SM, CV, cód. 18, 2, 6, doc. 192; Campelo to Governor, Cuieté, 4 Apr 1770, ibid., doc. 237; Governor to Jozé do Valle Vieira, Vila Rica, 4 Mar 1777, BNRJ, SM, cód. 2, 2, 24, fols. 87v–88v; Cambraia and Mendes, "A colonização," 143.

48. Petition of João Damaceno dos Reis Vidal and other landholders with Governor's reply, Vila Rica, 1 Nov 1794, APM, SC, cód. 260, fols. 42v–43.

49. The extent to which cannibalism in Brazil, the early modern Americas, and the non-Western world in general constituted a reality or a myth, propagated to justify conquest and enslavement, continues to divide anthropologists. Notable contributions to this debate include W. Arens, *The Man-Eating Myth: Anthropology & Anthropophagy* (New York: Oxford University Press, 1979); Frank Lestringant, *Cannibals: The Discovery and Representation of the Cannibal from Columbus to Jules Verne*, trans. Rosemary Morris (Berkeley, CA: University of California Press, 1997); Francis Barker, Peter Hulme, and Margaret Iversen, eds., *Cannibalism and the Colonial World* (Cambridge: Cambridge University Press, 1998); Laurence R. Goldman, ed., *The Anthropology of Cannibalism* (Westport, CT: Bergin & Garvey, 1999). Also see Barbara Ganson, *The Guaraní Under Spanish Rule in the Río de la Plata* (Stanford, CA: Stanford University Press, 2003), 22–23; Neil L. Whitehead, *Dark Shamans*, 191–95, 236–43.

50. Eschwege, *Pluto brasiliensis*, vol. 1, 43. Also see *idem, Brasil, Novo Mundo*, 240 n. 61. For comparable sixteenth-century images, see, for example, the figures of roasting human

body parts on spits drawn on the map by Diego Gutiérrez, "Americae sive quartae orbis partis nova et exactissima descritio ... " Antwerp, 1562, Lessing J. Rosenwald Collection, GMC, LC. In his famous account of life among the coastal Tupinambá in the 1550s, Jean de Léry noted the error of such portrayals of native cannibalism, which he corrected from personal experience, detailing instead a process of boiling, butchering, and then roasting not on spits but on a "*boucan*" or "big wooden grill." See Jean de Léry, *History of a Voyage to the Land of Brazil*, trans. Janet Whatley (Berkeley, CA: University of California Press, 1990), 79, 125–27.

51. Hemming, *Amazon Frontier*, 92; Eschwege, *Brasil, Novo Mundo*, 240 n. 61; Maximilian, *Viagem ao Brasil*, 126–27, 153, 313–15.

52. Maximilian, *Travels in Brazil*, 119.

53. Langfur, "Forbidden Lands," 304–05; Monteiro, "Entre o Etnocídio e a Etnogênese"; Whitehead, *Dark Shamans*, esp. 242.

54. Curt Nimuendajú, "Social Organization and Beliefs of the Botocudo of Eastern Brazil," *Southwestern Journal of Anthropology* 2 (1946): 93–115, quoting 115.

55. Maximilian, *Travels in Brazil*, 138. Still ritually consumed to this day by some of Brazil's native peoples such as the Araweté of the southern region of the state of Pará, cauim is a type of indigenous gruel, often fermented, made from cooked or masticated manioc, corn, or various fruits. For instance, see Eduardo Viveiros de Castro, *From the Enemy's Point of View: Humanity and Divinity in an Amazonian Society*, trans. Catherine V. Howard (Chicago: University of Chicago Press, 1992), 119–32.

56. On contested meanings of violence, see Whitehead, *Dark Shamans*; Brown, "On Resisting Resistance."

57. On the post-1808 conflict, see chap. 8 of this study; Barickman, "'Tame Indians,'" 360–65; Hemming, *Amazon Frontier*, 92–93, 99–100, 365–84; Paraíso, "O tempo da dor," 211–39.

58. João da Silva Pereira de Souza to Governor, Cuieté, 25 Nov 1769, BNRJ, SM, CV, cód. 18, 2, 6, doc. 264.

59. Campelo to Governor, Cuieté, 29 Sep 1769, BNRJ, SM, CV, cód. 18, 2, 6, doc. 193; [Manoel Vieyra Nunes], "Termo de reunião de conselho," Barra das Larangeiras, 5 Jul 1769, ibid., doc. 192. This was likely a case of Indians initiating an attack because soldiers were marching to a specific destination rather than tracking Indians in an effort to confront them. The source does not specify the ethnic group to which these Indians belonged.

60. Veloso de Miranda to Governor, [Presídio dos] Arrepiados, 23 Nov 1781, APM, SC, cód. 224, fols. 79v–80v.

61. Maximilian, *Travels in Brazil*, 323–25.

62. John Mawe, *Travels in the Interior of Brazil, Particularly in the Gold and Diamond Districts of that Country* (London: Longman, et al., 1812), 191–92.

63. Thomas S. Abler and Michael H. Logan, "The Florescence and Demise of Iroquoian Cannibalism: Human Sacrifice and Malinowski's Hypothesis," *Man in the Northeast* 35 (Spring 1988): 1–26; Oscar Lewis, "The Effects of White Contact Upon Blackfoot Culture" in *Anthropological Essays* (New York: Random House, 1970), 137–212; Kristine L. Jones, "Comparative Raiding Economies"; Neil Whitehead, "The Snake Warriors—Sons of the Tiger's Teeth: A Descriptive Analysis of Carib Warfare ca.

1500–1820," in *The Anthropology of War*, ed. Jonathan Haas (Cambridge: Cambridge University Press, 1990), 146–70; Ferguson and Whitehead, "The Violent Edge of Empire," 25–27.

64. Fonsêca's description of his expedition is found in Manoel José Pires da Silva Pontes, "Extractos das viagens feitas no deserto, que separa as povoações da provincia de Minas Geraes, e as povoações do littoral nas provincias do Rio de Janeiro, Espírito Santo, e Bahia," n.p., n.d., BNRJ, SM, cód. 5, 3, 40, fols. 17–19v.

65. Clearly, the drive to settle this portion of Indian territory came not only from Minas Gerais but also from the northeastern reaches of the captaincy of Rio de Janeiro.

66. See Paraíso, "O tempo da dor," 766–71; Hemming, *Amazon Frontier*, chap. 18; Barickman, "'Tame Indians'"; Judy Bieber, "The Aldeia System Reborn: Botocudo Communities on the Espírito Santo-Minas Gerais Frontier, 1808–1845" (paper presented at the Latin American Studies Association Conference, Chicago, September 24–26, 1998); *idem*, "Shifting Frontiers: The Role of Subsistence, Disease, and Environment in Shaping Indigenous Definitions of Frontiers in Minas Gerais, 1808–1850," (paper presented at the American Historical Association Conference, San Francisco, January 2002).

67. Governor, "Instrução que hade observar o Comandante distinado para o Districto do Cuyeté a respeito do Arrayal que nelle se estabalece e de todos os moradores que no mesmo quizerem rezidir," Vila Rica, 4 Jun 1765, BNRJ, SM, CV, cód. 18, 2, 6, doc. 203.

68. Governor, "Orden para a entrada dos corpos de gente para a civilização dos gentios silvestres Purîs e Buticudos," Vila Rica, 21 Apr 1766, APM, SC, cód. 118, fols. 148–50v; Governor to Antônio Pereira da Silva, Vila Rica, 28 Jun 1766, APM, SC, cód. 118, fols. 171v–72. A similar shift from defensive to offensive military policy characterized the colonial strategy adopted to counter Apache and Comanche raiders along New Spain's northern frontier during the same period. See Weber, *The Spanish Frontier in North America*, chap. 8.

69. For comparisons with Spanish American military policies regarding unconquered Indians, see Richard W. Slatta, "Spanish Colonial Military Strategy and Ideology," 83–96. In her study examining the transition from Spanish to Mexican rule in Sonora, Cynthia Radding observes that native resistance to conquest and incorporation "kept the frontier open and obliged the Spaniards to fight on Indian terms," which included the use of ambushes, hit-and-run tactics, and a high degree of mobility. Radding, *Wandering Peoples*, 275–79.

70. [Antonio Pereira da Silva] to Governor, n.p., ca. 1770, BNRJ, SM, CV, cód. 18, 2, 6, doc. 329.

71. Maximilian, *Travels in Brazil*, 185.

72. [Manoel Vieyra Nunes] to Campelo, Cuieté, [ca. May 1769], BNRJ, SM, CV, cód. 18, 2, 6, doc. 187.

73. The sources for the following account include Attestation of Antonio Cardozo de Souza and his soldiers, Vila Rica, 12 Dec 1769, BNRJ, SM, CV, cód. 18, 2, 6, doc. 299; and Souza to Governor, Vitória, 15 Sep 1769, ibid., doc. 301. Another reference to what appears to be the same ambush is to be found in [Antonio Pereira da Silva] to Governor, n.p., ca. 1770, BNRJ, SM, CV, cód. 18, 2, 6, doc. 329. Silva reported that Souza's company included tame Indians, and that they took six prisoners in the ambush, killing more than 50. I have opted to use the casualty figure presented by Souza himself, who led the attack.

74. Câmara to Prince Regent, Mariana, 30 Dec 1801, AHU, cx. 160, doc. 82.

75. Manoel de Jesus Maria to Governor, Rio Pomba, 27 Aug 1799, BNL, CP, cód. 634, fol. 573v; [Manoel Vieyra Nunes] to Campelo, Cuieté, [ca. May 1769], BNRJ, SM, CV, cód. 18, 2, 6, doc. 187. On ethnic soldiering, see Ferguson and Whitehead, "The Violent Edge of Empire," 21–3; Schwartz and Langfur, "Tapanhuns, Negros da Terra, and Curibocas."

76. Duro described this ambush in Duro to Governor, Antônio Dias Abaixo, 15 Jul 1802, APM, SC, cód. 277, fols. 111v–12v. Governor Lorena offered his congratulations for this action to Duro in Governor to Duro, Vila Rica, 13 Aug 1802, APM, SC, cód. 277, fols. 112v–13; and to Duro's commanding officer in Governor to Brandão, Vila Rica, 13 Aug 1802, APM, SC, cód. 277, fol. 113.

77. In the eighteenth century, the river passing through Antônio Dias Abaixo appeared on maps as the Piracicaba River. In the early nineteenth century, that name came to refer only to an upper tributary of this watershed, the Santa Barbara River to its lower reaches. See esp. the map "Parte da Nova Carta da Capitania de Minas Gerais," in Eschwege, *Pluto brasiliensis*, vol. 1, 34.

78. Private posses claimed rewards for the ears, scalps, and heads of hostile Indians as the Mexican government attempted to clear its northern borderlands of raiders during the first half of the nineteenth century. See Jeremy Adelman and Stephen Aron, "From Borderlands to Borders: Empires, Nation-States, and the Peoples in Between in North American History," *American Historical Review* 104:3 (June 1999): 814–41, citing 837.

79. Duro to Governor, Antônio Dias Abaixo, 15 Jul 1802, APM, SC, cód. 277, fols. 111v–12v.

80. Rugendas quoted in Hemming, *Amazon Frontier*, 100; Guido Tomás Marlière, "Vocabulario Portuguez-Botocudo," 1833, BNRJ, SM, cód. 1, 1, 3, fol. 7. On Marlière, see José, *Marlière, o Civilizador*. As noted, for the presence of dogs among the Puri Indians along the Muriaé River in 1812, see Manoel José Pires da Silva Pontes, "Extractos das viagens feitas no deserto, que separa as povoações da provincia de Minas Geraes, e as povoações do littoral nas provincias do Rio de Janeiro, Espírito Santo, e Bahia," n.p., n.d., BNRJ, SM, cód. 5, 3, 40, fols. 18–19. On the alleged absence of dogs among the Botocudo, see Robert H. Lowie, "American Culture History," *American Anthropologist*, New Series, 42:3, pt. 1 (July–September 1940), 409–28, esp. 415.

81. Souza to Governor, Vitória, 15 Sep 1769, BNRJ, SM, CV, cód. 18, 2, 6, doc. 301; Manoel José Pires da Silva Pontes, "Extractos das viagens feitas no deserto, que separa as povoações da provincia de Minas Geraes, e as povoações do littoral nas provincias do Rio de Janeiro, Espírito Santo, e Bahia," n.p., n.d., BNRJ, SM, cód. 5, 3, 40, fols. 17–19v.

82. Scholars have begun to identify a similar problem in conceptualizing the history of other colonial frontier zones. On the unsuitability of "contact zone" to describe the colonization of diverse Indian territories in Spanish America, see José Rabasa, *Writing Violence on the Northern Frontier: The Historiography of Sixteenth-Century New Mexico and Florida and the Legacy of Conquest* (Durham, NC: Duke University Press, 2000), 21; Guillaume Boccara, "Rethinking the Margins/Thinking from the Margins: Culture, Power, and Place on the Frontiers of the New World," *Identities: Global Studies in Culture and Power* 10 (2003): 59–81. On the imprudent application of the term *middle ground* to explain the settlement of eastern North American, see Gregory Evans Dowd, "'Insidious Friends': Gift Giving and the Cherokee-British Alliance in the Seven Years' War," in

Contact Points: American Frontiers from the Mohawk Valley to the Mississippi, 1750–1830, ed. Andrew R.L. Cayton and Fredrika Teute (Chapel Hill, NC: University of North Carolina Press, 1998), 118 n. 3. Mary Louise Pratt proposed the term *contact zone* to describe British imperial encounters in Latin America and Africa after the middle of the eighteenth century. See Pratt, *Imperial Eyes,* esp. 6–7; White, *Middle Ground,* esp. chap. 2.

83. Michael Taussig, *Shamanism, Colonialism, and the Wild Man: A Study in Terror and Healing* (Chicago: University of Chicago Press, 1987), esp. chap. 1; quotations, 4, 31.

84. The quoted phrase is from Silvio R. Duncan Baretta and John Markoff, "Civilization and Barbarism: Cattle Frontiers in Latin America," *Comparative Studies in Society and History* 20:4 (October 1978): 587–620, citing 590.

85. Colonists repeatedly made reference to Indian trails networks and communication from east to west and from north to south across the sertão. See, for example, Attestation (*atestação*) of Antonio Cardozo de Souza and his soldiers, Vila Rica, 12 Dec 1769, BNRJ, SM, CV, cód. 18, 2, 6, doc. 299; Souza to Governor, Vitória, 15 Sep 1769, ibid., doc. 301; Affidavit (*certidão*) of Captain Paulo Mendes Ferreira Campelo, Cuieté, 6 Feb 1770, ibid., doc. 234; João da Silva Pereira de Souza to Governor, Cuieté, 3 Feb 1770, ibid., doc. 267; Manoel José Pires da Silva Pontes, "Extractos das viagens feitas no deserto, que separa as povoações da provincia de Minas Geraes, e as povoações do littoral nas provincias do Rio de Janeiro, Espírito Santo, e Bahia," n.p., n.d., BNRJ, SM, cód. 5, 3, 40, fols. 17–19v.

86. Paraíso, "O tempo da dor," 781–811; Nimuendajú, "Social Organization"; Warren, *Racial Revolutions,* 64–83.

Notes to Chapter 8

1. For instance, see Wolf, *Europe and the People without History,* 88–100; Lockhart and Schwartz, *Early Latin America,* 55–57.

2. [Antonio Pereira da Silva] to Governor, n.p., ca. 1770, BNRJ, SM, CV, cód. 18, 2, 6, doc. 329.

3. "Petição que fizerão e assignarão os moradores das freguesias ostilizadas," ca. May 1765, APM, CC, cód. 1156, fol. 9.

4. Governor, "Instrução que hade observar o Comandante distinado para o Destricto do Cuyeté a respeito do Arrayal que nelle se estabalece e de todos os moradores que no mesmo quizerem rezidir," Vila Rica, 4 Jun 1765, BNRJ, SM, CV, cód. 18, 2, 6, doc. 203.

5. Settlers reported the abandonment of sesmarias in, for instance, petition of Joze Gonçalvez Vieyra and Joze Leme da Sylva, n.p., [ca. 1765], APM, CC, cód. 1156, fol. 10v. This then became a primary grievance of the government, justifying retaliation as in "Lista das pessoas que devem e tem obrigação de concorrerem para embaraçar o corso com que o gentio Sylvestre esta todos os annos entrando pelas fazendas e sesmarias da Beira do Rio Doce...," Vila Rica, 9 May 1765, ibid., fol. 4.

6. Governor to Treasurer, Vila Rica, 28 Jul 1764, APM, SC, cód. 118, fol. 65v.

7. Governor, "Para a expulção dos Indios de S. Jozé da Barra Longa...," Vila Rica, 20 Feb 1766, APM, SC, cód. 118, fols. 133–33v. Furquim and Barra Longa were devastated by several Botocudo attacks in the 1730s, leading the Count of Galveias to direct Colonel Matias Barbosa da Silva to arm and lead a large retaliatory expedition into the surrounding forests. Diogo [Luís de Almeida Pereira] de Vasconcelos, *História antiga,* 234.

8. Governor, "Orden para a entrada dos corpos de gente para a civilização dos gentios silvestres Purîs e Buticudos," Vila Rica, 21 Apr 1766, APM, SC, cód. 118, fols. 148–50v.

9. Governor to Antonio Pereira da Silva, Vila Rica, 28 Jun 1766, APM, SC, cód. 118, fols. 171v–72.

10. Campelo to Governor, Cuieté, 29 Sep 1769, BNRJ, SM, CV, cód. 18, 2, 6, doc. 193.

11. [Antonio Pereira da Silva] to Governor, n.p., ca. 1770, BNRJ, SM, CV, cód. 18, 2, 6, doc. 329.

12. Campelo to Governor, n.p., [ca. 1769], n.d., BNRJ, SM, CV, cód. 18, 2, 6, doc. 198.

13. Governor to capitães-mores, Vila Rica, 15 May 1777, BNRJ, SM, cód. 2, 2, 24, fol. 122; Governor to Colonial Secretary, Vila Rica, 31 Dec 1781, APM, SC, cód. 224, fols. 80v–81 (third letter of this date); Diogo Pereira Ribeiro de Vasconcelos, Breve descrição, 147–48. On Pataxó raids in Bahia, see Marquis of Valença to Francisco Nunes da Costa, Salvador, 23 Feb 1782, BNRJ, SM, II-34, 5, 93, doc. 1.

14. The events surrounding the attack are reconstructed from Governor to Antonio Paes de Almeida, Vila Rica, 4 Mar 1777; to Jozé do Valle Vieira, Vila Rica, 4 Mar 1777; to Jozé da Silva Pontes, Vila Rica, 4 Mar 1777; and to Ignacio Jozé de Souza Rabelo, Vila Rica, 28 Feb 1777, BNRJ, SM, cód. 2, 2, 24, fols. 87v–90v. Also Almeida to Governor, São José da Barra, 23 Feb 1777; Vieira to Governor, Abre Campo, 16 Feb 1777, BNRJ, SM, cód. 19, 3, 39, fols. 53v–55.

15. Quoted in Barbosa, Dicionário histórico-geográfico, 17.

16. Petition of João Damaceno dos Reis Vidal and other landholders with Governor's reply, Vila Rica, 1 Nov 1794, APM, SC, cód. 260, fols. 42v–43.

17. Petition of Jozé Bernardino Alves Gundim, Mariana, [1794], APM, SC, cód. 260, fol. 51v.

18. Diogo Pereira Ribeiro de Vasconcelos, Breve descrição, 147–48.

19. Rocha, Geografia histórica, 132–33.

20. Joam Pedro de Almeida to Senate of Vila do Principe, Peçanha, April 1792, RAPM 1 (1896): 781. Also see Matos, Corografia histórica, vol. 1, 187; Barbosa, Dicionário histórico-geográfico, 246–47.

21. Francisco Martins Penna to Governor, Tejuco (later Diamantina), 17 Dec 1801, APM, SC, cód. 277, fol. 100.

22. Petition of the residents of Santana de Alfié, 13 Dec 1806, BNRJ, SM, II-36, 5, 32.

23. Vasconcelos, Breve descrição, 53–54.

24. The historical geographies and dictionaries employed in the following analysis include: Rocha, Geografia histórica (1780); Vasconcelos, Breve descrição (1807); Araujo, Memórias históricas, vol. 8, pt. 2 (1822); Matos, Corografia histórica (1837); A. de Assis Martins and J. Harques de Oliveira, eds., Almanak administrativo, civil e industrial da Provincia de Minas Geraes para o anno de 1865 (Ouro Preto, Brazil: Typographia do Minas Geraes, 1864); Costa, Toponímia de Minas Gerais; Barbosa, Dicionário histórico-geográfico.

25. Hemming, Red Gold, 486. To be fair, Hemming would later author a book that documented persistent native resistance from the late eighteenth to the twentieth centuries. See idem, Amazon Frontier.

26. Matos, Corografia histórica, vol. 2, 73.

27. "Carta Régia (royal order) ao Governador e Capitão General da capitania de Minas Gerais sobre a guerra aos Indios Botecudos," 13 May 1808, *Legislação indigenista*, ed. Cunha, 57–60.

28. Ibid.

29. Ibid.

30. Quoted in Hemming, *Amazon Frontier*, 91–92, and Barickman, "'Tame Indians,'" 359. For Campos' published report, see Luiz Thomas Navarro de Campos, "Itinerario da viagem que fez por terra da Bahia ao Rio de Janeiro por ordem do principe regente, em 1808 . . . ," *RIHGB* 7:28 (1846): 433–64, quotation, 449.

31. Ottoni, "Memória," 313; Freire, "Informação da capitania de Minas Gerais," Sabará, 30 Mar 1805, BNRJ, SM, cód. 3, 1, 35, fols. 10–11; Vasconcelos, *Breve descrição*, 144–49, 157; Governor of Espírito Santo to Governor of Minas Gerais, Vitória, 7 Jun 1801, BNL, CP, cód. 643, fols. 587–87v; [Manoel Vieyra Nunes], "Termo de reunião de conselho," Barra das Larangeiras, 5 Jul 1769, BNRJ, SM, CV, cód. 18, 2, 6, doc. 192. For additional documents containing language later used in the war declaration, see Treasury Board, Report to Prince Regent on Botocudo hostilities, Vila Rica, 1 Feb 1806, AHU, Minas Gerais, cx. 179, doc. 36; Câmara to Queen, Caeté, 3 Dec 1796, AHU, Minas Gerais, cx. 142, doc. 53.

32. Governor, "Instrução que hade observar o Comandante distinado para o Districto do Cuyeté a respeito do Arrayal que nelle se estabelece e de todos os moradores que no mesmo quizerem rezidir," Vila Rica, 4 Jun 1765, BNRJ, SM, CV, cód. 18, 2, 6, doc. 203.

33. Governor, "Orden para a entrada dos corpos de gente para a civilização dos gentios silvestres Purîs e Buticudos," Vila Rica, 21 Apr 1766, APM, SC, cód. 118, fols. 148–50v; Governor to Antônio Pereira da Silva, Vila Rica, 28 Jun 1766, APM, SC, cód. 118, fols. 171v–72. A similar shift from defensive to offensive military policy characterized the colonial strategy on many other American frontiers. For example, this was true of the strategy adopted to counter the native inhabitants of northeastern Brazil at the beginning of the eighteenth century, as well as the one devised to deter Apache and Comanche raiders along New Spain's northern frontier during the second half of the same century. See, Puntoni, *Guerra dos Bárbaros*, 163–77; Weber, *The Spanish Frontier in North America*, chap. 8.

34. Stephen Greenblatt, *Marvelous Possessions: The Wonder of the New World* (Chicago: University of Chicago Press, 1991), 63–64. Also see Rabasa, *Writing Violence*, 6–7.

35. Coutinho to Governor, Rio de Janeiro, 27 Mar 1808; *idem* to Bishop of Mariana et al., Rio de Janeiro, 3 May 1808, AHEx, Livros da Capitania, Minas Gerais, 1808–1811, cód. I-1, 1, 34, fols. 2v, 6–6v. On Coutinho's role as a key member of the royal court in Lisbon and then Rio de Janeiro, see Silva, *Dicionário da história*, 222–25.

36. Coutinho to Governor, Rio de Janeiro, 4 Aug 1808, AHEx, Livros da Capitania, Minas Gerais, 1808–1811, cód. I-1, 1, 34, fol. 23v.

37. See Perrone-Moisés, "Índios livres e índios escravos"; Lepore, *The Name of War*, 106–13.

38. An initially desultory effort to exploit Botocudo labor intensified after 1830 as increasing numbers of settlers secured land in the region. Wright with Cunha, "Destruction," 344; Paraíso, "O tempo da dor," chaps. 5–6.

39. Maximilian, *Viagem ao Brasil*, 153.

40. Hemming, *Amazon Frontier*, 92–93, 99–100; Paraíso, "Os Botocudos," 417–23; Barickman, "'Tame Indians,'" 359–65. For Eschwege's estimate, see "Copia de huma Carta feita pelo Sargento Mor Eschwege (acerca dos Botocudos e das divisões da conquista) com notas pelo deputado da Junta Militar, Matheus Herculano Monteiro," n.p., 1811, BNRJ, SM, cód. 8, 1, 8, doc. 66. On Leão's expedition and subsequent controversial military activities in the region, see Chabert, *Historical Account*; Julião Fernandes Leão to Secretary of State, Rio de Janeiro, 18 Sep 1823, BNRJ, SM, DB, C-174, 37, doc. 6; Leão to Emperor, Rio de Janeiro, 24 Sep 1823, ibid., doc. 15; [Manoel Jozé Tellis] to Editor [*Diário do Governo*], [Rio de Janeiro?], [1823], BNRJ, SM, DB, C-177, 11, doc. 5.

41. [Johann Moritz] Rugendas, *Viagem Pitoresca através do Brasil*, trans. Sérgio Milliet, 5th ed. (São Paulo: Livraria Martins Editora, 1954), 123.

42. Hemming, *Amazon Frontier*, 365–84; Paraíso, "Os Botocudos," 417–23; Barickman, "'Tame Indians,'" 359–65; Bieber, "The Aldeia system." On the capture of Botocudo children by Pataxó Indians, see Chabert, *Historical Account*, 21. For a post-mortem estate inventory from even farther south in São Paulo listing numerous Indian slaves (all male) ranging in age from 13 to 60, many valued as highly as the property's African slaves, see Inventory of Manoel Jozé Machado, 1832, AN, Inventários, cx. 1420, no. 554. The natives are identified merely as "heathen" and thus may have been captured after the war policy was extended to São Paulo's Kaingáng Indians in November 1808. Legislation enacted in 1823 and 1824 created Indian directories and ordered directors to employ peaceful means to settle Indians into villages along the Doce River in Minas Gerais and Espírito Santo. See "Decisão 22," 20 Feb 1823; "Decisão 85," 24 May 1823; "Decreto 31," 28 Jan 1824, in *Legislação indigenista*, ed. Cunha, 111–14, 137.

43. Bieber, "The Aldeia System"; Paraíso, "Os Botocudos," 418; *idem*, "O tempo da dor." The population estimate by Marlière is from "Direção Geral dos índios de Minas Gerais," *RAPM* 12 (1907): 530. Also see José, *Marlière, O Civilizador*.

44. Rugendas, *Viagem pitoresca*, 123.

45. Francisco Manoel da Cunha, "Memoria sobre a navegação do Rio Doce, apresentada por Francisco Manoel da Cunha ao Conde de Linhares," *Publicações* [AN] 4 (1893): 4–6.

46. War Minister to Governor, Rio de Janeiro, 12 Apr 1809, AHEx, Livros da Capitania, Minas Gerais, 1808–1811, cód. I-1, 1, 34, fol. 93.

47. War Minister to Governor, Rio de Janeiro, 31 Jul 1810, AHEx, Livros da Capitania, Minas Gerais, 1808–1811, cód. I-1, 1, 34, fols. 203–3v.

48. War Minister to Governor of Bahia, Rio de Janeiro, 31 Jan 1810, AHEx, Livros da Capitania, Bahia, 1808–1811, cód. I-1, 1, 6, fol. 54v.

49. Governor to Julião Fernandes Leão, Vila Rica, 5 Dec 1812, BNRJ, SM, cód. 1, 4, 5, doc. 545.

50. Carlos Cezar Burlamaqui, "Esboço do estado atual das Comarcas de Porto Seguro e Ilheus," Rio de Janeiro, 5 Jul 1820, BNRJ, SM, I-28, 29, 11; Keane, "On the Botocudos," 205, 207; Paraíso, "Os Botocudos," 418–23; Hemming, *Amazon Frontier*, chap. 18; Izabel Missagia de Mattos, "'Civilização' e 'revolta': Os Botocudos e a catequese na Província de Minas," (Ph.D. diss., Universidade de Campinas, São Paulo, 2002); Carrara, *Estruturas agrárias*, 15; Paraíso, "O tempo da dor." The noted maps include John Luccock, "A Map of the Table Land of Brazil," London, 1820, in *idem, Notes on Rio de Janeiro*, between flyleaf

and title page; Carlos Krauss, "Mappa Geral das Colonias S. Leopoldina, S. Izabel, e Rio Novo na Provincia do Espirito Santo," Rio de Janeiro, 1866, GMD, LC; and *idem*, "Mappa Geral da Provincia do Espirito-Santo relativo as Colonias e Vias de Communicação," Rio de Janeiro, 1866, GMD, LC. As their legends and notations indicate, Krauss' maps were designed to lure European immigrants to settle Brazil's eastern forests.

51. Governor to War Minister, Vila Rica, 30 Jan 1811, BNRJ, SM, cód. 1, 3, 9, doc. 66; Governor, "Relação dos Regios Avisos recebidos no Correio," [Vila Rica], [1811?], BNRJ, SM, cód. 1, 3, 9, docs. 101–02; [Pedro Afonso Galvão de São Martinho?], "Mappa dos Novos Colonos a quem se demarcarão Sesmarias pelo Alferes Commandante da 1.ª Divisão do Rio Doce, desde Antonio Dias Abaixo, ate o Rio Corrente; e dos Habitantes, q. se empregão em cultivar estes terrenos, q. se achão presentem[ente] a Salvo das incursoens dos Botecudos, e ate [a]gora habitados por elles," BNRJ, SM, I-33, 30, 22, doc. 3.

52. Governor to War Minister, Vila Rica, 30 Jan 1811, BNRJ, SM, cód. 1, 3, 9, doc. 66. The governor's letter quotes extensively, without attributing authorship, from a report on the status of deployed troops by Pedro Afonso Galvão de São Martinho. See Martinho to Governor, Vila Rica, 29 Jan 1811, BNRJ, SM, I-33, 30, 22, doc. 1.

53. Governor, "Relação dos Regios Avisos recebidos no Correio," [Vila Rica], [1811?], BNRJ, SM, cód. 1, 3, 9, docs. 101–02.

54. Moraes, "Cronologia das cartas de sesmarias."

55. Câmara [Joaquim Joze Farneze, Antonio Felicianno da Costa, Manoel da Silva Pereira, Simeão Vas Mourão, and Antonio de Brito Teixeira] to Prince Regent, Vila do Príncipe, 9 Feb 1810, BNRJ, SM, cód. 8, 1, 8, doc. 1.

56. Jozé Joaquim de Barcellos v. Joanna da Rocha and her children Jozé Pinheiro and Joaquim Florianno and his wife Maria Joaquina, *ação civil* (civil action), 1824, ACSM, 1º ofício, cód. 450, auto 9734.

57. Chabert, *Historical Account*, 9–10.

58. Eschwege, "Copia de huma Carta feita pelo Sargento Mor Eschwege (acerca dos Botocudos e das divisões da conquista) com notas pelo deputado da Junta Militar, Matheus Herculano Monteiro," n.p., 1811, BNRJ, SM, cód. 8, 1, 8, doc. 66; José Bonifácio de Andrada e Silva, "Apontamentos para a civilização dos índios bravos do Império do Brasil," in *O pensamento vivo de José Bonifácio* (São Paulo: Livraria Martins, 1961 [1823]), 78–107. See also Manuela Carneiro da Cunha, "Pensar os índios: apontamentos sobre José Bonifácio," in *Antropologia do Brasil: mito, história, etnicidade* (São Paulo: Brasiliense/EDUSP, 1986), 165–73; *idem*, prologue to *Legislação indigenista*, 1–34.

59. Carta Régia to Governor of Minas Gerais, Rio de Janeiro, 4 Dec 1816, JCBL. Also see the slightly different Carta Régia to Governor of Espírito Santo, Rio de Janeiro, 4 Dec 1816, JCBL.

Notes to Conclusion

1. Limerick, *The Legacy of Conquest*, 23.
2. Turner, "The Significance of the Frontier." For a recent reassertion of Turner's periodization, broadening the period of frontier closure in the U.S. to the decades between 1880 and 1910, see Samuel M. Otterstrom and Carville Earle, "The Settlement of the United States from 1790 to 1990: Divergent Rates of Growth and the End of the Frontier," *Journal of Interdisciplinary History* 33:1 (Summer 2002): 59–85.

3. Turner, "The Significance of the Frontier," 1.

4. Ibid., 3.

5. For a characteristic statement by Bolton discussing common features of frontier expansion in the Americas, see Herbert E. Bolton, *Wider Horizons of American History* (New York: D. Appleton-Century, 1939), 1–54. Also see Webb, *The Great Frontier*, esp. 411–12; Alistair Hennessy, *The Frontier in Latin American History* (London: Edward Arnold, 1978), esp. 6–27; Roy Nash, *A conquista do Brasil* (São Paulo: Ed. Nacional, 1939); J.F. Normano, *Brazil: A Study of Economic Types* (Chapel Hill, NC: University of North Carolina Press, 1935), see esp. chap. 1. Normano's text was translated into Portuguese in Brazil in 1939 and reprinted in both Brazil and the U.S. in 1945 and 1966, respectively. See Normano, *Evolução econômica do Brasil*, trans. Theodoro Quartim Barbosa, Roberto Peake Rodrigues, and Laércio Brandão Teixeira. (São Paulo: Ed. Nacional, 1939). On the influence of Normano and Nash, see Souza, *A pátria geográfica*, 141–45.

6. On the response of Latin American historians to frontier historiography and Turner's thesis, see, Jane M. Rausch, "Latin American Frontier History: The Colombian Case," *Lateinamerika Studien* 19 (1985): 75–77; Hennessy, *The Frontier in Latin American History*, 6–27; Silvio Zavala, "The Frontiers of Hispanic America," in *The Frontier in Perspective*, ed. Walker D. Wyman and Clifton B. Kroeber (Madison, WI: University of Wisconsin Press, 1957), 35–58. Material specific to the Brazilian case includes Lombardi, "The Frontier in Brazilian History"; E. Bradford Burns, "Brazil: Frontier and Ideology," *Pacific Historical Review* 64:1 (February 1995): 1–18; Dean, "The Frontier in Brazil"; Janaína Amado, "The Frontier in Comparative Perspective: The United States and Brazil," in *Frontier in Comparative Perspectives*, Working Papers, no. 188 (Washington, DC: Latin American Program, The Woodrow Wilson Center, 1990), 28–55; Hebe Clementi, "National Identity and the Frontier," *American Studies International* 18:3-4 (1980): 36–44. Other comparative analyses I have found especially useful include Howard R. Lamar and Leonard Thompson, eds., *The Frontier in History: North America and Southern Africa Compared* (New Haven, CT: Yale University Press, 1981); A.L. Burt, "If Turner Had Looked at Canada, Australia, and New Zealand When He Wrote About the West," in *The Frontier in Perspective*, 59–77; W.J. Eccles, "The Frontiers of New France," in *Essays on Frontiers in World History*, 42–70; James Gump, "The Subjugation of the Zulus and Sioux: A Comparative Study," *Western Historical Quarterly* 19 (January 1988): 21–36; McNeill, *The Great Frontier*; David J. Weber and Jane M. Rausch, eds., *Where Cultures Meet*; Guy and Sheridan, *Contested Ground*.

7. Dean, "The Frontier in Brazil," 15. For an enthusiast assessment of Turner's ideas and their potential to explain and even guide Brazilian national development, see Fernando de Azevedo, *Brazilian Culture: An Introduction to the Study of Culture in Brazil*, trans. William Rex Crawford (New York: Hafner Publishing, 1971), 51–54, 129–30; for more critical views, see Holanda, *Caminhos e fronteiras*, vi–vii; Morse, *The Bandeirantes*, 28–34.

8. Lima, *Um sertão chamado Brasil*, 41–53, 57–62; Souza, *A pátria geográfica*, esp. introduction and chap. 1. As Souza notes, most of these intellectuals produced what she calls "sociographic" texts concerned with Brazilian national identity as opposed to academic histories based on archival sources. See pp. 28, 41–42. Prominent examples include Euclides da Cunha, *Rebellion in the Backlands*, trans. Samuel Putnam (Chicago:

University of Chicago Press, Phoenix Books, 1944 [1902]); Elysio de Carvalho, *O fator geográfico na política brasileira* (Rio de Janeiro: Monitor Mercantil, 1921); Victor Viana, *Histórico da formação econômica do Brasil* (Rio de Janeiro: Ministério da Fazenda, 1922), esp. 16–17, 141–45; Antonio José do Azevedo Amaral, *Ensaios brasileiros*, 2nd ed. (Rio de Janeiro: Omena & Barreto, 1930), 142–47; Cassiano Ricardo, *Marcha para Oeste: A influência da bandeira na formação social e política do Brasil* (Rio de Janeiro: Livraria José Olympio, 1940); Abreu, *Chapters of Brazil's Colonial History*, esp. chap. 9; Francisco José de Oliveira Viana, *Populações meridionais do Brasil: História, organização e psicologia* (São Paulo: Ed. Nacional, 1933), esp. chaps. 4–6; Nelson Werneck Sodré, *Oeste: Ensaio sobre a grande propriedade pastoril* (Livraria José Olympio, 1941); Nestor Duarte, *A ordem privada e a organização política nacional: Contribuição à sociologia política brasileira* (São Paulo: Ed. Nacional, 1939), esp. chaps. 2–3 and pp. 197–201; Martins de Almeida, *Brasil errado: Ensaio político sobre os erros do Brasil como país*, 2nd ed. (Rio de Janeiro: Organização Simões, 1953).

9. See Hannah Franziska Augstein, ed., *Race: The Origins of an Idea, 1760–1850* (Bristol, UK: Thoemmes Press, 1996), xiii–xv; Nancy Stepan, *The Idea of Race in Science: Great Britain, 1800–1960* (Hamden, CT: Archon Books, 1982), xii–xviii; Adam Lively, *Masks: Blackness, Race and the Imagination* (Oxford: Oxford University Press, 2000), 40–55; Ivan Hannaford, *Race: The History of an Idea in the West* (Washington, DC: Woodrow Wilson Center Press, 1996), chap. 7; Nancy Leys Stepan, *"The Hour of Eugenics": Race, Gender, and Nation in Latin America* (Ithaca, NY: Cornell University Press, 1991), 44–45; Thomas E. Skidmore, *Black into White: Race and Nationality in Brazilian Thought* (1974; reprint, Durham, NC: Duke University Press, 1993), esp. 28–34.

10. Da Cunha, *Rebellion in the Backlands*, 440, 464; *idem, Os sertões: Campanha de Canudos*, 35th ed. (Rio de Janeiro: Francisco Alves, 1991 [1902]). See also Robert M. Levine, *Vale of Tears: Revisiting the Canudos Massacre in Northeastern Brazil, 1893–1897* (Berkeley, CA: University of California Press, 1992), esp. chap. 1. On an earlier intellectual strain that romanticized the native as an icon of Brazilian national identity in the nineteenth century, see Ramos, *Indigenism*, 64–69; David T. Haberly, *Three Sad Races: Racial Identity and National Consciousness in Brazilian Literature* (Cambridge: Cambridge University Press, 1983), chaps. 1–3. On Da Cunha's views regarding race and geography, see Skidmore, *Black into White*, esp. 103–09; Dain Borges, "A Mirror of Progress," in *The Brazil Reader: History, Culture, Politics*, ed. Robert M. Levine and John J. Crocitti (Durham, NC: Duke University Press, 1999), 93–99.

11. Clodomir Vianna Moog, *Bandeirantes and pioneers*, trans. L.L. Barrett (New York: G. Braziller, 1964), 92, 182.

12. João de Lencastre to Crown, Salvador da Bahia, 12 Jan 1701, in *Os manuscritos do Arquivo da Casa de Cadaval respeitantes ao Brasil*, vol. 2, ed. Rau and Silva, 14–17.

13. See, for example, Jozé Joaquim de Barcellos v. Joanna da Rocha and her children Jozé Pinheiro and Joaquim Florianno and his wife Maria Joaquina, ação civil, 1824, ACSM, 1° ofício, cód. 450, auto 9734.

14. Sérgio Buarque de Holanda, *Monções*, rev. ed. (São Paulo: Ed. Brasiliense, 2000), 37, 67–68.

15. Michael P. Malone, "The 'New Western History,' An Assessment," in *Trails: Toward a New Western History*, ed. Patricia N. Limerick, Clyde A. Milner II, and Charles E. Rankin (Lawrence, KS: University Press of Kansas, 1991), 98.

16. Patricia N. Limerick, "What on Earth Is the New Western History?" in *Trails*, 85–86.

17. Cf. Michael P. Malone, "Beyond the Last Frontier: Toward a New Approach to Western American History," in *Trails*, esp., 139–56.

18. Boccara, "Rethinking the Margins," 64. Also see Said, *Orientalism*, 54–55.

19. João Severiano Maciel da Costa, *Memoria sobre a necessidade de abolir a introdução dos escravos africanos no Brasil...* (Coimbra, Portugal: Universidade de Coimbra, 1821), 19; Koster, *Travels in Brazil*, 460.

20. Usner, *Indians, Settlers, and Slaves*, 5. For other examples and discussion of this trend, see White, *The Middle Ground*; Thomas D. Hall, *Social Change in the Southwest, 1350–1880* (Lawrence, KS: University Press of Kansas, 1989); Steve J. Stern, "Feudalism, Capitalism, and the World-System in the Perspective of Latin America and the Caribbean," *American Historical Review* 93 (1988), 829–72; William Taylor, "Between Global Process and Local Knowledge: An Inquiry into Early Latin American Social History, 1500–1900," in *Reliving the Past: The Worlds of Social History*, ed. Oliver Zunz (Chapel Hill, NC: University of North Carolina Press, 1985), 115–90; Richard Graham, ed., *Brazil and the World System* (Austin, TX: University of Texas Press, 1991).

Bibliography

Archives and Manuscript Collections

Arquivo da Câmara Municipal de Mariana (ACMM)
Arquivo da Casa Setecentista de Mariana (ACSM)
Arquivo Eclesiástico da Arquidiocese de Mariana (AEAM)
Arquivo Histórico do Exército, Rio de Janeiro (AHEx)
Arquivo Histórico Militar, Lisbon (AHM)
Arquivo Histórico Ultramarino, Lisbon (AHU)
    Cartografia Manuscrita (CM)
Arquivo do Instituto Histórico e Geográfico Brasileiro, Rio de Janeiro (AIHGB)
Arquivo Nacional, Rio de Janeiro (ANRJ)
Arquivo Nacional do Torre do Tombo, Lisbon (ANTT)
Arquivo Público do Estado da Bahia (APEB)
    Seção Colonial e Provincial (SCP)
Arquivo Público Mineiro, Belo Horizonte (APM)
    Arquivo Casa dos Contos (CC)
    Junta do Governo Provisório (JGP)
    Seção Colonial (SC)
    Seção Provincial (SP)
Arquivo do Tribunal de Contas, Lisbon (ATC)
    Erário Régio (ER)
Benson Latin American Collection, University of Texas, Austin, TX (BLAC)
Biblioteca Nacional, Lisbon (BNL)
    Coleção Pombalina (CP)
Biblioteca Nacional, Rio de Janeiro (BNRJ)
    Seção de Iconografia (SI)
    Seção de Manuscritos (SM)
    Arquivo Casa dos Contos (CC)
    Arquivo Conde de Valadares (CV)

Arquivo Morgado de Mateus (MM)
Documentos Biográficos (DB)
John Carter Brown Library, Brown University, Providence, RI (JCBL)
Library of Congress, Washington, DC (LC)
Geography and Map Division (GMD)
Museu Regional, São João del-Rei (MRSJ)
Oliveira Lima Library, Catholic University of America, Washington, DC (OLL)

Published Primary Sources

The following list of primary sources excludes those published in *Anais da Biblioteca Nacional do Rio de Janeiro (ABNRJ)*, *Autos de devassa da Inconfidência Mineira (ADIM)*, *Documentos históricos (DH)*, *Documentos interessantes para a história e costumes de São Paulo (DI)*, *Revista do Arquivo Público Mineiro (RAPM)*, *Revista do Instituto Histórico e Geográfico Brasileiro (RIHGB)*, which have been cited in full in the notes.

Araújo, José de Souza Azevedo Pizarro e. *Memórias históricas do Rio de Janeiro e das provincias annexas a jurisdicção do vice-rei do Estado do Brasil.* 9 vols. Rio de Janeiro: Imp. Regia, 1820–1822.
Bowen, Emanuel. *A Complete System of Geography, Being a Description of All the Countries, Islands, Cities, Chief Towns, Harbours, Lakes, and Rivers, Mountains, Mines, Etc., of the Known World . . .* 2 vols. London: William Innys, et al., 1747.
Brazil, Minas Gerais, Câmara dos Deputados. *Autos de devassa da Inconfidência Mineira.* 2nd ed., 10 vols. Belo Horizonte, Brazil: Imprensa Oficial, 1976–1983.
Brito, Francisco Tavares de. *Itinerario Geografico com a Verdadeira Descripção dos Caminhos, Estradas, Rossas, Citios, Povoações, Lugares, Villas, Rios, Montes, e Serras, que ha da Cidade de S. Sebastião do Rio de Janeiro Até as Minas do Ouro.* Seville, Spain: Antonio da Sylva, 1732.
Brockwell, Charles. *The Natural and Political History of Portugal . . .* London: T. Warner, 1726.
Carrara, Angelo Alves (ed.). *Uma fronteira da Capitania de Minas Gerais. A freguesia de São João Batista do Presídio em 1821.* Mariana, Brazil: Universidade Federal de Ouro Preto, 1999.
[Casal], [Manuel Aires de]. *Corografia brazilica, ou relação historico-geografica do Reino do Brazil.* Vol. 1. Rio de Janeiro: Imp. Regia, 1817.
Chabert, X. *An Historical Account of the Manners and Customs of the Savage Inhabitants of Brazil; Together with a Sketch of the Life of the Botocudo Chieftain and Family.* Exeter, UK: R. Cullum, 1823.
Costa, João Severiano Maciel da. *Memoria sobre a necessidade de abolir a introdução dos escravos africanos no Brasil . . .* Coimbra, Brazil: Universidade de Coimbra, 1821.
Coutinho, José Joaquim da Cunha de Azeredo. *Ensaio economico sobre o comercio de Portugal e suas colonias oferecido ao serenisimo Princepe do Brazil, Noso Senhor.* Lisbon: Academia Real das Ciências, 1794.

Couto, José Vieira. *Memória sobre a Capitania das Minas Gerais; seu território, clima e produções metálicas.* 1799. Reprint with a critical study by Júnia Ferreira Furtado. Belo Horizonte, Brazil: Fundação João Pinheiro, 1994.

Cunha, Manuela Carneiro da (ed.). *Legislação indigenista no século XIX: Uma compilação (1808–1889).* São Paulo: Universidade de São Paulo, 1992.

Debret, Jean Baptiste. *Voyage pittoresque et historique au Brésil.* Paris: Didot Frères, 1834–1839.

Denis, Ferdinand. *Résumé de L'Histoire du Brésil, Suivi du Résumé de L'Histoire de la Guyane.* 2nd ed. Paris: Lecomte Et Durey, 1825.

Diário do Governo (Rio de Janeiro), 1823.

Eschwege, Wilhelm Ludwig von. *Brasil, Novo Mundo.* Translated by Domício de Figueiredo Murta. Belo Horizonte, Brazil: Fundação João Pinheiro, 1996.

Eschwege, Wilhelm Ludwig von. *Pluto brasiliensis.* Translated by Domício de Figueiredo Murta, 2 vols. Belo Horizonte, Brazil: Ed. Itatiaia, 1979.

Flaubert, Gustave. *Madame Bovary.* Translated by Mildred Marmur. New York: Signet Classic, New American Library, 1964.

Idade de Ouro do Brasil (Salvador, Brazil), 1811.

Koster, Henry. *Travels in Brazil.* London: Longman, et al., 1816.

Léry, Jean de. *History of a Voyage to the Land of Brazil.* Translated by Janet Whatley. Berkeley, CA: University of California Press, 1990.

Luccock, John. *Notes on Rio de Janeiro and the Southern Parts of Brazil; Taken During a Residence of Ten Years in that Country, from 1808 to 1818.* London: Samuel Leigh, 1820.

Mathias, Herculano Gomes. *Um recenseamento na Capitania de Minas Gerais, Vila Rica—1804.* Rio de Janeiro: Arquivo Nacional, 1969.

Martins, A. de Assis, and J. Harques de Oliveira (eds.). *Almanak administrativo, civil e industrial da Provincia de Minas Geraes para o anno de 1865.* Ouro Preto, Brazil: Typographia do Minas Geraes, 1864.

Matos, Raimundo José da Cunha. *Corografia histórica da província de Minas Gerais (1837).* 2 vols. São Paulo: Ed. Itatiaia, 1981.

Mawe, John. *Travels in the Interior of Brazil, Particularly in the Gold and Diamond Districts of that Country.* London: Longman, et al., 1812.

Maximilian, Prinz von Wied. *Travels in Brazil in the Years 1815, 1816, 1817.* London: Henry Colburn, 1820.

Maximilian, Prinz von Wied. *Viagem ao Brasil.* Translated by Edgar Süssekind de Mendonça and Flávio Poppe de Figueiredo. Belo Horizonte, Brazil: Ed. Itatiaia, 1989.

Menezes, Francisco Xavier de. *Relaçam da vitoria que os portuguezes alcançàraõ no Rio de Janeyro contra os francezes em 19 de Setembro de 1710.* Lisbon: Antonio Pedrozo Galraõ, 1711.

Ordenações e leys do reyno de Portugal confirmadas e estabelecidas pelo Senhor rey D. João IV. Lisbon: Mosteiro de S. Vicente de Fóra, 1747.

Pitta, Sebastião da Rocha. *Historia da America Portugueza, desde o anno de mil e quinhentos do seu descobrimento, até o de mil e setecentos e vinte e quatro.* Lisbon: Academia Real, 1730.

Pohl, Johann Emanuel. *Viagem no interior do Brasil.* Translated by Milton Amado and Eugênio Amado. Belo Horizonte, Brazil: Ed. Itatiaia, 1976.

Portugal, Luís de Almeida. *Cartas do Rio de Janeiro, 1769–1776*. Rio de Janeiro: Instituto Estadual do Livro, 1978.

Rau, Virginia, and Maria Fernandes Gomes da Silva (eds.). *Os manuscritos do Arquivo da Casa de Cadaval respeitantes ao Brasil*. 2 vols. Coimbra, Portugal: Atlântica, 1955–1958.

Reys, Manoel Martinz do Couto. *Manuscritos de Manoel Martinz do Couto Reys, 1785*. Rio de Janeiro: Arquivo Público do Estado do Rio de Janeiro, 1997.

Rocha, José Joaquim da. *Geografia histórica da Capitania de Minas Gerais*. 1780. Reprint with a critical study by Maria Efigênia Lage de Resende. Belo Horizonte, Brazil: Fundação João Pinheiro, 1995.

Rugendas, [Johann Moritz]. *Viagem Pitoresca através do Brasil*. Translated by Sérgio Milliet, 5th ed. São Paulo: Livraria Martins Editora, 1954.

Rugendas, [Johann Moritz]. *Voyage pittoresque dans le Brésil*. Translated by Mr. de Colbery. Paris: Engelmann, 1835.

[Sá], José d'Almeida [Correa de]. *Vice-reinado de D. Luiz d'Almeida Portugal, 2° marquez de Lavradio, 3° vice-rei do Brasil*. Vol. 214 of *Biblioteca Pedagogica Brasileira, Brasiliana, Serie 5.a*. São Paulo: Ed. Nacional, 1942.

Saint-Hilaire, Auguste de. *Viagem ao Espírito Santo e Rio Doce*. Translated by Milton Amado. Belo Horizonte, Brazil: Ed. Itatiaia, 1974.

Saint-Hilaire, Auguste de. *Viagem pelas províncias do Rio de Janeiro e Minas Gerais*. Translated by Vivaldi Moreira. Belo Horizonte, Brazil: Ed. Itatiaia, 1975.

Silva, Antonio de Moraes. *Diccionario da lingua portugueza*. 2 vols. Lisbon: Typ. Lacerdina, 1813.

Silva, José Carneiro da. *Memoria topographica e historica sobre os Campos dos Goytacazes com uma noticia breve de suas producções e commercio*. 1819. Reprint, Rio de Janeiro: Typ. Leuzinger, 1907.

Silva, José Bonifácio de Andrada e. "Apontamentos para a civilização dos índios bravos do Império do Brasil." In *O pensamento vivo de José Bonifácio* 78–107. São Paulo: Livraria Martins, 1961.

[Sousa], [Gabriel Soares de]. *Noticia do Brazil, descripção verdadeira da costa daquelle estado, que pertence á coroa do Reino de Portugal, sitio da Bahia de Todos os Santos*. 1587. Reprint, Lisbon: Typ. da Academia Real das Sciencias, 1825.

Taunay, Afonso de Escragnolle. *Relatos sertanistas*. Belo Horizonte, Brazil: Ed. Itatiaia, 1981.

Trindade, José da Santíssima. *Visitas pastorais (1821–1825)*. Belo Horizonte, Brazil: Fundação João Pinheiro, 1998.

Vasconcelos, Diogo Pereira Ribeiro de. *Breve descrição geográfica, física e política da Capitania de Minas Gerais*. 1807. Reprint with a critical study by Carla Maria Junho Anastasia. Belo Horizonte, Brazil: Fundação João Pinheiro, 1994.

Vide, Sebastião Monteiro da. *Constituições primeyras do arcebispado da Bahia*. Lisbon: Pascoal da Sylva, 1719.

Published Secondary Sources

Abler, Thomas S., and Michael H. Logan. "The Florescence and Demise of Iroquoian Cannibalism: Human Sacrifice and Malinowski's Hypothesis." *Man in the Northeast* 35 (Spring 1988).

Abreu, João Capistrano de. *Caminhos antigos e povoamento do Brasil*. Belo Horizonte, Brazil: Ed. Itatiaia, 1989.

Abreu, João Capistrano de. *Chapters of Brazil's Colonial History, 1500–1800*. Translated by Arthur Brakel. New York: Oxford University Press, 1997.

Adelman, Jeremy, and Stephen Aron. "From Borderlands to Borders: Empires, Nation-States, and the Peoples in Between in North American History." *American Historical Review* 104:3 (June 1999), 814–41.

Adonias, Isa (ed.). *Mapa: Imagens da formação territorial brasileira*. Rio de Janeiro: Fundação Emílio Odebrecht, 1993.

Aiton, Arthur S. "Latin-American Frontiers." In *Where Cultures Meet: Frontiers in Latin American History*. Edited by David J. Weber and Jane M. Rausch, 19–25. Wilmington, DE: Scholarly Resources, 1994.

Alden, Dauril. "Late Colonial Brazil, 1750–1808." In *Colonial Brazil*. Edited by Leslie Bethell, 284–343. Cambridge, UK: Cambridge University Press, 1987.

Alden, Dauril. *The Making of an Enterprise: The Society of Jesus in Portugal, Its Empire, and Beyond, 1540–1750*. Stanford, CA: Stanford University Press, 1996.

Alden, Dauril. "The Population of Brazil in the Late Eighteenth Century: A Preliminary Survey." *Hispanic American Historical Review* 43:2 (May 1963), 173–205.

Alden, Dauril. *Royal Government in Colonial Brazil with Special Reference to the Administration of the Marquis of Lavradio, Viceroy, 1769–1779*. Berkeley, CA: University of California Press, 1968.

Allen, John L. "Mapping the Plains and Prairies, 1800–1860." In *Mapping the North American Plains : Essays in the History of Cartography*. Edited by Frederick C. Luebke, Frances W. Kaye, and Gary E. Moulton, 41–62. Norman, OK: University of Oklahoma Press, 1987.

Almeida, Martins de. *Brasil errado: Ensaio político sobre os erros do Brasil como país*. 2nd ed. Rio de Janeiro: Organização Simões, 1953.

Almeida, Maria Regina Celestino de. *Metamorfoses indígenas: Cultura e identidade nos aldeamentos indígenas do Rio de Janeiro*. Rio de Janeiro: Arquivo Nacional, 2002.

Almeida, Rita Heloísa de. *O Diretório dos Índios : Um projeto de "civilização" no Brasil do século XVIII*. Brasília, Brazil: Universidade de Brasília, 1997.

Amado, Janaína. "Construindo mitos: a conquista do oeste no Brasil e nos EUA." In *Passando dos limites*. Edited by Sidney V. Pimentel and Janaína Amado, 51–78. Goiânia, Brazil: Universidade Federal de Goiás, 1995.

Amado, Janaína. "The Frontier in Comparative Perspective: The United States and Brazil." In *Frontier in Comparative Perspectives* 28–55. Washington, DC: Latin American Program, The Woodrow Wilson Center, 1990.

Amaral, Antonio José do Azevedo. *Ensaios brasileiros*. 2nd ed. Rio de Janeiro: Omena & Barreto, 1930.

Amoroso, Marta Rosa. "Corsários no caminho fluvial: Os Mura do rio Madeira." In *História dos Índios no Brasil*. Edited by Manuela Carneiro da Cunha, 297–310. São Paulo: Companhia das Letras, FAPESP/SMC, 1992.

Arens, W. *The Man-Eating Myth: Anthropology and Anthropophagy*. New York: Oxford University Press, 1979.

Armond, Louis de. "Frontier Warfare in Colonial Chile." In *Where Cultures Meet: Frontiers in Latin American History*. Edited by David J. Weber and Jane M. Rausch, 115–22. Wilmington, DE: Scholarly Resources, 1994.

Arruda, José Jobson de A. *O Brasil no comércio colonial*. São Paulo: Ed. Ática, 1980.

Augstein, Hannah Franziska (ed.). *Race: The Origins of an Idea, 1760–1850*. Bristol, UK: Thoemmes Press, 1996.

Azevedo, Fernando de. *Brazilian Culture: An Introduction to the Study of Culture in Brazil*. Translated by William Rex Crawford. New York: Hafner Publishing, 1971.

Balée, William. "The Ka'apor Indian Wars of Lower Amazonia, ca. 1825–1928." In *Dialectics and Gender: Anthropological Approaches*. Edited by David M. Schneider, Richard R. Randolph, and May N. Diaz, 155–69. Boulder, CO: Westview Press, 1988.

Balhana, Altiva Pilatti. "A População." In *O Império Luso-Brasileiro, 1750–1822*. Edited by Maria Beatriz Nizza da Silva, 19–62. Lisbon: Editorial Estampa, 1986.

Barbosa, Waldemar de Almeida. *A decadência das minas e a fuga da mineração*. Belo Horizonte, Brazil: Universidade Federal de Minas Gerais, 1971.

Barbosa, Waldemar de Almeida. *Dicionário da terra e da gente de Minas*. Belo Horizonte, Brazil: Imp. Oficial, 1985.

Barbosa, Waldemar de Almeida. *Dicionário histórico-geográfico de Minas Gerais*. Belo Horizonte, Brazil: Ed. Itatiaia, 1995.

Baretta, Silvio R. Duncan, and John Markoff. "Civilization and Barbarism: Cattle Frontiers in Latin America." *Comparative Studies in Society and History* 20:4 (October 1978) 587–620.

Barickman, B.J. *A Bahian Counterpoint: Sugar, Tobacco, Cassava, and Slavery in the Recôncavo, 1780–1860*. Stanford, CA: Stanford University Press, 1998.

Barickman, B.J. "As cores do escravismo: Escravistas 'pretos,' 'pardos' e 'cabras' no Recôncavo baiano, 1835." *População e Família* 2 (1999), 7–59.

Barickman, B.J. "'Tame Indians,' 'Wild Heathens,' and Settlers in Southern Bahia in the Late Eighteenth and Early Nineteenth Centuries." *The Americas* 51:3 (1995), 325–68.

Barker, Francis, Peter Hulme, and Margaret Iversen (eds.). *Cannibalism and the Colonial World*. New York: Cambridge University Press, 1998.

Barman, Roderick J. *Brazil: The Forging of a Nation, 1798–1852*. Stanford, CA: Stanford University Press, 1988.

Barthes, Roland. *Mythologies*. Translated by Annette Lavers. New York: Hill and Wang, 1972.

Bellotto, Heloísa Liberalli. *Autoridade e conflito no Brasil colonial: o governo do Morgado de Mateus em São Paulo: 1765–1775*. São Paulo: Conselho Estadual de Artes e Ciências Humanas, 1979.

Bergad, Laird W. "After the Mining Boom: Demographic and Economic Aspects of Slavery in Mariana, Minas Gerais, 1750–1808." *Latin American Research Review* 31:1 (1996), 67–97.

Bergad, Laird W. "Demographic Change in a Post-Export Boom Society: The Population of Minas Gerais, Brazil, 1776–1821." *Journal of Social History* 29:4 (Summer 1996), 895–932.

Bergad, Laird W. *Slavery and the Demographic and Economic History of Minas Gerais, Brazil, 1720–1888*. Cambridge, UK: Cambridge University Press, 1999.

Berger, Paulo. *Bibliografia do Rio de Janeiro de viajantes e autores estrangeiros, 1531–1900.* 2nd ed. Rio de Janeiro: SEEC-RJ, 1980.

Berlin, Ira. *Many Thousands Gone: The First Two Centuries of Slavery in North America.* Cambridge, MA: Belknap Press of Harvard University Press, 1998.

Bieber, Judy. "Postmodern Ethnographer in the Backlands: An Imperial Bureaucrat's Perceptions of Post-Independence Brazil." *Latin American Research Review* 33:2 (1998), 37–72.

Bieber, Judy. *Power, Patronage, and Political Violence: State Building on a Brazilian Frontier, 1822–1889.* Lincoln, NE: University of Nebraska Press, 1999.

Biolsi, Thomas. "Ecological and Cultural Factors in Plains Indians Warfare." In *Warfare, Culture, and Environment* Edited by R. Brian Ferguson, 141–68. Orlando, FL: Academic Press, 1984.

Bitterli, Urs. *Cultures in Conflict: Encounters between European and Non-European Cultures, 1492–1800.* Translated by Ritchie Robertson. Stanford, CA: Stanford University Press, 1989.

Boccara, Guillaume. "Rethinking the Margins/Thinking from the Margins: Culture, Power, and Place on the Frontiers of the New World." *Identities: Global Studies in Culture and Power* 10 (2003), 59–81.

Bodley, John H. "Hunter-gatherers and the Colonial Encounter." In *The Cambridge Encyclopedia of Hunters and Gatherers.* Edited by Richard B. Lee and Richard Daly, 465–72. Cambridge, UK: Cambridge University Press, 1999.

Bohls, Elizabeth A. "The Aesthetics of Colonialism: Janet Schaw in the West Indies, 1774–1775." *Eighteenth-Century Studies* 27:3 (Spring 1994), 363–90.

Bolton, Herbert E. *Wider Horizons of American History.* New York: D. Appleton-Century, 1939.

Borges, Dain. "A Mirror of Progress." In *The Brazil Reader: History, Culture, Politics.* Edited by Robert M. Levine and John J. Crocitti, 93–99. Durham: Duke University Press, 1999.

Boxer, C.R. *The Golden Age of Brazil, 1695–1750: Growing Pains of a Colonial Society.* Berkeley, CA: University of California Press, 1969.

Breen, T.H., and Stephen Innes. *"Myne Owne Ground": Race and Freedom on Virginia's Eastern Shore, 1640–1676.* New York: Oxford University Press, 1980.

Brooks, James F. (ed.). *Confounding the Color Line: The Indian-Black Experience in North America.* Lincoln, NE: University of Nebraska Press, 2002.

Brown, Kathleen M. *Good Wives, Nasty Wenches, and Anxious Patriarchs: Gender, Race, and Power in Colonial Virginia.* Chapel Hill, NC: University of North Carolina Press, 1996.

Brown, Michael F. "On Resisting Resistance." *American Anthropologist* 98:4 (December 1996), 729–35.

Bueno, Beatriz Siqueira. "Desenho e desígnio: O Brasil dos engenheiros militares." *Oceanos* 41 (January-March 2000), 8–38.

Bueno, Francisco da Silveira. *Grande dicionário etimológico-prosódico da lingua portuguêsa.* São Paulo: Edição Saraiva, 1967.

Burkholder, Mark A., and Lyman L. Johnson. *Colonial Latin America.* 5th ed, Oxford: Oxford University Press, 2004.

Burns, E. Bradford. "Brazil: Frontier and Ideology." *Pacific Historical Review* 64:1 (February 1995), 1–18.

Burt, A.L. "If Turner Had Looked at Canada, Australia, and New Zealand When He Wrote about the West." In *The Frontier in Perspective*. Edited by Walker D. Wyman and Clifton B. Kroeber, 59–77. Madison, WI: University of Wisconsin Press, 1957.

Cambraia, Ricardo de Bastos, and Fábio Faria Mendes. "A colonização dos sertões do leste mineiro: Políticas de ocupação territorial num regime escravista (1780–1836)." *Revista do Departamento de História—FAFICH/UFMG* 6 (July 1988), 137–50.

Canabrava, Alice P. "Uma economia de decadência: Os níveis de riqueza na Capitania de São Paulo, 1765/67." *Revista Brasileira de Economia* 26:4 (October-December 1972), 95–123.

Cardozo, Manuel. "The Brazilian Gold Rush." *The Americas* 3:2 (1946), 137–60.

Carrara, Angelo Alves. *Contribuição para a história agrária de Minas Gerais*. Mariana, Brazil: EdUFOP, 1999.

Carrara, Angelo Alves. *Estruturas agrárias e capitalismo; Ocupação do solo e transformação do trabalho na zona da Mata central de Minas Gerais (séculos XVIII e XIX)*. Mariana, Brazil: EdUFOP, 1999.

Carrato, José Ferreira. *Igreja, iluminismo e escolas mineiras coloniais*. São Paulo: Nacional, 1968.

Carvalho, Elysio de. *O fator geográfico na política brasileira*. Rio de Janeiro: Monitor Mercantil, 1921.

Carvalho, Theophilo Feu de. *Comarcas e termos: Creações, suppressões, restaurações, encorporações e desmembramentos de comarcas e termos, em Minas Geraes (1709–1915)*. Belo Horizonte, Brazil: Imprensa Oficial, 1922.

Castañeda, Antonia. "Women of Color and the Rewriting of Western History: The Discourse, Politics, and Decolonization of History." *Pacific Historical Review* 61 (November 1992), 501–33.

Castro, Celso Falabella de Figueiredo. *Os sertões de leste; achegas para a história da Zona da Mata*. Belo Horizonte, Brazil: Imprensa Oficial, 1987.

Castro, Eduardo Viveiros de. *From the Enemy's Point of View: Humanity and Divinity in an Amazonian Society*. Translated by Catherine V. Howard. Chicago: University of Chicago Press, 1992.

Chaves, Cláudia Maria das Graças. *Perfeitos negociantes: Mercadores das Minas setecentistas*. São Paulo: Annablume, 1999.

Clarke, G.N.G. "Taking Possession: The Cartouche as Cultural Text in Eighteenth-Century American Maps." *Word and Image* 4:2 (April-June 1988), 455–74.

Clementi, Hebe. "National Identity and the Frontier." *American Studies International* 18:3-4 (1980), 36–44.

Cook, Noble David. *Born to Die: Disease and New World Conquest, 1492–1650*. Cambridge, UK: Cambridge University Press, 1998.

Comissão Nacional para as Comemorações dos Descobrimentos Portugueses. *Brasil-brasis: Cousas notaveis e espantosas (A construção do Brasil: 1500–1825)*. Lisbon: Comissão Nacional para as Comemorações dos Descobrimentos Portugueses, 2000.

Cortesão, Armando, and Avelino Teixeira da Mota (ed.). *Portugaliae Monumenta Cartographica*. 5 vols. Lisbon: Imp. de Coimbra, 1960.

Costa, Emilia Viotti da. "Land Policies: The Land Law, 1850, and the Homestead Act, 1862." In *The Brazilian Empire: Myths and Histories* 78–93. Chicago: University of Chicago Press, 1985.

Costa, Iraci del Nero da. *Minas Gerais: Estruturas populacionais típicas.* São Paulo: EDEC, 1982.

Costa, Iraci del Nero da. *Populações mineiras: Sobre a estrutura populacional de alguns núcleos mineiros no alvorecer do século XIX.* São Paulo: Instituto de Pesquisas Econômicas, 1981.

Costa, Iraci del Nero da. *Vila Rica: População (1719–1826).* São Paulo: Instituto de Pesquisas Econômicas, 1979.

Costa, Joaquim Ribeiro. *Toponímia de Minas Gerais.* Belo Horizonte, Brazil: Imprensa Oficial, 1970.

Craib, Raymond B. "Cartography and Power in the Conquest and Creation of New Spain." *Latin American Research Review* 35:1 (2000), 7–36.

Cronon, William. *Changes in the Land: Indians, Colonists, and the Ecology of New England.* New York: Hill and Wang, 1983.

Cunha, Euclides da. *Os Sertões: Campanha de Canudos.* 35th ed. Rio de Janeiro: Francisco Alves, 1991 [1902].

Cunha, Euclides da. *Rebellion in the Backlands.* Translated by Samuel Putnam. Chicago: University of Chicago Press, Phoenix Books, 1944.

Cunha, Manuela Carneiro da (ed.). *História dos índios no Brasil.* São Paulo: Companhia das Letras, FAPESP/SMC, 1992.

Cunha, Manuela Carneiro da (ed.). "Pensar os índios: apontamentos sobre José Bonifácio." In *Antropologia do Brasil: mito, história, etnicidade* 165–73. São Paulo: Brasiliense/EDUSP, 1986.

Dean, Warren. "Ecological and Economic Relationships in Frontier History: São Paulo, Brazil." In *Essays on Frontiers in World History.* Edited by George Wolfskill and Stanley Palmer, 71–100. Austin, TX: University of Texas Press, 1981.

Dean, Warren. "The Frontier in Brazil." In *Frontier in Comparative Perspectives* 15–27. Washington, DC: Latin American Program, The Woodrow Wilson Center, 1990.

Dean, Warren. *Rio Claro: A Brazilian Plantation System, 1820–1920.* Stanford, CA: Stanford University Press, 1976.

Dean, Warren. *With Broadax and Firebrand: The Destruction of the Brazilian Atlantic Forest.* Berkeley, CA: University of California Press, 1995.

Delson, Roberta M. "The Beginnings of Professionalization in the Brazilian Military: the Eighteenth Century Corps of Engineers." *The Americas* 51:4 (April 1995), 555–74.

Delson, Roberta M. *New Towns for Colonial Brazil: Spatial and Social Planning of the Eighteenth Century.* Ann Arbor, MI: University Microfilms International, 1979.

Deutsch, Sarah. *No Separate Refuge: Class, Culture, and Gender on an Anglo-Hispanic Frontier in the American Southwest, 1880–1940.* New York: Oxford University Press, 1987.

Dicionário geográfico brasileiro. Porto Alegre, Brazil: Ed. Globo, 1972.

Dobyns, Henry F. "Military Transculturation of Northern Piman Indians, 1782–1821." *Ethnohistory* 19:4 (Fall 1972), 323–43.

Domingues, Ângela. *Quando os índios eram vassalos. Colonização e relações de poder no Norte do Brasil na segunda metade do século XVIII.* Lisbon: Comissão Nacional para as Comemorações dos Descobrimentos Portugueses, 2000.

Dowd, Gregory Evans. "'Insidious Friends': Gift Giving and the Cherokee-British Alliance in the Seven Years' War." In *Contact Points: American Frontiers from the Mohawk Valley to the Mississippi, 1750–1830.* Edited by Andrew R.L. Cayton and Fredrika Teute, 114–50. Chapel Hill, NC: University of North Carolina Press, 1998.

Duarte, Nestor. *A ordem privada e a organização política nacional: Contribuição à sociologia política brasileira.* São Paulo: Ed. Nacional, 1939.

Duarte, Regina Horta. "Facing the Forest: European Travellers Crossing the Mucuri River Valley, Brazil, in the Nineteenth Century." *Environment and History* 10 (2004), 31–58.

Dubofsky, Melvyn. "The Origins of the Western Working Class, 1890–1905." *Labor History* 7 (Spring 1966), 131–54.

Eccles, W.J. "The Frontiers of New France." In *Essays on Frontiers in World History.* Edited by George Wolfskill and Stanley Palmer, 42–70. Austin, TX: University of Texas Press, 1981.

Edney, Matthew H. *Mapping an Empire: The Geographical Construction of British India, 1765–1843.* Chicago: University of Chicago Press, 1997.

Edney, Matthew H. "Reconsidering Enlightenment Geography and Map Making: Reconnaissance, Mapping, Archive." In *Geography and Enlightenment.* Edited by David N. Livingstone and Charles W.J. Withers, 165–98. Chicago: University of Chicago Press, 1999.

Eltis, David. "Labour and Coercion in the English Atlantic World from the Seventeenth to the Early Twentieth Century." *Slavery & Abolition* 14:1 (1993), 207–26.

Farage, Nádia. *As muralhas dos sertões: Os povos indígenas no Rio Branco e a colonização.* Rio de Janeiro: Paz e Terra and Anpocs, 1991.

Faria, Sheila de Castro. *A colônia em movimento: Fortuna e família no cotidiano colonial.* Rio de Janeiro: Ed. Nova Fronteira, 1998.

Ferguson, R. Brian, and Neil L. Whitehead. "The Violent Edge of Empire." In *War in the Tribal Zone: Expanding States and Indigenous Warfare* 1–30. Santa Fe, NM: School of American Research Press, 1992.

Ferguson, R. Brian, and Neil L. Whitehead (eds.). *War in the Tribal Zone: Expanding States and Indigenous Warfare.* Santa Fe, NM: School of American Research Press, 1992.

Ferreira, Francisco Ignacio. *Repertorio juridico do mineiro. Consolidação alphabetica e chronologica de todas as disposições sobre minas, comprehendendo a legislação antiga e moderna de Portugal e do Brasil.* Rio de Janeiro: Typ. Nacional, 1884.

Ferreira, Mário Clemente. "Uma ideia de Brasil num mapa inédito de 1746." *Oceanos* 43 (July-September 2000), 184–95.

Figueiredo, Luciano. *O avesso da memória: Cotidiano e trabalho da mulher em Minas Gerais no século XVIII.* Rio de Janeiro: José Olympio, 1993.

Flaubert, Gustave. *Madame Bovary.* Translated by Mildred Marmur. New York: Signet Classic, New American Library, 1964.

Florentino, Manolo Garcia. *Em Costas Negras: Uma história do tráfico de escravos entre a África e o Rio de Janeiro (séculos XVIII e XIX).* São Paulo: Companhia das Letras, 1997.

Fonseca, Cláudia Damasceno. "Agentes e contextos das intervenções urbanísticas nas Minas Gerais do século XVIII." *Oceanos* 41 (January-March 2000), 84–102.

Foweraker, Joe. *The Struggle for Land: A Political Economy of the Pioneer Frontier in Brazil from 1930 to the Present Day.* Cambridge, UK: Cambridge University Press, 1981.

Fragoso, João Luís Ribeiro. *Homens de grossa aventura: acumulação e hierarquia na praça mercantil do Rio de Janeiro (1790–1830).* Rio de Janeiro: Arquivo Nacional, 1992.

Franco, Francisco de Assis Carvalho. *Dicionário de bandeirantes e sertanistas do Brasil: século XVI, XVII, XVIII.* Belo Horizonte, Brazil: Ed. Itatiaia, 1989.

Fraser, Valerie. *The Architecture of Conquest: Building in the Viceroyalty of Peru, 1535–1635.* Cambridge, UK: Cambridge University Press, 1990.

Freire, José Ribamar Bessa, and Márcia Fernanda Malheiros. *Aldeamentos Indígenas do Rio de Janeiro.* Rio de Janeiro: Programa de Estudos dos Povos Indígenas, Universidade do Estado do Rio de Janeiro, 1997.

Furtado, Júnia Ferreira. *O Livro da Capa Verde: O regimento diamantino de 1771 e a vida no Distrito Diamantino no período da real extração.* São Paulo: Annablume, 1996.

Ganson, Barbara. *The Guaraní Under Spanish Rule in the Río de la Plata.* Stanford, CA: Stanford University Press, 2003.

Garfield, Seth. *Indigenous Struggle at the Heart of Brazil: State Policy, Frontier Expansion, and the Xavante Indians, 1937–1988.* Durham, NC: Duke University Press, 2001.

Gerbi, Antonello. *The Dispute of the New World: The History of a Polemic, 1750–1900.* Translated by Jeremy Moyle, rev. ed. Pittsburgh: University of Pittsburgh Press, 1973.

Giraldin, Odair. *Cayapó e Panará: Luta e sobrevivência de um povo Jê no Brasil Central.* Campinas, Brazil: UNICAMP, 1997.

Goldman, Laurence R. (ed.). *The Anthropology of Cannibalism.* Westport, CT: Bergin & Garvey, 1999.

Gomes, Flávio dos Santos. "Seguindo o mapa das minas: Plantas e quilombos mineiros setecentistas." *Estudos Afro-Asiáticos* 29 (March 1996), 113–42.

Gomes, Mercio P. *The Indians and Brazil.* Translated by John W. Moon. Gainesville, FL: University Press of Florida, 2000.

Graham, Richard (ed.). *Brazil and the World System.* Austin, TX: University of Texas Press, 1991.

Graham, Richard. "Constructing a Nation in Nineteenth-Century Brazil: Old and New Views on Class, Culture, and the State." *Journal of the Historical Society* 1:2–3 (Winter 2000/Spring 2001), 17–56.

Graham, Richard. *Patronage and Politics in Nineteenth-Century Brazil.* Stanford, CA: Stanford University Press, 1990.

Greenblatt, Stephen. *Marvelous Possessions: The Wonder of the New World.* Chicago: University of Chicago Press, 1991.

Gruzinski, Serge. *The Mestizo Mind: The Intellectual Dynamics of Colonization and Globalization.* New York: Routledge, 2002.

Guimarães, Carlos Magno. *Uma negação da ordem escravista: Quilombos em Minas Gerais no século XVIII.* São Paulo: Icone, 1988.

Guimarães, Carlos Magno, and Liana Maria Reis. "Agricultura e escravidão em Minas Gerais (1700/1750)." *Revista do Departamento de História-FAFICH/UFMG* 2 (June 1986), 7–36.

Gump, James. "The Subjugation of the Zulus and Sioux: A Comparative Study." *Western Historical Quarterly* 19 (January 1988), 21–36.

Gutiérrez, Ramón. *When Jesus Came, the Corn Mothers Went Away: Marriage, Sexuality, and Power in New Mexico, 1500–1846*. Stanford, CA: Stanford University Press, 1991.

Guy, Donna J., and Thomas E. Sheridan (eds.). *Contested Ground: Comparative Frontiers on the Northern and Southern Edges of the Spanish Empire*. Tucson, AZ: University of Arizona Press, 1998.

Haberly, David T. *Three Sad Races: Racial Identity and National Consciousness in Brazilian Literature*. Cambridge, UK: Cambridge University Press, 1983.

Hahner, June E. (ed.). *Women through Women's Eyes: Latin American Women in Nineteenth-Century Travel Accounts*. Wilmington, DE: Scholarly Resources, 1998.

Hall, Thomas D. *Social Change in the Southwest, 1350–1880*. Lawrence, KS: University Press of Kansas, 1989.

Hannaford, Ivan. *Race: The History of an Idea in the West*. Washington, DC: Woodrow Wilson Center Press, 1996.

Harley, J.B, and David Woodward (eds.). *The History of Cartography*. 2 vols. to date. Chicago: University of Chicago Press, 1987.

Harvey, David. *The Condition of Postmodernity: An Enquiry into the Origins of Cultural Change*. Oxford: Basil Blackwell, 1989.

Hemming, John. *Amazon Frontier: The Defeat of the Brazilian Indians*. Cambridge, MA: Harvard University Press, 1987.

Hemming, John. *Red Gold. The Conquest of the Brazilian Indians, 1500–1760*. Cambridge, MA: Harvard University Press, 1977.

Hennessy, Alistair. *The Frontier in Latin American History*. London: Edward Arnold, 1978.

Henriques, José Cláudio. "O Bairro de Matosinhos no Inconfidência Mineiro." *Revista do Instituto Histórico e Geográfico de São João del-Rei* 7 (1992), 110–13.

Higgins, Kathleen J. *"Licentious Liberty" in a Brazilian Gold-Mining Region: Slavery, Gender, and Social Control in Eighteenth-Century Sabará, Minas Gerais*. University Park, PA: Pennsylvania State University Press, 1999.

Holanda, Sérgio Buarque de. *Caminhos e fronteiras*. Rio de Janeiro: J. Olympio, 1957.

Holanda, Sérgio Buarque de (ed.). *História geral da civilização brasileira*. Tomo 1, *A época colonial*, vol. 1, *Do descobrimento à expansão territorial*, 5th ed. São Paulo: DIFEL, 1976.

Holanda, Sérgio Buarque de. *Monções*. Rev. ed., reprint, 1945. São Paulo: Ed. Brasiliense, 2000.

Holanda, Sérgio Buarque de. "Movimentos de população em São Paulo no século XVIII." *Revista do Instituto de Estudos Brasileiros* 1 (1966), 55–111.

Holanda, Sérgio Buarque de. *Visão do paraíso: Os motivos edênicos no descobrimento e colonização do Brasil*. 4th ed. São Paulo: Companhia Editora Nacional, 1985.

Holloway, Thomas H. *Immigrants on the Land: Coffee and Society in São Paulo, 1886–1934*. Chapel Hill, NC: University of North Carolina Press, 1980.

Hostetler, Laura. *Qing Colonial Enterprise: Ethnography and Cartography in Early Modern China*. Chicago: University of Chicago Press, 2001.

Howe, John M. "The Conversion of the Physical World: The Creation of a Christian Landscape." In *Varieties of Religious Conversion in the Middle Ages.* Edited by James Muldoon. Gainesville, FL: University Press of Florida, 1997.

Hugon, Paul. *Demografia brasileira.* São Paulo: Universidade de São Paulo, 1973.

Jameson, Elizabeth. "Women as Workers, Women as Civilizers: True Womanhood in the American West." In *The Women's West.* Edited by Susan Armitage and Elizabeth Jameson, 145–64. Norman, OK: University of Oklahoma Press, 1987.

Jennings, Francis. "A Growing Partnership: Historians, Anthropologists and American Indian History." *Ethnohistory* 29:1 (1982), 21–34.

Johnson, Susan. "A Memory Sweet to Soldiers: The Significance of Gender in the History of the American West." *Western Historical Quarterly* 24:4 (November 1993), 495–517.

Jones, Kristine L. "Comparative Raiding Economies, North and South." In *Contested Ground: Comparative Frontiers on the Northern and Southern Edges of the Spanish Empire.* Edited by Donna J. Guy and Thomas E. Sheridan, 97–114. Tucson, AZ: University of Arizona Press, 1998.

José, Oiliam. *Historiografia mineira.* 2nd ed. Belo Horizonte, Brazil: Imp. Oficial, 1987.

José, Oiliam. *Indígenas de Minas Gerais.* Belo Horizonte, Brazil: Imp. Oficial, 1965.

José, Oiliam. *Marlière, O Civilizador.* Belo Horizonte, Brazil: Ed. Itatiaia, 1958.

José, Oiliam. *O negro na economia mineira.* [Brazil: n.p.], 1993.

Kagan, Richard. *Urban Images of the Hispanic World, 1493–1793.* New Haven, CT: Yale University Press, 2000.

Karasch, Mary C. "Catequese e cativeiro: Política indigenista em Goiás, 1780–1889." In *História dos índios no Brasil.* Edited by Manuela Carneiro da Cunha, 397–412. São Paulo: Companhia das Letras, FAPESP/SMC, 1992.

Karasch, Mary C. "Interethnic Conflict and Resistance on the Brazilian Frontier of Goiás, 1750–1890." In *Contested Ground: Comparative Frontiers on the Northern and Southern Edges of the Spanish Empire.* Edited by Donna J. Guy and Thomas E. Sheridan, 115–34. Tucson, AZ: University of Arizona Press, 1998.

Keane, A.H. "On the Botocudos." *Journal of the Anthropological Institute of Great Britain and Ireland* 13 (1884), 199–213.

Kicza, John E. (ed.). *The Indian in Latin American History: Resistance, Resilience, and Acculturation.* Rev. ed. Wilmington, DE: Scholarly Resources, 2000.

Kicza, John E. *Resilient Cultures: America's Native Peoples Confront European Colonization, 1500–1800.* Upper Saddle River, NJ: Prentice Hall, 2003.

Kiemen, Mathias C. *The Indian Policy of Portugal in the Amazon Region, 1614–1693.* New York: Octagon Books, 1973.

Klein, Herbert S., and Francisco Vidal Luna. "Free Colored in a Slave Society: São Paulo and Minas Gerais in the Early Nineteenth Century." *Hispanic American Historical Review* 80:4 (November 2000), 913–41.

Klein, Herbert S., Francisco Vidal Luna, and Clotilde Andrade Paiva. "Freedmen in a Slave Economy: Minas Gerais in 1831." *Journal of Social History* 29:4 (Summer 1996), 933–62.

Kraay, Hendrik. *Race, State, and Armed Forces in Independence-Era Brazil, Bahia, 1790s–1840s.* Stanford, CA: Stanford University Press, 2001.

Kraay, Hendrik. "Reconsidering recruitment in imperial Brazil." *The Americas* 55:1 (July 1998), 1–33.

Kraay, Hendrik. "'The shelter of the uniform': The Brazilian Army and Runaway Slaves, 1800–1888." *Journal of Social History* 29:3 (Spring 1996), 637–58.

Lamar, Howard R. "From Bondage to Contract: Ethnic Labor in the American West, 1600–1890." In *The Countryside in the Age of Capitalist Transformation: Essays in the Social History of Rural America.* Edited by Steven Hahn and Jonathan Prude, 293–324. Chapel Hill, NC: University of North Carolina Press, 1985.

Lamar, Howard R., and Leonard Thompson (eds.). *The Frontier in History: North America and Southern Africa Compared.* New Haven, CT: Yale University Press, 1981.

Lamego, Alberto. *A Terra Goitacá á luz de documentos inéditos.* 6 vols. Rio de Janeiro: Garnier, 1913–41.

Landers, Jane G. (ed.). *Colonial Plantations and Economy in Florida.* Gainesville, FL: University Press of Florida, 2000.

Langfur, Hal. "Moved by Terror: Frontier Violence as Cultural Exchange in Late Colonial Brazil." *Ethnohistory* 52:2 (Spring 2005), 255–89.

Langfur, Hal. "Myths of Pacification: Brazilian Frontier Settlement and the Subjugation of the Bororo Indians." *Journal of Social History* 32:4 (Summer 1999), 879–905.

Langfur, Hal. "The Return of the Bandeira: Economic Calamity, Historical Memory, and Armed Expeditions to the Sertão in Minas Gerais, 1750–1808." *The Americas* 61:3 (January 2005), 429–61.

Langfur, Hal. "Uncertain Refuge: Frontier Formation and the Origins of the Botocudo War in Late Colonial Brazil." *Hispanic American Historical Review* 82:2 (May 2002), 215–56.

Lara, Silvia Hunold. *Campos da violência: Escravos e senhores na Capitania do Rio de Janeiro, 1750–1808.* Rio de Janeiro: Paz e Terra, 1988.

Lauderdale Graham, Sandra. *Caetana Says No: Women's Stories from a Brazilian Slave Society.* Cambridge, UK: Cambridge University Press, 2002.

Lauderdale Graham, Sandra. "Honor among Slaves." In *The Faces of Honor: Sex, Shame, and Violence in Colonial Latin America.* Edited by Lyman L. Johnson and Sonya Lipsett-Rivera, 201–28. Albuquerque, NM: University of New Mexico Press, 1998.

Lenharo, Alcir. *As tropas da moderação: (O abastimento da Corte na formação política do Brasil, 1808–1842).* São Paulo: Símbolo, 1979.

Lepore, Jill. *The Name of War: King Philip's War and the Origins of American Identity.* New York: Knopf, 1998.

Lestringant, Frank. *Cannibals: The Discovery and Representation of the Cannibal from Columbus to Jules Verne.* Translated by Rosemary Morris. Berkeley, CA: University of California Press, 1997.

Levine, Robert M. *Vale of Tears: Revisiting the Canudos Massacre in Northeastern Brazil, 1893–1897.* Berkeley, CA: University of California Press, 1992.

Lewis, Oscar. "The Effects of White Contact Upon Blackfoot Culture." In *Anthropological Essays* 137–212. New York: Random House, 1970.

Libby, Douglas C. "Reconsidering Textile Production in Late Colonial Brazil: New Evidence from Minas Gerais." *Latin American Research Review* 32:1 (1997), 88–108.

Libby, Douglas C. *Transformação e trabalho em uma economia escravista: Minas Gerais no século XIX*. São Paulo: Brasiliense, 1988.

Lima Júnior, Augusto de. *A Capitania das Minas Gerais*. Rev. ed. Belo Horizonte, Brazil: Ed. Itatiaia, 1978.

Lima, Nísia Trindade. *Um sertão chamado Brasil: Intelectuais e representação geográfica da identidade nacional*. Rio de Janeiro: Revan, 1999.

Lima, Oliveira. *Dom João VI no Brasil*. 3rd ed. Rio de Janeiro: Topbooks, 1996.

Limerick, Patricia N. *The Legacy of Conquest: The Unbroken Past of the American West*. New York: Norton, 1987.

Limerick, Patricia N. "What on Earth Is the New Western History?" In *Trails: Toward a New Western History*. Edited by Patricia N. Limerick, Clyde A. Milner II, and Charles E. Rankin, 81–88. Lawrence, KS: University Press of Kansas, 1991.

Limerick, Patricia N., Clyde A. Milner II, and Charles E. Rankin (eds.). *Trails: Toward a New Western History*. Lawrence, KS: University Press of Kansas, 1991.

Lisboa, Karen Macknow. *A nova Atlântica de Spix e Martius: Natureza e civilização no viagem pelo Brasil (1817–1820)*. São Paulo: Hucitec, 1997.

Lively, Adam. *Masks: Blackness, Race and the Imagination*. Oxford: Oxford University Press, 2000.

Livingstone, David N., and Charles W.J. Withers (eds.). *Geography and Enlightenment*. Chicago: University of Chicago Press, 1999.

Lockhart, James, and Stuart B. Schwartz. *Early Latin America: A History of Colonial Spanish America and Brazil*. Cambridge, UK: Cambridge University Press, 1983.

Lombardi, Mary. "The Frontier in Brazilian History: An Historiographical Essay." *Pacific Historical Review* 44 (1975), 437–57.

Lowie, Robert H. "American Culture History." *American Anthropologist*, New Series, 42:3, pt. 1 (July-September 1940), 409–28.

Lowie, Robert H. "The Southern Cayapó." In *Handbook of South American Indians*. Edited by Julian H. Steward. Vol. 1, 519–20. New York: Cooper Square, 1963.

Luna, Francisco Vidal. *Minas Gerais: Escravos e senhores: Análise da estrutura popula-cional e econômica de alguns centros mineratórios (1718–1804)*. São Paulo: Instituto de Pesquisas Econômicas, 1981.

Luna, Francisco Vidal, and Iraci del Nero da Costa. *Minas colonial: Economia & sociedade*. São Paulo: Livraria Pioneira, 1982.

Luna, Francisco Vidal, and Herbert S. Klein. *Slavery and the Economy of São Paulo, 1750–1850*. Stanford, CA: Stanford University Press, 2003.

Otterstrom, Samuel M., and Carville Earle. "The Settlement of the United States from 1790 to 1990: Divergent Rates of Growth and the End of the Frontier." *Journal of Interdisciplinary History* 33:1 (Summer 2002), 59–85.

MacLachlan, Colin. "The Indian Directorate: Forced Acculturation in Portuguese America (1757–1799)." *The Americas* 28:4 (April 1972), 357–87.

MacLachlan, Colin. "The Indian Labor Structure in the Portuguese Amazon, 1700–1800." In *Colonial Roots of Modern Brazil*. Edited by Dauril Alden. Berkeley, CA: University of California Press, 1973.

Malone, Michael P. "Beyond the Last Frontier: Toward a New Approach to Western American History." In *Trails: Toward a New Western History*. Edited by Patricia N.

Limerick, Clyde A. Milner II, and Charles E. Rankin, 139–60. Lawrence, KS: University Press of Kansas, 1991.

Malone, Michael P. "The 'New Western History,' An Assessment." In *Trails: Toward a New Western History*. Edited by Patricia N. Limerick, Clyde A. Milner II, and Charles E. Rankin, 97–102. Lawrence, KS: University Press of Kansas, 1991.

Martin, Percy Alvin. "Minas Gerais and California: A Comparison of Certain Phases of Their Historical and Social Evolution." *Revista do Instituto Histórico e Geográfico Brasileiro, tomo especial, Congresso Internacional de História da América* 1 (1922), 250–70.

Martins Filho, Amilcar, and Roberto B. Martins. "Slavery in a Nonexport Economy: Nineteenth-Century Minas Gerais Revisited." *Hispanic American Historical Review* 63:3 (August 1983), 537–68.

Mattos, Hebe Maria. *Das cores do silêncio: Os significados da liberdade no Sudeste escravista – Brasil século XIX*. 2nd ed. Rio de Janeiro: Ed. Nova Fronteira, 1998.

Maxwell, Kenneth R. *Conflicts and Conspiracies: Brazil and Portugal, 1750–1808*. Cambridge, UK: Cambridge University Press, 1973.

Maxwell, Kenneth R. *Pombal: Paradox of the Enlightenment*. Cambridge, UK: Cambridge University Press, 1995.

McNeill, William H. *The Great Frontier: Freedom and Hierarchy in Modern Times*. Princeton, NJ: Princeton University Press, 1983.

McQuown, Norman A. "The Indigenous Languages of Latin America." *American Anthropologist*, New Series, 57:3, pt. 1 (June 1955), 501–70, esp. 60.

Mercadante, Paulo. *Os sertões do leste: Estudo de uma região: A mata mineira*. Rio de Janeiro: Zahar, 1973.

Merrell, James H. *The Indians' New World: Catawbas and Their Neighbors from European Contact through the Era of Removal*. New York: Norton, 1991.

Metcalf, Alida C. *Family and Frontier in Colonial Brazil: Santana de Parnaíba, 1520–1822*. Berkeley, CA: University of California Press, 1992.

Metcalf, Alida C. "Millenarian Slaves? The Santidade de Jaguaripe and Slave Resistance in the Americas." *American Historical Review* 104:5 (December 1999), 1531–59.

Métraux, Alfred. "The Botocudo." In *Handbook of South American Indians*. Edited by Julian H. Steward. Vol. 1, 531–40. New York: Cooper Square, 1963.

Métraux, Alfred. "The Purí-Coroado Linguistic Family." In *Handbook of South American Indians*. Edited by Julian H. Steward. Vol. 1, 523–30. New York: Cooper Square, 1963.

Métraux, Alfred, and Curt Nimuendajú. "The Mashacalí, Patashó, and Malalí Linguistic Families." In *Handbook of South American Indians*. Edited by Julian H. Steward. Vol. 1, 541–45. New York: Cooper Square, 1963.

Meznar, Joan E. "The Ranks of the Poor: Military Service and Social Differentiation in Northeast Brazil, 1830–1875." *Hispanic American Historical Review* 72:3 (August 1992), 335–51.

Mignolo, Walter D. "Misunderstanding and Colonization: The Reconfiguration of Memory and Space." In *Le Nouveau Monde, Mondes Nouveaux: L'experience americaine*. Edited by Serge Gruzinski and Nathan Wachtel, 271–93. Paris: EHESS/CNRS, 1996.

Minas Gerais, Departamento Estadual de Estatística. *Annuario estatístico, anno II (1922–1925)*. Belo Horizonte, Brazil: Imp. Official, 1929.

Monteiro, John M. "The Crises and Transformations of Invaded Societies: Coastal Brazil in the Sixteenth Century." In *The Cambridge History of the Native Peoples of the Americas*. Vol. 3, pt. 1, *South America*. Edited by Frank Salomon and Stuart B. Schwartz. Cambridge, UK: Cambridge University Press, 1999.

Monteiro, John M. "The Heathen Castes of Sixteenth-Century Portuguese America: Unity, Diversity, and the Invention of the Brazilian Indians." *Hispanic American Historical Review* 80:4 (November 2000), 697–719.

Monteiro, John M. *Negros da terra: Índios e bandeirantes nas origens de São Paulo*. São Paulo: Companhia das Letras, 1994.

Moog, Clodomir Vianna. *Bandeirantes and Pioneers*. Translated by L.L. Barrett. New York: G. Braziller, 1964.

Moreira Neto, Carlos de Araújo. *Índios da Amazônia: De maioria a minoria (1750–1850)*. Petrópolis, Brazil: Ed. Vozes, 1988.

Morse, Richard M. (ed.). *The Bandeirantes: The Historical Role of the Brazilian Pathfinders*. New York: Knopf, 1965.

Motta, Márcia Maria Menendes. *Nas fronteiras do poder: Conflito e direito à terra no Brasil do século XIX*. Rio de Janeiro: Arquivo Público do Estado do Rio de Janeiro, 1998.

Muldoon, James (ed.). *The Spiritual Conversion of the Americas*. Gainesville, FL: University Press of Florida, 2004.

Mundy, Barbara E. *The Mapping of New Spain: Indigenous Cartography and the Maps of the Relaciones Geográficas*. Chicago: University of Chicago Press, 1996.

Nash, Gary B. *Red, White, and Black: The Peoples of Early America*. 4th ed. Englewood Cliffs, NJ: Prentice-Hall, 1999.

Nash, Roy. *A conquista do Brasil*. Translated by Moacir N. Vasconcelos. São Paulo: Ed. Nacional, 1939.

Nazzari, Muriel. *The Disappearance of the Dowry: Women, Families, and Social Change in São Paulo, Brazil (1600–1900)*. Stanford, CA: Stanford University Press, 1991.

Nazzari, Muriel. "Vanishing Indians: The Social Construction of Race in Colonial São Paulo." *The Americas* 57:4 (April 2001), 497–524.

Needell, Jeffrey D. "Provincial Origins of the Brazilian State: Rio de Janeiro, the Monarchy, and National Political Organization, 1808–1853." *Latin American Research Review* 36:3 (2001), 132–53.

Neme, Mário. *Apossamento do solo e evolução da propriedade rural na zona de Piracicaba*. São Paulo: Fundo de Pesquisas do Museu Paulista da Universidade de São Paulo, 1974.

Nimuendajú, Curt. "Social Organization and Beliefs of the Botocudo of Eastern Brazil." *Southwestern Journal of Anthropology* 2 (1946), 93–115.

Normano, J.F. *Brazil: A Study of Economic Types*. Chapel Hill, NC: University of North Carolina Press, 1935.

Normano, J.F. *Evolução econômica do Brasil*. Translated by Theodoro Quartim Barbosa, Roberto Peake Rodrigues, and Laércio Brandão Teixeira. São Paulo: Ed. Nacional, 1939.

Novaes, Maria Stella de. *História do Espírito Santo*. Vitória, Brazil: Fundo Editorial do Espírito Santo, 1968.

Novais, Fernando A. "Brazil in the Old Colonial System." In *Brazil and the World System*. Edited by Richard Graham, 11–55. Austin, TX: University of Texas Press, 1991.

Novais, Fernando A. *Portugal e Brasil na crise do antigo sistema colonial (1777–1808)*. 2nd ed. São Paulo: Ed. Hucitec, 1981.

Nugent, Walter. "Frontiers and Empires in the Late Nineteenth Century." In *Trails: Toward a New Western History*. Edited by Patricia N. Limerick, Clyde A. Milner II, and Charles E. Rankin, 161–81. Lawrence, KS: University Press of Kansas, 1991.

Nuttal, Zelia. "Royal Ordinances Concerning the Laying Out of New Towns." *Hispanic American Historical Review* 4:4 (November 1921), 743–53.

Ortiz, Fernando. *Cuban Counterpoint: Tobacco and Sugar*. Translated by Harriet de Onís. Durham, NC: Duke University Press, 1995.

Paraíso, Maria Hilda B. "Os Botocudos e sua trajetória histórica." In *História dos índios no Brasil*. Edited by Manuela Carneiro da Cunha, 413–30. São Paulo: Companhia das Letras, FAPESP/SMC, 1992.

Pascoe, Peggy. *Relations of Rescue: The Search for Female Moral Authority in the American West, 1874–1939*. New York: Oxford University Press, 1990.

Peck, Gunther. *Reinventing Free Labor: Padrones and Immigrant Workers in the North American West, 1880–1930*. Cambridge, UK: Cambridge University Press, 2000.

Peres, Damião. *Estudos de História Luso-Brasileira*. [Lisbon: n.p.], 1956.

Perrone-Moisés, Beatriz. "Índios livres e índios escravos: Os princípios da legislação indigenista do período colonial (séculos XVI a XVIII)." In *História dos índios no Brasil*. Edited by Manuela Carneiro da Cunha, 115–32. São Paulo: Companhia das Letras, FAPESP/SMC, 1992.

Perrone-Moisés, Beatriz. "Inventário da legislação indigenista, 1500–1800." In *História dos índios no Brasil*. Edited by Manuela Carneiro da Cunha, 529–66. São Paulo: Companhia das Letras, FAPESP/SMC, 1992.

Pinto, Renato Venâncio. "Os últimos carijós: Escravidão indígena em Minas Gerais: 1711–1725." *Revista Brasileira de História* 17:34 (1997), 165–81.

Prado Júnior, Caio. *Formação do Brasil contemporâneo*. 20th ed. São Paulo: Brasiliense, 1987.

Pratt, Mary Louise. *Imperial Eyes: Travel Writing and Transculturation*. London: Routledge, 1992.

Price, Richard. *Alabi's World*. Baltimore, MD: Johns Hopkins University Press, 1990.

Priore, Mary del. *Ao sul do corpo: Condição feminina, maternidades e mentalidades no Brasil Colônia*. Rio de Janeiro: José Olympio, 1993.

Puntoni, Pedro. *A Guerra dos Bárbaros: Povos indígenas e a colonização do sertão nordeste do Brazil*. São Paulo: Hucitec, 2000.

Rabasa, José. *Writing Violence on the Northern Frontier: The Historiography of Sixteenth-Century New Mexico and Florida and the Legacy of Conquest*. Durham, NC: Duke University Press, 2000.

Radding, Cynthia. *Wandering Peoples: Colonialism, Ethnic Spaces, and Ecological Frontiers in Northwestern Mexico, 1700–1850*. Durham, NC: Duke University Press, 1997.

Raminelli, Ronald. *Imagens da colonizacão: A representação do índio de Caminha a Vieira*. Rio de Janeiro: J. Zahar, 1996.

Raminelli, Ronald. "Simbolismos do espaço urbano colonial." In *América em tempo de conquista*. Edited by Ronaldo Vainfas, 163–75. Rio de Janeiro: Jorge Zahar Ed., 1992.

Ramos, Alcida R. *Indigenism: Ethnic Politics in Brazil.* Madison, WI: University of Wisconsin Press, 1998.

Ramos, Donald. "From Minho to Minas: The Portuguese Roots of the Mineiro Family." *Hispanic American Historical Review* 73:4 (1993), 639–62.

Ramos, Donald. "Marriage and the Family in Colonial Vila Rica." *Hispanic American Historical Review* 55:2 (May 1975), 200–25.

Ramos, Donald. "Single and Married Women in Vila Rica, Brazil, 1754–1838." *Journal of Family History* 16:3 (July 1991), 261–82.

Ramos, Donald. "Vila Rica: Profile of a Colonial Urban Center." *The Americas* 35:4 (April 1979), 495–526.

Rausch, Jane M. "Latin American Frontier History: The Colombian Case." *Lateinamerika Studien* 19 (1985), 73–94.

Rausch, Jane M. *Latin American History: The Colonial Experience.* Rev. ed. New York: Markus Wiener Publishing, 1993.

Reis Filho, Nestor Goulart. *Contribuição ao estudo da evolução urbana do Brasil (1500/1720).* São Paulo: Livraria Pioneira Editôra, 1968.

Restall, Matthew (ed.). *Beyond Blacks and Reds: African-Native Relations in Colonial Latin America.* Albuquerque, NM: University of New Mexico Press, 2005.

Ricardo, Cassiano. *Marcha para Oeste: A influência da bandeira na formação social e política do Brasil.* Rio de Janeiro: Livraria José Olympio, 1940.

Rosa, Walter. "No primeiro dos elementos: Dados para uma leitura sintética do urbanismo e da urbanística portugueses da Idade Moderna." *Oceanos* 41 (January-March 2000), 40–58.

Rouanet, Sergio Paulo. "As Minas iluminadas: a Ilustração e a Inconfidência." In *Tempo e história.* Edited by Adauto Novaes, 329–45. São Paulo: Companhia das Letras, 1992.

Ruff, Julius R. *Violence in Early Modern Europe, 1500–1800.* Cambridge, UK: Cambridge University Press, 2001.

Russell-Wood, A.J.R. *The Black Man in Slavery and Freedom in Colonial Brazil.* London: Macmillan Press, 1982.

Russell-Wood, A.J.R. "Colonial Brazil: The Gold Cycle, c. 1690–1750." In *Cambridge History of Latin America.* Edited by Leslie Bethell, Vol. 2. Cambridge, UK: Cambridge University Press, 1984.

Russell-Wood, A.J.R. (ed.). *From Colony to Nation: Essays on the Independence of Brazil.* Baltimore, MD: Johns Hopkins University Press, 1975.

Russell-Wood, A.J.R. "Frontiers in Colonial Brazil: Reality, Myth and Metaphor." In *Society and Government in Colonial Brazil, 1500–1822.* Aldershot, UK: Variorum, 1992.

Russell-Wood, A.J.R. *The Portuguese Empire, 1415–1808: A World on the Move.* Baltimore, MD: Johns Hopkins University Press, 1998.

Sahlins, Marshall. *How "Natives" Think: About Captain Cook, for Example.* Chicago: Chicago University Press, 1995.

Said, Edward W. *Orientalism.* New York: Vintage Books, 1979.

Saletto, Nara. *Transição para o trabalho livre e pequena propriedade no Espírito Santo.* Rio de Janeiro: Universidade Federal do Rio de Janeiro, 1991.

Salomon, Frank, and Stuart B. Schwartz (eds.). *The Cambridge History of the Native Peoples of the Americas*. Vol. 3, *South America*. Cambridge, UK: Cambridge University Press, 1999.

Santos, Joaquim Felício dos. *Memórias do Distrito Diamantino da Comarca do Serro Frio (Província de Minas Gerais)*. 1868. 4th ed. reprint, Belo Horizonte, Brazil: Ed. Itatiaia, 1976.

Scarano, Julita. *Cotidiano e solidaridade: Vida diaria da gente de cor nas Minas Gerais, século XVIII*. São Paulo: Brasiliense, 1994.

Schultz, Kirsten. *Tropical Versailles: Empire, Monarchy, and the Portuguese Royal Court in Rio de Janeiro, 1808–1821*. New York: Routledge, 2001.

Schwantes, Carlos. "The Concept of the Wageworkers' Frontier: An American-Canadian Perspective." *Western Historical Quarterly* 18 (January 1987), 39–55.

Schwartz, Stuart B. "Brazilian Ethnogenesis: Mestiços, Mamelucos, and Pardos." In *Le Nouveau Monde, Mondes Nouveaux: L'experience americaine*. Edited by Serge Gruzinski and Nathan Wachtel, 7–27. Paris: EHESS/CNRS, 1996.

Schwartz, Stuart B. "Elite Politics and the Growth of a Peasantry in Late Colonial Brazil." In *From Colony to Nation: Essays on the Independence of Brazil*. Edited by A.J.R. Russell-Wood. Baltimore, MD: Johns Hopkins University Press, 1975.

Schwartz, Stuart B. "The Formation of Colonial Identity in Brazil." In *Colonial Identity in the Atlantic World, 1500–1800*. Edited by Nicholas Canny and Anthony Pagden, 15–50. Princeton, NJ: Princeton University Press, 1987.

Schwartz, Stuart B. "Somebodies and Nobodies in the Body Politic: Mentalities and Social Structure in Colonial Brazil." *Latin American Research Review* 31:1 (1996), 113–34.

Schwartz, Stuart B. *Sugar Plantations in the Formation of Brazilian Society: Bahia, 1550–1835*. Cambridge, UK: Cambridge University Press, 1985.

Schwartz, Stuart B., and Hal Langfur, "Tapanhuns, Negros da Terra, and Curibocas: Common Cause and Confrontation between Blacks and Indians in Colonial Brazil." In *Black and Red: African-Indigenous Relations in Colonial Latin America*. Edited by Matthew Restall, 81–114. Albuquerque, NM: University of New Mexico Press, 2005.

Schwartz, Stuart B., and Frank Salomon. "New Peoples and New Kinds of People: Adaptation, Readjustment, and Ethnogenesis in South American Indigenous Societies (Colonial Era)." In *The Cambridge History of the Native Peoples of the Americas*. Vol. 3, pt. 2, *South America*. Edited by Frank Salomon and Stuart B. Schwartz, 443–501. Cambridge, UK: Cambridge University Press, 1999.

Schwartz, Seymour I., and Ralph E. Ehrenberg. *The Mapping of America*. New York: Harry N. Abrams, 1980.

Seed, Patricia. *Ceremonies of Possession in Europe's Conquest of the New World, 1492–1640*. Cambridge, UK: Cambridge University Press, 1995.

Senna, Nelson de. "Principaes povos selvagens que tiveram o seo 'habitat' em territorio das Minas Geraes." *RAPM* 25:1 (1937), 337–55.

Shirley, Rodney W. *The Mapping of the World: Early Printed World Maps, 1472–1700*. London: Holland Press, 1983.

Silva, Maria Beatriz Nizza da. *A cultura luso-brasileira: Da reforma da Universidade à independência do Brasil*. Lisbon: Ed. Estampa, 1999.

Silva, Maria Beatriz Nizza da (ed.). *Dicionário da história da colonização portuguesa no Brasil*. Lisbon: Verbo, 1994.

Silva, Maria Beatriz Nizza da. *Sistema de casamento no Brasil colonial*. São Paulo: T.A. Queiroz, Universidade de São Paulo, 1984.

Silva, Maria Beatriz Nizza da. *Vida privada e quotidiano no Brasil na época de D. Maria I e D. João VI*. Lisbon: Editorial Estampa, 1993.

Silveira, Marco Antonio. *O universo do indistinto: Estado e sociedade nas Minas setecentistas (1735–1808)*. São Paulo: Hucitec, 1997.

Skidmore, Thomas E. *Black into White: Race and Nationality in Brazilian Thought*. 1974. Reprint, Durham, NC: Duke University Press, 1993.

Slatta, Richard W. "Spanish Colonial Military Strategy and Ideology." In *Contested Ground: Comparative Frontiers on the Northern and Southern Edges of the Spanish Empire*. Edited by Donna J. Guy and Thomas E. Sheridan, 83–96. Tucson, AZ: University of Arizona Press, 1998.

Slenes, Robert W. "Os múltiplos de porcos e diamantes: A economia escravista de Minas Gerais no seculo XIX." *Caderrnos IFCH UNICAMP* 17 (June 1985), 39–80.

Slotkin, Richard. *The Fatal Environment: The Myth of the Frontier in the Age of Industrialization, 1800–1890*. New York: Atheneum, 1985.

Slotkin, Richard. *Gunfighter Nation: The Myth of the Frontier in Twentieth-Century America*. New York: Atheneum, 1992.

Slotkin, Richard. *Regeneration Through Violence: The Mythology of the American Frontier, 1600–1860*. Middletown, CT: Wesleyan University Press, 1973.

Smith, Henry Nash. *Virgin Land: The American West in Symbol and Myth*. New York: Vintage Books, 1957.

Smith, Thomas R. "Cruz Cano's Map of South America, Madrid, 1775: Its Creation, Adversities and Rehabilitation." *Imago Mundi* 20 (1966), 49–78.

Sodré, Nelson Werneck. *Oeste: Ensaio sobre a grande propriedade pastoril*. 1941. Rio de Janeiro: Livraria José Olympio, 1941.

Souza, Candice Vidal e. "A noção de fronteira e espaço nacional no pensamento social brasileiro." *Textos de História* 4:2 (1996), 94–129.

Souza, Candice Vidal e. *A pátria geográfica e litoral no pensamento social brasileiro*. Goiânia, Brazil: Universidade Federal de Goiás, 1997.

Souza, Laura de Mello e. *Desclassificados do ouro: A pobreza mineira no século XVIII*. 3rd ed. Rio de Janeiro: Graal, 1990.

Souza, Laura de Mello e. *Norma e conflito: Aspectos da história de Minas no século XVIII*. Belo Horizonte, Brazil: UFMG, 1999.

Souza, Laura de Mello e. *O diabo e a Terra de Santa Cruz: Feitiçaria e religiosidade popular no Brasil colonial*. São Paulo: Companhia das Letras, 1986.

Souza, Laura de Mello e. "Violência e práticas culturais no cotidiano de uma expedição contra quilombolas, Minas Gerais, 1769." In *Liberdade por um fio: História dos quilombos no Brasil*. Edited by João José Reis and Flávio dos Santos Gomes, 193–212. São Paulo: Companhia das Letras, 1996.

Stein, Stanley J. *Vassouras: A Brazilian Coffee County: The Roles of Planter and Slave in a Plantation Society*. Princeton, NJ: Princeton University Press, 1985.

Stepan, Nancy Leys. *"The Hour of Eugenics": Race, Gender, and Nation in Latin America.* Ithaca, NY: Cornell University Press, 1991.

Stepan, Nancy Leys. *The Idea of Race in Science: Great Britain, 1800–1960.* Hamden, CT: Archon Books, 1982.

Stern, Steve J. "Feudalism, Capitalism, and the World-System in the Perspective of Latin America and the Caribbean." *American Historical Review* 93 (1988), 829–72.

Steward, Julian H. (ed.). *Handbook of South American Indians.* 7 vols. New York: Cooper Square, 1963.

Taunay, Afonso de Escragnolle. *História das bandeiras paulistas.* 3rd ed., 3 vols. São Paulo: Edições Melhoramentos, 1975.

Taunay, Afonso de Escragnolle. *História geral das bandeiras paulistas.* 11 vols. São Paulo: Typ. Ideal and Imp. Oficial, 1924–50.

Taussig, Michael. *Shamanism, Colonialism, and the Wild Man: A Study in Terror and Healing.* Chicago: University of Chicago Press, 1987.

Taylor, William. "Between Global Process and Local Knowledge: An Inquiry into Early Latin American Social History, 1500–1900." In *Reliving the Past: The Worlds of Social History.* Edited by Oliver Zunz, 115–90. Chapel Hill, NC: University of North Carolina Press, 1985.

Terán, Fernando de (ed.). *La Ciudad Hispanoamericana: El Sueño de un Orden.* Madrid: Centro de Estudios Históricos de Obras Públicas y Urbanismo, 1989.

Thornton, John. *Africa and Africans in the Making of the Atlantic World, 1400–1680.* Cambridge, UK: Cambridge University Press, 1992.

Trexler, Richard C. *Sex and Conquest: Gendered Violence, Political Order, and the European Conquest of the Americas.* Ithaca, NY: Cornell University Press, 1995.

Trigo, Abril. "On Transculturation: Toward a Political Economy of Culture in the Periphery." *Studies of Latin American Popular Culture* 15 (1996), 99–118.

Trindade, Raimundo. *Arquidiocese de Mariana: Subsídios para sua história.* 2nd ed. Belo Horizonte, Brazil: Imprensa Oficial, 1953.

Turner, Frederick Jackson. "The Significance of the Frontier in American History." In *The Frontier in American History.* 1–38. New York: Henry Holt, 1920.

Usner, Daniel H., Jr. *Indians, Settlers, and Slaves in a Frontier Exchange Economy: The Lower Mississippi Valley before 1783.* Chapel Hill, NC: University of North Carolina Press, 1992.

Vainfas, Ronaldo. *A heresia dos índios: Catolicismo e rebeldia no Brasil colonial.* São Paulo: Companhia das Letras, 1995.

Vasconcellos, Sylvio de. *Arquitetura no Brasil. Pintura mineira e outros temas.* Belo Horizonte, Brazil: Escola de Arquitetura da Universidade Federal de Minas Gerais, 1959.

Vasconcelos, Diogo [Luís de Almeida Pereira] de. *História antiga de Minas Gerais.* 4th ed. Belo Horizonte, Brazil: Ed. Itatiaia, 1974.

Vasconcelos, Diogo [Luís de Almeida Pereira] de. *História média de Minas Gerais.* 4th ed. Belo Horizonte, Brazil: Ed. Itatiaia, 1974.

Viana, Francisco José de Oliveira. *Populações meridionais do Brasil: História, organização e psicologia.* São Paulo: Ed. Nacional, 1933.

Viana, Victor. *Histórico da formação econômica do Brasil.* Rio de Janeiro: Ministério da Fazenda, 1922.

Voelz, Peter M. *Slave and Soldier: The Military Impact of Blacks in the Colonial Americas.* New York: Garland Publishing, 1993.

Waibel, Leo H. "As zonas pioneiras do Brasil." *Revista Brasileira de Geografia* 17 (October–December 1955), 389–417.

Warren, Jonathan W. *Racial Revolutions: Antiracism & Indian Resurgence in Brazil.* Durham, NC: Duke University Press, 2001.

Webb, Walter Prescott. *The Great Frontier.* Boston: Houghton Mifflin, 1952.

Weber, David J. *The Spanish Frontier in North America.* New Haven, CT: Yale University Press, 1992.

Weber, David J., and Jane M. Rausch (eds.). *Where Cultures Meet: Frontiers in Latin American History.* Wilmington, DE: Scholarly Resources, 1994.

Wegner, Robert. *A conquista do oeste: A fronteira na obra de Sérgio Buarque de Holanda.* Belo Horizonte, Brazil: Universidade Federal de Minas Gerais, 2000.

White, Richard. *The Middle Ground: Indians, Empires, and Republics in the Great Lakes Region, 1650–1815.* Cambridge, UK: Cambridge University Press, 1991.

White, Richard. *The Roots of Dependency: Subsistence, Environment, and Social Change among the Choctaws, Pawnees, and Navajos.* Lincoln, NE: University of Nebraska Press, 1983.

White, Richard. "The Winning of the West: The Expansion of the Western Sioux in the Eighteenth and Nineteenth Centuries." *Journal of American History* 65:2 (1978), 319–43.

Whitehead, Neil L. *Dark Shamans: Kanaimà and the Poetics of Violent Death.* Durham, NC: Duke University Press, 2002.

Whitehead, Neil L. "The Snake Warriors-Sons of the Tiger's Teeth: A Descriptive Analysis of Carib Warfare ca. 1500–1820." In *The Anthropology of War.* Edited by Jonathan Haas, 146–70. Cambridge, UK: Cambridge University Press, 1990.

Whitehead, Neil L. "Tribes Make States and States Make Tribes: Warfare and the Creation of Colonial Tribes and States in Northeastern South America." In *War in the Tribal Zone: Expanding States and Indigenous Warfare.* Edited by R. Brian Ferguson and Neil L. Whitehead, 127–50. Santa Fe, NM: School of American Research Press, 1992.

Wolf, Eric R. *Europe and the People without History.* Berkeley, CA: University of California Press, 1982.

Wright, Robin M., and Manuela Carneiro da Cunha. "Destruction, Resistance, and Transformation-Southern, Coastal, and Northern Brazil (1580–1890)." In *The Cambridge History of the Native Peoples of the Americas.* Vol. 3, pt. 2, *South America.* Edited by Frank Salomon and Stuart B. Schwartz. Cambridge, UK: Cambridge University Press, 1999.

Zavala, Silvio. "The Frontiers of Hispanic America." In *The Frontier in Perspective.* Edited by Walker D. Wyman and Clifton B. Kroeber, 35–58. Madison, WI: University of Wisconsin Press, 1957.

Zemella, Mafalda P. *O abastecimento da Capitania das Minas Gerais no século XVIII.* 2nd ed. São Paulo: Hucitec, 1990.

Theses and Unpublished Works

Almeida, Maria Regina Celestino de. "Os índios aldeiados no Rio de Janeiro colonial: Novos súditos cristãos do Império Português." Ph.D. diss., Universidade de Campinas, 2001.

Bieber, Judy. "The Aldeia System Reborn: Botocudo Communities on the Espírito Santo-Minas Gerais Frontier, 1808–1845." Paper presented at the Latin American Studies Association Conference, Chicago, September 1998.

Bieber, Judy. "Shifting Frontiers: The Role of Subsistence, Disease, and Environment in Shaping Indigenous Definitions of Frontiers in Minas Gerais, 1808–1850." Paper presented at the American Historical Association Conference, San Francisco, January 2002.

Carrara, Angelo Alves. "Agricultura e pecuária na Capitania de Minas Gerais (1674–1807)." Ph.D. diss., Universidade Federal do Rio de Janeiro, 1997.

Langfur, [Hal]. "The Forbidden Lands: Frontier Settlers, Slaves, and Indians in Minas Gerais, Brazil, 1760–1830." Ph.D. diss., University of Texas, 1999.

Mattos, Izabel Missagia de. "'Civilização' e 'revolta': Os Botocudos e a catequese na Província de Minas." Ph.D. diss., Universidade de Campinas, 2002.

Monteiro, John M. "Entre o etnocídio e a etnogênese: Identidades indígenas coloniais." Paper presented at the Latin American Studies Association Conference, Dallas, TX, March 27–29, 2003.

Moraes, Leonardo Pires B. de. "Cronologia das cartas de sesmarias concedidas em Minas Gerais." Uncatalogued TS in reading room, APM, 1991.

Paraíso, Maria Hilda Baquiero. "O tempo da dor e do trabalho: A conquista dos territórios indígenas nos Sertões do Leste." Ph.D. diss., Universidade de São Paulo, 1998.

Ramos, Donald. "A Social History of Ouro Preto: Stresses of Dynamic Urbanization in Colonial Brazil, 1695–1726." Ph.D. diss., University of Florida, 1972.

Resende, Maria Leônia Chaves de. "Gentios brasílicos: Índios coloniais em Minas Gerais setecentista." Ph.D. diss., Universidade de Campinas, 2003.

Sommer, Barbara A. "Negotiated Settlements: Native Amazonians and Portuguese Policy in Pará, Brazil, 1758–1798." Ph.D. diss., University of New Mexico, 2000.

Index

In this index an "f" after a number indicates a separate reference on the next page, and an "ff" indicates separate references on the next two pages. A continuous discussion over two or more pages is indicated by a span of page numbers, e.g., "57–59."

The authorized representative in the EU for product safety and compliance is:
Mare Nostrum Group
B.V Doelen 72
4831 GR Breda
The Netherlands